About Pearson

Pearson is the world's learning company, with presence across 70 countries worldwide. Our unique insights and world-class expertise comes from a long history of working closely with renowned teachers, authors and thought leaders, as a result of which, we have emerged as the preferred choice for millions of teachers and learners across the world.

We believe learning opens up opportunities, creates fulfilling careers and hence better lives. We hence collaborate with the best of minds to deliver you class-leading products, spread across the Higher Education and Test Preparation spectrum.

Superior learning experience and improved outcomes are at the heart of everything we do. This product is the result of one such effort.

Your feedback plays a critical role in the evolution of our products and you can contact us – reachus@pearson.com. *We look forward to it.*

Comparative Political Analysis

A Reader

Chetna Sharma
Department of Political Science,
Kamala Nehru College,
University of Delhi

Pushpa Singh
Department of Political Science,
Miranda House,
University of Delhi

Pearson

Senior Editor—Acquisitions: Anindita Malhotra
Senior Editor—Production: C. Purushothaman

ISBN 978-93-570-5645-8

First Impression

Published by Pearson India Education Services Pvt. Ltd, CIN: U72200TN2005PTC057128.

Head Office: 1st Floor, Berger Tower, Plot No. C-001A/2, Sector 16B, Noida - 201 301, Uttar Pradesh, India.
Registered Office: Featherlite, 'The Address' 5th Floor, Survey No 203/10B, 200 Ft MMRD Road, Zamin Pallavaram, Chennai – 600 044.
Website: in.pearson.com, Email: companysecretary.india@pearson.com

Compositor: MAP Systems, Bengaluru
Printed in India by Pushp Print Services

Table of Contents

Foreword

It is with great pleasure that I write this foreword to a book written by a group of rigorous scholars and teachers, who have chosen to put together a much-needed textbook on Comparative Politics.

In the overall teaching of Political Science, the transition from the old institutional perspective to a more dynamic, critical and alternative perspective—the study of comparative politics as it evolved in the 1950s, 1960s and 1970s—provided an important point of entry. At the University of Delhi, there had been a concerted attempt to change this in the mid-1980s, when new syllabi for the undergraduate degree were introduced by the parent Department of Political Science, under the dynamic leadership of Professor Manoranjan Mohanty. A range of new courses, in both scope and theoretical orientation, were formulated by a team of teachers from both colleges and the postgraduate department, introducing the perspectives of political economy and political sociology, and locating the analytical frame in a historical context. For years afterwards, generations of students were trained in them. Those of whom were able to absorb these ideas confidently subsequently became teachers. I am proud that so many of them have had the gumption to bring out a volume of this kind, talking of the relationship between the three sub-disciplines of Political Science (PS): Political Theory (PT), Comparative Political Analysis (CPA) and International Relations (IR), and addressing some of the problematic dimensions of teaching comparative politics in India.

The first is that there is practically no original research in this discipline in India. This is also true for much of the Global South, simply because of the practical considerations of funding and intellectual support being not available to scholars here. So the authors of this volume have had to rely on already-published material in order to produce a textbook which should be seen as a great point for initiating a thought process in the students and one that arouses curiosity to read and perhaps research further.

The second important challenge that underlies all three sub-disciplines, also referred to in the volume, is the question of Eurocentrism. The best way to meet this challenge would be to offer the findings of primary research in these areas. Without it, however, it is almost impossible to attempt a critique, but a broad critique is attempted here nevertheless to indicate a broad outline for students. Perspectives from ex-colonized countries, most of which constitute the Global South today, are slowly emerging and finding a place in well-known academic spaces—whether journals or institutions—and we need to find a way of making the next generation aware of them.

I hope that students and teachers alike are able to make good use of this book, and that its thorough and meticulous writing becomes the hallmark of the teaching–learning processes in our universities.

—Madhulika Banerjee
Department of Political Science,
University of Delhi

Preface

This book *Comparative Political Analysis:* A Reader is a culmination of our training, engagements and teaching in the field of Comparative Politics and Political Theory. The original inspiration for this book comes from our own student experiences long ago. We often found ourselves lost in the vast array of literature and always felt the need for a text that could provide us with a sound understanding of the core area of the discipline in a comprehensive manner. This problem has been endemic in the field of comparative politics, which is marked by the absence of a text that covers the syllabus in totality and produces the nuances of contemporary debates. When we started teaching, we noticed that the concerns remained the same, as we found our students in the same situation. We must confess that our approach and academic rigour has been highly enriched within and beyond classroom teaching and learning. This book explores the central ideas and questions that constitute the field of comparative politics with the aim of training young minds in the discipline and inspire them to engage with further studies in the domain. This text engages in critical thematic exploration, emphasizing the detailed study of important political institutions and their functioning in comparative perspective.

While the volume aims to provide an understanding of the core concepts of comparative politics, it also explores contemporary debates and critical perspectives in the field. Every chapter deals with the foundational theories, debates and their relevance in contemporary times. There is an intentional effort to move out of the confines of Eurocentric delimitations and incorporate perspectives from post-colonial societies. Spread over twenty-five chapters, the arguments explore the different dimensions of the subject, keeping in mind the intersectionality of gender, race and ethnicity. While the first, second and third chapters provide insights into the origin and development of the discipline of comparative politics, the fourth chapter discusses the gender question in the sub-discipline of comparative politics by analysing women and political participation from comparative perspective. Chapters five to twelve deal with the conceptual understanding of foundational concepts like capitalism, socialism, colonialism, nationalism, decolonization, constitutionalism and federalism in comparative terms. Following them are chapters thirteen to eighteen covering different states and regime types like authoritarian regimes, populist regimes, the capitalist state, the neoliberal state and the security state. The process of democratisation and the analysis discussed in chapter nineteen show how these processes have taken completely different trajectories in the context of developing societies. Chapter twenty and twenty-one discusses important institutions of the modern state such as electoral system and political parties. The last four chapters, from twenty-two to twenty-five, deal with four different political systems comprising Britain, Nigeria, Brazil and China to bring case studies of political processes representing four different continents. Studies of these countries that are geographically distant and politically different, provide us with myriad examples of how political phenomena are contingent and context bound. Their studies illustrate how very similar sets of political structures and institutions can yield very dissimilar outcomes in different countries. Interestingly, the study of political economy has been included to help us understand the working of a political system in totality. By delving deeper into the politics of these countries, we can learn about the intricacies and diversity of the ways in which political processes unfold itself in different regions. It also helps to understand the varying nature of politics in an increasingly globalized world.

All the chapters give valuable and relevant information related to the subject in the boxes to draw attention of the reader. Every chapter begins with a reader's guide that lays out the objective, structure and brief introduction of the content discussed within. Also included are the key words, glossary and review questions for the purpose of self-assessment. The ultimate aim of this volume is to provide a wide ranging, accessible and contemporary textbook to introduce students to the tradition of comparative research. We hope that this book proves to be useful for students, teaching community and for researchers in this field.

Writing for students is a long, continuous and exciting process. Students, peers and academicians are fellow travellers on this protracted journey. Their critical comments, feedback and ideas would definitely motivate us to improve. We dedicate this book to our teachers, from whom we have learned the art of engaging with the political and to our students who always inspire us to become better teachers.

Acknowledgements

We, Chetna Sharma and Pushpa Singh, are glad to be part of the academic fraternity at the University of Delhi that has shaped our ideas and thoughts to engage critically with the issues pertinent to the study of politics. The various academic interactions and explorations undertaken by us during our long journey as students and teachers at the University of Delhi have enriched us. This work is deeply informed by the interesting questions that we kept receiving from our students over the span of our teaching engagement of almost two decades. We are grateful to our students for bringing critical insights to classroom discussions and beyond. We thank our mentors and teachers from the Department of Political Science, University of Delhi, for their constant encouragement and support. We are especially indebted to our respective supervisors, Prof. Ashok Acharya and Prof. Madhulika Banerjee, for being a constant source of motivation and guidance. We are also grateful to our college and principal for providing us with a conducive space for academic growth and engagement. The lively discussion with our colleagues and their camaraderie always elevated our energy.

We are thankful to our reviewers for their valuable comments that enabled us to enrich this work. Many thanks to our contributors for their sincerity and timely submission.

Thanks are also due to our publisher, Pearson, and their team for their support. We would like to especially acknowledge the efforts of Ms. Anindita Malhotra and Mr. Sojan Jose for their constant support at various stages of this work.

We would like to recognise the firm support of our families, without which this work would have been impossible. Chetna Sharma would like to acknowledge her spouse, Dr. Neeraj Sharma, for his unfailing love, criticism, and encouragement. It gives her pleasure to express gratitude to her parents, Yogesh Sharma and Santosh Sharma, for their determined efforts in her education. She would like to thank her mother-in-law, Saroj Sharma, for her support. She will be happy to see the excitement of her daughters, Ananya and Advika, when they see the book in its final form.

Pushpa Singh greatly appreciates her spouse, Ravi Singh, for his love, encouragement, and support in all her endeavours. She is eternally grateful to her parents, Bidhu Mishra and father Vijay Mishra, for their love and blessings that keep her moving ahead. She also thanks her in-laws, Shail Singh and Parmanand Singh, and her brothers, Ashutosh Anand and Avinash Anand, for their constant support. Her children, Yajat and Keya, bring a spark to her life with their energy and smiles.

We would also like to state that this volume is a reflection of our long association and the beautiful bond that we share. Working together has been a sheer delight for both of us.

Chetna Sharma (Dr)
Pushpa Singh (Dr)

About the Authors and Contributors

Authors

Dr. Chetna Sharma teaches political science as an Associate Professor of political science at Delhi University's Kamala Nehru College. She was awarded her doctorate from the University of Delhi. She specialised in comparative politics and political theory. Her research interests include citizenship, multiculturalism, and minorities' rights. Various research papers have been presented by her at national and international conferences. She is a recipient of Junior Research Fellowship and Senior Research Fellowship from the University Grants Commission. She participated in a workshop on forced population displacement and the making of the modern world that was held in 2017 and was sponsored by the Brown International Advanced Research Institute at Brown University in Providence, USA. Comparative Government and Politics, co-edited by her, was published in 2019. Her papers and book reviews have been widely published in journals, including *Asian Ethnicity, Contemporary South Asia, Journal of Immigrants and Refugee Studies, Ethnicities, Journal of Polity and Society, Indian Studies Review*. Dr Sharma has been actively involved with curriculum development of University of Delhi and has also contributed to several online publications as a part of e-content generation by ILLL, University of Delhi.

Dr. Pushpa Singh is an Associate Professor in the Department of Political Science, Miranda House, University of Delhi. She has pursued her graduation, post-graduation, M.Phil. and Ph.D. from the University of Delhi. Her interest areas are comparative politics, political theory, development studies and gender studies. She has co-edited a book *Comparative Government and Politics* published in 2019. Her articles and book reviews have been widely published in several national and international referred journals such as *Asian Journal of Social Science, Studies in Indian Politics, Indian Journal of Public Administration, Journal of Rural Development, Contributions to Indian Sociology, Social Action, Journal of Polity and Society and Indian Studies Review.* She has contributed to many reference volumes published from Springer, Routledge, World Scientific, Thomson Reuters, Academic Press Elsevier, Palgrave, Orient Blackswan and Pearson. Besides, she has several online publications as a part of e-content generation by ILLL, DU and has been engaged with international and national projects in her research area sponsored by IDS Sussex, ICSSR and DU. Dr Singh has been actively involved with curriculum development of University of Delhi and has audited the Kings College of London Summer School (2013). She has presented in several international and national conferences and workshops. Promoting consumer education, she has been engaged with TULA, Miranda House Consumer Club since 2008, and contributes to publish *Santulan*, a journal on Consumer Education. Dr Singh has received several prizes and scholarship for academic excellence in her graduation and post-graduation from DR College and University of Delhi.

Contributors

Anusha is Assistant Professor (Senior Scale) at the Department of Political Science, Shaheed Bhagat Singh College, University of Delhi. She received a gold medal in BA and PhD degree from the University. Her domains of academic interest include political theory, comparative politics and resistance studies. The author's recent achievements include a book review in a published journal titled *Studies in Indian Politics*, a chapter in an edited book titled *Land Rights in India: Policies, Movements and Challenges* and an entry on Cold War in *The SAGE Encyclopedia of World Poverty*.

Alisha Dhingra is currently working as Assistant Professor in the Department of Political Science, at Satyawati College. She has earlier served as Assistant Professor at the Department of Political Science, Faculty of Social Sciences, University of Delhi from 2014 to 2016 and from 2017 to 2019. She has pursued her graduation and post-graduation from Hindu College and M.Phil. and Ph.D. from the Department of Political Science, University of Delhi. Her research interests include Indian and Comparative Constitutionalism. She has published ten research papers and two book reviews and contributed chapters in books published by Routledge, Sage, and Orient Blackswan among others.

Ankit Tomar has published widely in the fields of Indian and Western Philosophy and his three most recent co-edited books are *Ancient and Medieval Indian Thought: Themes and Traditions*, published by Sage, *Revisiting Modern Indian Thought: Themes and Perspectives*, published by Routledge, Reappraising *Modern Indian Thought: Themes and Thinkers*, published by Palgrave. He is presently working as a Research Assistant of the ICSSR project at Kalindi College, University of Delhi. He is also a senior doctoral research scholar of International Politics at Jawaharlal Nehru University, and holds an M.A. in Political Science from University of Delhi and an M.Phil. in International Politics from School of International Studies, Jawaharlal Nehru University. He has contributed number of chapters and articles in the national and international books as well as academic journals. He is an active participant of national and international level seminars, conferences, workshops and training programmes.

Babita Verma is Associate Professor at Department of Political Science, Lakshmibai College. She completed her PhD from the University of Delhi. Her specialization includes local self-government and gender. She has worked extensively in Uttarakhand and Rajasthan on different projects of National Commission for Women (NCW) and other nongovernmental organizations (NGOs). She has written several reports for NCW and other NGOs. She published a book titled *India's Foreign Policy under Rajiv Gandhi: Continuity and Change* in 2012.

Meena Kumari is Assistant Professor in the Department of Political Science, Miranda House, University of Delhi. She is pursuing her PhD from the Department of Political Science University of Delhi, Delhi and has been recipient of Junior Research Fellowship and Senior Research Fellowship. She has presented several papers in national and international conferences and seminars and has contributed Chapters in School of Open Learning, University of Delhi, Delhi.

Praveen Dhanda teaches at the Department of Political Science, Indraprastha College for Women, University of Delhi. He holds a PhD from Jawaharlal Nehru University, New Delhi, and his areas of academic interest include development studies, alternative intellectual traditions from Global South, modern Indian political thought and Gandhian thought. He has also received a research fellowship from University Grants Commission (UGC).

Rahul Chimurkar is Assistant Professor at Department of Political Science, Deshbandhu College, University of Delhi. He obtained his graduation and master's degree from the Department of Political Science, Hindu College, University of Delhi. He completed his PhD from Faculty of Social Sciences, Jamia Millia Islamia University, New Delhi. His research articles have been published in several peer-reviewed scholarly journals. His specialisation and areas of interest are Indian Government and Politics, Political Thought and Governance. His recent accomplishments in terms of publication includes a chapter '*Patel and Accession of Jammu and Kashmir*' in an edited book titled '*Patel: Political Ideas and Policies*' published by SAGE and 'Local Governance in Fifth Scheduled Areas: A study of implementation of PESA 1996 in. Bijapur district of Chhattisgarh' in an edited book titled '*Tribal Livelihood and Governance: Regional Concerns*' published by Rawat publications.

Rityusha Mani Tiwary is Assistant Professor (Senior Scale) at the Department of Political Science, Shaheed Bhagat Singh College of the University of Delhi. Currently, she is a Fellow at the Institute of Eminence at the Delhi School of Transnational Affairs, University of Delhi and an Honorary Fellow at the Institute of Chinese Studies, Delhi. Additionally, she is the Assistant Editor of the flagship journal of the Institute-*China Report: A Journal of East Asian Studies* (Sage). She holds a PhD in Chinese Studies from the School of International Studies, Jawaharlal Nehru University, New Delhi.

Her research and publications have focused on unpacking the interplay of power and hegemony in East Asia, regionalism, and China's role therein. Her broad research interests include studying foreign policy, diplomacy, borders, and conflict with a gendered comparative approach for India and China. Currently, she is working on her manuscript on power and hegemony in global politics and an edited volume on China's Domestic Governance.

She has been awarded Visiting Fellowships at the German Institute of Global and Area Studies, Hamburg, Shanghai Academy of Social Sciences, Shanghai and the Politics and International Studies Department, University of Cambridge, UK. In addition, she was the recipient of the Young Sinologist Fellowship by the Ministry of Culture, China, and the International Visitor Leadership Program of the Department of State, US.

Rohit Raj is currently working as an Assistant Professor in the School of Internal Security and Police Administration, Rashtriya Raksha University (An Institution of National Importance, Ministry of Home Affairs) Gandhinagar, Gujarat. He has received his Doctoral degree from the Department of Political Science, Jamia Millia Islamia University, New Delhi. He received UGC-Junior Research Fellowship in Public Administration and was promoted as Senior Research Fellow during his doctoral research. Dr Rohit Raj has taught papers on Security studies, Police Administration, Public administration and Public Policy.

Rounak Kumar Pathak is an Assistant Professor at Gargi College, University of Delhi. He is also pursuing his PhD from Department of Political Science, University of Delhi. He did his Post Graduation in Political Science (2011-13) from Centre for Political Studies, Jawahar Lal Nehru University. He did his Graduation in BA(H) Political Science from Hindu College, University of Delhi (2008-11). His area of interest is in Indian Politics, Party System, Electoral Politics, and Voting Behaviour etc. He has already published variety of research articles in various journals, in areas such as voting behaviour, party politics, economic & pandemic federalism.

Ruchi Shree teaches at the PG Department of Political Science, Tilka Manjhi Bhagalpur University (TMBU), Bihar from 2019. She taught at Janki Devi Memorial College, University of Delhi from 2012 to 2019. At present, she is also a research fellow at School of Law, SOAS (University of London), working on 'Fostering Ecocentric Community-led River Restoration and Conservation in the Ganga Basin (India)' supported by the British Academy Leverhulme Fellowship (2021–2023).

Shefali Manhas is presently pursuing PhD and working on a thesis titled 'Women's Activism and Resistance: A Study of Women's Organisations in Kashmir Since 1990' from Jawaharlal Nehru University, New Delhi. Her areas of specialization include political theory, comparative politics, gender and conflict studies. A scholarship holder from Indian Council Social Science Research, her recent accomplishments in terms of publication include entries on 'Domestic Violence' and 'Pollution' in *The SAGE Encyclopedia of World Poverty*.

Shivali Aggarwal teaches political science at Daulat Ram College, University of Delhi, from where she also received her BA (Hons) and MA degrees in political science. She was awarded the Shri Tilak Raj Memorial Award in Daulat Ram College for securing the highest marks in political science in graduation. She completed her MPhil and PhD from the Department of Political Science, University of Delhi. She has experience of four years of teaching at postgraduate level in the Department of Political Science, University of Delhi. Dr Aggarwal is credited with writing chapters for reputed publishing houses. She writes equally well in Hindi. She has the laurel of publishing three books on varied topics, namely Indo-Canadian relations, development issues in India and poverty in India. She presents research papers at international and national conferences. Her research interests include comparative politics, India's political economy, political theory and political thought.

Shivani Sharma is presently enrolled as a doctoral research scholar at the Centre for South Asian Studies, Jawaharlal Nehru University. She has taught at Hindu College, University of Delhi, and has been a fellow at the South Asia Democratic Forum. Her main areas of research include international politics, security studies and regional politics.

Skylab Sahu is currently a fellow at Uppsala University, Sweden and Assistant Professor at Miranda House, University of Delhi. Before joining Miranda House, she taught MA courses at the Department of Political Science, University of Delhi. She received her PhD from the Institute for Social and Economic Change (ISEC), Bangalore. Her teaching and research interests span political theory, gender studies, Comparative Politics, the Indian state, society and polity, and development studies. She has published her research in edited anthologies and several national and international refereed journals such as Studies in Indian Politics, Sociological Bulletin, Journal of Social and Economic Development, Journal of Health Management, Indian Journal of Political Science, Indian Journal of Human Development and Indian Journal of Social Work. She has authored books: "Gender, Sexuality, and HIV/AIDS: Exploring Politics of Women's Health in India", published in 2015 by Sage, and "Gender, Violence and Governmentality: Legal and Policy Initiatives in India", published in 2020 by Routledge.

Tripta Sharma teaches at Zakir Husain Delhi College, University of Delhi. She holds a PhD from Department of Political Science of the University. Presently, she is a co-director of a research programme—'Knowledge, Development and Politics: Contestations in State, Market and Civil Society'.

Vasavi teaches as an Assistant Professor in Lady Shriram College, University of Delhi. She is pursuing her doctoral research work from Department of Political Science, University of Delhi. Delhi. Her research areas broadly include fiscal federalism, gender budgeting, gender and federalism.

CHAPTER 1

Introduction: Understanding Comparative Politics

Pushpa Singh

Reader's Guide

The act of comparison is innate to human beings. Intentionally or unintentionally, we tend to compare everything around us. This is because comparison enables a better understanding of the world that we inhabit. In the field of Political Science, the sub-discipline of Comparative Politics is specifically modelled to provide the framework, methods and methodologies of comparison. The ambit of this sub-discipline is vast, covering a broad range of subjects like political regimes, political activities, political institutions, structures and processes. Its course has gradually evolved from the times of Greek antiquity to contemporary globalized world. This chapter introduces the sub-discipline of comparative politics and discusses its main features, methodologies and ambit of study. In that sense, it lays the ground for rest of the following chapters in this volume by briefly opening up the issues and concerns of the field. Subsequent lessons pick up these subject matters and engage with elaborate critical discussion on them. The effort is to produce a comprehensive understanding and outline the 'state of the art' of the discipline. Also, most of the studies in the sub-discipline of comparative politics are bereft of detailed discussion on methods and methodologies, which form the core element of this discipline. This chapter aims to engage meticulously with this pertinent area also, to attune the young minds to the nuances of the field of comparative research.

1.1 Introduction

Comparative Politics is a sub-discipline of Political Science that focuses on comparison as a method of political inquiry. It is one of the important sub-fields of politics where comparative analysis is well established. Comparative politics has been predominantly defined by means of its method. Most attempts to define its domain, especially vis-à-vis other sub-disciplines of political science, emphasize the primacy it places on comparison and case studies. Arend Lijphart spells this out very clearly in his statement 'among the several fields of sub-disciplines into which the discipline of political science is usually divided, comparative politics is the only one that carries a methodological instead of a substantive level' (1971, 682). Without any exception, all scholars of this field accept that comparison is the basic function of this discipline and it offers unswerving strategy of research. The essence of comparative politics lies in studying institutions and political processes by the method of comparison. In this sense, its boundary is primarily delineated on purely methodological basis. However, the domain of the discipline is not solely defined by its method, rather it is equally delineated by its substance and content, that is, the study of politics (Keman 2002, 33). The cardinal subject matter that concerns comparative politics is the study of political systems and their structures and functioning. Comparative politics can be seen as an approach that tries to explain political processes with the help of universal theoretical framework of reference, and the subjects of comparison are the macro-societal units of analysis (Ragin 1989, 6).

Kopstein and Lichbach (2005) think that comparative politics constitutes one of the three important poles in political science, the other two being the political theory and international relations. All these three sub-fields are closely related to one another, although their methods and subject matters may differ slightly. Political theorists are known to engage with the theoretical and philosophical underpinnings of a concept. International relations scholars focus more on what transpires between states, and comparativists concentrate on politics within countries and then try to find convergences and departures with other political systems to establish and explain the pattern. However, there is greater realization of the fuzziness of such compartmentalization of boundaries, as these sub-disciplines very often overlap and complement each other to make fuller sense of the subject matter. This division has become artificial and obsolete in the contemporary globalized world where every aspect of political system is mutually shaping and reinforcing each other. What transpires between nations is generally a response to the imposed global order that has immediate implication on what happens within these political systems. Therefore, the boundaries of comparative politics and international relations emerge as all the more fused. Yet, by training of their sub-disciplines, political theorists tend to make judgement about their subject matter; on the contrary, comparativists suspend their normative evaluation and are occupied with the description and explanation of the political world. For example, a researcher in comparative politics may not like authoritarianism, but her own judgement will not cloud her exploration of how and why some countries become autocratic and authoritarian. In that tradition, scholars in this field devote a great amount of time understanding and identifying the general conditions under which political phenomenon appears, gets distorted, fumble and fade away and sometimes also resurges possibly in a different form.

1.2 Nature and Scope

As the methods of comparison are deeply entrenched in comparative politics, this sub-discipline provides scientific rigour to the study of politics (Landman 2000, 20). Comparative method leads to creating propositions and a general theory to explain the event regularities in a political discourse. Scholars of comparative politics employ a lot of data work. But, unlike statisticians, their role extends beyond aggregation and cataloguing of these data. They interpret all these information and specific experiences and work out the correlations among all variables, meticulously obtained in order to conceptualize a meta-theory capable of explaining the world around. The domain and scope of comparative politics is very vast. Describing the range of critical political questions that lay in front of the field practitioners, Mark Lichbach and Alan Zuckerman state that 'the students of comparative politics explain electoral behaviour, political networks, political institutions, contentious politics, comparative political economies, welfare states, international-comparative linkages, and the state' (Lichbach and Zuckerman 2013, 1). Because of the panoramic engagements of students of this field, they are well equipped to explain the fundamental but complex questions about societies, such as: *Why do political phenomena unfold in a specific way in a particular society? Why do different countries have different kinds of regimes? Why do countries tend to develop in different directions and not in one? How do we explain the complete adherence of some Western practices or institutions by some of the non-Western countries and not others? What processes bring out the congruent pattern of development in some countries?*

The essence of comparative politics lies in comparing and investigating, and comparativists thrive on explaining variations they discover in their studies. Comparative politics owes a great deal to classical political philosophers such as Plato, Aristotle, Machiavelli, Montesquieu, Marx and Mill, who endowed the discipline with the initial framework of theorization and methods. However, hard currency to the discipline was brought by scholars such as James Bryce, Carl Friedrich and Herman Finer whose work provided a distinct and firm edifice to comparative politics in the early 20th century. Before 1900, the study of politics was largely dominated by philosophy, history and law (Ball 1971, 4). The prevailing temper of the comparative government studies in both Europe and the United States was heavily institutional, highly normative and hardly comparative. All the works in the field of comparative studies were basically studies of British and American political systems. Most of the works were in the tone of celebration of the paramountcy of British political institutions. From Bagehot (1867) to Bryce (1921) to Laxmi (1940) and Finer (1960), all the serious explorations revolved around the centrality of British and American systems. Although these works were identified as scholarships in comparative politics, in reality, they were specific history of some of the institutions of the West. Given the exclusionary nature of Western scholarship, it does not come as a surprise that these studies did not include the rest of the European democracies as they were seen as quaint and less significant. Other countries counted little, and their working was seen as irrelevant in the grand political analyses and at the most found their mention in folkloristic reporting of their existence. In those times, works in the field were little more than collections of country monographs that left the task of integration and comparison to the baffled reader (Rustow 1957, 536).

Special Insights

Eurocentrism

Eurocentrism has been one of the crucial challenges in the field of comparative politics. Most of the works in this discipline have originated from the scholars of the West, whose point of reference, yardsticks and framework of analysis were firmly rooted in the political systems and processes of Western Europe. It denotes a world view that presumes the superiority and universal applicability of the Western institutions and values. It shows the parochial temperament of the discipline and scholars who constitute it. Because of the Eurocentric bias, comparativists have failed to comprehend the new ways in which states, societies and human beings keep on reconfiguring themselves in contemporary times and throwing up new realities that are way too complex to be understood through the conventional framework.

Soon, however, such parochial proclivities diminished, giving way to development towards more genuine comparative understanding of a rather larger number of countries (Daalder 2011, 20). In the post-Second World War era, the appeal of the all-pervasive British model dwindled in the face of the rising supremacy of the United States. Gradually, young scholars from the other parts of Europe wanted to bring their own countries on the international scene. This brought more and more political systems on the map of comparative politics. Literature grew on cross-Atlantic comparisons, although their yardstick firmly remained British. Three kinds of work emerged in cross-national studies. The first category is denoted by the studies of different countries of Europe that were earlier not a part of the comparative political analysis. The second category of cross-national studies was the works dealing with massive survey analysis that arose in the decade of the 1960s and 1970s. In this league are the works of Almond Powell and Sidney Verba (1963) on political culture, Verba, Nie, and Kim (1978) on political participation, Ronald Inglehart (1977) on changing values, etc. The third type of cross-national analysis was reflected by the works based on social indicator data such as by Flora, Kraus, and Pfenning (1987) on the growth of welfare state and political modernization, etc.

When all the writings produced in the field were analysed, it was found that all the classical comparative literature were predominantly concerned with attainment, maintenance and defence of liberal democracy. Assuming that modernity will lead to democracy, these writings also strongly recommended modernization, either in explicit or in tacit ways. Most of these works were developed on the premise of the division of the world into three distinct categories: (a) modern democratic countries represented by the developed countries of the West, (b) modern non-democratic countries like that of Nazi, Fascist and totalitarian states, and (c) non-modern countries who were amorphous and expected to modernize and develop like the West. However, this categorization became obsolete in the wake of many global events that were neither expected nor could be explained by the scholarship and global discourse of comparative politics. By 1980, all these categories started dissolving as there were no more prototypes of either liberalism or Marxism to be followed by the developing societies as internal crisis started pervading the capitalist and socialist camps. This time onwards, a greater acknowledgement and acceptance of newer assertions and of the diversity of ways of knowing and being started getting noticed. The earlier conventional frameworks of understanding and analysing slowly faded away. The cost of modernity became apparently visible in the wake of environmental destruction and ecological crisis. The ambiguities were accentuated by the wave of postmodernism that left the world with no unequivocal answers or generalized solutions. Though the domain of postmodern theoretical discourse may be slippery and runs the risk of relativism, that may disintegrate into 'anything goes approach'. The world today is marked by fragmentation, heterogeneity and cosmopolitanism. The older forms of participation give way to newer forms of collective action and solidarity. This explains the global support for values such as human rights, peace, environmental concerns, women's rights and gays' rights.

Special Insights

Postmodernism and Comparative Politics

Postmodernism, an intellectual wave of the late 20th century, has hugely impacted all disciplines, including comparative politics. Under its influence, all categories that constituted the discourse of modernity such as homogeneity, universality, uniformity and standardization have increasingly come under fire. Postmodern literature confronts the one-sided, overoptimistic and self-congratulatory tone and tenor of modernist discourses that have so far guided comparative politics. These limitations have given way to the emergence of profound ambivalence about enlightenment project. Stringent critique of the discourse of modernity emanates from several and sometimes unrelated fields. Expressing doubts about the whole question of rationality, Richard Rorty proclaims to adopt what he calls 'frankly ethnocentric' position, stating that every culture is entitled to judge matters of rationality by its own light. Similarly, Alasdair MacIntyre emphasizes the need to look behind all questions of abstract rationality and inquires whose conception of rationality is operative in any situation.

Emphasizing on the positive achievement of this discipline, Charles Boix and Susan Stoke state that from the past few decades, the theory building in comparative politics has shifted from systemic broad explanations of countries to micro-foundations. Rather than developing a grand theory of a system, recent efforts in theorizing in the field tend to prioritize individual's interests, beliefs and context and then predict aggregate outcomes. This, Boix and Stokes believe, is truly a forward step in the discipline. Nevertheless, we still know little about the ways in which political institutions, social practices, norms and arrays of political interests originate and collapse (Boix and Stokes 2007, 21).

1.3 Why Compare?

The origin and development of comparative method is a very old one. Its legacy can be traced from Herodotus and Aristotle to Bodin and Montesquieu. A comparative study of societal phenomenon across countries helps to formulate a general theory about systems and processes that can be verifiable. Comparative approach is preferred as it deepens our knowledge of the political world by explaining the similarities and differences existing in it. It provides a wide range of factors for analysis, immediately widening the scope and accuracy of the study. Many scholars have emphasized the indispensability of comparison in political studies. Hague and Harrop (2013) think that comparison widens our understanding of the political world around us, therefore enabling us to come up with improved classifications, explanations and predictions. Similarly, Judith Bara believes that comparison is indispensable, as researchers cannot make an assertion about a specific feature of an event, institution or form of behaviour without comparing with others. Kenneth Newton and Jan Van Deth (2010, 1) state that the study of comparative politics and government is crucial as it serves three purposes. First, in order to understand our own country well, we must have knowledge of others. Second, we can understand other countries when we know their background, institutions and history. Third, we cannot arrive at valid generalizations about government and politics without the comparative method. Knowledge arising out of comparison assists in understanding, explaining and interpreting varied historical facts and processes for present institutional arrangements (Ragin 1989, 6). Comparative method makes research not only comprehensive but also systematic.

Special Insights

Tools of Analysis: Interests, Identities and Institutions

The primary focus of most of the comparativists remains the study of origin, characteristics and impact of different kinds of governments or 'regime types'. Kopstein and Lichbach (2005) identified three important tools of analysis for political regimes: interests, identities and institutions. People tend to support that political regime which they believe to represent their interest so they organize themselves in political parties, interest groups, trade unions, etc. Identity also determines political regimes and processes. Identities like religion and ethnicity also guide people's interest and political choices, which may be accommodated or rejected by the political order. Institutions and their functioning (parliament, judiciary, political party, elections and political party) are equally determinative of political regimes.

1.4 Methods of Comparison: How and What to Compare?

Among all the writings dealing with the issues, concerns and problems of comparative research method, most useful is the book by Todd Landman *Issues and Methods in Comparative: An Introduction* (2000) in which he discusses all nitty-gritties of comparative research in political science.

1.4.1 Process of Comparative Research

Comparative research is conducted in sequential processes that follow in a line: description, classification, hypothesis testing and prediction. Description provides an introduction of a country, classification helps all the samples to be organized based on certain features, hypothesis testing enables general theorizing by eliminating the rival explanations and ultimately, based on these theories, predictions can be made about future outcomes. The description, which is the first step in the process, must be systematic and appropriate to initiate a great research. Based on the nature of research, the classification may be simple or complex, capturing the greater degree of differentiation of the countries. Then, by hypothesis testing, researchers find explanation of the facts that they have gathered so far by seeing similarities and differences. This helps us to understand and explain the political phenomenon observed around and make inferences about them. These theories or models provide a yardstick to understand and analyse other systems as well. Testing is the stage that enables researchers to propose a general theory capable of providing broad explanations. Generalizations derived from the comparisons of some countries help to predict likely outcomes even for those countries that are not part of the comparison but have an almost similar situation. When this is done, based on the analysis of the targeted information generated so far, predictions are made about the regimes under study.

1.4.2 Levels of Analysis

Basically, there are two levels of analysis: (a) micro or individual level and (b) macro or system level. Przeworski and Teune (1970) explain macro-level research as studies dealing with systems (country or countries or global phenomenon) and micro-level research as those that deal with the intra-system level. Micro-political analysis concentrates on the individual unit of analysis, for example, a leader of a social movement, an important member of a political party and a respondent in a survey. It tries to capture the modes, orientation and aptitudes of individual political units. Contrarily, macro-level analysis focuses on bigger units that operate at a larger scale and cause wider repercussion such as specific communities, social classes and global protest movements.

1.4.3 Quantitative and Qualitative Methods

Quantitative method seeks to show differences in terms of numbers, data generation, interpretation and analysis. It deals with numerical value in terms of the objects of comparison that can be counted. Contrarily, qualitative methods explain the differences in kind. There are so many features of countries that cannot be measured in numbers such as the degree of protection of human rights, kinds of protest movements, nature of social mobilizations, features of political parties and nature of women's participation. They tend to take into account the attributes or different traits of the object of study. As quantitative method generates numerical data, exact facts and figures, it is especially helpful for the government to legislate policies accordingly and to publish the information as gazette and public records. Some examples of quantitative studies are the literacy rate of women, school dropout rates of girls, crimes against elderly and levels of agricultural production.

1.4.4 Kinds of Comparison

1.4.4.1 Comparing Many Countries

The methods of comparison also differ based on the number of countries taken for the study. The method of comparing many countries or sample cases is called **'large-n'** comparisons, where 'n' denotes the number of countries under the study. Comparing a large number of countries has great advantages in terms of having huge information from a wide variety of different conditions necessary for general theory building. This way of taking numerous countries for the study easily shows the general pattern across the countries and at the same time also brackets exceptions. This method was adopted by the behavioural political scientists and political sociologists. Their works tend to unravel broad generalizations based on enormous quantitative information that they generate exploring and explaining issues of political stability and political developments, etc.

Though the large-n comparisons do not spell out the exact number of cases, researchers in this method take more than 20 or 30 countries. The enormous data generated leads to empirical generalization. Some of the works of 'large-n' methods cover a range of countries over time and space and draw firm inference from them. One such example is *Democracy and Development* (2000) by Przeworski and others that compares 150 countries over a span of 40 years, that is, 1950 to 1990. The limitation of this method lies in the fact that it may not be very effective in generating specific information about societies or institutions.

1.4.4.2 Comparing Few Countries

The other way of comparison can be by comparing a small number of countries and is called **'small-n'** comparisons. It basically focuses on selected but detailed study of some features or events in a limited number of countries. This method takes five or six countries under its ambit of study. The goal of this method is to extract targeted information that can help the researcher to explain nuances in the understanding of different systems.

As there are lesser number of countries to be analysed, this method enables researchers to gather contextual evidence and explore complex processes which otherwise is not possible under large-n studies. The extensive study generates humongous country-specific information. It is also called case-oriented approach and provides researchers expertise in the countries studied.

This, however, does not mean that single case studies are less important. In fact, when the political context is very varied, complex and nuanced, a detailed analysis of the case study focusing on intra-system level makes more sense in the comparative analysis. It must be noted that case studies are qualitative works that provide very specific data and the link to reality which is usually missing in quantitative studies comparing a large number of countries.

Special Insights

Way Forward in Methodology

In recent times, there have been many interesting works that provide distinct methodological approaches to engage with the study of politics. Robert Chambers and K. Kar *Handbook of Community-led Total Sanitation* (2008), James C. Scott *Seeing Like a State* (1998) and Elinor Ostrom *Governing the Commons: The Evolution of Institutions for Collective Action* (1990) are example of works that stand out as they incorporate techniques of participatory rural appraisal and are informed by valuable forms of local knowledge and stable local institutional designs in their research.

1.5 Dilemma of Methods and Methodologies

Though it is clear that the general objective of comparativists is to explore similarities and differences among macro/micro-level units, there exist many ambiguities regarding its subject and content. The term comparative politics indicates the 'how' but does not specify the 'what' of analysis, giving rise to some amount of ambiguity in the field (Lijphart 1971, 682). While comparison remains the 'sine qua non' of comparative study, the object of the comparison remains undefined. The task of comparison has its own share of risks and challenges. There are almost always concerns about comparability of cases that are relatively dissimilar. This problem is highlighted by the predicament of comparing apples with oranges. Cross-national demonstrations are also not easy to be established as the variables in social sciences are too complex. The researcher may sometimes find it challenging to engage with non-Western societies for comparison as these are marked by fragmentation, cultural discontinuity and political ambivalence. The politics of these countries is tangled, perplexed, with political interests that are latent and unorganized, and with social and political institutions which, like the state itself, are in a process of gestation (Rustow 1957, 546). Religious, ethnic, gender and caste barriers may impose certain limitations in terms of a lack of appropriate units of comparisons. This state of affair has been a persisting problem for comparative political studies, but by no means is it insurmountable. Despite all the challenges, the discipline of comparative politics has come up with a conceptual framework to impel greater universality, keeping in mind the vastly extended global scale of its empirical investigation in contemporary times.

Comparative study is underpinned by two broad perspectives: (a) universalizing perspective and (b) relativizing perspective. The idea of universalist position implies that certain concepts can be applied everywhere. It presumes that these universal, well-developed frames of references can be used to study all political systems across the globe. However, many scholars contend the idea of universal applicability of the concepts. Concepts may bear different meanings in different cultures. Situational uniqueness, geographical location, local traditions, and so many other factors condition our research. It implies that the politics at a local level acquires special significance in the comparative research or for that matter in any research. This makes it extremely challenging to constitute a general theory of methodology in the discipline; hence, Landman and other scholars in the area think that a general science of comparative politics would be necessarily limited, if not impossible (Landman 2000, 33).

Restricting oneself to one of these two positions of extreme universalism or extreme relativism may defeat the purpose of comparative and empirical research altogether. Therefore, a middle path of synthesizing perspective of moderate universalism and moderate relativism is wisely advised (Van Deth 1998, XV). Cultural specificities of the contexts should be considered as determinative of its politics.

Additional Vignettes

Works like that of Hannah Arendt's *The Origins of Totalitarianism* (1951) was one of the most profound early works that discussed the use of racism as an ideological weapon by the forces of imperialism and colonialism. It examined the totalitarian regimes of Nazism and Stalinism. Needless to say, any honest comparative exploration has to address subjects of culture, racism, sexism, social and ethnic cleavages along with the particularities of the context in which they arise.

Two basic frameworks of comparative methodology (useful for the analysis of few countries) have been proposed by J.S. Mill in his book *A System of Logic* (1843): (a) the Method of Agreement and (b) the Method of Difference.[1] In the Method of Agreement, if the phenomenon is recurrent in two or more cases, then the reason for that phenomenon may be located in the common features of those situations. In other words, the presence or absence of common factors will determine the extent of agreement in the cases of comparison. For example, both India and Canada have been deeply influenced by British traditions, and this similarity might account for existence of democracy in both these nations. Contrarily, in the Method of Difference, there may be similar outcomes in two or more countries when compared, but the cause of those similarities can be traced to different sources or reasons. For example, both China and India are large countries; however, largeness does not account for the prevalence of democracy in India. As we can see, China is larger but not democratic.

These two strategies have been elaborated by Adam Przeworski and Henry Teune in their book *The Logic of Comparative Social Inquiry* (1970) as Most Similar Systems Design (MSSD) and the Most Different Systems Design (MDSD). MSSD is based on Mill's method of difference and compares systems with similar economic, political and cultural characters. In this method of comparison, there are lesser chances of differences to be found. Even if differences are found, they would be minimal and could be easily explained by the researcher as the variable will be limited. For example, it will be easier to compare the Anglo-American nations having a two-party system, due to the apparent similarities of the countries. At the same time, it may not be very comfortable to compare two systems having a number of variations in their systems such as Sweden and Japan. In this method, the focus of inquiry remains the system where the variations within the system are considered as explanatory variables. As the common characteristics are maximal, this method is called maximum strategy. Contrarily, MDSD is based on Mill's method of agreement and offers an alternate strategy of comparison. It takes into account the variations of traits of the subject of study at a level lower than that of a system, for example, of an individual or communities. In this approach, countries having very different traits but sharing a common characteristic (important from the perspective of study) are compared. For example, if we want to select cases for comparison to study democracy, Sweden and India may be chosen. They may be very different systems and have very little in common. However, both are consolidated democracies.

While comparing, the researcher should be mindful of the ways and basis of comparison in order to get a meaningful result. C.E. Black observes that there is greater value in comparing contemporary events and institutions than those that are widely separated in time. Also, the comparison of a smaller number of cases with similar features is more likely to lead to satisfactory conclusions than comparisons between societies existing many centuries apart (Black 1966, 39). In the end, one can conclusively say that every method has its own advantages and disadvantages. It is the task of researchers to be aware of them and adopt a particular method in accordance to the specific requirements of the subject of inquiry. The sample for study has to be carefully chosen depending on the problem of the research.

1.6 Evolution of Comparative Politics

The domain of comparative politics has evolved gradually with different theoretical discoveries and innovations. With changing context and time, it has gone through various phases characterized by the associated dominant approach of that period. It was the post-Second World War period that witnessed the retrenchment of the academic rigour of this sub-discipline, most particularly, under the leadership of David Easton in American Political Science Association. Comparative politics consolidated itself and was able to position as an independent and crucial area of inquiry from this time onwards. A critical account of evolution of the sub-discipline has been produced by Jean Blondel. He classifies it into three phases: the first phase extends till mid-18th century, second phase begins from mid-18th century and ends in 1914, and the third phase starts from 1914 and continues till now (Blondel 1999, 153). It is interesting to note that Klaus von Beyme's classification of comparative politics also resonates with that of Blondel (Von Beyme 2008, 28). He proposes three phases of development of the discipline in the categories of Premodern, Modern and Postmodern, which comes very close to the understanding of Blondel.

In its earliest days, the works in the field of comparative politics engaged with proposing blueprints for organizing societies. The feature of this phase is exemplified by the works of Aristotle and Thomas Aquinas who predominantly employed normative approach in their studies. These scholars laid the early foundation of this discipline. They identified different kinds of political order and produced treatises on the best form of government. Aristotle's classification informed all attempts to study and classify different types of political regimes. In his book *Politics* (Book 3, Chapters 6-7), Aristotle famously proposed the six-fold classification of political regimes where he divided them into monarchy, aristocracy, polity (pure types), oligarchy, democracy and tyranny (perverted types) based on the number of rulers and the quality of rule. For him, monarchy and aristocracy stood for the rule of the best, democracy was undesirable and tyranny intolerable. The works produced in the first phase, or traditional/classical phase, were marked by the predominance of philosophy, history and jurisprudence. Klaus von Beyme (2008) correctly reflects that the pre-modern or classical approach was normative, speculative, impressionistic and mostly ethnocentric. There was no attempt to systematically compare the subject of study and comparison in an anecdotal way. The works tend to produce a categorization of the whole political order, never paying attention to the details and particularities that distinguish one system from the other. Though this phase is thought to have severe limitations, yet the classical political theorists are still very relevant. As Alan R. Ball (1971) points out, the nature of questions raised by these classical thinkers will remain pertinent in all the times to come. Not to miss the fact that the first explorations in the field came from these scholars. Therefore, ignoring them will deprive the students of politics from all the communications and rich narratives available from such legacies. Also, historical enquiry continues to guide the more contemporary works such as that by Alexis de Tocqueville, Max Weber, Gabriel Almond, Seymour Martin Lipset and Theda Skocpol. Their methodologies are deeply informed by historical approach as they arrive to their conclusions by comparing the historical trajectories of different countries. In doing so, they have suggested that the roots of major political outcomes often rest most fundamentally with causal processes in the past. Moreover, they have maintained that to elucidate these causal processes, one must look closely at the unfolding of events over a substantial period.

The second phase or the modern phase is marked by scientific temperament and rigour and produced a meticulous account of political systems and their institutions. Von Beyme (2008) thinks that the works of Machiavelli, Montesquieu, Tocqueville and Mill paved the way for a modern phase. The 20th century witnessed prolific empirical works from a range of scholars. Especially the first half of it saw scholars engaging with different constitutions that had recently proliferated in Europe and America and were considered perfect subjects for the study. These works adopted a legalistic and constitutional framework of analysis as evident in the prominent scholarships of this period such as James Bryce's *Modern Democracies* (1921), Crane Brinton's *Anatomy of Revolution* (1937), Herbert Simon's *Administrative Behaviour* (1947), Herman Finer's *Theory and Practice of Modern Government* (1949), Maurice Duverger's *Political Parties* (1950) and K.C.'s Where *Legislatures* (1963). The decade of the 1950s was characterized by the behavioural movement guided by American scholarship.[2] Works such as David Easton's *The Political System* (1953), Gabriel Almond and James Coleman's *Politics of*

Developing Areas (1960), Gabriel Almond and Sidney Verba's *The Civic Culture* (1963) and Carl J. Friedrich's *Man and His Government: An Empirical Theory of Politics* (1963) further fuelled the quest for larger comparative studies. Behaviouralism gave rise to analytical framework of systems analysis under which countries were understood as political system constituted by the input, processing, output and a feedback loop that allowed the system to maintain a balance. Researchers were encouraged to aggressively seek data, interpret them and spot regularities in order to explain the system. It was believed that the systems analysis was a great breakthrough that aimed at studying the behaviour and functioning of institutions and people.

Unfortunately, despite too much stress on precision and scientific method, comparative politics failed to predict and explain a spate of political events since 1945 that shook the world. Its inability to anticipate the student movement of the 1960s, oil crisis of 1973, disintegration of Soviet Union in 1989, rise of new fundamentalism and such other crises brought a bit of embarrassment to the discipline. Consequently, the focus slowly shifted from the conventional framework of understanding confined to the state and its institutions to include a newer set of variables and determinants of the system like class, culture, race, ethnicity, gender, individual choices, intersectionality and so on. The behavioural phase was rendered as insufficient and therefore led to many new approaches such as modernization and development school, dependency theory, political culture approach and new institutionalism. The 1960s was the decade of modernization, institution building and development projects that held that by embracing development all societies can put their problem to rest. It pleaded that progress can be achieved by imitating all the patterns of development of societies of the West. As evident, the tone and tenor of modernization theory has been heavily ethnocentric. It offered some hope to the aspirations of newly independent countries that someday they might be able to lead modernized lives like that of the West. At the same time, it almost re-entrenched the superiority of the Western discourse of knowledge, somewhat also legitimizing the European colonial ventures and dismissing the emancipatory potential of epistemologies of the Global South. Interesting as it is, negating this overemphasized correlation between development and democracy, Przeworski and his co-authors in their book *Democracy and Development: Political Institutions and Well Being in the World 1950–90* (2000) have forcefully pleaded that development does not cause democratization although it may minimize the chances of democratic breakdown. Still plenty of other analyses continue to emphasize a directly proportional relationship between development and democracy.

It is in reaction to this deeply flawed understanding of world, societies and people that dependency school emerged. This approach had its roots in the non-West and held the pursuit of imperialism and colonialism responsible for inequality, underdevelopment and all other problems of developing societies. It conceptualized the globe to be constituted of two parts: core and periphery. The core is represented by the developed countries of the West whose colonial expeditions have ruined the periphery represented by developing societies. By constantly draining wealth, resources and labour of their colonies, these countries have become prosperous, whereas the developing countries have been exploited, robbed and ruined. This theory provided a good amount of ammunition to the scholars of developing societies to expose how the whole understanding of the world order was unjust and oppressive. However, it did not venture in the nuanced understanding of different variables and contingent factors that shape up political processes in developing countries. The critics drew attention to the replication of dependency syndrome in the peripheries where elite classes and crony capitalists prospered at the cost of poor marginalized sections living far away from cities.

On the other hand, political culture approach shifted the focus on people, their political orientation and attitudes and their set of beliefs and sought to explore how these factors shaped politics and the economy of a country. It took into account the social, psychological and historical accounts of people and the governing elite of a society. Political culture theorists were primarily focused on the question about the conditions that ensure the emergence, continuity and development of democracy. Their scholarship was defined by questions such as 'Individual political beliefs are shaped by what kind factors? What kinds of beliefs are politically important? In what ways political systems are determined by political beliefs? Do historical experience influence people's perception of politics?' (Verba 1980, 409). In order to answer these queries, they established a straight link between people's intrinsic commitment to democratic principles. Gabriel Almond and Sidney Verba in their path-breaking study *The Civic Culture* (1963) discussed the concepts of values, ideas, beliefs, norms, customs and knowledge that provided explanations outside of both Marxist materialism and structural functionalism.

In that sense, it definitely expanded the contours of the discipline of comparative politics, although it has been also been critiqued for overemphasizing stability and the Anglo-Saxon style of democracy. In recent times, Robert D. Putman's *Making Democracy Work* (1993) has renewed the interest in research rooted in civic culture approach, although in a different form. Putnam's work ushered the concept of capital with a completely new meaning that was beyond Marxist understanding of capital in terms of surplus value as well as its conventional association with physical and human capital. He conceptualized capital as 'social' that resides in the woven intricacies of organizational networks, norms and social trusts that enables coordination and cooperation for the benefit and smooth functioning of the whole society.

The third phase or the contemporary phase may also be taken to loosely represent Beyme's postmodern phase. It is characterized by many features, one of them being renewed interest in institutionalism. Neo-institutionalism got popularized by the works of James G. March and Johan P. Olsen, although it is quite different from the old institutionalism. 'The new institutionalism emphasis the relative autonomy of the political institutions, possibilities in efficiency of history, and the importance of symbolic action to an understanding of politics' (March and Olson 1984, 734). This approach brought the focus on institution back to the centre stage. Undoubtedly, the institutions and their functioning deeply influence organizations, associations and people. In present times, institutions have become larger, complex, resourceful and more interconnected; therefore, they are influencing collectives lives like never before. Neo-institutionalists have put the entire focus back on institutions. They capture the dynamics of its actions and interactions with other variables and determinants. Institutions stand for the long nurtured rules and formalization of political process in a society. Concerns with institution will never recede, rather they will magnify. Hence, the necessity to study them in the changed context. The institutions will continue to remain foundational even when different groups continue to fight for institutional designs as institutional matrix determines 'who gets what' of politics. Though the theory of neo-institutionalism is not coherent or complete yet, it has successfully reoriented the political studies towards a nuanced yet comprehensive understanding of institutions. Blondel and Landman believe that comparative politics has entered a new phase of eclecticism in 1990 that is specified by stress on institutions, individuals and cultural dimensions of politics. The significance of culture as the central aspect of comparative studies has been highlighted by ethnographic works like that of Donald Horowitz's *Ethnic Groups in Conflict* (1985). This study discusses how ethnicity can be foundational in shaping and determining all the spheres of institutional politics from party politics to military politics and affirmative actions as in the case of most of the African societies. The politics of Asia and Africa shows that culture is not only the setting but also the central theme of politics and can no more be treated just as a residual category.

1.7 Gendering Comparative Politics

As in any other domain of knowledge, there has been conspicuous absence of gender as a separate category of analysis in comparative politics. The reason for this omission is the very nature of the gendered world that we inhabit. The organization and functioning of a society is based on patriarchal assumptions about the role of men and women in society and politics. These prejudices are then replicated in our political attitudes and behaviour, resulting in gendered outcomes in development programmes and policies. For example, we have exclusive male institutions like military and nearly universal dominance of male actors in governments worldwide (Beckwith 2010, 159). Gender remains so central to the politics of a country and yet is systematically dismissed as a 'not so relevant' variable in the political analysis.

Resonating with the concerns of Judith Squires, who strongly advocates for gendering the study of politics in her work *Gender and Political Theory* (2004), there is a group of scholars in comparative politics, such as Teri L. Caraway, Leslie A. Schwindt-Bayer, Karen Beckwith and others, who plead for gendering comparative politics. All these scholars conceptualize their approach as developing and defining 'comparative politics of gender'. They argue that comparative political research must engage with gender as one of the pertinent tools of analysis. By encouraging a greater integration of gender in the discourse of comparative politics, we will be better equipped to answer questions like: *What is the relationship between women's rights and political stability? Does gender inequality explain the prevalence of dictatorship in the Muslim world? Is gendered leadership responsible for gendered public policy?* At the same time, scholars working in the area of comparative politics of gender also lament over problems they face while working in this framework. For example, they say that while they have wonderful careers, yet their work is seldom cited by scholars who do not work in the area, despite being engaged in similar theoretical debates. These are some of the vexing problems, although not particular to this field only. The challenge is how to make comparative politics take all these challenges in its stride and come up with a more plural and assimilative approach.

1.8 Comparative Politics in Contemporary Times

The text and subtext of politics have transformed drastically as nation states are no more the self-sustaining units that they were in the 17th and 18th centuries. This has happened in the wake of unprecedented changes that have been brought upon the world in the context of decolonization, global entrenchment of capitalism, regional economic integration, ever-changing politics of developing societies and international civil society bodies. After the Second World War, a large number of new countries that were earlier colonies emerged on the world map. These countries were remarkably different compared with the older democracies. Their state formation occurred in a very different environment, and hence, they were bound to diverge from the Western framework. In order to engage with these countries, the discipline needed to discover newer rules and tools of analysis. Similarly, the dissolution of a formidable block like the USSR gave rise to splintered fragile regimes that could not be comprehended by the traditional categories of understanding. All the countries could not be taken as undifferentiated masses. Widespread political changes in these countries need more dynamic framework to make sense of politics and the political system. Also, some of these countries have been marked by a high degree of instability and fluid nature of the state as in case of Somalia, Syria or Afghanistan. Changing structure, forms and features of states mould the nature of engagement in the discipline.

Politics increasingly is being conditioned by transnational forces in contemporary times. Multinational companies and global trade and supranational institutions have been constantly diminishing the power of the nation state. National economies have been sucked into world trading circuits, having very little space to manoeuvre their own interest. As result, the state is left debilitated and constantly negotiating to regain its space and control. There clearly emerges a tussle of power among all these sources of authority that are locked in a game of constant negotiation to draw and redraw their boundaries of power and authority. Therefore, it becomes critical for students of comparative politics to map ways and extent in which such processes of change are affecting the nature and scope of the discipline. Jeff Haynes points to the fact that the comparative political analysis cannot afford to neglect concerns arising from the impact of globalization on states, otherwise the discipline will run the risk of being analytically inadequate (Haynes 2003, 1029). The earlier literature in the field clearly looks uninformed of such changes or it may have failed to fathom the ways and degrees in which these transformations have impacted the political world altogether. Studies in comparative politics have primarily been engaged with conventional categories of analysis in politics such as the state and its institutions. However, in contemporary times, the domestic political-economic terrains of countries are defined hugely by transnational connections. Therefore, it becomes necessary to factor in globalization in all studies. In fact, all dimensions of globalization have to be analysed: technological, political, economic as well as cultural. Globalization has also given rise to asymmetrical distributions of development benefits across the world and within the countries, leading to strong currents of resistance against transnational corporations. On one hand, countries are eagerly getting globalized, and on the other hand, there are anti-globalization movements rampant across the world. Due to accessibility and easy dissemination of information, the grass-roots organizations from around the world have been collaborating to work against development projects that have resulted in grave environmental consequences.

The pertinence of comparative politics has grown all the more in the times when human rights have become an important yardstick to evaluate the efficacy of regimes. This field fits very well with the theory and practice of human rights. Todd Landman in his article on 'Comparative Politics and Human Rights' suggests that the field of comparative politics has much to contribute in this domain of research both in substantive and in methodological ways (Landman 2002, 890). The cross-cultural comparisons of different countries of the world can explicate inferences about determinants and variables that enable better protection and promotion of human rights in some countries while not so in case of other countries. With the rising wave of democratization, there is a more relaxed environment for campaigning, associating and tolerance for voices of dissent. This has also made it easier for people to channelize their demands and aspirations and assert them against the state and its paraphernalia. Therefore, new varieties of social movements sprung up and have been an all-pervasive phenomenon, particularly in postcolonial societies in the decade of the 1970s. These movements create huge ripple effects in the hyper-globalized world, where collective actions are mutually reinforced across porous borders. These are instances where micro-level dynamics may throw a serious challenge for macro-level global institutions such as the World Trade Organization, International Monetary Fund or World Bank. An example of this is the Battle of Seattle in which a massive number of protesters flooded the streets of the United States in a series of protest marches against the policies of economic globalization of the World Trade Organization in 1999. There are globalized protest movements backed by global civil society, which sometimes are held under the aegis of international non-government organizations that facilitate the support and exchange of ideas and projects such as those based on rights advocacy groups, issues of conservation, climate change, etc. In this light, it will be interesting for students of comparative politics to study the relation between social movements and democratic institutions and the conditions in which they supplement democracy or otherwise. Unfortunately, so far comparative research has shied away from the hard core engagements with alternative channels of political engagements, especially the demonstration and protest politics and transnational policy networks.

1.9 Conclusion

It may be observed that to retain its relevance, comparative politics has to constantly reinvent itself by persistent engagements with the variable that keeps on changing with time. Comparativists will always encounter many challenges when they engage in a truly comparative work. There will be differences in political patterns, endemic instabilities of the governments and volatility of institutions and structures, making systematic empirical investigation hard. As Lijphart aptly remarks, a 'conscious thinker' in comparative politics has to realize the limitations of the comparative method, but they should also recognize and take advantage of its possibilities (Lijphart 1971, 685). It becomes pertinent for the discipline to critically engage with all these problems. Also, it must be structurally and methodologically inclusive of categories such as gender, race and ethnicity (along with the conventional ones such as culture, institutions and policies) as critical categories of political analysis. On one hand, researchers must continue to revisit classical traditions to enrich their insights into the working of politics and inspire new works in the field. On the other hand, critical engagements in the discipline must bring forth methodological innovations and contingent tools to facilitate rigorous and profound research. In the backdrop of these far-reaching transformations, we must redefine how we do comparative political analysis.

Keywords

Comparativists
Comparative method
Comparative politics
Comparative government and politics
Cultural ambivalence
Method
Methodology
Residual category
Variables

Review Questions

1. What do you understand by comparative politics? Critically examine its nature and scope.
2. Do you think that act of comparison is the essence of the study of comparative government and politics? Describe some of the methods followed in the discipline and the problems associated with them.
3. Discuss the evolution of comparative politics. Also discuss the state of the discipline in contemporary times.
4. What do you understand by gendering comparative politics? Do you think that integrating gender research into the broader sub-field of comparative politics will make it truly comparative in its approach?

Notes

1. J. S. Mill (1843) in his book *A System of Logic* has proposed five methods of induction for testing causal hypotheses: the method of agreement, the method of difference, the joint method of agreement and difference, method of concomitant variation and method of residue.
2. For detailed analysis of different approaches in the discipline, kindly refer to the chapter 'Approaches to the Study of Comparative Politics' in this volume.

References

Almond, Gabriel, and James Coleman. 1960. *Politics of Developing Areas.* Princeton, NJ: Princeton University Press.

Almond, Gabriel, and Sidney Verba. 1963. *The Civic Culture: Political Attitudes and Democracy in Five Nations*. Princeton, NJ: Princeton University Press.

Arendt, Hannah. 1951. *The Origins of Totalitarianism*. New York: Harcourt, Brace and Co.

Ball, Alan R. 1971. *Modern Politics and Government*. London: Macmillan.

Beckwith, Karen. 2010. A Comparative Politics of Gender Symposium Introduction: Comparative Politics and the Logics of a Comparative Politics of Gender. *Perspectives on Politics* 8: 159–68.

Black, Cyril E. 1966. *The Dynamics of Modernization: A Study in Comparative History*. New York: Harper and Row.

Blondel, Jean. 1999. Then and Now: Comparative Politics. *Political Studies* XLVII: 152–60.

Boix, Charles, and Susan C. Stokes. 2007. *The Oxford Handbook of Comparative Politics*. New York; London: Oxford University Press.

Brinton, Crane. 1937. *The Anatomy of Revolution* (revised edition in 1965). UK: Vintage.

Bryce, James. 1921. *Modern Democracies* (2 Vols). New York: MacMillan.

Chambers, Robert, and K. Kar. 2008 *Handbook of Community-led Total Sanitation*. Brighton: IDS Sussex.

Chilcote, Ronald H. 1994. *Theories of Comparative Politics: Search for a Paradigms Reconsidered.*

Colorado: Westview Press.

_________. 2002. *Comparative Inquiry in Politics and Political Economy: Theories and Issues*. Colorado: Westview Press.

Daalder, Hans. 2011. *State Formation, Parties and Democracy: Studies in Comparative European Politics.* Colchester: ECPR Press.

Duverger, Maurice. 1950. *Les Partis Politiques.* Colin, University of Michigan.

Easton, David. 1953. *The Political System: An Inquiry into the State of Political Science.* New York: Cambridge University Press.

Finer, Herman. 1949. *Theory and Practice of Modern Government*. New York: H. Holt.

Flora, Peter, Franz Kraus, and Winfried Pfenning. 1987. *State, Economy and Society in Western Europe (1815–1975): A Data Handbook in Two Volumes: The Growth of Industrial Societies and Capitalist Economies*. Chicago, IL: St. James Press.

Friedrich, Carl J. 1963. *Man and His Government: An Empirical Theory of Politics.* New York: McGraw-Hill Book Company, Inc.

Hague, Rod, and Martin Harrop. 2013. *Comparative Government and Politics: An Introduction*, 9th edition. London: Palgrave Macmillan.

Haynes, Jeff. 2003. Tracing Connections Between Comparative Politics and Globalisation. *Third World Quarterly* 24: 1029–47.

Horowitz, Donald L. 1985. *Ethnic Groups in Conflict*. Berkeley; London: University of California Press.

Inglehart, Ronald. 1977. *The Silent Revolution: Changing Values and Political Styles Among Western Publics*. Princeton, NJ: Princeton University Press.

Keman, Hans. (Ed.). 2002. *Comparative Democratic Politics: A Guide to Contemporary Theory and Research*. London: SAGE.

Kohli, Atul, Peter Evans, Peter J. Katzenstein, Adam Przeworski, Susanne Hoeber Rudolph, and Theda Skocpol. 1995. The Role of Theory in Comparative Politics: A Symposium. *World Politics* 48: 1–49.

Kopstein, Jeffrey, and Mark Lichbach. (Eds.). 2005. *Comparative Politics: Interests, Identities, and Institutions in a Changing Global Order*, 1–5, 16–36, 253–290. Cambridge: Cambridge University Press.

Landman, Todd. 2000. *Issues and Methods in Comparative: An Introduction*. New York: Routledge.

_____. 2002. Comparative Politics and Human Right. *Human Rights Quarterly* 24: 890–923.

Lichbach, Mark I. 2013. *Democratic Theory and Causal Methodology in Comparative Politics*. New York: Cambridge University Press.

Lichbach, Mark I., and Alan S. Zuckerman. (Eds.). 2013. *Comparative Politics: Rationality, Culture and Structure*. New York: Cambridge University Press.

Lijphart, Arend. 1971. Comparative Politics and Comparative Method. *American Political Science Review* 65(3): 682–93.

March, James G., and Johan P. Olson. 1984. The New Institutionalism: Organizational Factors in Political Life. *The American Political Science Review* 78(3): 734–49.

Newton, Kenneth, and Jan Van Deth. 2010. *Foundations of Comparative Politics*. Cambridge: Cambridge University Press.

Ostrom, Elinor. 1990. *Governing the Commons: The Evolution of Institutions for Collective Action*. New York: Cambridge University Press.

Przeworski, Adam, and Henry Teune. 1970. *The Logic of Comparative Social Inquiry*. New York; London: Wiley-Interscience.

Przeworski, Adam, Michael E. Alvarez, Jose Antonio Cheibub, Limongi Fernando. 2000. *Democracy and Development: Political Institutions and Well-Being in the World, 1950–1990*. Cambridge, New York: Cambridge University Press.

Putman, Robert D. 1993. *Making Democracy Work*. Princeton, NJ: Princeton University Press.

Ragin, Charles C. 1989. *The Comparative Method: Moving Beyond Qualitative and Quantitative Strategies*. Berkeley, Los Angeles, CA: University of California Press.

Roy, Anupama. 2001. Comparative Method and Strategies of Comparison. *Punjab Journal of Politics* XXV(2).

Rustow, Dankwart A. 1957. New Horizons for Comparative Politics. *World Politics* 9(4): 530–49.

Scott, James C. 1998. *Seeing Like a State*. New Haven, CT: Yale University Press.

Simon, Herbert. 1947. *Administrative Behaviour: Study of Decision Making Processes in Administrative* (4th edn. in 1997). New York: The Free Press.

Squires, Judith. 2000. *Gender in Political Theory*. London: Polity Press.

Toulmin, Stephen. 1990. *The Hidden Agenda of Modernity*. New York: University of Chicago Press.

van Deth, Jan W. 1998. *Comparative Politics: The Problem of Equivalence*. London; New York: Routledge.

Verba, Sidney. 1980. *The Civic Culture Revisited: An Analytic Study*. The Little, Brown Series in Comparative Politics. New York: Little, Brown.

Verba, Sidney, Norman H. Nie, and Jae-on Kim. 1978. *Political Participation and Political Equality: A Seven-Nation Comparison*. New York: Cambridge University Press.

Von Beyme, Klaus. 2008. The Evolution of Comparative Politics. In *Comparative Politics*, edited by Daniele Caramani. New York; London: Oxford University Press.

Where, K.C. 1963. *Legislatures*. New York: Oxford University Press.

CHAPTER 2

Challenges to Comparative Government and Politics

Anusha and Shefali Manhas

Reader's Guide

The present chapter is an attempt to address the challenges posed to the discipline of comparative politics since its inception, that is, from the Aristotelian period to the contemporary globalized times. We will study how comparative politics has evolved itself as an independent and robust area of inquiry. The evolution of the field has not been a smooth one, and there have been different kinds of obstacles coming from various quarters such as the behaviouralists, dependency theorists, postcolonialism, postmodernism, eurocentrism and globalization. Nevertheless, it can be observed from the discussions of this chapter that even though comparative politics faced multiple challenges, it was able to sail through them by discovering newer approaches and tools of engagements. It was for these challenges only that comparative politics grew and flourished as an independent and distinct discipline.

2.1 Introduction

The importance of this chapter rests in highlighting the varieties of challenges that have jostled comparative politics from time to time, although the discipline has successfully managed to convert them into new opportunities to regenerate and emerge stronger. As already discussed in the preceding chapter, comparative politics has carefully positioned itself as an autonomous area of inquiry, although it remains very much rooted within the disciplinary boundaries of political science. Yet, it has never shied away from enriching itself by adopting the approaches and methodologies of other disciplines of social sciences like history, philosophy, law, sociology and, more recently, anthropology. The overdependence of comparative politics on some fields like history, philosophy and law in the beginning became the source of great trouble for the discipline. The overdoing of historicism and institutionalism, although must be acknowledged for their contribution to the early development of the field, led to an impending crisis in the later stage. It will be interesting to study how comparative politics has continued to evolve as a discipline by taking all challenges under its stride, overcoming crisis and eventually emerging strong as a discipline.

We will see that the concerns of comparative politics have transformed with changing context and time. The origin of comparative politics has been traced to the Greek political philosophy where the dominant mode of inquiry was not comparative. The classical tradition was preoccupied with how the society should be organized. It is only in the modern times that constitutional rule started to be perceived as the best foundation on which every country should be structured and governed.[1] The ambit of the study that concerned the classical tradition were: What is the best form of government? Who should rule? How many should rule? and so on. For a very long time, comparative politics remained entrapped within this overarching framework engrossed with the conceptualization of the best form of government. However, this 'ought' question had its own limitation. The normative approach could never venture beyond its comfort zone and confront politics 'as it is'. Unfortunately, this framework continued from the Aristotelian times to the beginning of modern world where the 'ought to' question was relegated to the backyard of comparative politics, and fresh attempts were made to capture the politics 'as it is'. The greatest drawback of the traditional approaches remains in its self-imposed confines of historicism, institutionalism and normativism.

The real breakthrough came to the discipline during the behavioural revolution. Under its influence, comparative politics reincarnated itself by adopting scientific approach and answering questions such as what determines the political behaviour of the citizens in a country and how is the voting pattern of one country different from another. The post-second world war period resulted in the reshaping of the global political dynamics. One of the immediate and most important phenomenon it led to was decolonization after which a multitude of newly independent countries jostled for their space in the world map. Comparative politics could not afford to ignore these countries, and yet had no tools to engage with them. The framework that it had employed to study the developed world so far could not work with these underdeveloped societies, as they were very different in all respects.

These developments made comparative politics to halt and ponder upon why the developed world is in the way it is. How can the underdeveloped world follow the path of development; whether it should be the same as that of the developed world or they should carve their own specific and contingent paths, etc. Comparative politics had to face strong critiques for being eurocentric and ethnocentric; further, dependency and postmodern currents left no stone unturned to shake the dominant modes of understanding in the field. For the first time, comparative politics had to grapple with a new perspective offering new lens of looking at things; for instance, dependency theorists raised the relation between the development of colonial countries based upon the underdevelopment of the colonized countries.

Globalization poses a fresh set of challenges to the methodologies of doing comparative politics. Consequently, the discipline had to evolve newer ways of conducting research studying various countries and their concerned issues. At the same time, there has also been a considerable expansion in the field of comparative politics, and comparativists now delve deeper into global issues like terrorism, environmental degradation, human rights violation and global protest movements. This is only a small reflection on the plethora of questions and issues that have concerned the discipline. The point of bringing them out here is only to understand how the field has confronted innumerable questions and challenges that changed with changing times. However, one thing that remained persistent was how comparative politics as a discipline has keenly adopted a comparative and problem-solving approach to the social, economic and political challenges that existed both at the national and international levels.

Even though comparative politics reformed itself with changing times, the evolution of the field was not always a smooth one. Every time there was a paradigm shift[2] in the field, the challenges faced by the subject took a new turn leading to an overhaul in the discipline. This chapter intends to focus on most of the challenges and crises faced by comparative politics. In order to serve the intentions of this chapter, the best way to study these challenges is to explore how every challenge/crisis generated revised methodology, theorizations and understanding. At present, the discipline is defined by these changing contours of the field. Precisely, it is for these challenges and crises that comparative politics has made a mark in the field of social sciences and harbours strong ambitions for fostering a better world.

Now, let us discuss the broad framework of the chapter. The chapter is divided into six broad sections: The first section is 'First Crisis in Comparative Politics: Macridis' Challenge to the Institutional Approach'.

This section first discusses how institutional approach answered the contextual questions that perturbed comparative politics only to make its stand stronger within social sciences. As the context evolved, Macridis questioned the traditional nature of the institutional approach. He brought about a paradigm shift in comparative politics and paved a way for a new set of approaches, theorizations and subject matter that concerned comparative politics.

This has been followed by the second section, namely 'Behavioural Revolution: Comparative Politics Turns Scientific', which talks about how comparative politics as a field revamped itself after the first crisis in response to Macridis' criticism of the traditional approach. It was in this era that the scientific approach (professed by the behavioural revolution) was adopted in almost all fields of social sciences. Scientific methods primarily look out for patterns and regularities that are repetitive, which helps us to predict and generalize the social norms which then become the social facts. As an extension of this phase, modernization theory conceptualized certain patterns and regularities in terms of charting out the development path of different countries. They opined that the developed countries of the West shall lead the path of development that shall have a particular structure and subsequent stages, whose trail the Third World shall follow.

The third section, that is, 'Post-Behavioural Developments: Modernization and Dependency Theories', engages with the challenges put forth by the modernization theory and its rebuttal by dependency theorists primarily emanating from Latin America. By this time, decolonization had reached near completion and postcolonial studies were important to fill in the interstices within such assertions.

Subsequently comes the fourth section that talks about the 'The Emerging Trends and Alternatives in Comparative Politics' and how they put up new challenges for the field with three points of discussions first on neo-institutionalism, second on postcolonial contestations and lastly on postmodern fragmentations. Neo-Institutionalists, by talking about the state, brought back the aspects of institutional approach that were somewhat lost during the behavioural revolution. Postcolonialists directly challenged the conceptualization of developing societies by parameters and perspectives that were thoroughly eurocentric. Postmodernists have challenged the very essence of comparative politics. By questioning the virtue of universalism, with which comparative politics has worked so far, it has decentred the very premises on which the core of this discipline rested.

The fifth section talks about 'Eurocentrism' and how it has been the perennial challenge for comparative politics that unrolls from the phase of institutional studies till the present globalized era. Eurocentrism is ethnocentric and results in mindless model building, crating archetypes and universal frameworks that may fall flat when applied to non-Western societies. One of the major reasons for this was that during the initial phases, comparative politics was primarily studied by the American political scientists. For obvious reasons, their perspective could not be a neutral one, as they thought themselves far superior than the Third World. The reason for this has been conjunctural which is explained later in the chapter.

Lastly, the sixth section engages with the concern about how a globalized world sets up new challenges to comparative politics. Since globalization has changed our very basic perception about the world, viz. the big world has become a 'global village', this has impacted comparative politics to a considerable extent. By this time, the basic categories of analysis of comparative politics, primarily the individual nation state, were meant to work with supra-national entities. Hence, many new actors like NGOs, both domestic and international, along with different kinds of grass-roots struggles emerged with which comparative politics had to deal with.

Now, we will study each section as it lays down the dominant ideas of the concerned phase, along with the challenges emanating out of the combination of the political context of that period and the nature of the discipline. Furthermore, it could be seen that different phases, starting from the 1920s till the present times, also provided comparative politics with the purpose to address the queries and the intent for survival.

2.2 First Crisis in Comparative Politics: Macridis' Challenge to the Institutional Approach

Before we discuss Macridis' challenge to the institutional approach which is taken as a first crisis in comparative politics (Chandhoke 1996, PE3), we shall study that for a long time, comparative politics was struggling to get established as a distinct field of study. The institutionalists played an important role in establishing comparative politics as a field of study by responding to the contextual challenges that had long made this recognition difficult. Now, let us study how institutionalists provided comparative politics with the acknowledgement that was long due.

The institutional approach, often called as the traditional approach, helped comparative politics achieve a distinct identity. Scholars such as Chandhoke and Mohanty are of the opinion that the period of institutionalism which could be traced from the 1920s till almost middle of the 1950s emphasized on the study of formal institutional structures which meant primarily the legal aspects, that is, the powers and functions of the institutions. The institutional approach studied forms of government, types of constitution, roles and functions of political party, legislature, judiciary, etc., of different countries independently or in a comparative perspective.

The institutional approach held its sway in the context of the First World War, European democratization and constitutional reforms happening in the 20th century. Individual countries of Europe and North America were the basic unit of the analysis. As the name suggests, this period of institutionalism emphasized on the study of formal institutional structures which meant primarily the legal aspects, that is, the powers and functions of the institutions, and it was the constitutional rule that was considered the worthiest.

This approach was exemplified in the major works of institutional period by Bryce, Laski, Finer, Barker, Jennings, Wheare and Duverger. They all were the 'institutionalists', as they studied political institutions such as legislature, bureaucracy, judiciary, federal systems, political parties and elections. They did not study factors that brought about economic growth and development in politics. In the words of Neera Chandhoke, 'The confidence in formal political institutions which had been the product of great revolutions such as the glorious revolution in England in 1688 and the French Revolution of 1789 was immense; therefore, analysis was formal' (1996, PE3). So, we could say that the formal legal approach was taken, but it was too narrow. There was a lack of systematic comparisons.

However, with time, Blondel (1999, 154) argues that it was realized that there were countries where the constitutional rule had failed. This made theorists work out the reasons that shook their trust on the constitutional rule. It was then that philosophers such as Tocqueville and Montesquieu said that contingency played a major role in deciding the future of every country. As the contingent conditions for every county differed, the parameters for the success of each country also diverged. So, then, experiences and observation took over mere deductive generalizations which paved the way for behavioural revolution that came much later. During this phase, apart from the state, other related aspects like geography, climate and parties were also taken into consideration.

Thus, this phase paved a way for the establishment of a distinctive subject matter for the discipline. So, it was during this institutional approach that it was realized that comparative politics was a separate discipline which had so many subjects to follow. Comparative politics became a new area of interest among theorists. One of the theorists who found institutional approach deeply problematic was Macridis, whose criticism of the institutional approach catapulted comparative politics far ahead of its times.

Therefore, one may say that it was during this phase that comparative politics could identify itself away from the discipline of political science. This phase also holds importance for the fact that it instigated theorists like Macridis who criticized the traditional approach and catapulted comparative politics far ahead of its times. So, to summarize, we could say that this phase of institutionalism provided comparative politics its own niche within the discourse that was trying to understand politics within and between countries.

However, the focus rested on the First World with an emphasis on the legal and institutional aspects and only on the comparison between the forms of government like whether the presidential form of government was better than the parliamentary form, federal versus unitary systems, and so on. Nevertheless, the institutional approach provided a strong base to comparative politics from where the behavioural revolution picked up, only to make the field more competitive and comprehensive.

Now, let us observe how the institutional approach could not provide comparative politics its due acknowledgement and appreciation, and it was only after Roy C. Macridis' criticism of comparative politics' institutional approach in 1955 that comparative politics underwent a major overhaul, leading to a better positioning as a discipline vis-à-vis political science. From then on, some theorists also agreed that comparative politics could be taken as a separate discipline.

In 1955, in a book entitled *The Study of Comparative Government* Macridis critiqued the traditional approach in comparative politics. Primarily, he pointed five shortcomings in the traditional approach. First, the traditional approach was parochial, as it studied and focused on the European countries. The main countries around which the studies revolved were Great Britain, France, Germany, Switzerland and to a lesser extent the Scandinavian countries. The issue here was that there were no differences or similarities made between these Western countries. They were referred to as having common historical and cultural ideologies with advanced capitalist systems. However, the commonalities were not pointed out and the ideologies were not studied in a proper perspective. The relationship between the ideologies and the institutions was not given its due importance. The non-Western world was studied from the perspective of the Western world. The institutions in the colonial countries were considered secondary and a prototype of the First World.

Second, Macridis said that the traditional approach was descriptive in nature as it only explained how political institutions worked. It was neither analytical nor explanatory, that is, issues related to political culture, political behaviour and the very basic question about why these institutions emerged were not addressed. Third, Macridis held that the traditional approach was formalistic and legalistic. Only institutions like legislature and judiciary were stressed upon, and other factors like interest groups and individuals were not considered. Fourth, Macridis insisted that the traditional approach emphasized on the study of the individual countries and individual cases. There was no comparison across different countries. Finally, Macridis explained that the traditional approach was 'essentially static', as it only talked about legal and institutional aspects. More so, it did not deal with the political changes as in how the state and its institutions would evolve over time and bring about a social change.

For Macridis, the task of the comparative politics is '... raising political questions, illuminating through parallel studies aspects of political behaviour and decision-making, providing us gradually with body of experience and data and sharpening our evaluation of governmental structures and policies'. To this, Macridis added, 'only in the long run could hypothesis be developed and tested, and only then could a scientific outlook in the proper sense of the term be discerned at least as a distant promise' (Macridis 1968, 80).

So, the critique by Macridis was considered as a 'renaissance' in the study of comparative politics by theorists like Samuel P. Huntington. Thereafter, comparative politics moved away from the legalistic-traditional, parochial, descriptive, Eurocentric and formalistic approaches to a more empirical one. In 'The Change to Change: Modernization, Development, and Politics', Samuel P. Huntington writes, 'Not until the mid-1950s did a renaissance in the study of comparative politics get under way. That renaissance began with a concern with modernization and the comparison of modern and traditional political systems. It evolved in the early 1960s into a preoccupation with the concept of political development, approached by way of systems theory, statistical analysis, and comparative history. In the late 1960s, the focus on political development in turn yielded to broader efforts to generate more general theories of political change' (Huntington 1971, 285).

2.3 Behavioural Revolution: Comparative Politics Turns Scientific

After the Second World War (1939–45), it was the behavioural revolution that made the survival stakes for comparative politics really high. Whatever transformations the behaviouralists brought about in the field of social sciences, comparative politics faced the impact in a way that left the critics of the field astounded.[3] Behavioural revolution can be seen as a major threshold in the study of the evolution of comparative politics. Munck (2007, 43) describes the relation between behavioural revolution and comparative politics as follows: 'Behaviouralism in comparative politics, as in other fields of political science, stood for two distinct ideas. One concerned the proper subject matter of comparative politics. In this regard, behaviouralists reacted against a definition of the field that restricted its scope to the formal institutions of government and sought to include a range of informal procedures and behaviours—related to interest groups, political parties, mass communication, political culture, and political socialization—that were seen as key to the functioning of the political system. A second key idea was the need for a scientific approach to theory and methods. Behaviouralists were opposed to what they saw as vague, rarified theory and atheoretical empirics, and argued for systematic theory and empirical testing. Thus, behaviouralists sought to bring about major changes in the established practices of Comparative politics' (Munck 2007).

Munck adds that the scientific vigour, through the abstract systems theory, that held the behavioural revolution was influenced by sociologist Talcott Parsons. Parsons tried to portray the society in terms of ideal typical patterns that moved along a trajectory of 'evolutionary universals' and this patterned trajectory was from an early primitive society to a modern one. Broadly, now, the behavioural revolution made attempts to invent value free and objective social science that could provide universal models through which different countries could be studied. Walton defines behaviouralism as 'the behavior, actions, and acts of individuals—rather than the characteristics of institutions such as legislatures, executives, and judiciaries—and groups in different social setting and explains this behavior as it relates to the political system' (Walton 1985, 2, cited in Wogu, 2013). So, there was a shift from the study of the state and notions of justice, equality and rights, as they were considered to be highly normative and contested in nature. The emphasis was now on what David Easton calls the 'political system'. According to Easton (1962, p. 9, cited in Wogu, 2013), there were eight major tenets of the behavioural revolution:

- Regularities: Discoverable uniformities in political behaviour which can be expressed in theory-like statements
- Verification: Validity of such theory-like statements can be verified
- Techniques: Means for acquiring and interpreting data
- Quantification: Precision in the recording of data
- Values: Objective scientific inquiry has to be value free or value neutral
- Systemization: Close interrelationship between theory and research
- Pure science: Directed towards forging a link between theoretical understanding of politic and application of theory to practical problem-solving
- Integration: Integration of political science with other social sciences

So, the subject matter of analysis was the political system, informal politics, political behaviour, political parties, interest groups, political culture and political socialization. Therefore, we see that there was an attempt at meta-theorizing with the help of approaches put forth by David Easton's 'input-output analysis' and later Almond's 'structural-functionalism'. Along with this, an effort was made to study mid-range theories like studying interest groups, political parties, bureaucracy and military and so on. The methodology adopted during this phase was the empirical and statistical analysis of cross-national units. The studies on comparative politics were primarily carried out in the United States.

So, we see that behaviouralism attended to the changing needs of the polities and the people. Heinz says, 'The behaviouralists' penetration of political science has had the effect of vitalizing and improving the older forms of writing and research. It has had a salutary influence on the quality of all political science' (Eulau 1973, 24–25, cited in Wogu, 2013, 9).

Behaviouralism in comparative politics was also criticized by some as a generalized theory whereby it could not answer specific issues in specific countries. For instance, the failure of democracy, and at times the regimes of totalitarianism, in some postcolonial countries could not be explained, as they did not follow the path of development that the West had ensued. The area specialists found the theories like the systems theory and structural functionalism, put forth during the behavioural revolution, were difficult to be applied, as every country had a contingent history, and these countries could not follow same or similar paths. Scholars like Schmitter also opined that the categories which emerged during behavioural revolution were often abstract, as they were not rooted in the realities of majority part of the world known as the Third World societies.

Precisely, what was happening was that the Western frames of reference were used for comparing the political systems based on Western values. The discipline of comparative politics evolved in terms of its methodology in response to the challenge put by Macridis, although new challenges came up. Blondel states that the universal models given by people like Easton and Almond were not only eurocentric but also worked on abstract categories which had no empirical connotations and hence not operational in terms of comparison. However, we also need to ascertain the contribution of these theories as it helped in the survival of the discipline by giving a global framework for comparative politics at a time when it was near impossible (Blondel 1999, 157).

Therefore, it may be suggested that the behavioural revolution brought about major transformations within comparative politics. It provided comparative politics with its own theory. Answering the ideas put forth by the behavioural revolution, David Easton gave the 'system's theory' and Almond proposed 'structural-functionalism'. All this was under the influence of the scientific vigour that heralded the behavioural revolution. Modernization theories were also the product of the behavioural era. They talked about the stages of development that every country, who is on the path of development, shall follow. This path was a linear one, and the stages shall be same for all. So, now, it was the modernization theories that left comparative politics in the field of challenges. Now, the main challenge for comparative politics was to accommodate the Third World. Modernization theories could not fit well for them; so, now the stage was ready for the new set of debates. In the next section, we shall study how dependency theory confronted the modernization theory.

2.4 Post-Behavioural Developments: Modernization and Dependency Theories

Many theorists from the Third World considered the modernization theories and development theories given by the West as inconsiderate and insensitive. They believed that the thread which runs through the works of this period like that of David Easton, Almond and Coleman and W. W. Rostow graded the political system in a hierarchical way; the Third World countries were believed to be in the primitive stages of development with a traditional political system. It was taken that they were yet to reach the final stages of development/modernity like the Western political system, by following a specific course of action.

Simultaneously, we also need to understand that power defines knowledge, and hence the 'developed/western' countries, that is, the United States, Britain, France and Germany ruled over the area of knowledge creation and modes of knowing. Therefore, the ruling political agenda of the theorists was to maintain the Western supremacy of political, economic and social institutions while dismissing the same of the non-Western world as unscientific, irrational, indigenous and so on. The tendency was to put the non-European world in a bucket of myths, traditions and superstitious practices which was downgraded and rendered worthless.

Therefore, we see that the modernization theorists were trying to frame universal models of development intending to fit the newly independent countries on the Western path of development. However, then, interestingly, the larger political canvas was witnessing youth uprisings, anti-war movements in the West, the cultural revolution of China, United Nations conferences on nation building, and so on. Even though some of the scholars who wanted to study them couldn't do so for the lack of framework to map them.

Elaborating further, the process of decolonization resulted in the overhauling of the erstwhile existing structures and deeply impacted upon the process of democratization taken up by these newly independent countries. Most of the countries of Asia and Africa were going through tremendous transformations. Gradually, even though in most postcolonial societies, constitutional governments and democratic institutions were established (though sometimes propped by the powerful nations of the world), military coup recurrently challenged their stabilities. Many of these countries unfortunately fell into different kinds of autocracies, especially in the African continent. This also raised a debate over the question of suitability of democracy as the form of government for such societies. Though, later on, we see an apparent wave of revival of democracies in many of these societies in the decade of the 1990s and onwards.

Also, these modernization theories had no explanation for the unexpected happenings, as they believed that the model of development should have been followed in a smooth and persuasive way. It was then held that generalizations or theory propositions cannot be done on the basis of study of the attitudes of only the Western world. There was a severe attack on the metanarratives. Both the subject matter and methodology hitherto adopted by modernization and political development theories were being challenged. They questioned the latter's methodology as being predisposed and flawed. This is because of the fact that colonialism and its aftermath were totally ignored by modernization and political development theorists.

Thus, with this kind of awareness arising in the Third World, the challenge before the discipline was to deal with the 'universal-particular dilemma' as worded by Manoranjan Mohanty. The sensitivity to the Third World was meant to expand the ambit of comparisons so that we do not just arrive at similarities and dissimilarities but to 'discover relationships' (Mohanty 1975, 26). Gradually, there emerged an understanding that the term development itself had different meanings in different societies. In other words, we could say that analysis was getting sensitized towards localized understanding. This gave a major challenge to the Eurocentric base of comparative politics. Thus, the postcolonial identity which was being shaped by non-Western scholars were creating new challenges for comparative politics.

Then, we had the emergence of dependency theorists in the mid-1960s who questioned the theories of the West. Some of these Latin American intellectuals who questioned the political development/underdevelopment in the context of colonial and semi-colonial countries were A.G. Frank, Samir Amin, Paul A. Baran and F.H. Cardoso. Andre Gunder Frank in his work 'The Development of Underdevelopment' talked about the relationship between 'metropolis' (developed areas) and 'satellites' (peripheral areas) in terms of how surplus is extracted from the satellites to the metropolis leading to the further polarization between the two. He says, 'these relations are an essential part of the capitalist system on a world scale as whole' (Frank 1972, 3). So, for Frank, underdevelopment is a 'world historical process' that results in development and underdevelopment at the same time.

One of the founders of dependency theory, Theotonio Dos Santos, describes dependence as 'a situation in which the economy of certain countries is conditioned by the development and expansion of another economy to which the former is subjected' (Santos 1970, 231–36, cited in Chilcote 1957). These theorists brought on the surface the argument that the colonialism practised by the First/European World had resulted in the underdevelopment of the societies of Asia, Africa and Latin America. The dependency school clubbed and defined them as the 'third world'.

Therefore, we see that the dependency theory provided comparative politics with a distinct enriched perspective. However, though the school of dependency brought sensitivity to the field, it was simultaneously accompanied by a problem. The clubbing together of all these societies as Third World somewhere brought insensitivity to the particular/peculiar trajectories of colonialism suffered by these countries.

2.5 Emerging Trends and Alternatives in Comparative Politics

Behavioural revolution was a good learning experience for the comparative politics. Since then, the subject has attracted various theorists working on the issues related to the subject of comparative politics. However, it had to face strong critiques for just being scientific and not addressing other issues like the state, state-society relations and political institutions. The new questions were on matters like state formation and revolution, varieties of authoritarianism and democracy, democratic breakdown, etc.

2.5.1 Neo-institutionalism: The State Is Back

The post-behavioural approach attempted to fill up the vacuums left by the behaviouralist revolution. It revived the relationship between institutions and political actors. The subject of study for comparative politics during this phase was the state and the state-society relations, formal political institutions and political behaviour. This was also known as the neo-institutional approach, as comparative analysis went back to political roots and emphasized upon political institutions.

It was now that the theories of the state were given their due importance. '*Bringing the state back in*' became a rallying cry in comparative politics (Skocpol 1985, 3–37). State was seen as an active agent that reshaped the societies; for instance, it was observed that in Asian countries like Japan and Singapore, the state had brought about changes. The behavioural approach had failed to engage with the political changes which post-behaviouralism tried to accommodate.

However, one has to keep in mind what B. Guy Peters points out, 'Institutions, however, do not act—the individuals within them act, so we need to understand how institutions and individuals interact in making decisions. Some individuals who may be very successful in some political settings would not be so in others' (Peters 2014). Peters explains his point by giving an example as to how the policies of Margaret Thatcher were successful in Britain but not in Scandinavian countries and in countries like Canada.

2.5.2 Postcolonial Contestations

The period of the 1950s onwards saw a proliferation of works that may be categorized as belonging to postcolonial literature. Basically, two different kinds of work are seen under this current first, the kind of works that emanated from the Western scholars who reflected upon the subject of colonialism and various kinds of impact it leaves on the colonized state and its masses. In other words, this kind of work is the Westerner's account of non-West. Second, there are works that explicate the meticulous account of colonialism from the perspective of the colonized. It is this kind of work that produces the alternate understanding of the West from the perspective of the non-Westerners. Notable in this league are the works by Gayatri Chakraborty Spivak, Homi Bhabha, Dipesh Chakrabarty and others.

What is interesting from the point of comparative politics here is that till now the discipline had comfortably set its parameters and created its framework of analysis that was typically based on the Westerners' views of the world, including the postcolonial world. The postcolonial literature made the researchers in the field of comparative politics aware of the requirements of different sensibilities and approaches to understand the politics and societies of such nations. In this way, any such intellectual current that presented a different understanding of the world posed a challenge for the discipline of comparative politics. In that sense, postcolonialism poses a similar set of challenge to the discipline as that by postmodernism which is equally or more so about decentring and anti-foundationalism.

However, on one hand, whereas these theories shook the base of comparative politics, leaving it baffled and grappling with the fluidity of ideas and understandings, at the same time, it created a ripple effect resulting in the changing of paradigms and creating a much higher level of tolerance for diversity in the area. For example, all the postcolonial societies who were typically identified as perversions or deviances or failed experiments of democracies were now started to be seen as distinct societies with their own particularities that needed to be studied thoroughly rather than ridiculed. In this way, these theories go a long way in making the discipline much more wide and accommodative of diversities of understandings and conceptualization.

2.5.3 Postmodern Fragmentation

Klaus Von Beyme writes, 'Thinking in fragments, as advocated by many postmodern theories, made the controlled comparison of Classical Modernity no longer possible' (Beyme 2008, 12). With the writings of Michael Foucault, Herbert Marcuse, Francois Lyotard, Luce Irigaray, Jacques Derrida, Richard Rorty, etc., a new vocabulary emerged. The most important within the emerging ideas was the delegitimization of grand theories or the metanarratives. It should be noted that this was seen for the first time, though, earlier, dependency theories had questioned the European tinge of universal categories, but their (dependency theories) own analysis was based upon categories as development, nation state, colonialism, and so on.

The postmodern thinkers argued that there are no transcendental theories or truths, instead there are shifting truths which are purely conjunctural in nature. Thus, the metatheories or the foundational theories were dismissed by these scholars; what emerged now was discourse analysis, that is, a set of power relations which produce meanings and knowledge systems. Henceforth, the universal theories which dwell upon a fundamental understanding of the social and political world were being interrogated. The world was taken in a state of flux, and the fluidity of human subjectivity was given prominence.

From the end of the 1970s, a major emphasis was placed upon sensitivity to specificities, in terms of banal forms of lives, where space and time both became important. As a result, localized forms of resistance, social movements, cultural assertions and right to land and resources or we could say right to 'commons' like air, water, and so on came into prominence. Therefore, an attempt was made to resurrect those ways of life/ knowledge systems which were diffused or scattered and not necessarily tied into the overall larger logic of the term development.

The scholarship which was emerging by now had a tendency to emphasize upon plurality of political processes and rejection of universal generalizations/uniformities. This gave a major jolt to the field of comparative politics. Hitherto, comparative politics was meant to look for commonalities rather than differences. However, now, the plurality of time and space assumed an important role. The issues like social movements including the grass-roots struggles challenged both the meaning of development and also the unit of analysis that is the nation state. The right to culture brought an understanding that cultures are different and not inferior or superior. Henceforth, the vocabulary of comparison started talking about cultures rather than countries.

The tendency to question 'totalizing categories' like modernization, development and nation state along with 'grand theories' posed a major challenge to the field. It was held that these categories had different meanings and relevance in different cultures, so it was raised that these categories cannot be applied universally. Further, it was considered unfair to look for uniformities across cultures based on these categories which had European origin. This in a way challenged the 'cognitive schemes' of the subject.

The postmodern phase turned out to be a major challenge for comparative politics as the entire established modes of comparing or the categories of comparison were turned upside down. The new lens of knowledge explained that differences, pluralism and fragmentation are important; and henceforth, the basic premise of the discipline was shaken. There were two things simultaneously happening, first there was a challenge to the western gaze of doing comparative theory and also to the hitherto meanings attached to the notions of modernity, development, progress and justice. Second, along with the challenge, varied meanings were being given to these notions in the non-western world Henceforth, the parameters of comparison became very diverse.

So we could say that comparative politics hitherto was working in a homogenizing and disciplinary framework had to deal with new dimensions. In a way, we could also say that this has further led the discipline to evolve and become rich by expanding on their levels of comparison.

2.6 Eurocentrism: All Time Pervading Challenge

The heading of this section shows clearly that Eurocentrism is not a new challenge, rather it has been there since the traditional approach of comparative politics. However, the recognition of Eurocentrism as a problem occurred much later.

A very basic understanding says that scholars who challenge the Eurocentric biasness of this field raise the issues of denial of agency and history to the non-Western world and that the West here basically means the United States, the United Kingdom, France and Germany. Stuart Hall says that eurocentrism has been used to mean 'putting Europe at the centre of things'. He explains that empirically if we see then Europe has been the primary centre of political and intellectual activities since the colonial times; however, the problem of eurocentrism arises when we attach superior values to the European ideas (Hall and Gieben 1992, 326). The basic premise of the challenges to Eurocentrism has been in terms of why/how far could the West provide models to understand development and values of non-Western nations. Are not the social base, political and cultural context of the non-western world relevant?

Eurocentrism could be seen, in order to start with, as a set of thoughts which challenge the superiority of the 'west' which over time has tried to dictate various forms of knowledge systems. It could be explained that an eternal West was created and this West also created an artificial 'other'. However, we need to understand that the Eurocentric mode of analysis was also a product of particular time, that is, it was conjunctural.

Along with this, we need to make it clear that there are no binaries like eurocentric and indigenous. So, while challenging the eurocentric framework, we cannot throw away the baby with the bathwater, that is, there are multiple strands within European theory and thoughts, which are different from the 'hegemonic eurocentic ideas' which provide the framework of cultural imperialism. The manifestations of eurocentrism are myriad; they could be seen in different disciplines, theories, and in fact in day-to-day relationships. So, what is problematic is the hegemonic prevalence of European ideas and not European ideas per se (Deshpande 2011, 87).

The entire understanding is made to dwell on the perception that the West is a place of perfection which encompasses values of equality, justice tolerance, democracy and so on, and if the other parts of the world want to develop, they would have to imitate this path. In the European ideas, for instance, models of political rule and governance and political systems are assumed to be 'superior' as Europe is considered the 'makers of history'.[4] The more problematic aspect is that the path laid down by the West for the non-West has to be followed by the latter and this is considered the 'natural/logical' way.

The traditional scholars of comparative politics, who were studying the powers and functions of the institutions, were basically rooted in the Anglo-American tradition. Their works were primarily aimed at providing models to the non-Western world, being completely oblivious to the social, political and economic situations in the non-Western world. This problem was catered by the new comparativists of the behavioural era, who held that the traditional way of doing comparative politics was parochial in nature and that the theorists should strive for a value free understanding of politics.

However, under the garb developing of value free notions of doing politics, again, the framework for comparisons was based upon the experiences of the Western world. Modernization and development theorists as discussed above were once again designing the path upon which the non-Western world had to walk. Thus, the universal categories of comparative analysis were based upon a complete ignorance of the history and culture of the non-Western world.

Comparative politics came into terms with the challenge of eurocentrism with the coming of the dependency theorists when for the first time it was recognized that the study of the postcolonial countries must take into account the fact that colonialism has affected the social, political and economic conditioning of those societies. So, it was held that these societies couldn't be abstracted from these layers.

Henceforth, from the 1970s onwards, myriad efforts were made to expand the ambit of comparative politics by encompassing various voices and identities and not just the Western ones. The sections on postmodernism and globalization discussed above illustrate direct and indirect ways through which eurocentrism was addressed in comparative politics.

2.7 Globalization and the Challenge for Comparative Politics

Webber and Smith notes, 'one of the most common descriptive labels of world politics in recent years has been that of transformation' (2002). This statement is loaded with many meanings, and one important factor for this transformation has been the phenomenon of globalization which has compelled comparative politics to take into account new actors which are primarily non-state.

With the advent of the 1990s, a new perspective was taking shape which was creating new vocabulary for understanding this field. As a result, old patterns and definitions within comparative politics were redefined to comprehend the existing scenario within and between countries.

Till the time of the post-behavioural revolution, the categories, unit of analysis, and the ways of studying were nearly fixed. For instance, the state was studied in terms of its nationality, population, territory, culture, democratization, etc. and the society was studied in relation to the state, political culture and behaviour. Hence, for major reasons in comparative politics, a comparative perspective was appropriated to understand the world which was primarily understood as a Westphalian model. However, by the 1990s, there was an 'expansion and intensification of all kinds of social relations across borders: economic, political, cultural, and so on', which Sorensen defines as globalization, which became a major challenge for comparative politics in contemporary times (Sorensen 2008, 606).

The explanation offered by Jeff Haynes (2003) could be employed to understand the growing interconnections between globalization and comparative politics. For this purpose, he lists five 'far-reaching processes of change' which altered the way of doing comparative politics.

First, there has been the emergence of many new countries. For instance, the member states of the United Nations today stands at 195. Second, we also need to account that these new nations have emerged amidst widespread political changes like decolonization, disintegration of the Union of Soviet Socialist Republic (USSR), and new wave of democratization in Latin America, East Asia and Europe. Third, with the growing influence of capitalism, the control of transnational corporations like Microsoft, Macdonald and Shell also increased. So, what we have now is a very important non-state actor, that is, transnational corporations which have been affecting the domestic politics in a significant way. The fourth process was the emergence of regional entities based upon the integration of different nation states such as the European Union, North

American Free Trade Agreement, South Asian Association for Regional Cooperation (SAARC), and The Association of Southeast Asian Nations (ASEAN) and the fifth process was the coming of transnational civil society like increasing regional economic integration and the growth of transnational political institutions[5] have also affected the domestic politics in major ways. The crux being that many actors have mushroomed in the globalized world.

As a result, the process of globalization is rapidly transforming contemporary societies whereby national boundaries have become open and interdependent on each other. It has led to the increase in trade in goods and services. It has brought about efficiency in the ways of living and the norms of social living have become intelligible to citizens of different nations.

Hence, in this era of globalization, we might say that governments have to face trivial and complex issues like accommodation of various identities, and granting them rights including citizenship rights. Along with this, there are various questions regarding to the economic growth and how the economies of the various countries are inextricably linked through the market, how economic trends in one country impact the other; there are also tensions between the states with regards to the distribution of natural resources like water, clean air, etc.

There also exists north-south divide between countries with regard to climate change, environment, diseases and epidemics; terrorism is a recurrent threat to all countries in the present times. There are global associations like the Greenpeace, National Rifle Association; there are various social movements that run across countries like feminist movement, LGBT movements, anti-nuclear movement, etc. So, we can say that now comparative politics has to deal with myriad actors, the state-centric approach has been completely decentred.

So, when the world becomes the global village, what should be the framework for the discipline? Do we need grand narratives or should we identify it with the heterogeneous particularities of each country?

Now, comparative politics is not restricted to politics from above like that of government and other power holders; but it is also politics from 'below' and politics from 'outside' like various social movements such as the World Trade Organization. In this context, we could also mention Wiarda who argues that in the changed context of state-society relations, comparative politics needs to study 'lower level' topics like public opinion, electoral behaviour, electoral strategies and so on (Wiarda 1998, 946).

2.8 Conclusion

Summing up the above given analysis, it would be apt to say that 'comparative politics has come full circle' as used by Todd Landman. He has described the discipline as showing an 'eclectic progressive' development where it evolved by encompassing major political, economic and social developments (Landman 2008, 302).

Therefore, we could say that interrogation in terms of both field of enquiry and its epistemology should be made a regular exercise so that the challenges faced by the discipline do not become a crisis. Broadly, we could say that getting sensitive to localities does not undermine the comparative method; what it dismiss is the comparison based on grand theories which works on the basis of inferiority and superiority. What we need is to redefine the way we compare and how to interpret the comparison.

The proposal is to make the theory of comparative study relevant to the changing times, in all the sense, that is, in terms of overall as well as context-specific political, social and cultural transformation and also to the new vocabulary getting evolved in terms of categories of analysis. Precisely, the need of the hour is to have a 'democratic' way of comparison. It would be apt to mention Cornel West and Bill Brown (1993) here, where they say that particularism should not be treated in opposition to universalism, rather the parameters of both should be combined to counter eurocentrism. Other scholars such as Stef Craps (2014) suggest 'cross cultural ethical engagement', where it is implied that the vocabulary of anyone, that is, modernist or indigenous framework can't be totally accepted or rejected, rather specificities should be open to 'diverse representations'.

Keywords

Behaviouralism
Comparative politics
Dependency
Eurocentrism
Globalization
Institutionalism
Post-behaviouralism
Postmodernism
Postcolonialism

Review Questions

1. How does eurocentrism pose a severe limitation to the field of comparative politics?
2. Describe the ways in which the discipline of comparative politics has addressed the contemporary challenges in the globalized world.
3. Discuss the development of comparative politics since the first major challenge labelled by Roy C. Macridis in 1955.
4. How have the major confrontations to comparative politics helped in the evolution of the subject? Illustrate with examples.

Notes

1. In fact, the classical tradition that talks about the first comparative study could be traced back to Aristotle, when he studied 158 constitutions, mainly from the Greek city-states, where he held that mixed constitution is the best form. He gave the classificatory basis for governments. Later, in the Roman period, Cicero and Polybius also employed comparative method in their understanding of political systems. However, by and large, it could be seen that studies were not comparative, rather there were in-depth analyses of countries.
2. This has been used in the Kuhnian sense, where he defines paradigm as a set of beliefs and concepts which define the methods and possibilities of the scientific community's perspective (Chilcote 2000: 31).
3. It was during the behavioural revolution that Macridis had critiqued the institutional approach.
4. An understanding has been made to prevail that Europeans are the most advanced in terms of history and that they have a civilization starting from the state of nature to modern times, and this belief makes them rate the non-Europeans as inferior and those who have to imitate the West to become modern. There are many literature which have dealt with the explanation that how Europeans have portrayed themselves as superior. See Amin (2009: 165–87). Also see Quijano and Ennis (2000).
5. They are of two kinds: one is international governmental organizations like the UN, WTO and OPEC and the other kind is international non-governmental organizations like Amnesty International, Red Cross and Greenpeace (Heynes 2003, 1029–31).

References

Amin, Samir. 2009. *The Culture of Capitalism, Eurocentrism, Modernity, Religion and Democracy: A Critique of Eurocentrism and Culturalism*. New York: Monthly Review Press.
Blondel, Jean. 1999. Then and Now: Comparative politics. *Political Studies* XLVII: 152–60.
Chandhoke, Neera. 1996. Limits of Comparative Politics. *Economic and Political Weekly* 31(4): PE2–8.
Chilcote, Ronald H. 1978. A Question of Dependency. *Latin American Research Review* 13 (2): 57.
———. 2000. *Comparative Inquiry in Politics and Political Economy, Theories and Issues*. Boulder: Westview Press.

Craps, Stef. 2014. Beyond Eurocentrism, Trauma Theory in the Global Age. In *The Future of Trauma Theory: Contemporary Literary and Cultural Criticism*, edited by Gert Buelens, Sam Durrant, and Robert Eaglestone, 45–61. Abingdon: Routledge.

Deshpande, Anirudh. 2011. Eurocentric Versus Indigenous. *Economic and Political Weekly* XLVI(30): 87–88.

Frank, Andre Gunder. 1972. The Development of Underdevelopment. In *Dependence and Underdevelopment*, edited by James D. Cockcroft, Andre Gunder Frank, and Dale Johnson. New York: Anchor Books.

Hall, Stuart, and Bram Gieben. 1992. *Formations of Modernity*. UK: Polity Press.

Haynes, Jeff. 2003. Tracing Connections between Comparative Politics and Globalisation. *Third World Quarterly* 24(6): 1027–47.

Huntington, Samuel P. 1971. The Change to Change: Modernization, Development, and Politics. *Comparative Politics* 3(3): 283–322.

Indian Political Science Association. 1976. New Dimensions in Comparative politics. *The Indian Journal of Political Science* 37(2): 116–21.

Landman, Todd. 2008. New Challenges for Comparative Politics. In *Issues and Methods in Comparative Politics (An Introduction)*. New York: Routledge.

Macridis, Roy C. 1968. Comparative Politics and the Study of Government: A Search for Focus. *Comparative Politics* 1(1): 79–90.

———. 1992. Major Characteristics of the Traditional Approach. In *Approaches to the Study of Political Science*, edited by Susser Bernard, 16–26. New York: Macmillan.

———. 2017. Comparative Politics and the Study of Government: The Search for Focus. In *Analyzing the Third World: Essays from Comparative Politics*, edited by Norman Provizer. New York: Routledge.

Mohanty, Manoranjan. 1975. Comparative Political Theory and Third World Sensitivity. *Teaching Politics,* vols. 1 and 2: 22–37.

Munck, Gerardo L. 2007. The Past and Present of Comparative Politics. In *Passion, Craft, and Method in Comparative Politics,* edited by Gerardo L. Munck and Richard Synder. Baltimore: The John Hopkins University Press.

Newton, Kenneth, and Jan W. Van Deth. 2010. *Foundations of Comparative Politics*, 2nd edition. Cambridge: Cambridge University Press.

Peters, B. Guy. 2014. Approaches in Comparative politics, in Daniele Caramani (ed.), *Comparative Politics.* Oxford: Oxford University Press (p. 43).

Quijano, Anibal, and Michael Ennis. 2000. Coloniality of Power, Eurocentrism, and Latin America. *Project Muse* 1: 542–43.

Skocpol, Theda.1985. Bringing the State Back In-Strategies of Analysis in Current Research, in P. Evans. D. Rueschemeyer and T. Skocpol (eds), *Bringing the State Back in.* New York: Cambridge University Press.

Shogien, Takashi. 2016. Dialogue, Eurocentrism and Comparative Political Theory: A View from Cross Cultural Intellectual History. *Journal of the History of Ideas* 77(2): 323–33. Accessed from http://www. academia.edu on September 11, 2023.

Sodaro, Michael J. 2001. *Comparative Politics: A Global Introduction.* New York: McGraw Hill.

Sorensen, Georg. 2008. Globalization and the Nation State. In *Comparative Politics*, edited by Daniele Caramani. New York: Oxford University Press.

von Beyme, Klaus. 2008. The Historical Development of Comparative Politics. In *Comparative Politics*, edited by Daniele Caramani. New York: Oxford University Press.

Webber, Mark, and Michael Smith. 2002. Problems and Issues in Foreign Policy Analysis. In *Foreign Policy in a Transformed World*, edited by Mark Webber and Michael Smith, 9–28. Harlow: Pearson Education.

West, Cornel, and Bill Brown. 1993. Beyond Eurocentrism and Multiculturalism. *Modern Philology* 90: S142–6.

Wiarda, Howard. 1998. Is Comparative Politics Dead? Rethinking the Field in the Post-Cold War Era. *Third World Quarterly* 5: 935–49.

Wogu, Ikedinachi Ayodele Power. 2013. Behaviouralism as an Approach to Contemporary Political Analysis. *International Journal of Education and Research* 1 (12, December): 4.

CHAPTER 3

Approaches to the Study of Comparative Politics

Skylab Sahu

Reader's Guide

An approach provides a particular direction or an angle to study politics in a comparative setting. This chapter analyses different approaches used to understand comparative politics and the importance of diverse approaches to study comparative politics. Two types of approaches, that is, traditional and modern, are used to study comparative politics. Philosophical, historical and legal approaches are some traditional approaches which remained predominant in the field of enquiry till the Second World War. New approaches such as system, structural–functional, behavioural, political–cultural and the new institutional approach became popular after the end of the Second World War.The traditional institutional approach placed the centrality of values, institutions and law in understanding comparative politics. On the contrary, modern approaches considered that the institutions no longer implicitly identified with the organizational structure, instead the focus of analysis moved towards the rules, norms, culture, individual behaviour and so on. It is also necessary to understand that no single approach is sacrosanct and instead all the approaches, both traditional and modern, have their own strengths and weaknesses. In such cases, the appropriate applicability of any approach or combination of approaches such as a 'triangulation' depends on the scholar's choice for the selected study.

3.1 Introduction

Comparative politics is concerned with studying and analysing political systems in a comparative way. In simple forms, scholars argue that comparative politics is not defined by the object of its study but by the method it applies to study the political phenomena (Lijphart 1971, 9). As a discipline, comparative politics has a long and prominent history that dates back to ancient Greece and especially to Aristotle who compared different forms of government.[1] Comparing the similarities and dissimilarities between the political phenomena across countries enables social scientists to understand if and how the experiences of some states are similar to that of others and to assess, for instance, whether the theoretical models of decision-making or the institutional practices have any universal applicability. The study of the individual countries as case studies has certain shortcomings in its approach, which comparative politics overcomes pertinently. Various approaches could be employed to study the political processes and institutions of various countries in a comparative manner. An approach is like an anchor or viewpoint or a way of thinking that provides tools to understand, analyse, evaluate and compare the subject of study. An approach trains a researcher to engage with the subject matter in a specific way, thereby enabling her/him to acquire a deeper and nuanced understanding of it. Various approaches used in the study of comparative politics can be seen as falling into two categories: traditional and the modern or the new approaches.

This chapter discusses the importance of the approach in the study of comparative politics. It analyses different approaches used by scholars to understand comparative politics. It focuses in detail on both traditional approaches and new or modern approaches. In the process, a critical analysis of the approaches is made to know both the advantages and disadvantages. It will enable the students now and in the future to use any approach in an appropriate way.

3.2 Traditional Approaches

The origin of the traditional approach is as old as the origin of the study of politics itself. Among traditional approaches, the philosophical, historical–legal and institutional approaches are well recognized. These approaches have been crucial in the field of enquiry till the Second World War and then subsequently lost their vigour. The normative approach represents a traditional tendency, dating to times before philosophy was separated from politics. The normative approach represents a traditional tendency, dating to times before philosophy was separated from politics. It looks for desirable cultural values in society and emphasizes norms in the form of rules or rights and obligations that are considered desirable. For example, an American political scientist would argue that democracy is premised on shared values looking for compromises, bargaining and consensus and not on the divisive values (Chilcote 2000).

3.2.1 Philosophical Approaches

This approach is one of the oldest, and its presence could be located in the writings of Plato, Hobbes, Marx and many others. The philosophy is the study of the science of truths or principles underlying all knowledge and being. Philosophical approach tries to explore the truth of political incidents or events. It also aims at discovering the objective of the writings and the purpose of writers. It is distinctly normative and ideological in nature and aims at building certain norms and universal standards. However, it strives to study the consequences of political events in a logical manner. For instance, while having an ideal state in mind, Plato prescribed concepts such as philosopher's king, communism of family and so on. The predominant ideas shaping this approach are justice, equality, liberty and the idea of the good. It follows the deductive method and there is acceptance for the researcher's own values and judgement. Scholars, who study from the philosophical point of view, intend to weave norms into the theory which is expected to be realized in practice. For example, Plato's advocacy of the philosopher king, Hobbesian faith in absolute monarchy, Lockian belief in constitutionalism and Marxian dream of communism apparently show a prominent streak of philosophical underpinnings in their works.

Many eminent scholars of the 20th century such as Laski and Barker worked in this frame while engaging with concepts such as equality, liberty, rights, justice and political obligation at great length. The strength of the approach lies in its intention of making an in-depth study of political phenomena and examining them impartially. It also follows the procedure of a logical analysis. However, this approach met with scathing criticism for being highly normative, descriptive and prescriptive. The works rooted solely in this tradition were idealist theories, which might feed the quest for discussion, but they remain far removed from ground realities. For example, pragmatists believed that Platonic conception appears more like utopia than a solid framework to structure, organize and actualize politics. The approach got a setback during the behavioural revolution.

3.2.2 Historical approaches

This approach emerged towards the last quarter of the 19th century. Some scholars believed that the study of the historical background of institutions and political phenomena would provide them with close and better insights of their working. It is important to know the historical context as the time, place and context in which the political phenomenon emerges explains lot many things about it. Theorists such as Machiavelli and Sabine viewed that politics should have a historical viewpoint. History explains the past political events and also links it with the present. Without studying the past, understanding of the present would remain largely incomplete. There are scholars who study the origin and the growth of political institutions in historical perspectives.

The historical approach to the study of politics has numerous challenges. One of the major challenges is to get proper documentation of the facts. There is a need to be careful in analysing and interpreting facts which may not be presented chronologically. Alan Ball has criticized the historical approach stating that 'the past evidence does leave alarming gaps, and political history is often simply recorded of great events, rather than a comprehensive account of total political activity' (Ball 1988). Very few historians interpret historical events and evidence broadly and freely.

3.2.3 Traditional Institutional Approaches

The first systematic thinking about political life was concerned with the question of the nature of governing institutions. The origin of this approach can be dated back to Aristotle, who came up with the classification of different types of governments such as monarchies, aristocracies and democracies and also tried to figure out the best form of government. Most interestingly, he had analysed 158 constitutions of the world. Institutions are important because they form such a large part of the political landscape and because the modern governance system is largely dependent on institutions (Roy 2001). Up to the middle of the 18th century, the main approach was normative and largely philosophical in sense. Montesquieu combined the legalistic and constitutional approaches as essential components of the traditional institutional approach which remained a dominant discourse up to the First World War (Blondel 1999, 27). They raised important questions about institutions and their goals. The major criteria of analysis concentrated around formal aspects of government, its various organs, rules or laws they followed, etc. The first generation of analysts of the constitutions were concerned mostly with the theories or principles of institutions and thus remained more deductive and normative. While in the later stage, scholars also became analytical and inductive, focusing how constitutional laws were implemented in practice.[2] Tocqueville was the first scholar to emphasize upon both theory and practice; he experimented this mixture of the approaches while engaging with American and European governments.

Comparative politics as a separate sub-discipline focusing on the study of institutions provided a new meaning through the works of James Bryce and A.L. Lowell, M. Ostrogorski, Mosca and Michels in the late 19th century. Bryce and Lowell focused on both the study of constitutions, that is, theory of governments, and actual practices of governments. While the first part required the study of documents and norms, the second part required the discovery and collection of facts or data. The usage and emphasis on facts appeared to be paramount in their approach. While disproving a critique coming from political systems, theorist David Easton, about hyper-factualism of the institutional approach, Bryce stated that any statement or argument without the backing of facts is mere speculation. Refuting the charge of hyper-factualism, the institutionalists held that contrary to a belief in an overload of facts, the real problem facing the discipline of comparative politics is the paucity of facts about many countries in the world, such as the Third World and the then communist countries. This search for data or facts led Bryce and Lowell to adopt quantitative methods, while balancing it with the use of qualitative method. They argued that any conclusion has to be supported both by qualitative assessment and quantitative data. Further, responding to a charge of legalism due to the emphasis that the institutional approach places on the study of laws and constitutions, it was asserted that laws too are facts, which are necessary to develop any theory. Furthermore, laws and constitutions should be crucial aspects of the study.

In addition, a few scholars mentioned that parties that were not mentioned in the constitutions were more important and significant in shaping the characters of politics. In 1902, Ostrogorski published a comparative study of political parties in Britain and America.

3.2.3.1 Features and Limitations of the Traditional Institutional Approaches

Looking at the works under the framework of the institutional approach, one can figure out an obvious pattern giving rise to some crucial concerns. As is evident, this approach is concerned with laws and constitutions. The traditional institutional approach places the centrality of law in understanding politics and society. It believes that political behaviour of actors is determined by government institutions and structures solely. It failed to realize that political processes are very dynamic and two-way in the sense that the state and its institutions are as much influenced by its people and other variables of the society as the state influences them. Under this approach, scholars studied institutions in the context of their historical development. Thus, for example, the British parliament would be studied through a detailed discussion of its historical evolution and would not be limited just to its present form and functions.

The limitations of this approach became more explicit in the light of Roy C. Macridis (1991) expressing dissatisfaction with the works done in the field of comparative politics. He complained that comparative study done in the traditional institutional way was comparative only in name and was more aptly a study of foreign governments focusing on governmental structures and formal organizations of state institutions. In addition, the approach primarily studied Western countries. The limited reach of such works prevented students from knowing about non-Western societies that were politically and culturally distinct from the West.

These works remained essentially descriptive; as discussions were conducted at length on formal political institutions of various Western countries, it was never clarified what prompted the choice of particular countries for comparison and not others. Further, while similarities and dissimilarities were highlighted, what factors possibly accounted for such similarities and differences were never examined.

Such descriptive studies were done mainly through two typical approaches: historical and legalistic. The historical approach traces the historical origin and growth of institutions and assumes that parallel historical accounts of institutions in different countries would indicate similarities and differences. The legalistic approach assumes that studying the formal-legal or constitutional powers of various branches of governments and their relationship with each other in the context of various countries is sufficient to call it a comparative study. Such studies do not attempt to examine the forces that influence and shape laws. Due to such preoccupation with formal-legal aspects of government structures, however, the approach loses a sophisticated awareness of the informal arrangements of society, which influence political behaviour and processes of decision-making to a great extent.

Traditional institutionalism remained essentially static. The traditional approach, Macridis claimed, had ignored dynamic factors which explain growth and change in a political system. Even when growth of new political institutions was studied, they were studied in terms of their 'political anatomy', that is, in terms of their legal status and configurations, and no consideration was given to changes that they caused to the organization of political power.

Starting from the 1930s to 1960s, the traditional institutional approach faced critique from various circles. While the need to expand the discipline to encourage studies of non- Western societies was seen as crucial, the influence of the behavioural revolution in the social sciences also pushed the scholars of comparative politics to develop a scientific method showing regular and predictable patterns of behaviour. Out of such dissatisfactions with the traditional institutional approach, strong need was felt to develop new approaches based on scientific method in the field of comparative politics.

3.3 Modern Approaches

The end of the Second World War brought several changes as the many countries of Asia, Africa and Middle East were decolonized and became new subject matter for study. With the expansion of the horizon of comparative politics, scholars felt that traditional approaches were inadequate to capture the complexities and nuances of political institutions and processes. This gave rise to many new approaches, which became popular, such as systems approach, structural-functional approach, behavioural approach, political cultural approach and the new institutional approach.

3.3.1 System Approach

In the post-1950s period, the need to study the politics of non-West was emphasized. This needed alternative frameworks that could capture new developments in the field such as 'modernization', decolonization, 'liberation', 'political development' and so on. This was the time that behavioural revolution heralded a new paradigm in social sciences. Behaviouralism claimed the possibility of prediction of behaviour of political actors in an objective and quantitative manner. The attempt was to model social sciences after natural sciences. The behavioural revolution brought in a clear departure in the field of comparative politics from the earlier study of constitutional and institutional structures (Pye 1966). The political systems approach has been identified with two patterns: the first one known as systems theory[3] is marked by the seminal contributions of David Easton and his followers such as Karl Deutch, Morton Kaplan and Herbert Spiro. The second one is known as structural functionalism, which resulted from the works of anthropologists Malinowski, Radcliffe-Brown, sociologist Talcot Parsons and political scientists Arthur Bentley and David Truman. Gabriel Almond brought together the divergent flows within the structural-functional theories and significantly contributed to the discipline of comparative politics.

David Easton developed the concept of a political system which he elaborated in his works *The Political System* (1953), *A Framework for Political Analysis* (1965a) and *A Systems Analysis of Political Life* (1965b). This approach stresses the need of studying the political system as a whole, thus making processes, policies and environment the major components of analysis. A political system operates within the social environment, so it will not be possible to understand the political events in isolation from other aspects of the society. System is composed of smaller units which are interconnected and interdependent. Scholars advocating systems approach assumed that, like in the animate environment, in the realm of the social or political too, there are many systems, each of which is made up of smaller systems and is in turn a part of a larger system. Easton proposed an understanding of political system in terms of input–output analysis; certain input in the form of demand and support is made that gets processed in the political system, and the output is produced in the form of policies. Support to the political system is expressed through various means such as voting, paying taxes, taking part in political life, taking part in wars and publishing public documents. Easton also identifies a 'feedback loop' operating between the political system and its environment to maintain its stability (Figure 3.1).

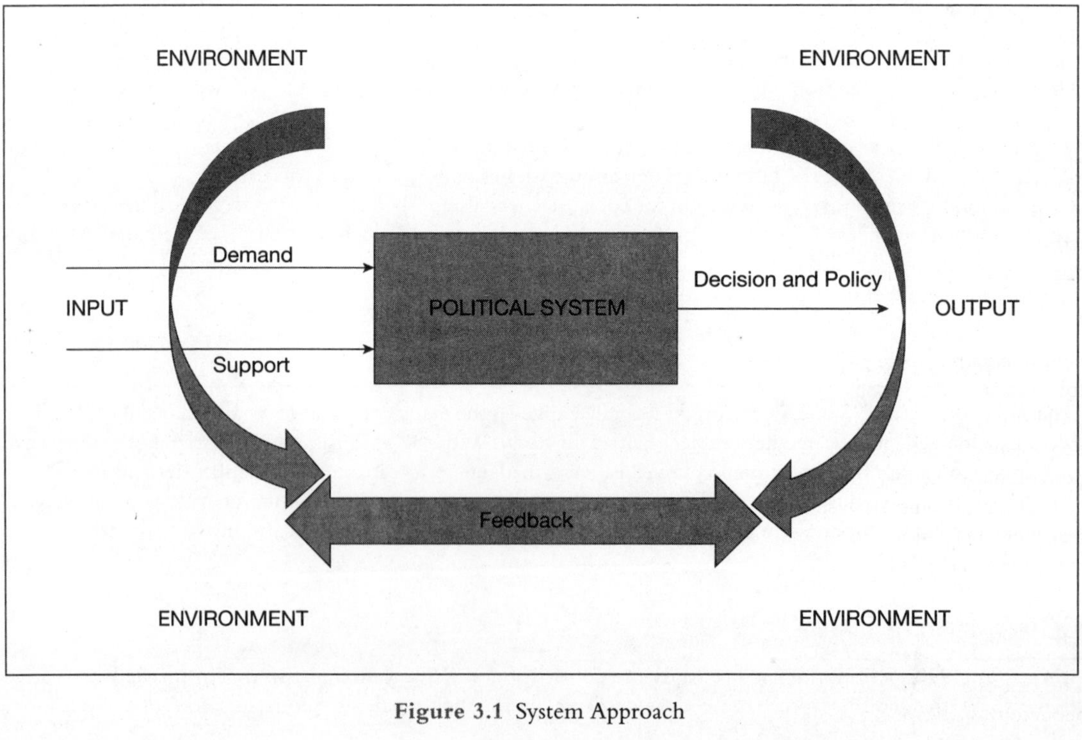

Figure 3.1 System Approach

However, the Systems Analysis faces many criticisms. It may not be able to capture empirical reality and other broader political aspects of the system. Behaviouralism has been unable to understand perceptions, expectations, formation and cognition of political actors. Further, other critics point out that it is impossible to understand political phenomena merely by looking at the present interactions between the system and its environment and by totally ignoring the past. Only the study of the evolution of a system and its historical strengths and weaknesses can tell us whether an event in the present is an urgent crisis or has a recurrent pattern. Input–output analysis has also little to say about the crisis in the political system, politics of decline, disruption and breakdown of the political system.

3.3.2 Structural–Functional Analysis

The most comprehensive formulations of the structural–functional approach in comparative politics are seen in the works of Gabriel Almond, G.B. Powell and James C. Coleman. On the first look, the structural–functional approach looks very similar to systems analysis: both focus on analysing inputs and outputs and both talk about maintaining equilibrium and the crucial role of feedback. There, however, is a small but crucial difference between these two variants of political systems approach. While the systems analysis focuses on the degree and nature of interactions between the environment and political system to explain the working of a political system, the structural–functional theory places emphasis on the specific nature of the structures and institutions and their functions in explaining political reality.

Almond, in the first phase of his work, rather than focusing on concepts of institution or organization, emphasized on the role and structure. Role signified the interacting units of the system, whereas structure represented the patterns in which interaction took place. Almond also introduced the concept of political culture, which later came to be identified as a separate approach to study comparative politics.

Structural-functionalists ask which structures perform what functions in a political system. In this way, they want to explain discrepancies between developed and developing countries. They point to the comparative lack of structural differentiation and the paucity of functional complexity, on the part of some states vis-à-vis others.

If a political system is 'developed', that is, if it is characterized by sufficient degrees of structural specialization and an ability to foster and expand political participation, then it can survive, whereas other systems crumble and fall. In the 1960s, Almond and Coleman were the first scholars to compare the political systems of 'developing' areas systematically according to a common set of categories.

Most of the criticisms of the structural–functional approach are same as those of systems theory. Easton's approach was overly concerned with equilibrium and avoided situations of stress, contradiction and conflict that generally characterize the 'normal' conditions of the modern state. Like Easton's theory, structural functionalism too is accused of having a conservative bias, as it merely describes what exists and what enables to maintain the existing rather than saying what ought to be. This is seen as a status quo in position. Though the political systems approach claims to bring in the non- Western world into the ambit of comparative studies, its framework has been more suitable to understand the democratic systems of the West only (Easton 1996).

The structural–functional approach was followed by the emergence of modernization theory that projected a common path of political development and institution building based on the model of the developed world to be followed by the developing societies. Then there was the emergence of the dependency school that challenged the proposition of modernization theory and its inherent Eurocentric superiority. However, the theoretical framework dependency also had its own limitations. Yet, it could provide an understanding from the perspective of the postcolonial societies.

This is the time that also saw the coming of the new school of thought that started analysing societies within the framework of political culture. The most contemporary of all approaches is the new institutional approach. The following sections are going to analyse the political culture and new institutional debates in detail.

3.4 Political Culture Approach

The rise of interest in the studies of political culture in the political studies is associated with the rise of the behavioural movement. Political culture has been defined by several scholars.[4] Gabriel Almond and Sidney

Verba defined 'political culture as the pattern of orientations to political objects among the member of the nation' (1963). By political objects, Almond and Verba meant institutions such as parliament and political parties. Political culture has been used as a conceptual umbrella that wraps around values, perceptions and beliefs, dealing with every political phenomenon. Political culture approach emerged out of the need, emphasized especially by Almond, to deepening and broadening the scope of political explanation. The goal of political culture was to explain the diversity among and continuity within states. The origins of the modern political and cultural analyses can be related to the political culture and political development. Political culture has also adopted a psychologist or individualist approach, for example, the Civic Culture by Almond and Verba (1963).

Special Insights

Political Culture: An Alternative Ideology

To understand why these revolutions did not take place in the Western capitalists states, one of the reasons was that the capitalists states could accommodate several demands of the working class adequately through welfare measures and in the process could pacify the potential revolutionary working class and could prevent the fall of capitalism. In the process, the capitalist regimes built consent for their ideology. The intellectual leadership helps in establishing the hegemony in state and civil society rather than coercive police or military which could help in the persistence of capitalist relations of production. Althusser in similar ways believed that the state survives through two key components: the repressive and the ideological state apparatuses. The ideological state apparatus works ideologically through religion, education, family, law, politics, trade unions, communications and culture (Althusser 1970).

Edmund Burke in his work *Reflection on the Revolution in France* (1982) stated that political culture has been essentially helpful to understand the regime stability and the structure of beliefs, values and traditions in any given time. It is believed that the political culture filters our perception, influences our attitude and has a large say in the extent and manner of our political participation. The civic culture was an extensive survey carried out in 1959 in five countries—the United Sates, the United Kingdom, Italy and Federal Republic of Germany and Mexico. The study intended to understand and gather data about people's opinion and understanding on political issues, their awareness about the political leadership, political discourse and so on. Based on the knowledge and opinion, the conclusion about the nature of the political culture was drawn. On the basis of the data, Almond and Verba identified three types of individual and collective political culture, and they are *parochial*, *subject* and *participant*. A *parochial* political culture was characterized by general ignorance about the political subject, and it also indicates a lack of involvement in the political activity. *Subject* political culture characterized widespread knowledge about political processes but disinterest of individuals to participate in the political processes. *Participant* political culture combined knowledge about politics, with a willingness of individuals to participate in political processes.[5] However, Almond and Verba argued that the best sort of political culture for a stable democratic system would involve a mix of subject and participant elements, and they named this mixture as *civic culture*. In this background of analysis, they concluded that the United States and Britain in their view had democratic political culture and stability as against Germany, Italy and Mexico.

Ronald Inglehart is one of the major contributors to the political culture approach. Inglehart tries to operationalize culture through levels of what he calls 'civic culture'. Civic culture refers to a coherent syndrome of satisfaction in personal life, political satisfaction, interpersonal trust and support for existing social order. In his 'The Renaissance of Political Culture', Inglehart hypothesized that societies that ranked high on this syndrome are much likelier to be stable democracies than those that ranked low. He also argues that the politics of different societies is characterized by durable cultural orientations that have major political and economic consequences which are closely linked to the viability of democracy (Inglehart 1988).[6] He found that 'wealthier nations and those with highly developed tertiary sectors are most likely to be long-established democracies, and the publics of these societies tend to show "civic" political culture, have less materialist values priorities'.

Special Insights

A Postmodern Approach to Study the Political Culture

The postmodern cultural analysis of politics critiques the behavioural political analysis. In cultural analysis, for example, interests are contextually and intersubjectively defined, and the strategies used to pursue them are viewed as context dependent. Narratives, stories, if one prefers that individuals and groups recount to make sense of their social and political world are grounded in interpretations held by people and groups, their motivations and events they experienced are central to the cultural analysis (Ross 2009b).

3.4.1 A Critique of Civic Culture

The *civic culture* of Almond and Verba receives several oppositions from different scholars. Lijphart stated that merely a consensual political culture may not ensure a strong democracy within a state. Rather, the institutional support could ensure the effective governance of societies that were divided in religious, ideological, linguistic, cultural and ethnic lines. This form of democracy was levelled as consociational democracy. Carole Pateman (1971) also argued that culture and structure are independent and are mutually interdependent and reinforcing. Hence, it is difficult to measure the political culture and the level of stability. Most importantly, the criticism by Kavanagh stated that the notion of the *civic culture* provides a false assumption of having a national political culture which is more or less homogeneous in nature. Actually, the *civic culture* is the probable coexistence of a range of subgroups within any given country.

Dennis Kavanagh (1972) identified four distinct bases on which *subculture* could be developed. They are (1) elite versus mass culture, (2) cultural divisions within elites, (3) generational subcultures and (4) social structure. The elite versus mass culture shows the attitudinal difference which might obtain between the political class as a whole and the reminder of the population. The second strand states that subculture is associated with the branch of elites which could also be divergent in nature. Political culture is also associated with dynamism, and the third categorization of the subculture indicates that political culture changes over time as particular generations become socialized into distinctive values or sets, reach political maturity and eventually die out to be replaced by a new generational political culture. Finally, there is much to be said for the approach which understands subculture as derivatives of a nation's social structure. This indicates that political subcultures are attitudinal expressions of the various classes, religious, linguistic and ethnic divisions which characterize any country.

Special Insights

The American political scientist Samuel Huntington (1993) in his article 'The Clash of Civilisations' argued that cultural differences are likely to be at the heart of future global conflicts. In this respect, Confucianism as a value system represents one of the most profound challenges to the ideological hegemony of the West. However, Huntington argues further that these alternatives will also collide with each other.

3.4.2 Limitations of Political Culture Approach

The political culture approach, like other approaches, faces conceptual problems. Scholars within have not reached a compromise in defining 'culture'. In 'Political Culture and Political Preferences', David Latin criticizes Wildavsky's definition of culture as 'shared values legitimating social practices' (Latin 1986). Latin argues that by focusing only on shared values, Wildavsky misses the point that people with strongly opposed views can share a culture and people with strongly similar views may come from different cultures. Latin proposes that we should see culture not as values that are upheld but rather as 'point of concern'. Latin argues that to share a culture means to share a religion, language or history. As one can assume, if the difficulties in reaching a common definition of culture are great, its operationalization is even greater.

Some of the weaknesses of this approach are (a) the conceptualization and operationalization of the concept is difficult, as discussed earlier, (b) there is inability to draw a clear distinction between subcultures and the overall political culture and (c) the inability to bridge the inferences made on the individual level to the state or system level.

Cultural approaches are less clear about exactly what domains of politics to examine, and there is even less of a consensus concerning the methods and tools to employ. Lichbach distinguishes between subjective and intersubjective views of culture—the subjective emphasizes how individuals internalize individual values and attitudes that become the object of study, while the intersubjective focuses on the shared meanings and identities that constitute the symbolic, expressive and interpretive part of social life. Cultural contributions to political analysis are relatively rare and far less developed. Few graduate students take culture very seriously, and if one peruses the annual list of dissertations in comparative politics over several years, it is difficult to place cultural analyses in the trinity of comparative politics, as the editors of this volume have done.

However, there are some strengths of the approach as well. One of the greatest strength of this approach is its potential to correct the rational choice theory conceptual flaw of not being able to identify the range of human goals. Marc Howard Ross is an advocate of the political culture approach, and he points out two features of culture relevant to comparative politics. First, people use culture to define meaning; second, culture is the foundation of social and political identity which affects individual behaviour.

3.5 New Institutional Approach

In the past 25 years, the field of comparative politics has experienced the emergence of the 'new institutionalism', which developed in reaction to the behavioural perspectives that exercise a significant influence on the field during the 1960s and 1970s. There are several scholars who have taken an 'institutionalist' approach which treat institutions as independent variables. It is argued that institutions have shaped political behaviour and social change. The institutions no longer implicitly identified with the organizational structure, instead the focus of analysis moved towards the rules and norms. In the 1970s, the environments of the organization were seen as critical and important in understanding the dynamics of any organization (Abrutyn and Turner 2011; Hannan and Freeman 1977). The new institutionalism is especially popular among the scholars of US politics since the late 1980s. More specifically, the new institutionalism is also about how the behaviour of political actors is shaped and conditioned by the institutional contexts in which they operate. Institutions also matter because they typically exercise power and mobilize institutional resources in political struggles and governance of relationships. Institutions are also important because they are seen as shaping and constraining political behaviour and decision-making and even the perceptions and powers of political actors in a wide range of ways. Therefore, students of politics have analysed several institutions such as party systems, the rules of electoral competition, government bureaucracies, parliaments, constitutions, the judicial system as well as large institutional complexes made up of the government and the gamut of public institutions that is called the 'state' (Bell and Head 1994). There have also been studies of 'non-state' institutions such as business corporations and trade unions. There have also been extensive studies of supranational institutional complexes such as the United Nations, the European Union and other international institutional regimes that help regulate economic relations, the environment or international trade and health, for example, the World Trade Organization, World Health Organization, and so on. The new institutional approach also has been increasingly applied in the analysis of politics in developing countries (Rakner and Randall 2000).

The perspectives on new institutionalism also discuss about 'hard' and 'soft' institutions. March and Olsen (2011) argued that under specific conditions actors behave according to the 'logic of appropriateness'. Institutions are seen as emerging within a particular sociocultural environment, and can be labelled as 'soft institutions' or 'social facts' (ideas, principled beliefs, social facts). It is often found that actors obey the rules set by soft institutions in the absence of legally binding rules. They often paradoxically accept and follow some norms and cultures such as administrative culture and co-operation on the one hand and some universally accepted norms such as human rights norms, environmental and labour standards and so on the other hand. Wiener (2006) has argued as stated by John Meyer that the types of public administration, constitutional practices, educational institutions, welfare state policies related to education or health and even the role of particular branches of defence ministries were taken in the diverse domestic context of a number of states despite an absence of a plausible necessity for the implementation of these norms and practices.

While new institutionalisms continue to produce useful insights, some scholars such as Abrutyn and Turner (2011) believe that older conceptualizations of institutional domains, like those provided by early functionalisms such as Herbert Spencer and Emile Durkheim, or by more modern-day functionalisms, like Talcott Parsons and Niklas Luhmann, and more current evolutionary approaches, such as those developed by Gerhard Lenski, Jonathan Turner and others, need to be reintroduced. The old institutionalism still has much to offer the new institutionalism because even those organizational analyses have a more general macro-conception of institutions.

The new institutionalism body can be divided into three analytical approaches: historical institutionalism, rational choice institutionalism and sociological institutionalism. These three theoretical islands developed independently from each other.

3.5.1 Historical Institutionalism

Historical institutionalism developed in the influence of the group theories of politics and structural functionalism prominent in political science during the 1960s and 1970s.[7] It borrowed from both approaches but aimed to go beyond them. The historical institutionalists define institutions as the formal or informal procedures, routines, norms and conventions embedded in the organizational structure of the polity or political economy. They can range from the rules of a constitutional order or the standard operating procedures of a bureaucracy to the conventions governing trade union behaviour. In general, historical institutionalists associate institutions with organizations and the rules or conventions promulgated by formal organization (Bell 1992). The historical institutionalist methodology is inductive, not deductive (Hay and Wincott 1998; Thelen and Steinmo 1992). Therefore, empirical investigations, through repeated observation, are the preferred strategy for inquiry. The re-emergence of the institutionalist tradition, for example, is well demonstrated in the current debate about government's proper role in promoting civil rights. The civil rights movement made a fundamentally institutionalist claim on American society where democratic political and economic ideals predominate and one chooses on the basis of merit, not on irrelevant criteria such as race (Blumstein 1981).

3.5.1.1 Characteristics and Weaknesses of the Approach

One could identify four features. First, historical institutionalists tend to conceptualize the relationship between institutions and individual behaviour in relatively broad terms. Second, they emphasize the asymmetries of power associated with the operation and development of institutions. Third, they tend to have a view of institutional development that emphasizes path dependence and unintended consequences. Fourth, they are especially concerned to integrate institutional analysis with the contribution that other kinds of factors, such as ideas, can make to political outcomes. Let us elaborate briefly on each of these points.

The actions of individuals working in the institutions shape the institutional outcomes. The assumption is that individuals seek to maximize the attainment of a set of goals given by a specific preference function and, in doing so, behave strategically, which is to say that they canvass all possible options to select those conferring maximum benefit.

Institutions provide moral or rational outlines for interpretation and action. The individual is seen as an entity deeply imbricated in a world of institutions, composed of symbols, scripts and routines, which provide the filters for interpretation, of both the situation and self, out of which a course of action is constructed. Not only do institutions provide strategically useful information, they also affect the very identities, self-images and preferences of actors.

All institutional studies have a direct association to power relations. But historical institutionalists were concerned to the way in which institutions distribute power unevenly across social groups. They are more likely to assume a world in which institutions give some groups or interests disproportionate access to the decision-making process, and, rather than emphasize the degree to which an outcome makes everyone better off, they tend to stress how some groups lose while others win. Steinmo (2008), for instance, explains cross-national differences in tax policy largely by showing the way in which political institutions structure the kinds of social interests represented in the policy process.

The historical institutionalists are also closely associated with a distinctive perspective on historical development. Institutions are seen as relatively persistent features of the historical landscape and one of the central factors pushing historical development. They have been strong advocates of an image of social causation that is 'path dependent' in the sense that it rejects the traditional claim that the same operative forces will generate the same results everywhere. They not only focus on the historical evolutions of the institutions but also take into account some abrupt historical cleavages or emergence situations. Many historical institutionalists also divide the flow of historical events into periods of continuity interrupted by 'critical junctures', that is, moments when substantial institutional change takes place, thereby creating a historical development moves onto a new path.

Special Insights

Case of Public Policy Applications of Institutionalism

A *policy network* can be defined as a *structured pattern of interaction* between the key actors in a given public policy arena, be it health policy, economic policy or whatever. Typically, the key actors in question are state actors (politicians and key bureaucrats) and non-state actors (business leaders, unionists, interest group leaders, etc.) who bargain and wield power and resources in patterns of policy contest and compromise. As such, a policy network—as a structured pattern of interaction between policy actors—is not an institution but a set of behaviours between actors. For our purposes, the critical thing about a policy network is that such interactions and behaviour are strongly influenced by *institutional* factors. These factors typically involve the nature of the state in a given policy arena and the institutional and organizational capacities of the major non-state actors or organizations in question. For example, in Australia—mainly because of our liberal political traditions—most policy arenas are characterized by 'pressure pluralist' policy networks. The institutional factors which typically underpin such a pattern of interaction include: the state was liberal and democratic and non-state sector was also fragmented with multiple groups and associations displaying relatively weak internal leadership and organizational capacities.

Although they draw attention to the role of institutions in political life, historical institutionalists rarely insist that institutions are the only causal force in politics. They seek to locate institutions in a causal chain that accommodates the influence of other factors, notably socioeconomic development and the diffusion of ideas. The historical institutionalists have been especially attentive to the relationship between institutions and ideas or beliefs. Goldstein (1993), for instance, shows how the institutional structure devised for making trade policy in the United States tends to reinforce the impact of certain ideas about trade while undermining others.

A few weaknesses of the approach include 'path dependence' claims that history matters. It believes that everything has cause, and sometimes different causes in history may lead to different outcomes. The concept 'path dependence', in the economic sense, could be subjective because it involves the judgement of the researcher in determining which historical cleavages had an effect on the outcome, thus it could not be based on the random selection. Lastly, it is not clear that focusing on multiple equilibrium (as the historical institutionalism focus on), one can have a clear picture in explaining the world.

3.5.2 Rational Choice Institutionalism

The rational choice institutionalism developed at the same time as historical institutionalism but in relative isolation from it. Williamson (2009) argues that the development of a particular organizational form can be explained as the result of an effort to reduce the transaction costs of undertaking the same activity without such an institution. The rational choice institutionalists recently have turned their attention to several other phenomena, including cross-national coalition behaviour, the development of political institutions and the intensity of ethnic conflict. Przeworski, Geddes, Marks and others analyse democratic transitions in game theoretic terms. Tsebelis and some other scholars of international relations have used the concepts of rational choice institutionalism to explain the rise or fall of international regimes, the kind of responsibilities that states delegate to international organizations and the shape of such organizations.

3.5.2.1 Characteristics and Weaknesses of the Approach

Hall and Taylor (1996) have discussed four characteristics of the rational choice institutional approach. First, rational choice institutionalists employ that individual actors are relevant actors, have a fixed set of preferences or tastes, behave entirely instrumentally so as to maximize the attainment of these preferences and therefore do extensive calculation.

Second, if all schools of thought tend to promulgate a characteristic image of politics, institutionalists also purvey a distinctive image of politics. They tend to see politics as a series of collective action surrounded with dilemmas. Political actors as individuals act to maximize the attainment of their own preferences and are likely to produce an outcome that is collectively suboptimal (in the sense that another outcome could be found that would make at least one of the actors better off without making any of the others worse off). Typically, what prevents the actors from taking a collectively superior course of action is the absence of institutional arrangements that would guarantee complementary behaviour by others. Classic examples include the 'prisoner's dilemma' and the 'tragedy of the commons', and political situations present a variety of such problems.

Third, one of the great contributions of rational choice institutionalism has been to emphasize the role of strategic interaction in the determination of political outcomes. That is to say, they postulate, first, that an actor's behaviour is likely to be driven, not by impersonal historical forces, but by strategic and rational calculations. Second, this calculation will be deeply affected by the actor's expectations about how others are likely to behave as well, leading actors towards potentially better social outcomes.

Finally, rational choice institutionalists have also developed a distinctive approach to the problem of explaining how institutions originate. Typically, they begin by using deduction to arrive at a stylized specification of the functions that an institution performs. They then explain the existence of the institution by reference to the value those functions have for the actors affected by the institution. This formulation assumes that the actors create the institution in order to realize this value, which is most often conceptualized, as noted above, in terms of gains from cooperation. Thus, the process of institutional creation usually revolves around voluntary agreement by relevant actors, and if the institution is subject to a process of competitive selection, it survives primarily because it provides more benefits to relevant actors than to alternate institutional forms.

Some of the weaknesses of the rational choice institutionalism include: (a) rational choice institutionalists are unable to provide an adequate predictive theory of action since it does not specify how preferences come about and why they vary from individual to individual; (b) rational choice institutionalism ignores social structure. Most qualitative- oriented scholars reject the idea of rationality and instead emphasize the idea that randomness and accidents matter in political and social outcomes.

3.5.3 Sociological Institutionalism

This approach emerged from organizational theory. The movement dates roughly to the end of the 1970s. These scholars wanted to challenge the view that some parts of the world reflect a formal rationality, while some others reflect culture. They argued that the 'institutional forms and procedures used by modern organizations were not adopted simply because they were most efficient for the task at hand instead these forms and procedures should be seen as culturally specific practices' (Hall and Taylor 1996). Sociological institutionalists define institutions more broadly than any other approach. Powell and DiMaggio define institutions not just as 'rules, procedures, organizational standards, and governance structures, but also as conventions and customs' (Koelble 1995). They go further and make the assumption that institutions define 'rational actors'. When it comes to the relationship between individuals and institutions, scholars use the cultural approach to explain outcomes. They argue that institutions affect behaviour of individuals by socializing individuals into particular institutional roles, and individuals consequently internalize norms related to these roles.

Institutionalists in sociology began to argue that many of the institutional forms and procedures used by modern organizations were not adopted simply because they were most efficient for the tasks at hand, in line with some transcendent 'rationality'. Instead, they argued that many of these forms and procedures should be seen as culturally specific practices, akin to the myths and ceremonies devised by many societies.

Several approaches used to explain institutional change as stated by Lowndes depend on understanding the relationship between agents and institutions. Existing arguments highlight that institutions matter because they shape the choices, behaviour, interests and identities of agents. However, this approach started adopting a determinist view about the institutions, resulting in a highly constrained view of agency. The 'new institutionalism' (rational choice, historical and institutionalism) is now under criticism from a new approach—constructivist institutionalism—claiming that established positions explain institutional change successfully, mostly because the agents in question are highly constrained by their institutional environments. Prominent institutionalists, such as Colin Hay, Mark Blyth and Vivien Schmidt, provide alternative accounts showing 'interpretive agents operating in relatively and discursive contexts to explain institutional change'. The critiques highlight how interpretive agents with institutional and wider structural contexts produce change (Bell 2011).

3.5.3.1 Features and Weaknesses of the Approach

Three features of sociological institutionalism exist. First, the sociological institutionalists tend to define institutions much more broadly than political scientists do. This approach tends to redefine 'culture' itself as 'institutions'. Second, the new institutionalists in sociology also have a distinctive understanding of the relationship between institutions and individual action, which follows the 'cultural approach'. An older line of sociological analysis resolved the problem of specifying the relationship between institutions and action by associating institutions with 'roles' to which prescriptive 'norms of behaviour' were attached. In this view, individuals who have been socialized into particular institutional roles internalize the norms associated with these roles, and in this way, institutions are said to affect behaviour. One might think of this as the 'normative dimension' of institutional impact. Although some continue to employ such conceptions, many sociological institutionalists put a new emphasis on what we might think of as the 'cognitive dimension' of institutional impact. That is to say, they emphasize the way in which institutions influence behaviour by providing cognitive scripts, categories and models that are indispensable for action because without them the world and the behaviour of others cannot be interpreted. Institutions influence behaviour not simply by specifying what one should do but also by specifying what one can imagine oneself doing in a given context. Here, one can see the influence of social constructivism on the new institutionalism in sociology. It follows that institutions do not simply affect the strategic calculations of individuals, as rational choice institutionalists contend, but also their most basic preferences and very identity. Finally, many sociological institutionalists emphasize the highly interactive and mutually constitutive character of the relationship between institutions and individual action. When they act as a social convention specifies individuals simultaneously constitute themselves as social actors, in the sense of engaging in socially meaningful acts, and strengthen the convention to which they are following.

One of the weaknesses of this approach is that it does not explain how institutions originate. Another weakness is the operationalization of culture. Some of the strengths of this approach are: (a) it is able to explain how institutions affect individuals' preferences or identities; (b) it provides an explanation of how actors choose strategies from culturally specific repertoires.

Special Insights

Traditional or Modern? Which Approach to Choose?

Triangulation is used to combine the advantages of both the qualitative and quantitative approaches. Each method offers specific advantages as well as disadvantages. Recent developments in social sciences have argued that the two traditions should not have a separate-but-equal status and should instead interact. Triangulation is not aimed merely at validation but at deepening and widening one's understanding. It is vital to get support of interdisciplinary research and its application in various disciplines such as comparative politics.

'By combining multiple observers, theories, methods, and empirical materials, researchers can hope to overcome the weakness or intrinsic biases and the problems that come from single-method, single-observer, single-theory studies. Often the purpose of triangulation in specific contexts is to obtain confirmation of findings through convergence of different perspectives. The point at which the perspectives converge is seen to represent reality.'—Jakob, Alexander (2001). The quotation is taken from Yeasmin (2012).

3.6 Conclusion

An approach provides a particular direction or angle to study the politics in a comparative setting. Broadly speaking, two types of approaches, that is, traditional and modern, are used to study comparative politics. Among the traditional approaches, the philosophical, historical, legal and institutional approaches are some well recognized traditional approaches. The traditional approaches remained predominant in the field of enquiry till the Second World War and then subsequently lost its vitality. With the end of the Second World War, the Third World nations were decolonized, and thus, there was an expansion of the universe of comparative politics. The scholars with emerging scientific approach felt that the traditional approaches were redundant and thus sensed the need of applicability of new approaches. A few new approaches which became popular were new institutional approach, system approaches, structural-functional approaches, behavioural approaches and political culture approaches. With the new approaches becoming a popular method of study, institutions no longer implicitly identified with the organizational structure, deductive and prescriptive, instead the focus of analysis moved towards understanding the process of policymaking, human behaviour, rules and norms. More specifically, the new approaches are more bored in nature. They indent to study the behaviour of political actors that is shaped and conditioned by the institutional contexts in which they operate. In the process, it studies different non-governmental institutions and its various implications on individuals and society and vice versa. It claims to be more scientific and yet claims to develop theoretical models such as systems approach or model. More specifically, the new approach such as culture approach intends to study how people's behaviour, attitude, belief and their inclination of participation also determine the stability of the state. On the other hand, scholars such as Dennis Kavanagh have argued that the political culture is not homogeneous, rather it is diffracted as subcultures.

It would be wrong to assume that the traditional approach has been totally redundant, rather even while adopting the new approach and making comparative analysis, some scholars may find it appropriate to understand the importance of the historical context, the role of traditional institutions such as the constitution, legislature, executive and judiciary, and their influence in shaping the behaviour of the individuals and vice versa. It is also necessary to comprehend that no single approach is sacrosanct and instead all the approaches, both traditional and modern, have their own strengths and weaknesses. The appropriate applicability of any such approach or combination of approaches such as a 'triangulation' depends on the scholar's choice who intends to make justice to the area of the study selected.

Keywords

Institutionalism
New institutionalism
Political culture
Rational choice institutionalism
Sociological institutionalism
Structural–functional approach
System approach

Review Questions

1. Discuss the new institutional approach to comparative politics.
2. Critically analyse the system approach and its criticisms.
3. Discuss various approaches to study comparative politics.
4. Define political culture. Do you think that the political culture is an appropriate approach to study comparative politics?

Notes

1. Richard Rose (1991) stated that comparative politics focuses on a combination of substantive focus on the study of the countries, political system and methods of recognizing, explaining similarities and differences between these countries using common models.
2. Some major works in the traditional institutional approach include James Bryce's *The American Commonwealth* (1888) and *Modern Democracies* (1921); A.L. Lowell's *Governments and Parties in Continental Europe* (1896); and Herman Finer's *The Theory and Practice of Modern Government* (1932).
3. Mexican political sociologist Pablo Gonzalez Casanova identified two types of works within the systems approach. The first one is functionalism, a major theoretician in this school being Talcott Parsons. The second one is generally known as systems analysis. The school Gonzalez Casanova focused on problems of decision-making and was influenced by the disciplines of operations research and mathematics in the post-Second World War period. What we understand as the political systems approach in comparative politics in the present day has been influenced by both these tendencies in systems analysis.
4. Wildavsky defines political culture as 'shared values legitimating social practices'. Ross (1997) defined culture is a system of meaning that people use to manage their daily worlds, large and small; culture is the basis of social

and political identity that affects how people line up and how they act on a wide range of matters. 'Culture is a framework for locating the self and others in it, for making sense of the actions and interpreting motives of others, for grounding an analysis of interests, for linking collective identities to political action, and for motivating people and groups towards some actions and away from others'. He further believes that in order to fully appreciate the role of culture in political life, it is necessary to know how the implication of culture interacts with interests and institutions.

5. Almond and Verba considered these three components to be ideal and applicable to individuals and political system as a whole.
6. Edward Muller and Mitchell Seligson (1994) developed a model that allowed them to make inferences about the possibility of unidirectional or reciprocal causation between civic culture attitudes and democracy. They found that most civic culture attitudes do not have any impact on changes in the levels of democracy. Their findings contrast with the assumptions made by Almond and Verba (1963) and later Inglehart (1988), as discussed earlier, that the viability of democratic institutions is affected by individual attitudes and beliefs.
7. The term 'historical institutionalism' was not coined until the early 1990 (Steinmo 2008).

References

Abrutyn, Seth, and Jonathan H. Turner. 2011. "The Old Institutionalism Meets the New Institutionalism." *Sociological Perspectives* 54(3): 283–306.

Almond, Gabriel A., and G. Bingham Powell, Jr. 1966. *Comparative Politics: A Developmental Approach.* Boston: Little, Brown.

Almond, Gabriel A., and James S. Coleman. 1960. *The Politics of the Developing Areas.* Princeton, NJ: Princeton University Press.

Almond, Gabriel A., and Sidney Verba. 1963. *The Civic Culture Political Attitudes and Democracy in Five Nations.* Princeton, NJ: Princeton University Press.

Althusser, Louis. 1970. *Ideology and Ideological State Apparatuses, Lenin and Philosophy, and Other Essays*, 127–88. London: New Left Books. Originally published in Ben Brewster, 1971. trans.

Ball, Alan R. 1988. *The Study of Politics: Modern Political Government*, 3–18. New York: Palgrave Macmillan.

Bell, Stephen. 1992. "Institutionalism: Old and New." Accessed from https://espace.library.uq.edu.au on September 12, 2023.

———. 2011. "Do We Really Need a New 'Constructivist Institutionalism' to Explain Institutional Change?" *British Journal of Political Science* 41(4): 883–906.

Bell, Stephen, and Brian Head. 1994. *State, Economy and Public Policy in Australia.* Melbourne: Oxford University Press.

Blondel, Jean. 1999. "Now and Then: Comparative Politics." *Political Studies* XLVII: 152–60.

Blumstein, James F. 1981. "The Resurgence of Institutionalism." *Journal of Policy Analysis and Management* 1(1): 129–32.

Bryce, James. 1888. *The American Commonwealth*, Vol. 1. Indianapolis: Liberty Fund.

———. 1921. *Modern Democracies.* New York: The Macmillan.

Burke, Edmund. 1982. *Reflection on the Revolution in France.* Penguin Classics.

Chilcote, Ronal H. 2000. *Comparative Inquiry in Politics and Political Economy: Theories and Issues.* Riverside: University of California.

Easton, David. 1953. *The Political System.* New York: Alfred A. Knopf.

Easton, David. 1965a. *A Framework for Political Analysis.* Englewood Cliffs, NJ: Prentice Hall.

———. 1965b. *A Systems Analysis of Political Life.* New York: Wiley.

———. 1966. Categories for the Systems Analysis of Politics, in *Varieties of Political Theory*, edited by David Easton, 143–54. Englewood Cliffs, NJ: Prentice Hall.

Finer, Herman. 1932. *The Theory and Practice of Modern Government.* New York: L. MacVeagh, The Dial Press.

Friedrich, Carl J. 1965. *Constitutional Government and Democracy.* Waltham, New York: Blaisdell Publication Co.

Goldstein, Judith. 1993. *Ideas, Interests, and American Trade Policy.* Ithaca and London: Cornell University Press.

Gramsci, Antonio. 1971. *Selections from the Prison Notebooks*, edited and translated by Quentin Hoare and Geoffrey Nowell Smith. London: Lawrence and Wishart.

Hall, Peter A., and Rosemary C.R. Taylor. 1996. Political Science and the Three New Institutionalisms. *Political Studies* XLIV: 937–57.

Hannan, Michael, and Freeman, John. 1977. The Population Ecology of Organizations. *American Journal of Sociology* 82(5): 929–64.

Hannan, Michael T. 1988. Organizational Population Dynamics and Social Change. *European Sociological Review* 4(2): 95–109.

Hay, Colin, and Daniel Wincott. 1998, Structure, Agency and Historical Institutionalism', *Political Studies* 46: 951–57.

Huntington, Samuel P. 1993. The Clash of Civilizations? *Foreign Affairs* 72(3): 22–49.

Inglehart, Ronald. 1988. The Renaissance of Political Culture. *American Political Science Review* 82(4): 221–44.

Kavanagh, Dennis. 1972. *Political Culture*. New York: Macmillan.

Koelble, Thomas A. 1995. The New Institutionalism in Political Science and Sociology. *Comparative Politics* 27: 221–44.

Latin, David. 1986. *Hegemony and Culture*. Chicago, IL: University of Chicago Press.

Lijphart, Arend. 1971. Comparative Politics and the Comparative Method. *The American Political Science Review* 65(3): 682–93.

Lowell, A. Lawrence. 1896. *Governments and Parties in Continental Europe*. United Kingdom: Longmans Green and Co Null.

Macridis, Roy C. 1991. Major Characteristics of the Traditional Approach, in *Approaches to the Study of Politics*, edited by Burnard Susser. New York: Macmillan.

Muller, Edward N., and Mitchell Seligson. 1994. Civic Culture and Democracy: The Question of Causal Relationships. *The American Political Science Review* 88(3): 635–52.

Pateman, Carole. 1971. Political Culture, Political Structure and Political Change. *British Journal of Political Science* 1(3): 291–305.

Pye, Lucian W. 1966. *Aspects of Political Development*. Boston: Little, Brown, and Co.

Rose, Richard. 1991. Comparing Forms of Comparative Analysis. *Political Studies* XXXIX: 446–62.

Ross, Marc Howard. 2009a. Culture and Identity in Comparative Political Analysis. Originally published in M. Lichbach and A. Zuckerman, Comparative Politics: Rationality, Culture, and Structure.

———. 2009b. Culture in Comparative Political Analysis, in *Rationality, Culture, and Structure*, edited by Mark Irving Lichbach and Alan S. Zuckerman. Cambridge: Cambridge University Press.

Roy, Anupama. 2001. Comparative Method and Strategies of Comparison. *Punjab Journal of Politics* XXV(2): 1–15.

Steinmo, Sven. 2008. What is Historical Institutionalism? In *Approaches in the Social Sciences*, edited by Donatella Della Porta and Michael Keating. Cambridge: Cambridge University Press.

Thelen, Kathleen, and Steinmo, Sven. 1992. *Structuring Politics: Historical Institutionalism in Comparative Analysis*. Cambridge: Cambridge University Press.

Yeasmin, Sabina. 2012. Triangulation' Research Method as the Tool of Social Science Research. *Bangladesh University of Professionals* 1(1): 154–63. ISSN: 2219-4851.

Williamson, Oliver E. 2009. *Markets and Hierarchies: Analysis and Antitrust Implications: A Study in the Economics of Internal Organization*. Berkeley, CA: Business & Public Policy Group, University of California.

CHAPTER 4

Gender and Comparative Politics: Women's Political Representation in Comparative Perspective

Chetna Sharma and Pushpa Singh

Reader's Guide

What do we mean when we talk about gendering comparative politics? Does comparative politics have any gaps regarding gender? How will studying comparative politics via the prism of gender help our comprehension of comparative analysis? These issues will continue to be the subject of our discussion in this chapter. We will talk about the concept of "gender" in the context of comparative politics and why it is crucial to address the gender gap in the field of comparative politics. The chapter makes a strong case for the inclusion of gender mapping and gender-specific analysis as a way to improve the narrative of comparative politics. The chapter is divided into two sections: the first half discusses the gender gap in comparative politics, places the concept of "gendering comparative politics," and describes the difficulties involved in doing so. In the second section, this very concept is attempted to be mapped using the analytical framework of political representation. The framework for the study of this issue is based on the idea that the level of political representation of women serves as the most crucial indicator of their political empowerment—or lack thereof.

4.1 Introduction

The goal of Gendering Comparative Politics is to make gender the primary area of study for the discipline of comparative politics. Discussing how gender as a category has been largely absent from the larger context of comparative political analysis will help clarify why it is necessary to establish it as both a dependent and an independent category of analysis, as well as how its inclusion will change the discipline. This would make it possible to capture the subtleties of comparative politics through the prism of gender because gender cuts across numerous political inquiry parameters. The discipline would become inclusive of cultural, racial, ethnic, and other specificities if research on gender from different nations were incorporated. This would demonstrate how marginalisation intersects, making some groups invisible and irrelevant. The goal of the chapter's discussion is to address historical biases in the field of political science by highlighting the exclusionary tendencies of political institutions, structures, and processes.

4.2 Gender and Comparative Politics: Meaning and Contestations

The term "gender" refers to the socially and culturally determined roles, behaviours, expressions, and identities of boys, girls, men, women, and gender nonconforming persons. It entails a multidimensional mapping of politically crucial, fluid identities, beliefs, norms, and practices that are seen as either feminine or masculine. These social conceptions shape how people see and interact with one another as well as how they should present themselves in terms of personality and outward appearances. Depending on the roles they play, the demands placed on them, how they interact with others, are the various ways in which gender is institutionalised in society.

Understanding gender involves analyses that consider how sexuality, masculinities, and femininities are produced. It also entails comprehending how gender norms affect connections between and among the sexes, how ideas of masculinity affect male behaviour, and how institutions and social practises favour or reward certain sorts of behaviour associated with privileged groups of men over other types of behaviour associated with women, persons of colour, or the poor (Weldon, 2006). The way that gender is understood in different communities varies over time and space. Gender norms, practises, and identities differ "across groups of women and men as well as across nations, regions, generations, and cultural groupings," having "multiple logics" (Beckwith, 2010:160). Recent gender studies research has emphasised women's heterogeneity and questioned the idea that women can be categorised in a single, cohesive way. The experience of white middle-class women has received too much attention, according to feminists from the Global South, which has prevented consideration of the distinctive and occasionally conflicting interests of women (Hooks 1984; Collins 1990; Smooth 2011). Similar to how gender non-conforming individuals question heteronormativity (Celis et al, 2013). Inequalities based on race, class, gender, ethnicity, and sexual orientation overlap to magnify the extent of marginalisation, making intersectionality another crucial idea of engagement.

A common language of gender must be established in order to advance knowledge in this area in comparative politics despite the fact that the concept of gender is used in a variety of empirical and theoretical investigations. According to Keren Beckwith, gender may be employed as a category and a process (Beckwith, 2005). While gender is a category that places an emphasis on its constructs, it is also a process that involves looking into the decisions made by individuals, groups, institutions, movements, and nations as well as the behaviours, customs, practises, and dynamics that underlie those decisions. In comparative political analysis, gender research is necessary as both a category and a process. Comparative, longitudinal, cross-sectional, and single-case studies can all be organised with gender as a focus (Beckwith, 2005). In comparative politics, gender can be used as a meta-concept, particularly in studies that examine the gendered implications of electoral laws, nomination processes, policy-making, and other decision-making processes, as well as the gendered outcomes of democratic transitions and other regime change, citizenship, and immigration law.

The concept of gender as a process emphasises how gender-based hierarchies are frequently the product of socially constructed gender-differentiated roles for men and women in different countries. Men are privileged in society and in politics, and this asymmetry and subordination are reflected in all political institutions and how they operate. The state reproduces gender hierarchies through its institutions, policies, laws, and other rules and regulations. For instance, Htun (2005) notes that analysing gender and the state necessitates taking into account how the state supports the major social structures and processes, such as the sexual division of labour, conventional heterosexuality, war, and militarism 'through its laws and policies, symbolic power, the statement and behaviours of officials, and subtle patterning of society' (Htun, 2005:162). The majority of the time, actions that seem to be gender-neutral are not the product of a conscious attempt by all males to oppress all women. Instead, they have emerged as a result of organisational norms, practises, policies, and discourses that have "rendered women, along with their demands and interests, invisible" within the state, normalising male privilege (Hawkesworth, 2005: 147).

4.3 Tracing the Gender Lacuna in Comparative Politics

An apparent gender gap can be seen in the field of political science when examining the legacy of political philosophy from the time of Plato to the time of Marx through the prism of gender. Many academics involved in feminist studies have brought this out, emphasizing how gender is often left out of most political studies (Okin 1979, Elshtain 1981, Eisenstein 1981, Pateman 1988, Squires 1999). Political science's several subfields exhibit gender bias, and there is a general excluding attitude. Even prestigious academic bodies, such as the Committee on Comparative Politics of the Social Science Research Council of Stanford University, did not analyze women as a category in 1958. At the same time, other variables including trade unions, corporate organizations, student movements, familial and lineage organizations, as well as religious and ethnic groupings, were seen to be important enough to understand the group interest representation in political systems. This omission was caused by the fact that neither gender experts nor mainstream scholars frequently raise the issue of gender's relevance to politics.

As the academic community continues to ignore a big and politically crucial minority, women, comparative and longitudinal studies from a gendered viewpoint are still lacking (Kang, 2017). Gender was not included in the primary framework of analysis in the volumes *Passion, Craft and Method in Comparative Politics* by Gerardo Munck and Richard Snyder, a scholarly contemporary and apparently complete volume, or the *Oxford Handbook of Comparative Politics* by Carlos Boix and Susan Stokes. The 2009 edition of Mark Lichbach and Alan Zuckerman's *Comparative Politics: Rationality, Culture, and Structure* contains more research examples on women and gender than the 1997 edition, but it does not consider gender analysis to be a valid theoretical perspective (Baldez, 2010). Gendered comparative politics was only a required course in three of the best political science departments' curriculum. In the Cambridge Studies in Comparative Politics series, there were over 30 new volumes published between 2005 and 2008, but none of them specifically compared gender (Caraway, 2010:173). Baldez called this omission of gender and comparative analysis a "gender lacuna" (Baldez, 2010). The comparative analysis needed to pay close attention to how political life is structured as well as how social norms, rules, practises, and institutions favour some groups and ways of life while disadvantage others across cultures and locales in order to find patterns of similarity and difference (Weldon, 2006). With the goal of "gendering comparative politics," a group of academics including Karen Beckwith, Terri Caraway, Louise Chappell, Leslie Schwindt-Bayer, Aili Mari Tripp, Lisa Baldez, Georgina Waylen, Milicaul Kittilson, Mona Lena Krook, Mala Htun, and Laurel Weldon are attempting to integrate gender perspectives.

4.4 Gendering Comparative Politics

Understanding the distinction between "gender and comparative politics" and "gendering comparative politics" is crucial when discussing gendering comparative politics. Research on gender and comparative politics would cover topics including women's movements, the role of women in the democratic transition, and the gendered character of political and economic institutions. However, the study is classified as gender and politics research because it places more emphasis on gender (Schwindt-Bayer, 2010). The drawback of this type of research is that it limits the examination of critical topics and does not provide a true comparative assessment (Schwindt-Bayer, 2010).

The goal of gendering comparative politics, on the other hand, is to compare and integrate gender studies with the more comprehensive discipline of comparative politics using cross-regional analysis. The goal is to shift from a study of a particular nation to a comparative research that proposes a broad theorization of several conceptual categories. With a focus on two crucial areas, this technique will more closely combine gender politics and comparative politics (Baldez, 2010). First, consider how fundamental ideas like democracy and gender have been kept apart by the various variables and key concepts used in the two domains. The second is to promote improved comprehension between the mainstream and gender experts.

Gender is not just another variable to be added to comparative analysis. Instead, gendering comparative politics entails creating in-depth studies for both large and small n using gender-specific concepts including representation, the electoral process, the state, and power. The goal is to increase the comparability of gender research with respect to the major analytical topics. Comparative analysis of various geographical and political contexts will highlight the diversity of gender, race, class, and other axes of dominance structures as well as the interactions between these structures and the many possibilities for resistance and reform (Weldon, 2006). In addition, it doesn't imply that every scholar has to research every nation and culture. Instead, it suggests that each gender scholar must take into account and show how the research that is relevant to a certain nation or region links with that of scholars in other locations. We need to show how gender cuts through and improves comparative politics while simultaneously advancing gender-specific ideas and better comparative research on gender (Schwindt-Bayer, 2010). Comparative analysis, both in terms of its methodology and topic matter, is what makes gendering comparative politics unique. Our understanding would be expanded both in terms of space and time if we conducted multidirectional study using both vertical and horizontal comparisons. It would be easier to comprehend the relationship between regime type and women's status if a range of regime types were included, such as non-democratic nations and former socialist systems.

4.5 Integrating Gender into Comparative Politics: Challenges and Prospects

As was discussed in the sections above, a lot of engagements with substantial number of works have recently appeared in comparative politics that address various aspects of gender and politics. The discipline is still quite far from the anticipated amount of involvement with gender on a larger scale. Although the conceptual change that included gender in comparative political analysis allowed for a significant expansion in the study's scope, "much of political science has been content to remain with its biases and blinders" (Lovenduski, 1998:351). In this section, we'll look at some of the challenges and opportunities that gendering comparative politics presents. The discipline's historical conditioning presents the first obstacle to gendering comparative politics (Caraway, 2010). In order to incorporate new research into areas that have already been defined in the canonical works, researchers and authors draw on the past. The absence of women and the gender issue from the canons or classic political science texts continues to define and shape the academic discourse in the subject.

The serious issue of a lack of data in this area presents the second difficulty. Furthermore, the scant information that is available is all derived from Western industrialised nations. At best, databases are inadequate, and for many categories, the data are just missing (Tripp, 2006). However, until we have a good grasp of how gender functions in less developed democracies and in non-democratic systems, we cannot properly understand the implications of gender. Concepts that have evolved in one context may not always translate well when used in comparison or may need to have their definitions expanded. As a result, research on gender and comparative politics still has a weak comparative component (Schwindt-Bayer, 2010).

The third challenge is constituted by the dilemma of the mainstream studies of "politics" and "gender and politics" barely engage or interact with each other. The broad areas of political inquiry often omit gender analysis unless it is mandated by the research topic itself. Therefore, despite a growing corpus of knowledge in the field, gender does not factor into the significance of political studies and is frequently confined to feminist circles. Lack of larger cross-regional studies makes it difficult to understand why semi-authoritarian and authoritarian states adopt policies that benefit women, when they could just as easily choose not to do so. Examples include establishing national organisations for women, instituting paid maternity leave, allocating one-third to half of parliamentary seats to women, and signing and ratifying the Convention on the Elimination of All Forms of Discrimination Against Women. Why do they carry out actions that seem to be in the interest of women, especially when they don't seem to care much about other civic, political, and human rights? Several of these questions raise doubts about the analytical work that has been done in democratic situations (Tripp, 2006).

The gendering comparative analysis opens up areas where our research and, eventually, our theories, could benefit from being informed by and reflecting real-world problems that needed to be solved. In this domain, the most substantial theoretical advancements can be made. What relationship, for instance, exists between women's rights and political stability? Is there a link between dictatorship's prevalence in the Muslim world and gender inequality? The methodological pluralism of comparative politics is well suited to research that uses the data already available to answer questions that have only recently been posed as well as to use primarily qualitative field-based data to establish a foundation of proof for identifying additional research questions, for purposes of generalisation, and for developing comparative theorization. It's critical to express the "added value" of gendered analysis in concrete terms, as well as to show how it produces new theories and sheds light on more extensive political processes (Beckwith 2005; 2010).

We urgently require quantitative and qualitative research on the political elements of a vast array of topics about which we know very little. Comparative scholars have hardly ever studied some of the most significant global phenomena associated with the feminization of globalisation and of labour. To address such intricate problem-driven issues, we must move beyond the disciplinary boundaries. Interdisciplinarity makes it simpler to connect knowledge with action because real-world problems often do not show themselves in disciplinary packages (Tripp, 2010). Tripp recommends problem-driven research as an alternative to method-driven research, which entails using multidisciplinary methodologies that are most effective at solving the complex, multidimensional challenges of the real world. The improved linkages between academics and practitioner/policy groups will help the emerging international research and collaboration models, especially those outside the US-European axis, better address the comparative issues of data gathering and theory creation (Tripp, 2010). The ability to examine politics from the bottom up, from the perspective of the underprivileged and marginalised, through the use of fieldwork, is one of the benefits and one of the specific contributions that gendered comparative politics can offer.

While there is a strong desire for comparative research of many case studies on various gender issues, there is still a need for regionally specific research. Small n approaches provide in-depth examination of specific characteristics of specific locations, allowing non-Western countries to contribute to the larger topic of comparative politics. By enabling the abundance of gender-specific case studies from other areas, the field can avoid the trap of Eurocentricism. Gender-specific case studies from various geographic locations must collaborate in order to develop a more complete understanding while keeping the particulars of their experiences.

This chapter's objective is to analyse the gendering of comparative politics as a discipline and show how politics is a gendered field; the following section will focus on how women are represented in politics. Understanding the historical, political, and cultural legacies as well as the various societal patterns that support or impede women's agency and power struggles will have an impact on the analysis. The party structure, institutionalisation, electoral rivalry, legal enforcement, and social attitudes toward women will all be investigated in relation to the significant role that gender quotas play in accelerating changes in representation.

4.6 Understanding Women's Representation in Politics from Comparative Perspective

Women's involvement in politics has increased dramatically over the past century, but cross-national scholarship on female leaders, their role, and access to various positions has to be investigated on a wider comparative platform. Political representation and tactics to increase the number of women in politics, serve as important yardsticks to assess how political spaces are gendered. Women are still disproportionately excluded from participation, and even when they do, their involvement rarely result in empowerment. However, it is important to critically examine the idea and practice of political representation in light of the unique contexts created by historical particularities, socioeconomic status, cultural attitudes, and patriarchal family norms of a nation or region that may thwart any attempt at women's political empowerment. It's equally crucial to draw attention to the ways in which these categories feed off one another and contribute to women's general exclusion from politics and society. Furthermore, because gender inequality is ingrained in all these spheres, simply increasing the number of women in legislatures and public offices won't be sufficient; rather, a deeper reform at the level of political practice as well as scholarly study is needed. With these efforts, political spaces' fundamental gender blindness will be corrected, and the discipline will become gender-equitable.

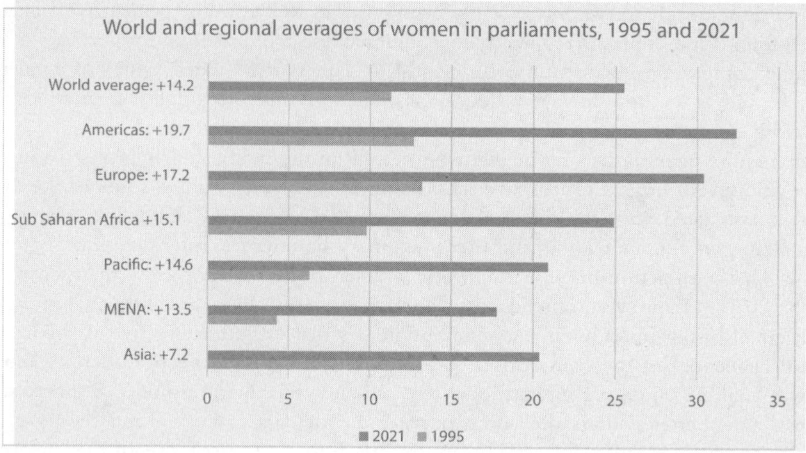

Source: Inter-Parliamentary Union.

4.7 Mapping Women's Political Representation: Some Reflections from Regions Across the Globe

Women continue to be underrepresented in national parliaments and high-ranking positions in governments around the world despite increased attempts in recent years to advance their political representation, a widely accepted measure of women's status in society. Women continue to be underrepresented in legislatures and in all high echelons of government worldwide. Neither the judiciary, political parties, nor the bureaucracy have been exempt from patriarchal biases. The correlation between sociological, cultural, and religious attitudes that appear to have an impact on women's political participation provides part of the answer (Ingelhart and Norris, 2003). The nature and degree of political representation of women, however, is also influenced by the sort of election system and voting behaviour. For example, the proportional representation likely to provide better possibility for women's participation compared to majoritarian systems. A broad analytical approach is required to comprehend the issues influencing women's political representation (Tremblay, 2007). In the section that follows, numerous parameters are used to discuss the nature of women's representation from various parts of the world.

Special Insights

Challenges Encountered By Women Parliamentarians: Some Facts

According to the IPU's most recent statistics, women make up little over 26% of parliamentarians globally. Despite recent advancements, they still face considerable barriers on the way to parity with their male counterparts. One of the biggest challenges is gender-based violence, harassment, and sexism. According to IPU studies of female lawmakers in Africa, Europe, and other parts of the world, these sentiments are widespread both within political parties and in parliaments as well as among the general public. These viewpoints encourage sexist abuse of female MPs. Additionally, where sexism intersects with ageism, racism, homophobia, ableism, and other prejudices, those who speak up for women's rights are more aggressively targeted, as are young women, women from minority groups, and women who are disabled. It is necessary to create or amend internal parliamentary policies and procedures that include clear definitions and prohibitions of gender-based violence as well as robust, capable, and independent grievance processes.

4.8 Political Institutions and Gendered Norms

The state, institutions, administration, and policy-making process are all markedly masculine, reflecting the strongly gendered nature of politics. Gender hierarchies are stratified and unassailable because all political institutions are gender regimes with specific beliefs about how men and women should act, think, and feel (Kronsell, 2005). The influence of gender on institutions can be seen in a variety of ways, including behaviour, workplace expectations, attire, family roles, and more. For example, women parliamentarians are frequently required to "do" the performance of a politician, which is coded as male, while also "managing" their femininity. This means that enacting formal and informal gendered conventions may imply something different for women than for men.

All of these factors have the ability to affect the political opportunities and limitations that women might face. They can help predict when and which institutions will be more receptive to demands for gender equality (Chappel, 2006). Women encounter structural impediments when they enroll in a male-dominated institution that restrict them from participating in the legislative process. Legislators are influenced by the unwelcoming irregular work schedules for women who have more than their fair share of home duties by the work norms established by masculine parameters (Kittilson & Schwindt-Bayer, 2012). It is harder for them to compete and win positions in public offices due to traditional roles, household duties, societal prejudices, power imbalances, and hierarchies. As stated in research by the Inter-Parliamentary Union (2016), women legislators are occasionally the target of harassment and violence in the form of sexist statements, online sexist assaults, and psychological harassment.

Women often have soft or low-profile portfolios, which suggests that women do not exercise equal political power, and they are frequently denied leadership positions and influential committee seats in legislatures (Tan, 2020). While gendered norms are present in political institutions around the world, these norms can be challenged to create new spaces for emancipation, as was the case in Australia, where Senator Larissa Waters became the first politician to breastfeed on the Senate floor thanks to a rule passed in 2016 that permitted breastfeeding in the Parliament (BBC News 2017). The prime minister of New Zealand, Jacindia Ardern, made history by being the first female head of state to attend the UN General Assembly with her three-month-old baby. Arden might be able to do this in light of the recently changed government policy that permits the prime minister or ministers to travel with a nanny when on an abroad assignment (Roy, 2018). However, such actions are not always regarded as "appropriate," as was the case when Pia Kjaersgaard, the speaker of the house, asked Danish MP Mette Abildgaard to remove her five-month-old daughter from the parliament (France presse, 2019). The Scandinavian countries are seen as supporters of gender equality and women's rights, as well as being family- and child-friendly countries with extensive parental leave, but they nonetheless uphold these gendered workplace practices.

The acceptance of women in politics is influenced by a number of non-political factors, including how they dress, behave, uphold moral principles, and perform domestic duties. These expectations place women politicians in a gender trap because they force them to exhibit traits that are both feminine and masculine. For instance, to appear non-militaristic and non-aggressive, the first politician in the Philippines dressed traditionally. In order to position themselves as contemporary leaders with whom the West will seriously engage, certain female politicians, including the presidents of the Philippines and Indonesia, Dr. Gloria Macapagal Arroyo and Megawati Sukarnoputri, have also embraced Western women's power suits. These women also made the decision to dress conservatively when travelling to rural or predominately Muslim areas. The majority of these women prefer to show their personal preferences when appropriate, but this constant juggling of their gender identities and professional appearance has not been simple for them. All female politicians must exhibit aggressive behaviour at some time, but in other circumstances, they must fulfil the conventional duties of being pleasant, capable, and tough.

It is interesting to note that androcentric political conventions and institutional norms have remained prevalent even in older democracies in Europe and America. When arguing a point of order, for instance, British parliaments until 1998 required both men and women to wear top hats because they symbolized the institutionalized masculinity that is characteristic of all-male organizations (Lovenduski, 2005). In the US Congress, women were also prohibited from wearing pants in the Senate, and Senate doorkeepers enforced this rule. Moseley-Braun, who showed up to the Senate floor in a pantsuit, contested this regulation. Aside from clothing, there are a number of additional elements that affect women and men extremely differently. For instance, family provides a support system for males in all occupations, but because of society's patriarchal training, it may bring stress or conflict for women.

A study by Olle Folke and Johanna Rickne (2016) found that this pattern of negative effect of family on women leaders' careers is prevalent throughout the world. According to their research, promoted women see an increase in divorce rates in the first three years after receiving their promotions, whereas promoted men did not exhibit a similar trend in their career graph (Folke & Rickne, 2016). There is always a subliminal expectation that women should remain in the home, which is sometimes reflected in national laws. For instance, the Japanese government's pension support programme gives non-working married women a greater pension than what working women typically earn, conveying a message to all women that taking care of the home and children is more suitable for them (Eto, 2008).

Special Insights

Rwanda Number One Since 2003 With Maximum Women Parliamentarians

The Rwanda Chamber of Deputies was the first elected national legislature where women held a majority in 2008. At 61.25%, the percentage of female MPs is significantly higher than the current global average of 26.4%. For years, Rwanda has topped the IPU's monthly rating of the number of women serving in national parliament. 2018 saw elections in Rwanda. The country has maintained its top spot in the global list, held since 2003, with 61.3% of women legislators, despite a decline in the proportion of women.

4.9 Women Leaders in Politics

Numerous structural, systemic, and ideological barriers prevent women from having adequate political representation. Women in politics still face challenges even after ascending to the highest levels of authority because institutional changes and legal reforms did not always result in changes to social, cultural, and gender norms. Asia has produced a number of influential female politicians who attracted attention from around the world. Their rise, however, denotes unique patterns in their ties to dynasty politics and familial bonds. Early female political leaders in Asia, notably in South Asia, acquired positions of power by inheriting them from their male relatives as their widows, wives, or daughters. They frequently possessed charisma that was passed down through the family and additionally served practical goals by stifling party factionalism. The political legacies of their male family members helped to legitimate the rise of women leaders like Bandaranaike and Kumaratunga in Sri Lanka, Indira Gandhi in India, Benazir Bhutto in Pakistan, Khaleda Zia and Sheikh Hasina in Bangladesh, and Aung San Suu Kyi in Myanmar. Similarly Yingluck Shinawatra in Thailand, Megawati Sukarnoputri in Indonesia, and Corazon Aquino in the Philippines were able to ascend to the top positions thanks to their familial ties to male politicians. Even while certain female politicians, such as Tanaka Makiko in Japan and Soong Ching Ling in China, did not hold the very highest positions, they were nonetheless able to maintain significant political influence thanks to their husbands' and fathers' respective legacies. The unique political quality of "moral capital," which female dynastic leaders intentionally employ, also contributes to their disadvantage because they are frequently held to high moral standards when dealing with allegations of corruption, scandals, and controversies (Chao and Louisa 2020).

Women's "partaking inclusion" but "participatory exclusion" is another common trend in several nations' political representation of women. Despite the fact that women actively participated in the anti-colonial campaigns and democratic transition against authoritarian governments, their issues are deemed unimportant in the post-transition phase. This exemplifies a participation paradox where involvement paradoxically does not lead to formal participation in political power, institution formation, and decision-making (Razavi, 2001; Waylen, 2007, 2010). Corazon Aquino in the Philippines, Benazir Bhutto in Pakistan, Khaleda Zia and Sheikh Hasina in Bangladesh, Megawati Sukarnoputri in Indonesia, Aung Sang Suu Kyi in Myanmar, and Wan Azizah Wan Ismail in Malaysia are just a few examples of the many women leaders who have spearheaded democratic uprisings against dictatorships.

However, overall women's political participation in these societies has slightly increased. Islamic precepts have been utilized by orthodox Muslim leaders in Bangladesh, Indonesia, Malaysia, and Pakistan to restrict the participation and ascent of women leaders (Thompson, 2002). It has been common practice to disparage women in politics as a means of undermining their standing as political participants.

4.10 Gender Quota

Increasing the percentage of female lawmakers, which can be done through quotas for women, is one strategy to bring about a gendered change of politics (Norris and Lovenduski, 1995). Therefore, many nations around the world have implemented various requirements like quotas, laws or regulations requiring candidate lists or representative bodies to include women, racial, ethnic, or religious minorities. The "incremental track" and "the fast track" are the two methods for ensuring equal participation of women in politics (Dahlerup and Freidenvall, 2005). The incremental track reflects a gradualist strategy, which presupposes that as society advances, so will the proportion of women in parliaments. This strategy is used in the politics of many post-industrial democracies, such as the Nordic countries, where one party's voluntary adoption of gender quotas causes a contagion effect that causes other parties to adopt them as well for electoral reasons, thereby consolidating women's representation through a ripple effect (Matland and Studler, 1996). The fast track strategy, on the other hand, establishes institutional requirements like mandated gender quotas through constitutional modifications at the policy level and is used by countries where it is more difficult to attain female parity in politics, such as several semi or non-democratic governments (Moon et al., 2008).

Party quotas, legislative candidate quotas, and reserved parliamentary seats are the three basic types of quotas. Some Asian nations, like Pakistan and Bangladesh, pioneered gender justice in politics by implementing gender quotas in the 1950s and the 1970s, respectively (Burghoon et al., 2008). Political party quotas exist in Singapore, Thailand, Malaysia, and the Philippines to guarantee a certain percentage of female representation, while legislative candidate quotas exist in Timor-Leste and Indonesia to guarantee the presence of female candidates on the party list. China has a combination of party quotas and reserved seats for women, but India adopted the reserved seat system at the local self-government level. To assure women's representation, Taiwan and South Korea both passed laws establishing reserved seats as well as candidate quotas. Despite the fact that these quotas do not ensure a shift in the political participation of women, countries that have implemented them fare better than those that do not, for instance Japan and Sri Lanka.

The numerous gender quotas, whether in municipal or national legislatures, or in party laws, show an increase in women's representation in nations including Afghanistan, Jordan, Cambodia, India, Pakistan, Indonesia, Nepal, Kyrgyzstan, and Timor-Leste. Between 1948 and February 1998, just sixteen women held cabinet positions in South Korea (Park, 1999). However, since the democratisation in 1987, when the gender quota was introduced, there have been more elected women than ever before, with the total reaching 57 in 2020. (Mobrand, 2018). From 1970 until 1984, there were no women in Singapore's parliament (Chew, 2008). Consequently, a voluntary 30% party quota was implemented to improve the representation of women (Tan, 2016). Similar patterns emerged in Indonesia following the adoption of a 30% gender quota. Following three decades of autocratic control, the nation reverted to democracy in 1999. Law reforms were implemented in 2004 and 2009, and as a result, there was an increase in the representation of women in the 2009 elections (Hillman 2017).

While some nations are keen to include women, others are not; in Taiwan's legislature, for instance, women hold 42% of the seats. China also shows a larger percentage of women represented, which is related to the communist party's implementation of gender quotas. However, in Japan, a country with a developed economy, only 10% of seats are held by women. Exploring the nuances of gender quota, the distinct effects of institutional norms on male and female representatives, the procedures for discussions, and other issues is crucial. In addition, the discussion of the success of gender quotas in democratic and non-democratic regimes offers novel insights on gendered involvement.

Special Insights

Does Gender Quota Help to Increase Women's Representation: Some Facts

Women were elected to parliament at rates of 7 points higher in single or lower chambers and 17 points higher in upper chambers in nations with well-designed gender quotas compared to nations without them. According to the IPU research, more than 130 nations now have quota policies in place, indicating that electoral quotas for women have extended to every continent. However, country-level quota experiences have demonstrated that not all quotas are equally effective. The majority of the time, imposing quotas alone, without any placement guidelines or sanctions, hasn't produced significant advancements in women's parliamentary representation. The IPU analysis also highlights how electoral systems affect women's representation, with the average share of women elected in proportional and mixed systems being noticeably greater (26.5%) than in majoritarian systems (20 per cent).

4.11 Mapping the Trajectory

The ideas covered in the aforementioned sections pose significant issues about the representation of women in politics. What effects, for instance, would reverse discrimination in the form of gender quotas have? Did it result in a significant increase in overall political representation and participation for women? What policy benefits can women expect that will empower them as a group? The Global Gender Gap Index 2021 measures the progression of gender-based gaps through time in four important areas: political participation, health and survival, educational attainment, and economic participation and opportunity. The largest of the four gaps continues to be the gender gap in political empowerment. It demonstrates that women hold just 22.6% of the more than 3,400 ministerial positions and just 26.1% of the 35,500 parliamentary seats around the world, with 81 nations having never had a female head of state. It would take 145 years to attain gender parity in politics (Global Gender Gap Report, WEF, 2021).

In its impact on determining the representation of women, gender quotas interact with party system institutionalisation, electoral rivalry, legal enforcement, and social attitudes toward women. Women struggle to hold key roles in all political parties and across all ideological spectrums, and they hardly ever hold positions of high leadership (Lovenduski and Norris 1993; Burghoon et al., 2008, Moon et al., 2008). In a political system dominated by men, the structure of party affiliations would also discourage women from proposing women-centric policies, and many of them are discovered to be giving up their seats to men in order to uphold party discipline. Women do not want to insult men and jeopardise their careers because men make decisions in parties. Women may be given the opportunity to lead when the party performs poorly or when the male political leader is embroiled in a scandal.

The opposition of male legislators to the growing number of female legislators also serves as a deterrent. Studies show that quotas alone are insufficient to secure the gendering of the political space and the empowerment of women as a group because, in practise, they hardly ever challenge the majority control of men in legislatures (Hughes, 2011). Without taking into account all of the challenges faced by women, adding women to current structures and procedures may not result in significant changes. According to Rosabeth Moss Kanter's (1977) "critical mass" hypothesis, which was adapted from physics to analyse organisational change, politics will alter once women make up a certain percentage of a parliament because some sort of tipping point will have been reached (Studlar and McAllister 2002). Recent scholarship, however, emphasises "critical acts" (Dahlerup 1988; Childs and Krook 2006, 2008). For instance, several of the women who were voted to seats in Nepal's local elections in 2017—where they made up 40.9 percent of the electorate—said that they required more training in political governance since they were having trouble managing finances (DFAT 2018). Due to socially imposed gender norms in families, Japanese women are hesitant to run for government (Kage et al 2019). In 2005, the Liberal Democratic Party's Koizumi Junichiro and the Democratic Party of Japan's Ozawa Ichiro supported a large number of female candidates for tactical reasons. Despite the fact that the number of female candidates and MPs in the 2009 election was the most ever in Japan, they were nonetheless seen as the party leader's subjects and were referred to as "Koizumi's female children" or "the Ozawa girls" (Kubo and Lee, 2017). Women in South Korea who benefit from gender quotas are expected to vote along party lines in order to return the party's favour (Shin, 2016). In addition, compared to 30% of their male counterparts, more over 50% of female PR members who served between 2008 and 2012 resigned from politics after their terms were up (Huang, 2019). In India, women who were elected to local self-government positions based on quotas were known as "proxy women," while their spouses—commonly referred to as Panchayat Patis (Panchayat spouse)—performed the actual administration. In many instances, women ran for election from reserved seats in place of their husbands (Rai and Sharma, 2000). Many Pakistani women councillors reported that they are frequently not even consulted on policy topics and are frequently not even invited to council meetings (Rai, 2005).

Women-centric policies have not emerged as a result of China's numerical growth in the number of women in politics or Bangladesh's presence of women in the top political posts. Due to quotas, a varied group of female lawmakers may not be motivated to advance women's problems because of political pressures (Krook, 2010). Even those nations with higher participation rates, like China, are only balanced at the middle levels, with no women in the highest positions due to the "glass ceiling effect" (Zeng, 2014). Women leaders were given opportunities primarily to represent gender stereotypes associated with docility, family values, morality, and portrayals as mothers or sisters of the oppressed nation. They are typically assigned softer portfolios, such as women's affairs, family and children's affairs, health, education, and culture. Additionally, events impeachment or accusations of power abuse against Yingluck Shinawatra in Thailand and Park Geun-hye in South Korea were interpreted as evidence of women's inefficiency in politics, which had a detrimental effect on their overall participation. Amy C. Alexander conducted a comparative study across 25 varied nations representing various areas and cultures to determine the relationship between the number of women in parliament and changes in women's confidence in their capacity to rule (Alexander 2012). The study came to the conclusion that having more women in legislatures has significant symbolic significance and increases women's citizens' confidence in their abilities to lead. Women may not always be represented by other women, but it is likely that when they hold leadership positions, they will advocate for pro-women measures more than men will. Gender-sensitive legislation has been introduced by female lawmakers in numerous nations, including the Netherlands, France, Sweden, Egypt, Rwanda, and South Africa. Reyes-Householder (2016) suggests that female presidents generally assure higher female cabinet representation by nominating more women to their cabinet than their male counterparts in her study on Latin America. In a related analysis, Tiffany D. Barnes and Mark P. Jones (2018) demonstrate that Argentina has approved a number of significant laws to advance women's rights, which have been made feasible by the increase in female representation in national and local legislatures over the past two decades. According to a research by Jennifer Piscopo (2014) women legislators in Mexico wrote and passed more laws concerning women's interests than their male counterparts across party lines. When moving various forms of motions and voting, Pakistani lawmakers have shown similar trends of cross-party coordination (Ahmed, 2020).

4.12 Conclusion

In conclusion, this chapter makes the case that gender mapping and gender-specific analysis can improve the narrative of comparative politics. By including gender-based analyses from all over the world, the field of comparative studies can become more diverse. The discussion in this chapter offers gender-perspective cultural and political insights and shows that gender exclusions must be researched in relation to regional specifics in order to improve the narrative of political discourse. The academic discipline, political structures and societal norms require re-engagement from a gender perspective.

Even though the discipline of Comparative Politics highly desires comparative research of large *n* case studies on various gender issues, the need of region-specific research also remains pertinent. The small *n* methods provide detailed study of selected features of specific regions, thereby opening opportunities for non-Western countries to become the part of larger discourse of comparative politics. The complexity and intricacies of industrialised and developing countries influence the nature and context of gender issues. The field can escape the trap of Eurocentrism by allowing the multiplicity of gender-specific case studies from other areas. Inclusion of cross-regional gender-based analysis would assure gendering of the field.

Keywords

Gender
Comparative Politics
Women's Representation
Gender Quota
Women Leaders

Review Questions

1. Why according to you gendering comparative politics will change the nature of the discipline?
2. Examine the possibilities and difficulties of gendering the field of comparative politics.
3. Discuss the various forms of gender quota adopted in different regions of the world to increase women's representation.
4. What factors determine the nature of women's political representation? Does adding more women in politics influence the nature of policies formed.

References

Ahmed, N. 2020. *Parliament in South Asia India, Pakistan and Bangladesh*. New York: Routledge.

Alexander, A.C. 2012. "Change in Women's Descriptive Representation and the Belief in Women's Ability to Govern: A Virtuous Cycle." Politics and Gender 8: 437–464.

Baldez, L. 2010. The Gender Lacuna in Comparative Politics. *Perspectives on Politics*, 8 (1):199–205.

Barnes, T. Jones. M. 2018. "Women's Representation in the Argentine National and Subnational Governments." In Ed. Leslie Schwindt-Bayer. Women, Representation, and Politics in Latin America. New York: Oxford University Press, 121–139

BBC News, "Australian politician becomes first to breastfeed in parliament" 10th May 2017 Available at https://www.bbc.com/news/world-australia-39853360

Beckwith, K. 2005. A Common Language of Gender? *Politics & Gender,* 1(1):128–182.

Beckwith, K. 2010. Comparative Politics and the Logics of a Comparative Politics of Gender. *Perspectives on Politics*, 8 (1):159–168.

Boix, C. Stokes, S. (Eds.). 2007. *The Oxford Handbook of Comparative Politics*. Oxford: Oxford University Press.

Burghoorn W., Iwanga, K., Milwertz, C. & Wang, Q. 2008. Gender Politics in Asia: Women Maneuvering within Dominant Gender Orders. Nordic Institute of Asian Studies Press

Caraway, T. 2010.Gendering Comparative Politics. *Perspectives on Politics*, 8 (1):169–175.

Celis, K. Kantola, J. Waylen, G. Weldon, L. 2013. Introduction: Gender and Politics: A Gendered World, a Gendered Discipline. In Waylen, G. Celis, K. Kantola, J. and S. Weldon L. Ed. *The Oxford Handbook of Gender and Politics*. Oxford: Oxford University Press.

Chappell, L. 2006. Comparing Political Institutions: Revealing the Gendered "Logic of Appropriateness" *Politics and Gender*, 2(2): 223–235. https://doi.org/10.1017/S1743923X06221044

Chao, C. Louisa, H., 2020. Asian Women Leadership: A cross-national and cross-sector Comparison. Routledge

Chew, P. 2008. "No Fire in the Belly': Women's Political Role in Singapore". In W. Burghoorn et al. (Eds.). Gender Politics in Asia: Women Maneuvering within Dominant Gender Order [p. 185–216]. Nordic Institute of Asian Studies Press

Childs, S. Krook, M. L. 2006. 'Should Feminists Give Up on Critical Mass? A Contingent Yes', Politics and Gender, 2 (4), 522–30

Childs, S. Krook, M. L. 2008. Critical Mass Theory and Women's Political Representation. Political Studies, 56: 725–736. doi: 10.1111/j.1467–9248.2007.00712.x

Collins P. H. 1990. *Black feminist thought: knowledge, consciousness and the politics of Empowerment*. Boston: Unwin Hyman.

Dahlerup, D. Freidenvall, L. 2005. Quotas as a "Fast Track" to Equal Representation for Women: Why Scandinavia is no longer the model. International Feminist Journal of Politics, 7(1), 26–48.

Dahlerup, D. 1988. From a small to large minority: Women in Scandinavian politics. Scandinavian Political Studies 11: 275–297

DFAT – TAF Australian Government Partnership on Subnational Governance in Nepal, 2018.

Eisenstein Z. 1981. *The Radical Future of Liberal Feminism*. New York: Longman.

Elshtain J. B. 1981. *The Public and the Private: A Critical Inquiry*. Princeton: Princeton University Press.

Eto, M. 2008. "Community Based Movements of Japanese Women: How Mothers in filtrate the Political Sphere From Below". In W. Lundström-Burghoorn. (Ed.). Gender politics in Asia: Women manoeuvring within dominant gender orders (pp. 43–67). essay, NIAS Press.

France-Presse, A. 2019. "Danish MP told her baby not welcome in parliament." *The Telegraph*, 20th March. Accessed from https://www.telegraph.co.uk on September 12, 2020.

Folke, O. Rickne J. 2016. All the Single Ladies: Job Promotions and the Durability of Marriage. IFN Working Paper No. 1146. https://www.ifn.se/wfiles/wp/wp1146.pdf

Global Gender Gap Report 2021, World Economic Forum. Available at https://www3.weforum.org. Accessed on August 16, 2023.

Hillman, B. 2017. Increasing Women's Parliamentary Representation in Asia and the Pacific: The Indonesian Experience. Asia and the Pacific Policy Studies, 4(1), 38–49

Hawkesworth, M. 2005. Engendering Political Science: An Immodest Proposal. *Politics and Gender*, 1(1):137–141.https://doi.org/10.1017/S1743923X0523101X

Htun, M. 2005. What It Means to Study Gender and the State? *Politics and Gender* 1 (1):157–166.https://doi.org/10.1017/S1743923X05241016

Hooks, B. 1984. *Feminist theory: from margin to center*. Cambridge, MA: South End Press.

Huang, C. 2019. "Gender Quotas and Women's Increasing Political Competitiveness," *Taiwan Journal of Democracy* 15 (1): 25–40.

Hughes, M. 2011. Intersectionality, Quotas and Minority Women's Political Representation Worldwide. American Political science Review, 105(3), 604–620

Inter-Parliamentary Union. 2016. Sexism, harassment and violence against women Parliamentarians. Accessed from https://www.ipu.org on August 2, 2023.

Inglehart, R. Norris, P. 2003. *Rising tide: Gender equality and Cultural change*. Cambridge: Cambridge University Press.

Kage, R. Rosenbluth, F. Tanaka, S. 2019. What Explains Low Female Political Representation? Evidence from Survey Experiments in Japan. *Politics and Gender* 15 (2): 285–309.

Kang, A. 2017. Women's Organizations and Substantive Representation in Africa. In Golder, M. Golder, S. Ed. *Comparative Politics Newsletter the Organized Section in Comparative Politics of the American Political Science Association*, 27(1). Accessed from http://mattgolder.com on August 12, 2023.

Kittilson, M.C. Schwindt-Bayer, L.A. 2012. *The Gendered Effects of Electoral Institutions: Political Engagement and Participation*. Oxford: Oxford University Press.

Krook, M. L. Childs, S. (Eds.). 2010. *Women, Gender, and Politics: A Reader*. New York: Oxford University Press

Kubo, M. Lee, A. 2017. "Electing Women to the Japanese Lower House: The Impact of the Electoral System." *Asian Women* 33(2): 69–99.

Lichbach, M.I. Zuckerman, A.S. 2009. *Comparative Politics: Rationality, Culture and Structure*. New York: Cambridge University Press.

Lovenduski, J. 1998. Gendering Research in Political Science. *Annual Review of Political Science*, 1: 333–356. https://doi.org/10.1146/annurev.polisci.1.1.333

Matland, R. E., Studlar, D. T. 1996. The contagion of women candidates in single-member district and Proportional Representation Electoral Systems: Canada and Norway. The Journal of Politics, 58(3), 707–733. https://doi.org/10.2307/2960439

Mobrand, E. 2018. On parties' terms: Gender quota politics in South Korea's mixed electoral system. Asian Studies Review, 43(1), 114–131. https://doi.org/10.1080/10357823.2018.1512554

Moon, K. Chun, K. Kim, M. Kim, E. 2008. A Comparative Study of Electoral Gender Quotas in Sweden, Germany, and South Korea: Focusing on the Interplay of the Main Actors in the Processes of the Implementation of Quota Policies. Asian Women, 24(1),75–100.

Munck, G.L. Snyder, R. 2007. *Passion, Crafts and Methods in Comparative Politics*. Baltimore: The John Hopkins University Press.

Norris, P. Lovenduski, J. 1995. *Political Recruitment: Gender Race and Class in British Parliament*. Cambridge: Cambridge University Press.

Okin, S. M. 1979. *Women in Western Political Thought*. Princeton, NJ: Princeton University Press

Pateman, C. 1988. *The Sexual Contract*. USA: Stanford University Press.

Park, K.-A. 1999. Political representation and South Korean women. The Journal of Asian Studies, 58(2), 432–448. https://doi.org/10.2307/2659403

Piscopo, J. M. 2014. Beyond hearth and home: female legislators, feminist policy change, and substantive representation in Mexico. Revista Uruguaya de Ciencia Política, 32(2), 87–110

Rai, S. M. Sharma, K. 2000. 'Democratising the Indian Parliament: the "Reservation for Women" Debate', in S. M. Rai. (Ed.). *International Perspectives on Gender and Democratisation*. Basingstoke: Macmillan

Rai, S. 2005. 'Reserved Seats in South Asia: A Regional Perspective', in J. Billington and A. Karam. (Eds.). *Women in Parliament: Beyond Numbers*, Stockholm: International Institute for Democracy and Electoral Assistance (IDEA)

Razavi, S. 2001. Women in contemporary democratization. International Journal of Politics, Culture and Society, 15(1), 201–224.

Reyes-Housholder C. 2016. President as rise: consequences for women in cabinet? Latin American Politics and Society 58(3), 3–25

Roy, E.A. 2018. "Jacinda Ardern makes history with baby Neve at UN general assembly." The Guardian, September 24. https://www.theguardian.com/world/2018/sep/25/jacinda-ardern-makes-history-with-baby-neve-at-un-general-assembly

Schwindt-Bayer, L. 2010. Comparison and Integration: A Path toward a Comparative Politics of Gender. *Perspectives on Politics*, 8 (1):177–182.

Shin, K. 2016. "Women's Mobilizations for Political Representation in Patriarchal States: Models from Japan and South Korea," in *Gender and Power: Towards Equality and Democratic Governance*. (Ed.). Mino Vianello and Mary Hawkesworth UK: Palgrave Macmillan, 344–65.

Smooth, W. 2011. Standing for Women? Which women? The substantive representation of women's interests and the research imperative of intersectionality. *Politics and Gender*, 7(3): 436–441.

Squires, J. 1999. *Gender in Political Theory*. Cambridge: Polity Press.

Studlar, D. McAllister, I. 2002. Does a critical mass exist? A comparative analysis of women's legislative representation since 1950. European Journal of Political Research 41: 233–253

Tan, N. 2020. "Women and Politics in East and Southeast Asia". In S. Maisel. (Ed.). Oxford Bibliographies in Political Science. Oxford University Press

Tan, N. 2016. Gender Reforms, Electoral Quotas, and Women's Political Representation in Taiwan, South Korea, and Singapore. Pacific Affairs, 89(2), 309–323

Thompson, M. 2002. 'Female leadership of democratic transitions in Asia', *Pacific Affairs*, 75(4): 535–55.

Tremblay, M. 2007. Democracy, Representation, and Women: A Comparative Analysis. Democratization, 14(4):533–553.

Tripp, A. M. 2006. "Why So Slow? The Challenges of Gendering Comparative Politics." *Politics & Gender* 2 (2): 249–263.

Tripp, A.M. 2010. Toward a Comparative Politics of Gender Research in which Women Matter. *Perspectives on Politics*. 8 (1):191–197.

Waylen, G. 2007. *Engendering Transitions: Women's Mobilization, Institutions and Gender Outcomes*. Oxford: Oxford University Press.

Waylen G. 2010. A comparative Politics of Gender: Limits and possibilities. *Perspective on politics*, 8 (1) 223–231. https://doi.org/10.1017/S1537592709992805

Weldon, L. 2006. The Structure of Intersectionality: A Comparative Politics of Gender *Politics and Gender*, 2 (2):235–248. https://doi.org/10.1017/S1743923X06231040

Zeng, B. 2014. Women's Political Participation in China: Improved or Not?. Journal of International Women's Studies, 15(1), 136–150

CHAPTER **5**

Capitalism: Origin, Growth and Evolution

Skylab Sahu

Reader's Guide

Capitalism emerged in Europe during the 16th and 17th centuries and evolved tremendously thereafter. Capitalism is defined as an economic system where private actors own and control the use of property as per their own interests, within a market economy determined by the principles of supply and demand. The capitalist society encourages competition and targets to achieve efficiency and productivity. Government is often expected to maintain peace, justice and tolerable taxes. Some liberal thinkers believe that capitalism and individualism are intimately related. They suggest that capitalism promotes economic and political freedom of people and thus defend individual against the state. However, in contrast, the socialist and specifically the contemporary Marxist thinkers believe that only a small group of people called as the capitalists have control over the economy and production and hence play a dominant role within the society as against the subordinate class. Capitalism as a socio-economic mode of life is not uniform in nature. Capitalism during the 17th century is different from capitalism in the 19th or 20th century and it is distinct in the era of globalization. Capitalism also varies across places; it is not the same in the United States as in China, not the same in Germany as in Scandinavia, Singapore or Thailand. This chapter highlights the origin, growth and development of capitalism, its implications and lastly it discusses how capitalism varies across nation states.

5.1 Introduction

Capitalism is a socio-economic system where the production and distribution is owned privately. The emergence of the Industrial Revolution introduced capitalism as the new economic form. The economic revolution which took place in the Western world during the Industrial Revolution, coupled with the imperialist rule, reinforced capitalism around the world in subsequent two centuries (Heller 2011). Capitalism was synonymously used for economic individualism and was viewed as a simple system of natural liberty. Economic individualism recognizes the pursuit of self-interest and the right to own private property which is morally and legally legitimized and accepted within the capitalist society. It can be explained as a system in which individuals compete with each other to accumulate wealth while having the right to use the land, labour and capital to produce goods and services for selling them to gain profit (Smith 1776, 75). The intention for profit makes capitalist enterprises to search for new markets, to develop new production and use new machines and technologies which can reduce their cost of production.

The capitalist society remains a society where the socio-economic system operates closely with the political system where the laws, rules and governance operate in favour of the capitalist endeavour and in tandem with capitalists. The state as a watchdog exists to secure and protect individuals and their rights, by making them free to decide where to invest, what to produce or sell, and what prices to charge. The government may impose restricted or limited charges for generating some revenues.

Diverse societies usually possessed varied economic attitudes and behaviours of people. When a particular pattern of the economic system operated through the dominant mode of production, a particular manner of the social relations also prevailed around the mode of production. The particular socio-economic relation of production functioned within the larger society, in correspondence to the institutions or the set of rules and behaviours that governs production and distribution of the society. Marx's argument was that when the society moved from the agrarian mode of production (landlord versus serfs) to the capitalism, not only the mode of production changed, but the production relations (capitalists and labours including both intra- and interrelationship) also changed. Subsequently, the attitude of people and the human behaviour accepted the prevailing forces of production. Values of the life that prevailed during agrarian economy changed within capitalism. For example, within capitalist society, individual-centric, need-based and materialist values became prominent.

Capitalism prevailed across centuries and spaces. The nature of capitalism in the 17th century is different from capitalism from the 19th to 20th century. The connotation of capitalism is totally different in the era of globalization. Capitalism may also vary across places; it is not the same in the United States as in China, not the same in Germany as in Scandinavia, Singapore or Thailand. Capitalism that persisted in the 19th-century England is not the same as it is continuing in the 21st-century England.

5.2 Theories of Capitalism

5.2.1 Liberal Theory of Capitalism

Adam Smith viewed capital improvement as the central aim of the economic and political system. In his book *An Inquiry into the Nature and Causes of the Wealth of Nations* (1776), he has tried to answer the question why some nations are wealthier than the others; it was not that other countries worked harder or have better resources. He then answered that the free trade followed in any country enhanced the economy. Smith argued that the barter system was restricted in nature; people had to wait to trade things that other people wanted through barter. The introduction of money removed that obstacle. He said that money made trade easier. In order to allow the trade to be free, there was further requirement of fewer regulations for a smoother economy. Buying and selling happened naturally and continued until the governing body stepped in to regulate this system. When governments stepped out of regulation, the capitalists could always work to make the biggest profit. When business owners have had a large vision of profit in mind, they would put out their best work. He gave the example of a butcher; if the butcher sold out bad cuts of meat, his customers would not come back. He might make a profit in the short term, but not in the long term. He further stated the invisible hand of the market ensured a prosperous system that worked for the good of the majority. Because of the free economy, Smith acknowledged that some would become extremely rich, and some would remain poor. For him, this was, however, inevitable for a thriving economy whereby the majority could pursue their happiness and goals, whereas the system unavoidably allowed for some measure of inequality.

In response to the economic theory of mercantilism, he stated that the economic system was a collection of winners and losers. For one country to get rich, it was necessary that another country became poor. Resources were limited, and it was right and just to benefit one's own country at the expense of another. This theory meant that countries tried hard to bring money and resources within their borders but blocked free exchange so that money stayed inside. Countries would levy large tariffs on goods coming from outside countries, sometimes at the expense of their own goods.

5.2.1.1 Neoliberal Thinkers and Capitalism

The modern liberal thinkers such as Nozick (2013) and A. Hayek believe that capitalism and individualism are intimately related. They suggest that capitalism promotes economic and political freedom of people and thus defends individuals against the state. However, by contrast, socialists and specifically contemporary Marxist thinkers believe that only a small group of people called capitalists have control over the economy and, hence, play a dominant role within the society. The subordinate class remains far from assimilated within the society as against the dominant class (Abercrombie, Turner, and Hill 2015).

David Ricardo's book *On the Principles of Political Economy and Taxation* argued trade as a development activity. Ricardo's idea on the international free trade was based largely on Adam Smith's idea of specialization of labour and specialization of the production. Smith famously wrote in *The Wealth of Nations*, 'If the wines of France are better and cheaper than those of Portugal, or its linens than those of Germany, it would be more advantageous for Great Britain to purchase both the wine and the foreign linen which it had occasion for of France than of Portugal and Germany'. Yet, Smith's argument was incomplete, as it relied on the notion of absolute advantage. Ricardo completed the argument with the idea of comparative advantage. He wrote that nations should focus on production in which they are efficient instead of just trading whatever was left out, such that states could build comparative advantages.

The liberal school, while propagating for the free trade, justified economic inequality and the presence of a gap between people who get benefited out of the economy and the poor. In fact, Adam Smith has gone to the extent of saying that some amount of inequality should be there and government may not intend to bridge the economic gap. Similarly, in the international context too, they have highlighted profit as the factor that should drive any nation for trade.

Special Insights

Max Weber on Capitalism and Rationality

Max Weber (1905) in his book *The Protestant Ethic and the Spirit of Capitalism* has discussed that capitalism evolved and developed when the Protestant ethic influenced large numbers of people to engage in work in the European world, which in turn helped individuals in developing their own enterprises and engaging in trade and accumulation of wealth. Weber defines that being influenced by the Protestant, people started showing dedication to disciplined work and acquisition, along with a life of denial of pleasure and spontaneity in enjoyment of life. 'Within capitalism the 'earning of more and more money, along with the strict avoidance of all spontaneous enjoyment of life, ... is thought of ... purely as an end in itself, ... Man is dominated by the making of money, by acquisition as the ultimate purpose of his life'. This is an example of what is meant by traditionalism. A man does not 'by nature' wish to earn more and more money, but simply to live, as he is accustomed to live and to earn as much as is necessary for that purpose. A shift to expansion of output on the basis of lower prices took place and, in general, the leisurely ways of conducting business gave way to the competitive struggle. And, what is most important in this connection, it was not generally in such cases a stream of new money invested in the industry which brought about this revolution ... but the new spirit, the spirit of modern capitalism, had set to work' (Weber 1905, 68).

5.2.2 Karl Marx and Theory of Capitalism

Marx's theory of modern capitalism was constructed as part of a more general theory of society. Marx conceptualized the proletariat as a unique element, and a major political force, in the capitalist society.

Marx understood capitalism as a system of production; for him each mode of production further consisted of particular relations of production, which in turn gave rise to a specific class structure. He stated that the economy did not consist of merely material things but was made up of relations between people who were connected to one another through the process of production. In a capitalist society, commodification started when things which were not traded earlier in the market become commodities for sale. For example, labour or skills of an individual become things that could be bought and sold. In earlier times, human beings themselves were bought and sold as slaves, but today it is considered immoral to treat people as commodities. But in modern capitalist society, almost everyone accepts the idea that a person's labour can be bought and other services or skills can be provided in exchange for money. Yet, in the capitalist economy, labourers are free to choose to work or to accept a circumstance of production, which was not the case with slaves.

Under the capitalist mode of production, labourers or workers sold their labour in the market to earn their wage. This gave rise to two basic classes—capitalists, who own the means of production (industries and factories), and workers, who sold their labour to capitalists. The capitalist class was able to get profit from this system by paying workers less than the value of what they actually produced, thus extracting surplus value from their labour. Marx's criticism of capitalism as discussed could be identified as two types: scientific criticism of capitalism and humanistic criticism of capitalism. Marx argues that capitalism is the last stage of the exploitation of individuals. In such exploitative condition, workers would be conscious of their position and exploitation and then the workers of all lands would unite and bring an end to the exploitative capitalist society. Followed by the revolution, the workers would be able to build a classless and stateless egalitarian society.

However, despite a scientific method of social change propagated by Karl Marx,[1] with the assumption that when the society will reach the highest form of capitalism, exploitation will be maximum, which would ultimately lead to the fall of capitalism. However, revolution occurred in the agrarian countries such as Russia and China is yet to be seen. Marxists had a challenge to explain the phenomenon and to reinterpret history.

5.2.2.1 Neo-Marxists on Capitalism

The question remained how the capitalist state could prevent the crisis of the state? In response, Gramsci (1970), who is often considered the theoretician of the superstructure, has discussed the cultural and intellectual hegemony within the society. It highlights how the state and ruling capitalist class use cultural institutions to maintain power in capitalist societies. In this regard, the civil society as the sphere of several religious and cultural institutions indeed helps to build consent towards the ruling party. The bourgeoisie, in Gramsci's view, develops a hegemonic culture using ideology, which helps to maintain the dominance. However, force remains dialectically related with the struggle for hegemony within the civil society. He stated that both persuasion and force was required for any revolution. Hegemonic culture propagates its own values and norms so that they become the 'common sense' values of all and thus maintain the status quo. Hegemonic power is therefore used to maintain consent to the capitalist order. The capitalist economic system survives as is accepted at the socio-cultural and political levels as a hegemonic order. The dominant class remain instrumental to establish such hegemony through their influence and intervention in civil society, political, legal and ideological institutions, which in return support the capitalist system and the capitalist state.

Miliband argued that liberal democracies retained capitalism openly. The social democracy, although achieved a lot of things, has not been able to make capitalism disappear. In return, the social democracies have made capitalists more tolerable for the working classes within the ambit of the capitalist system. The capitalist state works in close proximity of the state. The capitalist system, while aiming at profit, also caters to some of the basic needs of the workers such as health, housing, education, wages, industrial relations, social insurance, old-age pensions and so on. In the process, the capitalist system protects itself from crisis and prevents itself from the pressure of revolution or failure.

Poulantzas disagrees with Miliband's (1958) approach by adopting a structural position; he asserted that the state is objectively a capitalist entity, which can serve no purpose other than preserving the capitalist mode of production. The state reproduces capitalist relations irrespective of who is in power in the state. He further argued, 'the relation between the bourgeois class and the state is an objective relation. This means that if the function of the state in a determinate social formation and the interests of the dominant class coincide, it is by reason of the system itself: the direct participation of members of the ruling class in the state apparatus is not the cause but the effect'.

Special Insights

Schumpeter's View of Capitalism

Schumpeter's theory of capitalism has on one side Marx's ideas (and with some later Marxist views) and on the other side those of Max Weber. Its distinct feature, however, is Schumpeter's emphasis upon the role of the entrepreneur as the principal agent of capitalist development. In *The Theory of Economic Development* (1926), he perceives development or change as resulting from 'new combinations' of materials and forces in the sphere of production, a process which has three aspects. First, these new combinations 'are, as a rule, embodied ... in new firms which generally do not arise out of the old ones but start producing beside them ...'. Second, 'command over means of production is necessary to the carrying out of new combinations', and this is achieved above all by the use of credit, which Schumpeter sees as 'the characteristic method of the capitalist type of society ... for forcing the economic system into new channels'. The third element is 'the fundamental phenomenon of economic development', namely, the entrepreneur or 'captain of industry'.

Schumpeter summarized his view of capitalism as follows: 'Capitalism is that form of private property economy in which innovations are carried out by means of borrowed money, which in general, though not by logical necessity, implies credit creation' and the individuals who carry out these innovations 'we call entrepreneurs' (Bottomore 2010, 37).

5.3 Capitalism: Characteristics

Capitalism emphasizes on private ownership of the property, including assets such as land, industry or any other project and raw materials which are employed in producing goods and services for people. In no other system the right to private property is legally inviolable. The state cannot appropriate any property owned privately, except through the legal procedure. Moreover, it remains inescapable for the state to protect the right to own and accrue wealth legally without the fear of theft and plunder. In the pre-capitalist system, that is, in slavery and feudalism, wealth could be acquired either through heredity or through force. By contrast, within capitalism, wealth is accumulated through surplus value.

One of the ways to distinguish between the capitalist and socialist forms of government is to see the nature and pattern of the property right vested with private individuals or institutions or organizations. For example, in the former Soviet Union, the ownership of the property was with the state or the state authorities, and private individuals had no right to control. When a state moves from socialism to capitalism, one of the initial things is the restoration of right to private property. In 1991, this procedure of property reallocation from public to private had taken place in the states where the liberalization and privatization model was applied. In China too, in the mid-1970s onwards, the introduction of the special economic zone and many other initiatives enabled private people to invest in the economy and profit making. However, it does not mean that in capitalist states there would not be any state ownership. In capitalist states, most of the property is owned by private individuals, yet a few major sectors like gas, oil or electricity could be owned by the state. In the capitalist state, ownership by the state however remains minimal in comparison with private ownership. By contrast, in a socialist or communist state, the economy remains state owned.

Second, individuals have ownership over their own bodies, unlike slave system or feudal system where individuals may be owned by others and Marxist socialist system where labour can be directed by the state authority and they are generally not free to bargain over the level of remuneration. However, Marx stated that individuals who do not own any resources may have very less choices but to sell their brains or their muscle to an employer for a specific period. It does not mean a complete surrender of the individual to the employer or the employment condition; the workers retain the choice of employer and they also remain free to negotiate over the terms and conditions of their employment. The labour processes under capitalism are therefore based on contract rather than coercion, custom or duty.

The third characteristic of capitalism is that the economic pursuit in the capitalist society is undertaken for profit. The money system enabled capitalism to grow beyond individual locality. Raw materials and finished products are bought and sold for money in a relatively free and competitive market. The system of exchange is mostly based on the market price (price influenced by supply and demand). However, the market may not be totally free, rather it may be relatively free. In most of the countries, the government regulates the market; the state decides the amount of the tax that needs to be levied against any goods imported and so on. Therefore, the market cannot be totally free, yet it largely works in favour of capitalists. The capitalist market system also can be contrasted with the socialist system where the production and exchange are largely controlled by the state. In the communist state, the movement of products in terms of import and export is mostly restricted by the state.

Competition acts as a balance to excessive profits when producers strive with one another for attracting customers. During the early industrial capitalism, the trend has been towards less competition among companies. The early capitalism was monopoly capitalism. A classic example could be the virtual monopoly on oil held by John D. Rockfellwe's standard oil company. Competition was reduced by increasing concentration within a particular industry. An 'oligopoly' exists when several companies tremendously control an entire industry. An example is the music industry, in which four giant companies are behind many of the labels and artists. More specially, a shared monopoly exists when four or fewer companies supply 50 per cent or more of a particular market. Examples include US automobile manufacturers and cereal companies. In a capitalist economy, there could also be perfect competition where the market decides the price based on the supply and demand. However, in most of the capitalist economies, there is a possibility of having different economic sectors having diverse patterns of economies, that is, monopoly, oligopoly and perfect competition.

In advanced monopoly capitalism, mergers also occur across industries: corporation gain near monopoly control over all aspects of the production and distribution of a product by acquiring both the companies that supply raw materials and companies that are outlets for products. For example, an oil company may hold leases on the land where the oil is pumped out of the ground and own the individual gasoline stations that sell the product to the public. Corporations with control both within and across industries are often formed by a series of mergers and acquisitions across industries. These corporations are referred to as conglomerates—combinations of business in different commercial areas, all of which are owned by one holding company. Completion is also reduced over a long run by interlocking corporate directorates—members of the board of directors of one corporation who also sits on the boards of other corporations.

Wage labour is another characteristic of the capitalism system. In the primitive communal mode, there is no distinction between the owner and producer. Under slavery, the direct producer was a slave and, thus, was the part of the means of production. Labourers had not much freedom of mobility, and thus, they used to receive very little or subsistence. In capitalism, labourers are fully mobile both specially and occupationally as they were not physically compelled to work for the capitalist unlike the previous socio-economic system. But the proletarian labourer owns no property and depends merely on his own labour. The capitalist society is clearly divided into two classes: one who owns the means of production and the other as wage labourers. In pre-capitalist societies, labourers used to be paid by kind rather than cash, and the payment and work conditions used to be governed by customs and traditions. The labourers work to get their wages in capitalism and he or she is not compelled to work in a particular factory or under any particular capitalist. Rather, he or she is free to choose if to work or not to work and where to work. Wage in the capitalist system is determined by demand and supply of labour in the market (Suresh 2010).

The capitalist economy is market economy, and it does not mean that market existed within capitalism; rather it existed even in the pre-capitalist system. Those pre-capitalist markets were local markets or long-distance markets. However, the pre-capitalist markets were less competitive. In capitalism, the production is mainly for the market to gain more profit to get more value. Market economy is an economic system which is controlled, regulated and directed by the market itself (Suresh 2010).

5.4 Capitalism: Origin, Growth and Evolution

Some of the features of a capitalist system were present in many ancient societies. Trading between societies, nations and empires is as old as human civilization. There were private individuals who used to do trading in every era. However, all these were on a small scale. The economic system of capitalism is a modern system. One of the most important distinguishing features of this system is the centrality of market and dependence of people upon the system. Unlike earlier trading systems, capitalism envelops every sphere of human activity and guides production, distribution and consumption in totality.

5.4.1 Feudalism to Capitalism: A Phase of Transition

The socio-economic condition of a country is usually diverse in nature and also changes from time to time. However, despite a diverse trajectory followed by different countries in development, there remains some common tendency across all the countries, a tendency of shift from feudalism to capitalism. A few states although took the trajectory of socialism followed by feudalism or mixed agrarian and capitalist economy before they could be capitalist ultimately. Yet, till date, countries have remained either pre-capitalist or going to be a part of the capitalist economy soon.

In England, by the 11th century, there was growth in the productive forces, and there was technological advancement in the agrarian sector. One of the most important agrarian advancement made was the replacement of the two-field system of crop rotation with the three-field system. This change had several consequences including growth in production, growth of the population, the enclosure movement, growth of towns and cities and rapid increase of urban centres.

Capitalism began to start around the 13th century, substituting feudalism in England around the 16th and 17th centuries. High growth in agriculture achieved in the time increased the productivity, changed production and distribution pattern, and production and distribution relation or the mode of the production. This led to the social differentiation in agriculture such as the growth of the Kulak class, the substitution of labour renting to money renting. Farmers sold the surplus grain in the local market and remained profited. Peasants were able to rent land from landlords and retain the excess of their produce after paying the rent of the land. This led to the emergence of capitalist farmers in the European society also known as the Kulaks. They had incentives for improving the productivity because of having a fixed rent for the lands. This led to more marketing, trade and commutation. As a result, subsequently, these changing scenarios brought an end to the traditional agrarian economy. Search for market and profit became the guiding principle of production, leading to 'market feudalism' (Suresh 2010).

'The Enclosure programme' converted common resources to the encroached gazing land that led to the increase in sheep breeding and productivity of wool. In the process, the population of rural areas was displaced as it had no common resource to depend upon; people having inadequate entitlement to land also lost control over land. As a result, there was a sudden increase of landless labourers and unemployment (these unemployed people were the reserved army of unemployed). Simultaneously, the growing trade and town led to the rural–urban specialization and growth of trade between the rural manor and the city. Within agrarian societies, technological improvements led to the displacement of labour from agriculture. At the same time, manufacturing units and textile and mineral sectors developed, which were able to employ labour displaced from agriculture. Agricultural activity was located in rural areas, whereas industries were located in urban areas. This led to the subsequent migration of population from rural areas to urban areas. As the productivity increased in the agricultural sector, lesser amount of land was needed for feeding their population. This decreased the importance of land. Starting of industrial firms needed capital, which made the owners of capital the most important and powerful section of the population. Capitalism could be regarded as being present as soon as the act of the production and the retail sale came to be separated. For Karl Marx, the city signified the transition from feudalism to capitalism. It determined the territorial shift in the concentration of capital and the means of production to urban areas. There was decreasing feudal aristocracy and authority of the lords and rise of the bourgeoisie. The city was perceived as progressive because it exemplified the switch of historical, political and cultural parameters not present in the agrarian rural areas (Chandoke 1991). There was a rise of the capitalist class in towns and rural areas, and there was a subsequent increase of exploitation with feudalism. Due to unbearable exploitation, the surfs revolted against the feudal lords in the 13th and 14th centuries that led to the subsequent collapse of feudalism.

There were also other reasons which were responsible for the fall of feudalism in England. The Hundred years' War between France and England (1337–1453) created disorder and discontent within the societies. Then plague epidemic afflicted most of the Europe, including England (1348–49), which specifically witnessed the Black Death which reduced England's population from 4 million to 2.5 million by the early 15th century. Because of the plague in England, there was a high shortage of labour, which further augmented the exploitation of the serfs and peasants. This also led to the rise of discontentment and agitation. There was peasant revolt all over Europe from the late 14th to 16th century. The capitalists marked a change from its earlier forms of production such as agriculture and home-based rudimentary production to heavy industrialization and mass production (Suresh 2010).

Special Insights

Capitalism and Modernity

Since capitalism is a phenomenon of modern society, it is necessary to understand the emergence and features of modernity. The European history emerged after the medieval dark ages. The ideas, ideologies, institutions, politics and social and scientific changes that emerged during this period influenced the larger socio-economic condition. Renaissance (rebirth) spanning from the 15th century to 17th century was an important period, which marked the beginning of modern times. The renaissance scholars tried to break the fetters of religion, tradition and conformism. They stressed upon innovative scientific ideas. The Reformation of Christianity brought individuals at the centre of society. The emphasis of individual and freedom of will had long term and wider social implications too. There was a subsequent rise of individualism and the idea of sovereign individualism. Individualism became a defining characteristic for capitalism where self-interest, egoism and selfishness become the values. In the late 20th and early 21st centuries, capitalism and individualism divorced and became distinct discourses. Although individualism did not cause capitalism, there was some influence of one over the other. Furthermore, the scientific revolution between 1500 and 1700 was critical for the emergence of modern science and consequently for modern society itself. In the early modern period, both individualism and capitalism collided and shaped each other.

By the end of the 19th century, the making of the single capitalist world economy had been completed as capitalism reached every part of the world. Over time, this led to the growth of a world market for goods and services or an international division of labour. In the 19th century, the world trade grew about 11 times and continued to achieve the maximum profit. In the capitalist market, it is apparently neutral forces of supply and demand that determine the price of a product. The capitalist market economy was perceived or projected to be neutral. However, Marx has shown how the formal equality of the market could produce the socially structured inequality. The growing global capital also gave rise to structured inequalities in a greater way. Across the capitalist societies, there was division of classes between property owners, less wage earners and entrepreneurs who own capital (Hilton 1952). These inequalities, however, were not restricted to individual countries; as capitalism worked as a global system, the inequalities inherent with the system of capitalism got reflected at the international level. At the international arena, the core states achieved economic dominance and therefore used the political diplomacy, political coercion imposed the capitalist market economy for their own advantage. Wallerstein has rightly argued that the core–periphery hierarchy and the exploitation of the periphery by the core is in fact projected to be necessary for the reproduction of capitalism as a system.

There are disagreements about the origin and stages of growth of capitalism. However, most of the scholars of capitalism regard this as a modern phenomenon. Many scholars specifically discussing on the world system have referred to the periodization of the capitalist development. Neo-Marxist writers like Samir Amin, Andre Gunder Frank and Ernest Mandel have commonly identified the following stages of capitalist growth.

5.4.1.1 Pre-competitive Stage (1500–1800) or Mercantile Phase Expansion of Capitalism

Capitalist economy ensured a constant growth of the production within European countries. Followed by overproduction and an inclination towards gaining more profit, European merchants explored the coasts of Africa and Asia and the land of the South in search of gold, spice and slaves and in conquest of existing trade routes. Paul Baran, in *The Political Economy of Growth*, argued that 'the trading relationship of the phase was hidden form of looting and plundering', where European nations transferred all the economic surplus of the pre-industrial states to Europe. Such profits or surplus economy was directly used in Europe for the Industrial Revolution.

In the process of the unequal trading relationship, subsequently Europe developed as against the overseas Asian, African and Latin American states which lost the opportunity for economic advancement in the territories where the West traded. Their association with the Western states also had regressive effects on the level of the societal evolution they had already reached. This aspect is highlighted by Walter Rodney in the book *How Europe Underdeveloped Africa*. After 1800, because of increased industrial productivity, Europe was looking for extended market outlets in Asia and Africa to sale its products.

5.4.1.2 Colonial Phase of the European Expansion (1800–1880)

Between 1800 and 1878, the European rule increased from 35 per cent to 67 per cent. In addition, the new wave of invasion added 18 per cent between 1875 and 1914. The formal colonization between 1875 and 1914 witnessed an astonishing internationalization of capital. A few prominent states of Europe together with the United States contributed to 85 per cent of all international financial lending. Around half of the lending went to the countries of Asia, Africa and South America. They also build railways, excavated minerals and natural resources and connected it to ports and also established factories; all the activities further enhanced the wealth of the Western nations by subsequently making the other countries poor. The international financial companies also lend money (to a lesser extent though), and the multinational companies invested capital directly. In both the cases, the surplus economy strengthened the economy of the Western nations as against the peripheries. It was during this phase that the periphery was brought into the expanding network of economic exchanges with the core.

Moreover, some conscious and some unconscious efforts were made to support the process of colonialism ideologically. A few scholars argued that imperialism is a good necessity for a nation like England.[1] Back in the colonized states, the colonizer states were appreciated as they promised job and trade, forces that ensured civilization and universal progress and development through the establishment of railways, roads, post-office, printing machines and so on. The imperialist therefore found it as a part of their mission to disseminate law, order, justice, education, peace and prosperity. Colonies were regarded as national properties.

During the colonial capitalism, one can recognize Burke's thought about the historical tension between the liberal self-image of capitalism and its violent colonial predicaments in the late 18th-century British Empire. Burke has argued that under the British Empire, the East India Company lodged coercive processes of capital accumulation in the colonies. The self-image of capitalism was liberal values such as contractual freedom, equality and civilized manners of a commercial society; however, the manner adopted by the European commercial groups in the colonies indeed provided a contradictory nature of the capital and values akin to the socio, economic and political system.[2] B. Macpherson provides the most assertive articulation of this position.

5.4.1.3 Monopoly or the Imperialist Stage (1880–1960)

In the process of imperialism, Hobson[3] argued that capitalist societies save the capital or the money that they use to produce more goods or capital in future. Accumulation of capital is necessary for the development and progress of the state. It is also the capitalists' profit motivation, whereby the capitalists aimed at greater investment which can provide them a better hand in the competition with the rivals. For Hobson, imperialism did not serve the nation of small producers, tax-payers and workers, rather it served capitalist entrepreneurs or the small ruling class. Hobson highlighted the lack of investment at home, and the remedy he asked for was to improve the living standard of the home country. The solution he has provided here is to change the negative offshoots of imperialism which is basically reformist in nature and not structural.

Classical Marxist theorists such as Lenin, and Bukharin highlighted on Imperialism thesis. While analysing this theory, they have heavily relied on Marx's writing on the laws of motion of capitalism. The law believe in the concentration and centralization of the capital, leading to the monopoly of capitalism. The early writer while writing about imperialism believed that the monopoly of capitalism has arrived already or referred to the highest stage of the capital. There was a growing phenomenon of the internationalization of production. There were some massive companies from metropolitan countries that integrated mine-to-market production.

Vladimir Lenin argues in his book *Imperialism, the Highest Stage of Capitalism* (1917) that imperialism is a result of capitalists' search for greater profits outside their own country. This imperialism leads to the exploitation of people and the economy of the colonies. In the past one century, various Marxist thinkers have analysed and criticized the process of the capitalist economy.

Immanuel Wallerstein discussed that the concept of the World System Theory emerged in the 1970s which believes that the capitalist mode of production has shaped the world economy since the 16th century. Capitalism originated in Europe, but the search for profit and expanded production has extended to many o the countries in the world while taking into consideration two world classes. Such social contours have bee marked by ethno-national conflicts, internal inequality and revolt within nations. It is not a total theory o the world. It is rather a rejection of the social theory, which typically understands the nation and the nationa society as their frame of inquiry. The social theorist tried to understand the link between the developmen and the national, political and institutional arrangement. By contrast, Wallerstein and A.G. Frank argued tha national economic development and underdevelopment should be understood in the context of the internationa capitalist economy which systematically advantaged certain regions and the nations and deliberatively oppresse other countries, especially through colonialism and imperialism.

It has been argued how Marx has discussed two laws of motion of capitalism, and these laws referre to the processes of concentration and centralization. Concentration is also known as merger and takeover Centralization is associated with the enlargement of capital of an individual enterpriser using its accumulate profit. Whereas centralization refers to the processes where in a situation of competition, individual capitalis lose their independence and remain under the centralized control of one big firm or entrepreneur. Th financial capital and the industrial capital got interwoven with each other and the process of concentratio and centralisation of capital further helped in greater export and annexation of land, that ultimately affecte imperialism.

The economy in such a situation remains so powerful that it influences the respective political regimes t go against the principle of free trade and demand the imposition of protective tariffs.

5.4.1.4 Late Monopoly Capitalist or Neocolonization (1950–late 1980)

The Marxists believed the capitalist export to the periphery was tied with the import of raw materials to make industries run in the centre. Yet, their main aim was to achieve monopolies, protection, tariffs and so on in the manner in which protection hinders the export of goods while promoting the export of the capital.

After 1945, with the end of the Second World War, the Third World countries of Asia, Africa and Latin America became decolonized and free from the colonial rule. However, the economic relationship of these states with the colonizers did not break immediately.

Hoogevelt stated in the neocolonial period and especially after the Second World War, the Third World countries became independent; however, the newly independent countries remained dependent on the European countries. These states adopted a development model which was based on modernization, borrowed from the West, which also resulted in the transfer of economic surplus through developmentalism and technological rent. Developmentalism is an economic theory which states that the best way for Third World countries to develop is through adopting a strong internal market and to impose high tariffs on imported goods. Development was perceived merely as the economic development (basically those that were not regarded as sufficiently economically developed), especially in terms of growth of the gross domestic product (GDP). Development remained an elitist project as it was believed that the North was better off and developed economically; hence, it became the model than the South. It was further believed that the North knew how the South was to develop.

At the time of the Cold War, the approach of the world economy remained influential along with the dependency theory. Economic determinists stressed that imperialism was the inevitable product of capitalist expansion. Changes in the economies of capitalist countries forced Western powers to seek expansion of their markets by establishing colonies during the era of colonialism, and even after decolonization, the dependency of Western powers continued in the (periphery) postcolonial societies. International relations between core and periphery could thus be said to reproduce or reinforce domestic inequalities. These findings complement other recent studies, showing similar relationships with export-partner concentration. The core countries provided financial aid, investment and technological help to the underdeveloped states (Meyer and Hannan 1982).

5.4.1.5 Globalization and Neo-imperialism

James Fulcher calls the period after the 1970s as 'remarketized capitalism'. This period is marked by the rise of neoliberal beliefs in the free operation of market forces. The state was rolling back, and the welfare activities of the state were diminishing. The neoliberal capitalism growth, productivity and competition are presented as the major goals of human actions and development. As part of the liberalized and globalized economy, finance market and money were homogenized under the dominance of a few nations. The economic changes challenge the states to become competitive for ensuring economic development by accelerating the opportunity of investment between the states, to facilitate privatization, liberalization or deregulation, and the deterioration of labour legislation, trade union and welfare policies to attract the interest of transnational capital. While the capital and transnational corporations (TNCs) operated at a global or international level, the states were required to enforce political action at the national level.

Globalization could have diverse social, cultural and economic interpretation. Economic globalization includes the integration of national economies at the international level; it means free flow of trade, capital, direct foreign investment, short-term capital flows and international flow of workers; it also includes innovation and flow of technology and so on. TNCs are often seen as institutional drivers of globalization and growth. Globalization was further perceived as a decreasing world (the erosion of borders and geographical barriers to socio-economic activity). It identifies global integration, the reordering of interregional power relations whereby it is believed that the gap among developed and developing will reduce with a perspective consciousness of the global condition and the intensification of interregional interconnectedness (Giddens 1990; Harvey 1989; Held et al., 1999; Rosenau 1990).

5.5 Capitalism: Development and Underdevelopment of the Local

Globalization of the world productive system induces new forms of polarization. In the 19th century, industrial systems arose in the core countries of Western Europe, North America and Japan. The rest of the countries of the world remained mostly non-industrial and rural. There was a rapid expansion of the world economy and the collapse of colonial empires after the Second World War.

The IMF became an instrument to assert the US hegemony as the parity between gold and the US dollar was fixed. With the breakdown of the Bretton Woods system, instead of fixed rate of exchange, the currencies began to float freely in the capital market, which led to a substantial rise in the capital movements across the world. For instance, at this juncture, the value of the international capital movement is roughly 25 times more than that of the worldwide trade. According to Samir Amin, the crisis stemming from the continuous surplus of floating capital can be managed only with financial openness. As a result, the IMF encouraged borrowing after 1970. Indeed, the rising debt was useful for the management of the overabundance of capital. Borrowing by the nation state from the IMF, in turn, also allowed the IMF to put harsh conditionality in the form of structural adjustments on the recipient countries mostly from the Third World as also the former eastern bloc.

The World Bank (the United States took its loan for the management of Marshall aid programme in West Europe), even though is supposed to be apolitical, has displayed a distinct tendency to favour Washington and its allies, including non-democratic ones like Mobutu, Pinochet, Marcos, Suharto and Tontons Macoutes. In fact, the World Bank has been instrumental in the US hegemony built around the military industrial complex. Hence, it is constrained to work in the interests of transnationalism, a stance unprofitable to the US interests. For instance, the World Bank's interests in the mining sector were directly articulated with those of transnationals because the former provided a form of insurance to the latter against any form of nationalization. The bank's strategy in periphery acts through the structural adjustment programmes.

The institutionalized forms of dominance of the developed North acts over the developing South worked out through the international trading arrangements such as the General Agreement on Tariff and Trade (GATT) and later through the World Trade Organisation (WTO). New International Economic Order (NIEO) raised by a group of 77 had demanded transfer of credit and technology from industrialized northern countries to developing countries of the south on favourable terms. It is also assumed by many scholars that the Trade Related Investment Measures (TRIMS) and Trade Related Intellectual Property Rights (TRIPS) evidently carried the tendency to strengthen transnational monopolies.

In the era of globalization, several peripheral regions remain attractive for being the place for being labour intensive. The peripheral industrializing regions, on one hand, largely remained non-competitive and non-industrialized and, on the other, included the vast majority of the world's population. Partial industrialization could at best engross only a small portion of their tremendous labour reserves. Labour surpluses required need to adopt modern technologies in order to be globally competitive.

The capital accumulation globally is now largely regulated through TNCs and financial institutions. Mostly, goods, services and financial capital have become increasingly mobile, but most categories of labour remain confined to their country of origin. The national economic systems have had to adapt to the increasing penetration of world finance, goods and services and the world markets. Contrarily, the responsibility for ensuring social reproduction, such as the rules governing access to the means for meeting basic needs, provision of social services, political participation and the protection of the environment, is left to supposedly sovereign states.

Globalization brings an increased level of porosity of the territories, enables the international and transnational companies and industries to move to the areas which need less investment and have cheap labour to ensure the maximization of profit. A country which has more labour force and a good amount of the deposition of natural resources would be the place which would attract foreign capital investment more. India could be a classic example of such a condition where the labour is cheap and there are several states which have a reserve of natural resources. In addition to that, if the policy of a state government takes investment-friendly policies even at the cost of its biodiversity, environmental protection and so on, then it attracts the capital (industrial) investment in that state or region at a much faster rate. For example, the state of Himachal Pradesh,

Table 5.1 Contradicting Standpoints on Globalization

	In Favour of Globalization	Against Globalization
1	Technological communication and development help economic development.	The concept of globalization becomes so broad that it looks impossible to operationalize globalization.
2	Allows better integration across states or countries.	Lacks specificity with no geographical reference. It becomes difficult to distinguish regionalization to globalization.
3	Globalization may lead to achieve a global village without much barrier, having a system of global governance which will be equipped to solve tire global problems.	Internationalization is a much appropriate word than globalization. In the globalization era, it was believed that everything would be globalized and local centre of the power such as regional network (example SAARC). However, it is found that despite and globalization the regional level of networks still maintains its efficacy and most importantly, the state continue to play the dominant power structure that decides almost all decisions within boarders and cross borders.
4	Globalization pulls and pushes societies in different directions. It simultaneously stimulates cooperation as well as conflict, integration and fragmentation, exclusion and inclusion and order and disorder.	Globalization is an ideological construction that helps in justifying or legitimizing the neoliberal global economy. It also legitimizes the Anglo-American western capitalism.
5	Under globalization, it is not the size but tire power of elusive resources like intellectual property or skills that can matter more. Otherwise, it is difficult to explain the astonishing rise of companies like Microsoft, Cisco (computer) and Fresenius (dialysis treatment).	Globalization is usually discussed in the context of Washington Consensus of deregulation, privatization, structural adjustment programmes, limited governments and so on. Such processes have heavy negative implications over tire common people.
6	The interpretation of globalization is the globalist followed an open-ended conception of the global change, rather than a fixed or a singular vision of a globalized world.	The globalization of capital reflects the growth of a transnational capitalist class with backups such as tire World Trade Organization (WTO), the International Monetary Fund (IMF), and the World Bank, led by tire United States.
7	Globalization enables to bring a single world. This has affected many areas of life, especially economic and social. It is not a new force; in history, people have spread to different region, spread know-how, technology and ideas.	Americanization is a subtype of Westernization, and it has also involved imperialism, colonialism and commitment to development. Development which in fact gives rise to dependency is an output of globalization.

	In Favour of Globalization	Against Globalization
8	Globalization creates the opportunity for a new mode of social organizations, for example, tire global production network and regulatory regimes.	Capitalism as a social order has an expansionist approach. As in order to maintain tire profit, it needs to expand and find new markets. The history of the modem world is the history of tire Western capitalist powers, dividing and redevising tire world up into exclusive economic zones such as G-7.
9	Globalization provides an opportunity for the states to unite together and work for some common cause. For example, tire alliance of the OECD countries tackling tire economic issues and or the Kyoto Protocol addressing tire environmental issues.	The internationalization of the economic and social relations remains dependent upon great powers. Therefore, tire liberal order or equal treatment of nations within international arena is unlikely to endure.
10	The World Bank while supporting reforms is mindful of issues related to governance, participatoiy decision-making, social justice, human rights and environment. A plethora of empirical studies on tire impact of tire loan from tire Bank on recipient countries would, plausibly, help in placing tire Bank's role in a more positive perspective.	Globalization creates dependencies. The development projects generally reduce the independence of the southern states. Increased dependency on European state and specifically on tire World Bank and IMF. It has damaged tire environment, local industries and traditions.
11	Globalization provides opportunities to tire labour mobility. By 2004, around 200 million people worked outside their own country. These constituted people who opted for either high-profile or low-profile jobs.	When capital remains highly concentrated in the capitalist core and labour is located in the peripheral countries, then it remains further difficult for tire labour to negotiate for better.
12	In tire 21st century, tire Asian countries are growing fast, while having large markets, greater labour investment and better productivity and growth (China having fast rate of production and export). A few experts stated that if tire current trends continue, by 2014, Girina would have overtaken tire United States as tire world's largest economy (Gyngell 2004). The credit goes to tire global economy.	TNCs are seen as tire institutional driver of globalization. However, the TNCs represent a small number of all exporting firms, and yet, it monopolies tire global trade. As Leslie Skiair (2002) has highlighted, 15 per cent of tire US exporters in tire 1990s operated from diverse sites, yet these firms accounted for 80 per cent of all exports.
13	Globalization is broad in outlook which calls for the ethos of transnationalism.	In the era of globalization, scholars argue that the ideas of having a strong, sovereign nation state will wither away. There is no withering away of the state. There are some states or some organizations which reinforce nationality. For instance, the ideas of make in India, usage of indigenous as nationalism, etc. are such attempts intended to re-emphasise nationalism instead of internationalism

which is known for its mountain ranges and environmental uniqueness, declared an area of the Shimla district called Badi as a tax-free zone for little more than a decade because of which the place became a hub of many international and national companies' production houses. Undoubtedly, the nearby people of the region got employment opportunity in the region for a few years, but the environmental disservices that were the offshoot of this political economy were never assessed clearly. Moreover, recently, when the government also thinks to take back its decision on tax-free zone in Badi, the industrialists simultaneously are now thinking of shifting their industrial set up from the region to some other where they get a similar conducive position for expansion of their capital and labour.

Special Insights

Globalization and Women

The process of liberalization and globalization has adversely affected women (Krishnaraj 1999; Mohanty 2004). Many women have lost their jobs either to men or because of the introduction of technologies in the primary sector. Women were further treated as less efficient technically and less productive. With the process of liberalization and globalization continues, the formal sector is found to be disintegrated and the informalization of labour has grown in India which further made women's employment much more unsecured and irregular (Mohanty 2004).

There is a decline in the employment opportunities and access to social services, which has led to casualization and feminization of the workforce where women further face the burnt of declining job security and low wage (Jhabvala and Sinha 2002).

Capitalists attempt to maximize their financial returns on a world scale. This strive of maximization of the profit unavoidably creates social polarization and exclusion, which often encourages the excluded communities to lead an anti-systemic social movement. The antiglobalization movement has a diverse consequence on communities and groups led by traditional and autonomous labour unions, landless peasants, women groups, indigenous groups, socialists, communists, anarchists and autonomous groups. Several movements could be included in this regard such as parts of the ecology movement, the feminist movement, human rights groups, Third World initiatives and civil rights groups, students, religious groups, groups from the unemployment movement, traditional left-wing movements and so on from all over the world. While on one hand these groups contradict globalization, aim at democratizing globalization, reclaiming the common character of goods and services that are increasingly privatized by agreements such as the General Agreement on Trade in Services and the Agreement on TRIPS. The different issues and concerns of the involved groups are connected because they all consider problems that have been caused by the capitalistic globalization.

5.6 Capitalism and Diverse Experiences

Western Europe and the United States had long been seen the citadels of capitalism. But now, even a formerly communist country like China follows the capitalist path of development. Since more than around two decades, capitalism has further received leverage because of the process of globalization. In the era of globalization, capitalism started penetrating in every region of the world and affects the human life in many ways.

First, in the United States, free market-led capitalism persists, which experiences economic dynamism and higher rates of per capita income growth. There is less volatility and fewer inequities persist in market-led economies in comparison with other forms of capitalism. Second, corporatist or state-led capitalism, in which the government exercises substantial guidance and influences the distribution of private capital (e.g. China,

France and Japan in the 1980s). Third, managed capitalism, in which worker groups and broad social welfare issues exert significant influence on private corporate behaviour (e.g. Sweden, Germany). The fourth category could be a newly emerging capitalism of the East Asian regions which also can be called as Asian Style of capitalism.

The pace of growth of the capitalist economy in a country may not be persistent. It differs with time and with several economic and demographic variations. The United States experienced the longest expansion in its post-war history. In the 1990s, it became the engine of growth for the global economy and the instigator for economic performance in other industrialized nations. The unemployment rate fell to the lowest, 14 per cent, among the major industrialized nations, and the US inflation rate remained comfortably under control. Western Europe struggled with slow growth and insistently high unemployment, whereas Japan, whose economic system had been increasingly hailed as a model for others to imitate during the 1980s, became stalled in an extended marsh of economic stagnation. The fall of the Berlin Wall and the disintegration of the Soviet Union led Francis Fukuyama to declare not only the global triumph of capitalism but also the 'end of history'. It was also believed that it was not just capitalism in general but American (or Anglo-Saxon) style capitalism in particular that would dominate the global economy in the 21st century. However, the American economy slowed sharply in the mid-2000 and the unemployment rate overturned, reaching 6 per cent in early 2003. The collapse of the US stock market and the decease of many of the brightest shooting stars of the New Economy, interacting with a number of high-profile corporate humiliations, destabilized economic stability both at home and abroad. The US account deficit rose to a proportion of GDP unprecedented in the post-war era, sharply worsening the position as an international defaulter. The terrorist attack of 11 September 2001 has led the United States to take a variety of actions that appear inconsistent with its role as the leader of an open world economy and a major supporter of international institutions. And the pace of economic globalization, as reflected in the expansion of both trade and foreign investment in relation to global output, has reduced.

While China's government may be officially communist, the Chinese people express widespread support for capitalism. China began liberalizing its socialist command economy. In the late 1970s, under the leadership of Deng Xiaoping, after the death of the socialist leader Mao Zedong, the country has taken significant steps towards becoming a more market-oriented economy, which in turn has helped it achieve significant levels of economic growth and eradicate extreme poverty. With these changes came excessive economic growth—an average of 10 per cent since 1980. Since 2002, the Chinese have consistently been one of the strongest proponents of capitalism compared with others around the world, even more so than Americans and Western Europeans.

In the early 1800s, Sweden was one of the poorest countries in Europe. It was also a highly unequal society, with a small rich elite and a lot of very poor farmers. Like most countries, Sweden grew richer during industrialization. Two major education reforms (in the 1840s and 1950s) helped to create a more equal distribution of human capital, thus fostering equality of labour income. Swedish growth was higher than that of most other countries. As a result, Sweden ended up as the fourth richest country in the world in the 1970s (after the United States, Switzerland and Luxembourg, as measured by real GDP per capita). Sweden implemented high levels of labour market regulation, as well as high and progressive taxes.

The success stopped around 1970 when Sweden started sheathing behind other countries. Among economists, an agreement has emerged that a mix of failed macroeconomic policies, tax increases, labour market regulations and incentive changing social policies contributed to the problems. In the 1970s, policies became more anti-capitalist. In 1983, Sweden decided to implement a partial socialization of company profits, and the wage earner funds. Economic problems grew more and more severe, and when the boom of the 1980s turned into recession in the early 1990s, Sweden was hit much harder than other countries. Many expected the Swedish welfare state would lead to the collapse of economy. Instead, taxes remained high, public debt fell and economic growth returned. Today, *The Economist* describes Sweden as a North star and a Super model, and the *Washington Post* described Sweden as the Rock Star of recovery after the 2008 financial crisis. While taxes remain high by international standards, other areas of Sweden's economy are now very market friendly, and the country is well integrated into the global economy.

Hall and Soskice (2001) stated that some of the most important liberal market economies (LMEs) are the United States, Australia, New Zealand, Canada, Ireland and the United Kingdom. The LMEs have well-developed capital markets, 'outsider' forms of corporate governance. They use the market solution and contractual arrangements to regulate relations within and across sectors and industries. As far as employment relations are concerned, they have high levels of labour elasticity regarding hiring, firing and remuneration. By contrast, the LMEs and coordinated market economies (CMEs) have relatively more lenient forms of capital. The corporate governance includes non-market mechanisms for managing value chains (often industry-based regulatory associations) and horizontal connections within and across economic sectors. Employment relations in these countries include relatively less labour flexibility, widespread use of collective bargaining, comparatively more uniformity of wage outcome and greater employment security. Germany, Japan and Northern European countries are often touted as typical CMEs. The case of Sweden shows that a well-functioning capitalism can exist in a context with high taxes. Well-defined property rights, efficient government institutions, low corruption and low taxation on internationally mobile capital contribute to a market-friendly environment despite high levels of labour taxation and encompassing social insurance schemes.

The economies of Hong Kong, Singapore, South Korea and Taiwan experienced rapid industrialization and sustained exceptionally high growth rates (in excess of 7 per cent a year) between the early 1960s (mid-1950s for Hong Kong) and 1990s. In the early 21st century, all four countries had developed into high-income economies, specializing in the areas of competitive advantage. Hong Kong and Singapore have become world-leading international financial centres; South Korea and Taiwan have developed to be world leaders in manufacturing electronic components and devices. Their economic success stories have served as role models for many developing countries, especially of the Southeast Asia.

There were some major changes taking place; while the United States and Europe struggled with debt, unemployment and sagging competitiveness, most of Asia seems to prosper continuously (Schuman 2012). Many Asian companies became more and more prominent in the world, and hence, it is not surprising that many Asians have come to believe that their economic systems are superior to those of the United States and Europe. For decades, Asia had been learned and trained on free capitalism by the West and benefited tremendously. Now, many out there believe the time has come for the West to learn from Asia.

5.7 Conclusion

John Kay (fellow, Oxford) claimed that capitalism no longer exists. He then argued that in the 21st century, corporations have become obsolete without having significant fixed assets to buy or sell. Now the world economy is moving towards a network of relationships which is based on the global user base, whose loyalty often remain in question. Facebook, Uber and AirBnB represent nothing but structures of relationships. That network has no value unless a fragile complex of interactions and relationships stay in place. The value of the company is almost entirely intangible, unlike a steel mill or a railroad.

John Kay is appropriate to state that the contemporary capitalism has taken a new shape by being heavily dependent on the network and structures of relationship. However, it would be highly vague to state that 'capitalism no longer exists'. In taking a Marxist stand, one may argue that material base of any society as Marx stated is based on the modes of production which also determined largely the relationship of production. However, contemporary capitalism, as argued by Kay, is based on the networks or structure of relations, does not mean that it is not for economic purpose or profit. He fails to relate how social networks are used for the generation of the capital or for profit. Similarly, when we notice Google, Apple and so on, these firms had already put a huge amount of money and thus could get a large return.

Keywords

Capital
Labour
Competition
Property
Globalization
State
Imperialism

Review Questions

1. Examine the different stages of growth of capitalism in the modern world.
2. What are the various models of the capitalist system? How has globalization impacted capitalism?
3. Examine the salient features of capitalism in the context of globalization.
4. Explain the origin and development of capitalism.
5. Explain capitalism. What are the major challenges to the capitalist world order today?

Notes

1. The Marxists believe that the existing democracy in the capitalist countries is only a bourgeois democracy and there is no democracy for the majority of the people.
2. Scholars such as Hampsampsher-Monk and Marshall argue that Burke's argument revolves around the efforts to defend, retain and reform the British Empire soon.
3. Hobson was a liberal thinker whose analysis was Marxist.

References

Abercrombie, Nicholas, Bryan S. Turner, and Stephen Hill. 2015. *Sovereign Individuals of Capitalism (RLE Social Theory)*. New York: Routledge.

Antonio, Gramsci. 1970/1971. *The Prison Notebooks*. London: Lawrence and Wishart.

Bottomore, Tom. 2010. *Theories of Modern Capitalism*. London: Routledge.

Chandoke, Neera. 1991. The Post-Colonial City. *The Economic and Political Weekly* 26 (50, 14 December): 283–89.

Friedrich, Hayek. *Liberty, Capitalism and Austrian Economics*. Australia. Accessed from http://www.econlib.org on February 25, 2019.

Giddens, A. 1990. *The Consequences of Modernity*. Cambridge: Polity Press.

Gyngell, Allan. 2004. Lessons from the Parallel World. *The Australian Financial Review* (3): 3–4.

Harvey, D. 1989. *The Condition of Post Modernity*. Oxford: Blackwell.

Held, David, A. McGrew, D. Goldblatt, J. Perraton, et al. 1999. *Global Transformations: Politics, Economics and Culture*. Stanford, CA: Stanford University Press.

Heller, Henry. 2011. *The Birth of Capitalism: A 21st Century Perspective*. New York: Pluto Press.

Hilton, Rodney H. 1952. Capitalism—What's in a Name? In *Past and Present Society*, No. 1, 32–43.

Oxford: Oxford University Press on behalf of The Past and Present Society.

Jhabvala, Renana, and Shalini Sinha. 2002. Liberalisation and Women Worker. *Economic and Political Weekly*. 37(21): 2037–44.

Krishnaraj, Maithreyi. 1999. Globalisation and Women in India. *Development Practices* 9(5): 587–92.

Marx, Karl, and Friedrich Engels. 1848. *Communist Manifesto*. Translated by Moore. Chicago, IL: Charles h. Kerr & Company.

———. 1864. *The German Ideology*, edited by Simon Lawrence. Indianapolis, IN: Hackett Publishing Company.

Meyer, John W., and Michael T. Hannan. 1982. The Capitalist World-Economy by Immanuel Wallerstein. *International Organization* 36(1): 135–63.

Miliband, Ralph. 1958. *The Politics of Contemporary Capitalism*. London. Accessed from https://www.marxists.org on September 11, 2023.

Mohanty, Monoranjan. 2004. *Class, Caste and Gender*. New Delhi: SAGE Publishing.

Nozick, Robert. 2013. *Anarchy, State and Utopia*. New York: Basic Books.

Rosenau, J.N. 1990. *Turbulence in World Politics*. Brighton: Harvester Wheatsheaf.

Schuman, Michael. 2012. Can Asian-Style Capitalism Save the West? Accessed from http://business.time.com on March 25, 2012.

Schumpeter, Joseph A. 1926. *The Theory of Economic Development: An Inquiry into Profits, Capital, Credit, Interest, and the Business Cycle*. Cambridge, MA: Harvard University Press.
Sklair, Leslie. 2002. *Globalisation: Capitalism and its Alternatives*. Oxford: Oxford University Press.
Smith, Adam. 1776. *Wealth of Nations*. London: W. Strahn and T. Cadell.
Suresh, R.R. 2010. *Economy and Society: Evolution of Capitalism*. New Delhi: SAGE.
Vladimir, Ilyich Lenin. 1917. *Imperialism the Highest Stage of Capitalism*. Russia: Martino Fine Books.
Weber, Max. 1905. *The Protestant Ethic and the Spirit of Capitalism*. London: George Allen & Unwin Ltd.

CHAPTER 6

Socialism: Meaning, Growth and Development

Pushpa Singh and Chetna Sharma

Reader's Guide

Socialism has been a fascinating ideology that has guided and shaped the formation of many socialist regimes in the 20th century around the world. It has been seen as having tremendous scope in providing an alternative to the existing political and economic order. The beginning of 20th century saw the consolidation of socialist regimes that gradually became formidable in power and influence by manoeuvred projection, positioning and symbolism. Yet, in spite of the emancipatory promises and grand vision of their discourse, majority of these political systems began crumbling gradually. Why did it happen? What were the structural and institutional problems in such political regimes? Were such regimes based on inherent contradictions of the discourse itself? Does the end of socialist regimes like Soviet Russia in 1991 imply the end of socialism as an ideology? This chapter will engage with all these questions. It will discuss the various connotations of socialism, different strands of socialist philosophy, the rise of socialist regimes, and their problems that led to their decline and disintegration.

6.1 Introduction

As an ideology, socialism has occupied a major space in the intellectual political spectrum. For a long time in the discipline of politics, political debates couched their arguments in the semantics of socialism. It denotes a set of values or beliefs that is guided by the quest of equality, justice and freedom. There is no single definition of the term, as it has been subjected to different interpretations. In general, it refers to a system or arrangement based on social/community/state ownership of means of production and resources of the society. There are different variants of socialism like revolutionary socialism, state socialism, democratic socialism, etc. The common idea that connects them all is the espousal of community or public ownership of the resources. The term communism specifically refers to Marx's idea of socialism. It stands for creation of a society based on collectivization and should be devoid of any private property and individual ownership. Socialist ideas have inspired the establishment of many communist regimes in the 20th century. In general, we see an overwhelming inclination of countries of Western Europe to adopt a generous amount of welfarism and socialist provisions in their policies and governance in the post-Second World War period. Some scholars think that socialism denotes a stage of transition between capitalism and communism. In this stage, the working class will expropriate the means of production from the bourgeoisie class in the capitalist mode of production.

Communism, Marx's variant of socialism, has been the most pervasive international political movement of the 20th century. The first socialist regime that created a strong ripple effect was consolidated in Soviet Russia, thus converting a string of countries in Europe, Latin America and Asia as the Soviet satellites. All these developments started in the post-1950s where the whole world was ideologically polarized into two blocks, capitalists and communists. The capitalist block came to be known as the First World, whereas the communist world was seen as the Second World. The newly emerged countries came to be called as the Third World. Though this nomenclature does not hold relevance anymore in the wake of debilitating of communist societies and dismantling of the USSR and its satellites. The communist and the capitalist blocks entangled themselves in a prolonged conflict named the Cold War to influence and bring the postcolonial societies on their own sides. So profound has been the impact of socialist and communist thoughts that intellectuals all across the world have been drawn for a time to them.

6.2 Socialism: Tracing the Legacy

6.2.1 Early Socialists

Marx and Lenin were the most influential theorists of socialist ideology, although the idea did not originate with them. Marx has written prolifically on the emergence of industrial capitalism in Western Europe and envisaged a gradual demise of capitalism and its replacement by communism. Capitalism never met the fate that Marx predicted for it, but the most foundational critique of the system comes from Marxist analysis. No other political philosopher has been so influential in shaping the political order of the modern world as Karl Marx. A variety of socialist ideas have existed in the earlier times also, although they were markedly different from the version that appeared in the writings of Karl Marx. The early socialist pioneers were Henri de Saint Simon (1760–1825), Francois Marie Charles Fourier (1772–1837), Pierre-Joseph Proudhon (1809–1865) and Robert Owen (1870–1924). Though many trace the beginning of the idea to Plato's *Republic* (380 BCE) that discusses the concept of communism of property, Sir Thomas More provided an intellectually stimulating account of socialist ideas in his book *Utopia* (1516). His book portrayed imagined communist societies and inspired a range of works in the realm of utopian fictions. The term socialism has been applied by various theorists to illustrate varied meanings leading to a range of interpretations. Interestingly, this made Giovanni Sartori call it 'conceptual stretching' of socialism. Many countries claim to practice socialism, but they hardly exhibit the features or promises of emancipated society.

Special Insights

Origin of the Word 'Communism'

The term 'communism' was first used by French 'utopian Socialist' Étienne Cabet, in 1840. His idea of communism was influenced by Christianity and he was opposed to violent revolution. The word 'communist' was used in the English version of *Communist Manifesto* published in 1888, in which Engels explained the significance of using the term 'communist' rather than 'socialist'. He stated that different variants of socialism were associated with middle class movement and adherents of various utopian ideologies like Owenites in England, Fourierist in France, etc., who never questioned capital or profit. Far from this, communism was supposed to signify working class movement with commitment to the workers' problems.

Considerable disagreement can be observed among the thinkers of socialism. Though Marxist theorization dominates the socialist discourse, it will be interesting to engage with the history of origin and evolution of this concept. Robert Owen's strategy to bring these ideas into practice was to set up socialist communities that would present a model for the rest of the population to follow. Owenites favoured economically decentralized and city-based structures to overcome the effects of industrialization on environment. Karl Marx carefully read Charles Fourier (*The Social Destiny of Man*, 1808) and Pierre-Joseph Proudhon *The Philosophy of Poverty* (1846), the key figures of nineteenth-century socialist thought. He came up with scathing criticism of both of them in his book *The Poverty of Philosophy* (1847). Proudhon famously argued, 'Property is theft' and held that social harmony was natural and desirable. However, the prevalent economic system of that period prevented the flourishing of socialist thoughts. Proudhon did not offer the detailed framework of implementation of his ideas. He was the first one to use the term 'scientific socialism'.

Going by the details of the content and approach of these political theorists, we find apparent points of convergence and divergence. Marx emphasized the revolutionary overthrow of capitalism by the mass movement of urban working class. Radicals like Bakunin were ready to accept method of terrorism and assassination of officials to bring an end to capitalism. Bakunin proposed the notion of self-government by the people. Proudhon favoured a system of worker's control of factories. These scholars also held different understanding of the course of struggle against capitalism and the instruments used in this course. Surprisingly, Proudhon, Owen and Bakunin had greater following than Marx in the mid-19th century. Yet, the impact of Marx has developed to such an extent in the past century that Marxist thought has overshadowed other socialists.

6.2.2 Marx and Engels

Among all the theorists of socialism, Karl Marx (1818–83) is the most seminal. Marx called his ideas of socialism as 'scientific socialism', while branding other ideas as the utopian socialism. The entire political and economic philosophy of Marx is his reflection on his critical engagement with the process of growth and development of capitalism in Europe. Throughout his intellectual-philosophical journey, Friederich Engels (1820–95) remained the fellow companion who co-authored many seminal Marxist texts, including *The Communist Manifesto* (1848). Marx believed that capitalism is inherently an exploitative social, economic and political system that rests on the logic of oppression of the working or proletariat class by the capitalist class or the bourgeoisie. Marx has been a prolific writer explaining the rise of capitalism that caused overhauling, transformations in the society, economics and politics. He perceived the entire structure and logistics of capitalism to be deeply flawed and unjust. According to him, capitalism was a system of contradictions and antagonisms expressed in form of 'Class-Struggle' that he thought was the root of inequality and exploitation in the capitalist society.

The limitation of Marx lies in the fact that he did not work out the detailed plan for the operation of the socialist society, although there are some reflection in *The Communist Manifesto* about policies to be adopted after the overthrow of capitalism that include abolition of all rights of inheritance, centralization of means of communication, transport and state capital. Marx also proposed that there should be a combination of agriculture and manufacturing industries and equitable distribution of population between cities and countryside in a socialist society. Most important of all, child labour in factories to be abolished and compulsory education through public schools needed to be implemented. These changes were proposed for transitional phase of dictatorship of proletariat, a phase ahead of the final culmination of communist society. According to Marx, in a communist society, not just state but other institutional structures including police, military and bureaucracy will wither away, and the citizen's group would manage administrative responsibilities. An ideal society visualized by Marx would be a society, where all citizens would participate in governance in the absence of full-time bureaucrats and politicians. Marx had visualized international worker's revolution. However, Marx's conceptualization could not be implemented on grounds as proposed. It can be noticed that in the struggle against the capitalist mode of production, sporadic worker's protest against poor wages and bad working condition happened in many parts of the world supported by unions. However, all these movements were marked by the absence of a revolutionary potential and sustained commitment and strategy to bring these transformations. Since workers were able to manage some concessions from the capitalists, their revolutionary potential decreased. Capitalism devised the ways to counter the threat from the proletariat by co-opting them within the process of capitalist development. This resulted in the diminished revolutionary potential of the working class.

6.2.3 Lenin

Vladimir Ilyich Lenin (1870–1924) was the leader of Bolshevik, or majority party of Russian Social-Democratic Worker's Party. He found it necessary to revise Marxism in the light of prevailing condition of Russia and contributed many concepts to the communist doctrine. While he wanted to see revolution in Russia, he was also aware of the fact that Russia was a predominantly agrarian society. He knew that revolution in Russia required a different organizational structure, as it would not have offered an ideal ground for organized worker's struggle as proposed by Marx. Therefore, he redefined the terms, conditions and modalities of socialist struggle to suit the Russian context. He set new principles to organize the struggle and proposed the framework of the Soviet state that would follow this.

This gave birth to Lenin's idea of a **vanguard party**, a disciplined, organized army of revolutionaries. Lenin believed that the communist party will be the most important instrument of the working class and would carry out the revolution. The concept of vanguard originated from the observation that all revolutionary processes have had ideologically advanced sectors of the population who support radical change, backward sectors who supported the status quo and the middle sectors in between (Russell 1989, 170). Party, in this framework, is the only political entity, organized in a manner that it influences, guide and mould politics and political consciousness for the success of a socialist regime. Lenin's ideas were criticized because many believed that his ideas were vague, and revolution in an agrarian society like Russia was a premature idea. He was criticized for pushing revolution in a society where social and economic conditions were not conducive. Rosa Luxemburg found the idea of vanguard party problematic because she feared that the party would continue in power and will entrench itself as a new ruling class by replacing the old order. While Marx's dream of worker's revolution did not materialize, Lenin's vanguard party emerged as a powerful force to bring new development in socialist countries.

Another central idea of Lenin was **democratic centralism** to be followed by the party. The notion of democratic centralism is constituted by two core principles: democracy and centralism. The idea that underlies this concept is that once the decisions are taken by the communist party, it is binding on the entire members. Centralism was incorporated to enforce strict discipline of obedience in the party at all ranks and orders. The idea was to not allow the environment that could give rise to competing factions or small group activities in the party that could sabotage the functioning of the communist party and the state itself. There would be no space for doubts, questions or non-allegiances. The abrogation of this principle was to be punishable offence, and therefore all members refrained from expressing their uneasiness or disagreement. Though there were provisions for discussion, debates and hearing opinions of the other members on crucial issues in practice, none of these things was allowed. In fact, the socialist regimes developed zero tolerance for dissent. In other words, the party in the communist regimes projected itself to be democratic, yet it was highly centralized and autocratic. For example, party leaders were elected by members and regular reports were given by them, but strict obedience was enforced once the decision was taken.

One of the greatest contributions of Lenin lies in the fact that he produced one of the most detailed account of the theory of imperialism. It is one of the richest account of imperialism. In his famous essay *Imperialism, the Highest Stage of Capitalism* in 1916, Lenin explores the following questions: In what ways capitalism has developed, and what course of direction it is going to take in coming future? While doing so, he established a direct correlation between industrial capitalism, imperialism and colonialism. Lenin could foresee that capitalism as a system is self-replicable. He expanded this understanding in the form of a five-stage theory of imperialism, where he conclusively stated that imperialism is the highest stage of capitalism. The growing demand for the constant supply of resources under capitalism in the second half of the 19th century resulted in the intensification of the exploitation of the peripheral countries or the colonies. New sources of profit, cheap labour and access to resources of the colonies made life of people in Europe relatively easy and comfortable. Lenin believed that the anti-colonial movement, if successful, will disrobe the colonizers of their constant supply of resources, leading to the diminishing of their profits. It could culminate into the reemergence of worker's unrest in Europe. He also discussed that unfortunately, after independence, decolonized countries will try to replicate a similar capitalist system, giving rise to class struggle and the chain of exploitation associated with it in the peripheral countries. The capitalist development of the Western countries caused tremendous pressure on the peripheral areas. Within capitalist countries, these capitals brought from the peripheries were concentrated into large monopolistic corporations held by a few oligarchs. In the second stage, the industrial capital merges with the bank capital to constitute finance capital for monopolies. Instead of exporting commodities, in the third stage, the finance capital starts exporting finance. International capitalist association emerges that divides the world. It is accompanied by the territorial division of the world, thereby establishing imperialism.

6.2.4 Mao

Mao Zedong (1893–1976) is hailed as the founding father of People's Republic of China (PRC). Like Lenin, he tried to customize the Marxist philosophy according to the context of China in order to bring revolution there. For Mao, this term offered a platform to be experimented in his country in indigenous ways. Under his leadership, a mass movement for national liberation took an overtly communist tone and turned into another communist revolution. Mao created Chinese Communist Party in 1921. Mao has been very cautious about the tactics and strategy of the revolution. Lenin's idea of a communist party as the vanguard appealed to him, but he supplemented it with his own guerrilla warfare by forming a strong base of rural proletariat of Chinese peasantry. He worked out the modalities of the struggle in his own ways and clearly provided a local appeal to the concept, making it more practical and suitable for his own society. Though the communist revolution was to be carried out by the working class in a capitalist society, but this role was taken over by the farmers as China had not witnessed industrialization till that time.

Mao continued to hold leadership of PRC till his death in 1976. After that, for a brief period, China saw a nasty succession war in different competing factions known as 'Gang of Four'. Deng Xiaoping emerged as the leader who brought noticeable changes in the Chinese politics. He led China to adopt significant economic reforms that fetched far-reaching economic rewards. In a move to relax the rigid and stressed institutions, the older mode of strict state control was loosened. The commune system slowly started giving way to the private commercial enterprises and China took on the path of market economy. Interestingly, this was not seen as deviating from the ethos of socialist principles as China called this new experiment 'socialism with Chinese characteristics'. This strategy of extensive submergence in market economy proved to be a highly successful strategy for China. It has been able to climb up the scales of economic growth rate, and today, it is seen to constitute one of the formidable economic superpower in the multipolar world posing a great challenge to the advanced industrial states.

6.2.5 Evolutionary Socialism

While Marx and Lenin advocated a more revolutionary path of socialism, on the other hand, there emerged a new school of thought in light of the changing nature and circumstances of the capitalist world. This school of thought came to be known as evolutionary socialism. While revising Marx's ideas, theses scholars eventually abandoned the strategy of 'orthodox Marxism'. Realizing the unequal and exploitative nature and forces of capital, a group of scholars in the Western Europe revised Marx's ideas of socialism. They proposed revisionist or evolutionary socialism that believed in bringing gradual changes in the capitalist framework in form of higher wages, better socio-economic conditions and other reforms required for the betterment of the working class. Consequently, workers' groups started demanding certain reforms that were gradually introduced during this period in the countries of Western Europe. It gave rise to the feeling among workers that they were sharing the benefit of industrialization. In an attempt to promote national interests, the core idea of international class solidarity was abandoned. This was witnessed very clearly, when socialists in Germany, Britain, France, Italy and Austria gave their support during the First World War. The grand narrative of socialists' ideology was punctured by the new political dynamic, and the split was witnessed in the form of revisionist social democrats and revolutionary communists.

Fabian socialists emerged in Britain. The main theorists of this field were George Bernard Shaw, Sidney and Beatrice Webb and H.G. Wells and Graham Wallace. They were not convinced by the violent warfare of class struggle. Instead, they believed in education and persuasion as the method to achieve socialism. Fabian socialists came to wield significant influence in the labour party of Britain. Guild socialism also developed in Britain that was inspired by Samuel G. Hobson and G.D.H. Cole. They pleaded for public ownership of industries and their control by the guilds. In similar veins, syndicalism developed in France which was basically the product of the French trade union movement. Syndicalists such as Fernand Pelloutier and Georges Sorel wanted to replace the capitalist state with the federation of local workers group in France. Eduard Bernstein believed in evolutionary socialism. He thought that the condition of working class was not deteriorating as Marx proposed, rather it was improving in many respects due to trade union movements. This made him conclude that revolutionary overthrow of capitalism is neither necessary nor desirable. In place of that, a gradual peaceful transformation to socialism seemed more meaningful to him. Eduard Bernstein made people believe that socialism and equality can be established by ballot rather than bullets. In this way, all these scholars who were also known as democratic socialists rejected the extremist coercive violent modes of struggle. Instead, they supported evolutionary, peaceful and constitutional methods to regulate the capitalist economies.

6.2.6 Marxism Beyond Marx

The way socialist regimes were implemented across the world made many socialist thinkers and sympathizers warry of the orthodoxy, rigidity and the lack of transparency of the system. Dictatorship was disguised as democracy, movements were suppressed in the name of maintaining peace and order, and bureaucratic conservatism was encouraged, thus making the entire setup opaque and rigid. This was the reason that Western Marxists became disillusioned with the orthodoxy of Marxist-Leninism and gradually distanced themselves from the Soviet regime. They found the idea of rigid economic determination particularly repressive, and therefore, ventured beyond the confinements of Marxist orthodoxy in their conceptualization of Marxism. In context of these developments, Marxist ideas were reinterpreted and further extended by some scholars known as post-Marxist or neo-Marxists. As result, the Marxist philosophy was revised by a host of scholars such as Althusser, Gramsci, Lukacs, Miliband, Paul Baran and Paul Sweezy.

Louis Althusser elaborated the crucial role of ideology in fetching legitimacy and justification for of the state to ensure the domination of one class over another and to safeguard capitalism. He uses the term 'ideological state apparatuses' (non-violent institutions like educational system) as well as 'repressive state apparatuses' (violent institutions like military, police, etc.) that the state deploys to reinforce the acceptance and unquestioned obedience by the citizens. Marxists like Althusser points out that it becomes necessary for the state to create consent about the desirability of capitalism. This task of extracting consent is performed by the ideology.

Antonio Gramsci, the member of Italian Socialist Party, also focused on the role of ideology in maintaining the power of the dominant class. He emphasized the humanistic focus of earlier writings of Marx and came up with his own philosophical analysis of the role of ideology in shaping the functioning of the modern state by creating hegemony. The supremacy of the bourgeoisie is entrenched through economic, intellectual and moral dominance. It secures spontaneous consent of the subordinate groups by persuading them to accept its moral, political and cultural values in former's interest. The media plays a crucial role in manufacturing hegemony.

Ralph Miliband proposed the concept of relative autonomy of the state. He believed the state apparatus is not owned by the capitalist class as envisaged by Marx, rather the state is able to create a semi-autonomous space to manoeuvre its functioning. In this way, we can clearly see that all these Marxist scholars extend their theorization beyond the traditional base superstructure debate and advocated that the elements constituting the superstructure like religion, culture and law are equally significant in determining the dominance of one class over the other. Superstructure equally impacts the sub-structure or base rather than just being influenced by it. By insisting that there was a constant interplay between economics and politics, neo-Marxists were able to break free from the rigid 'base–superstructure' straitjacket and also from the stereotypical Marxist understanding of class struggle as the beginning and end of Marxist analysis.

In the contemporary intellectual discourse, Marxist economists of the 20th century Paul A. Baran and Paul M. Sweezy's work is significant. Sweezy discussed the concept of monopoly capital in unregulated market economy that would develop a system dominated by few companies. This system, on the one hand, would push prices of the products but also lead to stagnation in the economic system because of lack of competition. With the changing nature of capitalist system and in an attempt to find answer to the problems emerging in the society, interest in Marxist ideas continued taking various forms.

6.3 Structural Framework of State Socialism

6.3.1 Common Ownership and Collectivization

The aspiration for establishment of common possession instead of individual ownership is found in almost every form of socialism. It has been looked at as the most desirable goal for the society in the socialist thought. This idea finds resonance in many religious practices as well. For example, in Christianity, there have been huge support for common ownership and the early Christians held everything in common.

As a policy, collectivization was vociferously adopted by the socialist regime of Soviet Russia, particularly between the periods of 1929 and 1933. The pursuing of collectivization was possible by transforming the structure and pattern of agriculture in Russia. Soviet leaders thought it necessary to free the land from the hands of the rich peasant class in order to bring industrialization, though there were bitter disagreements often followed by political vendetta by these leaders as it happened between Stalin and Trotsky (1925–27) and between Stalin and Bukharin (1927–29). The faction that was supporting rapid industrialization pushed coercive collectivization in farming. They perceived that larger farms will efficiently use mechanized industrial methods leading to higher production. Moreover, it would have been easier for the state to monitor the agriculture sector and at the same time fetch greater revenue from it. Hence, the land was seized from the wealthy prosperous farmers called Kulaks, who were then forced to join the large collective farms called Kolkhozy. These cooperative agricultural enterprises were supposed to be owned by the state. Though the idea was conceptualized as the voluntary union of peasant, in the Soviet Union, the state started expropriating the private holding in highly contentious ways.

Under the drive of intensive collectivization, more than 20 per cent of total of Russian farmland was confiscated by the state under Stalin's order of 'liquidate the Kulaks as a class'. Those who resisted were severely dealt with harsh punishment and imprisonment. Nevertheless, many peasants defied the order and refused to abandon their private farm and be a part of Kolkhozy. In anger and frustration, they damaged their equipment and slaughtered their livestock. Stalin did not want this problem to overblow and create greater animosity in the rural hinterland, and therefore, decided to go little slow. Smartly, he shifted the blame of this chaos on the shoulders of overenthusiastic local officials in the piece 'Dizzy from Success' that he published in 1930. Owing to these violent policies, the overall agricultural output fell, though the state extracted the capital that it needed to carry out the heavy industrialization. The collectivization programme continued unabated sustaining the big industries that were developed at the cost of agriculture. The Kolkhozy was assigned a chairperson by the state to monitor its working strictly according to state provisions. The collectivization remained one of the central policies of the Soviet state till its demise in 1991. After that, the Kolkhozy was privatized.

Similarly, in case of China, a massive land reform programme was undertaken to bring out the rural collectivization of agriculture. Like in the Soviet Union, there were considerable debates between rural and urban development. However, overall, the programme was not very coercive as in case of the USSR. In the area of industry and banking also, the socialist transformation was brought out rather smoothly, although at times huge pressure was put on the private merchants and capitalists to offer their enterprises to create firms of state–private partnership. In this manner, the state was able to amass huge property and even the capitalists heavily depended on the state for their business by winning contracts. This made the capitalist class very unhappy from inside, though they could not express their resentment in fear of punitive actions of the state. The collectivization programme was gradually diluted in light of the increasingly marketized structure of the Chinese political system.

Special Insights

Religion in Socialist State

In most communist countries, religion was strongly suppressed. In Soviet Russia, religious places were used for other purposes as directed by the state. Marx called religion 'opium' of people, for he believed that it will be used to consolidate bourgeoisie domination. State atheism in the Soviet Union was known as *Gosateizan*. Members of Communist Party also professed atheism. In China also, party members were prohibited from practicing religion. Religious organizations were condemned as superstitious, and shrines were destroyed. However, since 1978, some reforms were introduced, and the freedom of religion started getting recognized by the constitution of these countries.

6.3.2 One-Party State

To ensure dominance in the political system and to consolidate its powers, most of the socialist states followed the model of one-party state. Communist party was at the apex of the political system. Organized on the principle of democratic centralism, policies were applied stringently leaving no space for dissent. Huge bureaucratic machinery was employed to implement the agenda and policies set by the party. As the sole ruling party, it was a leading guiding force controlling almost everything in the state. E.H. Carr cites Lenin's proclaimed support in 1919, 'the dictatorship of the working class is carried into effect by the party of the Bolsheviks which since 1905 or earlier has been united with the whole revolutionary proletariat' (Carr 1951, 230). In an attempt to create formidable state structures, civil liberties were compromised. Secret police and other organizations were used to monitor almost every aspect of people's life, from social to economic.

The communist party in all the socialist regimes was primarily concerned about the preservation of their all-encompassing control over the administrative and economic structures. Russell has rightly argued, 'As manipulated elections in capitalist countries can function to produce the form without the content of liberal democracy, corrupted one party system in socialist countries can function to produce the form without the content of socialist democracy' (1989, 171).

Communist party established its control through repression but also devised a system of allocating power. Important positions in society, economy, and state power were always given to people approved by the party. All important positions and appointments were also controlled by the party under the *nomenklatura* system which encircled important positions. For example, the head of university, editor and high officials were all pre-decided by the close coterie. The system was organized in a manner where party and its *nomenklatura* controlled key organizations and worked to legitimize communist ideology and authoritarian control. In case of PRC, the communist declared itself to be the 'guardian' of the state and society. This concept of guardianship is based on the practice of mass line. The party organization follows a strict hierarchy of different committees that flow from the top to the grassroots levels. Decision-making is stringently monitored by party rule of democratic centralism.

Special Insights

Women in Socialist Russia

The Bolshevik Revolution of 1917 established the legal equality of women with men in education, work and all aspects of life. As result, there were widespread employment opportunities for women in socialist Russia, and they contributed immensely in all sectors of economy; however, men were still preferred for some professions. A series of progressive legislations were promulgated to empower women. New marriage laws were introduced, and by 1918, under the 'First Family Code', state started conducting marriages instead of church. Men as well as women were free to dissolve the marriage at their will, and women had right to abortion. Generous maternity benefits, paid holidays, health care and insurance in case of illness were provided to women. A separate Women's Department *Zhenotdel* was created by the 1930s to specifically look into the concerns of women. However, all these progressive laws were reversed during Stalin's regime, instead the traditional role of women and their conventional duties were re-emphasized, pushing the women back to the confines of domesticity.

Special Insights

Hannah Arendt on Totalitarianism

In her classic text *The Origin of Totalitarianism* (1951), Hannah Arendt has produced the detailed account of structure, means and forms of totalitarian regimes like Nazism and Stalinism. She says that such regimes are able to reinforce total domination of human existence encompassing all aspects of their lives. Totalitarianism differs from other forms of political oppression such as despotism, tyranny and dictatorship, as it is more lethal and all pervasive. It radically shifts the existing political order to develop entirely new political institutions and destroys all social, legal and political traditions of the country. Totalitarian government always transformed classes into undifferentiated docile masses, created one party state to carry on its agenda, shifted the centre of power from the army to the police and aimed for world domination.

6.3.3 Centralized Planning and Economy

Socialist political system worked with a highly regulated economy. With state-owned monopolies and centrally planned command economy, it created a system of state control. Major means of production, including banks and factories, were under direct state control. Economic policy was also controlled by the party. To implement these in practice, five-year plans and annual plans were made. During the Stalin era, the Soviet Union experienced massive industrialization. By the 1950s, the Soviet Union gradually evolved from an agrarian economy to industrial economy. It was least affected during the great economic depression of the 1930s and presented as a formidable example of economic growth. Soviet's supply of oil and gas also helped in consolidating its economy during the 1970s when oil prices skyrocketed. However, the complex demands of modern economy, fall in oil prices and political turmoil affected its economic growth. The model of a centrally planned command economy was used in other socialist states. Council for Mutual Economic Assistance was an international organization to promote economic development of Socialist states that helped in planning, aid and technological help for rapid growth, but by the 1980s, crisis seems imminent. After the disintegration of the USSR and collapse of socialism in Eastern Europe, reforms were introduced for its transition to market economies. This transition was followed by institutional and political transformation. Privatization of enterprise, decentralization in decision-making, lifting of price controls and foreign trade became the new realities of the former socialist states.

6.4 Socialism in Practice: Some Case Studies

In the post-Second World War period, a large land mass was under the socialism. While in Eastern Europe, especially in countries like Poland, Romania and East Germany, it was the Soviet's support that established communist regimes, in some other like Yugoslavia and Albania, communist parties came to power with mass support of their own. In countries like Czechoslovakia, Hungry and Bulgaria, communist parties could manage with popular support and also with the help of Soviet Red Army. By the 1960s, the reach of the socialist system of rule extended to Asia, Africa and Latin America. From Latin America, Cuba presents a case of rise of socialism majorly because of American hostility and intervention. Similar was the case of Vietnam, Cambodia and Laos.

As the socialist regimes proliferated across the continents, multiple centres and models of communist politics emerged. Soviet authority was also challenged by Maoists. Stalin's ideas of restoration of capitalism and socialism in one country were perceived by Mao as betrayal of world revolution. While the USSR had plans for world domination, Mao was forming alliances primarily based on sentiments of anti-Soviet orientations. In order to protect its dominance, the USSR intervened militarily in Hungary, Czechoslovakia and Berlin, but it had to accept developments in Romania and Prague Spring in Czechoslovakia and the emergence of independent trade union solidarity in Poland. These developments indicate that gradually Soviet Russia was losing its hold in this region and that the Soviet model was rejected by different countries. Division and disagreements within communist world grew leading also to violent clashes, for example, border disputes between Vietnam and Cambodia, China and USSR and China and Vietnam. With this background, let's take a glimpse of some cases and try to understand the trajectory of socialist states in different continents.

6.4.1 Soviet Union (1917–91)

It is interesting to discuss the Soviet experience as a leading case study of Socialist regime. A socialist state under the command of Communist Party was established by Lenin in the USSR. Lenin died in 1924, leading to a tussle of power for control between Trotsky and Stalin. Stalin was in favour of continuing with the new economic policies introduced in 1921 by Lenin, favouring entrepreneurial peasantry and businessmen. He was inclined for establishing socialism in one country, and Trotsky was in favour of rapid industrialization referred to as 'New Course'. When Stalin came to power defeating Trotsky, he adopted extreme forms of industrialization reflected in the first five-year plan focusing on industrialization, collectivization and urbanization. 'Stalinism provide a model of centrally planned industrial revolution possible in a state that was backward and had no background forces like bourgeoisie class to support it' (Nagle 1985, 137). What followed was a path of faster economic development and the USSR emerging as an industrial giant. The regime's success in economic, military and space programmes won the support of people. 'Stalin had directed this industrial revolution with a dictatorial will and a pliant party apparatus in which open intra party factionalism and even individual dissent were forbidden' (Nagle 1985, 137).

The state machinery was heavily centralized. Since such regimes needed to distract the attention of the citizens from the approaching danger of political catastrophe, the suppression of social, religious and cultural freedom was used as a method. In the name of security of the state from the imagined spectre of capitalism, dissent was restricted and complete control of party was established. Many scholars feel that under the grab of socialism, political elites were serving their despicable motives. Most of the leaders in Soviet politics have been very repressive. Also, the leaders like Stalin, Trotsky and Bukharin publicly disagreed and could not generate any consensus on governance of the state, economy and society. Stalin has been notoriously known for his ruthless and repressive regime. Khrushchev as a successor of Stalin since 1955 embarked on a policy of de-Stalinization. Rejecting terror as an instrument of control, he also made an attempt to revive the party. When Brezhnev came in power in 1964, Stalin type of administration based on fear, terror and tight control was revived to instill allegiance. The political discourse was framed in a manner that common people seldom questioned its functioning. Election accepted in principle hardly made any sense in light of absence of an alternative party apart from the communist party. In Soviet Russia, criticism of system came to become equivalent to the disloyalty to the motherland.

Special Insights

Censorship and Soviet Regime

The Soviet regime was marked by tremendous social and political control and surveillance by the communist party, which was hierarchically organized, immensely powerful and remained sacrosanct. The political institutions were used as instruments to closely monitor the citizens by devising multilayered censorship system. The 'Department of Propaganda' deployed official censorship *Glavlit* in the Soviet Union that checked newspapers, journals and books and eliminated any unfavourable report on their society. Censorship remained one of the pillars on which communist states rested. The system also devised mechanism of rewards and punishments to ensure total allegiance of people. Extreme political violence and autocracy were normalized as order of the day. Stalin, particularly indulged in violent political vendetta causing mass execution of political opponents, human rights violations, and complete censorships in the 1930s called 'the Great Purge'.

The socialist principles for quest of liberation find no resonance in the Soviet politics. What emerged in the USSR was a single party rule with state control of economy and centralized planning. Developments in socialist states present us with a case which stand as the reversal of Marxism; the projection of an alternative system got distorted to a highly centralized, top-down, monolithic party state. The secrets behind the iron curtains got gradually exposed to the world, raising serious doubts about authenticity and morality of the system.

However, it needs to be admitted that the Soviet regime was able to provide improved services in housing, health, working condition and education. Mathematical and scientific education was preferred with the objective of making state the superior country in the world. Soviet Russia emerged as a world leader, a super power in the Cold War scenario. It was a territorially huge country, with powerful and technologically advanced military, and natural resources, thus a source of pride for its citizens. Russia's space programmes and victories in sports clear from Olympic medal tally were matters of envy for many. In the field of engineering and technologies, the progress was praiseworthy. This made people feel their society was prospering and that all was well under the communist party rule. However, these claims of success were often exaggerated. For example, even by 1939, barely 11 per cent of the population was able to get proper formal education. This system was also maintained with tight supervision, surveillance and control. Gradually, with the rising level of education, people started seeking information denied to them by the authorities. People also became politically aware by knowing whatever little they could about other political systems.

Since the late 1970s, it was getting difficult to control the system because economic stagnation was downgrading the quality of life. Fulfilling the aspirations of people increasingly became a challenge. Maintaining the super power status was equally becoming a burden. Moreover, with telecommunication revolution and liberalization in East-European states, maintaining censorship was becoming very difficult. The ethnic identity assertions by various groups further added to the national crisis, pushing the system almost to the verge of collapse. Gorbachev came into power in 1985 in this backdrop. He believed that the only way out would be to bring overhauling transformation of the system. He conceptualized reform programmes such as *perestroika*, *glasnost*, *demokratizatsiia* and new thinking. *Perestroika* focused on decentralization of economy and initiating programmes of individual involvement. *Glasnost* means lifting of tight control on public debate. *Demokratizatsiia* was Gorbachev's idea of democracy to increase political accountability within and outside party. New thinking was an initiative at the foreign policy level for better integration of the USSR with world economy and state system. The policies triggered changes in the USSR, and some citizen groups were formed challenging party monopoly. These pressures ultimately led to the first contested elections in Soviet parliament followed by election in the republic. A regime that was run on terror and fear witnessed competitive election. However, these change also catalysed the tremendous demand for autonomy by the federating country members of the USSR. The moment some relaxations were introduced, communist party lost the grip on the system and everything went haywire. Gorbachev's efforts to create a new socialist order for the Soviet Union failed, and so did his economic policies. In 1991, the coalition of conservative people attempted a coup d'etat to remove Gorbachev, and Yeltsin declared himself the leader. In the succeeding days in December 1991, the formation of Commonwealth of Independent States to replace the Soviet Union was announced. In the Soviet Union, reform produced crisis more than crisis forced reform (Brown 2004, 598).

The disintegration of the USSR changed the political map of the region with the emergence of 15 new states in 1992. Gorbachev's foreign policy had an important impact on the fate of communism in Eastern Europe. His policy of non-intervention and military minimization deprived the communist party of the USSR of its privileges and legitimacy. Though Gorbachev was under the impression that East European countries would follow his footsteps and introduce *perestroika* and *glasnost* types of policies, that did not happen. What happened was something no one had imagined, Soviet Union's disintegration replicated in other East European states.

With the disintegration of the USSR, the Soviet socialist system collapsed, raising important questions on viability of socialism in practice. It was also debated whether its collapse was determined because of economic policies adopted in the past 70 years or the authoritarian regime that was established in the name of the Communist party rule. However, economic factors cannot solely account for the failure of the system, as they by themselves are not sufficient conditions to explain failure of an authoritarian regime. Russia was confronted with various problems, and reforms were not initiated at the right time; thus, the system crumbled like a pack of cards. Collapse of communism was due to social as well as economic factors. On the economic front, the USSR was struggling with stagnant economy and excessive burden of military. On the social front, problems such as lack of freedom of religion, the suppression of culture, ethnic identity, the atmosphere of coercion and terror along with plethora of other problems had been accumulating since long. In one way, the disintegration of the USSR appeared inevitable, as aptly remarked by Brown, 'The task of holding together a democratized multinational state, in which each nation could point to a long list of grievances, was far harder than preserving the Union as a highly authoritarian state' (Brown 2004, 599).

Special Insights

Ethnic Conflicts and Soviet Union

The idea of nationalism worked both for and against the communist system at different times. In the USSR, almost 50 per cent population was Russian, so nationalism was referred to as Soviet patriotism. However, for other groups in the USSR, sentiments of a separate existence were simmering. In the post-1990s, these repressed nationalist groups surged in multinational USSR and started confronting the system. Though the right of secession was constitutionally granted to all federating member states, in practice, such demands were ruthlessly supressed. After disintegration of Soviet Bloc, 15 multi-ethnic states were created. All of them were struggling with the problems related to state-building and economic transformation, identities, boundaries and minorities. The ethnic conflicts had different sources, patterns and dynamics and made the entire process of transformation all the more complex.

6.4.2 People's Republic of China

Under the leadership of Mao, PRC was established on 21 September 1949. The Communist party of China under its chairman Mao initiated land reforms and consolidated its popularity among peasants. The 'Great Leap Forward' program was also initiated in the 1950s for major social and economic reforms.

Mao unleashed the Cultural Revolution in the late 1960s, and any institution that lacked revolutionary zeal or was associated with pre-communist China was attacked. Till 1978, PRC had followed command economic system, but even then, this variant of economic system was more decentralized. The economic reforms initiated by China around the 1970s had a slogan 'to get rich is glorious'. These economic reforms though, not accompanied by political reforms, increased the legitimacy of the regime as the goal of economic growth was achieved. Since 1992, PRC has called itself a socialist market economy following its own version of socialism. PRC or China is one of the countries in Asia that is characterized by spectacular growth, but government control clearly remains intact. The communist party commands the reins of power, whereas the state banks and state firms set the direction of economy. It is a unique market economic system with combination of substantive government ownership and control.

Special Insights

People's Republic of China: A Unique Case

Interestingly, PRC is the only socialist regime that has managed to survive, although with considerable modifications. With focus on growth, major achievement of the system is its ability to fulfil the desire of rapid growth. China represents the case of 'state capitalism', the term used by Lenin to describe a state that pursues its own interest in the market economy. It is a system that uses market for political gains. Chris Patten, Britain's last governor of Hong Kong and an astute observer of China, puts it as, 'There is no Marxism left in China, though there are bits of Leninism' (Brown 2004, 605).

China is considered a case of miraculous growth, but the benefits of this growth has not percolated to the bottom layers. However, in the post-1990s, government has initiated low-cost and low-benefit programmes to cover rural population of the country. Yet, there has not been trickle-down effect, making the society very unequal. PRC represents a distinct combination in which the political system still remains autocratic, while the economy has undergone tremendous shifts towards market economy. Like any other socialist regimes of the world, the communist party of China is elitist in its formation, though it has developed some unique features of leadership rotation, regular promotions and a system of term limits.

The Chinese model of economic growth with authoritarian political system had its own problem of inflation, corruption and growing inequality. The rapid development of China no doubt is impressive. However, it is yet to be seen how long it will continue and in what ways. China is already perceived by many as a formidable economic power, giving a good competition to the advanced industrial societies of the West. However, the discomfort and languishing anxieties and contradictions of the system are quite apparent in the form of unemployment, corruption, repression of political dissent and environmental concerns.

6.4.3 Cases from Eastern Europe and Latin America

Many countries in Eastern Europe, Asia and Latin America adopted communism at one point of time. Soviet Russia actively supported the establishment of socialist regimes and made many attempt to sustain them world over. The most noticeable were its effort in Eastern Europe where it superimposed socialist policies by deploying coercive methods and repression. In most of Eastern Europe, Communism was seen as an alien system, emanating from the Soviet Union and people could not associate with it. However, the perceived Soviet might have suppressed all oppositions in most of the East European countries. Armed resistance was also checked by integrating the forces into Soviet-dominated Warsaw Pact. Since 1968, the USSR used Breznev Doctrine based on the idea of 'right and duty' to intervene in any 'fraternal country' to preserve socialism. The Cold War politics, the fear of mutual assured destruction and the possession of nuclear weapons compelled all to accept Soviet dominance. No matter how hard the regimes tried to produce a narrative which projected communism as 'most progressive' part of the nations' history, it failed. The support base of communist system was missing in these countries. Only Bulgaria and, to some extent, Yugoslavia shared pro-Soviet sentiment but that too started waning by the 1960s. Like the USSR, the economy of Eastern Europe also started crumbling. Therefore, in the post-1989 period, the Communist movement gradually gave way to international de-Communizing movement.

The case of Cuba and Vietnam suggests that anti-imperialist sentiments were important first in establishing communist regime and then in its continued existence. Communist regime survived for a long time in these countries. Cuba became a communist regime in 1956 under the leadership of Fidel Castro, supported by the Soviet Union. Socialism in Cuba is deeply rooted as it continues to retain socialist order, though in recent times has greatly relaxed its economy and promoted self-employment and small business venture. In 2002, a plebiscite was held in Cuba in which the majority of the population supported socialism. Vietnam became a socialist regime in 1941 under the leadership of Ho Chi Minh. Heavy industrialization, collectivization of agriculture and farmers' cooperative were made the key features of the system. However, in recent times, Vietnam has allowed small- and medium- scale business enterprises and has been trying to become part of globalized economy.

Poland witnessed communist seize in 1945 by the Soviet Union which continued till 1989 even though people remained dissatisfied with the system. The system staggered due to political repression and economic crisis. Communist party imposed martial law, imprisoned prominent leaders and used military power to control. However, things started changing with decreased influence of the USSR. Constitutional reform began with round table talks, and elections were announced with massive public support. In October 1989, communism in Poland ended. The transition process came to an end when in 1991 Lech Walesa was elected the president of Poland.

Special Insights

Prague Spring

Czechoslovakia came into being in 1918 after getting independence from the Austro-Hungarian Empire. It remained under German occupation between 1939 and 1945. After a coup d'etat in 1948 by the Czechoslovak Communist Party, it became a communist state and remained so till 1989. In the late 1960s, the leadership and the people wanted to relax the system from communist strongholds which came to be called Prague Spring. It refers to the reforms related to decentralization of economy and democratization of the society started by the leader Alexander Dubcek in Czechoslovakia. This effort to liberalize the political institutions and practices in 1968 was stopped by Soviet leadership in its middle by deploying troops to seize the developments. Under the influence of Brezhnev, the Czechoslovak Communist Party restored all the earlier laws of censorship and strict control. Dubcek was expelled from the party and replaced by Gustav Husak. Later, in 1989, Czechoslovakia witnessed 'Velvet Revolution', in which 41 years of communist party came to end without any bloodshed or violence. By 1993, Czechoslovakia split into two countries, the Czech Republic and Slovakia.

Yugoslavia also presents an interesting case of study. It came into being in 1918 after getting independence from the Austro-Hungarian Empire. In 1946, a communist government was established there, though Yugoslavia wanted to keep away from Soviet and create its own version of communism under the leadership of Josip Broz Tito. After death of Tito, the country fell to irreconcilable ethnic strife. The transition process in Yugoslavia was the most cataclysmic in Europe. Disintegration, civil war and ethnic cleansing were all part of this process. Though communist party was the only legal party in Yugoslavia, by the 1970s and 1980s, new parties mushroomed. Tensions between ethnic groups and regions got accentuated by economic, political and ethnic crisis. Slovenia and Croatia were the richest and bore a grudge for being levelled down to help Macedonia and Montenegro, on the other side, Kosovo enjoyed autonomous status resisted by others. There was a vast difference in the economic status of people in different regions. Ideologically, it became difficult to keep the country united. By the end of 1991, all six Yugoslav republics—Serbia, Slovenia, Croatia, Bosnia, Macedonia and Montenegro—held competitive elections. By December 1991, the whole of Yugoslavia was no longer Communist. Ultimately, Yugoslavia dissolved into its seven constituent states (Serbia, Croatia, Bosnia and Herzegovina, Macedonia, Slovenia, Kosovo and Montenegro) in 1992. Ultimately, the combination of new ideas, pressure of social and economic situations and political choices triggered processes that led to the end of Communist rule in Europe.

Special Insights

Women and Post-Communist Societies: Some Insights from Contemporary Times

After nearly 30 years of disintegration of the USSR and demise of communism in Eastern Europe, we find that the status of women in these countries remains worrisome. The basic rights of women enshrined in the erstwhile Soviet constitution, right to vote, ownership of property, right to education, right to divorce and right to equal pay for equal work, have all vanished away with the disintegration. The post-communist societies such as Uzbekistan, Tajikistan and Turkmenistan have witnessed resurgence of conservative, reactionary and religious forces in recent times resulting in a backlash on women's rights and autonomy. These states are struggling to maintain their unity and existence and issues related to women are least important for them. The market economy further exacerbates this gender inequality by favouring men in employment opportunities. Even if they are employed, women are the first one to be fired during financial crisis. Certain conservative groups have also questioned the legitimacy of women working outside the home.

6.5 Conclusion

It can be conclusively observed that the functioning of socialist regimes depicts a clear disjunct between the prophecy and practice of the Marxist tenets. When the grand vision of socialism was implemented, there arose inevitable complexities and distortions, raising doubts about the viability of the system, and also palpable were inherent contradictions of the system. However, the failure of Soviet regime cannot be taken as a signifier of failure of socialism. The greatest contribution of the discourse of socialism is in its ability to provide an alternative, a moral corrective to the flaws of capitalist system. Moreover, the world in the contemporary times has seen increasing decline of the ideological confrontations between the capitalist and socialist regimes. Rather, the new ideological confrontations and disagreements have been happening on the basis of religion, gender, environment, etc. Also, the new Left that emerged in the 1960s–70s shifted the discourse of Marxism to engage with newer, pertinent issues such as the gender rights, gay rights, environmental issues, anti-war movements, etc. Therefore, the discourse and narrative of socialism has also been reinventing itself to provide alternative ways of thinking, theorizing and organizing the world around.

Keywords

Command economy
Communism
Cold War
Leninism
Maoism
Vanguard Party

Review Questions

1. What do you understand by socialism? Critically analyse the reasons for the rise and fall of socialism in the former Soviet Union.
2. Do you think that after the demise of socialism in most of the countries in recent times, communism is still a useful analytical tool to study comparative politics?
3. Trace the development of socialism in and out of Europe with the help of some case studies.
4. Do you believe that Marxist analysis is still pivotal in the understanding of our society, economy and the world?

References

Amin, Samir. 2007. *Empire of Chaos*. Delhi: Aakar.

Brown, Archie. 2004. *Rise and Fall of Communism*. New York: HarperCollins (e-book).

Carr, E.H. 1951. *The Bolshevik Revolution 1917–1923*, Volume II. New York: The Macmillan Company.

Chattopadhyay, Paresh. 2016. Twentieth Century Socialism a Minority Rule. *Economic and Political Weekly* 51(20): 52–60.

Hannah, Arendt. 1951. *The Origins of Totalitarianism*. New York: Harcourt, Brace and Co.

Heywood, Andrew. 2002. Chapter 3: Political Ideologies. In *Politics*, 51–59. London: Palgrave.

Hyle, Gil. (1996). Analytical Marxism: Socialism without class struggle. *Gil Hyle reviews Analytical Marxism by Tom Maye.* Sage Publications, California, 1994. Accessed from http://www.fifthinternational.orgv on September 14, 2023.

Marxists Internet Archive. Introduction. Available at https://www.marxists.org. Accessed on September 14, 2023.

McCormick, John. 2007. Communist and Post-Communist States. In *Comparative Politics in Transition*, 195–209. United Kingdom: Wadsworth.

Meek, Ronald L. 1957. The Definition of Socialism: A Comment. *The Economic Journal* 67(265): 135–39.

Nagle, John. 1985. *Introduction to Comparative Politics.* Chicago, IL: Nelson Hall.

O'Neil, Patrick. 2004. *Essentials of Comparative Politics (Chapter on Communism and Post Communism)*. New York, London: W. W. Norton & Company.

Robert, Andrew. 2009. The State of Socialism: A Note on Terminology. *Slavic Review* 63(2): 349–66.

Russell, James W. 1989. *Modes of Production in World History*. London: Routledge.

Wolff, Jonathan and David Leopold, "Karl Marx", The Stanford Encyclopedia of Philosophy (Spring 2021 Edition), Edward N. Zalta (ed.). Accessed from https://plato.stanford.edu on September 14, 2023.

CHAPTER 7

Colonialism in Comparative Perspective: Forms and Dimensions

Ruchi Shree and Pushpa Singh

Reader's Guide

The chapter attempts to unravel the complexities of colonialism as a conceptual category as well as its practice in comparative perspective. It highlights the contestations over its meaning and the problems arising due to its proximity with other concepts such as imperialism and capitalism. Colonialism as a historical process with its time span of around five centuries affected almost every part of the world. It is said to have profound impact on the socio-political, economic, cultural and psychological aspects of life of the colonized people. The emergence of postcolonialism as an interdisciplinary area of study could be seen in this light. Many countries of Latin America, Asia and Africa have been under some form of colonial rule, and the variation in terms of their experience of colonialism makes it an important area of study in the discipline of comparative politics. Colonial impacts were inevitably multidimensional. This chapter aims to trace the historical legacy of colonialism and explore its multidimensionality. To do so, the chapter is divided into three parts: the first part unpacks the conceptual underpinnings of the subject by engaging with its political, economic, cultural, psychological and environmental dimensions. The second part traces the historical development of colonialism as a world system, rise of colonial powers, the interlinkages between colonialism and capitalism and also elaborates upon the forms of colonialism, viz. settler colonialism, formal and informal colonialism, etc. The third part captures the narrative of postcolonialism and neocolonialism in the wake of changed global milieu in post-Second World War period.

7.1 Introduction

Colonialism has long remained a crucial engagement in the explorations in social sciences. It is particularly significant for comparative politics as colonial legacies deeply influence the process of democratic consolidation and overall nature of state. As it is the subject matter of the discipline of comparative politics to do a comparison of a range of countries, study of phenomenon like colonialism enables the researcher to understand the specific contexts and peculiarities of postcolonial societies. Colonialism could be seen as an exceptional global moment in the world history in terms of its unprecedented pursuit of control and oppression of the masses of the lesser known parts of the world. Colonialism has been a pervasive, brutal and deeply entrenched system of territorial acquisitions and control that ruled many countries belonging to Latin America, Asia and Africa. By design, it has been aggrandizing, repressive and unjust. Under this system, colonial powers like Britain annexed and created its vast expanses that sprawled uninterrupted over almost four centuries. It led to a system of white supremacy and colonial regimes of power and knowledge that made them dismissive of indigenous people and their culture. Colonialism has affected the world history significantly and continues to influence and shape the identities, anxieties and aspirations of the postcolonial societies. As an ideology, it gave rise to a plethora of new concepts, viz. decolonization, internal colonialism, neocolonialism, postcolonialism, etc. Scholars often debate about the forms and nature of colonialism, that whether the experience of colonialism was transformative or transitory and whether its impact was direct or indirect or both. Ronald J. Horvath states that academic establishments have not unanimously agreed on definition of colonialism. People feel strongly about it, either criticizing it or praising it, depending on their location, giving rise to myriad connotations of the term. We find rich and extremely nuanced understanding of the subject from scholars like Fanon, Ngugi and Gandhi who argue that colonialism was not only about the socio-political and economic domination, but its entrenchment has been pervasive in all realms of existence of the colonized people. It also colonized the mind and psyche, dismissing the culture and civilization of such people as either obsolete or secondary as discussed by Edward Said. Postcolonial thinkers ranging from Mahmood Mamdani, Bernard Cohn, Nicholas Dirks and many others have documented the colonial and postcolonial experiences of various countries. For instance, Diderot turned the debate of colonialism as a civilizing mission almost upside down while criticizing the European colonization. He not only challenges the view that the indigenous people are benefitted by the European civilization but also argues that the European colonists were the uncivilized ones. To him, the colonial empires often become the sites of extreme brutality because the colonists are far away from legal institutions (Muthu 2003). Since the experience of colonialism is spread over almost five centuries and across all parts of the world, it is expected that there will be not one, but many forms of colonialism. In this context, it is pertinent to understand the subject in a comparative perspective, the conceptual underpinnings of colonialism highlighting its varied implications and different understanding in the eyes of the colonizers and the colonized.

7.2 Conceptual Underpinnings

In the broadest sense, colonialism is a practice of domination but the nature and extent of this domination brings nuances to its meaning. There is a lack of unanimity among scholars as the term has been interpreted in numerous ways over a period of time. The root word of colonialism originated from Latin American word *colonia*[1] meaning such a property which is created among the foreigners in a planned way. Most commonly, colonialism is understood as a policy in which a country (colonizer) rules over the other country/countries (colonized) and develops trade for its own benefit. For example, Britain established colonialism over 13 original colonies in North America before these colonies achieved independence in 1776. The independence of these 13 colonies materialized the creation of the 50 states in the United States.

7.3 Political Dimension: Colonialism and Imperialism

To understand the political dimension of colonialism, let us explore the categories of colonialism and imperialism. These two concepts are at times even used as synonyms. However, their meanings clearly unleash the difference between them. Colonialism comes from the Latin word *colonus* meaning farmer and is used in the sense of transfer of population from one territory to another; imperialism has its roots in another Latin term *imperium* meaning command with an implied reference of one country exercising control over another (*Stanford Dictionary* 2010). Both colonialism and imperialism were forms of conquest and expected to benefit Europe economically as well as strategically.

Some scholars have distinguished between the different categories of colonialism based on their purpose of establishment in the host country/countries, for example, for settlement or for economic exploitation only. Others distinguish between colonialism and imperialism. To them, while in colonialism, the dependencies are directly governed by a foreign nation, imperialism is a more direct form of domination. So, we may say that there is a lack of unanimity among the scholars in terms of the meaning and usage of these two terms. Robert J.C. Young (2015), a British postcolonial theorist, writes that the term 'imperialism' should not be confused with 'colonialism'. He goes on to explain that imperialism operates from the centre as a state policy which is developed for ideological as well as financial reasons, whereas colonialism is nothing more than development for settlement or commercial intentions (Young 2015). One may interpret from this that imperialism always has an element of colonialism which may not be the case with colonialism. In other words, colonialism does not necessarily imply imperialism. Scholars such as Ronald J. Horvath (1972) argue that at times it is possible to use colonialism and imperialism interchangeably. He gives substantive examples to prove his point. He writes that although China and the Soviet Union condemn the United States for being an imperialist power, at the same, these two countries have been and still are colonial and imperial powers in their own ways. It is in this context that he says that there is no need to distinguish between colonialism and imperialism. To him, the history of Russia is full of aggressive and exploitative colonialism and so is the history of China with respect to Tibet as a conquered colony. Thus, we may say that the meaning and usage of these two concepts have often been overlapping.

The case of British East India Company's rule in India is understood as the case of colonialism as well as imperialism. The company came to India for doing business but eventually started controlling the country politically. India was made a part of the British empire by the British government. As Michael Doyle writes, 'empires are relationships of political control imposed by some political societies over the effective sovereignty of other political societies ... Imperialism is the process of establishing and maintaining an empire' (Doyle 1986, 19). The political control connotes the ability to dominate the process of policymaking. Starting from 1757 to its end in 1947, for almost two centuries, the East India Company ruled in India and is considered as one of the most devastating experiences of colonialism.

7.3.1 Economic Dimension: Colonialism and Capitalism

7.3.1.1 Some Reflections from Marxist Discourse

Colonialism and capitalism have an inevitable link; however, the nature of this link is open to different understandings. Ellen Meiksins Wood, a noted Marxist political scientist in his book *An Origin of Capitalism: A Longer View* (2002, 2013), writes that the connection between capitalism and colonialism is simple and straightforward. Wood even uses the concepts of colonialism and imperialism interchangeably. He states that a large part of the 16th- and 17th-century history of Europe is full of colonial ventures and conquests. Wood further argues in favour of the agrarian origin of capitalism and capitalist imperialism. This process further helped in shaping the formation of nation state, marked by specific features of territoriality and sovereignty.

Although, much before Meiksin Wood, it was in the early 20th century when scholars such as Hobson, Lenin and Luxemburg wrote about the relation between colonialism/ imperialism and capitalism in different ways. Hobson's book *Imperialism: A Study* (1902) classifies the capitalists who benefitted from imperialism into three categories: first, the financiers; second, big firms engaged in building warships, manufacturing guns, etc.; third, the great manufacturers of export trade. He argues that imperialism was required for these capitalists to make profits, as they could not invest and buy or sell products at home. It was a necessity to control a non-capitalist culture for economic reasons. However, he also argues that imperialism did not benefit the capitalist nation as a whole. Apparently, it benefitted the wealthy class much more than the working class and poorer sections of the society.

Lenin developed his analysis of Western economics and political domination in *Imperialism: The Highest Stage of Capitalism* (1917). He argues that imperialism provided the greatest opportunity to the European countries to avert their domestic crisis. The European countries could do so by feeding their faltering economies resources from the colonies. Lenin argues that the late-19th century imperialism was primarily driven by the demand of constant raw materials to run the wheels of late capitalism. As profit plummeted, the colonial powers panicked about the economic crisis that was looming large and could only be resolved through territorial expansion outside the national borders. Like Hobson, Lenin also emphasized on the massive industrial concentration in capitalist countries. He talks about the five essential features of capitalism, namely (i) concentration of production and capital in the subsequent stages establishes monopolies; (ii) financial oligarchy is created when bank capital merges with industrial capital; (iii) during the third stage instead of export of commodities, export of capital becomes significant; (iv) these developments lead to creation of international cartels and capitalist monopolies; and (v) the final stage culminates into territorial division of whole world among the capitalist powers. In this way, imperialism and capitalism directly feed to the colonial expeditions as discussed by Lenin.

Lenin's understanding resonates with Marx, who viewed European colonialism as internal and external aggrandizement of territories across the continent. The capitalism of Europe could sustain itself by bringing more territories under control for extraction of resources. Gradually, the structure and function of the capitalist mode of production consolidated colonialism in all parts of the world. This vicious cycle of extraction continued unabated and was fortified with the military control and complete repression of such societies.

Marxist theorists such as Rosa Luxemburg, Karl Kautsky and Nikolai Bukharin also elaborate on imperialism in different contexts. Kautsky's analysis and his concepts bear a significant meaning in the world-systems theory as well as postcolonial studies. He negated the idea that imperialism would result in development of the areas subjected to economic exploitation and argues that imperialism is a relatively permanent relationship structuring the interactions between two types of countries (Young 2001). It is interesting to note that imperialism in its earlier phase generated military competition between capitalist countries. However, later it resulted in an arrangement between colonial powers to frame a steady system of exploitation of the non-developed world (at present, developing countries). Immanuel Wallerstein is the most renowned thinker for the world-systems theory. According to him, the world-system is a relatively stable set of relations between core and peripheral state *World-System Analysis: Theory and Methodology* (1982). In the globe, the division of labour is marked in such a way that it benefits the core states and siphons resources from the periphery to the core.

Rosa Luxemburg in *The Accumulation of Capital* (1913) wrote that foreign imperialist expansion was essential for the survival of capitalism. She further writes that 'capitalism arises and develops historically ... amidst a non-capitalist society' (Hunt and Lautzenheiser 2011). The imperialist struggle to control the nonmarket/non-capitalist economies has four broad aims: first, to attain the raw materials; second, to wipe out the indigenous methods of production; third, to transform the natural economy into a commodity, or market; and fourth, to isolate industry, trade and agriculture which were earlier part of an interconnected economy. She partly disagreed with Marx on the process of primitive accumulation.

Paul Baran and Paul Sweezy, American political economists, take up Marxian framework in their book *Monopoly Capital: An Essay on the American Social and Economic Order* (1966) to analyse the nature of the American capitalist society. They point out the paradoxes of the economy—a tendency towards stagnation and at the same time powerful strides in technology and productivity. They do not make claim for universal character and experience of capitalism, rather highlight the distinguishing features of capitalism in America. The large corporations are the centres of economic power and decision-making there. The book provides a critique of militarism and imperialism and is considered an important text even today.

Noted scholar Samir Amin argues that 'colonialism is inseparable from capitalism'.[2] He gives examples from the 16th century when parts of America were colonized by colonial powers like Spain, Portugal, Britain and France for capitalist gains. Later, during the 17th–20th centuries numerous other countries of Asia, Africa and Latin America also became colonies for the very similar purposes. To him, even the present phase of globalization is a new avatar of capitalism which is adding to the inequality in the world.

7.3.1.2 Some Reflections from Liberal and Alternate Understandings

The aforementioned discussions have been representative of the Marxist interpretations of colonialism and capitalism by various scholars and theorists. Now, let us look at some of the non-Marxist/alternative understanding of colonialism for a complete view. Works of Alexis de Tocqueville and J.S. Mill discussed in the next paragraph provide the locus standi of liberalism and show how the idea gets comfortably accepted in the discourse of civilizing missions of the West. On the other hand, Indian nationalists and freedom fighters such as Dadabhai Naoroji and M.K. Gandhi and economic historians like R.C. Dutt talked of economic drain theory that robbed the colonies. Gandhian historian Dharampal provides nuanced and erudite implications of the colonial rule. Environmentalists like Ramchandra Guha and Madhav Gadgil and ecofeminists like Vandana Shiva highlight the nefarious and irreversible impact of colonialism on environment.

Tocqueville not only supported the French colonization of Algeria, but was also actively engaged in advancing the project. Though he recognized the fact that colonialism did not necessarily bring good government to the colonized population, he did not oppose the process of colonialism. Mill as a life-long employee of British East India Company had a close experience of colonialism. He believed in normative legitimacy of imperial rule, though his understanding about its nature and justification changed over time. Mill thought that colonialism would bring civilization, peace and prosperity for the colonized people and to the entire humanity as discussed in his book *Considerations on Representative Government* (1861).

However, an alternative understanding of colonialism has come up from those exploring the legacy of the inevitable link between colonialism and poverty and have engaged with the anti-colonial struggles in their countries. Dadabhai Naoroji propounded the theory of economic drain, discussed in his book *Poverty and Un-British Rule in India* in 1871. He detailed how the British colonial rule in India was draining out the wealth of the country to the benefit of the Britishers. Naoroji pointed that, at first, the internal drain takes place when the material resources are transferred from the rural remote areas to the cities. Then, the external foreign rule drains and exhausts gradually all the resources of the colonies by siphoning them back to their countries to feed their drive for industrialization. He concluded that the exploitative and extractive policies of the colonial rule were responsible for the increasing impoverishment of the people. Naoroji saw mass poverty in India as the immediate consequence of the British rule in the country. His proposition was corroborated by others studying the economic implications of colonial rule in India as well. Economic historian R.C. Dutt in his classic work *Economic History of India*, Vols. I and II (1902, reproduced in 2001 by Routledge) further highlights how the British rule deliberately sabotaged the Indian art and crafts by their policies. It resulted in the destruction of Indian loom supplies in the external market in Europe and Asia and made communities of weavers and other artisans unemployed and obsolete. This was done by Britishers to benefit the rising manufacturing textiles and others sectors in Britain and to make India its perpetual supplier of the raw material. In this way, there occurred a systematic structural and institutional economic exploitation. The economy of the villages in India had been more or less self-sufficient in the pre-colonial era, but the colonial rule ruined it all, pushing the agrarian system in a perpetual crisis. The disintegration of indigenous market and deindustrialization of economy forced these workers to move to farming that already was under pressure due to adverse agricultural policies of British. In contemporary times, Amiya Bagchi in his work *The Political Economy of Underdevelopment* (1982) elaborates the vile consequences of British colonialism on the Indian economy. In similar veins, Prasannan Parthasarathi's *The Transition to a Colonial Economy: Weavers, Merchants and Kings in South India* (2001) revisits the association between poverty and colonialism in India, tracing an apparent decline in standards of living due to the 19th-century deindustrialization and drain of resources caused by the colonial rule.

Gandhi produces the most comprehensive critique of the narcissistic British colonial rule in India. He emphasized the inextricability of colonialism, Western modernity and economic exploitation of the colonies. In his book *Hind Swaraj* (1905), he provides a detailed account of what is wrong with the Western civilization, its structures and institutions. Gandhi lamented the parasitical temperament of the industrial economy of British colonial empire that was sprawling its paraphernalia at the cost of the poor colonies. Like Naoroji, Gandhi also analysed the colonial rule in terms of economic drain theory that was making India poorer, debilitated and completely helpless. He quashed the theories proposed by the Western scholars who justified the colonial rule and its policies doing good for the masses. Gandhi was a vehement critic of the economic policies of the Britishers which were responsible for uprooting of the self-sustained indigenous economies of the small villages. He questioned the moral authority of the British rule for continuing its repressive regime in India. He was particularly repelled by the synthetic textiles of Britishers that flooded the Indian market and rendered the native workers jobless. This prompted him to proclaim the Swadeshi Movement that strongly advocated the use of indigenous cloths and other goods. In order to visualize the aim of Swadeshi, Gandhi called upon the people to regain the lost pride in their culture and themselves. The profoundness of his ideas led to advocacy of widespread local village-based small-scale industries. This model of economy stood as sharp contrast to the centralized and homogenized mass production of commodities by big industries of the industrial societies. Significantly, he took everyone's attention towards the gigantic hidden cost of such mode of production that takes huge toll on the environment and ecology.

In fact, Gandhi found the entire conceptualization of life, living and society of the West as deeply flawed as it was rooted in insatiable quest for unbridled materialism. As the resources on our planet are finite, the extravaganzas of the indulgence will cost us all dearly. Entire humanity is sustained by the same planet and its resources; no country or community has a right to plunder it in order to fulfil its gargantuan materialist appetite. This pattern of the West, he believed, will eventually destroy it under its own burden. However, older civilizations like India have a lot to offer to the West. The traditions in such societies are based on sharing, renunciation and control over the self to exonerate oneself of all allurements and solicitations of the gloss of materialistic West. It is in this context that he thought it pertinent for the current generations to revisit and nourish their strong roots.

Gandhian historian Dharampal has produced meticulous account of deleterious colonialism. Through his epic works *Indian Science and Technology in Eighteenth Century* (1971) and *The Beautiful Tree* (1983), he brings to our notice how indigenous systems of education, local governance, agriculture, science and technology were destroyed by the British rule. These systems were rooted in the indigeneity and were highly effective and efficient in many respects. However, the colonial invasion subverted the existing systems and rendered these modes of knowing and doing as outmoded. Colonialism constantly fabricated web of lies to prove their superiority in front of the colonized people and to justify their domination. The Britishers imposed English education system that was myopic and ill-fitted for the Indian masses. It mocked the indigenous education system without even bothering to know it. Hence, it comes as no surprise that the rooting out of the indigenous system of education in India was a result of the imprudent colonial policies. Such explorations in the misadventures of colonial rule expose the banality of the claimed 'moral and political supremacy' of the hegemonistic colonial empires.

7.3.2 Cultural and Psychological Dimensions

In continuation with the thoughts of Gandhi and Dharampal, now we will engage with the writings of scholars such as Franz Fanon, Ashis Nandy, Ngũgĩ wa Thiong'o and others who have underlined the cultural and psychological aspects of colonialism. For instance, Ngũgĩ wa Thiong'o, a postcolonial literary and social activist from Kenya, has analysed the experience of colonialism in the African context. He writes that colonialism not only robbed the people of their natural resources, but also enslaved them by colonizing their values. By imposing their language on the natives of the colony, colonizers also colonized the imagination of the colonized people. This colonization of the culture, language and imagination had deep, debilitating impact on the colonized masses. His writings such as *Decolonising the Mind: The Politics of Language in African Literature* (1986) and *Something Torn and New: An African Renaissance* (2009) highlight the dilemma before the Third World intellectuals in choosing between the colonial language and their mother tongue.

Ashis Nandy's book *Intimate Enemy* (1983) narrates the experience of colonialism in India through the lens of psychology. Nandy's writing touches upon a range of diverse issues including language, personality, traditions, etc. He writes, 'English is not my language. Though I have developed a taste for it, it was once forced upon me. Even now I often form my thoughts in my native Bengali and then translate when I have to put them down on paper'. He points out that even after 30 years of toil, though he has acquired reasonable competence in the language, but it is not his first language. He has been told that his forefathers taught him the wrong English, thus he must now relearn the language (Nandy 1983, 19). He admits himself being too old to do that now. Colonial rule has induced a lack of confidence and loss of bearing among the colonized people. The aftermath has been so overwhelming that these people, even when politically independent now, are largely ignorant of the society and culture that sustain them.

Nandy seems to be resonating with Ngugi's concerns. Deviating from the issue of language, Franz Fanon shifts our attention to 'race' as a major factor in the experience of colonialism. Across the world, racial discrimination was a major characteristic of colonialism. His books *The Wretched of the Earth* (1963), *Black Skin, White Masks* (1952) and *A Dying Colonialism* (1959) reflect the multidimensional orientation of colonialism. His books played an important role in motivating the process of decolonization. On one hand, his writings highlighted the problem of racism, and on the other, they also underline the hegemony of capitalism as a model of political economy.

Dipesh Chakrabarty (2007) and Vivek Chibber (2013) have taken up these issues in their writings in different ways. In his book *Provincializing Europe*, Chakrabarty argues that concepts such as disenchanted space and secular time are distinctively European and may make little sense in the peculiar context of non-European societies. Posing them as universal ideas makes the 'other' belonging to a different culture feel and appear as incomplete or lacking these categories. Colonialism has been a predicament of paradoxes, as Europe has been preaching Enlightenment humanism to the colonized and yet simultaneously denied it in practice. However, Chibber challenges Chakrabarty's position by advancing a critique of Subaltern Studies. He also defends universal categories such as capitalism, class, rationality and objectivity. Chibber further states that a universal understanding of these categories helps in explaining the realities of a political actors and the system as a whole.

Worldwide, the colonial powers often used the administrative structures and policies to favour themselves. The colonial state introduced changes in various areas such as agriculture, industries, education and administration, to name a few. However, the extent of any country getting affected by colonialism was dependent upon several factors. For instance, Manoranjan Mohanty in his article 'Colonialism and Discourse in India and China' (1999) tries to make sense of colonialism in a comparative perspective. He argues that in China, political movements evolved in such a way that the Chinese people did not internalize the colonial worldview. They understood the importance of unifying role played by the Chinese language. Contrary to that, in India, the Eurocentric worldview and English as a language was given much importance by the Indian elite. This dominion of the language of the colonizer and the politics behind it was neither resisted or nor even seriously questioned. Interestingly, people facing subjugation devise ways and means to get out of this entrapment and recover the 'self'. The colonized 'self' is constantly embattled searching for its identity. This leads to constant negotiations within the mind of the colonized, with the self and others to generate a sense of the 'self'. One example is Aime Cesaire's concept of 'negritude'[3] which is a construction of identity by appropriating the term 'nigger' used in a derogatory sense for racial discrimination. A literary movement arose from the 1930s to 1950s to create a Pan-African racial consciousness by taking pride in being blacks. So, while for a long time, the Negro people were made to feel ashamed of themselves by their colonizers, forced to live in a state of rejection, Cesaire's idea of negritude came as a hope. It gave the blacks a new sense of history, identity and culture. Colonialism also ruined the linguistic and cultural diversity of the colonies that served as a strong source of identity for them.

The monstrosity of injustice pervades all aspects of colonialism. Its entrenchment transgresses all imaginable boundaries impinging upon all reals of life of the colonized. It is relevant to point out how this subjugation conditions the practices associated with food habits in the colonized world. Traditional food and farming were coercively replaced by cash crops like indigo, sugarcane, cotton and tobacco in all colonies. Routinely, the food patterns and the farming systems of the indigenous communities were ridiculed. On the other hand, food products emanating from the European markets were projected as the objects of aspirations. For example, there are many works that are now questioning the epistemological hegemony and sanctity of products like white crystalline sugar and the colonial politics that fanned the production of such things that were positioned as representative of modernity, purity and progress. Most of the medical interventions by now have established how the indigenous systems of food consumption and indigenous crops carry higher nutritional value compared with the imported hybrid crops brought in by the colonial masters. Understanding of colonialism should be mindful of all these asymmetries of power generated out of subtle policies and acts of the colonizers.

7.3.3 Colonialism and Environment

In the times when we are moving towards an impending environmental crisis, it is pertinent that we should analyse the relationship between colonialism and environment. One must be informed of the ways in which colonialism caused great damage to the natural resources across the world and caused the environmental tragedy. In particular, contemporary concerns and initiatives on environmental degradation, deforestation and species extinction or anxieties about climate change continue to draw deeply from the misadventure of the colonial empires.[4] The discussion in the preceding sections has already pointed out that colonial ventures were guided by the demands of industrial capitalism. Colonialism perpetuated as it was the greatest source for supply of natural resources for the empire. Colonial empires left huge ecological footprints. The ecological shadows of the empire are still lurking in the darkness of their deeds.

Scholars such as Ramchandra Guha and Madhav Gadgil have explored the environmental aspect of colonialism. Their writings discuss rampant destruction of environment cause by the colonial rule. Guha thinks that the foreign rule is never desirable or suitable for the land or the people. The colonizers are unlikely to have the knowledge of local conditions and, therefore, may not be able to resolve the problems of public policy effectively. Also, due to cultural, linguistic and often religious differences between colonizers and colonized, the colonizers are unlikely to sympathize with the native people. They are also likely to act tyrannically. Even if the colonizers really try to treat the native people fairly, their natural tendency is to sympathize with those similar to themselves (other foreign colonists or merchants) and is likely to lead to distorted judgement in cases of conflict. The colonial rulers and merchants go to the colonies in order to acquire wealth with little effort or risk, so their economic activity often exploits the colonized country rather than developing it. Colonial conquest and control mark an ecological watershed by most environmental historians like Guha, Gadgil and others, as it brought unparalleled destruction of environment in the colonies. Scholarships in the field show how the colonial empire drove their industrial economy by ensuring a relentless chain of supply of raw materials, resources, commodities, crops and minerals from the natural world (Kumar, Damodaran, and D'Souza 2011, 2). When Britain ran out of its supply of English oak, it started ravaging forests of its colonies to procure woods. Massive destruction of forests in the Indian sub-continent resulted from the transfer of Indian teak to Britain for ship-building.

Another viewpoint comes from the ecofeminists, viz. Vandana Shiva, who find great semblance between modernity, colonialism and patriarchy (Shiva 1988). In her views, colonialism appears as one of the projects of Western modernity and modern science that subjugates women and nature in the similar fashion. She highlights the reductionism of modern science and industrial capitalism that fueled the colonial expeditions and its pursuit of plunder of natural resources to sustain its industrialism.

7.4 Colonialism: Historical Development

James Chiriyakandath (2008) in his article 'Colonialism and Postcolonial Development' writes that two-thirds of the world experienced colonialism in some or the other form. Different countries experienced colonialism at different points of time. We may classify the countries into three categories: first, there are countries who colonized others and thus called colonial powers (Britain, France, Germany, Spain, Portugal, etc.); second, those who were colonized (India, Algeria, South Africa, etc.) named as colonies; and third, those who experienced colonialism as well as colonized others (the United States) when they got independence from colonialism.

7.4.1 Rise of Colonial Powers

The period from 16th- to 20th century is marked as the phase of European colonialism. The countries experienced being the colonial powers and the colonies in numerous ways. Some countries even became colonies of two to three countries at different points of time or even simultaneously. For instance, while some part of India was under Portuguese control, the major part of its territory was British colony. The period from 1870 to 1914 has often been termed as 'age of imperialism'. During this phase, the hunt for colonies was at its peak, and its prominent feature was 'scramble of Africa'[5] in 1884, in the Berlin Conference. Britain, France, Germany, Portugal and Belgium divided their share of influence. This was followed by intense colonialism and warfare in the world.

The rivalry between major European colonial powers like the United Kingdom, France, Germany and others was largely responsible for the colonial rule. There were ups and downs in the status of colonial powers. For example, Germany was hardly a colonial power before its unification in 1871. Being a neighbour of France and Britain, it was eager to participate in the colonial race, but Germany not yet had the chance to control overseas territories, mainly due to its late unification and its lack of experience in modern navigation. Eventually, Germany called for the 1884–85 Berlin Conference to set the rules of effective control of a foreign territory, and the arrangement for territorial division of power was worked out. Britain, the oldest colonial power, colonized a large territory of the world from Asia to Africa to Latin America. Even the United States was a British colony till its independence in July 1776. However, later, the United States as a colonial power ruled over countries such as Hawaii, Cuba, Puerto Rico and Philippines. In the 16th and 17th centuries, Spain, Portugal, Holland, England

and France were the major colonial powers. In the 19th century, the club was joined by the European countries like Belgium, Germany and Italy and also the non-European powers, namely the United States and Japan. France expanded its colonial regime in northern Africa and Indo-China. Portugal, an old colonial power, was controlling many countries from Africa like Angola, Mozambique and others. Similarly, Germany and Italy were also making colonies in other parts of Africa.

Competition for colonies led to numerous wars in the 17th and 18th centuries. The colonial powers were squabbling among each other to control the large tracts of land. By the end of the 19th century, the fights were intensifying, and the countries started making groups. In 1899, the United States had a quarrel with Spain, and it not only annexed Philippines and Puerto Rico but also turned Cuba into a protectorate. In 1904–1905, Japan defeated Russia in a war over Manchuria. Italy seized Libya in 1911 which led to Italy's war with Turkey. Eventually, the two world wars of the 20th century were also a product of the colonial ambition of few powerful nations.

7.4.2 Forms of Colonialism

Worldwide, the colonial patterns can be classified in terms of time span, its geographical outreach, its impact, etc. Some scholars have used the terms, settler colonialism and exploitation colonialism. Others have discussed the category of internal colonialism, formal and informal colonialism, etc. This section intends to unravel these concepts and emphasize that the motives of all these forms of colonialism were economic. Although different forms of colonialism functioned in different manners.

7.4.2.1 Settler and Exploitative Colonialism

Robert Young writes that colonialism 'involved an extraordinary range of different forms and practices carried out with respect to radically different cultures, over many centuries' (Young 2001, 17). He also lists examples of three different types of colonialism. The first category is of settler colonies such as British North America and Australia and French Algeria; second are the administered territories established without significant settlement with the aim of economic exploitation, such as British India and Japanese Taiwan; and third, the maritime enclaves, such as Hong Kong, Malta and Singapore.

The settler colonialism is about large-scale immigration usually motivated by religious, economic or political reasons. For security and prosperity, the settlers tend to economically as well as politically exploit their colonies.[6] For example, the settlers from Holland, Portugal, Britain and Germany colonized the various parts of Africa such as Angola, Mozambique, Namibia, Zimbabwe and Zambia. Similarly, Algeria was a colony of France. While some colonial powers tried to assimilate the local cultures, others concentrated only on their economic gain.

In exploitation colonialism, a country establishes control over another country to access its natural resources for its own benefit. There are numerous examples of such colonialism, and the most notable among them are the British empire in India, Egypt and South Africa. The British rule set up a colonial administration in its colonies to exploit the raw materials and other finished goods to export to the motherland. This process also destroyed the handicrafts, agriculture and pre-colonial social setup in the colonies.

7.4.2.2 Formal and Informal Colonialism

Ronald Horvath distinguishes between formal colonialism and informal colonialism. He writes that 'formal colonialism' refers to a form of inter-group domination in which the settlers migrate from the colonizing powers to their colonies in a significant number. In 'informal colonialism', the inter-group domination occurs due to the voluntary migration of permanent settlers from places other than the metropolis. For example, one can see the migration of Asians to Africa, the Chinese migrating to Southeast Asia, etc.

7.4.2.3 Internal Colonialism

The term 'internal colonialism' is used to denote that exploitative relationship as colonialism can exist within societies as well as between them. It may happen in numerous ways. For example, dominant ethnic or religious groups may exploit the groups in minority or the industrial regions may dominate and exploit the agricultural regions. The term was first used by Marxists such as Lenin and Gramsci to explain how capitalist exploitation operates on a regional level. Later, it was used in different contexts. It has been applied in Latin America, between urban populations with largely European backgrounds and indigenous native population; economic and political inequality in Canada; race relations in the United States.

A.G. Frank theorized internal colonialism as a form of uneven development. Few scholars have differentiated between internal colonialism and neocolonialism. In the former, the control comes from within, but in the latter, a country is controlled from outside. Examples of internal colonialism are countries like Algeria, Ireland, etc. In Algeria, French culture is so dominant that it has created a core-periphery where the French-speaking Christians constitute the core while the Arabic-speaking Muslims are at the periphery. Ireland remained a part of United Kingdom for a long time. Now, it is divided into two parts. While one part is united with the United Kingdom, the other part is independent, but it is difficult to distinguish between the British and Irish cultures.

In this way, we see that different colonies went through different forms of colonialism that bore slight difference in terms of the nature of rule and extent of repression. Nevertheless, all forms of colonialism were thoroughly oppressive and exploitative. In the following section, we will discuss the developments in the world after the end of colonialism. Transformations in the post-Second World War period generated ground for the end of colonial rule through decolonization. The end of colonialism ushered in an era of emancipation, though the colonial past heavily informed the identity, institutions and politics of postcolonial societies. The last sub-section discusses the phenomenon of neocolonialism as an extension of the old colonial project in terms of its politics of accumulation, though disguised.

7.5 Colonialism and After: Decolonization, Postcolonialism and Neocolonialism

7.5.1 Decolonization

By the 20th century, the colonial rule all across the continents were becoming weak and fatigued. They were finding it hard to explain the duality in their conduct in terms of preaching the political values of Enlightenment and at the same time forcefully containing their colonies. The world also witnessed two deadliest world wars that were the result of the bickering of colonial powers for colonies. League of Nations created after the First World War failed miserably to avert the looming Second World War. Soon, the world witnessed the worst holocaust of its lifetime. Countries, across the globe, realized the extent of tragedy and pledged to establish an effective system of international supervision to subvert any such event in the times to come. Consequently, UNO was established in 1945 that catalysed the world public opinion in favour of emancipation of erstwhile colonies. The colonizers were also heavily burdened and no longer capable of continuing their colonial rule in the wake of many factors, most important of them being the rising intensity of the independence movements in the colonies. The 'Right to Self-Determination' proclaimed by General Assembly on 14 December 1960 under the declaration on 'Granting of Independence to Colonial Countries and Peoples' strongly upheld the idea of political freedom of colonized people. It inevitably led to the strong wave of decolonization. Further, non-alignment movement expedited this process. It is because of these developments in the international milieu that a large number of erstwhile colonies got independence in the decades of the 1950s and 1960s. Decolonization resulted in emergence of many new countries after their long anti-colonial struggles (please refer Chapter 6 for the details). Unfortunately, many of these countries reverted to authoritarian regimes and military rule by 1970, for example, Brazil, Nigeria and others; this will be discussed in detail in the chapter on democratization in the second section of this book.

7.5.2 Postcolonialism

Postcolonialism as a multidimensional concept is used in different contexts to mean a range of diverse experiences. Broadly, it rejects the colonial interpretation of non-Western societies and re-narrates the account of the colonized through the lens of postcolonial scholars. The method of postcolonial scholars engages the present and simultaneously revisits the past. There is strong urge to remember, illuminate, reflect and reproduce the account of the past, from the perspective of colonized masses. It is a form of deconstructive reading most usually applied to works emanating from the colonizers (Ashcroft, Griffiths, and Tiffin 2009, 192). It is an act of recovering past legacies, a painful remembering of the past to make peace with the present.

The term postcolonialism connotes postcolonial theory (high theory of Derrida, Lacan and Foucault), postcolonial practice (Said, Spivak and Bhabha[7]), postcolonial literature (Frantz Fanon, Mahatma Gandhi, Ngũgĩ wa Thiong'o and Chinua Achebe), and many other scholars have their interdisciplinary connotations. Most of the scholars in social sciences trace the roots of postcolonial theory in Edward Said's book *Orientalism* (1978). Said highlights the hierarchy of knowledge in which the societies of the East are portrayed as secondary, trivial and non-significant. The secondariness of colonized people and their culture makes them appear as irrelevant and redundant in the eyes of West. This complete dismissal of any possibility of identity and agency of the colonized preserves the perverse domination of the colonizers. While Said's work has focused on the experience of colonial representation and cultural stereotyping in the Middle East, other scholars like Mahmood Madani, Bernard Cohen, Homi Bhabha and Dipesh Chakrabarty further expanded the field of postcolonial studies. These scholars show how the non-Western cultures and ways of living and knowing are systematically projected as exotic, anachronistic and obsolete, beyond the comprehension of the rational enlightened West. The colonized is represented as belonging to the realm of unknown, dark and mysterious like the nature itself and colonizers as the agents who have moral burden of helping these 'wretched' masses to transcend to the realm of civilized existence.

Another major turning point in postcolonial theory comes with Gayatri Spivak's 'Can the Subaltern Speak?' (1988). She questions the very idea of transparent sub-altern speech and her writing emphasizes that it is very difficult for those at the periphery to get heard. She argues that power is everywhere, even in the language itself; therefore, it is impossible to have transparency and authenticity. However, Spivak's writings have been criticized for being so theoretical and complex. To use San Juan's expression in his analysis of Bhabha and Spivak, who alleges their writings for 'metaphysics of textualism' that 'void[s] the history of people's resistance to imperialism, liquidate[s] popular memory, and renounce[s] responsibility for any ethical consequence of thought' (Juan 1998, 22).

Bhabha's work *The Location of Culture* (1994) calls upon rethinking questions of identity of the colonized masses. He discusses concepts such as 'mimicry' and 'hybridity' that have been used as methods of struggle against the colonial rule. Postcolonial scholars like Bhabha and others capture the dilemma and peculiar identity of the people subjected to colonial subjugation. Bhabha claims that the 'East' internalized the images and practices of their former colonial masters, though with unease, and fell prey to both cultural and psychological ambivalence. This caused an internal strife and a sort of psychological split that was best resolved by its resorting to mimicry—among others—as a means of resistance (Tion 2017). The understanding of the self-as-other and the other-as-self both serve to make colonialism quite a problematic category in which 'slippage', 'excess' and 'difference' between binaries cannot be easily dismissed (Bhabha 1994, 86). His conceptualization of categories such as 'hybridity', 'syncretism' and 'ambivalence' are important to make sense of ethnicity and nationhood in this new global cultural world.

7.6 Neocolonialism

Neocolonialism is an indirect control over the developing countries by the developed countries. Kwame Nkrumah's book *Neocolonialism* (1965) explains on the basis of his experience of Ghana, how neocolonialism is colonialism in disguise. Despite being politically independent, a country under neocolonialism cannot afford to act autonomously. Its institutions, structures, trade and foreign relations are always influenced and directed from outside. In this way, the economy of most of the Third World countries cannot act independently and are heavily guided by the international institutions like the World Bank and International Monetary Fund. Neocolonialism appears as an extension of colonialism, though it is more complex, indirect and nefarious; both are guided purely by the capitalist interest. The chapter on capitalism in this volume covers the concept of neocolonialism in detail.

Apparently, after decolonization, while the direct colonial rule came to an end in countries of Latin America, Asia and Africa, instead they are now controlled by the international organizations who manoeuvre trade and commerce policies, global arrangements and Intellectual Property Rights in such a way that leave little space for autonomy. Nkrumah (1965, 1) writes, 'where neo-colonialism exists the power exercising control is often the State which formerly ruled the territory in question, but this is not necessarily so. For example, South Vietnam was previously under French power, in the neocolonial era, it is now under the control of United States'. He argues that neocolonial control may be exerted by a group of financial interests which may not be part of a specific country as such. As example, he cites the case of Congo's economy that is run by powerful international financial bodies.

Cold War politics that emerged in the post-1950s period also became a ground for domination of the decolonized countries of the world. Britain was relegated to the secondary position in front of the United States and USSR that emerged as the supreme powers. The Cold War engulfed the world for five decades that witnessed bizarre zero-sum game between the United States and USSR, making these postcolonial countries Cold War pawns. The newly independent countries were allured to join either of the power blocs in lieu of the aid and assistance package. In this process of wooing them on their side, Eastern and the Western camp continued to dole liberal financial and military assistance to postcolonial countries for decades. With the disintegration of Soviet Union, the Cold War ended, and there was a complete withdrawal of aid and assistance from outside. This led to increased clamour and complexity at the domestic front; these newly independent countries have been trying hard to sustain their economy and polity. Many scholars feel that in the post-Cold War phase, these states have been reduced to political irrelevance in the new world order. The asymmetries of power and resources sharing still remain unequal and unjust. The terms of the trade and commerce in globalized world have ensured the continuity of such inequality and keep these postcolonial societies at the end of the ladder of hierarchized world. In fact, global capital devises newer ways to continue its politics of accumulation, backed by treaties of World Trade Organization, regimes of Intellectual Property Rights and Patents. The postcolonial societies may find it increasingly difficult to negotiate with the new world order to their benefit.

7.7 Conclusion

To sum up, colonialism is a system of domination and subjugation. Ronald Horvath writes, 'it seems generally, if not universally, agreed that colonialism is a form of domination—the control by individuals or groups over the territory and/or behaviour of other individuals or groups' (Horvath 1972, 47). The wide range and scope of comparative politics as a discipline helps us in making sense of colonialism as a concept as well as a process. The multifaceted nature of this concept requires a much-nuanced approach to study it. Earlier, colonialism was merely understood as a socio-economic and political process. In recent times, especially with reference to postcolonialism as a new field of study in social sciences, colonialism is now being understood more in embedded sense. The role of language, culture, territoriality, ethnicity, race, gender and other ascriptive identities in conditioning the determinants and the variables of comparative politics are increasingly identified as crucial and are studied henceforth.

Keywords

Colonialism	Imperialism
Capitalism	Neocolonialism
Decolonization	Postcolonialism

Review Questions

1. Critically analyse the different conceptual underpinnings of colonialism. Discuss briefly the implications of the different dimensions of the concept.
2. Do you think colonialism as a concept could be understood better in a comparative perspective? How do scholars use comparative perspective to understand the colonial politics in different states?
3. What are the various forms of colonialism? Give a brief account of experience of colonialism in Asia or Africa.
4. How do you differentiate between settler colonialism and exploitative colonialism? Give examples to make your case.

Notes

1. Such areas usually had very poor living conditions as they lacked basic amenities, viz. potable water, sanitation, road, etc., for example, the Mexican-Americans in the United States.
2. His interview 'Samir Amin: Colonialsm is Inseparable from Capitalism', accessed on 4 November 2017, http://www.humaniteinenglish.com.
3. In his book *Discourse on Colonialism* (2000/2010, 90–91).
4. Kumar, Damodaran and D'Souza (2011) discuss in detail how the colonizers had a penchant for conquest of the natural world of the colonies that led to irreversible alteration in the ecology and environment. Later, they came up with the solution in terms of policies on conservation and protection of flora and fauna to mitigate the effects of their misdoings. However, these policies turned out to be of cosmetic nature and hardly rescued the environment.
5. It did not happen suddenly but had a background of fight among the colonial powers to share the benefits from colonies/colonialism. Boer War of 1899–1902 was an outcome of that. For details, see http://originalpeople.org, accessed on 3 November 2017.
6. To know more about settler colonialism, one can read an article on American Settler Colonialism on the following link: http://nativeamericanhistory.about.com accessed on 3 November 2017.
7. Their writings and commentaries are intrinsic to colonial discourse analysis.

References

Amin, S. (1990). Colonialism and the Rise of Capitalism: A Comment. Science & Society, 54(1), 67–72. http://www.jstor.org/stable/40403048.

Ashcroft, Bill, Gareth Griffiths, and Helen Tiffin. (Eds.). 1995. *The Post-Colonial Studies Reader.* London, New York: Routledge.

Bagchi, Amiya K. 1976. De-industrialization in India in the Nineteenth Century: Some Theoretical Implications. *Journal of Development Studies* 12: 135–64.

———. 1982. *The Political Economy of Underdevelopment.* Cambridge: Cambridge University Press.

Baran, Paul, and Paul Sweezy. 1966. *Monopoly Capital: An Essay on the American Social and Economic Order.* New York: New York University Press.

Bhabha, Homi. 1994. *The Location of Culture.* London, New York: Routledge.

Cesaire, Aime. 2000/2010. *Discourse on Colonialism.* New York: Monthly Review Press; New Delhi: Aakar Books.

Chakrabarty, Dipesh. 2007. *Provincializing Europe: Postcolonial Thought and Historical Difference.* Princeton: Princeton University Press.

Chibber, Vivek. 2013. *Postcolonial Theory and the Specter of Capital.* New York: Verso.

Chiriyakandath, James. 2008. Colonialism and Post-Colonial Development, in *Politics in the Developing World*, edited by Peter Burnell, 31–45. New Delhi: Oxford University Press.

Dharampal. 1971. *Indian Science and Technology in Eighteen Century: Some Contemporary European Account.* Delhi: Impex India.

Dharampal. 1983. *The Beautiful Tree: An Assessment of Indigenous Education in the Colonial Context.* New Delhi: The Biblia Implex.

Doyle, Michael W. 1986. *Empires.* Ithaca, New York: Cornell University Press.

Dutt, Romesh Chunder. 1902. *The Economic History of India, Vol. I, Under Early British Rule*, 2 vols. London: K. Paul, Trench, Trübner & Co. ltd.

Fanon, Franz. 1952. *Black Skin White Mask* (translated by Charles Lam Markmann). New York: Grove Press.

Fanon, Franz. 1959. *A Dying Colonialism* (translated by Haakon Chevalier). New York: Grove Press.

Fanon, Franz 1963. *The Wretched of the Earth* (1963 translation by Comstant Ferrington). New York: Grove Weidenfeld.

Fanon, Franz. 1967. *The Wretched of the Earth.* Harmondsworth: Penguin.

——— 1986. *Black Skin, White Masks.* London: Pluto.

Gandhi, Mohandas Karamchand. 1905. *Hind Swaraj.* India: Navajivan Publishing House.

Guha, Ramchandra. 2000. *Environmentalism: A Global History.* New Delhi: Oxford University Press.

Horvath, Ronald J. 1972. A Definition of Colonialism. *Current Anthropology* 13(1): 45–57.

Hunt, E.K. and Mark Lautzenheiser. 2001. Chapter 13: Theories of Imperialism: The Writings of Hobson, Luxemburg, and Lenin, in *History of Economic Thought: A Critical Perspective*, 347–70. New Delhi: PHI.

Jackson, Abraham Valentine Williams, 1862–1937. (Ed.).; Dutt, Romesh Chunder, 1848–1909; Smith, Vincent Arthur, 1848–1920; Lane-Poole, Stanley, 1854–1931; Elliot, Henry Miers, Sir, 1808–1853; Hunter, William Wilson, Sir, 1840–1900; Lyall, Alfred Comyn, Sir, 1835–1911. *History of India*. Accessed from https://archive.org on September 18, 2023.

Juan, E. San. Jr., 1998. *Beyond Postcolonial Theory*. New York: St. Martin's Press.

Kumar, Damodaran, and D'Souza. 2011. *The British Empire and the Natural World: Environmental encounters in South Asia*. New Delhi: Oxford University Press.

Kumar, Deepak, Vinita Damodaran, and Rohan D'Souza. 2011. *The British Empire and the Natural World*. New Delhi: Oxford University Press.

Lenin, Vladimir. 1917. *Imperialism: The Highest Stage of Capitalism*. New York: International Publishers. Luxemberg, Rosa. 2013. *The Accumulation of Capital* (reprint 2003). London/New York: Routledge.

Mill. 1861. *Utilitarianism*. West Strand, London: Parker, Son and Bourn.

Mohanty, Manoranjan. 1999. Colonialism and Discourse in India and China. Accessed from http://www.ignca.nic.in on September 12, 2023.

Muthu, Sankar. 2003. *Enlightenment Against Empire*. Princeton: Princeton University Press.

Nandy, Ashis. 1983. *Intimate Enemy: Loss and Recovery of Self under Colonialism*. New Delhi: Oxford University Press.

Nkrumah, Kwame. 1965. *Neocolonialism: The Last Stage of Imperialism*. London: International Publishers, Michigan University Press.

_______. Neo-Colonialism, the Last Stage of Imperialism 1965: Introduction. *Marxism in Africa*. Accessed from https://www.marxists.org on September 18, 2023.

Parthasarathi, Prasannan. 2001. *The Transition to a Colonial Economy: Weavers, Merchants and Kings in South India, 1720–1800* (Cambridge Studies in Indian History and Society). Cambridge: Cambridge University Press.

S, P. (2011). Difference Between Colonialism and Imperialism. *Difference Between Similar Terms and Objects*. (July 28, 2011). Accessed from http://www.differencebetween.net on September 18, 2023.

Said, Edward. 1978/1995. *Orientalism*. London: Routledge.

Sethi, Rumina. 2011. *The Politics of Postcolonialism: Empire, Nation and Resistance*. London: Pluto.

Shiva. 1988. *Staying Alive: Women Ecology and Survival in India*. Delhi: Women Unlimited.

Spivak, Gayatri. 1988. Can the Subaltern Speak? in *Marxism and the Interpretation of Culture*, edited by Cary Nelson and Lawrence Grossberg, 271–313. Urbana: University of Illinois Press.

Stanford Dictionary. 2010. Accessed from http://plato.stanford.edu on 12 May 12, 2014.

Stuchtey, Benedikt. (2011). Colonialism and Imperialism, 1450–1950. *European History Online*, January 24, 2011. Accessed from http://ieg-ego.eu on September 18, 2023.

Thiong'o, Ngũgĩ wa. 1986. *Decolonising the Mind: Politics of language in Africal Literatute*. Harare: Zimbabwe Publishing House.

Thiong'o, Ngũgĩ wa. 2009. *Something Torn and new: An African Renaissance*. New York: Civitas Books.

Tion, Lucian. 2017. The Postcolonial Self and the Other, in *Werckmeister Harmonies*, edited by Béla Tarr. Accessed from http://www.acta.sapientia.ro on September 13, 2023.

Wood, Ellen Meiksin. 2002/2013. *The Origin of Capitalism: A Longer View*. New Delhi: Verso and Aakar Books.

Young, Robert. 2001. *Postcolonialism: An Historical Introduction*. Oxford: Blackwell.

——— 2015. *Empire, Colony and Postcolony*. Hoboken: Wiley Blackwell.

CHAPTER 8

Decolonization

Rohit Raj

Reader's Guide

'Decolonization' is a multifaceted process that led to the emergence of new nation states in the aftermath of the Second World War. Decolonization was the most significant epoch in the world history that witnessed events unfolding in Asia, Africa and Latin America. It entailed a change in the world order and its serious implication on economy, culture and society, at both global and domestic levels. Its background is rooted in the development of imperialism and the response it attracted in the national movement of the colonies. It becomes crucial for us to understand the nuances of decolonization and the effect it produced worldwide. An in-depth analysis would help the students of political science, especially of comparative politics, to understand the parallels and divergence in the making of a nation state, the evolution of institutions and the effects it had on the society. The chapter is divided into four parts. The first part covers the background, the second part discusses different perspectives, the third part elucidates conditions in post-independent nation states and the fourth part discusses the state and society in the Third World. The chapter also includes some case studies on India, Algeria, Indonesia and Vietnam.

8.1 Introduction

8.1.1 Decolonization: Background

The empires which have been built throughout the four centuries experienced rapid decolonization after 1945. During the previous two centuries, the European imperialism kept changing its character. This helped the imperial powers to expand their colonies and facilitated their shift from one continent to the other. The economic condition of Europe in the mid-18th century was relatively weaker than those in the rest of the world. By 1830, Western Europe had relatively advanced than the rest of the world. The five phases of imperialism as discussed by Rothermund (2006) are described further.

The first phase witnessed the early maritime expansion to the occurring of the 7-year war that ended in 1763. The second phase experienced the consolidation of the colonial rule till 1870 in which the British dominated. The third phase saw the high tide of imperialism until 1914 when the First World War began. The fourth phase was the period between the First World War and the Second World War. This period also witnessed the Great Depression of 1930 which forced the imperial powers to change their economic policies in their interest. The last phase was contradictory. This was the post-war imperialism as an action against the inevitable decolonization. Great Britain was bankrupt at the end of the Second World War and depended upon the credit of the United States and some of its colonies. France and the Netherlands struggled to protect their control over their territories and tried to regain control over them. The phases and their analysis can be termed as 'Eurocentric', as they explain the changing character of imperialism over some time. A 'Eurocentric' explanation does not take into account the activities at the peripheries within the empires. For the explanation of the agency of the people at the periphery, 'Excentric theory' was propounded. 'Excentrism' also explains the systemic coercion and the conditions in which the people lived in colonies. Sometimes, the outright military interventions by the colonial administration were termed as an institutional arrangement. Mahatma Gandhi was an early proponent of 'Excentrism'. He argued that the Indians cooperated with the British to help them establish their rule. He used this understanding to mobilize the masses and launched the Non-Cooperation movement against the British government. The understanding of the different phases and perspectives on imperialism helps us to understand the contexts that set the conditions for decolonization. The process of decolonization should be read as an interactive process that saw the setting of the agendas of colonial rulers and the counter agendas and mobilization, as to shift the arena of political action.

The process of decolonization began towards the end of the First World War and was accompanied by national historical consciousness. It is interesting to analyse that how the happenings in one region, whether core (advanced) or periphery, spread to another region of the world.

Decolonization refers to the 'process of transfer of legal and institutional control over the territories and dependencies to the indigenous, formally sovereign nation-states' (Duara 2004). Duara explains that the movement for decolonization was not only confined to legal sovereignty but also built up the claims for moral justice and political solidarity against imperialism. Therefore, the decolonization movement carried two objectives: to carry out the anti-imperialist movement and to understand the processes and events of the action as emancipatory ideology and its expression.

A historiographical understanding of decolonization was fundamentally shaped by the writings of the nationalist leaders and historians. Western historians who were sympathetic to the process also contributed to the cause. Postcolonial writings were also sensitive to the historical experience of the people in different colonies.

The imperialism was spread across Asia and Africa and extended to the Caribbean and the Pacific Islands. The colonialism of the Western nation states and later the rise of Japan imposed very brutal and dehumanizing conditions in colonies. This is a well-documented fact and is reflected in the graphic analysis of the independence movements in the colonies. Karl Marx noted that the whole project of imperialism is to incorporate the regions into the modern capitalist system.

Colonial projects of the capitalist nation states were motivated by their urge to control global resources and markets. Britain, France, Netherlands, Germany, Italy, United States and Japan were competing for their share over the resources. 'Social Darwinism', that is, survival of the fittest, was extended to the races and nations to justify the domination of imperial powers. It is assumed that if a nation or a race does not dominate, it ends up being dominated. The two world wars were the result of the competition between other powers. The arrival of the two latecomers on the scene, Japan and Germany, for the share in world resource further aggravated the situation. The perspectives of the colonized explain the process of 'incorporation' into capitalism in a subtle manner. Imperialism led to the erosion and fragmentation of existing communities. The indigenous populations were negatively affected by the incorporation since the concept of modern education, society and family were opposite and conflicting with their language, religion, caste, lineage and solidarity. Capitalism deepened its roots, and alien cultural values were introduced in the colonies. The project of imperial incorporation also took into consideration the historical resources and social position. This led to the development of a dualistic kind of societies in the colonies. Imperialism led to the integration of urban centres and modernization of urban spaces though relatively on unequal terms. Contrarily, in rural areas, the social life was distorted, economic organization devastated and exploitation continued. This may be related to the Dependency theory and can be explained as the articulation of the mode of production; it mainly describes the pattern of the utilization of the non-capitalist mode of production by modern capitalism and its exploitation for the production of capitalist value.

This served the metropolitan economy, but the rural areas never received its benefit. This has not merely been seen as traditional and modernity but should be read as the different kinds of incorporation in a capitalist system. This difference and intensity of incorporation shaped the course of decolonization.

Anti-imperialist sentiment and nationalism emerged particularly from the modern urban sector where capitalistic offshoots forms of knowledge, technology and capitalism spread more widely. The resistance in the colonies was modelled upon traditional and indigenous patterns. The 1857 war of independence in India, Taiping rebellion in China and Senussi uprising in Tunisia are some of the examples of early resistance. The colonial masters ensured that the natives stay in constant denial and humiliation. The colonial actions contradicted the Western values of humanism and rationality.

8.1.2 Decolonization: Meaning, Nature and Scope

The total membership of the United Nations has gone from 51 member states in 1945 to 193 at present. This was mostly possible as an after-effect of the collapse of European imperial powers. This shift from colonial empires to nation states is a product of historical churnings. Arguably, the empires of some sorts endure and exert their influences on the international system. The characteristics of a territorial integrity and sovereignty premised on legitimacy from the people have privileged the nation states to counter exert their preferences. 'Colonialism' has become an unacceptable word in the lexicon of the modern international system. It connotes the full or partial control over another country with its settlers and exploiting it economically. The unacceptability of colonialism is more evident in the series of UN resolutions. More significantly, the resolution no. 1514 in the year 1960 denounces colonialism as 'serious abuse of human rights' and makes the self-determination as legally binding. Such resolutions had a profound effect in revisiting the norms of governing the relationship between politics and the people. This, in turn, enabled a transformation by shaping the contemporary history with its scrutinizing ability and overt analysis of events, decisions and policies. The process that gave effect to this transformation is decolonization. It signifies the disappearance of the empire as a political power and end of the racial hierarchy that accorded it an international character and a governing principle of structuring the world order. The credit of its resurrection may be attributed to Moritz Julius Bonn, a German social scientist at London School of Economics. This term was virtually lost in the political parlance to reappear in the early 1960s.

Multiple definitions with a subtle degree of variation can be found in the textbooks of social science. The *Oxford English Dictionary* defines it as 'the withdrawal of colonial power from its former colonies; the acquisition of political and economic independence by such colonies'. The terms 'withdrawal' and 'acquisition' have been used with 'transfer' and 'agreement' in some cases, which can be debated. In *Decolonisation: A Short History* (2017), the authors Jan Jansen and Jurgen Osterhammel explain the term as:

1. The simultaneous dissolution of several intercontinental empires and the creation of nation states throughout the Global South within a short period of roughly three post-war decades.
2. The historically unique and, in all likelihood, irreversible delegitimization of any kind of political rule that is experienced as a relationship of subjugation to a power elite considered by a broad majority of the population as alien occupants. It can be described as a moment in history with a bearing on the process that is in flux.

The peculiarities and specifications of decolonization varied significantly from one another. The anti-imperialist movements across continents witnessed a degree of inconsistency in the appeal. These movements witnessed a critique of the West and its imperial justification through several layers and standpoints. Not every movement critiqued the West, culturally. China's anti-imperialist struggle drew more inspiration from the socialist emancipator ideas and values rather than directly confronting the power. While in its neighbourhood, in India, confrontation with the colonial power was a significant feature of the movement. Critique ranged from social, political, economic and cultural, which had a contagious effect on the struggles and campaigns against the imperial powers.

8.1.3 Decolonization and Its Waves

Conventionally, decolonization refers to the political upheavals that challenge and brought an end to the European colonial powers and established almost a hundred new nation states across Asia and Africa. Though the events unfolded in the late 20th century in Asia and Africa, the stage was set in the late 18th and 19th centuries in the larger part of the Americas. The first wave of decolonization took place in Americas and resulted into the creation of the United States of America. A similar anti-imperialistic struggle took place in the other parts of the Americas, namely Haiti and Brazil. However, in case of the United States of America, the situation flared at multiple levels. First, the war between France and Britain was at its full swing across different theatres of the empire, and the rebels found the situation favourable. Second, Britain freeing its colony was a risky decision as the threat of being annexed was imminent. The transfer of power and the United States emerging as an independent nation with its sovereignty was a very significant political development.

Another phase of this wave witnessed Napoleonic wars and French invasions. The series of political developments included issuing of declaration similar to American declaration. Similar happening in Latin America resulted in the determination of landlords, merchants and other local powers. The first wave of decolonization featured violent undertones, and the process was accompanied with disorders. The disagreements over the nature of the state among the colonists featured as an undercurrent in the struggle.

Jeffrey Haynes has discussed four waves of decolonization (Haynes 1996). The 'first wave' of decolonization began in the early 19th century with the independence of the former Spanish and Portuguese colonies in Latin America. More than 20 countries emerged in the wake of two major revolutions, namely American Revolution (1776) and French Revolution (1789), and also Napoleonic Wars. This wave was facilitated by Napoleon's success in the Peninsular War (1807–14).

The 'second wave' began after the First World War (1914–18). The demise of the Ottoman Empire led to decolonization in the Middle East and North Africa including Yemen, Egypt and Oman.

The 'third wave' of decolonization began after the Second World War. The colonial powers Britain, Japan and France relinquished their colonies after 1945, and this speeded up in the next 20 years. This wave mainly swept out the colonial powers from Asia, Africa and the Middle East.

The 'fourth wave' was characterized by the creation of new states at the end of the Cold War after 1989 when Yugoslavia fell apart into small states. Further, by balkanization of Soviet Union in 1991 and the birth of new states in Sub-Saharan Africa like Namibia and Somaliland.

The whole process of decolonization gaining momentum after 1945 had several reasons. First, the international climate no more favoured the colonial powers to continue their presence in their respective colonies. Second, the colonial powers, mainly Britain and France, became weak after the Second World War. Third, the unequivocal demand for independence by the nationalist leaders gave a strong resistance to the colonial rule.

In Africa, the colonial powers were looking to exit with dignity. This was complemented by the generation of self-assurance among the people of the continent and the emergence of confident nationalist politicians with a pressing demand for political and economic independence. Decolonization gained speed after Sudan got independence in 1956 and the rest of the countries followed in the next decade.

In South and Southeast Asia, determination of the local people along with the defeat of British by Japanese, Resistance to French by North Vietnamese and the popular resolve to force the Dutch to quit Indonesia were some episodes in the narrative of decolonization in the region. The dropping of atom bomb on Japan in 1945 and the aftermath could not help the British or French to reinstate their control.

French authorities did try to regain territory but met with stiff resistance from the anti-imperialists. Freedom for Laos (1949), Cambodia and later Vietnam assisted the decolonization process. Although Vietnam continued to fight successive aggressions, it successfully emerged victorious in its resolve to decolonize the territory.

Anti-colonial lobby gave a strong resistance to the colonial and the imperial powers both domestically and internationally.

Fifty years after the Russo–Japanese War (1905), a real culmination of the decolonization in the 19th century was the Bandung Conference (1955), held in Bandung, Indonesia. Representatives from 29 newly independent nation states, from Asia and Africa, met to set their agendas in the backdrop of the independence movements in other parts. The conference's agenda was to express solidarity against imperialism and racism and to promote economic and cultural cooperation among the nations. This conference was against colonialism and neocolonialism that was being spread in the backdrop of the erupting Cold War tensions. China, India and Indonesia played an active role in the conference. The conference finally led to Non-Aligned Movement in 1961. It was also decided to maintain distance and remain neutral of the two blocks—the United States and Soviet Union. However, Indo-China war in 1962 eroded the Bandung spirit and solidarity.

The international factors supported decolonization process by providing it with the necessary conditions. The world war was fought against racism and totalitarian regimes, and it was not agreed by the superpowers to return to the pre-war situations. Second, it was in the interest of the United States to remove the economic control of the colonial powers from their colonies that would facilitate its home-grown transnational business corporations to expand their trade. After the Second World War, the establishment of United Nations as an International security organization through consensus led to support the idea of self-determination.

8.2 Decolonization: Major Perspectives and Debates

8.2.1 Different Perspectives on Decolonization

Delavignette (1977, 131) states that decolonization fundamentally means rejection of the civilization of the 'white man'. Decolonization is a process of diplomatic negotiation and military engagement between the two contending parties: colonial and anti-colonial.

Gardinier (1968, 269) suggests that the first use of the word decolonization was probably made in Moritz Joseph Brown (1932) in his article 'Imperialism', appearing in the *Encyclopedia of Social Sciences*.

Dutch authors Gert Oostindie and Inge Klinkers (2004) in *Decolonizing the Caribbean* discussed two forms of decolonization: (i) a classic model of armed conflict ending around 1960 and (ii) negotiating towards independence between the contending parties.

Where Dutch and the British determined that their possessions were no longer of value and sought the means to retreat from them. The Marxist historian Jean Suret Canale (1982, 476) dissented from such interpretations and wrote: 'The empires did not deliberately decide upon the retreat, did not desire decolonization and did not prepare for it.'

Henry Labouret (1952, 20), a French administrator, explained that modern colonization necessarily led fatally to this inevitable end that historic circumstance only speed up or slowed down.

Majority of the authors concentrated their analyses on the upheaval beginning with the end of the Second World War. W.B. Yeats summed up the prevailing condition in 1921 in *Things Fall Apart; the Centre Cannot Hold.*

(Chinua Achebe's novel *Things Fall Apart* is named after a line from W.B. Yeats poem the *The Second Coming*)

Turning and turning in the widening gyre;
The falcon cannot hear the falconer;
Things fall apart; the centre cannot hold;
More anarchy is loosed upon the world.

The breaking away of the colonies attracted considerable attention of authors and produced diverse literature on the subject. In the 1970s, the theme of decolonization was prevalent, and much texts carried the word 'decolonization' as their title. A prominent text by Rudolph von Albertini (1971) appeared as *Decolonization: The Administration and the Future of the Colonies 1919–1960.* This volume analysed the history of the colonial world and also the former national empires. Henry Grimel's work *La de decolonization* also got attention. Most of the studies on decolonization were done in a regional or national context with the phenomenon in Sub-Saharan Africa getting frequent attention. The most provocative of the critical study on decolonization followed the disassembling of French West Africa and the violent resistance by the National Liberation Front in Algeria. Frantz Fanon's book *The Wretched of the Earth* became one of the most widely read books on decolonization. The author's thesis gets underlined in the first sentence of the book as:

> Decolonization is always a violent phenomenon. The naked truth of Decolonization evokes for us the searing bullets and blood-stained knives, which emanate from it. (Fanon 1966, 29–30)

Fanon was inspired by a French writer, George Sorel, whose *Reflexions sur la Violence* (1908) finds 'therapeutic' essence in violence. Fanon found in it a cleansing effect, expunging of colonial experience, achieved through the use of violence. He explains that the colonized were disinherited or the wretched are 'new men', rising against the system. These new men are gaining authority and dignity, which were previously denied to them by the colonizers. Fanon explains that there will be a change in the social order, with the previously oppressed people getting free and control of their destinies. In his preface to this book, French philosopher Jean-Paul Sartre poses a challenge to the Europeans as: 'Europeans, you must open this book and enter into it.'

Decolonization offered a lot more than a political perspective. In the process to reconfigure the world and constitute it along the egalitarian lines, the intellectual exercises called for *Provincializing Europe* (Chakrabarty 2000). The text discussed the linkages between historical thinking and postcolonial perspectives.

Europe has been discussed in the text as a myth which is considered as the original sight of the 'modern'. Also, the text attempted to pluralize the sites of global political modernity. He argued that the Eurocentric vision must not become a mindset. The rhetoric of the empire was formed upon the base of modernity. Modernity emphasized upon the rational and the order and celebrated technological improvements. This ensured the colonial powers establish their superiority and created separate categories of primitiveness and backwardness opposed to progress and betterment, respectively. This age-long myth helped the Empire to maintain their cultural prowess in the world at large. However, Chakrabarty maintains that the task of 'provincializing' Europe is not to discard or reject the European thought but to revise the thoughts from and for the margins; the thought being everybody's heritage. Decolonization was considered a foremost event that was the most intense and successful globally.

8.2.2 Decolonization and Dominant Ideologies

The ideals of decolonization and anti-imperialist movement were based on two pillars— 'socialism' and 'the evolving discourse of alternative civilization'. 'Socialism' was opposed to imperialism and argued for socialist equity through state control over society. China, Vietnam, North Korea, and Tanzania adopted the idea completely. Other decolonized nations experimented with the socialist principles of equity, market restrictions and state-sponsored distribution and redistribution. This idea was borrowed even by the non-communists like Sun Yat-sen, Jawaharlal Nehru in India, Kwame Nkrumah in Ghana and others. The Third Communist International (Comintern) debated the possibility of the socialist revolutions in the colonial world. Exploring the scope of accompanying the decolonization process to establish a non-capitalist state based on egalitarian principles was discussed. The European and Russian Communists leaders decided to reverse the Marxist doctrine and pronounced that the road to evolution will emerge from Calcutta and Shanghai rather than Paris and London. The communists found out that the proletariat or industrial working class were not strong and organized and were in the minority in the colonial world. Therefore, they changed the strategy and decided to support the progressive bourgeois nationalism. Socialist ideas and their support in national movements in colonies also produced tensions. For example, the African working class movement saw the subordination of the socialist agendas in favour of the nationalist forces. Despite shortcomings in the idea, socialism dominated as an idea in shaping the political and economic imaginations in the colonial world before and after their political independence. It was rather customized by being part of the national ideology and programme. In the 1950s and 1960s, Jawaharlal Nehru, a nationalist leader and the first prime minister of India, experimented with the idea of 'Mixed Economy'— State ownership of economic enterprise with the element of the regulated private property. In the 1960s, Kuo-Min Tang (KMT) regime in Taiwan also retained a strong state control in the late 1960s. The regions where the socialist forces became dominant against capitalism appealed for a larger national coalition that also included the native elites and intermediate class. Mao in his *On New Democracy* mentioned that the communist democratic republic which we now desire to establish can be a democratic republic only under the joint dictatorship of all the anti-imperialist and anti-feudal people, and this common front included the proletariat, peasantry, intellectuals, petty bourgeoisie and even the section of capitalist bourgeoisie opposed to imperialism (Mao 1967, 89).

The vision itself was tested after Mao achieved his power in 1949. He became intolerant to people who did not subscribe to his versions on communism. As a part of the Cultural Revolution, he demoralized the entire generation of people by paralysing China politically, economically and socially.

The rapidity of the retreat from modern colonial empire impressed all as it was happening. The colonizers introduced both administrative and political changes to reinvigorate the colonial system, anticipating a long stay.

But the future of the colonizers was doomed to a large extent. Dutch left the East Indies in 1949; British left India in 1947; French followed the same fate followed by the Dutch in 1954. Resistance to the colonial rule grew all around the world. And the two major colonizers lost the status of 'Great Powers'. A weak Britain was left with very little wealth and saw quick defeat and surrender of Singapore to the Japanese. France was defeated. The purpose of the colonial empire was now being questioned.

Post-war Europe witnessed the process of recovery and rebuilding followed by the consolidation of the colonial powers in the continents. Their power was faced by the rise of two superpowers—soviet unions and the United States. Interestingly, both were opposed to the colonial powers. NATO Defence Treaty (1949) was one indication of a new European Cooperation, characterized by the dilution of the colonial rivalry. An essential factor in the process of decolonization was the United Nations.

Its membership grew from 51 (1945) to 99 (1960). Surprisingly, the largest number of members were from Africa (16 of 17). The United Nations adopted the 'Declaration on decolonization of granting independence to colonial countries and people'. The UN further asserted that the process of liberation is both 'irreversible' and 'irresistible' and colonialism must be put to an end.[1]

8.3 Decolonization: Post-War Developments and Important Themes

8.3.1 Decolonization: Economic Imperatives and Challenges

Subsequent considerations of decolonization were broadly described in Frantz Fanon's *The Wretched of the Earth*. Amidst the political and the economic factors shaping the world globally, the book becomes a part of the rich resource for the vast array of ideas and theories on decolonization. Notably, in the 1950s and 1960s, the popular concepts of modernization and underdevelopment entered the glossary of political economy. The prevalence of disparity among former colonizers and the colonized were subjected to analysis. Exploitation became synonymous to underdevelopment. Guyanese author Walter Rodney in his book *How Europe Undeveloped Africa* described the situation as 'one-armed Bandit'. Exploitation and benefits to the indigenous population were extended in lieu of one another. He further stated that 'underdevelopment', as a comparative advantage of one nation above the other, is a product of capitalist, imperialist and colonialist exploitation (1974, 14). In *Neo-Colonialism: The Last Stage of Imperialism*, Kwame Nkrumah made a similar argument as of V.I. Lenin's work *Imperialism: The Highest Stage of Capitalism*. Nkrumah explained neocolonialism as the worst form of imperialism. He explained that economic exploitation during the colonial period continued unabated even after the retreat of European flags. He saw this phenomenon as having no takers for this kind of exploitation. He argued that development is 'exploitation without redress' (Nkrumah 1970, xi).

Neocolonialism was surpassed by the 'Dependency Theory' of which Samir Amin and Andre Gunder Frank are the major proponents. In his book titled *Decolonization and Dependency*, Aguibou Y. Yansané argues that the 'political decolonization benefitted a few among the indigenous population'. He further states that the middle class collaborated with the transnational corporations to get the control of local economies and made them a part of globalization. Fanon in *Wretched of the Earth* termed the middle class as 'underdeveloped middle class'. He elaborates that the underdeveloped middle class has a 'psychology of a businessman, not that of the captain of the industry. It was an intermediary between the nation and capitalism, which today puts the masque of neo-colonisation' (Fanon 1966, 122–24).

As discussed above and pressed by many scholars, national independence was just one of the satisfying conditions for decolonization. Economic independence and control was another condition. The political and economic aspects of decolonization were very analytical and descriptive. To add a scholarly understanding of the cultural aspect to decolonization was very significant and an unavoidable task. Kenyan novelist Ngũgĩ argued that the biggest weapon wielded and daily unleashed by imperialism against that collective defiance is the cultural bomb.

8.3.2 Decolonization and Culture

The cultural bomb unleashed the destruction of culture. It annihilated the culture of the native people through the colonial power's cultural regime. Ngugi in his provocative book *Decolonizing the Mind* argues for decolonization at the level of the mind. As against the idea that the writer should be faithful to his imagination, and language need not constrain cultural authenticity, Ngugi is greatly concerned with language and argues that its uses are central to people's definition of themselves (1986, 4). Therefore, people should use their system of communication and not an alienating language, the one imposed by the colonial power. Ngugi considered himself a part of the anti-imperialist struggle movement. He wrote in Gikuyu, his mother tongue. He also suggests that African things must be seen from the African perspective (1986, 94). Ngugi's argument has further been used in postcolonial thought. Some scholars state that in many postcolonial societies, it was not the English language which had the greatest effect, but the writing itself. They also argue that both the seizing of the means of 'communication' and 'adaptation' of the written language are crucial to the independence from the colonial situation (Ashcroft, Griffiths, and Tiffin 1989, 82). Essentially, 'postcolonialism' is a literary phenomenon and helps to describe the condition of the Asian and African literature. Predominantly, it opposes the colonial rule and its domination. It has helped to reorganize the masses against the colonial characterization of power. The central objective of the literature was to replace this imperial gaze. Also, it questioned the European perspective of colonies as the 'Master of all the surveys'. This had a bearing upon the novels and paintings that superficially depicted the rich landscape of Asia and Africa and ignored the deep characterizations (Ridely 1993, 653).

8.3.3 Decolonization and Other Aspects

Decolonization reversed the flow of immigrants, thus shifting the European migratory patterns. In the first phase, the European settlers and administrators, who had previously lived in the urban centres, deserted them, as a retreat from the colonies, for example, Bombay in India and Algiers in Algeria.

This was an important phase followed by the decolonized people themselves sweeping into the European continent in search for a better economic condition and opportunities. A quick recovery from war and a miraculous economic transformation attracted a large number of immigrants, although in menial positions.

This saw a substantial number of people migrating from former colonies to Great Britain, Suriname to the Netherlands and Morocco to France in the early 1990s. This had a mixed effect. Racism became a problem and led to different politico-cultural developments. The conservative parties became stronger in the European countries. The advantage in this process was the cultural exchange that took between the people of different countries. Kriston Ross's *Fast Cars, Clean Bodies: Decolonization and Reordering of French Culture* (1995) helps us understand this phenomenon.

Decolonization has gained continuity as a concept, though it has a subtle ramification on the politics, society, culture and other areas. The idea is closely linked with literature, films, music, imagination, etc. The coupling of the theories of postmodernism and postcolonialism has helped to develop new perspectives to understand the world. The commanding position of Europe or Euro-centrism is being challenged to create new perspectives and methods to interpret the worldly phenomenon.

Neocolonialism also has subtle manifestation amidst the process of decolonization. For example, it is evident that in a free market economy, sovereignty has been co-opted by the market institutions that have vested interests in postcolonial nations. Transnational and multinational corporations are controlling the economy to an extent. These passive colonial instincts have a large bearing upon the postcolonial states and the postcolonial societies. It is so much apparent that movies, literature and architectural designs that draw inspiration from European civilization are still celebrated as antiquities and glorified to the extent of providing them exotic and aesthetic value. For example, some hotels in Africa, Vietnam and India even praise the signs and symbols of the imperial age. It somehow glorifies the empire and its rich past.

Brutal aspects of decolonization have appeared time and again through postcolonial film-making. The film industry in Europe has portrayed the brutalities in the process. *The Battle of Algiers* (1965) and *Indochine* (1992) are some of the movies. On the other hand, film industry in former colonies and postcolonial states also depicted the complexities at multiple levels, from politics to the life of the less ordinary and all. Movies like *Mandabi* (the money order) portray the ordeal in the life of a native struggling with his identity and conflicting life versions. Satyajit Ray through his *Apu Trilogy* (*Pather Panchali*, *Aparajito* and *The World of Apu*) has exhibited the intimate and complex life of young men and women in the early 1950s and the struggle in a very socio-psychological framework.

The retreat of Europeans is also linked to the civil war in different countries of the world. The ethnic riots, especially in African countries, are portrayed in some movies. *Hotel Rwanda* (2004) depicts the civil war between Hutus and Tutsis and the complexities in the ordinary lives of the natives.

8.3.4 Decolonization and the Role of Women

The relationship between the national movements and women movements has remained a complex and debated topic. In the writings of Frantz Fanon and Jiweon Shin, the role of women and gender in the movements of decolonization has been discussed.[2] Fanon has discussed the role of women in Islamic societies under the colonial rule. The colonial reformers championed the rights of native women. Fanon analyses the patterns through which colonialism enters the domestic spaces of colonized societies on the pretext of liberating the women on the one hand and garnering the support of women for the colonial powers on the other. He states that this was an attempt to divide the men and women of the nation. The feminists believe that this critique is not only confined to the Islamic societies, but also other parts of Africa, India and other Southeast Asian regions. They mentioned that nationalist movements kept women within the patriarchal structures.

Decolonization did not perceive the return of traditional forms of patriarchy. Rather, it produced new women who were to be educated. This would have contributed to the national service by rearing healthy children. Women were also expected to participate in the national movements, but ideally, they were to cherish and maintain the family values and be less involved in public discourses. The desire to change gender relationships and the cause to equal status was subordinated in the making of the nation as envisioned by men. Partha Chatterjee has also termed this new patriarchy as 'National patriarchy'. Women issues and their status in the society have primarily been contested in the domain of the colonizers versus the nationalist man across the continents. The primacy of nation over its constituting communities largely assumed that the nation was founded on a broad historical tradition consisting of civilizational values and it cannot be challenged. Any serious attempt to radically transform the value system by the colonial administration was seriously resisted by the nationalist who revered the ancient structures and its value system.

8.4 State And Society in the Third World

8.4.1 The Challenge of Governance in Decolonized Countries

The process of decolonization succeeded the two world wars. Global wars acted as a catalyst to the process of decolonization. Violence became very integral to the process of transition. Amidst the developments, there were contending and competing versions of the political order. Moreover, the redrawing of political boundaries, territorial dimensions and ethnic compositions led to civil war followed by ethnic cleansing and refugee population. The process of decolonization was not strong enough to uproot the colonial empire in all its forms. On the other hand, serious attempts were made to reconstitute the empires in other forms. The First World War had a shattering effect on the imperial powers. It balkanized the empires into several nation states. With the establishment of the League of Nations (1920), the assertion of sovereignty became the chief instrument of nation states in the New World order. An interesting phenomenon was noticed when the victorious empires reconciled with the concept of nation states within their empires. This resulted in the formation of metropolitan cores and colonial peripheries. The colonial peripheries were given the status of states rather than nations and did not enjoy popular sovereignty.

The nationalist movements in various colonies had a mixed strategy of resisting with force, violence, education and peaceful mobilization. Nkrumah and Gandhi mobilized the rural masses relatively peacefully though the period was marred by lack of institutional measures from the colonial administration like economic programmes like redistribution and land reforms. Revolutionaries like Mao Zedong and Ho Chi Minh carried the policy of restructuring the rural societies on egalitarian lines at the cost of mass violence. In Indonesia, Sukarno was prevented from carrying any significant movement by the Dutch colonial administration.

Nationalists in the colonies mobilized the masses and built the narratives to what Benedict Anderson refers to as 'imagined communities of the nation'. Here, the imagined communities refer to the people who are differentiated by language, class, culture and distance imagine themselves as one community assisted by modern communication. He states that a nation is a social construct. The project of national awakening involved celebrating the primordial unity of the nation and its glorious past that went into slumber from ancient to modern. Nationalist historians, in particular, challenged the modern European capitalistic foundations. They claimed the indigenous capitalist structure and alternative modernity that existed in China, India and Southeast Asia. This challenged the Western assumption and claimed a cosmopolitan view that existed before the arrival of the West. Decolonization was a result of a series of waves in a continuum. It offered the possibility of nation states with the right of self-determination. This may be varied in degree, but it captured the political imagination of the people.

The domestic and international developments led to a large number of newly independent countries after 1945. Many, especially in Africa, were very small, underdeveloped and required competent governments that would help to improve the prevailing conditions. The prerequisite for the colonial transfer of power was the early sign of adoption of the forms of democracy by the nationalist leaders. Leaders were not convinced with the alien politics that developed in authoritarian colonial rule. To them, the acquisition of power was more important. The challenge in the newly independent countries was to reconcile the multilayered differences existing among different social groups. Huntington (1968) notes that cultural mistrusts prevail between people who feel no affinity to each other; yet, they are forced to coexist in states with inflexible boundaries, which nearly always leads to incapacity to build strong and durable political structure. This observation did fit in with the states that chose to adopt the democratic foundations and challenged the foundations in due course. Mouzelis's (1986) analysis of the communist states in Asia—North Korea, Vietnam, Laos and China—was successful in weeding out the cultural mistrust between different social groups and communities and also developed strong political institutions.

Postcolonial states also witnessed the emergence of a new generation of indigenous leaders who were capable of dealing with domestic and international affairs. The model they chose was of their colonial predecessors. In this regard, Engel and Marx (1994) noted that irrespective of the claims of the civilizing imperative, the colonial states were imposed systems, vehicles of victorious over the vanquished.

The colonial precedence of a high degree of autonomy is a very significant perspective to understand the relationship between the postcolonial states and its society. Challenges in Third World postcolonial states can be classified as, first, the social and political and, second, the economic. The social problems relate to the maintenance of control over the citizens and settle the various 'ascriptive' and 'acquired' differences to maintain the social order. The economic challenge relates to planning the economy and sustaining economic growth. By the time, the new nations got their independence from the colonial rule, the global financial system was already established. The Third World countries automatically got absorbed in this inevitable grand international system with less bargaining powers in policy matters.

This hostile international environment has led to the domestic calibrations of the policies in accordance to the international norms. This has fuelled cynicism and despair among the citizens and questioned the probity and competence of the governments. This further aggravates when the state uses various techniques of cajoling, persuading and threatening or uses force to maintain the social order. The impression that gets generated is a self-serving motive of the tiny political elites.

8.4.2 States in the Third World

The state is a compulsory association claiming control over territories and people within them. The function of a state includes administrative, legal, extractive and coercive. Mainly, the state maintains political order and also deals with external states and international agencies.

The essential statements of the state are a monopoly over the legitimate use of force, territoriality, administration, sovereignty, the rule of law and the capability to regulate economic development.

The Third World countries are artificial constructions. In Western Europe, the nation created the states, but in the Third World, the state formation preceded the nation and nation-building. The existence of a state depended to the extent of legitimacy and authority perceived by the social groups and classes. Migdal (1988, 22) mentions that the successful imposition of the state's will depended upon the means of social control and the effectiveness of the means in achieving the goals. The challenge faced by the postcolonial state was to maintain interaction between different social groups and to interact with the social groups. Huntington (1968) attributed the frequent breakdown of the democratic political system in Third World countries to the weak institutionalization of political controls during the mushrooming of mass politics due to societal tensions and divisions. Haynes (1996) also described the manner in which the institutional weakness has resulted in the collapse of the state capacity. He suggests the example of African countries like Zaire, Angola, Mozambique and Sierra Leone where the weakening of the political institutions led to the collapse of the state. Hayden (1983) explains the African society's ability to deflect the power of the state regarding non-adherence to the state laws and policies. State capacity and its realization in the Third World society have been limited by the scope of the enforcement of the states' will on their citizens. Also, the failure to develop a societal consensus or a universal sense of national unity poses a challenge to the pattern of interaction.

The domestic politics is confined around the capture of power and its sustenance. This has led to the development of 'political clientelism' in these societies. The patron–client relationship gets established for mutual exchanges. Clientelism in the Third World has led to the exclusion of the masses from politics. Monopolization of political spaces by a small group becomes antithetical to any attempts to democratize the society. The phenomenon has ultimately resulted in the blurring of the social boundary between the state and society.

8.4.3 Civil Society

The groups of non-state organizations, interest groups and associations such as trade unions and professional associations maintain a check and balance on the power of the state. Rudolph (1987, 34) states that in the West, France and Britain have successful and strong civil societies.

In Africa and the Middle East, Haynes (1993) states that civil society is weak because of clear and deep divisions on ethnic and religious lines. These divisions serve to weaken the ability to confront the power of the state.

In the region of the Middle East, the situation is different from the Third World because of three peculiar reasons: first, the region is rich in oil reserves; second, Islam is a cultural referent and third, Middle East was colonized by the Ottoman Turks. In the absence of a state with a shared sense of purpose, the civil society is weak and fragmented. There is a tendency among the political elites to use political positions for amassing wealth for personal purpose.

In Asia, the distinctively rich social, cultural, ethnic, linguistic and religious diversity produced the states whose politics reflect their historical past. There was no common colonial outcome in Asia. Mitra (1990, 3–4) argues that 'there was not a complete discontinuity in the state tradition as a result of the alleged wasting away of the pre-colonial political institutions, but rather colonial creations were … subject to multiple acts to reappropriations by indigenous social groups' (Bayart 1991, 52).[3] The civil society in Asia has variations from weak to the strong in Asian States which also reflects the level of economic development. Special interest groups also emerged as a result of modernization.

In Latin America, the level of industrialization has surpassed the other countries of the Third World. This led to the emergence and growth of politically active working class and organized trade unions. The effect of the world war and the great economic depression led to strong and significant political effects. Post-1945, it involved widespread democratization followed by new authoritarianism. This phase also witnessed massive industrialization and urbanization coupled with strong population growth. This generated a strong popular pressure for greater public spending and political participation. The call for democratization was reversed, and a military coup was witnessed between 1964 and 1976. Bureaucratic authoritarian regimes (undemocratic) were set up who steered the future of many of the countries, and this developed a broad coalition of landowners, capitalists and the military. In the late 1980s, the fortune of Latin America declined because of growing indebtedness. The next decade saw the attempts to democratize in the wake of the popular demands to hold elections and international pressure.

Over the period, the civil societies have played a crucial rule in checking the state power. Most of the countries in Asia, especially India, have a robust civil society. The character of the civil society in India is mainly frictional, not associational (Jayal 2001). The role played by the civil society in one country is contagious to the civil society in the other nations.

Case Studies

Case Study 1: India

India was one of the oldest colonies of Britain and was regarded as the jewel in the British crown. It was destined to get its independence in 1947.

English East India Company came for the purpose of trade. After the disintegration of the Mughal Empire, corporate power manifested its most commercial prospect. East India Company knew how to manage its financial organization and its military. The British administered India with the help of the expatriate civil servants. They also educated a large number of lawyers and introduced courts. This should not be seen as an altruistic measure. To mention, the courts were a source of revenue for the British as well as it provided a platform for political debates. In this manner, litigation was introduced in the system. The political discussions in the bar helped to enrich the early nationalism during this period.

The first organised mass uprising of 1857 is also regarded as the first war of independence. It was supported by the landlords and peasants. Though Britishers were able to suppress the uprisings, they got a clear sign of decolonization. In the year through the 'Government of India Act 1858', the power of the company was transferred to the queen, thus began the institutionalization of the colonial power in India. Repressive policies were drafted as to keep control of the native population with some conditional concessions. The major concern of the colonial power was to extract maximum wealth from the region. Dadabhai Naoroji discussed the concept of the drain of wealth in his book *Un-British Rule in India*. Indian National Congress was formed in 1885 with an aim to raise questions and secure the interests of native Indians. Over the period, it grew to become a pan Indian organization with representations from all sections of society. Political movements were carefully calibrated to respond to the policies of the British government. This also gave a chance for the new generation of leaders to groom themselves and serve the interests of the people. Mahatma Gandhi was a very prominent figure who returned to India after experiencing the conditions of the natives in Africa. His weapon against the British Government was *Ahimsa* (non-violence), and the strategy was named as *Satyagraha* (holding unto the truth). He was an instrumental figure in mobilizing the masses against the British and gradually rose to the status of a mass leader of a larger section of the Indian society. During the world wars, the Indian response was very much thought about and was fruitful when the struggle culminated into the independence of India in 1947. Post-independence, the decolonization of the princely state was a challenge. The Union of India was able to unify the different princely states that were earlier under the paramountcy. The constituent assembly was very successful in framing an Indian constitution that could spell out the objective and aspirations of the newly independent nation. Overall, India's struggle for independence was a very rich epoch in the history of decolonization of India. The movement not only had an auspicious timing but also inspired the other nations to launch a struggle against the colonial imperial powers.

Case Study 2: Algeria

The French captured Algeria in 1830. It exterminated about one-third of the local population in its fights against the Algerian resistance. The French were so brutal that their celebrated intellectual Alex De Tocqueville suggested the plans of starving the Algerians to death. There was an increase in population from 3.5 million to 5 million between 1891 and 1921. In 1947, Algeria had 1 million European settlers and 7.8 million Algerians. The French raised the concern of populations. The White settlers feared that they would be swept away by the increasing population of Muslims. Also, during this period, the production of food crops declined, and wine was produced in large quantities by the settlers. Algerian peasants were forced to move towards dry highlands. Various personalities such as Messali Hadj and Ferhat Abbas were inspired by the nationalist leaders of the other countries like Nehru, Ho Chi Minh and Kemal Ataturk of Turkey. The nationalist leaders adopted constitutional methods at the beginning which was responded violently by the French authorities. Though French authorities offered meagre concessions like French citizenship, this could not impress the nationalist leaders. Various armed factions resorted to violent struggle owing to mistrust and attitude of the authorities. The French were committed to preserving its colony even after the historic defeat by Vietminh at Dien Bien Phu and accepting the verdict of Geneva Conference in 1954. This led to the Battle of Algiers which France finally won. They won the battle but lost the war. The approach of the French was very brutal and oppressive. There was so much cruelty that the war drew a line between the race relations and rendered the relations irreconcilable. An interesting fact and a paradoxical situation emerged. A considerable number of Algerians migrated to France to fill the workforce gap since a large number of French soldiers were stationed in Algeria. Though there was a transfer of power at a later stage to the nationalist political parties, it could not sustain the popular government. Algeria passed into the hands of a military dictatorship, which stressed Islam rather than its cherished republican secularism.

The violence by the French authorities left a profound mark on the French intellectual life. This act was against the French universal civilizational value. Debates on Algeria became more intense in France. The French decolonization was a philosophical challenge posed to the French Civilization unlike the Britishers, who felt no philosophical dilemmas.

Case Study 3: Indonesia

The Dutch colonial rule in Indonesia was different from the British rule in India. The Dutch did not introduce a legal system in Indonesia. They carefully documented the Indonesian Customary law, and the instruction was left to native authorities. The Dutch did not promote Western education leaving a very few people who had the privilege of getting one. Dutch kept the administration under very tight controls and left no scope for nationalism to emerge. Despite the challenge, a young group of people organized their struggle to declare their native language as a national language. This was the first step towards decolonization. During the Second World War, Indonesia was captured by the Japanese who were ruthless in their colonial adventures. They committed serious war crimes but also promoted the national language and culture. The Japanese also supported the secular nationalists and Muslim political parties to grow. They also helped to raise the army which had a significant role to play in political development. Soon after the dropping of atomic bombs on Japan, Indonesian nationalists were hopeful of independence. The Dutch again tried to regain its control but was forced to acknowledge an independent status to Indonesia. The nationalist movement saw the serious political contemplations of Sukarno and his opponents, both young and old. In the late 1950s, Sukarno moved from democracy to authoritarianism. Soon, Sukarno was outmanoeuvred by coup, and General Suharto took over as president of Indonesia.

Case Study 4: Vietnam

The French took a long time to colonize Vietnam. By 1900, the whole area of Vietnam was under foreign control. Primarily, the region was rich in agriculture. The French ruled the region with a heavy hand and did not allow any national movement to erupt. They propelled the region to a most exploitative form of a capitalist enterprise. They encouraged extractive economic activity towards export of agro-based products. French policy of tying the rice market to the world market upset the native peasants and aggravated the condition of subsistence farmers. It led to major unrest in the region and motivated insurgent groups by the late 1940s.

Ho Chi Minh, who went to France for his education, founded the Communist Party of Indo China. Initially, he started a struggle against the Japanese control of Vietnam. He united the different factions of communist parties in Vietnam under the umbrella party of Communist Party of Indo China or Vietminh. After the successful August revolution of 1945, Ho Chi Minh proclaimed the independence of Vietnam. In 1950, it was recognized by the British and the United States. Soviet Union, China and several East European states had recognized the Republic of Vietnam much earlier. This contention became the cause of Vietnam's involvement in the Cold War. The conflict occurred between North Vietnam and South Vietnam. North Vietnam was supported by the Soviet Union, China and other communist allies, whereas South Vietnam was assisted by the United States, South Korea, Australia and other non-communists. The war ended in April 1975, with the North Vietnamese army capture of Saigon. North and South Vietnam unified in the following year. The US military involvement ended with a scar in its military history. The war witnessed the worst human rights violations and huge fatalities. This war changed the dynamics between the Eastern and the Western blocs, affected the North-South relations and altered the norms of international politics. The decolonization's violent manifestation was at display.

8.5 Brief Comparative Study of Decolonization in British and French Colonies

Decolonization is seen as a historical movement. Britain and France, in their respective colonies, developed a respective imperial tradition and developed governing abilities of their domestic political institutions. The post-Second World War period witnessed the material hardships faced by the empires coupled with the emergence of 'anti-imperial' United States and Soviet Union and the growing level of maturity among certain sections throughout Asia and Africa. The trajectories of imperial powers did not involve the question of who would be granted independence first, but the decisive issues in shaping the future of their colonies such as supporting the factions in the colonies and procedure of governance based on geographical, political, economic and cultural lines. This helped Europeans to exercise a significant degree of control.

Additional Vignette

Though Britain and French were the two competing imperial powers in the early 19th and 20th centuries, Britain had advantages over French in certain respects.

First, Britain was already experienced in organizing a response to the pressure for decolonization because of the set precedents of the imperial rule before the Second World War. This symbolized their institutional potency in dealing with the nationalist responses. Second, Britain had a good relation with the United States in the Second World War. Third, Britain's domestic political institutions were more capable, prompt and decisive, the reason being the two-party system in Britain and a multi-party system in France. Fourth, relation of the empire with the national stakeholders. Britain's long experience in dealing with colonial discontent in its colonies through a multipronged approach helped it to maintain relatively a favourable position than France. French ad hoc policy of violence and violent confrontation was embedded in their response to the Algerian and Vietnamese movements.

8.5.1 Decolonization: Continuities

It is essential to acknowledge and examine the trajectory of continuities between the colonial past and postcolonial present. The Western countries have continued to affect the domestic policies of the Third World countries. This has initiated ideological and cultural debates in contemporary times. The nationalist leaders knew the limitations of the national independence. Kwame Nkrumah coined the term neocolonialism to refer to the Western means to exert its influence over its previous colonies. For example, the relationship of France with its former colonies in West and Central Africa testifies the concept of neocolonialism. For a long period, former French colonies continued to peg their currency to the French franc. The natural resources of the countries were exploited under a raw deal by the French companies. France continued to retain its control over its military bases in Africa under peculiar arrangements.

The most striking example of intervention in a postcolonial state was the British and French Invasion of Egypt for Suez in 1956. Postcolonial coercions also came from the International Monetary Fund, World Bank and GATT (now WTO). These institutions furthered the cause of the Western powers under the garb of neo-liberalism. There were numerous instances when the IMF and World Bank framed socially destructive policies for the poor countries in return for the financial assistance in the form of development aid and loans. To escape the neo-imperialist phenomenon, the leaders sought to forge transnational alliances in the form of regional federations and Pan-ethnic groups. It started with the Bandung Conference and culminated into Non-aligned Movement. It has also taken shapes of the regional economic alliances, for example, OPEC, SAFTA, APEC, ASEAN and BRICS. The political economy of development in contemporary times is very much being influenced by the invisible hand of the market economy, and the balance has tilted in favour of the Western states. A clear categorization is apparent and has generated concern among the postcolonial states that are still struggling with the management of their domestic issues.

8.6 Conclusion

Decolonization as a process has continued to shape world history. The emergence of newly independent states in Asia and Africa forms the colonial rule after a series of waves of decolonization has multiple implications. Colonialism and its characterizations have shaped not only the world politics but also the psyche of an ordinary human being. The nation states have ushered into 'triumph' and 'tragedy' owing to the decolonization movement. As 'triumph', it has seriously asserted the principle of national self-determination that becomes the bedrock of political sovereignty and international relations. The 'tragedies' in the process of nation-building involved conflict by ethnic, linguistic and cultural lines. These conflicts have led to the loss of human lives and forced migrations. Decolonization is succeeded by democratization that is a dominant political ideal of the contemporary world. It promises a stable and quality experience to the ordinary.

Keywords

Decolonization
Imperialism
National movement
Third World State and Society

Review Questions

1. Explain the theoretical underpinnings of decolonization.
2. Discuss the different waves of decolonization.
3. Critically analyse the different perspectives of decolonization.
4. Discuss the position of women in the process of decolonization.
5. Critically analyse the characterizations of postcolonial state and society.

Notes

1. For further details, visit http://www.un.org/en/decolonization/declaration.shtml
2. Refer to the chapter by Jiweon Shin, entitled 'Social Construction of Idealized Women in Colonial Korea: The 'New Woman' Versus 'Motherhood', in Duara (2004).

3. For more details, read 'Finishing with the Idea of the Third World: The Concept of the Political Trajectory' by Jean-Francois Bayart in Manor (2013).

References

Amin, Samir. 1977. *Imperialism and Unequal Development*. New York: Monthly Review Press.

Ashcroft, Bill, Gareth Griffiths, and Helen Tiffin. (Eds.). 1989. *The Empire Writes Back: Theory and Practice in Post-Colonial Literature*. London, New York: Routledge.

———. 1995. *The Post-Colonial Studies Reader*. London, New York: Routledge.

Betts, R. 2012. Decolonization: A Brief History of the Word. In E. Bogaerts and R. Raben. (Eds.)., *Beyond Empire and Nation: The Decolonization of African and Asian societies, 1930s–1970s* (pp. 23–38). Brill. Accessed from http://www.jstor.org on February 27, 2019.

Chakrabarty, Dipesh. 2000. *Provincializing Europe; Postcolonial thought and Historical Difference*. Princeton, NJ: Princeton University Press.

Delavignette, Robert. 1977. *Robert Delavignette on the French Colonial Empire: Selected Writings*, edited by William B. Cohen. Chicago, IL: University of Chicago Press.

Rothermund, Dietmar. 2006. *The Routledge Companion to Decolonization*. New York: Routledge.

Duara, Prasenjit. (Ed.). 2004. *Decolonization; Perspectives from Now and Then*. London: Routledge.

Fanon, Frantz. 1966. *The Wretched of the Earth*. New York: Evergreen.

Frank, Andre Gunder. 1979. *Dependent Accumulation and Underdevelopment*. New York: Monthly Review Press.

Gandhi, Mohandas Karamchand. 1905. *Hind Swaraj*. India: Navajivan Publishing House.

Gardinier, David. 1968. Decolonization, in *Handbook of World History: Concepts and Issues*, edited by Joseph Dunner, 268–72. London: Owen.

Haynes, Jeffrey. 1993. *Religion in Third World Politics*. Chicago, IL: University of Chicago Press.

Haynes, Jeffrey. 1996. *Third World Politics*. Oxford/Cambridge: Wiley Blackwell.

Huntington, Samuel P. 1968. *Political Order in Changing Societies*. London: Yale.

Jancen J.C., and Osterhammel Jurgen. 2017. *Decolonization: A Short History*. Princeton, NJ: Princeton University Press.

Jayal, Niraja Gopal. (Ed.). 2001. *Democracy in India*. New Delhi: Oxford University Press.

Kennedy, Dane. 2016. *Decolonization: A Very Short Introduction*. New York: Oxford University Press.

Labouret, Henri. 1952. *Colonisation, Colonialisme, Décolonisation*. Paris: Larose.

Manor, James. (Ed.). 2013. *Rethinking Third World Politics*. London: Routledge.

Migdal, Joel S. 1988. *Strong Societies and the Weak States*. Princeton: Princeton University Press.

Mitra, Subrata K. 1990. *The Post-Colonial State in Asia: Dialectics of Politics and Culture*. New York: Harvester Wheatsheaf.

Mouzelis, N. 1986. *Politics in the Semi-Periphery: Early Parliamentarism and Late Industrialisation in the Balkans and Latin America*. London: Macmillan.

Ngũgĩ wa Thiong'o. 1986. *Decolonizing the Mind: The Politics of Language in African Literature*. London: Currey.

Nkrumah, Kwame. 1970. *Neo-Colonialism: The Last Stage of Imperialism*. New York: International Publishers.

Oostindie, Gert, and Inge Klinkers. 2004. *Decolonising the Caribbean: Dutch Policies in a Comparative Perspective*. Chicago, IL: University of Chicago Press.

Ridley, Hugh. 1993. *Images of imperial rule*. London: St. Martin's.

Ross, Kristin. 1995. *Fast Cars, Clean Bodies: Decolonizaton and the Reordering of French Culture*. Cambridge, MA: MIT Press.

Rudolph, L.I., and S.H. Rudolph. 1987. *In Pursuit of Lakshmi: The Political Economy of the Indian State*. Chicago, IL: University of Chicago Press.

Suret-Canale, Jean. 1982. From Colonization to Independence in French Tropical Africa: The Economic Background. In Prosser Gifford and Wm. Roger Louis (eds), *The Transfer of Power in Africa: Decolonization 1940–1960* (pp. 445–81). New Haven, CT: Yale University Press.

Sorel, Georges. 1908. *Réflexions sur la violence*. Paris: Pages Libres.

Tse-Tung, Mao. 1967. *On New Democracy*. Peking: Foreign Language Press.

von Albertini, Rudolf. 1971. *Decolonization: The Administration and Future of the Colonies, 1919–1960*. Garden City: Doubleday.

CHAPTER 9

Nationalism: Perspectives and Contestations

Pushpa Singh and Meena Kumari

Reader's Guide

The purpose of this chapter to analyse the idea of nation and nationalism through a variety of connotations available in the intellectual arena. Generally, any discussion on nationalism tends to focus primarily on the European discourse, however, the discussion here will include diverse perspectives emerging from different parts of the world like Mahatma Gandhi in India, Mao Zedong in China, Fratz Fanon and Amilcar Cabral from Africa. All these figures and many others have played crucial role in enthusing anti-colonial and nationalist sentiments in erstwhile colonies in the post-Second World War period. In context of the colonised countries, the rise of nationalism was in response to repressive and hegemonic colonial regimes. Gandhi, Zedong, Fanon and Cabral could unite the colonised masses in their countries by not only presenting a thorough critique of Western civilization and colonial governance, but also providing the possible alternatives.

9.1 Nation and Nationalism: An Introduction

Nation and nationalism are interlinked but difficult terms to define. Nation denotes a community of people who view themselves as a part of a cohesive group premised on shared culture, geographical territory, language, religion and such other factors. The member of this community is bound together by common customs, traditions, a sense of unanimity, solidarity and the national consciousness. State is the physical embodiment of the idea of nation, binding together people with such affiliations with same set of beliefs and practices (Hugh Seton-Watson 1977). The idea of nationalism is based on national identity, generally associated with common history, culture, ethnicity, language, religion and other attributes that bind people and provide them a sense of collective identity. However, none of these attributes singularly are sufficient or necessary as the contemporary nations are based on a variety of social bases. In reality, the contemporary nations are an "amalgam of historical communities that possess a fairly clear sense of separate identity in the past but have been brought together by various economic, social and political developments" (Birch, 2001, p.8). The notion of nationalism gained momentum in eighteen and nineteen century Europe and played a crucial role in the development of the modern nation states. Propelled by the French Revolution and British Industrial Revolution, nationalism is primarily a "political principle that emphasises the congruence of political and national unit" (Gellner, 1983, p.1). Nationalism provided the ideological criteria for the nation-state to emerge and exist and hence preceded the nation. Numerous factors contributed to the spread of nationalism like imparting primary education at a large scale "the centralisation of bureaucracy, codification of law, unified market to serve mercantile class" and so on (Mondal, 2003). J. S. Mill defined nationalism as "A portion of mankind is said to constitute nationality if they are united among themselves by common sympathises which do not exist between them and another-which makes them cooperate with each other more willingly than with other people, desire to be under same government and desire that it should be government by themselves or a portion of themselves exclusively." Mill believed that the feeling of race, decent, language religion, territory or a common enemy allows a community to forge nationalism. However, the trajectory of nationalism has been different in Europe and in rest part of the world. French Revolution has been seen as the precursor of nationalism and the idea swept all over Europe in waves, uniting people based on national identity and culture. In some contexts, resistance and separatist agitations against large Empires ignited nationalist feelings like in case of Greece, while in some others, steps towards unification produced nationalism as in case of Italy. As a political doctrine nationalism catalysed the formation of new states in nineteenth century like Greece in 1830, Belgium in 1831, Italy in 1861, Germany in 1871 and so on.

The idea appears to have developed in different phases-in its early stage nationalism was greatly influenced by religion as was the case in Protestant England in 16th century, the second phase can be identified with commercial capitalist state resulting in 'proto-nations, third phase signify domination of militarism in state that propelled nationhood towards the end of 18th century and finally the fourth phase is that of industrial capitalism (Mann, 1995). However, in comparison to the other ideas such as state, justice, democracy, the debates on nationalism developed little late due to marginal significance accorded to it by the scholars particularly from the discipline of political science. One of the reason for this has been the inclination to reduce the concept to its extreme expressions-manifestating either in form of separatist movements challenging territorial cohesion and probity of the prevailing states or bolstering right-wing ultra-nationalistic politics, creating a highly centralised, heirarchised state (Özkırımlı, 2017). Both these interpretations proved devastating for the growth of the nationalism as an ideology.

9.2 Civic and Ethnic Nationalism

Two important variants of nationalism are the ethnic nationalism and civic nationalism. Civic nationalism is based on the principles of liberalism and rationalism and promotes liberal values of citizenship, democracy, liberty, equality and rights. It is premised on democratic and inclusionary norms that supports free will of individuals (Lecours, 2000). Michael Ignatieff states "civic nationalism maintains that the nation should be composed of all those-regardless of race, colour, creed, gender, language and ethnicity-who subscribe to nation's political creed," projecting itself as a "community of equal, right bearing citizens, united in patriotic attachment to a shared set of political practices and values" (Ignatieff, 1994, p.3-4). On the other hand, ethnic nationalism is constituted by linguistic, religious or ethnic factors and are relatively closed and exclusionary to outsiders. The nation is understood to be pre-political, meaning nations have been existing since antiquity and membership to this communion is available by virtue of being born in these close knit ethnic groups as a part of ancestry. In other words civic nationalism is based on civil values, promotes multiculturalism and are open to all citizens of a nation, ethnic nationalism is based on close socio-cultural ties requiring shared ethnicities and supports cultural homogeneity. Johann Herder (1773-1803), the German philosopher is closely associated with the idea of ethnic nationalism. Some examples of such ethnic communities are Jews, Persians, Japanese, Chinese and Armenians as they continue to retain the central identifying features like name, religious and customary practices, language, and territorial associations despite overwhelming socio-economic and cultural changes across the world (Smith, 1981). Similarly various ethnic groups have been flourishing from time to time in parts of the world like northern India, Balkans and Ethiopia and also gradually dissolving due to conquest, absorption and fragmentation (Smith, 1981). Nations have been existing much before the creation of modern states and are bound by history, language, culture and blood ties. For ethnic nationalism symbols, shared history, collective memories, festivals, habitats, customs, sacred places act as the factors that differentiate them from others. However, all forms of nationalism can be exclusionary in face of challenges such as migration (Spencer, 2001).

9.3 Theories of Nationalism

A number of theories try to trace the intellectual origin of nationalism by ascribing certain characteristics to the term. This section will discuss some of the prominent theories in this domain.

9.3.1 Primordialist and Perennialists Theories of Nationalism

Primordialist theory foregrounds the pre-modern ethnicity, kinship, collective symbols, legends and such affinities as the core constitutive elements of nationalism. It is believed that ethnic bonds are natural and human beings associate with each other with basic shared experiences. Primordialist approach believes that all societies derive their common identity from some primordial affiliations based on blood, religion, language, race and territoriality. Shared cultural traditions result in close proximity of members belonging to a community and bind them deeply. For perennialists, nation and the sentiments of nationalism is perennial, signifying that it has always been there among close knit people and precedes the nation state. Nations are perennial, possessing an essence and have always existed as a product of historical processes. Emphasising the naturalness of ethnic bonds, Edward Shils states that family attachments and ties of blood are fundamental and ineffable (Shils, 1957). In similar league, C. Geertz stresses on the naturalness of primordial identities and feeling of affection. Johann Gottfried Herder emphasised cultural nationalism and believed that members of a nation are tied to the whole by cultural bonds, providing a shared meaning and sentiments that constitute people's collective soul. He believed nationalism to be 'inborne and self-nourishing' and that a nation denotes one people and displays a national character. Elaborating on Herder's definition Johann Gottlieb Fichte proposed a cultural definition of nation as "those who speak same language are linked together, before human intervention takes a hand, by mere nature with a host of invisible ties." Among the contemporary writings on the subject, Walker Connor's scholarship is informed by the ethnic perennialism. He argues that nationalism primarily evokes psychological and non-rational sentiment, is beyond reason and provides constituting members a sense of belonging to an extended family (Connor, 1995). However, the premises of primordialism has been extensively questioned. For example, Paul Brass critiques perennialism by stressing that nationalism and ethnic identities are very much product of modernity, fabricated and processed by the elites to ensure their political and economic benefits (Brass, 1991).

9.3.2 Modernist Theories of Nationalism

In opposition to primordialists and perennialists, modernist theories believe that nation and nationalism are product of process of modernisation resulting from transition of traditional to modern industrial societies. Industrialism and modern state created new political, socio-economic and cultural conditions that buttress nationalism. Modernist approach believe that nationalism is a cultural and political ideology of modernity. Modernisation and nationhood are interlinked and modernisation offers the best context that fosters national identity. The Renaissance, Enlightenment and Scientific Revolution ushered in unprecedented development with immense transformative effects in all aspects of politics, economy and society. Modern times is also defined by the rise of mass communication that served nationalism and nation states as highlighted by Karl Deutsch. Simultaneous developments in mass literacy, industrialisation, urbanisation, social mobilisation and mass communication entrenched the feeling of nationalism among communities in modern times.

Though nationalism has not been the subject of engagement for Marxism, some Marxist reflection are found in the writings of Miroslav Hroch, Wallerstein and Hobsbawm. Hroch's book *Social Preconditions of National Revival in Europe* (1968) presents a class analysis of emergence of modern nation. Immanuel Wallerstein produces a weak theory of nationalism that suffers from economic reductionism and provides limited understanding. He believes that ethnic consciousness is a garb to disguise economic interest of classes and nation is a "historical product of the capitalist world-economy" (Wallerstein, 1987, p.387). Eric J. Hobsbawm and Terence Ranger's *The Invention of Tradition* (1983) offers a class-specific and Euro-centric analysis of nation and nationalism. These categories, according to him are relatively recent construct in human history. The state and capitalist class utilised tradition to assimilate lower classes and preserve social order creating conducive conditions for expansion of capitalism and market. Hobsbawm cites examples of state's creation of symbols of national identity and celebrations such as the British coronation ceremony, national military parades, annual May days, national sporting associations and so on that nation states use to solicit, rekindle and entrench citizen's faith and support for themselves. He further suggests that nationalism developed in two phases; the first phase denotes the liberal-bourgeoise nationalism that took shape in pre-democratic stage. The second phase (1870-1914) was dominated by rise of ethno-nationalism marked by ethnic and linguistic exclusivity in groups like Armenians, Albanians, Georgians, Macedonians and so on, leading to greater demands by lower classes for participation and representation.

Benedict Anderson's *Imagined Communities* (1983) offers a psychological and cultural perspective on the rise of nationalism. Even though his conceptualisation falls into modernist frame, it also provides a postmodernist analysis of nation and nationalism. Calling nation 'imagined' does not imply that it is unreal; rather nation is constructed from various processes such as same language, cultural and traditional roots, eventually leading to creation of a national identity. He defines the nation as an "imagined political community that is imagined as both inherently limited and sovereign" (Anderson, 1983). According to him a nation is an imagined political community as the inhabitants of even small nations would never know or meet their fellow members. Nonetheless, the members of a particular nation feel bounded, affiliated and close to their fellow-members whom they never meet and never heard of and the image of their communion stays in their minds. As result, a strong and positive spirit of community has arisen in contemporary time nurturing fraternity and deep emotional values among people who view themselves as part of a nation. A 'deep horizontal comradeship' is sensed by people despite the general state of dissent and inequality in the society. People enjoy their sense of imagined alliance and affinity to community inspiring patriotic feelings and nationalistic sacrifices. Nations with memorials like 'Unknown Soldier' tombs claim these soldier as their own even if the tomb may be empty or hold unidentified remains imbuing nationalism. This gives rise to the culture of not to kill rather to die for the imaginations that they have (Anderson, 2006).

Nations are sovereign but 'limited' as all nations have finite boundaries and beyond that lies the boundaries of the other state. This separation by boundaries is apparent in people's mind. On the one hand, geographical map determines the physical space of a nation on the other hand, states are also marked by existence of separate culture, language, ethnicity and so on. These borders are not fluid but real, as people cannot cross them specially in modern times and must be respected recognising other nations' sovereignty. Nation is perceived as sovereign as it symbolise freedom from the stranglehold of religion as was the case in medieval Europe when states were subordinate to church and the clergy. Nationalism arrived with the backdrop of enlightenment and therefore was opposed to the traditional religious structures as well as the divine rights of monarch with hierarchical dynastic rule. Renaissance instilled the fervour of scrutinising all traditional hierarches leading to decline in the unquestioning conviction in church and religious dominance. This was accompanied with a series of changes in the society like the demotion of sacred, exclusive script languages like Latin which served as the language of religion and the state administration. As the sacred language was not available to the ordinary masses, there emerged secular languages or vernacular that made communication and information so easily available. The emergence of nationalism was possible in a big way in modern times due to the convergence of capitalism and print technology developed in 16th century that enabled imagining of the nation. Print capitalism changed European consciousness forever by making mass communication possible through newspaper circulation, use of vernaculars and expansion of book markets. Such standardised vernacular became national language, uniting people who now imagined themselves as members of the national communion setting the stage for emergence of modern nation (Anderson, 1983). People who spoke different dialect like French, Spanish and English started seeing themselves as embodying united community. Vernacular became the language of vast majority, who now through newspapers and other printed information became aware of numerous people sharing their nation and language. People no more wanted to organise power around the centralised absolute monarchies; instead they preferred to create an orderly society with which they could associate and find a reflection of their own.

However, Anderson's conceptualisation has also been critiqued on various points. Like a modernist, he see the demise of religion and resurgence of state's sovereignty in its place denoting a lesser degree of significance to religion. In reality this has not been the case, as in many Arab countries, not only religion defines life of people, but Arabic in classic form survived in face of other vernaculars (Rafeedie, 2016). Many scholars like Partha Chatterjee find his explanation as too simplistic. The adoption of a vernacular as the national language in context of diverse and multilingual colonial context with specific power dynamics appears problematic at several levels (Chatterjee, 1993). Anderson's ideas are also subject of feminist critique. His idea nationalism appears to be androcentric with men's fraternity as its edifice while completely ignoring gender, class, racial structures and a complexity of power relationships that regulate them (Mayer, 2000). National identity is also acquired through "articulation process, a creation and is created again and again, through the cognition of one's actions and physical behaviour" (Keyser, 1997, p.64). However, Anderson's definition fails to capture nationalism as a lived idea and experience.

Earnest Gellner *Nations and Nationalism* (1983) also emphasise the significance of industrialisation and associated developments such as modernisation, urbanisation, labour migration and public education for emergence of nationalism. Nationalism unfolded in modern times as industrial societies work best with certain level of uniformity in terms of languages, cultures and skills. Public education and culture industries fosters homogeneity and assimilation, hence are promoted by the state. Modern industrial societies are in flux, mobile and constantly transforming in terms of occupational requirements, skills and technological necessities and need changing nature of labour. Unlike the earlier times, this creates a need of constant communication and coordination with large masses, hence nationalism becomes essential necessity for binding people in unison. It was difficult for nation and nationalism to emerge in premodern times as in those times a small minority of elites maintained their social, political and economic hegemony and differentiated themselves from the general masses. However, modern conditions ushers in standardisation, homogenisation and uniformity by the very logic of its mode of production and structure of the market. In the new context, unlike the exclusionary 'high culture' of elite of the premodern times, now a pervasive and homogeneous culture attaches entire population. For him, it is not nationalism that reins in modernity, instead, it is industrial society that creates and sustains nationalism. However, many critics find Gellner's theory to be overtly materialistic and ignorant of cultural component of nationalism.

Anthony D. Smith states that in the beginning nationalism was a liberating force that disentangled people from parochial localism of region, customs, clans to create formidable nation-states. Centralised market and organised and democratic political administration based on popular sovereignty replaced the feudal oppressive regimes through 19th and early part of 20th century. However, the idea of nationalism was also subjected to contortions by imperial and colonial rulers to meet their own ends as in case of Tzarist Russia, Ottoman Empire and Meiji Japan (Smith, 1998). A range of small scale mini-nationalist thoughts based on language and cultural variances fuelled ethnic cleavages posing new set of challenges for the earlier unifying version of nationalism. Such cleavages culminated in redrawing the map of Europe since early 20th century and acted as a perpetual threat to the fragile unities of nascent states. For Anthony Giddens, nation and nationalism are inherent part of modern states and is reflexively monitored by it (Giddens, 1985).

9.3.3 Postmodern Understanding of Nationalism

The scholarships in the area that highlight the fragmentation, contingencies, plurality of national identities, challenges put by feminism, forces of globalisation and so on are identified as postmodern analysis on the subject. Such explanations also emphasise the emergence of 'post-national' discourse of identity politics and global culture, implying that people may be governed by a variety of sentiments, associations and commitments that is not border driven. Some of the important scholars of this paradigm are Homi K. Bhabha, Partha Chatterjee and Yuval-Devis. Deconstructing the discourse of orthodox nationalism, postmodern analysis problematise the centralisation, homogenisation and standardisation that feed the ideologies of absolute sovereignty of nation states. This narrative captures the dissenting voices, transcendental characters of categories and identities, the diversities of stories within grand theories that questions the hegemonic interpretations. Local concerns, regional associations, multiplicity of identities, traditions and viewpoints, uncertainly and changing nature of people, group formation and problems are all factored in as significant markers of politics. Linear models of understanding history and development process is replaced by the multidirectional and plural and varied perspectives.

9.4 Anti-colonial Nationalism (Gandhi, Mao, Fanon and Cabral)

The rise of nationalism in post-colonial societies has a complex historical context and specificities resulting from its unique political, economic and cultural configuration. However, most of the scholarships on the subject are ignorant of this fact and tend to put all in the grand narrative of historical transition (Mondal, 2003). However, a closer look at particular processes, pressures and dynamics that shaped the ideological development of nationalist thoughts reveal a nuanced understanding of colonialism and decolonisation in these countries. Industrialization in Europe drove the imperialist expedition for the raw materials, resources, cheap labour and the market, culminating in the settlement of colonies in the resourceful territories of the world. Colonialism was naturalised and accepted in such a way that by early 20th century for most people in the capitalist countries "imperialism became a natural order of things, just like Cold War would be two generations later" (Westad, 2012, p.73). During colonial rule all the colonies were transformed into the supplier of raw material and market for finished products. The invasion and occupation of these regions led to imposition of a violent and oppressive rule, and its brutality was fearful. It resulted in vicious exploitation, cultural subjugation and racial oppression. In fact a great deal of socio-economic problems of those times, that might appear resulting from natural disasters were directly or indirectly the making of colonial powers. Widespread unrest and resistance ensued that took the form of formidable anti-colonial struggle for independence. Colonised countries employed diverse techniques, processes and methods to achieve self-determination. Some nations have fought a long independent struggle, others relatively small, some relied on violence others relatively on non-violence. However, emancipation could be possible because of the waves of nationalism that swept the colonies and served as the edifice of national liberation movement in the colonies. Basically, nationalism manifested in form of anti-colonial movements in these countries. Many scholars hold the view that colonialism has been the chief source of nationalism and nationhood in developing societies (Smith, 1983). By the end of nineteenth century, nationalist ideas spread in Asia that mobilised people against the colonial rule. Anti-colonial nationalism denotes the last wave of nationalism that ended in liberation of the colonised world. Liberation nationalism has also highlighted the role of women in these societies.

Special Insights

Colonialism and Holocausts

Colonialism has much devastating and denigrating impact on the colonised land and masses than it is often realised. While a range of post-colonial scholars emphasised about the deep rooted and irreversible impact on the psyche of subjugated people, there are others who critically analyse the orchestration of such nefarious forces that resulted in death of millions causing a colonial holocaust. Unfortunately, such discussion are seldom part of Western discourse on human rights and justice. The works such as by Mike Davis *Late Victorian Holocaust: El Niño Famines and the Making of the Third World* (2001) demonstrates that famines in erstwhile colonies like India, China, Vietnam and Brazil in 19th and 20th century were result of interplay of forces of colonialism and capitalism, in which colonisers intentionally neglected and caused insurmountable miseries to their colonies.

In Latin America decolonization took the shape of nationalist revolts in 18th century. It resulted in the freedom of Brazil from Portugal in 1822 and Columbia, Bolivar, Argentina, Chile Uruguay, Peru, Paraguay and Venezuela by the year 1824 from the Spanish colonialist. Africa was predominantly ruled by the French colonizers which was more rigid and stringent. Despite the constant demand for freedom the decolonization drive in Africa only begin post World War II. Here the freedom was not granted in the same manner as in other colonies. In place of giving the complete autonomy as British did, French drew these colonies even closer to deal with the booming anti-colonial sentiments in Africans (Irom, 2018). Indonesia fought against the Dutch colonizer's brutal and violent suppression of the Indonesian voice. Even with this much oppression the movement further intensified and more or less remained non-violent, under the leadership and guidance of Dr. Sukarno who formed the National Indonesian Party.

In India, there were numerous popular revolts and resistances against the Britishers during more than 200 years of exploitative colonial rule. Within the country, some regions like Maharashtra and West Bengal became the hub of nationalist activities in the initial independent struggle. Slowly the movement spread to whole country leading to the emergence of mass movement with increasing participation from the women and men. Leaders like Surendra Nath Banerjee, Mahadev Govind Ranade, Gopal Krishna Gokhale, Bal Gangadhar Tilak, Vivekanand, Mahatma Gandhi and many others strategically mobilised people against the callous and unjust British rule. They projected glorified picture of pre-British India, promoted Indian made goods, boycotted British manufactured goods and gave a clarion call for *Swaraj* or self-rule and independence. Developing indigenous ideas about nationalist, earlier Tilak and later Gandhi proclaimed *Swaraj* and extended the movement to the far countryside. Tilak thought of religion as an essential element in nationality. He believed that Hindu religion provided for a moral as well as a social tie; and it binds nationality (Tilak, 1906). However, in order to neutralise the counter religious assertions, a composite nationalism and creation of secular state was envisioned by the Indian nationalist leaders. Mahatma Gandhi, by mobilising all women and men against British rule, galvanised one of the greatest anti-colonial movements in the world. While Gandhi produced a profound critique of Western civilization, Eurocentric ideas and beliefs; Tilak, Vivekanand and others offered a rich spiritual-material debate while evoking the rich legacy of Indian spirituality and culture. They visualized India as a cultural unit and evoked cultural nationalism.

The feeling of common identity and newly found nationalism served as the anchor and paved the way for creation of the Indian National Congress in 1885 with the help of Allen Octavian Hume, a reformist, retired British official. In a short span of time, Congress gained considerable Indian support and became an organisation with 600 delegates. Gandhi viewed colonialism and imperialism as sinister exploitation of other nations. This exploitation has caused a chaos and anarchy not only in India but in all other colonies. As Gandhi believes that the whole world is one and there should be harmony among all nations of the world, he argued that this exploitation was not the exploitation of the weak by strong. But it was the ill treatment, victimization and enslavement of one sister nation by the other. And ultimately it is the machinery which allowed these nations to exploit others.

9.4.1 Gandhi on Nationalism

Through his seminal work *Hind Swaraj* Gandhi reflects his idea on the subject of nation and nationalism. Through scattered throughout the text, these ideas can be seen as highlighting four fundamental question/observations on the subject according to Anthony J. Parel (Parel, 1991). It is with reference to these points that Gandhi presents his views. He begins by responding to those who claimed that India is not a nation. In the second place, he addresses the relationship between religion, language and nation. As third point of address on the question, Gandhi discusses the contribution of Indian National Congress in promoting Indian nationalism while also assessing the strength and shortcomings of moderate and extremist factions. Lastly, Gandhi also expounds his thoughts on professionals like doctors, lawyers and the class of newly educated Indian intelligentsia.

Colonial rulers persistently attempted to undermine Indian nationhood and its national identity by questioning its civilizational worth and over popularization of their own idea. Gandhi's first concern is with those people who thought that India was not a nation prior to British rule and that Indian nationalism is purely the product of colonial rule. In this regard Gandhi said "India has been a nation right from pre-British time which is evident from two inherent attributes of Indian civilisation - one is its accommodating capacity and the other is existence of certain places of pilgrimage scattered throughout India" (Gandhi, quoted in Rai, 2017). India's exposure to liberal political values, nationalistic thoughts and English education sowed the seeds of nationalism. However, Gandhi contends that the national sentiments have been there in pre-British India and it has been a nation much before the colonial rule. This fact is evident from two features of Indian civilization-from its accommodating propensity and the existence of pilgrimage places in different parts of India. People of this subcontinent already had the feeling of community and shared cultural traits despite a great diversity. India inherently displayed the attribute of an absorbing and inclusive culture, religion and different practices arriving from foreign land and people. In other words, there has been fusion of cultures and people, providing grounds for the feeling of commonality, bonding and nationalism. Indian nation signify all people of the country irrespective of the religion, region, language and the caste they belong to. According to Gandhi, the 'acharyas' or ascetics, monks and hermits have greatly contributed to creating an accommodative character of Indian civilization. They travelled through the whole country, spreading messages of faith, peace, harmony and creating a common consciousness. Wherever they went, they developed deep connection and bonding with the local people and also created pilgrimage places.

Gandhi's second argument states that India has been inhabited by multilingual and multireligious people. To outsiders it may look differentiated, heterogenous and dissociated masses. Because of this reason, many believed that India would cease to exist as a country when Britishers leave. Gandhi strongly detested this opinion as he stressed that "India cannot cease to be one nation simply because people belonging to different religion live in it" (Gandhi, 1909, p.42). He believed that despite their external appearances, all religions are constituted by similar ethical core. Once people realise this, there will be no communal discord and harmony will prevail in the society. If religion would have been the basis of nationalism then entire Europe had been one nation, but that is not the case. Gandhi further states that "in no part of the world are one nationality and one religion synonymous terms" (Gandhi, 1909, p.43). His idea of nationalism starts with nation and then consistently moved to province and eventually to locality. In this sense at the very first place, he was an Indian, then only he was a Gujrati and the local identity was the endmost thing. All Indians are essentially members of a single nation while their other identities derived from religion, caste or sect are of secondary importance and should be in consonance with the national identity. So, for Gandhi the common identity of population is the Indian identity whom he identified as *praja*, (nation), the term introduced in *Hind Swaraj*. Gandhi's nationalism was greater than sectarianism and, in this sense, the first and foremost identity of every individual is of an Indian and then only a Hindu or Muslim or Parsi or a Christian (Gandhi, 1922). Reflecting on English language, he says that this language has become a hegemonizing tool in the hands of new elite who use this language to gain administrative posts and privileges. Therefore, this language should not be continued, instead, the country should think of lingua franca that could serve as a channel of communication among the multilingual society. People should also try to learn other's language for greater understanding and to create a cohesive culture.

Next, Gandhi discusses the immense significance of Indian National Congress in streamlining the national consciousness and uniting people's voice and aspirations. Congress reflected the microcosm of the country and its membership was constituted by people like Nairoji, Gokhale and Taiyebji who belonged to different religions like Parsi, Hindu and Muslim. The plural ethos of the country has been its strength and must be protected and promoted. Unlike some Hindu and Muslim nationalists, Gandhi has never used 'nationalism' in narrow sense and mobilized masses as 'Indians', not associated the idea with any particular religion (Nandy, 1994). Gandhi addresses the debate between the moderate and extremist faction within the Congress. He raises objection to the violent methods of extremists as it might be successful in replacing Colonial rule, but it will inevitably create a violent and unjust nation. Gandhi believed that the notion of nation and nationalism should never validate and permit use of violence for national salvation and liberation (Parel, 1997). He says that nationalism in itself was not evil but the selfishness, narrowness and exclusiveness associated with modern nations were actually dangerous and evil. As it allows one to think about their own or self-profit at the extent of others and at the growth and degeneration of our fellows in other countries (Gandhi, 1922).

The goal should not be just getting rid of Britishers but to achieve Swaraj or self-rule which will be based on fairness, justice and complete freedom. In Gandhi's words our nationalism is non exploiting, injuring or harmful to anyone's interest. "Our nationalism can be no peril to other nations in as much as we will exploit none, just as we will allow none to exploit us, through Swaraj we will serve the whole world" (Young India, 1931 p.21). The extremists were inspired by the violent nationalism of European countries, but their brand of nationalism is sectarian and exclusionary according to Gandhi. Instead, India should strive to adopt nationalism that display inclusiveness and diversity. He opposes European version of nationalism and wanted to develop an Indian kind of nationalism free from western influence, a far more accommodative and rooted in Indian cultural traditions and values. Through Hind Swaraj, Gandhi produces a strong critique of a newly emergent national elites such as doctors, lawyers and other professional classes. These classes are self-seeking and do not stand for the welfare of general masses. These symbols of modern civilization engage in deceiving, oppressing and amassing wealth for themselves. He believed that independent India should have constructive village programmes and Panchayat system or village local self-government.

Gandhi also expounded his views on nationalism and patriotism that reflect individual's relation towards nation. Patriotism is far more inclusive and accommodative of plurality in opposition to nationalism which is inherently intolerant towards pluralism (Nandy, 1994). On the other hand, patriotism is positive because it shows love for one's own country without any suspicion and fear towards others. Gandhi was both a nationalist and patriot and his nationalism was based on anti-imperialism, not on chauvinism and hatred against others. In *Hind Swaraj* he himself claims that by patriotism I mean the welfare of the whole people. Thus, his conception of patriotism and nationalism was based upon the acceptance of India's diversity and affirming it. Gandhi said he was living and probably would die also for India's freedom because it was a part of his idea of Truth which he wanted to achieve. He associated truth with God and thought, only a free nation can worship the true God in real sense. This nation has a claim over every individual who are born here and inherited the beautiful tradition and culture of this land. Serving this land was real patriotism for him. In this sense his patriotism was not exclusive, not based upon the calculated interest to injure other's. Patriotism thus for Gandhi simply means humanitarianism which was inclusive to the broader human race, it was all embracing, oppose any exploitation and distress of other nationalities (Gandhi, 1931). For Gandhi patriotism was like an oceanic circle because he believes just as a variant of patriotism teaches the individual to always ready to die for the family, the family for the village, the village has to die for the district, further the district for the province, the province for the nation, and further this sacrifice should be entrenched for the wellbeing of the whole world. In same way Gandhi's passion for nationalism and his idea of nationalism gives primacy to nation over individual because he believes that for the benefit of nation and the humankind, if necessary, individual life or identity can be compromised. So, he wants a nationalism free from any malice or ill will towards other individual or other countries

Gandhi's idea of nationalism also included elements of internationalism as Indian conception is supportive of inclusiveness and tolerance towards other identities and views. Gandhi revived *Vasudhaiva Kudumbakam* a famous Sanskrit phrase from the *Maha Upanishad*, signifying that the whole living being on this earth is a family. It is an extended conception of family which is all inclusive and all encompassing. For Gandhi it was impossible to be an internationalist without being a nationalist. Internationalism can only be achieved when people belonging to diverse identities and different nations organized themselves as one and act as one. Emphasising mutual respect, tolerance and sacrifice, he believed that India's freedom should not be based upon the degradation, extermination and vanishing of the other nations and communities. Rather it should be based upon a positive will so that other nations may pick up some good lessons and utilize its knowledge and resources for benefit of the human race. "Indian nationalism is not exclusive, nor aggressive, nor destructive. It is health-giving, religious and therefore humanitarian. India must learn to live before she can aspire to die for humanity" (Gandhi, 1931, p.113). *Poorna Swaraj* which was an integral constituent of his idea of nationalism was according to him was not isolated freedom but flourishing and noble autonomy. He argued that he believes in what he calls the perpetual truth *'sic utere tuo ut alienum non laedas'* literally means 'Use thy own property so as not to injure thy neighbour's (Gandhi, 1931, p.17). Unlike the common belief that Gandhi would not have supported military arrangement of the independent India, he was assured and spirited about a militarily strong nation and discussed the military arrangement for the future India (Mishra: 2014). Thus, though Gandhi wanted a peaceful, tolerance and non-aggressive nation but at the same time wanted a strong state for the safety and security of nation as he knows probably the implication of a militarily weak nation.

9.4.2 Rabindranath Tagore on Nationalism

Rabindranath Tagore the first noble laureate from Asia was not much comfortable with the idea of nationalism because for him nationalism of west has expressed itself in form of imperialism. For him imperialism was actually an external expression of the nationalism. He found nationalism to be narrow in its approach, instead, was a supporter of the idea of 'internationalism.' The source of his disillusionment with the idea of nationalism were three incidents. First, Europe's constant participation in creation of global chaos, instability and bloodshed including the first World War from 1914-18. Second, fatal and destructive war between Japan and China and third the sudden eruption of 'revolutionary terrorism' in India. All these incidences made Tagore an intense critic of the idea of nationalism.

Tagore argued that nationalism was against the highest values of humanity and it gave birth to separation and segregation. It was based upon the plunder and loot of the other's resources and wealth. Nationalism thus is not liberating, rather bounding in the name of self-autonomy and freedom (Rai: 2017). Most of Tagore's contemporaries were confused over his contrasting opinion over nationalism and imperialism as they believed that anti-imperialism naturally translates into nationalism and patriotism. However, Tagore remained opposed to the idea of nationalism without comprising the spirit of anti-imperialism (Nandy: 1994). Tagore stressed the destructive capacity of nationalism as it inspires states to accumulate power and become a self-seeking 'geographical demon.' The values and bonds that create nationalism undermine harmony, cooperation and peace and promote conquest and conflict in the name of national interest (Rai: 2017).

Tagore was indeed a poet and writer of great vigour. His idea of nation and nationalism also found some expression in the various poems, novels, and other literary works. Ashis Nandy says that three well known novels of Tagore-*Gora* (1908–09), *Ghare-Baire* (1916) and *Char Adhyaya* (1934) depict his ideas of nation and nationalism. In *Gora* the character of problem was politico-psychological, in *Ghare-Baire,* the nature of problem was politico sociological and in *Char Adhyaya* the issue he faced was at politico-ethical level (Nandy: 1994). Tagore proposed a unique and constructive idea of *'swadeshi samaj'* which was opposed to mechanical, artificial and impersonal notion of nation and nationalism. For him, a nation should be a real embodiment of the social relations based on the cooperative spirit, love, compassion and care towards each other. In this sense Tagore's nationalism was a sort of internationalism and cosmopolitanism which synchronize not only the nation but the world (Rai: 2017).

9.4.3 Mao and the Nationalism in China

Despite the fact that as a historical civilization, China's legacy dates back to thousands of years, its nationalism is comparatively a new phenomenon. The early forms of nationalism and unifying societal force came from its own culture in China which was able to resist and assimilate external threats. China was never fully and officially colonised but its sovereignty was compromised due to the presence of several foreign powers, more specifically European powers on its land in late 19th century. Further events intensified the conflict between British and Chinese resulting in first Opium War from 1839-1842. In year 1911 a revolution overthrew the Manchu dynasty which mark the starting of a long revolutionary process. Following this development, a struggle between the Chinese Communist Party and the *Kuomintang* (Nationalist) was stated which ended with communist control over China.

It was the humiliation from war with Japan and the Opium War that led to awakening of the Chinese spirit of nationalism. Leaders in China, both from the right and the left, started organising people and gradually mobilised to build a modern nation-state that could provide defence against imperialism. For example, an appeal to create a nation state based on ties of families, clan and village were evoked by nationalistic leader Sun Yat-sen. Confucianism was attacked and rendered obsolete in May Fourth Movement in 1919 due to perceived external threats mostly from Japan and US (Liew and wang, 2004). People were expected to become patriots and modern science and democracy was identified as the instruments to establish China as a nation-state. However, the early nationalist mobilisations were limited to small segment of the society. Collective mobilisation of Communist Party of China and the Chinese peasantry in response to second Sino-Japanese war of 1937 made its nationalism a mass phenomenon. Mao Zedong, a communist and a nationalist, diffused Marxist ideology and anti-feudalism into organisational potential of nationalism to establish People's Republic in 1949. He asserted that "the Chinese nation is known throughout the world not only for its industriousness and stamina but also for its ardent love for freedom and its rich revolutionary traditions" (Zedong, 1965, p.314). A powerful export from the West, nationalism was given indigenous guise and vivid colours of socialism to counter the domination of the capitalist world. Strong streaks of Marxism and Leninism were supplemented with domestic call for economic development and nation building.

In post-1949 China, nationalism can be broadly classified into four stages or waves. First, from (1949–1976) the phase of Centric or State controlled nationalism under the leadership of Mao Zedong. Second, from (1976–1989) the phase of pro-western liberal nationalism which was represented by the thinking of 'learn from the west.' Third, from (1989-2008) the phase of 'anti-west pragmatic nationalism' started with the infamous and brutal Tiananmen Square incident and continued till Chinese hosting the was summer Olympics in 2008. Fourth, from (2008 onwards) is the stage of 'expression of nationalist sentiments' in China. This period is characterised by the high access and reach to internet services providing opportunity to sentimental expression for the young population (Modongal, 2016).

Mao Zedong was immensely influenced by the Marxian idea of class struggle that believed in revolution as the remedy against the capitalist exploitation. Mao's nationalism was highly spirited with the sentiments of patriotism, anti-feudalism and anti-imperialism. It generated the ethos of collaboration and partnership between the Communist Party of China and other classes and political parties. In his famous article "The Chinese revolution and the Communist Party of China," Mao Zedong argued that eventually the vision of the Chinese revolution was surely to adopt communism and socialism and never capitalism. Mao's nationalism is this way was the establishment of a nation along the socialist lines and national independence (Zhang, 2014). Mao was known for his ruthless, brutal yet popular rule in China. His revolutions are characterised by four common objectives. The first objective for Mao was the unification of China through the elimination of the warlords and erasing down the foreign influence. Second aim for him was the revival of China's freedom and the deterrence of foreign invasion on Chinese soil. Third goal of his revolution was establishment of China's respect as a sovereign party in the international order. Final and the ultimate aim for him was the restoration of China's prosperity and well-being. (Freeman: 2020).

It can be observed that generally, it is the right wing leadership and politics that raises the question of nationalism, as it has been the case in Europe. Left politics remains critical of nationalism as it suspects nationalism to be one of the tools of capitalist class to create false consciousness and to maintain the inequality and exploitation of working class. Various scholars like Rosa Luxemburg and Michael Hardt and Antonio Negri in contemporary times have questioned the creditability of nationalism. In fact, some scholars also hold the view that nationalism was manipulated by Chinese Communist party to gain legitimacy from people and to continue its hold on politics and society (Nelson, 2000, Unger, 1996). Even though Deng Xiaoping introduced reforms from 1978 in China, the economic liberalization fetched further legitimacy for Chinese Communist party. The democratic uprisings of 1978, 1987 and 1989 were treated severely by the party leadership. Within the government, a debate between the liberal Chinese intellectuals and neo-authoritarian faction unfolded from 1980s. While the liberals supported democratisation and political reforms, neo-authoritarians advocated for recentralization of economic reform for making China strong. It can be conclusively remarked that the debate over nationalism, democracy and national identity are discussed, construed or misconstrued informed by two decisive factors of politics in China namely-Chinese Communist party and perception of West, particularly US (Liew and wang, 2004).

9.4.4 Frantz Fanon and African Nationalism

Africa and Latin America have also witnessed the nationalist assertion during their liberation movements. Colonial rule proved most devastating for Africa and Latin America and accentuated the racial discrimination and segregation. Two prominent thinkers Frantz Fanon and Amilcar Cabral proposed a profound critique of colonial dominance and exploitation by imperial forces. Fanon captures the oppressive colonial subjugation and exploitation that dehumanised African people. Such injustices and brutalities have given rise to the quest for national liberation in the African continent. British, French and Portuguese colonizers tried to inscribe it in the minds of colonized masses that they had no history and were incapable to rule themselves. Their native culture and history were distorted and they were made to believe that their well-being depended on assimilation in the European culture. As in all the other colonized parts of the world, the pursuit of self-rule, self-governance and the national freedom was dominant during the colonial rule in Africa.

The colonialist followed racial segregation to alienate the native people and destabilise them psychologically. They imposed the intellectual poverty by deriding the culture, people and practices of Africa. Fanon developed 'psychological model of national liberation' to overcome the psychological and intellectual alienation of the native Africans (Dada: 2010). In *Black Skin, White Mask* (1967), he questions the racial superiority of the Europe and projected inferiority of the African people. He attacks the white supremacist notion that "all person of African origin and descent were subhuman, sub persons or downright savages" (Fanon, 1967, p.114). This book captures the humiliation, anguish and desperation of the black people who through their performance of 'Whiteness' manage to sustain themselves in the world defined and determined by Whites. The inferiority of the colonised are not inherent or innate or natural, but it is a result of and response to superimposition of white supremacy of the colonisers, hence he states "The feelings of inferiority in the colonized are correlative to the feelings of superiority in the European..." (Fanon, 1967, p.83). In his *The Wretched of the Earth* (1961), Fanon justifies the adoption of violence by the colonised masses in order to defend themselves and to overthrow their oppressors. He emphasised that as the colonisers did not considered the African colonised masses as human beings, therefore these people are not bound by normal rules of civility and principles of humanity. Fanon emphasised that the African nationalism programme must also include planning of overall development of native people through imparting education, knowledge and skills. Influenced by Marxist idea of alienation, Fanon formulated the concept of 'colonial alienation' and 'bourgeois nationalism'.

The bourgeois nationalism in Africa was associated with the emergence of a class who were not only loyal to the colonial institutional structures but also shared their belief. This kind of nationalism was promoted by the African pseudo bourgeoisie. The reflection of bourgeois nationalism was also evident in pre-independent India. The English-speaking elite who has supported English as a medium of instruction and considered the British rule as helpful and enlightening to India suffered from same syndrome. According to Fanon, the African pseudo bourgeoisie were not alike the European bourgeoisie. Because the European bourgeoisie were at least productive, transformant, and parasitical. But the pseudo-bourgeoisie in Africa were only parasitical in nature. Hence for Fanon, the national independence in Africa not represented the victory of nationalism over imperialism, rather a kind of coalition and compromise between the international imperialism and national pseudo-bourgeoisie (Magubane: 1971). Fanon's argument has the similar connotation for post-independent India as independent India was ruled by the elites, landlords and upper class, neglecting the representation of lower classes.

9.4.5 Amilcar Cabral

Born in 1924, Amilcar Cabral was the revolutionary and the central figure in the Cape Verde and Bissau-Guinea's national liberation struggle. His rich body of writings deals with radical politics and critical social theory, discussing subjects like social transformation, history, violence, oppression and liberation. Cabral's thoughts and texts inspired revolutionary action across continent catalysing anti-colonial struggles and attaining of decolonization. From a non-violent student studying agriculture in Lisbon, Cabral transformed to become one of the greatest and internationally acclaimed revolutionary leader (Rabaka, 2014). His ideas display influence of Frantz Fanon and Negritude Movement, providing a vehement critique of imperialism, colonialism, racism and capitalism. All these phenomenon interlock, intersect and overlap each other, producing an extremely exploitative social, political and economic structure of domination and extraction. Advocating 'Pan-African Unity' and African nationalism, his thoughts inspired people to reclaim their right to self-determination in different regions in Africa. Colonialism was based on pathological, sadistic and viciously violent suppression of people, and Portuguese colonialism was one of the most exploitative and divisive among these. It was this primitiveness, brutality and savagery of this repressive discourse that led to the mass resistance against ultra-colonialism of Portuguese which contextualise the Cabral's theoretical formulations (Anderson:1962).

Special Insights

Negritude Movement

This literary and ideological movement by Francophone intellectuals was started as an expression of anti-colonial, anti-racial, cultural and political movement asserting the values of Blackness and African culture, history, beliefs, traditions and glory. This movement was product of encounter of Aimé Césaire, Senghor, and Léon-Gontran Damas who came from different French colonies to study in Paris in 1920s. These scholars vehemently denounced the exploitation of Africa by European colonial powers and the inhumane characteristics of colonial discourse that projected African people as sub-human. To resist and liberate Africans, these scholars stressed on developing 'black consciousness' that took pride in African heritage. They started a journal *"The Black Student"* in 1935 that became a mouthpiece of Black anti-colonial and anti-racial movement. The Negritude Movement was also inspired by the Harlem Renaissance Movement centred in Harlem, Manhattan, New York City in 1920s for intellectual and cultural revival of art, culture, music, dance, fashion, traditions and practices of African American origin.

Based on their self-professed superiority, European colonisers dominated and oppressed the rest of the world. The colonial rule in Africa hampered and obstructed the development of the native Africans. Colonialism obstructed the natural growth of these counties and took away the self-autonomy of these nations. To get rid of this system Cabral proposed 'political model of national liberation' to attain self-determination, progress and development of African countries (Dada: 2010). The anti-imperialist, anti-colonial and anti-racial thoughts of Cabral are also suffused with the ideology of Marxism, leading to creation of Black Marxism. National freedom is basic right of people that also includes the freedom of the productive forces and the process of progress and development (Cabral, *Unity and Struggle,* p.143). African people must arise to reclaim their history and culture and should take control of means of production to stop the appropriation of the surplus value. African territories were witnessing a 'violent superimposition of European historicity' by the colonizers over the Africans (Dada: 2010). For Cabral the real liberation of Africa was directly linked to the valid reclaim of the means of production and the native history.

9.5 Nations and Nationalism: Challenges

Nationalism is not beyond its own set of problems. The very first set of challenges emanate from the ambiguity and fluidity that surrounds the concept leading to the notorious terminological difficulties in defining the subject. Along with the absence of even preliminary agreement on defining the central concepts, the domain is informed by deep divisions between "basic paradigms and methodological approaches in the field" (Smith, 1983, p.221). Scholars are not even agreed to the core concepts and substantive elements constituting the subject. For example, many a times, writing in this area reflect different value-orientations and opposed ideological position on questions of ethnicity and nationalism. This further leads to the challenge of outlining the relevant question in this area of study. Despite a range of theories available, there is paucity of genuine dialogue and debate as all these theories are focused on quite different objects of explanations, forbidding the assessment of rival theories and models. Different theoretical explanations seek to answer different questions, emphasising separate dimensions, hence emerge as monologues on nationalism. They do not even cover complete range of crucial questions/concerns of the field like "formation of ethnic groups, conditions of ethnocentrism, the basis of ethnic communities, nature of ethnic identity, gendered, class and cultural character of ethnic identity" and so on (Smith 1998, p.222).

Besides, the Eurocentric theories of nationalism appear to be prejudiced in not only their conceptualisation but also in the way define the terms. For example, Smith differentiates between ethnocentric and polycentric nationalism associating them with eastern and western nationalism respectively. He states that in the western context, "nation were seen as cultural communities, united by common historical memories; in Eastern Europe and Asia, nation is an ethnic conception, emphasising community of birth and native culture" (Smith, 1983, p.11). There are implicit values and judgements in the ways in which western nationalism is distinguished from its eastern counterpart. "Western nationalism is non-biological, rational, civic and able to overcome its tribal loyalties of blood and ancestry, and therefore is polycentric, resembling the dialogue of many actors on a common stage" (Smith, 1998, p.158). In opposition to this, eastern nationalism is "biological, pathological, emotional, irrational, primordial and ethnocentric" (Smith, 1998, p.158). Clearly seen here is the polarised lens of Western scholarship that advertently evaluates and stereotypes all categories in terms of good/bad, West/East and so on.

A host of developments towards the end of twentieth century raises reasonable doubts about the earlier models of nationalism. The conventional model of nation-state is increasingly altered by the rising aspirations of federalism and regionalism. Economically integrated, hyper globalised world has eroded the position of nation state as the singular unit of political power and sovereignty. National identity is under a continuous process of reconceptualisation in light of external culture, language, practices and porousness of state's boundaries. As a consequence of these shifts, individuals are becoming more conscious of their multiple identities, transnationalism and cosmopolitanism that tend to dissociate them from nationalism (Putri et al., 2017). Nationalism by itself is not sufficient to hold and sustain a nation through times, as demonstrated by many decolonised countries of Africa that fell into the cycle of authoritarianism and reversal of democracy in 1980s. Nation states hold together and are governed by a multiple and complex network of materiality, networks of interdependence and support structure, shared objectives of the populace and an efficient and responsive administration, to name a few.

Also, the forces of nationalism holding territories and identities together, started losing out to other cleavages and mobilising factors in the post-colonial world in the 1960s and 1970s. For example, India and Algeria though founded on secular credentials of the West, were countered by cultural and religious mobilisations. Even the newly created countries out of old Ottoman Empire found it difficult to maintain stability. Parts of Middle-East and Africa witnessed sweeping cultural forces challenging its newly found independence and statehood. On the other hand, in Iran the politicisation of Islam took shape of national ideology after the removal of Shah. In general, there has been increase in inter-ethnic conflicts, religious fundamentalism and nativistism in all parts of the world in contemporary times. The inclusive and bounded nature of nationalism faces further challenges due to events like the civil wars in Burundi and Rwanda in the 1990s, the splitting of Yugoslavia by 1992 and the genocide that followed these events highlighted the exclusionary racist and ethnic cleavages. In fact most part of the globe are rampant with separatist or autonomy movement driven by the nationalism of smaller groups who view themselves as separate and want to exist independently. These countries present the dilemma of the 'smaller nationalism' of such groups versus the 'larger nationalism' of the state and has no apparent solutions. Territories like the Flanders with Flemish movement, French Basque country with Basque people, Northern Catalonia with Northern Catalan people, Bavaria in Germany with Bavarian people and many such regions in Bosnia and Herzegovina are puzzles for nationalism. On the other hand, there has been upsurge in nationalistic sentiments in some countries like Japan in 21st century in the form of 'reactive nationalism', which can be seen as Japan's reaction to the rise of China.

9.6 Conclusion

Based on the discussion in the chapter, it can be concluded that the idea of nationalism continues to remain seminal in the contemporary scholarships. The world is constantly undergoing realignment, which to a great extent, will be shaped by nations and nationalism. There has been a varieties of theories illustrating its various dimensions, but the modernist explanation appears to find greater acceptance. However, in reality the concept of nation and nationalism are highly contested. The trajectory of genesis and evolution of nationalism also varies world-wide. So far, the dominant literatures on the subject always gave space to capturing its unfolding and associated debates only from Western European view point. However, this chapter attempted to bring in some of the non-Western perspectives along with the earlier existing debates.

A comparative analysis of discourse of nationalism as witnessed in the European context and in the anti-colonial context shows interesting divergences and some convergences. As nationalism in colonised societies fuelled the national liberation movement, and overlapped and interlocked with the critique of racism, capitalism and Western culture. Even though material realities and new solidarity networks reconstitute identity and political affiliation, in many ways the nationalism of post-colonial world continues to strongly shape the contemporary understanding of politics, society and self in these countries.

Keywords

Nationalism
Anti-colonial nationalism
Civic nationalism
Political nationalism

Review Questions

1. Discuss the different theories of nationalism. How does the Western perspective on nationalism differ from the nationalism that emerged in the colonised territories?
2. Illustrate the features of anti-colonial nationalism with the help of suitable case studies. In what respect it is different from the discourse of nationalism that emerged in Europe?
3. Critically analyse how the anti-colonial nationalism of Gandhi, Fanon and Cabral presents a comprehensive critique of cultural, racial, political and economic hegemony of European colonial powers.

References

Anderson, B.: Imagined Communities. London, New Left Books, 1983.

Birch, A H., (2001) *The Concepts and Theories of Modern Democracy*, (2nd Edition), London: Routledge.

Brass, P.: Ethnicity and Nationalism. New Delhi, Sage, 1991.

Chatterjee, Partha *The Nation and its Fragments: Colonial and Postcolonial Histories* (Princeton: Princeton University Press, 1993), 5.

Dada S.O. 2010. "Fanon And Cabral on Culture and National Liberation", *Lumina*, Vol. 21, No.1, ISSN 2094-1188.

Davidson, B. Cabral, A. the PAIGC, & Wolfers, M. 1979. Introduction, In *Unity and Struggle: Speeches and Writings of Amilcar Cabral* Vol. 3, pp. ix–xvii. NYU Press. http://www.jstor.org

Davis, M. 2001. *Late Victorian Holocaust: El Niño Famines and the Making of the Third World,* New York: Verso.

Deutsch, K. 1953 Nationalism and Social Communication. New York, MIT Press.

Freeman, C.W. Mao Zedong: Nationalist in Spite of Himself, Remarks to the SAIS China Forum Ambassador Middle east policy council. https://mepc.org/speeches/mao-zedong-nationalist-spite-himself

Gandhi, M.K. 1931. *Young India*, Gandhi Heritage Portal.

Gandhi, M.K. 1947. *India of My Dreams* Compiled by: R. K. Prabhu Navajivan Mudranalaya.

Gellner, E.: Nations and Nationalism. Oxford, Blackwell, 1983.

Geertz, C.: The Interpretation of Cultures. New York, Free Press, 1973.

Giddens, A. 1981. *A Contemporary Critique of Historical Materialism*, London, Macmillan.

Giddens, A. 1985. *The Nation-State and Violence*, Cambridge: Polity Press.

Hobsbawm, E.: Nations and Nationalism Since 1780. Cambridge, CUP, 1990.

Hroch, M. 1968 Social Preconditions of National Revival in Europe. Cambridge, Cambridge University Press.

Ignatieff, M. 1994. *Blood and Belonging: Journeys into the New Nationalism*London: Vintage.

Lecours, A. 2000. "Ethnic and Civic Nationalism: Towards a New Dimension", *Space and Polity,* 4(2): 153–166. DOI: 10.1080/13562570020013672

Liew, Liong H. Wang S. 2004. *Nationalism, Democracy and National Integration in China* London and New York: Routledge.

Magubane B. 1971. "Amilcar Cabral: Evolution of Revolutionary Thought", *Ufahamu* Vol. 2, No. 2: 71–87.

Mann, M. 1995. 'A Political Theory of Nationalism and its Excesses' in S. Periwal ed.) *Notions of Nationalism,* Budapest, London and New York: Central European University, pp. 44–64.

Misra, M. 2014. "Sergeant-Major Gandhi: Indian Nationalism and Nonviolent "Martiality" *The Journal of Asian Studies* Vol. 73, No. 3: 689–709.

Mondal A. A. 2003. *Nationalism and Post-colonial Identity: Culture and Ideology in India and Egypt*, London & New York: Routledge Curzon.

Modongal, S. 2016. "Development of Nationalism in China", *Cogent Social Sciences*, 2:1, 1235749, DOI: 10.1080/23311886.2016.1235749

Nandy, A. 1994. *The Illegitimacy of Nationalism: Rabindranath Tagore and the Politics of Self,* Delhi: Oxford University Press.

Nielsen Niels, Kayser 1997. Welfare-Nationalism? Comparative Aspects of the Relation Between Sport and Nationalism in Scandinavia in the Inter-War Years, The Sports Historian, 17(2): 63–79. DOI: 10.1080/17460269709445789

Parel, A.J. 1997. *Hind Swaraj and other Writings.* Cambridge University Press.

Putri, P. I. Nasruddin, E. & Wahab, J. A. 2017. Defining the Concept of national Identity in Post Modern Society, Proceedings of the 3rd International Conference on Transformation in Communications 2017 (IcoTiC 2017), Atlantic Press.

Tagore, R.N. 2009) *Nationalism*, New Delhi, Penguin India.

Tilak, B. G. 1906. *Kesari*, 24th April, 1906, cited in Kumar ed. Selected Document.

T. Mayer, 2000 "Gender Ironies of Nationalism: Setting the Stage," *Gender Ironies of Nationalism: Sexing the Nation* London: Routledge.

Rabaka, R. 2014. *Concepts of Cabralism: Amilcar Cabral and Africana Critical Theory*. NY, London: Lexington Books.

Rai, S.K. 2017. Nation and Nationalism: Revisiting Gandhi and Tagore *"Gandhi Marg"* Volume 39, Number 2&3, July-September & October-December 2017.

Rafeedie, Fadia "Review of Imagined Communities by Benedict Anderson," July 19, 1999, accessed March 8, 2016, http://socrates. berkeley.edu/~mescha/ bookrev/Anderson,Benedict.html.

Seal A. 2001. *The Emergence of Indian Nationalism, Competition & Collaboration in Later 19th Century.* Cambridge University Press.

Shils, E.: "Primordial, Personal, Sacred and Civil Ties", British Journal of Sociology 7/1957, p. 13–45.

Smith, A.D. 1983. *Theories of Nationalism*. London, Duckworth.

Smith, A.D 1998. *Nationalism and Modernism: A Critical Survey of Recent Theories of Nations and Nationalism*. Routledge.

Spencer, P. 2001. Civic Nationalism, Civic Nations and the Problem of Migration. In: Ghatak, S. Showstack Sassoon, A. eds. Migration and Mobility. Palgrave Macmillan, London. https://doi.org/10.1057/9780230523128_6

Wallerstein, I. 1974. *The Modern World-System I*. New York, Academic Press.

Wallerstein, I. 1979. *The Capitalist World-Economy*. Cambridge University Press.

Wallerstein, I. 1980. *The Capitalist World-System II*. New York, Academic Press.

Wallerstein, I. 1987. "The Construction of Peoplehood: Racism, Nationalism, Ethnicity", *Sociological Forum*, 2/1987, pp. 373–388.

Westad, O. 2005. The revolutionaries: Anticolonial politics and transformations, In: *The Global Cold War: Third World Interventions and the Making of Our Times* pp. 73–109. Cambridge: Cambridge University Press. doi: 10.1017/CBO9780511817991.004

Zhang Y. 2014. "Analysing the Connotation of Mao Zedong's Nationalism" *International Journal of Social Science Studies* Vol. 2, No. 1; pp. 65–69.

CHAPTER 10

Comparative Constitutionalism

Alisha Dhingra and Rounak Kumar Pathak

Reader's Guide

The chapter attempts to expose students to the multitudinous sites of constitutionalism by distinguishing between constitutions as historical texts and constitutionalism as ideological sites which justify specific constitutional theory and practices. The chapter explores questions such as: What is a constitution? What is the process through which constitutionalism evolved? For adequate investigation to these questions, the chapter traces the diverse historical experiences of constitutional development and their forms, and the conception of transformative constitutionalism in societies transitioning from colonial to postcolonial constitutionalism. Moreover, it also delves into the specificities of constitutionalism in South Asia. The chapter also engages with the recent literature on feminist constitutionalism and environmental constitutionalism stressing on the need to rethink and reshape the contours of comparative constitutionalism.

10.1 Introduction

The roots of comparative constitutionalism may be traced to a period as far back as the time of Aristotle. Despite this, the field of this research saw a surge in interest after the 1990s. This came about as a result of the drafting of new constitutions and the reforming of existing ones in a number of different countries. A significant portion of the literature on comparative constitutionalism emerged within the setting of African nations, Post-Soviet countries, and more recently, Asian countries. The study on constitutionalism that emerged in the 1990s began to undermine the dominance of liberal constitutionalism includes such terms as "global south constitutionalism," "postcolonial constitutionalism," "transformative constitutionalism," and "post-liberal constitutionalism." It investigates the relationship between constitutionalism and such aspects of society as (faith, ethnicity, and gender), among others. In doing so, it moves even farther and further away from the foundation of liberal constitutionalism. (Dhingra 2017: 99).

It is important to investigate and consider the implications of the fact that more than half of the constitutions of the world's nations were written after the decade of the 1970s. A number of these constitutions came about as a direct consequence of a change of government in the respective nations. Iraq and Afghanistan are two illustrative instances of such states that have recently enacted new constitutions. As a direct result of the conclusion of the cold war, a great number of new constitutions were written and adopted. (Irving 2008).

10.2 Understanding Constitution and Constitutionalism

In its most basic sense, the constitution is defined as the highest law of the land. But we need to understand that a constitution is not only a legal document but also an ethical and political document. Upendra Baxi (2018) distinguishes among 'three interactive meanings of constitutions as texts, constitutional law, and theory/ideology ("constitutionalism"). Despite the fact that many constitutional affirmations are presented in one kind of legal language or another, a constitution also includes crucial symbolic statements (Irving 2008: 25). In comparison to what is considered to be a "actual" depiction of social interactions, the constitutional public may be portrayed in a manner that is more "egalitarian and inclusive" if the constitution is given the opportunity to do so. These statements may further and plainly bring out many downsides, as well as pinpoint towards the ones who have been "excluded" or "condensed legally opaque" in the previous periods.

Shefali Jha draws attention to the fact that a constitution serves at least two purposes: the first purpose is that it outlines the powers of the government, thereby establishing the form that the government will take, and the second purpose is that it exempts certain topics from the authority of the government (Jha 2008: 351). To ensure that people's rights are protected, liberal constitutionalism necessitates that certain limits be placed on the powers that the government has. This is done for the aim of protecting people's freedoms. She contends that "liberal rights-based constitutionalism" fails to recognise the fact that the "safeguard and awareness of rights" cannot solely originate from "letting rights to supersede the normal political mechanism," but rather is "correspondingly a substance of organisational design of that political mechanism." She says this is because "liberal rights-based constitutionalism" is not successful in recognising this fact. Even though there is now published material on constitutionalism in non-liberal democratic countries, liberal academics are unsettled by this development. Constitution and constitutionalism are two distinct concepts, according to the liberal academics. They hold the view that constitutionalism does not exist in a nation if the state's authority is not constrained by the nation's governing document and that such a nation does not have a constitution.

The concept of constitutionalism, as 'theory as well as practice' may be recognized as an appreciation of the requirement to confine the unrestrained power of the state. (Dhingra 2014: 135). The said description nevertheless cannot fully comprehend the meaning of constitutionalism. In addition to it, this description can continue to be more appropriately chosen as a 'liberal constitutionalism'. The leading goal of the liberal constitutionalism is to protect rights as well as freedom of the citizens. Also, for the purpose of attaining this objective, organisational differentiation of power has been stressed upon for attaining this goal of liberal constitutionalism. In the framework of liberal constitutionalism, the state seems as a neutral mediator wanting in the competence to guide the lives of the citizens. In the post-colonial and the post-soviet situation, what went to the background was the emphasis on organisational outlining of power and an impartial state and the transformative potential of the state is underscored. Constitutions have not only the assigned work of organising the political structure but also the assigned task of changing the social structure for making the social structure in resonance with the political structure.

For a good number of years, constitutionalism was considered to be equivalent to judicial review (Kahana and Stephenson 2012:240). This discourse was included because the conservative view emphasised the dominating aim of the constitution, which was to control majorities of people as well as the legislators. As a result, this narrative was included in the document. It was believed that the courts would be the institutions that would carry out this primary responsibility in connection with the constitution. The arguments of Tsvi Kahana and Rachel Stephenson suggest that there has been a significant shift in the traditional constitutionalist movement's focal point. The concept that may be referred to as "democratic constitutionalism" is supported and advocated for by a large number of constitutional experts originating from a variety of countries all over the globe (ibid). The establishment of what is now known as "democratic constitutionalism" is distinct from both the version used in the United States, which asserts the supremacy of the court, and the model used in Britain, which states that parliament is sovereign. The establishment of constitutional supremacy and parliamentary sovereignty is the fundamental tenet of a kind of constitutionalism that is often referred to as democratic constitutionalism.

10.3 Evolution of Constitutionalism from Ancient to Modern

"Mcllwain (1947)," traces the historical evolution of constitutionalism all the way back to the days of Primordial Greek and continuing on into the early 20th century. This modern conception of the constitution sees it as the "cognisant origination by the people of the fundamental law," which stands in contrast to the much more traditional understanding of the constitution, which sees it as "functional values to be inferred from a country's real organisations and their improvement".

Some modern formulations, such as that of Thomas Paine, consider a constitution to be a "antecedent," in the sense that it exists temporally before the foundation of a country and is necessary to and a "conclusive historical entity". In contrast to the formation that is British constitutionalism and the manner in which it is portrayed via words and averments made by Bolingbroke, it exists in its own right. These definitions are far closer to the original ones given for the term in ancient times.

Mcllwain suggests that constitutionalism is a historical process and it basically denotes legal limitations on governments. He believes constitutionalism to be like a living tradition that is free to adaptations and changes with time, context and usability. Some of the important elements that constitute the core of constitutionalism are the principle of law and popular consent.

The traditional Greek structure is the most primitive one. This has resulted in the coining of the word "Politeia," which describes "it signifies above all the state as it truly is... its complete economic and social texture as well as concerns governmental". The primary flaw of medieval constitutionalism is that it was unable to impose any kind of consequence or penalty, other than a warning or the use of revolutionary force, against any prince. The prince was the one who genuinely trampled such rights underfoot and destroyed them using jurisdiction. It was unavoidable that religious factions of each faith, if fetched under the king's punishment for rebelliousness, should come to consider the ruler not as a real king but as an oppressor, who by being aggressive against God had abandoned his legitimate authority. This was because the Protestant reformation and religious schism brought about transformation.

According to Mcllwain, the doctrine of separation of powers makes the government weak, whereas the permissible curbs of authority do not need to do such a thing - this can really authorise it about the domain connected with gubernaculum – during this time, autonomous courts may get entrusted with protecting authority by guarding the privileges of the individuals. Mcllwain believes that this topic is important to him on a fundamental level because of the circumstances surrounding it. He attributes the rise of fascism throughout Europe to the "incompetence of constitutional governments." By substituting some practical parting between courts, decision-making executive people, and the government having gubernaculum-jurisdiction distinction, the modern world has not only guaranteed the deleterious constraint of the sphere of government, but it has also ensured that there is no room for reform within the sphere of government.

The aforementioned story needs to become a basic component of contemporary constitutionalism, which Mcllwain describes as "the legal limitations to arbitrary authority and a total political duty of the government to the governed." (Mcllwain 1947: 146).

10.3.1 Constitutionalism in Various Settings

Since the origins of modern constitutionalism in Britain and the United States, constitutionalism in the setting of post-decolonization third world contexts, and constitution in the framework of post-cold war situations have all brought about significant changes in the nature of constitutionalism. Uday Mehta differentiates between the constitutionalism of the United States of America, which follows a pattern associated with the constitutionalism of the 18th century, and the constitutionalism of India, which follows a pattern associated with the constitutionalism of the 20th century (Mehta 2010: 25). The concept of "distrust of authority" is deeply ingrained in the foundations of the American constitutionalist tradition. The essential idea associated with constitutionalism subsequently served a role to constrain political power to be wary of this, and to fix the domain of it. Uday Mehta's position can be summarised as follows: "This kind of embarrassing construction of control and politics is obviously not the condition with constitutionalism prevalent most of the time in the 20th century, more specifically and graphically within India." Mehta's argument is based on the fact that constitutionalism was prevalent throughout the majority of the 20th century. One of the things that constitutionalism does is the establishment of control, and another of its accomplishments is the expansion of the sphere in which control may be exercised. Mehta contends that the Constitution of India can be regarded as the "truly ground-breaking programme of rupture" because the constitution interjected the relationship of the politics with time, history, and customary rituals like caste as well as religion. These ties were then transformed into objects of governmental control, which necessitated their renovation at its hands.

Baxi (2013) places a strong emphasis on the uniqueness of the emergence of "constitutional and social we-ness" in the formative instances of three states, namely South Africa, India, and Brazil. Because it is based on an image of future society and, as a result, embodies a temporal discontinuity from the past, the development of a sense of "we-ness" is a process that may be described as transformational.

The constitution of South Africa was the driving force behind the change, which consisted of a transition away from a racist government and society and toward an institution that was established on non-racism and non-sexism. As a result, Justice Langa's analogy of "crossing the bridge" is an apt one to describe the process of formulating and writing the South African constitution.

Baxi contends that it may be compared and then contrasted with the formation of the constitution of India. The Indian constitution was written in the background of the partition of the country. Hence, the Indian constitution was short of 'therapeutic' as well as 'diagnostic' dimensions. These two dimensions showed the passage and gave guidelines to the framing of the constitution of South Africa. The constitutive time in India was made of opposing ideas. Nehru laid stress on the elimination of obstacles. Ambedkar averred about the 'dialectic contradictions' connected with the founding moment in India. Ambedkar stated:

> "On the 26th of January 1950, we are going to enter into a life of contradictions. In politics we will have equality and in social and economic life we will have inequality. In politics we will be recognizing the principle of one man one vote and one vote one value. In our social and economic life, we shall, by reason of our social and economic structure, continue to deny the principle of one man one value." (CAD Debates, 25th November, 1949) (http://parliamentofindia.nic.in/ls/debates/vol11p11.htm cited in Baxi 2013)

By drawing inspiration from the story of "K.G. Kannabiran and Upendra Baxi," the author Kalpana Kannabiran (2012) promotes the ideology known as "transformative constitutionalism." The meaning of "transformative constitutionalism" was given a broader scope by Kannabiran. According to Kannahiran, it does not just consist of constitutive moments but also include "a vision inherent in the constitution that motivates movements for social reform." (Kannabiran 2012: 444). The meaning of the phrase "transformative constitutionalism," which is one that is obliquely articulated in Kannabiran's work, aligns more closely with the notion of "transformative constitutionalism" as conceived by Karl Klare. The following are the terms that Klare uses to define "transformative constitutionalism.":

> "a long-term project of constitutional enactment, interpretation, and enforcement committed (not in isolation, of course, but in a historical context of conducive political developments) to transforming a country's political and social institutions and power relationships in a democratic, participatory, and egalitarian direction" (Klare 1998:146).

The development of constitutionalism in South Asia has followed a different path, and this difference cannot be explained within the framework of Western-liberal constitutionalism. Instead, the constitutionalism of South Asia needs to be understood in the context of its very own unique context and framework. When compared to the constitutionalism practised in nations of the West, the problems and issues that are central to "South Asian Constitutionalism" are distinctive. It is a well-known fact that arguments concerning constitutionalism in the countries of the West centre on the use of diverse informational approaches and the role of the judicial system in cases involving constitutional issues. On the other hand, the demands for constitutional plans and arbitration are the primary sources of concern for the countries of South Asia.

The work "the Comparative Constitutionalism in South Asia" (Khilnani et al., 2013), which is considered to be a pioneering work on South Asian constitutionalism, places an emphasis on similarities that can be found within the constitutions, similarities that can be found within party-political edifices, and similarities that can be found within the legal arrangements that are already in place in the region of South Asia. The editors of the book are troubled by the fact that the legal scholars and courts in these countries have become used to looking towards the nations of the countries of the West. This has caused them to feel uneasy. This notion of South Asian culture, which Upendra Baxi argues was a product of colonisation, is challenged by the author. Therefore, he favours using the principles of post-colonial constitutionalism in his work. This book makes an effort to dismantle the Eurocentrism that is associated with constitutionalism and its related fields. The project to challenge the Eurocentrism associated with the field of constitutionalism had by that time begun along some opulent writings regarding constitutionalism prevalent in the nations of the African continent, and the aforementioned book is most certainly one step onward and upward toward the aforementioned path in the direction of which it is heading.

The book "Unstable Constitutionalism: Law and Politics in South Asia" (Tusnet and Khosla 2015 is an additional ground-breaking work in the field of South Asian constitutionalism. Tushnet and Khosla have adopted the fundamental principles of an ideology known as "unstable constitutionalism." This term denotes that there is a divergence with regard to the institutional type, the one that may exemplify the form of constitutionalism, despite the fact that many of the political actors in the aforementioned nations are dedicated to the idea of constitutionalism. This is because this term refers to the fact that there are multiple constitutions in existence. The development of unbalanced constitutionalism seeks to clarify the alteration between law and socio-political authenticities, as well as the method by which the law strives to arbitrate this alteration and strengthen the soul of constitutionalism by finishing the civil malady. To put this another way: how does rule function for the purpose of achieving the raison d'être of rules regarding achieving steadiness? In addition, Tushnet and Khosla argue that the law may further outline or guide socio-political authenticities, and that the only place one can find some singularity of unstable constitutionalism is in dialogue between rules and politics. These editors are also of the opinion that although each and every stakeholder in South Asia has faith in the concept of a contract regarding constitutional matters, that stakeholder is unable to give their approval regarding the conditions connected with that contract. They bring attention to the fact that every stakeholder has faith in the concept of a single state. On the other hand, neither the editors nor the authors of these books initiated any kind of discussion with the works on transformative constitutionalism, insurgent constitutionalism, post-colonial constitutionalism (with the exception of Baxi), and post-liberal constitutionalism.

10.3.2 Locating Gender in Constitutionalism

Literature associated with the framework ofliberal constitutionalism has not given sufficient attention to the repercussions of constitutionalism in the process of defining gender-related dealings and the possibility of constitutionalism regarding the redesigning of gender relations. This is because the literature has not paid sufficient attention to the liberal constitutionalism framework (Dhingra 2020). In literature that deals with gender issues, the ideas of "power" and "change" have received a lot of attention. When the constitution is being written, there will be a focus on the "play of power," which will result in an expansion of the scope of constitutionalism. This will be done in order to pay attention to the "play of power." The importance of power should not be limited to identifying the power of male members in organisations that make constitutions based solely on the total numerical power they hold in those organisations. This emphasis on power should also be placed on the power of discourses on womanhood and how they shape the agenda and debates during the process of creating a constitution. Any emphasis on 'change' can become worthwhile for locating the collective modification imagined in the constitution, particularly in relation to gender-related relations, so long as the emphasis is placed in the right place. According to Menon's definition of feminism, the term refers to an acknowledgment of the fact that "hierarchical organising of the world around gender is key to maintaining social order" (Menon 2012: viii). Because of this, it is absolutely necessary for us to investigate whether the provisions in the constitution and constitutional standards upset the "hierarchical organising of the world around gender" in order to fulfil a purpose that is connected with determining whether or not the constitution possesses any transformative probability in relation to the shifting of the social order.

The women have been subjected to a pattern of subjugation that is both persistent and deeply rooted in their past (Irving 2008: 36). Irving contends that feminists have a responsibility to be conscious of the fact that constitutional laws may function as instruments for either "conserving or defying the aforementioned subordination," and that this is something that they must be aware of. Irving argues that constitutions need to be considered historically 'gendered' by making the point that they are gendered. This word, "gendered," suggests that even though a particular constitution may seem to be neutral with regard to gender, the contents and language of that constitution may have an unequal influence on women. She maintains that an examination of the constitution from a "gender audit" perspective needs to take precedence over an exclusive concentration on equal rights. This so-called "gender audit" has to focus on the language and analysis of the constitution, as well as the rules regarding citizenship, the mechanism of representation, and the question of whether or not the constitution recognises global and conventional law. A gender audit in connection with the constitution should not be limited to investigating simply the subject matter that a constitution designates as being relevant to gender equality. This gender audit should investigate if the provisions included in the constitution may help create gender equality and institutions or whether they can hinder these efforts.

Irving contends that the subordination of women is not completely dependent on the structure and provisions of the constitution; however, the contents of the constitution can play a significant role in "either reinforcing the historical-socio-cultural inhibitors or assisting in mitigating them."

The mission of feminist constitutionalism is to investigate whether or not there is a connection between feminism and the laws that are outlined in the constitution. This investigation, contestation, and redefinition of the basic concept of constitutionalism from a feminist point of view. (Baines, Barak-Erez and Kahana 2012: 1). In feminist constitutionalism, it is not enough to just revisit familiar topics from fresh angles; the subject matter must also be reexamined. Feminist constitutionalism, on the other hand, implies more prominently to offer new questions and provide unique refrains and to assume responsibility for altering the alignment of discussion about the constitution and debates regarding constitutional concerns.

It is important to recognise the status of constitutional law because of the support it provides for feminist investigation. It is imperative that the framework of constitutionalism that is inextricably tied with feminism be maintained in order to bolster and promote feminist valid theory. The majority of countries' judicial systems are underpinned by constitutional law, which shapes "fundamental expectations in connection with nationality, privileges, and accountabilities." Constitutional law plays a significant foundational role in many judicial systems. Therefore, feminists who participate in the analysis of legal issues have a duty to realise that legal structures cannot be transformed without first paying attention to the constitutional underpinnings upon which they are based.

The goal of feminist constitutionalism is not restricted to only reviewing existing constitutional biases and making feminist modifications; rather, it seeks to establish an academic arena that can be used for evaluating constitutional preparations as well as experimentalism. It's possible that constitutional changes won't always take the form of amendments to the constitution; rather, these reforms might become apparent in the wake of the introduction of innovative approaches to feminist constitutional debate as well as court decisions.

According to Mackinnon, "Constitutions are artefacts of special masculine legal action defining countries and creating states as they root the government of those nations and states." The plan is to put in writing the conditions under which the men engaged and have agreed to keep each other accountable. Mackinnon asserts, by arguing that in the traditions of the Anglo-Saxon people, the law is some way by which social control is transported, Mackinnon is making his case. In addition, she argues that the Constitution sits atop the authority hierarchy of the country. It leads one to a profound interest in a variety of constitutions on the one hand, but on the other, it leads one to a lack of interest in investigating its organisation. In addition to this, she asserts that liberation fighters from the formerly colonised countries embraced the form even if they altered the substance of their struggle for independence.

Mackinnon contends that female constitutionalism requires the stimulation provided by a variety of ideals. The problem of male dominance will be addressed strategically, but the stimulation must be carried out in a direct manner. This stimulation calls for not just the constitution, but also for the social command to be saturated with functional parity for the members of the society who identify as female. In addition to this, it is necessary to have an active meeting with society, which is generally accepted to be unequal on the basis of sex as well as gender.

Mackinnon argues further that the project of feminist constitutionalism should not be derailed by 'essentialist questions' such as the discussion of 'sameness versus dissimilarity' or 'traditional relativist questions' regarding many culturally related practises that are founded on the idea that the subordination of women should be tolerated. The presumption that a private range that is delineated around a dwelling unit and household is a habitation that contains sex equality has to be thrown out. As a result, this presumption is impermeable to public processes, thus this presumption needs to be discarded. The substances, in which there does not exist a good alternative to differ or guide to affect the outline of choices or consequences that already exists, such as the form of government or sexual access, as well as forms of force ranging from socialisation to physical aggression, would not be rationalised as consenting if they were to be considered.

Jennifer Nedelsky is certain in her assertion that one of the main responsibilities of contemporary constitutionalism is to find a way to ensure that democratic decision-making processes are held accountable to fundamental principles (Nedelsky 2012: 15). She contends that

> "feminist constitutionalism invites us to 1) reimagine the scope of practices and institutions that should be held accountable to core values 2) reimagine the forms of deliberation about those values and their practical meaning, and 3) reimagine multiple forms of accountability- so that judicial review becomes only one highly specific and democratically limited mechanism (ibid)."

According to Nedelsky's argument, in order to ensure the fulfilment of fundamental rights like parity, there must be a profoundly "transformative discourse addressing gender-based separation of labour". It is necessary to re-evaluate our guiding principles so that different layers of norms, practices, and organisations, as well as laws, may be held accountable to those standards. She encourages individuals to consider moving outside state organisations in order to engage in new kinds of conversation around vital criteria and answerability to them. As a consequence of this, the fundamental principle of constitutionalism has to be stretched beyond its bounds in order for it to achieve its primary objective.

In their article, Beverley Baines and Ruth-Rubio-Marian argue that a "feminist constitutional agenda" should investigate the following topics: "(1) constitutional agency, (2) constitutional rights, (3) constitutionally structured diversity, (4) constitutional equality, with special attention to (5) reproductive rights and sexual autonomy, (6) women's rights within the family, and (7) women's socio-economic development and democratic rights." (Baines and Marin 2004: 4).

Special Insights

Drafting of a Feminist Constitution

Kathleen Sullivan, raises the question: "What options would a hypothetical group of feminist drafters confront if they were to constitutionalise women's equality from scratch?" (Sullivan 2002: 747)" Her answer is that those drafters will have to make some choice about as stated hereunder:

"(1) between a general provision favouring equality or a specific provision facing sex equality, (2) between limiting classifications based on sex or protecting the class of women, (3) between reaching only state discrimination or reaching private discrimination as well, (4) between protecting women from discrimination or also guaranteeing affirmative rights to the material preconditions for equality, (5) between setting forth only judicially enforceable or also broadly aspirational equality norms."

Irving maintains that Sullivan's proposal cannot be considered a complete constitution since it consists of just "A Bill of Rights," as opposed to other sections of a constitution (Irving 2008: 29). Irving maintains that we are obligated to shift away from a rights-centred strategy that has not addressed the "structurally prior concerns" that remain unanswered. These questions include the appointment of judges, how they carry out their duties, the process by which laws are produced, as well as the criteria and procedures that are used to choose those who will craft those criteria, and so on.

Irving contends that focusing solely on the provisions for the rights and the declaration about parity is to bind constitutionalism to the process of judicial review, while at the same time ignoring issues relating to the manner in which constitutional interpretation can be controlled, along with any constitution itself.

One of the most significant achievements of feminist activism and practises has been to challenge the public-private divide. This has been accomplished via a variety of different strategies. Due to the establishment of this division, a lot of concerns relating to women were relegated to the realm of private concerns. In this way, the topics relating to the problems faced by women were introduced into the realm of political discourse. In recent years, the feminist idea and crusading movement has been working toward the goal of constitutionalizing issues that are relevant to the sphere of the family. The patriarchal system is based on the presumption that the wives and mothers of the members of a society are simply responsible for the upkeep of their household or family. This house is assumed to include the wives and mothers' husbands, as well as their children and other elderly members of the household. (Dhingra 2021).

A number of these most recent constitutions have come a long way toward challenging this postulation, which is quite encouraging to see. For example, Article 27 of the Constitution of Rwanda offers equal rights and equal answerability to both the mother and the father in reference to the process of parenting their kids. This provision was included in the constitution in order to promote gender equality. It goes on to require the state to develop an adequate law in order to construct essential institutions for the protection of the family in general, and especially for the protection of the women and children. (Republic of Rwanda Constitution, 2010) In Colombia's constitution, Article 46 mandates that the government, families, and communities all have some responsibility for ensuring the safety of the country's elderly residents. It orders the state to make certain resources, including social security and food assistance, accessible to them in the event that they experience difficulties and destitution. In precisely this way, the constitution of Colombia includes provisions for the protection of women, as well as babies, children, and adolescents of all ages (Constitution of Colombia, 1991).

10.4 Environmental Constitutionalism

Environmental constitutionalism is the study of the formulation, implementation, and efficacy of integrating environmental rights, processes, and policies into constitutions across the world (Kreilhuber 2017). Environmental constitutionalism is also known as green constitutionalism. It is impossible to overstate how surprising it is that environmental constitutionalism has emerged. It is widely believed that the Stockholm Convention on the Human Environment in 1972 was the global impetus that sparked the exponential growth of international, regional, and national environmental law regimes, including their rights related aspects. Although it is possible that the 1948 Universal Declaration on Human Rights and the twin international covenants on Civil and Political and Economic, Social and Cultural Rights in 1966 were the origins of environmental rights, the term "environmental rights" did not enter the lexicon until 1972.

Although it is impossible to pinpoint the precise year in which the first environmental provision of any type was included in a constitution, the current wave of environmental protection legislation started in the wake of the Stockholm conference. From that point on, constitutional incorporation proceeded at a modest but consistent pace during the 1970s and 1980s, continued unabated throughout the 1990s, and has been widespread ever since. At this time, fifty percent of all the constitutions that have ever been written on our planet either explicitly or indirectly acknowledge a basic right to the environment. A little less than a third of countries additionally have procedural environmental rights clauses that clearly state rights to knowledge, participation, and access to justice in environmental concerns. Some provisions are more common than others, such as those that expressly recognise a right to a beneficial or healthy environment. On the other hand, provisions that recognise the rights of nature, require environmental education, advance sustainability, or incorporate human dignity as an essential component of environmental protection are less common. Countries are aware of the currents that are bringing environmental constitutionalism to all regions of the globe, regardless of whether or not they are actively mimicking the policies of one another. Some constitutions have environmental provisions that are directive principles of public policy, encouraging governments to care for the environment. Other constitutions insist that the government owns environmental resources in trust for the benefit of the people and must care for them accordingly for present and future generations. Still other constitutions' guarantee environmental rights as an indivisible aspect along with other rights, such as the right to free expression, the right to racial equality, and the right to privacy. This rights-based approach denotes a shift away from the conventional understanding of environmental protection, which has primarily taken place at the international level through multilateral treaties on pollution, biodiversity, climate change, and so on, or by domestic statutes that seek to secure clean water or air, for example. This shift is signalled by the use of the term "rights-based."

There are many different ways in which environmental constitutionalism may be expressed; it can take the form of substantive rights, procedural rights, directive policies, reciprocal responsibilities, or any combination of these and other characteristics. There are certain characteristics that are quite typical. For instance, about one half of the world's nations have constitutional provisions that either explicitly or implicitly acknowledge a person's right to a healthy environment. Roughly the same amount imposes a moral obligation on people to act in a manner that is protective of the natural world. Certain clauses are fairly precise, such as those that provide for rights of nature or rights to drinkable water or other natural resources. Other provisions provide for rights to other natural resources. Some of them are more ephemeral than others; they acknowledge trust duties over natural resources or toward future generations, or they address connected topics like sustainability or climate change. Stewardship of the environment is seen by some as an issue that should be addressed at the national level. The majority of constitutional provisions that address environmental concerns are written in narrative form; however, some include numerical outcomes, such as maintaining a percentage of prescribed tree cover. Countries like Bhutan (60 percent) and Kenya include such provisions in their constitutions (10 percent). There has also been an increase in the number of clauses that are aimed to provide rights to specialised procedural safeguards in environmental disputes. In most cases, environmental procedural rights include requirements for environmental assessment, the right to obtain information, or the right to petition or participate in environmental decision-making. Such rights are helpful in maintaining the vitality of opposing substantive rights. When stakeholders have the right to obtain information that is both free and timely, when they can engage in debates, and when they may legally challenge environmental decision making, there is a greater chance that a constitutional guarantee to a positive environment can take root. Procedure environmental constitutionalism is also important in its own right, and it has the potential to be as effective as, or even more effective than, substantive environmental rights. This is due to the fact that courts are more likely to impart additional process than they are to impose substantive remedies. Some nations, such as Brazil, have adopted all or the majority of the principles of environmental constitutionalism, whilst other nations have taken no such steps. The majority of nations are located somewhere in the middle. The proliferation of environmental constitutionalism around the world, both in terms of the number of such documents and the significance of the issues they seek to address, is attested to by the myriad of provisions that seek to protect various facets of the environment through a variety of frameworks and enforcement mechanisms. The environmental constitutionalist movement is expanding at the subnational level as well, helping to bridge holes in the federal structure. Most notably by states in the Americas in general, and Brazil in particular, subnational governments around the globe have deemed it appropriate to constitutionalize substantive and procedural environmental rights, environmental duties, and sustainable development for present and future generations, frequently with a great deal more specificity and enforceability than is provided in national constitutions. The recognition of constitutional environmental rights at the subnational level may also be of particular significance in nations that have not yet accorded environmental rights the status of a fundamental human right at the national level. Environmental constitutionalism is an essential node in the web of national management of the environment. Other essential nodes include adherence to international, multilateral, and regional treaties and norms; dialogue with subnational and local governments; and environmental impact assessments and water framework legislation as examples of national statutory schemes. As a consequence of this, it has the potential to serve as an imprimatur for the purpose of ensuring and promoting complementarity of diverse regimes at the various levels of governance. Incorporating environmental rights, protections, and processes into legal systems has beneficial implications that go beyond the decisions reached by courts. It has been shown that nations that have implemented environmental constitutionalism have lower ecological footprints per capita, have greater performance on various environmental indices, and are more likely to ratify international environmental accords. There is also some evidence that environmental constitutionalism encourages the creation of domestic environmental laws and regulations. Environmental constitutionalism may also represent the climax of domestic environmental laws, rather than the prelude to such legislation. To summarise, environmental constitutionalism is not a replacement for current international and national legal systems; rather, it is an intrinsic part of these institutions, serving to support and scaffold them. It is an issue that needs to be examined and considered by the judiciary as it contributes to the advancement of constitutionalism in general. In point of fact, environmental constitutionalism is playing an increasingly more significant complementary and supplementary role in the effort to solve the kind of environmental issues that are experienced most intensely by people who are often disregarded or mistreated by the current legal frameworks. Existing international and local laws and legal systems do not, on their own, provide either the protection of human rights in the environment or the conservation of the environment. Treaties, concepts, and customs at the international level don't contribute much to the advancement of environmental rights at the local and subsidiary level. There is not currently an international convention that protects environmental rights. In addition, the benefits that people might get from multinational and bilateral accords that aim to address environmental issues are sometimes minimal at best. And despite the fact that many countries' domestic statutes and regulations give environmental protection and resource conservation, these laws seldom strive to improve environmental rights. This is despite the fact that domestic statutes and regulations are fairly advanced in many countries. In addition, international human rights regimes come the closest to the idea that individuals have a fundamental right to a quality environment; however, these regimes are frequently out of reach to individuals who would benefit from the recognition of environmental rights at the constitutional level. This is despite the fact that international human rights regimes come the closest to the idea that individuals have a fundamental right to a quality environment. The environmental constitutionalist movement has the potential to assist fill the voids that are left by other legal systems (Daly, Louis Kotzé, James R. May 2017).

The relationship to human rights, climate change as the most emblematic environmental challenge of our time, and the 2030 Sustainable Development Agenda, which aims to leave no one behind on the path to a better and more sustainable future, will all play a role in the development of the new frontiers for environmental constitutionalism, which will be played out in this very context. The discussion of human rights in relation to the environment, as well as constitutional protections for environmental rights, is especially pertinent in Africa. There was a time, not so long ago, when the idea that the rest of the world stood to learn from an examination of human rights legislation in Africa could have been deemed to be bizarre. However, in recent years, this idea has gained traction. However, throughout the last several years a significant amount of change has taken place, not just on the ground in Africa but also in the opinions that are generally held towards the continent. It is also important to remember that several "Western" courts have previously used the African Charter in their judgements, which is something that should be taken into consideration. This should not come as a surprise given that this instrument has contributed a number of novel ideas to the field of international human rights. The African Charter is the only regional human rights instrument that incorporates economic, social, and cultural rights as well as civil and political rights into a single document and subjects them all to the same complaints procedure. This is in addition to the African Charter's one-of-a-kind enforcement mechanism, which makes it the only regional human rights instrument. Because of this, it is very significant that these rights (such as the right to health, water, and food, for example) clearly have a strong overlap with environmental rights. As a result, it is possible for individuals to bring cases relating to the environment before the African Commission on Human and Peoples Rights and the African Court. Therefore, the human rights protection body established by the African Charter is the very first human rights body that is competent to decide on numerous violations of first-generation human rights as well as second-generation human rights in a single judgement. In terms of advanced environmental constitutionalism, South Africa has been a pioneer not only on the African continent but also throughout the globe. The chapters that are included in this edition were presented at the New Frontiers conference in April 2016 in South Africa. In addition to having a forward-thinking constitution that protects environmental rights, South Africa also has an unusual and fascinating set of comprehensive environmental laws that make substantial provisions for public involvement in environmental policy and decision-making.

Special Insights

Environmental Rule of Law

In order for environmental rule of law to be effective, the following conditions must be met: 1. Environmental laws that are just, clear, and can be put into practise; 2. Public participation in decision-making, as well as access to justice and information in environmental matters, in accordance with Principle 10 of the Rio Declaration. 3. The accountability and integrity of institutions and the people who make decisions, particularly via the active participation of environmental audits and enforcement; 4. Mechanisms for the settlement of disputes that are easily accessible, fair, unbiased, prompt, and responsive. This includes the cultivation of specialist knowledge in environmental adjudication, as well as the development of new environmental processes and remedies. 5. Acknowledgement of the symbiotic link between respect for human rights and protection of the natural environment; and 6. Particular guidelines for the application of environmental legislation (May and Daly 2017).

The 2030 Agenda for Sustainable Development and the Sustainable Development Goals (SDGs) offer a once-in-a-generation chance to make significant strides toward the establishment of environmental rule of law. This can be accomplished by ensuring that sustainable development is founded on rights and that it provides all people with equal access to environmental protection. In addition to this, they provide a mechanism for putting into practise the hundreds of environmental promises that have already been made, including the many articles included in constitutions all over the globe.

10.5 Conclusion

The theory and practice of constitutionalism have progressed throughout the course of time, and several constitutional frameworks have formed as a result of the varied cultural and political circumstances that have existed throughout history. Western-Constitutionalism that adheres to liberal principles cannot effectively account for the nature and operation of constitutionalism in various regions of the globe. Although the concept of limited government control is the foundation of liberal constitutionalism, the pervasive role that governments play in the societies of many Asian and African nations makes it impossible to ignore the existence of such institutions. Is it accurate to say that the politics associated with the nations in the Asian and African area provide us with an opportunity to rethink the concept of constitutionalism?

One major framework of analysis is provided by the concept of transformative constitutionalism. In contrast to liberal constitutionalism, which places an emphasis on restricting the power of the state, transformative constitutionalism places an emphasis on empowering the state to reshape society in a way that eliminates class distinctions. According to this school of thought, burdened people are unable to exercise their freedom if the state does not intervene in their lives. On the other hand, these burdened people require the active participation of the government in order to be liberated from the historical oppression they have endured.

In today's context, it becomes pertinent to locate gender and environment in constitutionalism and rethink and reshape the contours of comparative constitutionalism in recognition of the emerging trends.

Keywords

Constitution
Constitutionalism
Environment
Gender
Feminism
Liberal Constitutionalism
Transformative Constitutionalism

Review Questions

1. Distinguish between constitution and constitutionalism.
2. Discuss the evolution of constitutionalism. How is modern constitutionalism different from ancient constitutionalism?
3. What are the different alternative frameworks of constitutionalism that have emerged in the non-Western context? Do you think they have challenged the hegemony of Western-liberal constitutionalism?

References

Baines, Beverley and Ruth-Rubio-Marin. (2005). 'Toward a Feminist Constitutional Agenda'. In *The Gender of Constitutional Jurisprudence.* (Eds.)., Beverley Baines and Ruth Rubio-Marin. Cambridge: Cambridge University Press. pp. 1–21.

Baxi, Upendra. (2004). 'The (Im)possibility of Constitutional Justice: Seismographic Notes on Indian Constitutionalism' *In India's Living Constitution: Ideas, Practices and Controversies.* (Ed.). Zoya Hasan, E. Sridharan and R. Sudarshan. pp. 31–63 New Delhi: Permanent Black.

Baxi, Upendra. (2008). 'Outline of a "Theory of Practice" of Indian Constitutionalism'. In *Politics and Ethics of the Indian Constitution.* (Eds.)., Rajeev Bhargava. New Delhi: Oxford University Press. pp. 92–118.

Baxi, Upendra. (2013). 'Preliminary Notes on Transformative Constitutionalism'. In Transformative constitutionalism: Comparing the apex courts of Brazil, India and South Africa. (Eds.)., Oscar Vilhena. Johannesburg: Pretoria University Law Press, pp. 19–47.

Constitution of Colombia, 1991, online available at: https://www.constituteproject.org

Constitution of Rwanda 2010. Accessed from http://aceproject.org on November 14, 2014.

Daly, Erin Louis Kotzé, James R. May. (2017). 'Introduction to Environmental Constitutionalism in New Frontiers in Environmental Constitutionalism'. United Nations Environment Programme (UN Environment). Accessed from https://www.informea.org on November 12, 2014.

Dhingra, Alisha (2017). Review of three books in Studies in Indian Politics. June 2017. Sage.99–102.

Dhingra, Alisha. (2014). 'Indian Constitutionalism: A Case of Transformative Constitutionalism'. *Asian Journal of Multidisciplinary Studies,* 2(7), pp. 135–139.

Dhingra, Alisha. (2020). 'Gendering Constitutionalism: A Comparative Study of India and South Africa', *Studies in Humanities and Social Sciences,* IIAS Shimla, 27(2), 103–120.

Dhingra, Alisha. 2021. "Feminist Constitutionalism: Women in Making and Working of Constitution". *Bihar Journal of Public Administration.* Vol. XVIII, No. 1., Jan.-June, 2021. 120–132.

Irving, Helen. (2008). *Gender and the Constitution: Equity and Agency in Comparative Constitutional Design.* New York: Cambridge University Press.

Jha, Shefali. (2008). 'Rights Versus Representation: Defending Minority Interests in the Constituent Assembly' In *Politics and Ethics of the Indian Constitution.* (Eds.)., Rajeev Bhargava. New Delhi: Oxford University Press. pp. 339–352.

Kahana, Tsvi and Stephenson Rachel. (2012). 'The Promise of Democratic Constitutionalism: Women, Constitutional Dialogue and the Internet'. In *Feminist Constitutionalism: Global Perspectives.* (Eds.)., Beverley Baines, Daaphne Barak-Erez and TsviKahana. New York: Cambridge University Press. pp. 240–259.

Kannabiran, Kalpana. (2012). *Tools of Justice: Non-Discrimination and the Indian Constitution.* New Delhi: Routledge. Kalpana Kannabiran (2012).

Klare, Karl. (1998). —Legal Culture and Transformative Constitutionalism, *South African Journal on Human Rights,* 14, pp.146–168.

Kreilhuber, Arnold (2017). 'New Frontiers in Environmental Constitutionalism in New Frontiers' in *Environmental Constitutionalism.* United Nations Environment Programme (UN Environment), Available at: https://www.informea.org

Mackinnon, Catherine. (2012). 'Foreword'. In *Feminist Constitutionalism: Global Perspectives.* (Eds.)., Beverley Baines, Daaphne Barak-Erez and TsviKahana. New York: Cambridge University Press. pp. ix-xii.

Maneesha Tikekar. (2014). *Constitutionalism and Democracy in South Asia; Political Developments in India's Neighbourhood.* New Delhi: Oxford University Press.

May, James R. and Erin Daly. (2017) *Judicial Handbook on Environmental Constitutionalism.* United Nations Environment Programme (UN Environment), Available at: https://www.iucn.org

Tushent, Mark and Madhav Khosla (2015), *Unstable Constitutionalism: Law and Politics in South Asia.* New York: Cambridge University Press.

McIlwain, Charles H. 1947 (1940). *Constitutionalism: Ancient and Modern.* Ithaca, NY: Cornell University Press

Mehta, Uday. (2010). 'Constitutionalism' In Oxford Companion to Indian Politics. (Eds.)., Niraja Jayal and Pratap Bhanu Mehta. New Delhi: Oxford University Press. Pp. 15–27.

Menon, Nivedita. (2012). Seeing Like a Feminist. New Delhi: Zubaan and Penguin Books India.Baines, Barak-Erez and Kahana.

Nedelsky, Jeniffer. (2012). The Gendered Division of Household Labor: An Issue of Constitutional Rights In Feminist Constitutionalism: Global Perspectives. (Eds.)., Beverley Baines, Daaphne Barak-Erez and TsviKahana. New York: Cambridge University Press. pp. 15–47.

Sullivan, M. Kathleen. (2002). —Constitutionalizing Women's Equality. California Law Review, 90, online available at: http://scholarship.law.berkeley.edu/californialawreview/vol90/iss3/3

Sunil Khilani, Vikram Raghavan and Arun K. Thiruvengadam. (Eds.). 2013. Comparative Constitutionalism in South Asia. New Delhi: Oxford University Press.

Tushnet, Mark and Madhav Khosla. (Eds.). 2015 *Unstable Constitutionalism—Law and Politics in South Asia.* Cambridge University Press.

Vickers, Jill. 2013. 'Is Federalism Gendered? Incorporating Gender into Studies of Federalism'. *Publius: The Journal of Federalism*, Vol. 43, no.1

CHAPTER 11

Federalism in Comparative Perspective: Nature, Meaning and Emerging Trends

Rahul Chimurkar and Vasavi

Reader's Guide

Comparative politics in the past remained confined to the study of political institutions only. In recent times, however, one could witness the expanding contours of the discipline as it is increasingly becoming inclusive of the crucial new dimensions of engagements that enable it to capture a rich narrative in comparative political analysis. It is in this sense that this chapter on federalism is discussed here. The concept of federalism has evolved over a period of time in the study of comparative politics. In simple terms, federalism implies the existence of two levels of government. Today, most of the countries of the world have adopted different variants of the federal system. The nature of federalism varies from country to country depending on the nature and importance of the underlying political economy, social diversities, geographical factors, cultural conditioning, international influences and other determinants of the political system. In contemporary times, the study of comparative federalism has been gaining grounds. This chapter attempts to cover the different dimensions of federalism. It will discuss the nature of federalism and explore the differences between federalism, federation and confederation. Section 11.2 will engage with the various models of federal governance followed by debates related to the distribution of power in the federal set-up in different countries. The concluding section underlines some of the challenges faced by federal systems in the era of globalized world.

11.1 Introduction

The term 'federal' is derived from the Latin word 'foederatus', which is derived from two terms, that is, 'foedus' (treaty) and fidere (trust). Preston King's *Federalism and Federation* (1982) describes federalism in a normative way as an ideology and federation to mean this ideology's institutional manifestation. Since federalism is the driving force behind the establishment of federation, 'there may be federalism without federation but 'no federation without some matching variety of federalism' (King 1982, 76). Ronal Watts in his book *Comparing Federal Systems* (1999) further elaborates the concept by differentiating categories of federalism, federation and federal political systems. A large number of countries encompassing a considerable amount of the world have adopted a functioning federation. It also needs to be mentioned here that there is no single archetype or universal model of federation. Countries have adopted federalism and created federations by customizing the concept in accordance to their own suitability and contextual requirements. Federations vary in terms of their allocation of legislative, executive responsibilities, taxing powers, degree of symmetry or asymmetry of constituent units, economic and social diversities, etc.

11.2 Federalism and Federation

Elliot Burner defines federalism as a constitutional mechanism for dividing power between different levels of government so that federating units can enjoy substantial constitutionally guaranteed autonomy over certain policy areas while sharing power in accordance with agreed rules over other areas (Burner 2017, 3). Generally, there are two major levels within a federation: (a) a central or federal level and (b) a state or provincial level. However, there are also examples of federal systems with constitutionally recognized three levels of government, with the third one being at the local level. The major examples of this type are South Africa and Belgium. Elliot argues that the question of whether federalism is suitable for a given country chiefly depends on the balance between common interests or identities, on the one hand, and divergent interests and identities, on the other (Burner 2017, 5).

In order to understand the concept, we may distinguish three terms: 'federalism', 'federal political systems' and 'federations'. Federalism is used as a concept as well as a form of government. It is a system of government that represents the existence of dual government at the same time. The term federation is used for such countries which have adopted federalism as a system of governance in one or the other ways, viz. countries like Canada, Australia, United States, India and Russia. 'Federalism' is basically not a descriptive but a normative term and refers to the advocacy of multi-tiered government combining elements of 'shared rule' and regional 'self-rule' (Watts 2008, 1–2). It means combining both unity and diversity and also accommodating the different identities within a larger union. It is also based on non-centralization, which implies that both the levels of government are treated as equal partners in the distribution of powers. 'Federal political system' and 'federation' are descriptive terms applying to particular forms of political organization. The term 'federal political system' refers to the broad category of political systems that have two or more levels of government which combine elements of shared rule with common institutions and regional self-rule for the governments of constituent units (Watts 2008). In contrast to the decentralized model of federal government, unitary systems have a single source of authority that encompasses a whole spectrum of more specific non-unitary forms, that is, species ranging from quasi-federations and federation to confederations and beyond. Within the genus of federal political systems, federations represent a particular species in which neither the federal nor the constituent units of government are constitutionally subordinate to the other, that is, each has sovereign powers derived from the constitution rather than another level of government; each is empowered to deal directly with its citizens in the exercise of its legislative, executive and taxing powers and each is directly elected by its citizens.

Comparison between Federal and Unitary Government

Federal Government	Unitary Government
1. Powers are distributed between different levels of the government.	1. All powers are concentrated in one central authority.
2. Separate legislatures could be found at the central and state levels.	2. Legislatures may be bicameral (Britain) or unicameral (China).
3. Citizens have to abide by two sets of laws.	3. Unitary system of law prevails.
4. It is marked by the presence of an independent judiciary to resolve conflicts between the centre and states.	4. Judiciary may be independent or may not be independent.

Federal Government	Unitary Government
5. Rigid constitution	5. Constitution may be rigid (France) or flexible (Britain).
6. Written constitution.	6. Constitution may be supreme (Japan) or may not be supreme (Britain).
7. Examples: United States, India and Canada.	7. Examples: China, France and Britain.

11.3 Confederation

Both confederation and federalism signify an association of states, but there is a vast difference between the two. Confederation is an association of states, but this association is voluntary in nature. In a federation, states agree to give up a part of their powers and follow the national laws and policies defined by the constitution. In a confederation, states enjoy a larger degree of autonomy and could freely leave the union when they decide to do so. In a confederation, the central government derives its power from the component states, whereas in a federation, all powers of the central government are derived from the constitution. In a confederation, one could not see the presence of a strong legislature, whereas in a federation, there is a dual government, each having its own legislature, executive and judiciary.

Confederation is a conglomeration of independent states which create a union or central government for some common purposes. At the same time, the confederating units retain their cardinal powers of government, and the very existence of the central government depends on the cooperation and understanding of the member states. What is no less important is that in a confederation, the central government has no direct authority over citizens in several states; whatever power it possesses has to be exercised through the component states. A confederation owes its existence not upon the terms of the constitution, but upon a loose agreement, which they are free to leave at will. The central authority in a confederation is a mere agency of the member states, and the latter have powers superior to that of the agency. The central agency has a direct relationship with the people, and the commands of the agency would operate upon the people in each individual states only to the extent the state government so permits (Basu 1987, 6–7).

The best example of confederation is the United States (in its early years of political formation), which was later turned into a federation once its constitution came into force. Another example could be the European Union (EU), which is composed of many countries that willingly decided to give up a part of their independence but still maintain their sovereignty in order to create a supranational body and present a united front on the global fora. The EU operates under a single economic market, a common currency adopted by most member states. But at the same time, there are some member states that resist transferring some key powers which they hold as sovereign states. For example, Britain and France have not shared their defence powers.

11.4 Livingston on Nature of Federalism

William S. Livingston in his article 'A Note on the Nature of Federalism' (1952) argues that the classical definition attempts to explain federalism in juristic and legalistic terms. For them, federalism is a system of government whereby the power is divided between central and state governments in such a manner where each level of government is independent of the other. But the boundary between the units and extent of their powers may vary from country to country. Therefore, studying federalism merely on the basis of the law enshrined in it will not help. One needs to take into account the use of extra-constitutional forces that also shape and influence the government process in a federal system.

He argues that it is the federal nature of the society that gives birth to a federal political system. According to him, 'the essence of federalism lies not in the constitutional or institutional structure but in the society itself. Federal government is a device by which the federal qualities of the society are articulated and protected' (Livingston

1952). Societal forces are more important to him. He introduced the concept called 'instrumentalities' to explain the non-constitutional matters such as habits, attitudes and acceptances which facilitate the adoption of federalism. Livingston also noted that his 'instrumentalities' could, after a period of time, become 'rigidified and acquire a status of their own'.

11.5 Evolution of Comparative Federalism

Federalism as an idea, and practice is widely implemented in countries worldwide in the present day. However, it is imperative to reflect on the origin of the idea and gradual evolution of the concept. It was initially an independently explored practice in a less cohesive and coherent manner. One cannot just trace back the idea to any time or place. A federation is characterized by a common union which integrates its constituents in a manner preserving their autonomous identities. A typical ancient example of this union is the Amphictyonic League of ancient Greece, which integrated indigenous tribes to preserve and protect their customs and religious practices in a loose manner. Another example which needs to be mentioned is Israel, which typically integrated the 12 tribal groups in ancient times for several years. It was characterized by a written constitution, which is a notable feature of federations. Since the 13th century, Israelites were united for more than seven centuries under the Torah of Moses as a common constitution that integrated all the tribes. Such unions were not just confined to Israel and Greece but were evident in other parts of the world also. There were few tribal groups such as the Bedouin tribes and Iroquois league in America which were good examples of such unions. The key factors behind the formation of such groups were protection of religious rites and aggregation of military powers.

The middle ages saw a rise of confederations in several European cities. It was a new age of federalism. The smaller self-governing cities combined into larger cities to serve common economic and military purposes. The best examples were the Lombard League (1167–1250) and the Hanseatic League (1250–1669) in Europe. However, confederations were not just confined to the continent of Europe. In North America, the United States was established under the Articles of Confederation (1781–1788). It was the colonial government's inadequate economic policies and legislation through far away parliament which sourced dissatisfaction that eventually culminated into the American revolutionary war (1775–1783) and the Declaration of Independence (1776). It was to accomplish the revolutionary task of removing the colonial government that the 13 states together formed a confederation. However, very soon a sense of dissatisfaction was understood in the prevalent set-up of confederation. Under the Articles of Confederation, each state had an equal vote in Congress, with state delegations subject to recall by state legislatures; consequently, representatives were tied mostly to the interests of their states (Tarr 2005, 383). At the same time, the confederal government was confined to selective responsibilities with no say in the matters of constituent units. The absence of adequate national authority reduced the United States, in the words of Alexander Hamilton, 'the last stage of national humiliation' (Tarr 2005, 383). The congress could only make requests to the states but could barely enforce them. Whereas the legal design of the confederation still allowed for success in the revolutionary war, it turned out to be unfit to solve the problems of the post-war period, especially those of an economic nature, with each state creating trade obstacles by passing protectionist legislation and issuing its own currency (Palermo, 2017, 71). At the same time, the constitutions of the states never proved to be able to contain the unaccountable activities of the state legislatures. The state legislatures functioned in a manner hampering individual liberty. It was in response to these issues that the first federal state of the United States was formed in Philadelphia Convention in 1787. The framers of US constitution were already familiar with the confederacies existing in Germany, Switzerland and Netherlands. All these confederacies seemed to have displayed the same inefficiency and instability of government that had plagued their own confederation since independence. So, the framers came together in Philadelphia in 1787 to think of a new order that would guarantee both individual freedom and collective security. Montesquieu's three principles, namely recognition of intermediate powers between people and government as necessary for political stability, constitutional separation of powers among the branches of government and organization of a large state as a federal republic, subdivided into smaller units on the basis of mutual agreement (Hueglin and Fenna 2006, 99) helped the American constitution framers in establishing their desired new order. The third principle, that is, federal republic, was only related to federalism. It would provide the best of both worlds—the smallness necessary for democracy to function and the largeness necessary for both internal and external security (Hueglin and Fenna 2006, 100). A compromise was reached in Philadelphia where everyone agreed on the principle of 'shared sovereignty'.

As early as 1787–88, Alexander Hamilton, John Jay and James Madison were able to clearly identify the distinctive characteristics of the new proposed constitution. The principle of separation of power between the three organs of government, that is, legislature, executive and judiciary, became the cornerstone of this new era of federalism. At the same time, the idea of judicial review with a system of checks and balances became highly significant. This federation was nowhere a result of confederation but was in itself an independent revolutionary incident. Achievement of both economic and political objectives through a federal set-up and not a unitary one became important. Hence, the creation of a stable federal government with preservation of necessary individual freedoms against the orders of such strong federal government was the main driving force. Also, the protection of order, security and property through a system of shared responsibility between a stable central government and accountable state governments became highly significant. Some of the key features of the federal set-up in America which marked it as different from the earlier model of confederation are the adoption of principle of constitutional supremacy, direct importance of central legislation over individuals and establishment of a strong senate or the house of representatives.

Very soon, the formation of a federal state was witnessed in the other parts of world. In Europe, two such examples were Switzerland and Germany with their distinct federal systems. Even before the establishment of a federal system, Switzerland had been working on a confederal system. In 1291, initially only the first three cantons, that is, Schwyz, Unterwalden and Uri, founded a confederal alliance. Later, other parts joined this alliance, like Lucerne in 1332, Zurich in 1351, Glarus and Zug in 1352, Berne in 1353, Fribourg and Solothurn in 1481, Basle and Schaffhausen in 1501 and Appenzell in 1513. After the defeat of Napoleon, the last three cantons of Geneva, Neuchatel and Valais joined in 1815. Hence, the integration of Switzerland was a gradual process. The federal constitution of 1848 which established a federal government in Switzerland occurred after the war of Sonderbund between the Protestants and the Catholic separatist league in 1847. Hence, federalism in Switzerland was majorly inducted as a lasting solution to the conflict between these communities. It established the right to freedom of religion in Switzerland. Although, not as famous as their American counterparts, the founding fathers of the Swiss Confederation pursued a worthy and noble goal: to bring peace, security, freedom and reconciliation of diversity to their country by means of a modern federal constitution (Kincaid 2005, 351). Similar to their American counterparts, in Switzerland, this constitution of 1848 was to serve as the highest law of the land. At the same time drawing from the American example, a strong Council of States was established with effective representation of the cantons. Two very distinguished features of this constitution were dual membership in legislatures at both federal and provincial levels and unequal representation of the cantons in the second chamber. At the same time for the first time it was in Switzerland that the idea of direct democracy was merged with that of federalism. The Philadelphia convention had failed to introduce instruments of direct democracy, already existing in municipalities and some states, equally at the national level (Palermo 2017, 77). While the 1848 constitution established modern Switzerland, it has been completely modified two times, that is, in 1874 and in 1999. In 1848, the main principle for the distribution of powers was to give to the confederations the minimum of powers necessary to survive as a union of cantons. The Swiss constitution has at its foundation the theory of classical liberalism with special focus on the negative conception of liberty, where the individual functions freely with least interference of the state.

Talking about Germany, it was by the constitutions of 1867 and 1871 that the first German federation was established, which was very different from the American and Swiss models. It was in itself a distinct model of federalism with several asymmetrical features and weak central powers. Among all the units, it was Prussia which played the dominant role in terms of territory, polity and economy. Formation of federation was a response to the simultaneous power accumulation by several bodies like principalities, cities, businesses and corporations. The formation of modern state in Germany occurred over the foundation of federalism. Federalism with asymmetrical features in the constitutions of 1866 and 1867 had the history of rivalry between Prussia and Austria. After Prussia won over Austria in the 1866 war, the 37 German-speaking regions decided to form a confederation without Austria. It led to the establishment of the North German Confederation in 1867 and later the German Empire in 1871. After the First World War, when Germany lost badly, the Weimar Republic was established, which also carried forward the same tradition of federalism with asymmetrical relations due to the predominance of Prussia, having several antithetical elements to the conceptions of democracy and republic. There was a lot of dominance of the monarchic governments of the states at the federal level. They even exercised authority over crucial matters such as foreign affairs and military. Unlike the US Senate and Swiss Council of States, the Bundesrat or second house in Germany was composed of chosen members of the monarchic state governments and not elected representatives. It was in 1949 after the end of the Second World War that the constitution of the Federal Republic of Germany was passed and formed by the Parliamentary Council, which was composed of 65 members selected by the lander or state parliaments. The main goal of the majority of founding fathers was to establish a Western-style democratic federal state that would guarantee freedom, peace and security and enable a free-market economy to come into existence (Kincaid 2005, 145). At the same time, a distinguishing feature of German federalism was the overlapping of centralized and decentralized state units with a sense of shared responsibility between both tiers of government.

Federalists versus Anti-Federalists Debates

<table>
<tr><th colspan="2">Federalist vs Anti-Federalist Debates</th></tr>
<tr><td colspan="2">The greatest contribution to federalism was given by three fathers of the United States—Alexander Hamilton, James Madison and John Jay. These authors issued 85 articles for promoting the ratification of the constitution of the United States. After the constitution was approved by the convention in 1787, it had to be ratified by nine states. The ratification process became a lively debate between the Federalist and Anti-Federalist in each of the states.</td></tr>
<tr><th>Federalists</th><th>Anti-federalists</th></tr>
<tr><td>1. Supported the constitution, wanted a strong government.</td><td>1. Opposed the ratification of the constitution.</td></tr>
<tr><td>2. They believed that the national government should have the power and control the country—that only a strong government can deal with the challenges facing this new nation.</td><td>2. Believed that government would have too much power and infringe on people's liberty.</td></tr>
<tr><td rowspan="2">3. Alexander Hamilton argued that the constitution protects American liberties. It is the perfect balance between liberty and power. For example, the checks and balances and separation of powers make it impossible to have tyranny.</td><td>3. In favour of state's rights—states should have more power.</td></tr>
<tr><td>4. Believed that the new government only protects the interests of wealthy merchants, not the commoners.</td></tr>
<tr><td>Proponents—Alexander Hamilton, John Jay and James Madison.</td><td>Proponents—Sam Adams, Patrick Henry, John Hancock and Thomas Jefferson.</td></tr>
</table>

11.6 Features of Federalism

It has been evident that there has been an enhanced interest worldwide in adopting federalism as the basic framework of government or adopting federal political institutions. There are a number of countries inhabiting a big share of the population exhibiting the fundamental characteristics of a federation. A notable characteristic of this significant expansion of federalism as a system across boundaries is that it has been adopted in varied forms incorporating distinct innovative mechanisms. Having said this, one should also not deny that there are certain common features of federal systems worldwide, making them federal, hence different from unions and confederations or any other type.

A fundamental feature of all federations is that there is simultaneous existence of two determining motives, one of uniting for certain purposes and other to retain autonomy for fulfilment of other purposes. Hence, federalism is about establishing harmony along with diversity. This phenomenon is evident in the structural design of federations, wherein powers are allocated between the federal government, responsible for common objectives, and regional governmental entities, tasked with expressing regional identity (Watts 2008, 83). Nevertheless, the manner and pattern of power distribution in federations have diverse characteristics due to their unique circumstances. Various factors, including geographical, historical, economic, ecological, security, linguistic, cultural, intellectual, demographic, and international elements, as well as their interconnectedness, significantly contribute to the strength of incentives for both unity and regional distinctiveness. Consequently, these factors influence the specific allocation of powers within different federations (Watts 2008, 84). It has also been understood that there is a direct relation between the degree of homogeneity and the nature of distribution of power, whereby a considerable degree of homogeneity leads to more powers apportioned to the federal government, and greater diversity leads to greater powers assigned to the regional governments. Another feature that has been a part of federations is a balance between dependence and interdependence of the federal government and the constituent units. The above statements however do not explain sufficiently, the significant features of federalism. The following paragraphs elaborately explain the distinguishing features of federal systems worldwide:

- **Separating governments:** In a Unitary state, there is only one government, that is, National or Federal government. In a federal state, there is simultaneous existence of not less than two levels of government exercising upon the same set of citizens. These tiers of government majorly being at the federal level are commonly called as federal/national/central government and at provincial level are commonly called as regional/state/constituent units. Hence, the central feature of federalism is the manner in which sovereignty is divided between two or more levels of government. While the federal government in federations is elected directly by the electorate of the entire federation, the provincial governments are elected by the electorates of the respective provinces. The federal government exercises legislative, executive and taxation authority over the entire federation, while the provincial government exercises them over the respective state.
- **Distribution of powers and responsibilities:** Federal constitutions are characterized by formal division of powers and responsibilities between the different levels of government. In the process of distributing powers, the constitution makers in various federations took note of certain dynamics; they had to see the mechanism in which different responsibilities were to be demarcated, what responsibilities had to be assigned to which level and how to give constitutional recognition to such division. A good example of the constitutional division of powers and responsibilities is of India, where the three lists of union, state and concurrent (seventh schedule) have incorporated the powers of both federal and the state levels of government.
- **Constitutionality:** A very important characteristic of federal systems is a written constitution, defining the competence and resources of the two orders of government, and not unilaterally amendable in its fundamental provisions by only one order of government (Saxena 2006, 33). As Hueglin mentions, federal systems require codified constitutions, that is, constitutions superior to the normal processes of politics and lawmaking and able to demarcate the relationship between two contending levels of government (Hueglin and Fenna 2006, 275). The role and status of the constitution vary from defining supreme law, to exercising judicial review through law courts, to enabling referendums, to safeguarding individual and collective rights, to evolving itself through formal amendments. Federalism involves a collaboration between different forces, forming the relationship of shared sovereignty, which is inherently constitutional. Federalism requires the utmost authority of a single document regulating the relationship between the federal government and its constituent units. The constitution in all federal systems is an authoritative text or document. A very significant feature of federal constitution is that it contains rules not just about the political system, but also about itself, that is, it also contains provision for its own amendment. Hence, federal constitutions are also flexible constitutions.
- **Constitutional interpretation:** Federal constitutions are not just about codification of rules and regulations, but they are also about interpretation of them. This necessitates establishment of an umpire to interpret and implement those rules. In most of the federations, this umpire has been the judicial umpire that is a final court providing the meaning of constitutional provisions in various contexts and situations. Some major examples are the supreme court of the United States, Canada, Australia, India, Malaysia, etc. Other alternatives to such final courts have been the constitutional courts or also some forms of electorate acting through a referendum. For example, Switzerland conducts referendum where the electorate plays the adjudicative role. The constitutional courts have been the adjudicators in Germany, Belgium and Spain.

- **Intergovernmental arrangements:** The inevitability within federations of overlaps and interdependence in the exercise of powers of governments has generally required the different orders of government to treat each other as partners (Watts 2008, 117). It is here that the necessity of constant deliberation, consultation and discussion towards forging cooperation and coordination between different levels of government has been considered essential. To realize this cooperation, within federations, structures, institutions and processes for intergovernmental relation have been considered relevant. Intergovernmental relations serve the dual purpose of interaction between the federal government and constituent units and also interaction between the units. Both purposes have been considered important within the intergovernmental mechanisms functioning within federations. Intergovernmental interaction is carried out at both formal and informal levels. A typical example of formal institution facilitating intergovernmental interaction is the Inter-State Council in India, which is a non-permanent constitutional body, established by a presidential order on the basis of provisions in Article 263. The council has been formed to cater discussions and deliberations amongst states over policies, issues of common interest and dispute. The various informal mechanisms to facilitate intergovernmental relation across federations have been ministerial-level meetings, ad-hoc meetings, department-level meetings, etc. A noteworthy feature, especially in parliamentary federations where first ministers and cabinet ministers responsible to their legislatures tend to predominate within both levels of government, is the prevalence of 'executive federalism', that is, the dominant role of governmental executives in intergovernmental relations (Watts 2008, 118). Such federal institutions have largely developed outside the constitution. It has been evident in federations like Canada, Australia, Germany and India. A good example is of First Minister's Conferences in Canada.

11.7 Michael Burgess' Five Bases of Comparison

The advent of behavioural revolution during the 1950s has led political scientists to identify similarities and differences between the different federal systems. Burgess defines federalism in a novel manner where he examines five principal bases acting as lenses which can help understand and explore similarities and dissimilarities between different federal systems. The five foundations encompass the framework of federations: the structural dimension, the sociological underpinnings, the political economy driving ideologies, the dynamics of political parties and party systems, and the realm of constitutional reform and judicial review (Burgess 2006, 136). The different bases can further be explained as follows:

- **Structure of federations:** Initially studies over federations have relied on their demarcation into the Westminster model, presidential model and a blend of both the types. The federations of Canada, Australia and India are the oft-cited examples of Westminster type, while the United States is the most prominent example of the republican-presidential type. Hybrid examples have been Germany and Switzerland. These sets of typologies very well explain the internal structures of federations. On the other hand, the study of distribution of powers in federations enhances the understanding about the federations. It should be noted that the division of powers and competences can be organized on a territorial and non-territorial basis (Burgess 2006, 136). The particular patterns of distribution of powers have differed with respect to the context of federations. This can be explained using the examples of the diversified societies of India and Malaysia. In India, the federal government has been provided an upper hand in terms of power distribution, which is evident from the constitutional provision with respect to emergency (Articles 352–360 of part xviii) and the emergency situation from 1975 to 1977. This specific distribution of power tilted towards the union government exemplifies India as a new federal model attuned to its typical needs. Similarly, in Malaysia, the constitutional allocation of power has been worked in favour of the desires and wants of the federal government. For example, Article 75 of the constitution establishes federal supremacy in the event of state law being inconsistent with federal law. This constitutional provision becomes significant when there is inconsistency between state and federal governments, whereby the federal government gets an opportunity to barge into state matters. These powers have been resorted to on numerous junctures to encounter multiple crises that have materialized in the life of the federations.

- **Sociological bases of federations:** The societal configuration and relations have deep imprints on the nature of the federal system. It has been an area that has been explored by scholars deeply. At the same time, the significance of societal cleavages for the federal systems has never been discounted. Social cleavages have been having varied degrees of political prominence in different federations at different points of time. Some of these cleavages have been based on nationalism, linguistic and ethnic diversities, territorial differences and religious identities. The crucial stability of the constitutional and political order hinges on the territorial distribution of the diverse social divisions within the federal state and the extent to which this distribution undergoes change. (Burgess 2006, 140). It is the nature of such cleavages and their distribution across the federation that impact their federalism. At the same time, territoriality interacts with the social cleavages that construct political identity. Territoriality incorporates social, economic, political and cultural-ideological forces, and an understanding of all such forces in the decision-making processes establishes that territoriality fluctuates across policy arenas. At the same time, there also has been the idea of non-territorial federalism, which has been characterized by personalized autonomy and authority that cut across territorial boundaries and national unity where no nationality or ethnic group could claim to a fixed territory. When it comes to social cleavages, religious distinctiveness and disparity has been very important as it has caused both violent and non-violent conflicts. Therefore, religious difference has been understood as a very important cleavage within federations. For example, India is multireligious in nature, with the majority group being Hindus and minorities composed of Muslims, Christians and all other religious groups. It creates a cultural pattern where religious disparities communicate with all other cleavages like regionalism, ethnicity, language and caste system. It can also be concluded that religion has a very important role to play in the public affairs of ethnically and linguistically diverse modern nation states. At the same time, since the authenticity of federations lies in recognizing and accommodating diversity, they are expected to include new territorial and non-territorial political agencies. The nature and degree of such incorporation and accommodation helps in differentiating the federations.
- **Political economy within federations:** The communication between politics and economics has a significant effect over the relationship between federal governments and constituent units within federations, which becomes important to understand and identify differences among federations. It therefore becomes crucial to study the nature of disbursement of financial power and resources within the federation. It has also been evident that capitalism is the economic base of federation, and federations therefore in turn are liberal democratic capitalist states based upon capitalist values, beliefs and goals (Burgess 2006, 145). Therefore, the manner in which federations are organized to fulfil this objective becomes another lens to differentiate federal systems. The political economy approach proves valuable as it delves deep into the core connection between economics and politics, allowing us to precisely examine how federalism and federation operate with the primary goal of optimizing economic prosperity and overall well-being in its widest scope. (Burgess 2006, 145). At the same time, the political economy within federation helps in further analysing necessary adjustments within the constitution, political processes and decision-making. In Canada, the interaction between the national economy and the federal system has produced both centralization and decentralization of economic and political power resources. While at some point, there has been the central government controlling the financial policy, in other instances, there has been more of provincial autonomy and role in terms of economic powers. At the same time, greater reciprocity between political economy and constitutional reforms and structural changes has been evident across federations. The constitutional reform agendas and changes have been proposing for newer mechanisms in terms of fiscal arrangements within federations. Therefore, what has been obvious in the functioning of federations is larger constitutional engagement in terms of disbursement of finances, raising of taxation powers and sharing of taxes between the federal governments and the constituent units while keeping in mind their expenditure responsibilities. Having said this, federations have also constituted constitutional and statutory organizations to realize the aforementioned commitment. For example, in India, the Finance Commission, which is a constitutional body, has been constituted under Article 280, while a statutory body named Planning Commission had been established to undertake planned development across the country. The Planning Commission got changed into National Institute for Transforming India (NITI)

Aayog in the year 2014. The changing nature of fiscal federalism from the era of planned development in the 1950s to liberalization, privatization and globalization (LPG) in the 1990s has impacted the centre-state relations. Fiscal federalism is, in various respects, shaped by the national political economy. It brings to the forefront several fundamental characteristics of federation that deserve more than a passing consideration. (Burgess 2006, 148).

- **Political parties, party systems and federations:** The instrumentality of political parties and party systems for comparing federal systems and federations has been confirmed by political scientists and scholars. The relevance and importance of parties and the organizational capacity of party systems within federations have been studied by them numerous times. Different studies have paid attention to the relationship of internal organizations of political parties and the layout of party system with the performance and functioning of federal systems. Political parties serve as vehicles and tools for organized vested interests, acting as conduits for specific values, beliefs, and aspirations. These interests and values evolve over time, enabling parties to direct or channelize them through the diverse structures and institutions of the state. (Burgess 2006, 150). Within federations, the parties and party systems can provide a conceptual lens which can help in analysing their impact over different sections of the political system. It has also been concluded that the capacity of regional governments to dissent and bargain with the central government has depended on the party configuration and interaction between parties at the two levels of government. For example, it has been suggested by the mainstream literature that there is a positive correlation between centralized party system and centralized federations and decentralized parties and decentralized federations. One can accomplish the task of weighing federalism within federations by analysing parties, their structure, their function and their evolution. Both the United States and Canada serve to be perfect examples of highly decentralized federal polities, with the former having the presidential form of government and the latter having parliamentary 'Westminster' form of government. The origin and evolution of these non-centralized parties has been referred to the organization of the constitutional set-up.
- **Constitutional reform and judicial review:** Constitutional reform has been an important and a difficult task within federations. Federations have been said to being made in a continuous manner, where a sequence of activities like bargains and accords comes into play. At the foundation of such bargains and agreements lie principles, morals and beliefs that are institutionalized within a codified constitution. At the same time, despite the federation being accomplished in an evolutionary manner accommodating varied communities and interactions amongst them, the idea of constitutional agreement being a historical consequence does not get minimized. Therefore, it is through constitutional modification that federations assimilate and conciliate communities and groups by bringing together the dual ideas of concurrence and heterogeneity. It is this established relevance of constitutional reform which is an unnerving task for federations; it has a lot to reciprocate to the federal society and vice versa. At the same time, changes in constitutions are evident and obvious as they respond to changing social, cultural, economic and political circumstances and conditions. Thus, constitutional reform in federations is firmly predicated on the legitimate assumption and expectation that basic federal values will be respected and protected (Burgess 2006, 157). Also, constitutional reform does not mean relinquishing the basic principles adopted at the time of formation of the federation, as they always serve to bedrock the changes established. It is through these requisite changes that the federations adapt to changing times, needs and demands. The study of constitutional reforms provides another important lens to distinguish federations and enhance understandings around federalism.

11.8 Varieties of Federal Governance: Case Studies

It is understood that federalism has been witnessing growing popularity in all these years. Worldwide it has been seen as an institutional instrument towards warding off separatism and fissures within states. It is in the light of this growing popularity of the concept that Rekha Saxena in her notable work *Varieties of Federal Governance* tries to draw the origin and development of the idea of federal governance in various countries of the world. She initiates the process by classifying the various well-known federal political systems into presidential federations, British Commonwealth parliamentary federations, non-commonwealth parliamentary federations and European parliamentary federations. This classification has been further enhanced by the addition of devolutionary systems and confederal supranational organizations of the EU.

The US American constitutions of 1777 and 1787 have been the first written constitutions presenting the modern idea of federalism. The powers of the government have been subjected to checks and balance through the dual mechanisms of vertical separation of power between the different levels of government and horizontal division of power between the three hands of the government, that is, legislature, executive and judiciary. The establishment of federalism in America was followed by its further adaptation in Switzerland in 1848. A major difference between the two was Switzerland unlike America comprises a collegial executive having seven presidents. It then spread to Germany, Canada, Australia, India, Malaysia, South Africa, etc., emerging as a global idea. The gradual spread of federalism saw modifications with experiments in new places and contexts.

Presidential federations comprise the federations of the United States, Switzerland, Latin American countries, post-communist Russia and African countries like Nigeria. All these federations maintain the separation of powers between three organs of government, with each having its constitutionally defined jurisdictions more or less independent of each other. The second classification of countries is grouped under parliamentary federations. The examples are Canada (1867), Australia (1901), India (1950) and Malaysia (1957). They functions like Westminster form of government where cabinet is accountable to the legislature, that is, parliament. One could find a 'fusion of powers' in parliamentary federations. Another model that has been discussed is of the parliamentary federations. The major examples are Canada (1867), Australia (1901), Germany (1949), India (1950) and Malaysia (1957). They all function with Westminster form of government with the cabinet being responsible to the legislature, that is, the parliament. On the contrary, in presidential federations, the executive is not responsible to the senate.

There is also a remarkable difference in the evolution of various federations in the world. In the formation of early federations like America and also the later ones like Germany and Australia, cultural diversity did not acquire the centre-stage responsibility, rather it was more a result of territorial diversity. Federalism was adopted to accommodate geographical and historical diversity in an attempt to unite various indigenous communities. On the other hand, in federations like Switzerland, Canada, India, Belgium, Malaysia, Spain and Russia, cultural federalism played a dominant role, that is, federalism was more to accommodate the cultural and linguistic diversity within society. Though territorial dimension was not absent in these federations, what became prominent was the cultural characteristics attached to regional and geographical variations. Protection and preservation of cultural identities became a necessary objective of all such federations.

The two significant typologies of 'legislative federalism' and 'executive federalism' have further been employed to differentiate various federations. The presidential federations of America, Switzerland, Russia, etc. have features of legislative federalism, for example, strong federal second chamber, separation of power, executive presidency and judicial review. On the other hand, parliamentary federations like Canada, Australia, India, Germany and South Africa are examples of 'executive federalism' where executive bodies like the cabinet play the most important role in conducting intergovernmental relations, division of powers and judicial restraint. However, there are exceptions, for example, India, which has recently developed and strengthened its judicial institutions through the mechanism of judicial review, and South Africa, which has incorporated legislative federalism.

Parliamentary federations could again be classified into commonwealth parliamentary federations and non-commonwealth parliamentary federations. Prominent examples of commonwealth parliamentary federations are Canada, Australia, India, Malaysia and South Africa. All these parliamentary federations had the common history of British colonialism with Queen being the head of the state. Canada and India have been said to be originally having very centralized structure but eventually moving in the direction of pure federalism from the quasi-federal features. At the same time, Australia has been seen adopting a few features of presidential federations like a directly elected federal second chamber and employing referendum for making constitutional amendments. It has also emulated some example from the American federal model, like residuary powers being handed over to the constituent units. The federations of Ethiopia and Nepal have been classified as non-commonwealth federations as both escaped the colonial rule. A separate category of European parliamentary federations could also be noticed with the major examples being Germany, Austria, Spain, Belgium, Portugal, etc., as they are characterized by distinctive and distinguished features and internal variations, like constitutional courts as the federal umpires and Kelsenian judicial review. The constitutional courts in Germany and Austria are solely responsible for adjudication of intergovernmental disputes.

The aforementioned typologies could be supplemented with two other systems, that is, devolutionary systems and supranational confederal integration. Devolutionary systems could be witnessed in those countries wherein the different states/provinces have been amalgamated into unions through royal acts or through colonial rules but eventually have witnessed demands for territorial autonomy and secession. Examples of this systems are Scotland and Sri Lanka. Scotland underwent the devolution of domestic powers through a referendum in 1997. On the other hand, post-independent Sri Lankan government followed Sinhalese linguistic majoritarianism and Buddhist religious majoritarianism, which escalated conflicts between the Sinhala community and Tamil community. It saw demands by Tamilians for greater autonomy which further aggravated into violent secessionist demands for a separate state. On the other hand, the EU could be identified as the best example of confederative organization at the supranational level. The EU is the economic and political union of 28 member states located in Europe. It is a political entity with decision-making involving intergovernmental mechanisms. These classifications of different federations signify that federalism cannot be identified and defined through a single system and the task of comparative federal theory is to identify such variegated models of federalism.

11.9 Variations in Distribution of Powers

The distribution of powers between the different levels of government is one of the main features of a federation. As Watts says, what distinguishes federation from other forms of federal systems such as decentralized unions or confederations is the constitutional guarantee of autonomy over a range of assigned functions for each order of government (Watts 2008, 83).

Different factors such as security, cultural, geographical, historical, international, concern to maintain a balance between independence and interdependence, have impacted on the distribution of powers. Three other main factors play a crucial role in affecting the distribution of powers in offered federations. The first factor is the period in which the constitutional distribution of powers occurred (Watts 2008, 85). For example, the United States and Switzerland distributed powers in equal terms, whereas newer federations like India have mentioned the clear-cut distribution of powers and functions in the form of three lists, that is, union, state and concurrent lists, demarcating function at different levels. The second factor is prevailed common law tradition (as in the United States, India and Malaysia), a mixed common law and civil law legal system (as in Canada and South Africa) or a civil law tradition (as in Switzerland, Brazil and Mexico) (Watts 2008, 85) impact the way in which the constitutional law is applied and interpreted. The third factor is the character of the federal legislative and executive institutions (Watts 2008, 85). The nature of institutions like presidential or parliamentary affects the manner in which the legislative powers will be distributed between different levels of the government.

With regard to the 'Exclusive legislative authority', allocation of powers to the federal government is limited in the case of the United States but extensive and detailed in case of India, Malaysia, Brazil, etc. The powers are constitutionally defined in these federations. A large number of concurrent jurisdiction is also present in these federations. The only exception is Canada where the areas of concurrent jurisdiction are clearly defined like agriculture, old-age pensions and immigration. In some federations like India, Brazil and Venezuela, one could clearly identify the constitutional powers allocated to the local governments too. There is something called 'shared authority' (Watts 2008, 88), which implies both orders of government have related powers and neither of the two could supersede each other. For example, both levels of government in Canada have got powers over environmental matters, and any policy on it requires the consent of both orders as neither of the two can have supremacy over each other.

Special Insights

Gender Budgeting

Gender budgeting is the process of integrating gender into almost all aspects of the decision-making process, especially those dealing with resource allocation and revenue generation. The objective remains to integrate gender perspectives into government budgeting at both national and subnational levels. Keeping a gender perspective in mind while making policies also involves not just resource division between the centre and states as per their responsibilities but also federal government interacting with the regional governments in terms of grants and aids. This has been given constitutional and extra-constitutional status in federations. An often-cited example is of the Finance Commission in India, which is a constitutional body formed under Article 280.

At the same time, with respect to gender budgeting, there have been examples of how federations have engaged themselves into multiple novel practices. For example, in Canada, gender analysis has been a process where policies at all stages, be it in their initial formative stage or when they have been implemented, undergo evaluation to estimate their gender inclusivity and their understanding of gender differences. At the same time, in Canada, there has been ample stress on the importance of gender disaggregated data. On the other hand, since in Switzerland, federal, cantonal and local levels all have considerable autonomy in public finance, gender budgeting has been important at all levels. In India, the launch of the Gender Budget Statement in the union budget of 2004–2005 was the first step in this direction, followed by the formation of Gender Budgeting Cells (GBCs) in all departments. Since then, we have made efforts in bringing gender-specific schemes. However, we need to reform ourselves in terms of evaluation of the programmes and ensure greater transparency and accountability to remove gender injustices.

11.10 Distribution of Finances

Parliamentary systems like Canada, Australia, Germany, India and South Africa follow the Westminster model of government. They have a few common elements in terms of federal and fiscal arrangements but not in entirety. They also have peculiarity in their respective set-ups owing to their varied contexts.

The Canadian federal system represents the textbook best-practice system of fiscal federalism, as provincial and municipal governments share with the federal government unrestricted access to all the major tax sources and are responsible for raising a high proportion of their own revenues (Boadway 2007, 99). The Canadian model of fiscal federalism can very well be defined as a balanced federalism. Constitution has clearly divided powers between both levels of government. The federal government is free to utilize any form of taxation, and at the same time, it is free to spend, borrow and lend as it finds suitable. A notable feature of Canadian fiscal federalism is that the residual power rests with the provinces. The main source of taxation is available to both orders of government so as to enhance their revenue-raising capacity. The expenditure responsibilities are divided between both types of governments; however, expenditure programmes that have some effects beyond the respective provincial boundary are shared responsibilities. In Canada, the federal government raises revenue through three tax bases, namely personal income taxation, sales taxation and payroll taxation.

When we talk about the expenditure responsibilities in Australia, the constitutional arrangement clearly demarcates expenditure responsibilities between the federal and state governments. In practice, there is a difference due to the larger intervention of the federal government in key areas falling under the state government. As per the constitution, each state government has freedom to decide its economic policy within its jurisdiction. And henceforth, the federal and state governments have individual responsibility to make their revenue and expenditure decisions, with their budgets being decided independently. However, there is a heavy reliance of the states on transfers from the federal government. A distinctive feature of revenue raising assignments in Australia is that most taxes are exclusively available to one tier of government with minimal sharing of tax bases. The federal government has ultimate authority over all growth taxes and therefore a predominant position in the financing of public services (Braun 2010, 178). There is no tax piggybacking (Morris 2007, 53). In Australia, the federal government collects all federal taxes including value-added tax (VAT) whose revenues are raised for the states (Anderson 2010, 29). There are no formal limitations for the federal government to use its tax revenues and offer contracts to member states with conditions attached (Erk and Swenden 2010, 178). Only the goods and services tax (GST) which was introduced in 1999 remains the federal tax not at the whimsies of the federal government and constitutes half of transfers to provincial governments. There is evident vertical fiscal imbalance between the orders of government due to some mismatch between their revenue-generating capacity and expenditure responsibilities. It is henceforth required to maintain a mechanism of transfer of funds from federal government to the states. Transfers in Australia, both general purpose and specific purpose, are tied to particular objectives. With the introduction of GST, all revenues collected under it are transferred to states and territories in the form of untied grants within horizontal fiscal equalization principles. The federal government makes transfers to state in specific arenas called Specific Purpose Payments (SPPs), with an intent to implement national priorities.

German federation is another significant illustration of parliamentary federation. German fiscal federalism is characterized by high cooperation and centralization. The German constitution called the Grundgesetz established two orders of government, that is, the federal and the lander/state governments. The Grundgesetz guarantees existence of the lander and provides them with a strong constitutional position. The Grundgesetz establishes Germany as a federation with strong states and local jurisdictions (Feld and Von Hagen 2007, 128). A half of federal laws requires the approval of both houses of parliament and hence Bundesrat which represents the landers. Each level of government has been constitutionally allotted fiscal powers. Tax order in Germany is based on tax sharing. Revenues generated are fixed to be shared in an equal manner between the federal government and the provincial governments. The Grundgesetz enlists the exclusive responsibilities of both the federal government and subnational government; however, it is through the concurrent power that the federal government takes control of many other responsibilities. There is a unique relationship between both the governments, where the federal government cannot take decisions without the lander, and the lander being not completely independent to carry on with their own policies. Both governments are highly interdependent. This institutional arrangement has led to a 'Spaghetti Bowl' of internal relations (Feld and Von Hagen 2007, 133). None of the governments can make alterations to their respective tax revenues without consent of the other. Hence, lander governments become very important. When a mismatch between spending behaviour and revenue income occurs, the member states cannot overcome this problem by a simple redistribution of tax shares as they cannot raise taxes individually because they lack tax sovereignty and flexibility (Erk and Swenden 2010, 175). They are left with alternatives like borrowing, equalization payments and vertical transfers. On the spending side, responsibilities are shared between the governments, and only a small number is undertaken exclusively by any particular government. However, almost half of the spending responsibilities are undertaken by the federal government. The major taxes, namely income tax and VAT, are joint taxes as the revenue is being shared not just between the federal and provincial governments but also between the local jurisdiction. Thus, German fiscal federalism is about joint taxation, and those joint rights are constitutionally guaranteed (Hueglin and Fenna 2006, 326). Hence, the states' own source revenue does not match to their expenditure responsibilities. Also, there is consistency in the tax base and tax rate across the landers, what we call as tax harmonization. Germany also follows a systematic variant of fiscal equalization in a three-step manner. Initially, after distributing revenues from the joint taxes as per a formula, unconditional grants are provided as part of fiscal equalization policy, which is again formula based. It is strongly egalitarian and lifts the fiscal capacity of all the below-average states. After that the federal government makes conditional vertical transfers. The unconditional grants are larger than the conditional grants. Overall, we can conclude that the German financial constitution, though predominantly based on joint taxes, gives the lander a strong bargaining position by requiring the Bundesrat consent to most of the relevant legislation (Saxena 2006, 316).

Special Insights

Capturing the Intersectionality of Ethnicity, Language, Race and Religion in Federal Discourse

Classic models of federalism like the United States and Germany have mainly emphasized on the division of powers between the two levels of government, written constitution, sources of revenue, independent judiciary, and so on. These features have served well in those countries with a core national identity like that of the United States and Germany. These federations have never bothered to take into account the various dimensions of language, religion, race and gender in the discourse of federalism. Postcolonial states like India, Sri Lanka and Pakistan have faced surmounting challenge to the national unity because of the diversity of languages. The competition between different languages to prove their superiority became one of the challenges for these federal countries. The success of these states in managing the linguistic diversities lies in using federalism as a means to accommodate these diversities as well as good political management by coming up with social, political and economic policies to ensure group rights are guaranteed in our constitution. For example, Official Language Act (1963) lays down that English should be used as a link language between the union and non-Hindi states, and regions can have one or more official languages. Article. 350 (b) also provides for the appointment of an officer for linguistic minorities to protect their constitutional rights.

The issue of racial and ethnic variations has been very important for the discussions on federalism. If federalism is about the division of power amongst different levels of the government, it is very much about the representation and inclusion of people belonging to diverse backgrounds. The question of race and ethnicity has been addressed by the federations in varying degrees and manners. When we talk about the oldest example of the United States, the grave concern of racial inequality still can be located in the questions of federalism. The federal structures and processes have not proven very efficient when it is about welfare policy outcomes for the African-Americans.

Another example is of Canada. Apart from the English- and French-speaking people, Canada comprises 'native' people, for example, the status Indians (who live on Indian reserves), the Metis and non-status Indians (who live off reserves) and the Inuit or Eskimos. There is evidence of these groups not being well assimilated into Canadian life and structures. There remains the issue of reconciliation of their interests within the federal regime.

On the other hand, federalism has served to solve the questions of several multi-ethnic countries of Asia and Africa. Though there have been failed examples, the role of federalism in balancing the ethnic variations in some of these countries like Malaysia, Nigeria and India can never be discounted. In India, the structures and processes of federalism have catered to the coexistence of ethnically and linguistically diverse communities. However, there still remains other issues of development being very important in such federations.

The issue of religion becomes another important thing in the discussions of federalism. Since the older federations of America, Switzerland, Canada and Australia never were multi-religious in nature, their federal constitutions never really paid much attention to religious questions. On the other hand, the newer ones like India and Malaysia, with India being the best example, had to deal with the multireligious fabric of the country. The Indian constitution incorporated the ideals of secularism, justice, equality, liberty and fraternity, which included the freedom to practice and propagate any religion.

11.11 Conclusion

Federalism as a concept was born to serve the economic and military purposes. It was aimed at bringing together the autonomous constituents or units that were not capable of defending their economic and military interests alone. Notable examples of this have been United States and Switzerland. The political success of the idea of federalism led to the adoption of the federal system of government by a number of countries in the 20th century because of its ability to encompass complexities and voices of assertion and ascriptive identities arising from ethnic diversity, cultural plurality, territoriality, cleavage politics, etc. But the challenges have increased in the era of globalization due to the pressure for 'managing pluralism'. Hence, the EU appears to be a more pragmatic framework to accommodate the new, diverse and dissenting identities existing in different federal political systems rather than more rigid frameworks like that of the United States. In the present times, non-institutional instruments like interest groups, non-governmental organizations, other civil society associations, social movements and campaigns supplement the practical necessities of the federal dynamics in substantial ways. Multi-tier levels of governments in a federation can better ensure participatory democracy. However, ensuring the representations of marginalized and excluded groups specifically from rural remote cities will remain a challenging task in coming times. The need for coordination among different levels of government is bound to increase. Just like any other set of institutions and procedures, federalism is only as good as the intentions and abilities of those putting it to use (Hueglin and Fenna 2006, 357).

Keywords

Comparative federalism
Confederation
Cooperative federalism
Federalism
Federation
Multilevel governance
Self-rule

Review Questions

1. What do you mean by federalism as a theory and practice? Describe its nature and meaning.
2. Discuss the various bases of federations by Michael Burgess.
3. Differentiate between federation and federalism. What are the different models of federations? Explain any one model.
4. Do you think that federalism as a concept could be understood better in a comparative perspective? Give the reasons to substantiate your argument.
5. Is federalism the wave of the future? Why have various states adopted federalism (e.g., Belgium, Spain and Mexico)?

References

Anderson, George. 2010. *Fiscal Federalism: A Comparative Introduction*. New York: Oxford University Press.

Basu, Durga Das. 1987. *Comparative Federalism*. New Delhi: Prentice hall of India.

Braun, Dietmar. 2010. Making Fiscal Federalism Self-enforcing: Germany, Australia and Switzerland Compared, in *New Direction in Federalism Studies*, edited by Jan Erk and Wilfried Swenden. London, New York: Routledge.

Boadway, Robin. 2007. Canada, in *The Practice of Fiscal Federalism: Comparative Perspectives*, edited by Anwar Shah. London: McGill-Queen's University Press.

Burgess, Michael. 2006. *Comparative Federalism: Theory and Practice*. London, New York: Routledge.

Burner, Elliot. 2017. *Federalism*. Stockholm: International Institute for Democracy and Electoral Assistance.

Feld, Lars P., and Jurgen Von Hagen. 2007. Federal Republic of Germany, in *The Practice of Fiscal Federalism: Comparative Perspectives*, edited by Anwar Shah. London: McGill Queen's University Press.

Francesco, Pallermo, and Karl Kossler. 2017. *Comparative Federalism: Constitutional Arrangements and Case Laws*. Oregon: Hart Publishing.

Hueglin, Thomas O., and Alan Fenna. 2006. *Comparative Federalism: A Systematic Inquiry*. Canada: Broadview Press.

King, Preston. 1982. *Federalism and Federation*. London: Croom Helm.

Livingston, William S. 1952. A Note on the Nature of Federalism. *Political Science Quarterly* 67: 81–95.

Morris, Allan. 2007. Common Wealth of Australia, in *The Practice of Fiscal Federalism*, edited by Anwar Shah. London: McGill-Queen's University Press.

Pallermo, Francesco, and Karl Kossler. 2017. *Comparative Federalism: Constitutional Arrangements and Case Laws*. Oregon: Hart Publishing.

Saxena, Rekha. 2006. *Situating Federalism: Mechanisms of Intergovernmental Relations in Canada and India*. New Delhi: Manohar Publishers.

Saxena, Rekha, eds. 2011. *Varieties of Federal Governance*. New Delhi: Cambridge University Press.

Shah, Anwar. 2007.Introduction: Principles of Fiscal Federalism. In *The Practice of Fiscal Federalism: Comparative Perspectives*, edited by Anwar Shah. London: McGill-Queen's University Press.

Steytler, Nico. 2005. Republic of South Africa. In *Constitutional Origins, Structure and Change in Federal Countries*, edited by John Kincaid and G. Alan Tarr. Canada: McGill University Press.

Tarr, G. Alan. 2005. United States of America, in *Constitutional Origins, Structure, and change in Federal countries,* edited by John Kincaid and G. Alan Tarr. London: McGill-Queen's University Press.

Watts, Ronald L. 2008. *Comparing Federal System*. London: McGrill-Queen's University Press.

CHAPTER 12

Nation State: Historical Evolution in Western Europe and Postcolonial Context

Chetna Sharma

Reader's Guide

We live in states; the state plays an important role in our lives, it collects taxes, provides education, security and welfare and promotes economic growth. Virtually anything can be done by the state. State entails defined territory, population, government and sovereignty. This chapter traces the historical evolution of modern state, its present form and some significant developments in the globalized world that has initiated a debate on its future.

12.1 Introduction

Every part of earth is divided into states, so much so that not just land but also the air space above it as well as its coastal waters are under the jurisdiction of states. At the same time, this constellation of states changes when new borders are drawn and new states emerge on the world map. The current ambitions in Scotland and Catalonia and the process of federalization in Belgium or secession in some others may change the numbers of states from present 195 to more or maybe less. The changing world map tells us that the process of state-building is complex and volatile. However, how do we recognize a state? What are its core features? A state entails a defined territory, people, government and sovereignty. Since people live together in a state, it is important that they must have something in common, for example, language, religion, common history and culture. Every state uses symbolism like the national anthem, a flag, a national currency and national holidays to instil a sense of political belongingness and membership in its citizens. However, in contemporary times, all these categories of shared belonging are deeply contested, for example, minorities may not speak the dominant language and may not belong to the dominant religion or culture. Moreover, all individuals living in a state may not be recognized as citizens of that state—they could be migrants (legal/illegal), refugees or asylum seekers. We will engage with these debates in the rest of the chapter, but to begin, we could say that it is an organization that makes and administers rules for a territorial, that is, defined area, binding for people residing in it.

12.2 Origin of State: A Brief History

Human history shows that there have been times when the state as we know it today, controlling all important aspects of our life, did not exist. However, to maintain social order and control, people use to live in a group formed on the basis of clan, kinship or tribe. The well-documented accounts from the Greek classics such as Plato's *Republic* and Aristotle's *Politics* provide us detailed discussion on the different kinds of political system prevalent in Greek city states. The different types of states existing in those times were monarchy, aristocracy, polity, oligarchy, democracy and tyranny. The decline of city states gave way to emergence of new empires in succeeding times. Hence, we see the making of the Roman Empire where consolidation of the administration and governance appears apparent. With the emergence of feudal economy based on the relationship between lord and serf, the nature of political rule changed. The medieval history is characterized by the tripartite struggle for power and authority among the king, feudal lords and church where monarch always made an attempt to establish its superiority vis-à-vis other parallel authorities. Power diffusion played itself in a manner where lords used their economic and military power and church used their religious authority to establish papacy. The conflict between church and monarch on the boundaries between spiritual and secular continued from 12th century to the reformation. With the advent of renaissance and new developments in the area of science in the 15th and 16th centuries, economic transformation in the form of industrialization and change in nature of trade and war led to a crisis in feudalism and its gradual decline. This strengthened unified territorial rule with power under sovereign head that consolidated the prevalent regimes into absolute monarchy.

The modern state established a centralized supreme authority and rightful claim to obedience from its subjects. The notion of state power rooted in law led to establishment of Constitutional government based on depersonalized governance. This narration captures the history of state formation merely of western hemisphere. States originated in many different ways in different places. There was never a linear pathway of state-building, but three general patterns could be captured in trajectory of state formation.

The first pattern is represented by states mostly in medieval monarchies like Britain and France that arose on the basis of the gradual transformation of existing political units. It was a gradual process that took centuries. In Europe, the final triumph of state can be signalled with the Treaty of Westphalia. It also settled the borders of many states. The second pattern predominant in the 19th century comes from those states that mainly emerged with unification of different dispersed political units, for example, Germany and Italy. The third pattern of states formation is reflected by those states that emerged with the breakup of empires and heterogeneous states. After the First World War, Ottoman and Austro-Hungarian Empires disintegrated. After the Second World War, many new territories gained statehood in Asia and Africa.

Special Insights

Thoughts to Ponder

There are various kinds of states ranging from the United States (one of the largest states) to Montenegro (one of the smallest states). However, nearly all these 193 states share specific features that put them into the box with a label 'State'.

Some supranational organizations may look like state in some respect but they are not, for example, the European Union.

- Why are there disputes regarding the boundaries of the state and their origin?
- Did states exist in Africa or Asia before colonization? If not, then what kind of political organization did they have, and if yes, why new borders were drawn?

A further reading of the chapter would help us to solve the matrix and answer some of these questions.

12.3 State Formation and Nation-Building

According to Flora et al. (1999), the formation of modern states proceeded in several phases. The first phase was the formation of state institutions, for example, an army, a bureaucracy and its gradual consolidation. While police and courts were established to provide internal order, armed forces were needed for external security. Revenue and taxes provided monetary support for this system. This phase of state-building was defined as penetration. The second phase of nation-building was referred to as standardization that involved connecting the people and inculcating a shared sense of belonging. Common language, religion, education, historical heritage and culture were used as medium in this process. In the process, national myths about shared experiences and historical destinies were created, and education system became one of the means to spread them. The third phase referred to as mass democracies helped in establishing democratic states with larger participation of population. Later, welfare state characterized by redistribution and equality of opportunity was created particularly in north-western Europe after the Second World War (Newton and Van Deth 2011, 24–26). These phases help us to understand and develop comparative perspective on the process of state- and nation-building. However, Rokkan himself mentions that this process was not uniform even within Europe. In some cases, it was interrupted by revolution, and in some others, war or foreign occupation (as for Germany) changed the whole process resulting in phases being overlapped or coincided. Thus, while this was the story of one part of the world the other part also saw the rise of Fascist State, Mussolini in Italy, Hitler in Germany, Franco in Spain, Salazar in Portugal and communist State in Russia. The last phase defined by Rokkan as welfare state in Europe also changed by the late 1970s. From being an impartial referee, it became an interventionist state responsible for providing welfare and interfering in different aspects of life. Welfare benefits led to the problem of overload; thus, by the mid-1970s, the same interventionist state was criticized for too much bureaucratic interference and inefficiency, thus initiating debate on roll back the state. Policy change in different parts of the world with the rise of globalization and liberalization very soon gave birth to the idea of decline of state. This small summary of state and nation-building raises an important question: Why did the nation state flourish across the world reaching to a number of nearly 200? To understand the whole trajectory and debates, let's begin with how the modern nation state emerged.

12.4 Idea of Nation

In the different phases of its history, nation was interpreted as bearing different meanings in different contexts such as group of foreigners, a community of opinion, an elite, a sovereign people and a unique people. With the French Revolution, nation as a community of citizens and political entity emerged. Nation has thus become at once a cultural entity (the original connotation of the term) as well as a political entity in Europe.

12.4.1 Are Nation and State Intertwined?

The nation and the state are not synonymous to each other yet; when we consider the elements they share or the way they are defined, it appears that since modern times, nation and state are strongly tangled. Most of the times, nation is referred in the connection to 'nation state'. Nation emphasizes the (collective) subjectivity of the community; it is about identity, shared history, language and culture. The state is objective; it concerns people, territory and institutions. However, if we cannot speak about nation and state as distinct entities, how can we understand their mutual relation? Also, if they really are intertwined, how can we understand the linkages in both directions? To understand this, let us first discuss the questions in the next section.

12.4.2 Does the State Presuppose a Nation?

To create legitimate structure of authority when people voluntarily accept laws and policies and pay their taxes inculcating an idea of belonging is important. However, the related question is whether in a multicultural and globalized world with extensive migration it is important to share nationhood. If the state is able to provide security, justice and social services, wouldn't that be enough to build the necessary loyalty. Examples from contemporary world suggest migration and diversity do not make nationhood obsolete; they make belonging more complex and challenging. For the stability, it is important for a nation state to be inclusive. The symbols of identification should be the result of a deliberative process of all who live in and are its member.

12.4.3 Does the Nation Presuppose a State?

The inquisitive minds of our readers would raise another question with reference to the discussion in the previous part of this chapter. Can we imagine a nation to exist without the state? The scholars who adhere to a more primordial perspective on the nation claim that the nation is a reality apart from the existence of the state. The legitimacy of a nation lies in a shared identity of its people, distinct from other groups. With reference to shared identity, Adrian Hasting gives the example of British identity that developed gradually from the 12th century onwards, long before the state in its present form came into existence.

12.4.4 Nation State

A type of state that connects the political entity to the cultural entity and derives its political legitimacy to rule as a sovereign is a nation state. The term 'nation state' implies that the nation and state concur in a manner that state prefers to adopt and endorse a specific cultural group in order to have a stable system. The model of the nation state infers that people of state establish a nation. They were united by shared culture, history, language and common descent, and whenever shared features were absent, the nation-state often tried to produce it. However, this understanding raises many questions because concepts are contested with reference to different contexts. For example, if in Europe nations are seen as essentially cultural construct, in ex-colonies nations are viewed as political units.

Postcolonial states encapsulate several nations, and the process of state formation is not yet complete. Stability of state is often a challenging task largely because of their multinational composition. Further, identity assertions based on religion, language, region, tribe, etc., are viewed as 'communal', 'parochial' and even 'anti-national'. African nation states emerged through the incorporation of many tribes with multiple differences. While race is the most prominent feature, even this condition is not widespread in nation formation as exemplified in the case of multi-racial state South Africa. In South Asia, virtually every state is multireligious and multilingual. Similarly, in Latin America, the population is multiracial, multilingual, multireligious, or all of these. In North America and Australia, national population was created largely by migrants from Europe, and differences were so specific that they not just spoke diverse languages but also followed different Christian denominations. This suggests that the meaning of the term nation and the experience of the national population vary vastly across the continents. In past many years, states from Western Europe, which were conceived as culturally homogeneous, gradually became culturally heterogeneous because of migration. This signifies the importance of context and history that give different connotations to concepts. The 'people' of the United States did not have a pre-existent 'nation' (in the European sense) to latch on to their nationalism and yet American nationalism led to the formation of a state. On the other hand, 'nations' may not always clamour for their sovereign states as borne out by the experience of India (Oommen 2002–2003, 263).

Neera Chandhoke argues that there is something vexatious about the construction of the hyphen between the nation and the state. The idea that every nation should have its own state, with reference to European experience is problematic in other contexts. Tracing history, it appears probably it is the state that demands a nation. If we hyphenate the nation with the state, the problem of political allegiance to the state is solved and establishing effective political institutions becomes possible. The formulation proved so attractive that the hyphen, which connects the conceptual worlds of the nation and the state (the nation state), came to rule politics across the world (Chandhoke 2002–2003, 83).

T.K. Oommen discusses different situations represented by 'nation-states'. It could be one nation, one state, citing this as an ideal Japan is referred as an example. There is a possibility of different nations forming state for geopolitical reasons, for example, Switzerland. Nation states are also formed when one nation is divided into two; Germany until 1990 is an important case. Another possibility with reference to history is when part of a nation is established into one sovereign state, for example, Bangladesh or the Republic of Ireland. Indian Punjab and Pakistan

Punjab are excellent examples to suggest how a nation may be divided between two sovereign states. Number of nations could also constitute a state, for example, India, the United Kingdom and the Soviet Union before the break up. A set of migrants drawn from a multiplicity of nations could also constitute a state, for example, the United States (Oommen 2002–2003, 264).

This discussion makes it clear that the meaning and content of nation and state have transformed substantially over time. The content of the concept of nation was essentially cultural, and it compressed a variety of attributes. However, when nations started to establish themselves as states, following the maxim 'one-nation, one state' primarily in Western Europe, the hyphenated term nation state came into trend. As argued by T.K. Oommen, it is often forgotten that the nation state implies a process, and it is possible and historically true that the process can even be reversed. Not only can a nation be constituted into a state, a state can dismantle and destroy nations (Oommen 2002–2003, 265).

12.5 Approaches to Understand Nation State

As suggested by most of the scholars, the range of explanations for the formation of nations is wide and different perspectives are debated.

12.5.1 Primordialist

The primordialist approach to study nation is based on the belief that nations have existed since time immemorial having overwhelming and affective significance for the members (Geertz 1973; Shils 1957; Van den Berghe 1978, 1979, 1995). The important representative of the primordial approach Anthony D. Smith argues that the roots of the idea of nation and identity can be traced even before the creation of modern nation state. Anthony Smith has proposed a synthesis between what he calls 'gastronomy' and 'geology' (Smith 1998, 3–23), the instrumentalist and the archaeological theories of nationalism. Rejecting theories that either trace nation state as something that has evolved or something that was invented, he proposes in some situations nationalists act as archaeologists while in some others as manipulators. They uncover the past and then use it freely (Ben-Israel 2011, 67). However, this explanation fails to explain how and why ethnic and nationalist expressions and their intensity varied over times.

12.5.2 Perennialism

Scholars supporting perennialism argue that the idea of nationalism has been with us for many centuries, and nations existed as a historical reality. They support the historical antiquity of the nation, and to explain it further, two positions have emerged. Continuous perennialism argues some nations have continuous history, while recurrent perennialism supports the argument that there was a change in nations over time. They trace the origin of nation through history but do not consider it as natural or organic.

12.5.3 Modernism

Modernists believe that nations are the result of some phenomena defined as modern. The idea of common memory, language and claim over a homeland are associated with some political and economic changes obtained in the modern times. Thus, it would mean that nation has emerged recently and its past goes back to just one or two century. It also specifies that it is a creation of some completely new developments related with modern period.

It is referred to as a modern phenomenon because it is a product of modern processes like capitalism, industrialism and so on. Starting with capitalism, Marxists like Eric J.F. Hobsbawm argued nationalism served as a bourgeois ideology by uniting the dominant classes and the masses in a community which was portrayed to be egalitarian. Hobsbawm recognizes two prime senses of nation in the modern period—first, with reference to citizenship, it emphasizes on common political participation and, with reference to ethnicity, it emphasizes on common bond based on shared culture, identity, history and language. According to Hobsbawm, to get the support of masses and serve the interests of elites, 'invented traditions' are used as a mechanism. However, it needs to be argued with reference to 'invented tradition' that a completely new tradition would not work to mobilize people. Existence of some cultural resources and relations is a prerequisite for ethnic forces to work upon.

According to Gellner (1983), the origin of nation state could be traced with changes in social and economic systems from agrarian to industrial. Industrial society needs standardized and homogenized culture for better communication and that need is fulfilled by the education system that also inculcates common language. Political boundaries are reorganized along cultural lines, and nation states are formed. Nationalism unites the population because the process of industrialization, urbanization and capitalism requires advanced forms of communication for which uniform language is required. Greater mobility of people and urbanization bring in sociodemographic changes, and in this process, a common language generates greater cultural identification. This could be represented as follows:

industrialization → nationalism → nation

Gellner's theory could be criticized for being explicitly instrumentalist and functionalist in orientation, that is, Gellner looks at nationalism as being functional for modernization (Benedict Anderson 1991, 207). It seems without a shared culture, modernization would not be effective. It explains the causes of a phenomenon in terms of the needs it serves. This explanation has no role for passions and emotions that are also associated with nationalism. Third, as some would argue, Gellner is wrong on his thesis that nationalism is a product of industrialization; contrarily, nationalism existed before industrialization (see Armstrong 1982; Smith 1986). We could cite numerous examples where industrialization has happened without being complemented by nationalism. There are also societies where nationalism occurred without industrialization. With reference to this, Nicos Mouzelis (1998, 158) discusses proto-industrialization of several regions in Western Europe where industrialization happened without being accompanied by nationalism. The Balkans and Latin America in the 19th century could be cited as cases where nationalism happened without industrialization. Scholars such as M. Mann and Anthony Giddens have argued that nationalism has not occurred because of the development of markets and industry; rather it was because of the development of the state and its institutions such as military and bureaucracy and advanced forms of tax structure which resulted in the destruction of political, economic and cultural localism (Kumar 2010, 392–406).

Political modernization theories of Tilly (1994), Mann (1995) and Hechter (2000) shift our attention to the system of governance. Governmental control became more effective and efficient with war in Europe during the 16th and 17th centuries. State elites in order to legitimize their rule used their position and circumstances to homogenize the population over the course of the 19th century (Hechter 2000; Tilly 1994). The political variety of modernism argues that nations and nationalism emerge out of the changing dynamics of the relations between the state and society (Kumar 2010, 395).

The constructivist school of researchers contend that the nation is a construct, built and altered by people to define the identity of a political community in ever-changing circumstances. The constructivist approach discusses importance of historic and legendary myths and heroes serving as a foundation for identity. The constructivist position is probably best reflected in Benedict Anderson's definition of the nation as 'an imagined political community'. For Anderson, national consciousness is created among a community of people, connected to each other without necessarily knowing each other.

12.5.4 Cultural and Political Nation

Another way to comprehend nation could be seen in terms of cultural and political nations. This kind of understanding was given by German historian Friedrich Meinecke. Cultural nations are seen to be characterized by an inherited ethnic identity shaped by high level of ethnic homogeneity; for them, the membership of community is not dependent on political adherences or civic loyalties. Meinecke (2015) gives the examples of the Greeks, Russians and Germans as cultural nations. We could say that this understanding overlaps with the primordialist approach to understand nation which have been discussed in the preceding paragraphs. The understanding of political nations intersects with those of the modernist school of thought, which we have also discussed before. Political nations could be understood as those which are formed primarily by shared citizenship, irrespective of cultural, ethnic and other loyalties.

12.5.5 Civic and Ethnic Dimension

The exclusively civic definition of the nation is associated with Ernest Renan's argument, founded upon the will of people, that the nation is a sovereign state. According to this position, nation is a free association of individuals that form a state and the state creates the nation. The ethnic definition is associated with Johann Herder. German nationalism and its emphasis that to belong to the same ethnic nation, one must share the same language, history and culture and or believe that they share the same ancestry is the perfect example. However, both the views are related with a certain theoretical monism. The central idea of both the approaches is the nation must be either civic or ethnic, thus mutually excluding each other. Actually, the traditional ethnic and civic views of the nation are just like two sides of the same coin, because both give rise to nationalisms which favour the nation state as the only adequate political arrangement (Seymour 1999, 414).

12.5.6 World Polity Theory

According to Meyer (1997), neither nationalism nor nations are a necessary condition for nation states to emerge. Emphasizing external factors, Meyer's diffusion theory traces the origin of nation state as part of a world culture that emerged over the past 200 years. Nationalism was adopted as the most legitimate form of statehood by state elites because of pressures operating at world level. The principal argument of this theory is that, with increasing connections and exposure of a state to global culture, elites got attracted to adopt world cultural patterns and create a nation state. Second, the probability of a change to the nation state also increases with the adoption of nation state by more and more regions of the world.

12.5.7 Postcolonial Perspective

Partha Chatterjee (1993) draws a distinction between nationalism as a political movement, which contests the colonial state, and nationalism as a cultural construct, which empowers the colonized to postulate their difference and autonomy. He argues anti-colonial nationalism makes an effort to create its own sphere of sovereignty within colonial society. His analysis is based on division between material and spiritual world. The material world constituted of the economy, statecraft, science and technology and a spiritual world of culture, religion, customs and family. While the hegemony of the West is accepted in the material domain, the spiritual world is protected and defended. Ernest Renan (1992) in his essay 'What is a Nation?' had stressed a similar position that 'a nation is a soul, a spiritual principle'. The communities that are imagined by anti-colonial nationalism often invoke a shared past or a cultural essence that is regarded as synonymous with a religious or racial identity. It is interesting that when Nehru wrote his book on India, he called it 'The Discovery of India', for he was conscious of the fact that he was making a discovery, and not an invention, in the sense of an intellectual or imaginative construction (Aikant 2006, 170). We can see how this projection perpetrates the ideology of a dominant common world where the West leads and the East follows. This neat distinction between the spiritual and the material, in effect, does not exist. Even a cursory glance at India's historical past will reveal that a holistic approach has characterized its 'world-view in which the tenets of dharma, artha, kama and moksha are interwoven' (Aikant 2006, 169–70).

Approaches discussed in the preceding pages trace the reasons for emergence of nation state emphasizing different positions of scholars. Significantly, almost all trace modern nation state from Europe. Certain significant developments accelerated the process beginning with treaty of Westphalia.

Special Insights

The French and American revolutions of the late-18th century gave birth to the ideal of the modern nation state. What emerged gradually was the idea of an independent state with a written constitution, ruled in the name of a nation of equal citizens.

12.6 Legacy of Treaty of Westphalia

The origin of a modern nation state is traced in Europe, and the Treaty of Westphalia is referred as the landmark. The Thirty Years' War in the Holy Roman Empire and the Eighty Years' War between Spain and the Dutch Republic were the major triggers behind signing the Peace of Westphalia: The Thirty Years' War was fought almost all over central Europe from 1618 to 1648. It was also a war between Protestants and Catholics. Many nations of Europe, big and small, including German states, the Austrian Empire, Sweden, France and Spain, took part in it. The triggering factor for war was an attempt of Roman Emperor, Ferdinand II, to impose Roman Catholicism on its peoples. Another important development was the war referred to as The Eighty Years' War or Dutch War of Independence (1568–1648). It was a revolt of the 17 provinces against the political and religious supremacy of Philip II of Spain, the sovereign of the Habsburg Netherlands.

These wars devastated entire regions. Due to war and famine, the population of Germany, Italy and the southern Netherlands decreased significantly. Political order of European powers changed remarkably with the rise of France and Sweden and decline of the Habsburg Empire.

This state of affairs of frequent wars and conflict made it clear that a solution should be grounded on a 'packaged deal' between different sides. With Peace of Westphalia, war came to an end and certain important decrees developed. It established the principle of sovereignty that gave the state power over all essentials of nation and the state, including religion.

Numerous territorial changes were also decided that included trade relaxations and free navigation on the Rhine. It established an example of peace achieved by diplomatic congress and also ingrained the system of political order based upon the notion of coexisting sovereign states. With increasing European influence on the world, these Westphalian principles, specifically the concept of sovereign states, became vital to international law and to the prevalent world order. However, in the 18th and 19th centuries, during colonization of Asia and Africa and world wars, these principles were vividly undermined.

Nation states that emerged gradually with the 'Westphalian system' were also associated with certain very specific developments. The significant factors to accelerate the process in Europe were as follows:

1. **Centralization:** The centralization of law and policymaking helped offshoot the development of nation states. Quick economic development became permissible with single central authority of nation state. Without the barriers of local taxes and regulations, trade throughout the nation became easy. Militarily, the nation-state was much stronger, and with the creation of national armies, the dependency on nobility decreased.
2. **The importance of Napoleon:** Importance of Napoleon Bonaparte in the development of nation state also needs to be acknowledged. During this period, most medieval and feudal laws were reversed, giving way to national law code. In response to Napoleon's military victories, seeing him as a challenge, many groups rallied together as a nation to defeat him.
3. **Warfare:** The long period of wars and struggle for supremacy of territories was a significant aspect behind the emergence of the modern state. Technological and military development changed the nature of warfare. Instead of mounted cavalry, states deployed paid troops. With the establishment of regular large armies, dependence on nobility decreased. The successful deployment of massed infantry was followed by introduction of gun powder. All these developments in military technology necessitated greater centralization, administration and central revenue system (Spruyt 2007, 214).
4. **Modern economy and rise of capitalism:** The advent of capitalism expedited the emergence of the modern state. The infrastructure required for the success of capitalism included roads, bridges, harbours, canals and railways, education and health facilities. It was also important to have police to protect goods and belongings of people. In the capitalist economic system, efficient legal system was required to regulate and manage commercial clashes. For emerging capitalist, kings were attractive as contracting parties as bearer of the large, centralized and efficient system. Centralized administrative system was also advantageous for traders because of standardization of weights, coinage, property rights and legal codes (Spruyt 2007, 217).
5. **Modern technology, economy and media:** Technological advancement specifically print, telegraph and the railways facilitated state control over population. It also enabled it to cast its networks over entire countries

and in some cases continents. Later, telephone, teleprinters, computers (first put to use in calculating the results of the US census), highways and better means of transportation and communication changed the system forever. Technology gave the government tools to control their countries and populations something never ever witnessed in history.

6. **Role of ideology:** When we trace the emergence of nation state in Europe, ideologically, we realize that in the new economic and political system new ideological position developed. The long conflict between monarch and pope and also between monarch and feudal lord resulted in the final triumph of monarch favouring absolute power to the state.

12.7 Nation State in Postcolonial Context

Historical developments and reasons for the emergence of Western nation states establish a linear path of their development. It universalizes a particular experience, the Western, for the others. The received version of the story tells us that the nation states originated some 500 years ago with the breakdown of the imperial states system in Europe. However, how could we understand evolution of state in other parts of the world. Since the end of Second World War, the number of independent states has increased. While decolonization in Africa and Asia was the reason for creation of new entities in the post-Second World War phase, the end of communist domination and disintegration of USSR after the Cold War increased the number of states further. Tracing the development in Western Europe and North America, it becomes clear that in most of the situations the nation nearly always created the state. However, the reverse of it, state formation preceding nation-building, is reflected from the study of postcolonial states. The existence of culturally and ethnically separate groups and their political interaction is often characterized by conflict because they find it difficult to regard the state as their primary source of political allegiance. The challenge is to establish and then uphold control over citizens, in other words, to build nation states from often different groups sharing a space drawn during colonial times.

Most postcolonial societies gained independence when colonial powers withdrew their control after the Second World War, but elites in an attempt to expand their own powers have embraced the borders created arbitrarily. Discussing the problem of borders that separate different groups, Herbst writes, 'The fundamental problem with the boundaries in Africa is not that they are too weak but they are too strong' (Herbst 2000, 253; Spruyt 2007, 224).

In postcolonial states in Africa and Asia, what most of them inherited was arbitrarily created colonial borders, feeble economies, widespread corruption, crumbling administration and infrastructure. This has affected their capability to control means of violence to an extent that in some areas different groups vie with each other for some control. Warlordism, drug trafficking, conflict diamonds, ethnic conflicts, mass killing and ethnic cleansing emerge in the absence of a legitimate state structure. Thus, whereas European states witnessed a gradual monopolization of violence and the gradual eradication of armed private actors, some areas in Africa are witnessing the opposite trend (Spruyt 2007, 225). Most of the postcolonial states have failed in their principal task of developing viable economies, controlling law and order within borders and providing public services to the people. According to Joel Migdal, while the governments of such newly independent countries affected many spheres of social life, they lack the ability to direct these societies, weak states confront strong societies (Migdal 1988; Spruyt 2007, 224). These states are facing different challenges in the process of nation- and state-building. To follow the Western state model in a mere couple of decades, they have to build a nation state that can play its role in the international community according to internationally adopted standards (following International Human Rights Laws and democratic standards) that perform the basic functions towards its citizens; so, what they lack is the time to sort out internal rivalries to find new and stable configurations in the power sharing (Grotenhuis 2016, 34). Thus, in the pressure to maintain stable state structure, they face different types of challenges and dilemmas.

12.8 Should Postcolonial Societies Follow Western Model of State?

The fundamental question with reference to the discussion in the preceding paragraph is, whether nation- and state-building in rest of the world should take European nation state as a benchmark. The unique historical process in terms of cultural, religious and socioeconomic circumstances that led to the Western European nation state should be considered as non-replicable. There should thus be space for different trajectories of nation- and state-building taking place today with different outcomes.

The Western nation states influenced nation state making in the rest of the world, and continue to do so. The colonial rulers built state institutions in the colonies that were a blueprint of the institutions back home. Later, in the 1990s, the international development community's good governance agenda tied aid to building governments and state institutions according to the models of the Western European state. Development aid came with clear political and economic conditions. The system of aid with strings attached has not helped in establishing a stable structure. Some space for development according to national convictions and political ideas of the recipient countries need to be considered:

- **Economic challenges:** Newly emerging states are facing a very different economic environment. Warfare, modernization and economic and technological progress had an important link in state making in Europe. However, with the spread of liberal capitalism, changing nature of war, the nature of challenges for state making has changed. Richard Stubbs (1999) argues East Asian states succeeded in establishing simultaneously neo-mercantile economic policy, state development and authoritarian government. Nonetheless, that is true for very small part of the world; rest all of them in Asia and Africa are struggling with weak economic structures and different types of challenges with liberalization and globalization of economies.
- **Ideological questions:** For most of the postcolonial societies, territorial identification has not displaced affinities based on language and religion. For example, whether the idea of territorially demarcated authority is compatible with theocratic organization in the Muslim world still remains a matter of debate (Piscatori 1986; Spruyt 2007, 228). In newly independent states of Central Asia, traditional loyalties are considered more important. While Czechoslovakia and Yugoslavia disintegrated, Romania, Hungary and other countries in Eastern Europe face multiple challenges in state- and nation-building. In most of the states of Asia and Africa, nationalist elites after independence have failed to create a sense of national identity.
- **Vibrant civil society and state:** In contrast to the situation in the West, civil society is weak and often fragmented in the states of Africa and the Middle East. The postcolonial societies are struggling to come out of a logic of the nation state in which every ethnic entity aspires for itself a separate state. The task of nation-building is transforming a multiethnic society into a national society that involves reordering of old equations among the ethnic groups into a new one dominated with the logic of national identity. Thus, as referred by Professor D.L. Sheth, the state, rather than addressing itself the creation of civil society (in which several social categories could participate in one political system), became largely a mediator of ethnic political equations (Sheth 1989, 621).
- **Clientelism and the absent state:** When elites in the postcolonial societies failed to build nation state, they explored other ways of increasing their constituencies and to remain in power. In the process, one of the most common and easiest is to develop patron–client relations, the relationship of mutual advantageous nature that also leads to a situation where state at best is absent and at worst part of the problem. In many fragile contexts, some elites or groups control political process while large segments of society remain unrepresented. This leads to a situation when state as a formal authority exists but effective control is exercised by few powerful groups, for example, national armies of the state. This present a very different context because we need to acknowledge the different processes of nation-building in fragile contexts, where on the one hand state is absent and on the other 'different actors, networks, and loci of power fill the void of the absent nation-state' (Haynes 1996, 42).
- **Authoritarianism:** To escape from the chaotic and difficult situation of negotiation, accommodation of varied groups, ethnic tensions and stagnant economy that challenged the stability of their regime, political elites relied on authoritarian. The new variety of statism was invented having distinct clannish, military-dictatorial character. With strong state structures, integration into the international order was achieved but civil order within state was lost. Some postcolonial states persisted with political democracy, but lower growth rates and frequent ethnic conflicts erode the legitimacy of the state from within and lead to a demand for a strong state and a strong leader leading to some kind of authoritarianism.
- **Question of legitimacy:** The very logic of super imposing a nation state on ethnically plural societies undermines the legitimacy of the state in many Third World countries. People have become disillusioned because they do not see any role for themselves as citizens neither in domestic nor in international sphere.

The dilemma is that there are forces that drive the countries to 'integrate' into the already established system of world economy and culture but the participation is not on equal terms. These very forces of integration operate in a manner that poses a challenge to the existence of these countries as sovereign nation states. It is another matter that the old established nation states of the West in the process of creating structures of international or regional cooperation are proceeding to introduce changes in the established structures. However, as argued by Professor Sheth, the countries of the Third World clung to the 19th-century concept of the state in the last decades of the 20th century (Sheth 1989, 620).

12.9 Decline of State Debate

With changing role of state, there is a very significant debate among scholars that has constantly engaged the attention on the question, are we moving away from a system of sovereign states towards less distinct, more hierarchical and in many ways more complex structures? It appears that, gradually, it would become challenging for the state to protect the political, military, economic, social and cultural life of citizens. Whether the direction of change is necessary as some expect or unwanted as others comprehend remains to be seen. It is undeniably true that in the globalized world in the economic domain, the free movement of capital and the flexibility of transnational corporations have influenced the regulating role of the nation state. The financial crisis in the second half of the 1990s and early 2000s is one such instance. With reference to these changes by the mid-1990s, Kenichi Ohmae predicted 'the end of the nation-state' (Grotenhuis 2016, 37). It is argued with reference to Ethiopia, Liberia, Rwanda, Sudan and Zaire that in much of sub-Saharan Africa, the state has already collapsed. Some success stories could be cited with reference to states such as Japan, South Korea and Singapore, as they have achieved internal order, stable economies and have delivered efficient services for their natives. However, some states such as Afghanistan, Burma, Iran and Iraq are facing enormous challenge as they have lost control that varies from clashes between disparate groups to full-scale war. The need for a political authority of some kind legitimated either by coercive force or by popular consent, or more often by a combination of the two, is the fundamental reason for the states existence but many states are coming to be deficient in these fundamentals (Strange 2004, 128). There are three major positions in the debate about globalization and its impact on states. First, there are scholars who argue that as a result of globalization, states are losing authority and influence. The prominent argument is 'the domain of state authority in society and economy is shrinking and what were once domain of authority exclusive to state are now being shared with other loci of sources of authority' (Strange 1996, 82), globalization erodes the power of the states (Julius 1997, 454). Kenichi Ohmae, John Noisbitt and Susan Strange are in this group. State-centric scholars have trust in state powers even in changed scenario of globalization (Hurst and Thompson 2000; Weiss 1998). Linda Weiss, Robert Gilpin and Ethan Kapstein are scholars supporting state-centric arguments (Sorensen 2008, 605). Certain groups of scholars also take a position that in the globalized world, states are becoming stronger in some respects and weaker in others and the process of state transformation plays out differently in different states (Brenner et al., 2003; Held and Mcgrew 2002; Jessop 2002). Decline of state theory is largely argued from the following perspective:

Trade and weapons: After the end of the Cold War, the threat of nuclear war destroying life has lost its significance; moreover, the confidence that state could avert nuclear war by defensive strategy has also waned. Thus, technology has punctured one of the crucial aim for the existence of the state, that is, its ability to resist attack by others. With reference to economic changes and its global nature, one very significant development is governments have lost their grip over their own currencies; the value of currencies is subject to fluctuations, often beyond the power of states. Some commercial groups are more affluent than states and are able to influence economic developments of a state. They are in position to set their own terms because the mobility of their capital gives them great locational flexibility.

Territorial boundaries: Capital's unusual movement enables it to transfer from areas of higher to lower taxation, thus diminishing state control over their revenue and industrial base. The increased flow of capital and populations has produced the phenomenon of transnationalism challenging the idea of boundaries. Geographer and social theorist David Harvey claims that the new world order is one in which finance capital rather than bounded nation states will play the chief coordinating role (Katherine 1993, 44).

Competition for market not for territory: The role of territory in defining power of state has changed because control over large land mass is no longer considered as a means to increase affluence. In this changed scenario, the search for allies among other states goes on, but for the added bargaining power conferred by a larger economic area. MNCs may be persuaded, in exchange for access to the national market, in most developing or ex-socialist countries, the prospect of new jobs and extra export earnings brought by such investments have become powerful reasons for a change of attitude towards the so-called 'multinationals' (Strange 2004, 131).

Rise of international NGOs: NGOs are either funded privately or receive financial support from other states or international organizations. In some states, NGOs also provide important services. It is useful for government to have organizations that provide public services with the help of public finance known as quasi-autonomous non-governmental organization (QUANGO) (QUANGO are organizations that are partially or wholly funded by the government to perform public service functions but not under direct government control). Public broadcasting is the classic case where QUANGOs operate in public sector at arm's length from government. Like NGOs, it is exceedingly difficult to estimate the exact numbers, but what is certain is the rising influence of these actors in policies (Newton and Van Deth 2011, 388).

Internet: Internet, satellite communication and developments in the virtual world are sometimes difficult but sometimes impossible for states to control. Customarily, no state has ever been able to influence and control the thought process of people. What has changed with new and sophisticated technology is that the barriers created by language and borders have been crossed, and with just a click, huge amount of information could be transferred to almost the whole world. With the advent of computer networks and the consequent reach of information and knowledge to larger audience, the battle between freedom and control was irreversibly lost by the latter.

Changing nature of conflicts: The principal function of state to fight in an attempt to protect its interest or offensively to extend them has lost its significance. Violent interstate conflict has decreased, and in most of the established democracies, national borders are no longer disputed challenging the age-old justification for the military might of the state. At the same time, the intra-state conflicts cannot be handled by the conventional armed forces.

State sovereignty and decline debate: Globalization has an impact on state structure influencing its different aspects. With technological advancement and worldwide trade, the mobility of people, capital and goods across national boundaries has increased. Discussing declining authority of states Susan Strange argues that the polarization of states between those who retain some control over their destinies and those who are effectively incapable of exercising any such control does not add up to a zero-sum game. The diffusion of authority away from national governments has left a yawning hole of non-authority, ungovernance it might be called (Strange 2004, 133).

Importance of international organizations: In the domain of international law, there is increasing space for citizens to claim their rights beyond the confines of national law. The European Court of Justice and the European Court for Human Rights are well-known examples of institutions used by citizens to challenge national jurisdiction. As the intensity and scope of relations between states have increased so has the number of international organizations. As a result, states are increasingly caught up in a web of directions, advice and instructions (Newton and Van Deth 2011, 390).

Environmental threats and rise of global civil society: In the postindustrialized world, we are struggling with environmental degradation, population growth, soil and plant erosion, water shortages and climate change. Since this has emerged as a global problem, the solution also lies in global cooperation. Different national and international networks in an attempt to seek solution and global cooperation use the most modern and global means of communication. In manipulating these, they sometimes outflank national government and international capital alike. It seems that it is the global civil society that is knocking on the doors of nation state, challenging its conventional role and extending the reach of global forces.

12.10 Debate on Resurgence of State

State role is challenged, and it seems as if its influence has decreased due to the process of globalization, but what is also visible is no other actor has taken the responsibility for providing security, justice, basic social services and infrastructure to the citizens of a nation state. The state is responsible for maintenance of internal law and order, to decide who will live and work within their borders and to issue passport and travel documents to their citizens.

The European Union (EU), widely seen as the most ambitious project of intergovernmental governance, continues to struggle with its domains of authority. Ever since the problematic 2005 referendum about the European constitution, member states have become increasingly reluctant to hand over more responsibilities to it. The exit of Britain from the EU, the result of referendum, signifies that national interest and nation state remain the most powerful organizations even to form and continue an international association. While the average state budget in European countries equals 40 per cent of GDP, the budget of the EU is only 1 per cent of the total European GDP. Issues that are vital to citizens, like health, education and welfare, have remained national. Also, the modern nation state remains the most important source of power and wealth in our globalized world. Although in most developing countries and in fragile states especially, the state's share of national GDP is much smaller (between 10% and 20%), the state is nevertheless an important and powerful actor in the economy of a country. The capacity to impose taxes and levies on citizens and companies and the authority to give out contracts and concessions give the state access to collect large amounts of money and economic power; the state formally is still the sole legitimate executer of physical (military) force. From an international perspective, the nation state has access to international networks of aid. State continues to be the main actor in modern warfare (Afghanistan, Iraq and Caucasus) to create international and supranational agencies of government such as the EU and the UN and control them (Newton and Van Deth 2011, 390).

1. **Nationalism:** The decline of the state argument underrates the rising forte of nationalism. Technology at one level stimulates global integrations and weakens national boundaries at another making it easier to endure nationalism. Communications technology helps to preserve minority languages and culture with local radio and TV station and desktop publishing (Newton and Van Deth 2011, 391).

   New power dynamics have emerged in the changed scenario with political power shifting from weak states to stronger states. The United States is in position to influence policies of different states, France tried to have some control in North and West Africa, and, of course, Russia in central Asia. Locus of power has also shifted from states to markets, strengthening the giant MNCs. Some scholars prefer to use the term governance rather than government because the changed realities of world require role of coordination of many actors in the political system. It is no longer a requirement on the part of government to control every aspect of our life. Some political powers have evaporated in the sense that state power is exercised weakly or not at all, examples include some areas of the former Soviet Union and some parts of Africa and Asia (Afghanistan) (Newton and Van Deth 2011, 391).

   The state is not withering away but changing and increasing its power to deal with new settings.

Special Insights

States in the 21st century

Conventional states: Conventional states remain sovereign within their own borders, and in most of the cases territory, people and sovereignty are not disputed.

Proto states: These states are threatened by uprisings, insurrections, separatist movements, ethnic clashes or civil wars, but the label proto state suggests that conventional state may emerge in these places.

Supranational states: The EU is the only clear example of a supranational organisation. Nonetheless, we should not forget that important policy matters such as foreign affairs, defence and taxation still remain with the national government.

2. **Changing role of state and economy in globalized world:** The result of what Sassen calls the 'denationalization' of the state fosters economic globalization by making it easier for companies to operate across national borders. One of the roles of the state vis-à-vis today's global economy has been to negotiate

the intersection of national law and foreign actors, whether firms, markets or supranational organizational (Sassen 2006).

With reference to the present global economic system, it could be argued that global economy and the national states are not operating in the mutually exclusive domains. There is no clear line of division between the national economy and global economy. It is a zone of politico-economic interactions that produce new institutional forms and alter some of the old ones (Saskia 2006, 92).

3. **Citizenship and identity:** Globalization has not intensely challenged the continuing relevance of citizenship. Collective solidarity at global level is missing. Sense of world citizen cannot be guaranteed by market forces. As regards with nationhood and identity, the modern state is based on two kinds of community, a community of citizenship and a community of sentiments. According to Anthony Giddens, the creation of identity is increasingly becoming an individual project because we reflect and then accept or reject religious or other beliefs. Simultaneously, some collective identities above the nation are in the process of emerging. For instance, 'Western civic identity' the essential component of the Western political order around a set of norms and principles most importantly political democracy, constitutional government, individual rights, private property-based economic systems and toleration of diversity (Deudney and Ikenberry 1999, 193).
4. **Conflict and war:** The traditional state of war is still significant with special reference to regional explosion in the Middle East and in East Asia. The world nonetheless remains conflict-ridden, with a substantial place for 'hard' geopolitics. Rising ethnic separatism, conflict between potentially nuclear states like India and Pakistan, China's geopolitical role, the politics of Russia and some smaller well-armed powers, the prevalence of military regimes in the world, the likely proliferation of nuclear weapons and the largely uncontrolled current spread of chemical and biological weapons through the world are the realities of today's world.
5. **State sovereignty or empire:** Sovereignty has taken a new form; this new global form of sovereignty is what is referred to as Empire. The declining sovereignty of nation states and their increasing inability to regulate economic and cultural exchanges is in fact one of the primary symptoms of the coming of Empire. The boundaries defined by the modern system of nation states were fundamental to European colonialism and economic expansion. The territorial boundaries of the nation delimited the centre of power from which rule was exerted over external foreign territories through a system of channels and barriers that alternately facilitated and obstructed the flows of production and circulation (Hardt and Negri 2004, 116). It is a decentred and deterritorializing of rule that progressively incorporates the entire global realm within its open frontiers. Empire manages hybrid identities, flexible hierarchies, and plural though modulating networks of command (Hardt and Negri 2004, 117).

   Empire not only manages a territory and population but also creates the very world it inhabits. The object of its rule is social life in its entirety, and thus Empire presents the paradigmatic form of biopower (Hardt and Negri 2004, 118).
6. **Environment protection and role of nation state:** Even in the domain of environmental protection, one of the key concerns in a globalized world, the key participants, those who could implement coordinated policy decisions, are representatives of nation states. 'Soft geopolitics' is becoming denser in this arena too. The other main delegates are the 'experts' (NGOs, experts and global civil society), but they also approach the nation state. Thus, environmental issues mainly encourage dual networks of interaction, one a potentially local/transnational civil society, the other inter-national, in the form of 'soft' geopolitics. The former may transcend the nation state, the latter coordinate states more tightly together, though perhaps in partly consensual terms which are not incompatible with a gradual spread of a civil society, again it is a mixed story (Mann 2004, 143).
7. **New social movements and state:** The 'new social movements' are usually concerned with the 'new politics' of identity of sexuality, lifestyle, religion and ethnicity. It is debated this new politics of identity weaken national (and nationally regulated class) identities, replacing or supplementing them with local cum transnational sources of identity. Ethnic politics may fragment existing states, but they take the form of nation states. To realize their demands, different groups address states. For implementation of their demands, state support is required whether to restrict or liberalize abortion, provide positive mechanism for single parenting or to clarify harassment, child abuse and rape, and the evidence needed to prosecute them. Thus, Michael Mann argues class politics will decline but not national politics in general (Mann 2004, 143).

12.11 Conclusion

The evolution of a nation state in the world is volatile and complex and has not followed a linear path. Some nations are old, and some are new; some were shaped by the physical environment which isolated them and made possible an evolutionary process, while others grew out of tribal or ethnic conflicts. Nations were created to fulfil some political purposes, but some were inspired by bond provided by common religion or by texts. Origins of nation states were driven by the economic needs of industry or changing nature of war. Many new nations had not thought of themselves as nations until it happened because of colonial constructions. World history, by definition, could not have blueprinted one plan along which all bounded groups proceeded to form themselves into nations. Thus, economic differences, tradition, politics, the urge for self-rule, and many more need to be recognized as separate forces working in different ways in different places and different contexts. The trajectory of origin and evolution of nation state has gone through different phases encountering different challenges from different forces.

Keywords

Globalization
Identity
Industrialization
Nation state
Postcolonial state

Review Questions

1. Discuss the decline of state debate with reference to globalization.
2. Industrialization and war played a significant role in the evolution of modern state. Comment.
3. Discuss the challenges of nation- and state-building for postcolonial societies.
4. With reference to the Treaty of Westphalia, discuss the prime factors that accelerated the development of a nation state in Europe.

References

Aikant, Satish C. 2006. Rethinking the Nation. *Indian Literature* 50(5): 169–78.

Armstrong, Alexander. 1982. *Nations Before Nationalism*. North Carolina: University of North Carolina Press.

Anderson, Benedict. 1991. *Imagined Communities: Reflections on the Origin and Spread of Nationalism*. London: Verso.

Ben-Israel, Hedva. 2011. The Nation-State: Durability Through Change. *International Journal of Politics, Culture, and Society* 24(1/2): 65–74.

Chandhoke, Neera. 2002–2003. Holding the Nation Together. *India International Centre Quarterly* 29(3/4) India: A National Culture? 80–94.

Chatterjee, Partha. 1993. *The Nation and its Fragments, Colonial and Post Colonial Histories*. Princeton, NJ: Princeton University Press.

Deudney, D, and J. Ikenberry. 1999. The Nature and Sources of Liberal International Order. *Review of International Studies* 25 (2): 179–96.

Geertz, Clifford, 1973. *The Interpretation of Cultures Selected Essays.* New York: Basic Books, Inc., Publishers.

Gellner, Ernest. 1983. *Nations and Nationalism*. New York: Cornell University Press.

Grotenhuis, René. 2016. *Nation-Building as Necessary Effort in Fragile States*. Amsterdam: Amsterdam University Press.

Hechter, Michael. 2000. *Containing Nationalism*. Oxford: Oxford University Press.

Hardt, Michael, and Antonio Negri. 2004. Globalization as Empire, in *The Global Transformations Reader: An Introduction to the Globalization Debate*, edited by David Held and Anthony Mcgrew, 2nd edition, 116–19. Cambridge: Polity Press.

Haynes, Jeff. 1996. *Third World Politics: A Concise Introduction*. Oxford: Blackwell Publishers.
Jessop, B. 2002. *The Future of the Capitalist State*. Cambridge: Polity Press.
Kumar, D.V., 2010. Gellnerian Theory of Nation and Nationalism: A Critical Appraisal. *Sociological Bulletin* 59(3): 392–406.
Mann, Michael. 1995. A Political Theory of Nationalism and Its Excesses, in *Notions of Nationalism*, edited by S. Periwal (pp. 44–64). Budapest: central European University.
Mann, Michael. 2004. Has Globalization Ended the Rise and Rise of the Nation-State? in *The Global Transformations Reader: An Introduction to the Globalization Debate*, edited by David Held and Anthony Mcgrew, 2nd edition, 135–46. Cambridge: Polity Press.
Mcgrew, Anthony, and Held David. 2002. *Governing Globalization: Power Authority and Global Governance*. USA: Wiley.
Meinecke, Friedrich. 2015. *Cosmopolitanism and the National State* (trans. Robert B. Kimber). Princeton, NJ: Princeton University Press.
Meyer, John W., John Boli, George M. Thomas and Francisco O. Ramirez. 1997. World Society and the Nation State. *American Journal of Sociology* 103 (1, July): 144–181.
Migdal Joel, S. 1988. *Strong Societies and Weak States, State Society Relations and State Capabilities in the Third World*. Princeton, NJ: Princeton University Press.
Mouzelis, Nicos. 1998. Ernest Gellner's Theory of Nationalism: Some Definitional and Methodological Issues, in *The State of the Nation* (pp. 158–65), edited by J.A. Hall. Cambridge: Cambridge University Press.
Newton, Kenneth, and Jan W. Van Deth. 2011. *Foundations of Comparative Politics Democracies of the Modern World*, 2nd edition. Cambridge: Cambridge University Press.
O'Conner, Walker. 1994. A Nation is a Nation, is a Sate, is a Ethnic Group, Is a …., in *Nationalism*, edited by John Hutchinson and Anthony Douglas Smith, 36–46. Oxford: Oxford University Press.
Oommen, T.K. 2002–2003. Demystifying the Nation and Nationalism. *India International Centre Quarterly* 29(3/4) India: A National Culture?: 259–74.
Peter, Flora, Stein Rokkan, Stein Kuhnle, and Derek Urwin (eds). 1999. *State Formation, Nation Building and Mass Politics in Europe: The Theory of Stein Rokka*. Oxford: Oxford University Press.
Piscatori, James. 1986. *Islam in a World of Nation States*. Cambridge: Cambridge University Press
Pierre L. van den Berghe. 1978. Race and Ethnicity: A Sociobiological Perspective. *Ethnic and Racial Studies* 1(4): 401–411.
Renan, Ernest. 1992. What Is a Nation? Text of a conference delivered at the Sorbonne on 11 March 1882, Ernest Renan, Quest-ce Quune nation, Paris, Presses-Pocket (trans. Ethan Rundell). ucparis.fr/files/9313/6549/9943/What_is_a_ nation.pdf
Sassen, Saskia. 2006. The State and Globalization, in *Readings in Comparative Politics Political Challenges and Changing Agendas*, edited by Mark Kesselman and Joel Krieger, 89–94. Boston: Houghton Mifflin.
_________, 2003. The Participation of States and Citizens in Global Governance; *Indiana Journal of Global Legal Studies*; Bloomington Vol. 10, Iss. 1, (Winter 2003): 5–28.
Seymour, Michel. 1999. On Redefining the Nation. *The Monist* 82(3): 411–45.
Sheth, D.L. 1989. Post-Colonial Societies and Rise of Nation State: State. *Nation and Ethnicity: Experience of Third World Countries Economic and Political Weekly* 24(12): 619–21, 623–26.
Shils, Edward. 1957. Primordial, Personal, Sacred and Civil Ties. *British Journal of Sociology 8*: 130–45.
Smith, Anthony. 1986. *The Ethnic Origins of Nations*. Oxford: Blackwell.
Smith, Anthony D. 1998. *Nationalism and Modernism: A Critical Survey of Recent Theories of Nations and Nationalism*. London: Routledge.
Sorensen, Georg. 2008. Globalization and the Nation State, in *Comparative Politics*, edited by Daniele Caramani, 601–24. Oxford: Oxford University Press.
Spruyt, Hendrik. 2007. War, Trade and State Formation, in *The Oxford Handbook of Comparative Politics*, edited by Charles Boix and Susan C. Stokes. New York: Oxford University Press.
Strange, Susan. 2004. The Declining Authority of States, in *The Global Transformations Reader: An Introduction to the Globalization Debate*, edited by David Held and Anthony Mcgrew, 2nd edition, 127–34. Cambridge: Polity Press.
Stubbs, Richards, 1999. War and Economic Development: Export—oriented Industrialization in East and South East Asia. *Comparative Politics* 31(3): 337–55.
Tilly, Charles. 1994. States and Nationalism in Europe, 1492–1992. *Theory and Society* 23: 131–46.
Van Creveld, Martin. 2006. The Fate of the State, in *Readings in Comparative Politics Political Challenges and Changing Agendas*, edited by Mark Kesselman and Joel Krieger, 70–81. Boston: Houghton Mifflin.
Weiss, Linda. 1998. *The Myth of Powerless State*. New York: Cornell University Press.

CHAPTER 13

The Capitalist State

Chetna Sharma

Reader's Guide

The many states share the fact that they are all founded on contemporary bourgeois society in one way or another, despite their odd diversity of form. They vary in degree of capitalist growth, degree of liberation from feudal amalgamation, degree of modification by the unique historical development of each country, and degree of development. In light of this, they share a few crucial traits. In this chapter, we'll talk about a few key issues with a focus on the characteristics of the capitalist state. We'll try to discuss issues like whether a capitalist system necessitates a capitalist government. Does the state, as an institutional constellation, give effect to the capitalist economic entitlement claims by granting them major rights? We shall make an effort to comprehend the intricate relationships that exist between the capitalist system, acquisition tactics, and shifting governmental structures.

13.1 Introduction

Compared to other systems that produce products and services for sale, capitalism is unique. This comprises the historical growth, replication, and expansion of a labour market in which employees sell their labour to business owners in a formally free and equal commercial exchange. The influence of capitalism on the development of technology and the amassing of wealth is unparalleled in human history. In terms of pure production, creativity, abundance, and dynamism, capitalism is unmatched by any other economic system. Capitalism offers an amazing system for producing options, disseminating knowledge, and advancing some forms of equality and freedom. Moreover, capitalism is prone to socially destructive concentrations of wealth and inequality, accumulation crises, and periodic economic collapse, often on a global scale. Uncertainty, instability, and inequality are also key traits of capitalist systems, and all three have a negative impact on our social and natural environments. Long ago, Marx and Engels noted that capitalism permanently transforms the communities in which it exists. Also, it produces what economist Joseph Schumpeter referred to as "creative destruction," leaving a trail of chaos in its wake that we have seen at various points in history. People's livelihoods were severely disrupted by the decline of the old industrial sector, the oil shocks of the 1970s, the housing bubble of 2008, the Eurozone crisis, and the global financial crisis.

A particular type of state was established as a result of capitalism, which had an impact on nearly every element of human life. In order to handle uncertainties, smooth out booms and busts, and provide a framework of shared economic stability in which capitalist risk-taking might flourish, capitalism needs a set of opposing forces that are formed in an institutionalised and functional form. The state's genius is in its ability to deploy magic to make market capitalism friendly to people and consistent with contemporary democracy. Let's begin our journey to understand the capitalist state with this backdrop.

13.2 Origin and Evolution

State, or at least state-like, institutions existed before industrial capitalism rose to prominence in Europe, and they had a significant impact on the dynamics of the later global growth of capitalism. Early state structures and practises reflected capital accumulation, a key aspect of capitalism. According to McMichael, 'if the capitalist world market which unifies various production systems depends upon states to secure and regulate its operation, then it logically follows that the world history of capital is embedded in the history of states' (McMichael 1987: 188). There is no reason to predict a convergence across states in capitalist societies because history is a necessary component in the growth of any particular state. They will change with changes in the balance of class forces as well as with national forms of growth and their shifting insertion into the global market.

The state is capitalist to the extent that it establishes, upholds, or rectifies the conditions necessary for capital accumulation in a particular circumstance. As a result, state administrators cannot have a single, clear point of reference for determining how best to satisfy the requirements and interests of capital. In fact, unless capital continues to be accumulated in whatever self-substituting form develops from the competitive hunt for added value, there is no such reference point for external observers like state theorists to assess whether the state succeeds in doing so. The general path of accumulation is a complex outcome of the tactics used at many levels and locations within a specific context.

According to Hirsch (2005), capitalism and "the state" are two interrelated historical phenomena. The mercantile state served as a conduit for the capitalist economy's rise historically as a power that eventually became a capitalist state. 'Civil society' cannot exist without the state, according to the 'thought experiments' about the 'state of nature' made by British classical political philosophers Hobbes (1651). Civil government, to the extent that it is created for the security of property, is actually instituted for the defence of the rich against the poor, or of those who have some property against those who have none at all, according to Adam Smith (1776). When the labour market, as well as trade and the manufacturing process, came to be controlled by the financial aspect and profit, capitalism was born. About 1800 was the beginning of this in Britain and France.

Special Insights

Capitalist state's relevance for enduring capitalism

States are vital for capital; it is a myth that capital can or wants to "escape the state" by moving offshore. Investors face obstacles rather than incentives as a result of the temporary deterioration or dissolution of nations on certain territories (such as in Somalia during the early 1990s, Lebanon between 1975 and 1990, and the Solomon Islands between 2000 and 2003). Large international firms and other capitals nevertheless rely on nations to provide infrastructure, regulate business activity, safeguard them from threats, and defend their interests in states ruled by competing capitals. Yet, imperialism—the enlargement of the activities of the most powerful nations throughout the world—has been a characteristic of capitalist expansion, from the English conquest of Ireland under Cromwell to the US invasion of Iraq in 2003. In addition to directly exercising their influence through the use of force and diplomacy, the ruling classes of the biggest, richest nations also reinforce this by the use of international institutions. The governments of wealthy nations, who are the IMF and World Bank's largest creditors, have direct authority over both institutions. The World Trade Organization and the United Nations have always supported the interests of their wealthiest members or been rendered ineffective by disputes among them.

The functioning of the capitalist system depends on a number of fundamental rights, including the right to private property, the right to private property in the means of production, and the right to employ labour and appropriate the surplus value (profit) that is generated by that labour. These demands are granted in the form of legal rights by the capitalist state, an institution that forms unity with the capitalist system. It is the state, however, that must continuously seek its legitimacy and that of the capitalist system throughout this process and inside full-fledged capitalism. The most important formal characteristic of the capitalist state is its particularization, or its institutional isolation from the capitalist circuit. This division also lends legitimacy to the state's use of its legalised monopoly on violence. The state justifies its activities by arguing that they are in the supposed general interest of everyone, which results in the actors' compliance. The State also places itself above and outside of the specific economic interests and upholds the law through adjudication and punishment. The state's enforcement of rights by legislation inevitably necessitates their material reproduction. The state depends on the economy for that material reproduction. As a result, the state is forced to use taxation to take money out of the economy.

Hence, taxes serve as a foundation for state action. The tax base, which determines the possible action radius of the state, must be expanded in order to reach realistic tax rates. This can be done by enhancing the environment for capital accumulation and, by extension, the conditions for economic growth. Krätke notes that "the idea of a general duty on the part of each individual citizen to pay taxes to the state, which cannot be contested, whatever his (her) own judgement about state activities or the specific tasks to which they are applied, is a very modern one" (1987: 57–58).

The state's responsibility to care for and safeguard property rights necessitates the restriction of those rights as well. With this restriction, any concretization of taxation is further problematic since it always forces the government to take a position on how income and wealth are distributed. Furthermore, the state's obligatory actions, such as advancing the conditions for capital accumulation and offering social security benefits, imply that the state controls a sizeable portion of the economy. Property rights and taxes by the state appear to be at odds with one another, supporting the interests of some, and endangering the legitimacy of the state. The capitalist system's very survival and perpetuation, however, depend on the legitimacy of the state.

In the name of advancing the general interest, the state sought justification for upholding its definition of granted rights, and if there was a conflict between rights or a requirement to give one right priority over another, the issue was settled in terms of the ostensible best interests of everyone. Although the concept of "general interest" is intrinsically ambiguous, the state frequently uses it in practise to justify its actions and inactions. Hence, the reference to abstract common interest ultimately refers to the granting and upholding of the fundamental economic entitlement claims made in the form of rights, which in turn refers to the de facto continued existence of the capitalist system. To gain legitimacy, the state places itself above and apart from the competing economic interests as an impartial adjudicator and exceptional social institution. Nonetheless, the replication of the capitalist system is the de facto goal of the state. Because it upholds the constitutional rights to life and property, the state is crucial to the operation of the capitalist system. It also offers the framework required to uphold security, law, and order. In a social formation that is socially divided and pluralistic, the state has overarching political responsibility for ensuring social cohesion (Garland, 2016).

In a democracy, these "governing groups" must obtain a majority of the vote in order to stay in power. They attempt to balance the demands of the electorate with the needs of capital accumulation. This calls for a special kind of politics that allows the needs of capital to be represented as the interests of all people. It also calls for some self-control on the side of specific capitalist interests as well as a constant stream of concessions to keep the support of other interests. The needs of capital accumulation and the requirements of popular support are kept in a careful balance by the state.

Empirically, the OECD (Organisation for Economic Development and Cooperation) members Australia, Austria, Belgium, Canada, Denmark, Finland, France, Greece, Germany, Ireland, Italy, Japan, Netherlands, New Zealand, Norway, Portugal, Spain, Sweden, Switzerland, United Kingdom (of Great Britain and Northern Ireland), and United States of America are the main examples of fully developed capitalist nations. Yet, not all of those nations from 1870 to 2015 can be categorised as capitalist. (Reuten, 2019: 327).

The maintenance of the monetary, legal, and administrative foundation for competitive capitalism throughout the years when capitalism was consolidating required the minimal state, or "night watchman" state, in order to provide the broad external circumstances for capital accumulation. The capitalist class was forced to focus on market prospects for profit and industrial management with less government interference. Yet, the Great Depression's impact on the growth of larger governments and the consolidation of totalitarian nations during the years between world wars resulted in a different understanding of the state. The expansion of capitalism was thought to depend on state intervention. In the revised scenario, it became clear that government economic involvement is necessary for capitalism to survive. It was an economic system in which the government actively interfered with economic activity and market operation using a variety of tactics. State interventions are possible both domestically and internationally, for diplomatic and domestic business interests. States have the ability to influence the economy through controlling a sizeable portion of productive assets through a variety of statisms, such as subsidies, investments, consumption, and other regulatory tools, as well as through official and informal coordinating mechanisms (Wright et al., 2021). These actions influence economic activity in ways that might or might not put private businesses under pressure. These include unconventional monetary policy actions as well as protection for oligopolistic businesses. The majority of the means of production are owned privately, and the economy's primary mechanisms for coordinating action are markets and pricing. Furthermore, rather than a political system in and of itself, the ultimate impact of state interventions on the private sector is decided by the political objectives of the governments as well as by the amount and scope of public support for private economic activity.

The capitalist state found itself in a new position where more extensive intervention was necessary for the capitalist system to function. As a result, adjustments were made to several state regulations. The French government nationalised a number of industries, including aviation, railroads, and other businesses. After World War II, the role of the state in the economy grew. According to Megginson (2005); p.11), the "economic and industrial mobilization that occurred during World War II dramatically increased the power (and prestige) of national governments as economic managers." Moreover, nationalisation of industries including coal, steel, air travel, power, and gas continued on a global scale. The pinnacle of state ownership of profitable businesses most likely occurred between the late 1970s and the early 1980s (Musacchio & Lazzarini, 2014). The effectiveness of government ownership became a major topic of discussion in intellectual and political circles in the 1970s and 1980s. The economic difficulties in the Communist bloc prompted concerns about the effectiveness of state ownership, but the two recessions brought on by the oil shocks and stagflation in the 1970s and 1980s led to financial crises in many state-owned businesses in the Western world State capitalism was viewed as ineffective and a threat to enterprises during this time period. This description and governments' need for money to lower their debt loads and current expenses served as the primary drivers of the wave of privatisations (Musacchio & Lazzarini, 2014). Bremmer (2010) argues in this system "the state...use markets to create wealth that can be directed as political officials see fit...The ultimate motive is not economic (maximizing growth) but political" (4–5). Advance capitalism's recent crises have demonstrated that there are occasions when markets cannot function effectively without extensive state intervention. The discussion has now changed to how government assistance should be used and whether or not those who receive state funding can be trusted to use the money appropriately (Grimshaw & Rubery, 2012).

A significant rearticulation of the economic and extra-economic took place as a result of the shifting competitive dynamics brought on by knowledge-based, globalising economies, which also altered the dynamics of the state's role (Jessop, 2002). This is related to the wide restructuring, rescaling, and re-temporalizing of market-state-civil society linkages as well as shifting types of state intervention that have an impact on how market forces are defined, regulated, and operated. Due to the shifting nature of capitalism and the expanding internationalisation of the capitalist economic system, the government continued to have little influence over many crucial issues affecting domestic economic performance. The state was supposed to uphold both home and foreign trust in the economic climate and the likelihood of successful investment. This restriction was particularly closely linked to changes in the balance of payments during the era of the gold and gold-dollar exchange standards and fixed exchange rates, and it was enforced by the dominant global financial powers (at first, Britain, then the USA), as well as by international capitalist organisations like the IMF and World Bank.

The pressure on the state to maintain investment-friendly conditions or face the effects of capital flight is increased by the growing international mobility of capital. It also gives multinational corporations the opportunity to get around many political restrictions and controls at the expense of fixed, domestic capital and wage labour. State intervention is now regarded as crucial for the growth of capitalism, despite the fact that the minimal state, or "nightwatchman" state, could secure the broad external conditions for capital accumulation. With the evolving forms of capitalism, the nature and function of the capitalist state have also altered. Politics has grown too important to be left to politicians and the whims of the populace as a result of the complexity of the economic and political systems. The deliberate shielding of crucial economic ministries and boards from legislative control and/or the active participation in policy-making and implementation for a new breed of industrial statesmen thereby enhance the indirect, external restraints on democratic politics.

The division of the political and economic spheres and the state's ultimate reliance on the capitalist economy's continuous prosperity place restrictions on it. The management of the economy is also a political activity, and because bourgeois societies are pluralistic, capital cannot forcibly impose its interests on other classes or groups. This is important to keep in mind. The modern state is more than a tool for interclass dominance; it is also a tool for intraclass rivalry. This rivalry manifests itself in a variety of ways, such as through trade, international investment, imperialist dominance, conflict, diplomacy, etc (Barker, 1978). The relative size of the capital(s) that are located inside each country's orbit also determines its capacity to compete.

Special Insights

Illusion of Equality in the capitalist state

People frequently turn to the state when they wish to affect social change because they believe that the state should be above social conflicts and a guardian of all citizens' interests. It's a mistake, though. The state and the capital have tight links. The internal structures of the state are being shaped by an even closer link between them. State and federal welfare, education, and health policies make sure that the capitalist class has access to a sufficient supply of labour. Employers require or may need employees with the general abilities and specialised skills that the educational system provides. More crucially, given that these competences could be developed in quite diverse ways, the educations system prepares people to obey commands and accept of the status quo. Even major multinational firms nevertheless depend on states to provide infrastructure, regulate business activities, safeguard them from below-the-belt threats, and defend their interests in states ruled by competing capitals.

13.3 Approaches to understand the capitalist state

13.3.1 Karl Marx and the capitalist state

For a period of almost 40 years, Marx critically engaged with bourgeois society and examined the state. Overall, he examined the regular form of the capitalist type of state as well as some of its exceptional forms, including Bonapartism, and related state power to particular state forms and the shifting balance of powers. He also emphasised the importance of the institutional separation of the economic and political in capitalist social formations.

Two fundamental notions of his work have been cited by numerous observers. One views the state as a tool of class rule (instrumentalist perspective) that the economically dominant class or classes use more or less successfully to uphold its political authority and economic exploitation. The Communist Party's Manifesto, which asserts that the "executive is a committee for managing the common affairs of the whole bourgeoisie," is sometimes cited as the source of the instrumentalist viewpoint. The other emphasises its function as a somewhat autonomous authority (autonomist view) or maybe a totally autonomous authority that could control the class conflict in the public good or even manipulate it to the private benefit of the political strata. Marx's assessments of the class battles in France in the 1850s highlight state autonomy most famously—and inspirationally. In fact, he even asserted that Bonaparte had created a "praetorian state," wherein the army under Bonaparte III begins to act in its own right against society rather than on behalf of one segment of society against others. This moment was, however, as Marx noted, short lived (Carens & Mares, 2007).

Some commentators attempt to reconcile these divergent interpretations by arguing that the first perspective holds for "regular" periods of class struggle and the latter for "special" periods when class struggle is stalled and/or threatens a social disaster. This instrumentalist-autonomist dichotomy, which is not found in Marx but is an artefact of subsequent attempts to develop the Marxist theory of the state, is the basis for this argument. A third perspective on the state exists as well, and it offers Marx's critique of the state a more genuine line of direction. Marx's comments on the Paris Commune of 1871 make this retention particularly evident. He read related works on political and constitutional theory as well as books on the histories of states in France, Italy, Poland, England, Germany, Sweden, and the United States in 1843. He also researched the English and French revolutions. His critique of Hegel's doctrine of the state was influenced by these in-depth investigations. Marx argued that the contemporary state could only represent a "illusory" community of interest, refuting Hegel's assertion that it could and would represent the common, organic interests of all members of society (Carens & Mares, 2007). The ongoing hostilities, vulgar materialism, and egoistic conflicts of a society founded on private property ownership and waged labour are concealed beneath this deceptive communal fiction. Since the state is founded on the division of rulers and ruled, Marx views it as an alienated type of political organisation (Thomas, 1994). This division manifests itself differently depending on the class-based modes of production, the stage of capitalism growth, the kind of capitalist formation, and the degree of integration into the global economy.

13.3.2 The Capitalist State Understanding of Miliband and Poulantazas

Modern Marxists Miliband and Poulantzas focus less on the needs and requirements of capital accumulation and more on political and ideological issues. Miliband contends that a major source of political influence and social order is the indoctrination of people into the ideologies of the ruling class. (Jessop, 1991). Poulantzas rejects all forms of instrumentalism and contends that because the state is a complex social structure, classes should not be viewed as merely economic forces that exist apart from the state and independently of it and are capable of influencing it passively. He argued, specifically, that the separation of the political and economic spheres created a space for the dominant classes to achieve hegemony by looking beyond their particular economic concerns, sacrificing short-term economic gains when necessary, defining the functions of state power, and presenting a more expansive national-popular vision. The institutional makeup of the state and the outcomes of state power determine the political impact of class. Additionally, the class conflict is not only present in civil life but also at the very centre of the state machinery. In order for capital accumulation to proceed unobstructed, the state has an objective duty to ensure social cohesiveness.

Poulantzas suggested that the new type of capitalist state is "authoritarian statism" in his book State, Power, Socialism (1978). This type of state has a democratic outward appearance, but it has very distinct special characteristics that limit the ability of the lower classes to influence politics and policy and provide the upper classes more leeway to deal with escalating crisis-tendencies. The primary trend in this state is "intensified state control over every aspect of socioeconomic life combined with the radical demise of the institutions of political democracy and with harsh and multifaceted restrictions on so-called "formal" liberties" (1978: 203–4). Poulantzas concentrated on the "irresistible rise of the state administration" while discussing "authoritarian statism." He primarily connected this to the expanding economic role of the state as this is over determined by the political situation.

13.4 Neo Ricardian and the Capitalist State

The economic aspect of state is a topic that the neo-Ricardian theorists are specifically interested in. They emphasise how government intervenes in the economy to maintain or increase corporate profits at the expense of workers and how it affects the distribution of income amongst social classes. The state is typically only included in neo-Ricardian analysis as a third force that can intervene or as an instrument that can be used to one's advantage. Although these ideas take on many shapes, they nonetheless share the same basic presuppositions about how capitalism develops over time and what its most recent stage is like. Competition during the era of laissez-faire capitalism inexorably leads to capital concentration and centralization, creating a new regime where monopolies control the whole economy. Monopoly capitalism is characterised by an increasing propensity for the rate of profit to decline and a corresponding stagnation in production. More government involvement in the economy is necessary to counteract this tendency and sustain the dynamism of capital creation. Such intervention can take a variety of shapes, including the nationalisation of foundational industries, the centralization of financial and credit control, state support for investment, state support for technological research and development, and the establishment of international economic organisations. Monopoly capitalism becomes state monopoly capitalism as a result of the expansion of such interference. It states that state can be used to shift the base by reducing it to an epiphenomenon of an economic system (Jessop, 1991).

13.5 The Capital Logic School

The capital logic school, which has its roots in West Berlin, has attempted to extrapolate the overall structure and primary functions of the capitalist state from the existence and mode of production of pure capitalism. They contend that the nature of generalised commodity production is what leads to the separation of state and civil society that is a hallmark of bourgeois social formation. A non-market organisation is required to offer the fundamental prerequisites for capital accumulation. The state is an ideal collective capitalist (Altvater, 1973). The legal and monetary framework required to support the production and exchange of goods as well as the accumulation of capital is the most broad, abstract requirement for the existence of capitalism that is assigned to the state. The bourgeoisie law mandates the establishment of officially equal legal subjects with transferable property rights in commodities, including labour, as well as the creation of a legal system capable of deciding legal disputes and enforcing these rights. A monetary system that facilitates trade and allows for logical economic calculations must also be established by the state in order to ensure labour force reproduction, which is not achievable through market forces and is accomplished through industrial legislation, education, and social welfare. The government will need to ensure the provision of those goods and services that are indispensable for capital accumulation but whose private production is unproductive. This may involve nationalisation or some form of government assistance (Jessop, 1991). The propensity of profit rates to decline is significant in this context because it necessitates political action to harness opposing inclinations to restructure capital and reorganise the labour process. This means that it is not only asserted that the state is necessary for capitalism (and cannot, therefore, be impartial in the class conflict) but also that the quantity and scope of its intervention tend to grow as the process of capital accumulation gradually progresses (Altvater, 1973; Yaffe, 1973).

The capitalist state is enmeshed in the capitalist mode of production and is unable to escape its paradox and crises. The capital logic school contends that while the government increasingly steps in to maintain demand and reorganise production, it is unable to override market forces or stop the inevitable decline in the rate of profit. As it cannot directly influence the choices made by private capital, the capitalist state's power in this area is constrained. The conflict present in capital accumulation serves to strengthen this restriction. So, it is claimed that keynesian-style intervention to preserve full employment demand comes at the cost of escalating inflation. As a result, there may eventually be no choice but to abandon such measures, which will cause a severe slump and widespread unemployment. More state spending is required if the state is to find a solution to this conundrum. It resembles a trap in certain ways. The problem is that the "need of capital" continues to be the only basis of explanation, and that capital logic approach can only identify the probable forms of state and specify the broad bounds within which variations can occur without seriously endangering the process of capital accumulation.

13.6 The Frankfurt School

The analysis of the capitalist state is enhanced by Frankfurt-based Marxist scholars who emphasise historical specificity and the importance of class struggle. The only way to comprehend the capitalist state is through the shifting roles it plays in the class conflict over how the labour process is organised and who gets to keep the surplus value (Hirsch, 1974; Holloway & Picciotto, 1977). The broad evolution of the contemporary interventionist state from its inception in the feudal absolutist state in Europe is analysed. To ensure the broadest possible opportunity for capital growth in the early stages of capitalism, the capitalist state must assume a laissez-faire role. But, it must also take action to control fierce competition's harmful characteristics, such as factory legislation. The socialisation of production and the declining rate of profit necessitate greater state intervention as the process of capital accumulation progresses. To ensure the ongoing restructuring of social relations in favour of capital accumulation on a global scale, the internationalisation of capital brings new challenges and necessitates new types of state machinery and state intervention. Legislation and forms of representation alter as a result of these events. The best starting point for the transition from feudalism to capitalism is royal absolutism that implements mercantilist policies. It transitions to bourgeois parliamentary democracy throughout the liberal capitalism era. The shift from absolutism to parliamentary government and the expansion of the vote to the dominated classes continue the class struggle. In the era of monopoly capitalism, the state must establish direct contact with private capital and broaden the scope of its interventional tools in order to mobilise resistance against the tendency of declining profit margins. The state bureaucracy must exercise discretion in this situation. The shrinking influence of parliament in light of major capitalists' desire for direct access to the executive and administration reflects this development. The capitalist state evolved into a powerful state with a weak parliament as accumulation continued.

13.7 Neo Gramsician

Neo Gramscians emphasise that the capitalist state is not a straightforward tool that can be controlled by a single bourgeois class. The organisation of the bourgeoisie's political and ideological dominance depends critically on the state. A power bloc is a relatively stable alliance of dominant classes whose dedication to a shared professional viewpoint and a certain amount of reciprocal self-sacrifice of immediate interests are what keep them together. Success in transforming popular democratic struggle into an ideology that upholds the authority of dominant classes is essential to the power bloc's ability to maintain its hegemony. Their legal equality as economic agents is complemented by the constitution's equal rights guarantees, which likewise promote their atomization and individuation and conceal the real disparities in political power. The creation of nation states not only relates to the requirement for a perfect collective capitalist, but it also entails the existence of a collective national interest that represents the interests of all of its residents, regardless of their class affiliation. This is supposed to support the idea of a neutral state that can end class conflict and support capitalist dominance. In contrast, if the working class wants to establish its counter hegemony over the populace, it must isolate the power bloc and transform the popular democratic fight into a large-scale movement led by a populist political party.

Free elections, powerful legislative institutions, and welfare policies all contribute to the political dominance of the bourgeoisie. A certain amount of flexibility is guaranteed by the right to vote, rival political parties, the separation of powers, and parliamentary administration. In a democracy, the dominant group can preserve social harmony and establish the conditions for ongoing capital accumulation. The new Gramscian School holds that the dominance of capital is conditional on the constantly shifting interplay of class forces. The power of capital is seen in its capacity to profit from economic downturns in order to restructure production and boost capital accumulation.

In capitalist society, economic, political, and ideological levels appear to be institutionally separated, but they are actually much interconnected. A reform of the state as a system of political dominance may be a prerequisite for resolving an economic crisis because economic crisis has effects on other levels and vice versa (Jessop, 1991). The explanation above makes it abundantly evident that while Marxist theories use a variety of approaches, they are all united by a shared interest in a certain mode of production, their state of existence, and their impacts on social formations. Let's talk about the key components of a capitalist state after these caveats.

13.8 Features of the Capitalist State

It is vital to understand that the capitalist state differs from states in pre-capitalist or non-capitalist formations as well as from atypical political regimes, such as predatory military dictatorships. The peculiar, form-driven strategic selectivity of the capitalist state has significant effects on the structure and efficacy of state intervention. The following are the capitalist state's four key characteristics:

1. Its institutional detachment from the heart of capitalist production and the resulting monopoly on the means of coercion, which is also "constitutionalized."
2. Its structure as a tax-state and the function of money as the foundation of its economic system.
3. The function of law and logical legal bureaucracy as the organisational framework
4. The state has a responsibility to establish the conditions required for accumulation because capitalism is neither self-governing nor self-sufficient.

Each of these characteristics is both compatible with and maybe beneficial to the capitalist economic system. The economic function of the state and its institutional structure have changed, nonetheless, in line with how capitalism is evolving. The state serves as a conduit for the socialisation of capital, and it is also restructured to take into account changing economic conditions. Class dominance does not appear as class dominance in capitalist regimes in its numerous forms. This is reflected in Stanley Moore's aphorism: "When exploitation takes the form of exchange, dictatorship may take the form of democracy" (1957: 85). Hence, a political system based on the rule of law, equality before the law, and a single, sovereign state "fits" or "corresponds" naturally with an economic system based on private property, the wage relation, and profit-driven, market-mediated exchange. In other words, they have a relationship of "formal adequacy" with one another. When this is established, economic conflict typically follows the logic of the market (i.e., concerning wages, working hours, and prices), and political conflict generally follows the logic of the representative state based on the rule of law (i.e., concerning defining the national interest, balancing the specific interests of citizens and property owners within a "illusory" general interest). As a result, class isn't explicitly an organising principle of the capitalist sort of state (Jessop, 2019). The dominant class is forced to compete for power on formally equal terms with members of lower classes since it has no legal monopoly and no exclusivity of political power.

The state also ensures the fictional commodification of land, money, labour, and knowledge while adjusting their future demand commodification in light of the shifting patterns of appearance of the structural difficulties and tactical conundrums that face capitalism as well as the shifting power dynamics that fight the scope and effects of such fictitious commodification. This pertains to managing the supply of labour, the labour markets, and the employment terms throughout the labour process.

In the ideal-typical instance, individual capitals are restrained from utilising direct coercion when engaging in rivalry with one another and during the labour process. In contrast, the state is permitted to employ coercion to safeguard private property, the honour of contracts in the labour market, and other kinds of capitalist transaction. This makes it possible for capital to insist on having the authority to control the hiring process, take advantage of surplus labour, and enforce agreements with other capitalists (Jessop, 2019). Here, a dual relation is at play. The rights to freedom, equality, and property seem to exist formally in the labour market, but there is economic exploitation and despotism within the employment process. Despite being excluded from the production process, the government often steps in to deal with crises and economic difficulties like high inflation, high unemployment, or trade deficits that have no clear or consistent connection to the actual process of capital accumulation.

The state itself may offer products and services when the market fails. While the state and its managers plainly vary from the capitalist economy and give the appearance of official neutrality, how these economic demands are manifested in economic policy depends on the balance of political forces inside the state system. Usually, state interventions serve as a conduit for and a means of state activity. The purgative impacts of market-mediated rearrangement must be replaced by the state's own policies when it steps in to ease structural economic crises.

The state's function is essential for capital accumulation since economic crises cannot be resolved by merely withdrawing or refraining from intervention. Hence, it faces a political conundrum when attempting to fix the issue on behalf of capital. If its crisis management consciously favours one segment of capital at the expense of others, it runs the risk of escalating economic issues for capital as a whole and undermining its own credibility. But, even if it is successful in garnering support for policies that are in the interests of capital as a whole, it will still be impossible to avoid favouring some capitals over others. This will alter the power dynamics and may upset the initial alliance that supported such programmes. The fact that there are numerous nation-states and they must contend with a growing global capitalism only serves to exacerbate all of these restrictions. The transnational reach and adaptability of capital make it challenging for individual nation-states to track and regulate the process of capital accumulation. Contrarily, the need for governmental intervention does not disappear as a result of the globalisation of finance. It only makes achieving it more challenging.

The pre-capitalist and capitalist states are a diverse group, with varying powers to affect the world market at various stages of its development. This results in a tendency towards ever-greater integration and unification of the world market. Thus, the shape of the emerging world market is related to "the particular pre-existing territorial features of the pre-capitalist system of reproduction and the structure of its administrative apparatus of rule" (von Braunmühl, 1978: 167; see also Gerstenberger, 2007). There is no global state to oversee the international market, even though it is obliquely connected and interwoven through the logic of profit-driven, market-mediated competition. They frequently coexist as acrimonious adversaries, if not deadly foes. However, the world of states is not just a collection of independent nations; some of them engage in center-periphery and other hierarchical relationships, making them less equal than others, the diversity of states, each with a varied size and capacity to protect the interests of its own capital and/or the capitals functioning in the economic space(s) it seeks to rule. While having separate logics, the world of states and the global market interact to shape the developing global dynamic of capital accumulation.

Competition among capitals prohibited any one capitalist from being the first to cut hours, decrease female and child labour, and improve working conditions. Yet, fierce rivalry led to rising new-born and adult mortality, a declining population, and environmental damage. The rivalry on the global market and the challenges of being an early adopter in the fight against climate change are examples of this phenomenon in the twenty-first century. Referring again to Marx, progressive capitalists (who could profit from relative surplus value) and trade unions joined forces to pressure the state to enact laws against the wishes of many individual capitalists. This is an example of what Engels would later call the state's role as the "ideal collective capitalist." He wrote that "the modern State, no matter what its form, is essentially a capitalist machine, the state of the capitalists, the ideal personification of the total national capital" (Engels, 1989: 319).

Special Insights

State and Market Relation

In the end, categorising the world into "market capitalist" and "state capitalist" camps is an unhelpful oversimplification. The majority of nations, in actuality, are spread out over a spectrum with varying degrees of economic state intervention, both in terms of goal and scope. The only people who claim that the government has no place at all in the economy are the most ardent libertarians. Yet, given the different ways in which this relationship is manifested today, the question of whether the state or the market should be in charge is no longer relevant. Denmark (27%) and Germany (18%), for instance, are the two European countries that have the largest economic influence as buyers, while the United States has a 17 percent share, China has a 13 percent share, and Hong Kong has an 8 percent share. Nobody really contests the state's involvement in economic affairs. The issue is what that function should be and how it can be carried out in a way that simultaneously improves economic efficiency and reduces the type of rent-seeking behaviour, or "corruption," that frequently occurs anywhere the public and private sectors collide (Ferguson, 2012).

13.9 Varieties of Capitalist State

All capitalist regimes interfere with their economies for political reasons, while the motivations behind and scope of these interventions differ (Ferguson, 2012). Governments can influence economies through licencing, taxation, regulation, or economic redistribution. The terms "state ownership" and "statism" refer to various ways in which the government might influence economic activity. The former is based on the ownership rights that the state can use to steer businesses in the direction of particular goals established by the state's political agenda, which may differ greatly for developmental, welfare, predatory, and regulatory states (Witt & Redding, 2013). The ability of the state to conduct business with the company forms the basis of the latter mechanism, or "statism." The state can serve as a buyer, paying for goods and services from businesses, or as a lender, giving businesses access to low-interest loans (Wright et al., 2021). The way that governments use these instruments or processes to interfere in economic activities is the third aspect of state capitalism that the "non-threatening government" element captures. Countries that are close to one another on the "state ownership" or "statism" dimensions but far apart on the "non-threatening government" dimension exhibit a startling contrast. For instance, Singapore and Kazakhstan both have extremely comparable low scores on the "statism" category and nearly identical high scores on the "state ownership" part, showing that both countries significantly rely on ownership. At the same time, Singapore scored significantly better than Kazakhstan on the "non-threatening government" dimension, indicating that the Singapore government's economic interventions are seen favourably because they take place within clearly established institutional boundaries (Wright, et al., 2021).

State ownership is a tactic used by all governments to some extent; in the US, for example, the government owns the land, the airports, and the mail service. Additionally, the US has a number of oligopolistic industries, including telecommunications and military hardware (Wood & Wright, 2015). Every country safeguards its resources, imposes some limitations on foreign ownership, and supports its national heroes. Countries with significant state ownership of businesses, market intervention, and governmental presence might be extremely efficient (like Singapore), only moderately efficient (like Norway), or extremely inefficient (like Italy). In a similar vein, the majority of Asian countries, such as those of China, Japan, Korea, Singapore, and Chinese Taipei, did not initially subscribe to market fundamentalism and relied extensively on state intervention, including widespread state ownership of businesses, to further economic development (OECD 2015:19).

The character of capitalist state involvement has changed as a result of capitalism's evolving nature. China has emerged in recent decades as a successful example of an expanding state intervention in the economy. China has established itself as the second-largest economy in the world—or, by some metrics, the largest—as well as a major exporter. Even while China's overall state ownership has been dropping for four decades, the largest corporations are still state-controlled, and the size of China's economic growth has increased the model's appeal and global image (Milhaupt & Zheng, 2015). To build Sino-centric global production networks, China in particular has consistently depended on State Owned Companies (SOEs) and policy banks (Schindler & Kanai, 2021). According to the IMF (2020:1), "the recent increase of SOEs on the global arena mainly reflects the emergence of China's economy—where SOEs still play a significant role—along with other emerging market economies." China "plays a major role in this story, which is partially the outcome of a purposeful policy, known in Chinese as the "going out strategy,"" the OECD argues (2015:36).

From the early 2000s, the advent of contemporary state capitalism in both of its forms has drastically changed the world's development landscapes. More specifically, the geographic contexts of finance, manufacturing, infrastructure, and government have become increasingly dominated by statist interventionism and state-capital hybrids (Alami et al., 2021). Governments still own and run national commercial companies in important industries, according to a policy brief from the International Finance Corporation (the World Bank's private arm). State-owned industries have survived and grown in a number of high-income nations, significant emerging market economies, and low- and middle-income countries (IFC 2018). The 2020 IMF Fiscal Monitor dedicates a whole chapter to State Owned Enterprise (SOEs). It takes stock of their increasingly widespread prevalence in "virtually every country", with "many governments relying on them to serve their citizens and to foster economic and social development", and notes that "SOE cross-border activity has diversified and increased in this century" (IMF 2020:1–3). Infrastructure investment and project implementation, including those in the water, mining, energy, ports, and rail and road transportation sectors, have shown to be one area where state-capital hybrids have been most successful. According to a research co-authored by the World Bank and the Public-Private Infrastructure Advisory Facility (PPIAF), 83% of infrastructure investments in developing countries were made in 2017 by SOEs and government-sponsored organisations (World Bank-PPIAF 2017).

Three types of statism—techno-industrial policy, national development plans, and economic nationalism—have grown in scope with the rise of state-capital hybrids, adopted more forceful and combative modes, and increased their visibility in the geographic contexts of policymaking. The legitimacy of national development strategies has "recovered" (UNCTAD 2018:130). According to a recent survey, "from roughly 62 in 2006 to 134 in 2018 there were more than twice as many countries with a national development plan" (Chimhowu et al., 2019). According to the UNCTAD report (2018:129), "developed countries are under pressure to adapt to increased competition in trade, investment, and technology due to the success of fast-growing economies in East and South-East Asia. In order to compete at the technical forefront of the Fourth Industrial Revolution, states have created a range of programmes, specialised types of government-business cooperation, as well as new types of technology and innovation policies (Werner, 2021; Yeung, 2016).

Also, it has encouraged low- and middle-income economies to build on their past successes and advance industrial development, particularly in light of the Anglo-Saxon liberal capitalism's current crisis of legitimacy following the global financial crisis of 2008 and the post-Washington Consensus's repeated failures to produce meaningful development advances (Sheppard & Leitner, 2010). After the global financial crisis of 2008, multilaterals have also embraced regional and territorial development strategies as a readymade component of contemporary development policy and "an antidote that can fix market and governance shortcomings" (Schindler & Kanai, 2021:45). In a volatile geopolitical environment, the rise of various types of economic nationalism and neo-mercantilism has been intertwined with the restoration of industrial and spatial planning programmes. There are three notable cases (Alami et al., 2021). First, ideas of national security and geo-economics statecraft are becoming more and more entwined with technological and innovation policy. One example is the rivalry over 5G technology between the US and China. The promotion of investment opportunities in developing nations is intended to provide an outlet for the excess capital of the various private sectors. Second, aid and development policy has been employed more and more as a sort of "export stimulus." (Mawdsley et al., 2018). These policies have also been designed to achieve geostrategic goals, which has led to the restoration of geographic spheres of influence and the advancement of national interests in global development. Finally, geo-economics and geopolitics have played a significant role in the resurgence of spatial planning techniques (Anguelov, 2020; Kanai & Schindler, 2019). States and corporate actors fight to reorganise areas through the financing, construction, and control of expansive infrastructure in the developing world in a process known as the "infrastructure scramble," according to Kanai and Schindler (2019).The objective is to "enhance economic competitiveness through enhanced connectivity to transnational value chains" (Kanai & Schindler, 2019:303).

13.10 Crisis and Contradictions

There may appear to be more room for government participation in promoting financial development in less developed economies. Yet, a less effective institutional structure is frequently present along with less development, which raises the possibility of ineffective interventions. In other words, there is a particular geography to the risks of state capitalism. If its unbridled spread is recognised as a general source of worry, it is seen as a particularly hazardous risk in non-western, poorer nations, where the separation of the political and economic spheres is seen as more fragile than in western liberal states. Expanding direct state ownership and engagement in developing nations is presumably risky because it could lead to a shift away from liberal government structures.

In the current geopolitical climate of escalating tensions between the United States and China, the emergence of state capitalism may result in a politicisation of economic relations and protectionist responses. The OECD (2015:12, 21) states that governments all around the world are working harder to develop laws for handling foreign investment from SOEs. Additionally, there is a chance that these actions will provoke a protectionist response elsewhere. This is also noted by the IMF (2020:21), which argues that "as SOEs have grown in scope and size, their drawbacks have spilled over to other countries, leading to calls for protectionist measures". The IMF underlines that these risks are compounded by the absence of a global governance framework in the matter: "Domestically, some countries have frameworks that seek to promote fair competition between SOEs and private firms for example, in Australia and the European Union. At the global level, however, there is no common framework" (IMF 2020:1). This is also recognised by UNCTAD (2018, 2020:xi) as a significant risk. It emphasises that many advanced economies have implemented "more rigorous screening of investment in strategic industries on the basis of national security considerations" over the past few years, and that one-third of national investment policies adopted in 2018 introduced restrictive measures on FDI (the highest proportion in 20 years).UNCTAD argues that this trend towards "growing economic nationalism" and "towards more interventionism, rising protectionism" is one of the main challenges to "the system of international production", "global investment and investment policymaking", particularly in a context of "geopolitical and financial risks and continuing trade tensions" (2020:x–xi, xiii).

These categories reflect a deep concern for the direction that the political form of global capital accumulation may be rapidly taking, namely, a direction in which the unchecked spread of statism and non-market conforming state-capital hybrids may weaken competitive value-disciplines, spark a shift away from liberal Western-dominated market-centric governance, politicise economic relations, and exacerbate geopolitical and geo-economics tensions between countries. There are several practical arguments against the government getting overly involved in the financial systems (Alami et al., 2021).

During the 2008 financial crisis, there was some uneven new growth that made many people poorer and more unsecure than before, which led to right-wing populist backlashes (Cumming, Wood, & Zahra, 2020). Also, there has been a rise in curiosity about the function of unorthodox monetary policy, the unequal results of quantitative easing, and the COVID-19-driven rescue round in the US and UK. Recent data suggests that this may be advantageous to huge financial institutions because their portfolio companies are financially fragile and leveraged too much, making them eligible for financial relief programmes set up by governments to help struggling enterprises. (Wiggens et al., 2020).

13.11 Conclusion

The chapter's conclusion states that even if market failure and environmental damage, two of rising capitalism's major issues, could be addressed by intricate regulation, the expansion of social security payments and the number and complexity of regulations must continue to rise in order for the capitalist system to work. We have discovered a subtle yet essential shift in the official agendas and discourses around the state, which increasingly acknowledge the state's complete range of roles in development, including those of promoter, manager, and capital owner. The emergence of state capitalism today, which we recognise as a global phenomenon, has its roots in the expansion and globalisation of capitalism. State-capital hybrids have grown in number as a result of the state's political mediation of this capitalist restructuring process on a number of different levels and across the worldwide North-South divide. Second, the rapid development of China and the escalating rivalry between established players and up-and-coming rivals have politicised the expansion of state capitalism and heightened geopolitical tensions. As capitalism changes and takes on new forms, the function of the capitalist state will also change.

Keywords

Capitalist state
Capital accumulation
Market
General interest

Review Questions

1. Discuss the features of the capitalist state.
2. Discuss the evolution of the capitalist state with special reference to the changing forms of capitalism.
3. The expanding worldwide mobility of capital increases the pressure on the state to maintain investment-friendly conditions or face the consequences of capital flight. Describe the characteristics of a capitalist state in today's globalised society.

References

Alami, I. Dixon, A. Mawdsley E. 2021. State Capitalism and the New Global Development Regime Antipode. 53(5): 1294–1318. Doi: 10.1111/anti.12725

Altvater, E. 1973. Some Problems of State Interventionism. Kapitalistate, 1:96–108 and 76-83. Cited in Jessop B. 1990. State Theory Putting the Capitalist State in its place. UK: Polity Press.

Anguelov, D. 2020. Banking "Development": The Geopolitical–Economy of Infrastructure Financing. Area Development and Policy. https://doi.org/10.1080/23792949.2020.1799717

Barker, C. 1978. A Note on the Theory of Capitalist States. Capital & Class 4 (1), Spring.

Bremmer, I. 2010. The End of the Free Market. Who wins the war between states and Corporations. London: Portfolio Penguin Random House.

Carens, M. Mares, I. 2007. The Welfare State in Global Perspective. In Boix, C. Stokes, S. The Oxford Handbook of Comparative Politics. USA: Oxford University Press.

Chimhowu, A. O. Hulme, D. Munro, L. T. 2019. The "new" National Development Planning and Global Development Goals: Processes and Partnerships. *World Development* 120: 76–89.

Cumming, D. J., Wood, G., & Zahra, S. A. 2020. Human resource management practices in the context of rising right-wing populism. Human Resource Management Journal. https://doi.org/10.1111/1748-8583.12269.

Engels, Friedrich 1989. Socialism: Utopian and Scientific. MECW 24, 281–325.

Ferguson, N. 2012. We're All State Capitalists Now. Foreign Policy, February 9. Accessed from https://foreignpolicy.com on September 12, 2023.

Garland, D. 2016. The Welfare State: A Very Short Introduction. UK: Oxford University Press.

Gerstenberger, H. 2007. Impersonal Power: History and Theory of Bourgeois State. Leiden, The Netherlands: Brill.

Grimshaw D. Rubery, J. 2012. Reinforcing Neoliberalism: Crisis and Austerity in the UK. In S. lehndorff. (Ed.). A Triumph of Failed Ideas European models of Capitalism in the Crisis Brussells: ETUI: 41–58.

Hirsch, J. 2005. Materialistische Staatstheorie; Transformationsprozesse des kapitalistischen Staatensystems, Hamburg: VSA-Verlag.

Hirsch, J. 1974. Staatsapparat und Kapitalreproduktion, Frankfurt: Suhrkamp. Cited in Jessop B. 1990. State Theory Putting the Capitalist State in its Place. UK: Polity Press.

Hobbes, Thomas 1651, Leviathan. Accessed from http://files.libertyfund.org on September 11, 2023.

Holloway, J. and Picciotto, S. 1977. 'Capital, Crisis, and the State', Capital and Class, 2: 76-101. Cited in Jessop B. 1990. State Theory Putting the Capitalist State in its place. UK: Polity Press.

IFC, 2018.The State of Governance at State-Owned Enterprises. Corporate Governance Group, International Finance Corporation, World Bank Group.

IMF, 2020. Fiscal Monitor—April 2020. International Monetary Fund. Accessed from https://www.imf.org on September 14, 2023.

Jessop, B. 1991. *State Theory putting the capitalist state in its place.* Pennsylvania: The Pennsylvania State University Press.

Jessop, B. 2019.The Capitalist State and State Power. In Vidal, M. Smith, T. Rotta, T. Prew, P. The Oxford Handbook of Karl Marx. New York: Oxford University Press.

Jessop, B. 2002. The Future of the Capitalist State. UK: Polity Press.

Kanai, J. M. Schindler, S. 2019. Peri-Urban Promises of Connectivity: Linking Project led Polycentrism to the Infrastructure Scramble. Environment and Planning, A51(2): 302–322.

Krätke, M. R. 1987. Die Kritik der Staatsfinanzen: Zur politischen Ökonomie des Steuerstaats. Hamburg, Germany: VSA Verlag. Cited in Vidal, M. Smith, T. Rotta, T. Prew, P. 2019. The Oxford Handbook of Karl Marx. New York: Oxford University Press.

Mawdsley, E. Murray, W. E. Overton, J. Scheyvens, R. Banks, G. 2018. Exporting Stimulus and "Shared Prosperity": Reinventing Foreign Aid for a Retro Liberal Era. Development Policy Review, 36(S1): O25–O43.

McMichael, P. 1987. 'State formation and the Construction of the World Market', in M. Zeitlin. (Ed.). Political Power and Social Theory, 6, Greenwich, Ct: JAI Press. 187–237.

Megginson, W.L. 2005. *The Financial Economics of Privatization.* New York: Oxford University Press.

Milhaupt, C. J. Zeng, W. 2015. Reforming China's State Owned Enterprises: Institutions not Ownership. In C. J. Milhaut and C. J. Zeng. (Eds.) Regulating the Visible Hand? The Institutional Implications of Chinese State Capitalism. Oxford: Oxford University Press. 175–201.

Moore, S. W. 1957. The Critique of Capitalist Democracy. *An Introduction to the Theory of the State in Marx, Engels and Lenin*. New York: Paine Whitman.

Musacchio, A. Lazzarini, S. G. 2014. Reinventing State Capitalism. Harvard University Press.

OECD 2015.State-Owned Enterprises in the Development Process. Organisation for Economic Co-operation and Development. Accessed from https://www.oecd.org on September 12, 2023.

Poulantzas, N. 1978. *State, Power, Socialism*. London: Verso.

Reuten, G. 2019. *The Unity of the Capitalist Economy and State A Systematic-Dialectical Exposition of the Capitalist System*. Leiden: Brill.

Schindler, S. Kanai J. M. 2021. Getting the Territory Right: Infrastructure-led development and the re-emergence of spatial planning strategies. Regional Studies, 55(1): 40–51.

Schindler, S. Kanai, J. M. 2021. Getting the Territory Right: Infrastructure led Development and the Re-emergence of Spatial Planning Strategies. Regional Studies, 55(1): 40–51.

Sheppard, E. Leitner, H. 2010. Quo vadis Neoliberalism? The Remaking of Global Capitalist Governance after the Washington Consensus.Geoforum, 41(2): 185–194.

Smith, Adam 1776. An Inquiry into the nature and causes of The Wealth of Nations, Edited by Edwin Cannan, from the 5th 1791 edition, London: Methuen & Co. Accessed from http://www.econlib.org on September 12, 2023.

Thomas, P. 1994. Alien Politics: Marxist State Theory Retrieved. London: Routledge.

UNCTAD 2018. World Investment Report, 2018. United Nations Conference on Trade and Development. Accessed from https://unctad.org on September 12, 2023.

Von Braunmühl, C. 1978. On the Analysis of the Bourgeois Nation State within the World Market Context. In State and Capital, edited by John Holloway and Sol Picciotto. London: Edward Arnold. 160–177.

Werner, M. 2021. Geographies of Production II: Thinking through the State. Progress In Human Geography, 45(1):178–189.

Wiggens, K., van der Velde, M., & Wigglesworth, R. 2020. Coronavirus: Private equity's bailout, 14 April Available at: Financial Times. Accessed from https://www.ft.com on September 12, 2023.

Witt, M. A. Redding, G. 2013. Asian Business Systems: Institutional Comparisons, Clusters and implications for Varieties of Capitalism and Business Systems theory. Socio Economic Review, 11(2): 265–300.

Wood, G. Wright, M. 2015. Corporations and New Statism: Trends and Research Priorities. The Academy of Management Perspectives. 29(2): 271–286.

World Bank-PPIAF, 2017. Who Sponsors Infrastructure Projects? Disentangling Public and Private Contributions. The World Bank and the Public-Private Infrastructure Advisory Facility. Accessed from https://ppi.worldbank.org on September 12, 2023.

Wright, M. Wood, G. Musacchio, A. Okhmatovskiy, I. Grosman, A. Jonathan P. 2021 State Capitalism in International Context: Varieties and Variations. Journal of World Business. https://doi.org/10.1016/j.jwb.2020.101160.

Yaffe, D. 1973. 'The Marxian Theory of Crisis, Capital, and the State', Economy and Society, 2(2): 186–222.

Yeung, H. W. C. 2016. Strategic Coupling: East Asian Industrial Transformation in the New Global Economy. Ithaca: Cornell University Press.

CHAPTER 14

The Welfare State

Chetna Sharma

Reader's Guide

This chapter lays out the characteristics of the welfare state in concrete terms to help us grasp how it differs from a capitalist or neoliberal state. The welfare state is a system aimed to steer the capitalist juggernaut along a more socially acceptable track, whereas the capitalist economy is a dynamic machine for producing private profits through competitive production and market exchange. The term 'welfare state' has led to some of our misconceptions about it. Welfare states do not focus solely on 'welfare.' They deal with social protection, social rights, social provision, and the social control of economic activity, all of which have a wider range of beneficiaries than only the poor. At its core, the market economy is moralised and modified by a series of social safeguards imposed on capitalist economic processes. These safeguards can be funded by payroll deductions, general taxation, or government borrowing and come in a variety of shapes and sizes depending on the state.

14.1 Introduction

After consolidating their territory and sovereignty, modern states went through a number of developmental stages. The first goal was to offer a minimal safety net, but over time, states extended public services to broader sections of the population and provided equal civil and political rights to all citizens. Most states steered clear of "too much" social and economic involvement for a very long period. Physical security was deemed to be the state's primary function according to the prevalent liberal conception of government. Yet, the Great Depression of the 1930s and the turmoil of the post-war economy in the late 1940s altered the old laissez-faire beliefs that were connected to growing capitalism in many nations. Democratic states gradually came to terms with the notion that markets did not always operate efficiently and that intervention by the government was required to address these inadequacies. Several states started to take on a bigger role in caring for the very young and very old, the sick and disabled, the jobless and the impoverished. After the Second World War, primarily in Western Europe but also in other parts of the world, state extended its role and reach to different sectors and welfare states emerged.

The simplest definition of a welfare state may be one in which the government is responsible for providing its residents with at least a basic level of welfare. Such a definition avoids questions like what exactly is meant by "basic," if social policies are in fact emancipatory, whether they aid in system legitimation or not, and whether they work to counter or support the market process. Would it not be more appropriate to demand of a welfare state that it satisfy more than our basic or minimal welfare needs? (Esping-Andersen, 1990:19). In the interests of the general populace, answers to these intriguing issues were necessary.

Furthermore, it's critical to comprehend whether the welfare state concept should only be seen as a specific period in post-war history. According to David Garland (2016), the concept of welfare is an essential part of modern government that is present in all advanced nations in some capacity and serves as a vital tool for ensuring the social and economic sustainability of capitalist economies. The idea of welfare state and its functions are contested by many. Progressives claim that it is a poor substitute for a major redistribution of wealth and property. Conservatives contend that it weakens entrepreneurship, demoralises recipients, and establishes an oppressive, tax-and-spend state by being overly charitable and insufficiently punitive. Welfare users contend that they would prefer to have a well-paying job over the embarrassments that come with receiving means-tested benefits. The burden of paying for people who choose not to work is something that taxpayers frequently lament. In contrast to anyone's ideal social interaction, the welfare state, according to David Garland (2016), is a tool for problem-solving and damage control. Let's try to comprehend the welfare state and the types of difficulties it faces in various parts of the world against the backdrop of this contentious understanding of the welfare state.

14.2 Origin and Evolution of the Welfare State

At the end of the 19th century, western countries began to develop unique sets of socio-economic structures and modes of government. By the middle of the 20th century, these states had been firmly established. Nonetheless, throughout human history, societies have exhibited some type of collective social provision. Certain forms of governmental social participation date back to the sixteenth century. A relief programme known as "the Poor Law" was developed by the early modern English state. Starting in the late 16th century, Parliament passed laws that sought to modernise the religious dole system and set it up on a more consistent, secular foundation. Authorities from the local government now disbursed alms that had previously been given by churches, monasteries, and charity hospitals. Local administrations in Britain were still in charge of providing poor relief at the turn of the 20th century. Yet, as time went on, the national government became more involved. Both in colonial America and Great Britain, where analogous poor law institutions were eventually founded, the relief and regulation of the poor was one of the pillars upon which the modern state was built.

By the late 18th century, market capitalism, urbanisation, and industrialization had begun to weaken the traditional safeguards supplied by local churches, monasteries, and charitable organisations. The new political economy pushed for the commodification of land, labour, and money as well as the repeal of regulations and practises that restricted the free flow of goods and services on the market (Jessop, 2002). With the emergence of capitalism, new ideas about political economics and possessive individualism emerged that posed a threat to the pre-existing protective relationships. Individualism replaced community in the new socio-economic system, contract took precedence over status, and the economy was seen as a separate realm from the social.

To address the problems that arose under a system dominated by capitalism, several sorts of state action and involvement were necessary. During a time of scarcity and food riots brought on by the Napoleonic wars, Berkshire magistrates implemented a system known as "Speenhamland" (after the town in which it was originally developed) in 1795. To help workers feed their families during a time when salaries were low and bread was expensive, Speenhamland was a system of allowances and grants-in-aid of wages. The system's impact, which quickly expanded to other rural areas, was widely acknowledged to be disastrous. Due to the availability of allowances for employed labourers, employers were forced to reduce pay, endangering the financial stability of nearby residents whose property taxes supported the system. The fury it caused fuelled calls for the repeal of the Poor Laws, a demand that claimed the concepts of Thomas Malthus, David Ricardo, and Adam Smith as supporters. Yet, no political economist completely supported such a radical position. A Royal Commission of Investigation was established in 1832, and two years later it issued a report outlining the frightening scale of the new pauperism and the failure of the system designed to combat it. The old Poor Laws were not completely repealed, despite the Report's extensive criticism. A significant opposition movement of collectivist advancements and new social protections was posing a threat to the laissez-faire revolution by the middle of the 19th century. Industrialization brought employees together in massive mines and factories and aided in the development of labour unions. The first trade union federations emerged in Germany and England, but they gradually spread to all developed nations. After this, workers' parties began to emerge, first in Germany around 1870, then in other European nations, and eventually in Britain, where the British Labour Party was founded in 1900. The power dynamics between social classes changed as a result of the workers' increasing organisational strength, giving labour's representatives newfound sway. According to Karl Polanyi (1944), welfare states were created as a result of the broad opposition to the laissez-faire philosophy and economic system.

Although British governments upheld their belief in the free market, they acknowledged "extraordinary circumstances" where protective measures were required and laissez-faire principles should be disregarded. Intervention by the central government was justified in a variety of areas, including the regulation of railroads, mines, and factories; the provision of public education; the advancement of public health; and many more. Even more was done by city governments, including giving access to clean water, sewage, and sanitation; controlling the housing market; establishing public restrooms, libraries, and parks; and instituting a 'municipal socialism' that was in direct opposition to free market ideas.

This historical dialectic is known as the "double movement" by Polanyi (1944). On one side, the forces of laissez-faire liberalism triumphed, creating a new society based on market freedom, individual interests, and a limited state; on the other, a widespread, diffuse reaction was sparked by the pragmatic collectivism of various authorities who took action to deal with emergencies, fix market failures, and manage the social upheavals brought on by the capitalist juggernaut. A similar dynamic played out in the USA, where local public welfare laws and sporadically distributed massive disaster aid from the federal government balanced out the country's ideological commitment to laissez-faire and market individualism.

Around the middle of the nineteenth century, a new system of social and economic governance spread over the developed world with surprising speed. The first social insurance legislation were enacted by German Chancellor Bismarck in the 1880s. Ten years later, the first old age pension programmes were introduced by the governments of Australia, New Zealand, and Denmark. Workmen's compensation, old-age pensions, labour exchanges, and a nascent system of National Insurance for sickness, invalidity, and unemployment were all implemented by liberal governments in Britain at the beginning of the 20th century. Western nations were driven towards a universal vote by the rise of organised labour as an industrial and political power, which in turn gave rise to new demands for economic security and redistributive policies. The principles of liberalism were updated by intellectuals like T. H. Green and L. T. Hobhouse starting in the 1880s and 1890s, advocating a more optimistic image of the state and rethinking the connection between social and economic policy. This brand of liberalism believed that the greatest way to promote individual freedom was to provide individuals with the education, welfare, and security they need to practise true autonomy rather than leaving them to fend for themselves.

Several areas of the world's welfare state founders subscribed to a variety of ideologies: Bismarck was a conservative, Beveridge and Keynes were liberals, Atlee and Bevan were democratic socialists, Roosevelt was a pragmatic populist with a patrician background, and trade unions created the welfare state in Sweden. Few of them were fervent opponents of traditional family values or staunch critics of capitalism. They pushed for a welfare state because they were worried by the persistent evidence of economic instability, unpredictability, market failures, family disintegration, home squalor, and the misery and calamities that capitalism brings with it. Their argument always depended on an understanding of contemporary issues and the need for real-world solutions, not on idealistic utopias or radical ideologies.

The political and economic disasters of the 1930s and 1940s compelled post-war governments to establish welfare states as the cornerstone of their nation-states and to create an international monetary system to support that objective. Following the Great Depression, capitalists also recognised the advantages of managed economies. The more forward-thinking capitalists understood and accepted this since welfare governments provided the social structures and human capacities that were necessary for market capitalism to function. Welfare measures also resulted from demands made by large coalitions made up of farmers, members of the middle class, and professionals. Following fascism and the problems caused by the lure of communism and Soviet propaganda, it was crucial to connect various social groups to the democratic state by providing social benefits that would benefit everyone. In the midst of World War II, the Provisional Government of the French Republic and the British government both published expansive welfare state proposals. Every industrialised country had a core of welfare state institutions in place by 1960, and every government had taken on the duty of overseeing the economy.

Political scientist Harold Wilensky (2002:211) noted that the welfare state has transformed into "one of the great structural uniformities of modern society" in a relatively short amount of time. The welfare state was created as a practical solution to the issues that plagued urban, industrial, market society, particularly the additional risks and uncertainties brought on by unrestrained market capitalism. According to economist John Maynard Keynes, welfare states are a set of collective action strategies for the more effective control of capitalism's market processes rather than a method of abolishing them. National governments across the industrialised world had passed laws governing social insurance, income tax, old-age pensions, and child welfare by the early decades of the 20th century, establishing new administrative networks that linked the state to the populace. The new approach saw government take control of controlling labour markets and guaranteeing economic outcomes, as opposed to laissez-insistence faire's on limiting government and opening up markets.

Many facets of society received benefits from the welfare state. Wealthier households benefited from policies like healthcare, better education, and the home mortgage tax deduction. Women from the middle class have access to higher education and professional professions. Companies benefited from a skilled and healthy work force and collaborated with unions to negotiate salary and productivity agreements that brought about industrial peace, enabled longer-term planning, and improved competitiveness. In many countries, trade unions started to promote integration rather than confrontation, and they were rewarded with a seat at the economic governing table. Full employment, growing real earnings, and improved public services brought about an improvement in security and living standards for the working class. Reducing poverty, fostering equality of opportunity, encouraging individual autonomy, promoting social stability, and promoting social integration were, in general, the five main objectives of welfare states.

The post-World War II decades saw the expansion of welfare states made feasible by a booming global economy, the supremacy of western manufacturing, affordable energy, a secure global monetary system, and a Fordist regime of mass production and mass consumption. Additionally, they were made possible by the framework of economic and financial ties established at Bretton Woods in 1944. This system of institutions promoted trade, provided funding for development, and upheld fixed exchange rates while giving national economies some degree of control over their own futures. Individual governments could restrict the cross-border flow of capital and money under this form of "embedded liberalism," shielding their economies from the full impact of global competition. Additionally, it permitted governments to control labour markets and raise money for social spending because domestic investors, producers, and consumers had few departure choices.

Bretton Woods lasted until 1971, when the US administration, under pressure from the costs of Vietnam (an unpopular war that was fought without tax increases to pay it), a significant trade imbalance, and recurrent runs on its currency, devalued the dollar and revoked its convertibility into gold unilaterally. This move destabilised the international system and loosened the restraints that had restrained national economies. At the same time, the expansionist era of the global economy came to an end and a period of contraction began, which was characterised by deep recessions, slow economic growth, and high unemployment rates, all of which had a negative impact on the funding of welfare states. Western economies suffered when OPEC countries doubled the price of oil in 1973, thereby ending the era of cheap energy.

Special Insights

Welfare State: The Dilemma of Name

An issue has always existed with the term "welfare state." The phrase was least popular when it initially became widely used in the 1950s and 1960s. The man widely considered as the founder of the British welfare state, William Beveridge, was vehemently opposed to the word. He disagreed, saying that it suggested a "something for nothing" or "Santa Claus state," which was at variance with his emphasis on the value of employee contributions, volunteer labour, and personal responsibility. The author of the current concepts of social rights and social citizenship, T. H. Marshall, likewise shied away from the phrase. Marshall never once used the phrase in his well-known speech on citizenship and social class, and he subsequently said, 'the welfare state is a term for which I have developed a very strong dislike'. Even Richard Titmuss, the foremost intellectual advocate for Britain's post-war social policies, believed that the term "welfare state" was hostile and was more often employed by opponents of social policy than supporters. Beveridge, Marshall, and Titmuss recognised the tendency of the phrase "welfare state" to conjure up images of a beggarly population receiving unfair advantages from an overbearing state. These negative associations still exist and are all-too-easily recalled because the term finally gained acceptance and was used by both supporters and opponents. It would be more true and less Anglo-centric, according to David Garland (2016), to speak of "the social state" and "welfare capitalism," if we could just wave a magic wand and change the vocabulary.

14.3 Approaches to Understand Welfare State

The welfare state raises several important moral questions concerning social justice, the character of the contemporary state, and how it interacts with its people. The nature of welfare state and social security expenditures, as a form of citizen redistribution, varies greatly between governments and is typically the cause of major social, political, and economic turmoil. Regarding how the welfare state operates, there are two fundamentally different perspectives. Liberal viewpoints view the welfare state as a left-wing organisation that taxes the wealthy, infringes on their liberties, and promotes worker dependency and laziness. According to socialist perspectives, the welfare state is a right-wing tool used by the capitalist system to maintain a healthy, educated workforce without resorting to coercion or excessive expenditures. The other ideas centre on the reasons why very distinct social security programme models developed in various nations. Esping-Andersen, a Danish political scientist, offers one of the most thorough analyses of welfare state programmes and the numerous organisational models. He makes distinctions between various welfare state forms based on eligibility for benefits, levels of assistance, the extent of redistribution, and efficacy in reducing or fostering inequality. Esping-Andersen provides three categories based on these characteristics.

Social democratic welfare capitalism: Scandinavian nations have a form of welfare capitalism that is social-democratic. The objective of social security is equality based on the highest standards, not equality of "minimum needs." It follows that everyone participates equally in the system on the basis of the principle of universal entitlement and that monetary payments are generous and of a high standard. The objective is to emphasise individual independence as much as possible rather than the market or the family. High degrees of decommodification, extensive universalist benefits, strong cross-class solidarity, reliance on public rather than private provision, and a dedication to equality characterise this system.

Conservative Welfare capitalism: Continental Europe, which includes Austria, France, Germany, and Italy, is home to a conservative kind of welfare capitalism. This style is characterised by corporatism, in which governments, employers' groups, and unions work closely together to plan social security programmes. The degree of redistribution is often low, and entitlements are based on status and class. The government mainly relies on the cooperation of industry and labour organisations. Social security programmes emphasise traditional family values since the church has a significant influence on corporatist regimes. This system demonstrates a dedication to subsidiarity principles, modest levels of decommodification, the preservation of occupational hierarchies, and a desire to maintain traditional family relationships.

Liberal welfare Capitalism: Liberal politics, capitalist economics, and residual social policies form the foundation of the liberal welfare state. In Anglo-Saxon nations, particularly in Australia, Canada, and the USA, a liberal form of welfare capitalism is prevalent. Benefits are limited and primarily provided to low-income populations. Traditional standards of labour ethics are significant, and entitlement laws are severe. The government supports social security initiatives from the business sector. Low levels of decommodification, meagre benefits, a preference for private means of social support, and a general interest in bolstering markets are all characteristics of this system.

The welfare state arguments of the 1990s revolved around Esping-Andersen's typology. Although his typology has many serious drawbacks, including the omission of gender concerns, the distinctive characteristics of southern

Europe, the interdependence of "welfare capitalism," and discussions over benefits between unions and employers' associations, his typology is nevertheless crucial. Its key benefit is that it organises a lot of dissimilar systems into a few useful and comprehensible categories.

14.3.1 Functionalist Explanations

The earliest analyses of social security system diversity place a heavy emphasis on functionalist justifications. State intervention is necessary in emerging capitalism to protect workers and stabilise families. This point of view contends that variations in social security between nations are mostly due to varying degrees of socioeconomic growth. According to a recent resurgence of functionalism, welfare policies help modern nations transition from industrial to post-industrial economies, allowing, for instance, the closure of coal mines and textile factories by pensioning miners and textile employees or retraining them for other careers.

14.3.2 Institutional Approaches

They emphasise the significance of institutional frameworks. According to the theory, large social security arrangements become more challenging to develop as more institutions become involved in policymaking. States with complicated federal systems and those that hold referendums the most are less developed than unitary states, where the ability to make decisions is consolidated and centralised. The endurance of welfare states after they are formed may also be explained by institutional inertia since these states are surrounded by bureaucracy and institutionalised interests that prevent reform. Depending on each country's decision-making structures in the welfare sector, two variations of the institutional approach can be used. First, there's the concept of policy networks. In general, policy networks involve a greater range of interests and, as a result, more disagreement and conflict than communities since they are looser and more open. Government officials, senior welfare department officials, a wide range of welfare professionals and staff, and a wide range of pressure groups representing welfare service users are all included in welfare policy networks. The network of committees, working groups, and consultative bodies established within governmental institutions and commercial organisations like think tanks brings these together. In the welfare sector, policy networks are present in Britain, France, and Italy, with a lesser degree in the USA.

The formulation of welfare policies in other nations is heavily formalised inside corporatist institutions. In accordance with these arrangements, the government and a select group of business interests collaborate closely within the official structures that develop and carry out public policy. This entails that all parties concerned at the highest levels of the corporatist structure are free to bargain and negotiate in the knowledge that the decision made about the implementation of the policy will be supported by those at lower levels of the system. It has the benefit that judgements can be taken that have legal force, and that steady, predictable rules can be followed. The system's downside is that it is more exclusive and closed off than policy networks, which precludes organisations outside of the corporatist system from participating in decision-making. Austria, Luxembourg, The Netherlands, Norway, and Sweden throughout the 1960s and 1980s were among the countries with the most established corporatism. At the same time period, less pure versions were discovered in Belgium, Denmark, Finland, West Germany, Ireland, and Switzerland.

14.3.3 International and Transnational Dependencies

There are methodologies that emphasise global and transnational dependencies. They, like Lenin's theory of colonialism, explain the multiplicity of social security systems in terms of relationships between states. More recently, a contentious discussion regarding whether globalisation requires nations to decrease their welfare programmes in order to boost their economies' competitiveness in the global market has erupted. New Zealand is occasionally cited as the paradigmatic example of a nation that transitioned from having a protected economy and a robust welfare state to having a market economy and a more restrained welfare state. There is a claim that pressure is mounting to change welfare policy in small or weak economies. They must slash costs, including their welfare costs, in order to defend themselves against the effects of global capitalism. Theories focused on the influence of the European Union on the social policies of its member states are also included in this group of explanations.

These varied techniques initially appear to be competing theories. But none appears to be adequate on its own. Because one explains only a portion of the riddle, a much better explanation incorporates all of them. As an illustration, the emergence of the welfare state has usually resulted in intense friction between employers and employees who have distinct financial resources and varied capacities for organising support. This conflict has also been acted out simultaneously in many institutional settings, inside various legal frameworks, and in accordance with various laws. International conditions, especially those in which developed economies, particularly colonial powers, had higher surpluses to dedicate to welfare, undoubtedly had an impact on the outcomes. Finally, it is important to note that there are numerous distinct methods to establish a welfare state, just as there are numerous and equally viable ways to establish a democratic political system. Monetary transfers are not inherently better or worse than the direct delivery of services, while they may be more appropriate for some situations or goals than others. As a result, various welfare state features are used by various states.

14.3.4 Welfare State Sectors

Welfare states are also tax states since they must pay for the benefits, which necessitates the transfer of resources. In many nations, the 1960s and 1970s saw the rapid expansion of social security programmes with relatively little complaint or opposition. The social and economic security programmes contributed to the development of a just and fair society, which improved the legitimacy of the state and its social structures. In most nations, a comprehensive list of welfare state policies would be lengthy, and even the most basic of them are extremely difficult to administer. The varieties of welfare sectors in different countries are as follows:

Social Insurance: Social insurance programmes are often legally required, state-administered, more-or-less comprehensive programmes that are aimed at safeguarding workers and their families against financial loss as a result of illness, injury, old age, disability, or unemployment. The insecurity of wage employees and their families—the fundamental issue with capitalist labour markets—is addressed by these programmes through a system of shared risk that generalises security. Employees are required to make regular contributions (supplemented by employer contributions made on their behalf) to programmes like National Insurance in the UK or Social Security in the USA in order to be eligible for benefits like sickness and disability payments, unemployment benefits, retirement pensions, and other benefits.

Social Assistance: Social assistance is the umbrella term for non-contributory, income-support programmes that provide relief to people whose incomes are insufficient to meet their fundamental requirements. Benefits from social assistance are often selectively offered to just those who can prove their need. Examples include the General Assistance, Food Stamps, Earned Income Tax Credits, Child Tax Credits, Supplementary Security Income, and Medicaid programmes in the United States, as well as the Income Support (formerly known as "National Assistance" and "Supplementary Benefits" and currently transitioning to "Universal Credit"), Housing Benefits, Council Tax Allowance, Rent Rebates, Free School Meals, and Means-Tested Jobseeker's Allowance programmes in the United Kingdom. Social assistance is minimally redistributive and funded by general taxes.

Publicly-funded social services: These services offer free or reduced-cost access to things like day-care, healthcare, public transportation, legal help, and so on. Moreover, local government earnings are used to pay for amenities like parks, libraries, museums, sports and recreation centres, affordable housing, and other public spaces for use by the public. Hence, social rights and services offer "decommodified" answers to urbanisation and marketization-related issues.

Social Work and Personal Social Service: Social work and individual social services make up a fourth sector. Welfare states offer individualised forms of support like social work with families, children's services, social care for the elderly, community care for the mentally ill, and probation and aftercare supervision for offenders, in addition to insurance benefits, social assistance, and public services.

Economic management: The government's role in the economy is crucial, to sum up. The functioning of extensive government restrictions over economic life is necessary for welfare state programmes to function.

Industry nationalisation, economic planning, property rights distribution, tax laws, fiscal and monetary policy, consumer credit policy, labour market policies, corporatist agreements, prices and incomes policies, farming and food subsidies, industrial policy, training initiatives, regional investment initiatives, financial rules, and minimum wage laws are all currently being used or have historically been employed as instruments of economic management in welfare states.

Hidden Welfare State: David Garland (2016) emphasises the "hidden welfare state" as a key component of the welfare programme. It comprises of social assistance payments that are distributed either through the tax code or through independent contractor agreements. For instance, the US house mortgage tax allowance is a significant government assistance and stimulus programme, whose expenditures are higher than those of the country's public housing. The government subsidises and regulates corporate welfare programmes that offer certain employees improved retirement, healthcare, and other "fringe benefits," but which are offered by businesses as a form of tax-exempt remuneration. These social welfare programmes, which are the least egalitarian of all, are mainly hidden in the tax system and are rarely the subject of political discussion.

Special Insights

Social Security Provisions in Different States

Many countries have quite varied systems in place for social security. Certain countries, such as Denmark, the Netherlands, or Sweden, have very comprehensive risk management programmes. Others, including the USA, UK, and Japan, offer more constrained coverage. In 2001, state social security costs in Denmark and Sweden accounted for about 30% of GDP. Korea and Mexico are at the other end of the scale, with social security spending at 6.1% and 5.1% of GDP, respectively. A quarter of the national budgets of several European nations, notably France, Germany, Italy, and Norway, are allocated to social spending. In comparison to other regions of the world, Europe spends more overall. The services that states offer highlight the differences between them even more. The elderly receive around 45% of social security payments in Greece. In European nations, health typically comes in second. In almost every nation, health care and pensions are the two biggest spending priorities. Combined, they cover nearly two-thirds of social security costs in several European nations and more than three-quarters in the United States. (Newton, 2010: 370–371)

14.3.5 Welfare State in Different Parts of the World

Understanding the welfare state is essential for comprehending modern politics, which exhibit complex systems with a variety of organising principles that change and adapt, whether at the level of administration on a daily basis or at the more fundamental level of policies and goals (Kersbergen; Manow; 2020). The American welfare state was formed by Franklin D. Roosevelt's New Deal. Yet Johnson's Great Society reforms altered and expanded FDR's welfare state, and then Clinton's "welfare to work" legislation redesigned it. The welfare state in America is primarily liberal or "market-conforming," although it provides almost socialist-style benefits to veterans and their families, and government spending on education has traditionally been rather significant. Despite the fact that these countries are frequently lumped together as having "liberal" welfare regimes, America's welfare institutions are substantially distinct from those of Canada, Australia, or New Zealand. America's welfare state differs between itself as well, with each of the fifty states and many local governments implementing various programmes and services for its citizens. In a similar vein, the welfare state established in the United Kingdom by post-World War II Labour administration figures like Clement Atlee and Nye Bevan has undergone substantial revision and change in the intervening decades. The social democratic system in Sweden has neoliberal components and certain privatised services. The relatively modest, market-oriented form that exists in the USA contrasts sharply with the large, egalitarian welfare state of social democratic Sweden. The welfare states of other social democratic countries, especially those of Sweden's Nordic neighbours, with whom it is typically grouped, also differ from Sweden's welfare state in significant respects.

Although in Britain, social insurance programmes were created on the basis of universalistic ideas, with everyone contributing at the same flat rate and receiving benefits at the same flat rate. In order to ensure that labour market disparities were replicated in welfare costs and benefits, Germany, Austria, and France tied contribution and benefit levels to earnings. Federal nations with weaker states, most notably the USA, ceded many of these responsibilities to local government. France and Britain, two governments with strong centralization, gave authority to central government institutions to oversee the system.

Some countries, like the Netherlands and Germany, relied on religious institutions and non-profit organisations to provide social services. In order to modernise industry, train employees, guarantee full employment, and maintain price stability, governments in Germany, France, and Sweden constructed corporatist structures that enlisted employer federations and trade unions as "social partners." The establishment of public daycare and assistance for the elderly by Nordic welfare nations increased the independence and equality of women. Countries like Italy, Germany, and France focused on the requirements of the industrial male worker while attempting to preserve traditional family systems.

The Nordic region spends up to 30% of GDP on social programmes; continental governments spend an intermediate 25%; and Anglophone countries spend the least, with the USA and other countries in the region spending less than 20%. Large spending, however, may not always be a sign of the system's generosity. For instance, during Thatcher's administrations, unemployment costs rose, not because services were better, but rather because the rate of unemployment had dramatically grown.

In Nazi Germany, Vichy France, Fascist Italy, and Peronist Argentina, welfare states existed and contributed to the politics of nationalism, populism, and even racial eugenics that characterised these regimes. The communist welfare states that existed in countries like East Germany, Hungary, and Yugoslavia up until the 1980s guaranteed full employment, the right to work, a large range of low-quality public services, and heavy subsidies for necessities like food and housing. There are quite affluent welfare states today in Middle Eastern oil nations like Saudi Arabia, United Arab Emirates, Oman, Kuwait, and Qatar as well as in Asian states like Hong Kong and Singapore. Nevertheless, these states only provide benefits to their own citizens and do not accept migrant workers. China, Brazil, and India have similarly created systems of social insurance, pensions, and healthcare to cover their vast populations.

14.4 Crisis and Criticism of the Welfare State

The socioeconomic environment in which the welfare state operates is dynamic. Welfare state programmes are impacted by changes in the labour markets, demographics, household structure, cultural values, and citizen expectations. The welfare state has faced several crises at various times in an effort to adjust to socioeconomic developments. Each new policy creates a new front in the ongoing battle for limited resources that characterises welfare reform and mobilises a diverse range of interest groups. There are competing interests in these conflicts for employers and employees, pensioners and young people, families with and without children, taxpayers and welfare recipients, high earners and the low paid, etc. Arguments over welfare often involve tensions over issues of race, class, gender, and migration, making them emotionally fraught and weighted in terms of symbolism. The spectre of inflation and slow growth posed a serious challenge to the welfare state in the 1950s. It was excessive bureaucracy, excessive control, and the continuance of poverty a decade later. Stagflation (high unemployment, high inflation, and low growth) was the main issue in the 1970s; unemployment and "dependence culture" were the main issues in the 1990s; cost containment and public debt are the current issues.

Welfare fraud affects all welfare systems. Individuals make misleading claims. When they are healthy enough to work, they make up illnesses or say they are taking care of dependents who don't exist. They pretend to be looking for work when they are really avoiding it or get unemployment benefits while working "off the books." Employees who are physically fit retire on disability benefits after being declared unfit by conspiring doctors, and so on. These are actual issues that damage the system's reputation.

Large-scale fraud by welfare providers is a more serious issue, particularly in welfare states where services are acquired by public agencies and delivered by private companies. American journalists expose doctors who defraud Medicaid, nursing home owners who overpay the government, and even judges of juvenile courts who are bought to send minors to private detention institutions.

Welfare services are frequently criticised for giving benefits to people who are not eligible and can be rigid and inattentive. Another issue is the propensity of welfare organisations to make application procedures onerous and humiliating in order to deter clients from claiming their legitimate benefits. Instead of encouraging customers to become autonomous, overbearing bureaucracy can demoralise and weaken them.

Special Insights

Changing Demography: Challenge for the Welfare State

Welfare states must give the highest consideration to population dynamics and traits. Western countries saw low rates of elderly population and high rates of working-age population in the 1950s and 1960s, resulting in a favourable "dependence rate"—that is, a favourable ratio of many contributing workers to few welfare state recipients. These actuarial benefits vanished in later decades. Humans lived longer, which resulted in an increase in the elderly population as well as the number of really old people. Life expectancy was 48 years for males and 49 years for women in 1907 when old age pensions were first offered in Britain. Few individuals lived long enough to be eligible for the pension at age 70.

The population of retirees receiving pensions has increased significantly, and the average life expectancy today is 75 and 80 years, respectively. In 2009, 13% of Americans and 16% of Britons were 65 or older, with the latter population group expected to double in size during the ensuing 35 years. The birth rate has decreased in Western countries as well. Women today have fewer children than they did in the middle of the 20th century, which has led to a decline in population growth throughout several European and Scandinavian countries. The age distribution of the populations in Europe has significantly changed as a result of these trends, with fewer workers having to support an increasing number of pensioners.

Excessive spending is another issue. It is alleged that public entities do not follow the same cost-control rules as the private sector. They are accused of being wasteful with other people's money and having a greater interest in growing their budgets and bureaucracies than in keeping costs down. Government transfers are compared to a "leaky bucket," with money being lost as a necessary by-product. Even when social organisations run well, they frequently become victims of their own success, leading to the development of new requirements, raised expectations, and greater expenses. For instance, expenses rise in the healthcare industry as more advanced technology and treatments become accessible and as people start to demand higher standards of care.

Another important criticism is that assistance programmes have unexpected repercussions and "perverse" impacts, which worsen the situation rather than make it better. A typical example is when government agencies try to decrease local poverty by making benefits freely accessible, only to discover that their kindness draws more claims from other areas. This "magnet effect" issue also occasionally results in foreign migrants claiming social benefits, which causes "benefit tourism." Welfare regimes have hidden moral costs that outweigh their advantages. For instance, if individuals start to believe that the government is the only one in charge of solving social issues, then their willingness to volunteer their time may decline. Giving welfare assistance may diminish autonomy, making people more reliant mentally while improving their financial circumstances. Dependence on benefits over an extended period of time may demoralise claimants, discouraging initiative and effort, lowering self-respect and responsibility, etc.

Special Insights

Migration, Cultural Change and Welfare State

Western countries have seen significant waves of immigration in recent years, increasing their ethnic and religious diversity (Xu, 2007). Moreover 10 million residents of the EU at the beginning of the 1990s were citizens of non-European countries, and a further 5 million were EU citizens who had relocated among member states. Solidarities that welfare regimes rely on are getting harder to maintain. Political unrest is being caused by assertions that immigrants steal benefits intended for citizens. Stories about migrant labourers from Eastern Europe and "benefit tourists" in the UK have outraged the public and fuelled anti-EU sentiment.

As the Crash of 2008 starkly shown, the government's de facto position as the last-resort insurer and willingness to rescue huge corporations from bankruptcy may encourage high-risk behaviour. Some economists believe that the welfare state is a significant contributor to moral hazard because it protects market participants from danger, which causes them to be less cautious, inventive, and entrepreneurial. The welfare state also unintentionally perpetuates particular types of racial, ethnic, and patriarchal dominance. The resident national population, as well as its constituent families and individual citizens, were seen as the main targets of welfare and social reproduction policies. Several of these programmes were based on the supposition that stable, two-parent households were more common, in which men could expect lifetime employment, if not necessarily a job for life, and were paid a "family wage." Welfare state provisions have been based on the male breadwinner model of household and employment because welfare states presuppose the stability of the patriarchal family form (Pateman, 1989). Additionally, this ignored other sexualities and various family or household structures (Carabine, 1996).

Welfare states have faced significant, and occasionally insurmountable, challenges that have sparked discussion about the welfare state's demise.

Special Insights

Gender, Family and Welfare State

The idea behind post-war welfare regimes was to protect male breadwinners by assuming that their "family salary" would cover the needs of wives and kids. And they took it for granted that there were stable households with women taking care of the home, the kids, and the elderly. A feminist analysis of the welfare state was presented by Alva Myrdal. She claimed that what needs to be protected is "working women's right to marry and have children," rather than "married women's right to work" (1945:121).

In modern times, the supply of unpaid welfare is considerably reduced as more women enter the workforce, as fewer men's salaries can support a family, as more marriages terminate in divorce or separation, and as more people choose to live alone or as single parents, as well as the fact that fewer men's earnings can support a family. Again, these trends have major implications for welfare states, particularly in liberal benefit regimes in the Nordic countries where the rates of divorce and unwed pregnancies are high. In Scandinavia and the United States, more than half of all children grow up without both biological parents. Together with divorce laws being liberalised, benefits for single parents, and improved social services, the main result of women entering the workforce has been to decrease women's dependence on men and increase their level of autonomy. Concerns about the effects of family breakup, the demands of working women, and the issues of an increasingly diversified range of households are some of the issues that welfare states are attempting to address.

14.4.1 Decline of the Welfare State

Post-war development and the creation of welfare states were made possible by expanding markets, affordable energy, and stable money. Nevertheless, starting in the late 1960s, signs of global economic slowdown emerged, including dropping profit margins, declining productivity, balance of payments issues, budget deficits, and recurrent fiscal crises. The 1973 oil shock that sparked the crisis was the beginning of a sharp and protracted economic slump, but Bretton Woods' earlier collapse—a system of global monetary restrictions that had made it possible for national governments to control their economies and foster welfare states—was also crucial. Without the restraint of the system's fixed exchange rates, governments increased their spending and fuelled inflation, which resulted in unpredictability in the currency markets. Government efforts to boost demand led to a decline in investment and an increase in unemployment, which caused an inflationary cycle. By the middle of the 1970s, US inflation rates had reached 10%, and by the end of the decade they had reached a peak of 13.5%. In the UK, rates increased even more, reaching 24% in 1975. As unemployment increased, it put pressure on the welfare state's financial stability by increasing benefits while decreasing tax and insurance contributions. Attempts to increase taxes to close the budget gap were met with fierce opposition. When Mrs. Thatcher was elected in 1979 (with a 5.4% unemployment rate), there were approximately 1.5 million unemployed Britons; by the conclusion of her first term, that figure had more than doubled to over 3 million (11.9 per cent). Early in the 1980s, the US jobless rate doubled from earlier decades, reaching about 10%. In addition, manufacturing jobs relocated to low wage economies in developing countries after the 1970s, benefiting from cheaper transportation and the newfound flexibility to invest abroad. Advanced production methods reduced the number of workers and elevated the value of highly skilled personnel in the industries that survived.

As a result, opposition parties launched a prolonged campaign against welfare states in the late 1970s in support of free markets and traditional family values in one nation after another. The welfare state has long been hated by libertarians as it interferes with both individual freedom and the functioning of markets. Classics like Hayek's "The Road to Serfdom" and Hilaire Belloc's "The Servile State" depicted it as a road to tyranny; this perspective was echoed by Milton Friedman and Chicago School economists. According to the Marxist view of the state, welfare states were to blame for halting growth and causing the economic crisis. (Holmwood, 2000). In the critical attacks of the 1980s, issues related to consumer choice, cost, and efficiency were frequently raised.

There also came new issues like pollution and risk categories, which proved harder to control, regulate, or manage under the pre-existing structures. Education prices are rising disproportionately, medical expenditures have gone up due to advancements in medicine, and one-parent families need additional assistance. As a result, the welfare state also ran into societal issues with providing everyone with access to healthcare, housing, and education. Also, at this time, issues including demographic imbalance, social isolation, and mental illness, as well as single families and single parents, developed.

Immigration led to its own set of social and political issues. The welfare state was stated to be in crisis, whether as a result of the excessive demands placed upon it, a lack of resources to meet them, a shortfall in state capacities to achieve objectives, a loss of political coherence, eroding faith in the legitimacy of government, or plain overload. One suggestion that was frequently made was that in order to relieve the burden on an overburdened state apparatus, state functions should now be shared by non-state groups. Another argued that the liberal, night watchman state should be reinstated so that it could focus on performing its few, essential duties more successfully. The neoliberal reforms of recent decades have promoted market mechanisms and introduced performance metrics, budget limits, and purchaser-provider agreements as numerous ways to incentivize efficiency in the public sector.

14.4.2 The Changing form of Welfare State

The neoliberal, "deregulating" approach of economic governance and a market-oriented reworking of social policy emerged through time, changing the nature of welfare states to create a less expansive, more austere version. Even in the USA, where welfare state government has historically been most criticised, New Right reformers failed to completely eliminate the welfare state despite their political hegemony in the 1980s and 1990s. In fact, the failure of their protracted onslaught could be seen as evidence that, at least where democratic institutions are still in place, a welfare state is essential.

The neoliberal challenge has an effect on welfare states worldwide. Germany changed its approaches to the labour market, cut back on unemployment insurance, and lowered government spending. Sweden reduced taxes, partially privatised social security, and accepted historically high jobless rates. Neoliberal reform, however, has its roots in the liberal English countries, particularly in America and Britain, as well as in Canada, Australia, and New Zealand. Leading the way were Margaret Thatcher and Ronald Reagan, who both attacked the post-war order with strong rhetorical attacks combining neoliberal economic prescriptions with neoconservative nostrums intended to reassert national "greatness" and undo the cultural shifts of the 1960s. They aimed to change the state by strengthening its armed forces while minimising its influence in social and economic matters. The New Right state was intended to be minimal in certain ways yet robust in others, much like the minimalist state of the classic liberal movement. By the 1990s, a new "Washington Consensus" that pushed for globalisation, free trade, unrestricted capital flows, and unregulated labour markets had replaced the post-World War II welfare state settlement. It was argued that tax breaks and benefits for the wealthy will eventually "trickle down" and benefit everyone.

Treasury departments in need, dealing with more unemployment and lower tax revenues, received a bonanza from privatisations. Another significant development in policy was the liberalisation of banking and finance. Governments started making small cuts, such as reducing payments, the range and calibre of social services, and tightening eligibility requirements. Instead of retirement or healthcare, cuts primarily affected discretionary social assistance programmes. Reformers aimed to eliminate all traces of the "dependence culture" that would deter receivers of benefits from seeking employment. Government expenditures increasingly favoured tax credits for the working poor over help for unemployed people, forcing those who are extremely destitute to rely on food banks, relatives, and various survival techniques.

In Britain, unemployment benefits were renamed "Jobseeker's Allowances" and "welfare to work" was given more attention. The Personal Responsibility and Work Opportunity Reconciliation Act (1996), signed by US President Clinton, replaced the federal programme that provided aid to dependent children and their parents with a more stringent, state-run programme called Temporary Assistance to Needy Families (TANF). The original intent of such help, which had been to enable widows and single mothers to stay at home and care for their children, was reversed by TANF, which obliged single moms to find job in order to receive welfare benefits. However, job cuts also affected positions in the public sector, particularly in the USA where a goal of succeeding Republican governments was to shrink the size of the federal government. In terms of relative size, President George W. Bush lowered the size of the federal government to its lowest level since 1940. This programme to eliminate jobs had a disproportionately negative impact on minorities and significantly diminished the capabilities and competency of the American state.

Neoliberals have long argued that the market can provide services like housing, health care, education, and pensions more effectively than the government. Their chosen course of action was to reorganise welfare institutions such that they behaved more like market players because it was impossible to abolish the welfare state and go back to unregulated markets. Internal markets and competitive methods were then implemented to end the "monopolies" held by public housing, hospitals, schools, and universities and to encourage the operation of these institutions cost effectively.

During the 1990s and early 2000s boom years, the USA and the UK displayed affluence. Yet, neoliberal policies strongly favour dominant market actors. These immediate, direct advantages favour the wealthy over the poor, employers over employees, and capital over labour. It is notable that the foundational institutions of the original welfare state have largely survived and are still in place despite these fundamental changes, the decline in social assistance, and the focus on choice, consumption, and competition. Moreover, the evidence from other countries demonstrates that the main welfare state programmes of healthcare, unemployment and sickness benefits, and pensions offer a wider range of coverage. The welfare state has been under attack by neoliberalism, although it has mostly affected people who are in need rather than those who are working (Koch and James 2020). But after 30 years of political hegemony, neoliberalism has not replaced nor destroyed the core components of welfare state governance, nor has it lessened the electorate's continued support for them. Instead, taxes and social spending as a percentage of GDP have plateaued at varying rates under various regimes, and reforms have largely been based on steady state funding as opposed to the fast increase of the earlier period. In the face of fierce criticism, welfare states have shown to be extremely robust and enduring.

The task for all governments is to implement future-focused improvements and establish reforms to welfare states that successfully handle current threats while also boosting economic efficiency. Regarding pension reform, the UK is bringing the retirement age up to 68 by the middle of the 2030s, when the gender pay gap will be eliminated, from the long-standing limits of 65 (for males) and 60 (for women). In the USA, the complete Social Security pension eligibility age will increase from 65 to 67; however, partial payments may be accessed as early as age 62. According to David Garland (2016), we are not free to embrace or reject the welfare state as a possible form of government policy. It's also not a part of the post-war era that we are now putting behind us. Instead, the welfare state is an essential component of contemporary governance and is crucial to the social and economic well-being of capitalist societies. A welfare state of some kind is an essential component of each contemporary country. Welfare regimes can take a variety of different shapes and can be more or less effective. Every industrialised society with an industrial or post-industrial economy has some form of the welfare state even after three decades of attacks.

14.5 Conclusion

Capitalist societies with advanced technology require a favourable social climate as well as a supportive physical infrastructure. It needs the well-functioning families, communities, schools, and healthcare systems that generate socialised, educated, healthy workers. Climate change, the depletion of natural resources, and population health are all terrible outcomes of capitalist processes and technological progress. Capitalism needs a set of countervailing forces to prevent self-destruction. And welfare states are the institutionalised, functional manifestation of these pressures. Beveridge, Keynes, and their contemporaries realised that capitalist processes produce uncertainty, instability, and antisocial repercussions. They created a system to control these unforeseen events, smooth out booms and busts, and create a foundation of economic security for everyone so that capitalist risk-taking could continue. Since then, social regulation of markets, social insurance of employees, and public provision of social services and protections—in other words, the welfare state in one or more of its variants—have established itself as our go-to tools for containing the anti-social dynamics and the negative externalities that are the inherent corollaries of free-market capitalism. The genius of the welfare state lies in its ability to make market capitalism liveable for people and conducive to contemporary democracy by harnessing the power of averages and communalizing risks. The history of the past century demonstrates that welfare state governance can be successful in democratising and civilising the incredible power of capitalist enterprise.

Keywords

Welfare State
Neoliberalism
Capitalism
Welfare benefits

Review Questions

1. 'Economic inequality as a result of capitalism and political equality promised by democracy interact to produce the welfare state.' Comment.
2. All welfare state regimes deal with diverse internal and external obstacles and dangers, yet they have demonstrated an amazing potential for survival. Consider the evolving welfare state ideas in light of this assertion.
3. Why does the welfare state's expansion not inevitably result from globalisation?

References

Carabine J. 1996. A Straight Playing Field or Queering the Pitch? *Centring Sexuality in Social Policy. Feminist Review,* 54(Autumn): 31–64.

Esping-Andersen, G. 1990. *The Three Worlds of Welfare Capitalism.* Cambridge: Polity Press.

Garland, D. 2016. *The Welfare State A Very Short Introduction.* UK: Oxford University Press.

Harvey D. 2005. *A Brief History of Neoliberalism.* New York: Oxford University Press.

Holmwood, J. 2000. Three pillars of Welfare State Theory. T.H. Marshall, Karl Polanyi, Alva Myrdal in Defence of the National Welfare State. *European Journal of Social Theory,* 3(1): 23–50. DOI: 10.1177/13684310022224660

Jessop, B. 2002. *The Future of the Capitalist State.* UK: Polity Press.

Kersbergen, K. Manow, P. 2020. *The Welfare State.* In Caramani, D. Ed. Comparative Politics. Fifth Edition. Uk: Oxford University Press. 376–393.

Koch I. James D. 2022. The State of the Welfare State: Advice, Governance and Care in Settings of Austerity, *Ethnos,* 87(1), 1–21. DOI: 10.1080/00141844.2019.1688371

Myrdal A. 1945. *Nation and Family: The Swedish Experiment in Democratic family and Population Policy.* London: Routledge and Kegan Paul.

Newton, K. Van Deth, J. 2010. *Foundations of Comparative Politics Democracies of the Modern World Second Edition.* Cambridge: Cambridge University press.

Pateman C. 1989. *The Patriarchal Welfare State in the Disorder of Women: Democracy, Feminism and Political Theory.* Stanford: Stanford University Press.

Polanyi, K. 1944. *The Great Transformation.* Boston: Beacon Press.

Wilensky H. 2002. *Rich Democracies, Political Economy, Public Policy and Performance.* Berkeley: University of California Press.

Xu, Q. 2007. Globalization, Immigration and the Welfare State: A Cross-National Comparison. *The Journal of Sociology & Social Welfare,* 34(2). Accessed from https://scholarworks.wmich.edu on September 18, 2023.

CHAPTER 15

The Neo Liberal State

Chetna Sharma

Reader's Guide

The welfare states covered in the previous chapter, which experienced nearly three decades of expansion after 1945, have faced difficulties in the decades following the 1970s. Starting in the late 1970s, welfare states were consistently attacked in a series of nations under the pretence of fostering dependency culture and inefficiency. The changes that were originally felt as an economic crisis and later as a change in the dominant forms of production and social organisation must be adapted by states all over the world. Politicians and decision-makers found it difficult to modify welfare state programmes to satisfy post-industrial society's needs. Neoliberal critiques and post-industrial adaptations, in their various forms, came to be as reactions to socioeconomic changes driven by late 20th-century capitalism. This chapter discusses the numerous neo liberal state that appeared around the globe after the 1980s and the difficulties they met with.

15.1 Introduction

Social scientists acknowledge some of the fundamental elements of neoliberalism even though they have not come to a consensus on a single, universal definition. Its main tenets are laissez-faire economics, which advocates for free markets, free trade, and minimal government intervention. It also emphasises the importance of individual freedom against excessive government power and the notion that human welfare and the social good will be maximised by extending market and property relations into all aspects of human interaction (Smith 2017, Gardie and Harvie 2011). Neoliberalism is a theory of political and economic behaviour that contends that the greatest way to enhance human welfare is to liberate each individual's capacity for entrepreneurship within an institutional setting marked by robust private property rights, open markets, and free trade. A suitable institutional structure for such behaviours must be developed and maintained as part of the state's responsibility. The state must provide things like monetary integrity and the establishment of the military, police, defence, and legal institutions and functions needed to protect private property rights and to ensure that markets operate as intended. In addition, markets must be developed if they don't already exist in sectors like land, water, education, health care, social security, or environmental damage, maybe through government action (Harvey, 2005). Neoliberalism is a term used to describe new political, economic, and social structures in society that place an emphasis on market interactions, redefining the role of the state, and promoting individual responsibility (Springer et al., 2016). The state is a key means of advancing neoliberal agenda, and the following section explores the neoliberal state in various global contexts.

15.2 Origin and Evolution

The welfare state's rise throughout the decades following World War II was made feasible by a developing and expanding global economy that experienced steady economic development. The fordist regime of mass production and mass consumption, cheap energy, the supremacy of the western manufacturing sector, and the stable international monetary system gave the necessary framework to launch welfare state initiatives. Additionally, they were made possible by the framework of economic and financial ties established at Bretton Woods in 1944. This system of institutions promoted trade, provided funding for development, and upheld fixed exchange rates while giving national economies some degree of control over their own futures. As a result of the limited exit choices available to domestic investors, producers, and consumers, governments were able to control labour markets and finance social spending. Bretton Woods remained in place until 1971, when the US government, under pressure from the Vietnam War's expenditures, a sizable trade imbalance, and recurrent runs on its currency, unilaterally devalued the dollar and abolished its convertibility into gold. This move destabilised the global financial system and loosened the restrictions that had restrained national economies. The age of inexpensive energy came to an end when the Organization of the Petroleum Exporting Countries (OPEC) doubled the price of oil in 1973, sending western economies into a severe recession. At the same time, the expansionist era of the global economy came to an end and the period of contraction began. This period was characterised by deep recessions, slow economic growth, and high unemployment rates, all of which had a negative impact on the funding of welfare states.

A severe and protracted economic downturn that affected welfare states worldwide started in the middle of the 1970s. Growth and the expansion of welfare states were made possible by expanding markets, affordable energy, and stable money after World War II, but starting in the late 1960s, problems with the balance of payments, budget deficits, and recurrent fiscal crises indicated that the global economy was slowing and that welfare states might have reached their growth potential. The 1973 OPEC oil shock set off the crisis, but the earlier breakdown of Bretton Woods—a system of global monetary regulations that had made it possible for national governments to control their economies and foster welfare states—was just as significant. Governments spent more and fuelled inflation without the restraint of the system's fixed exchange rates, which led to instability in the currency markets. Government efforts to boost demand led to a decline in investment and an increase in unemployment, which caused an inflationary cycle. By the middle of the 1970s, US inflation rates had reached 10%, and by the end of the decade they had reached a peak of 13.5%. In the UK, rates increased even more, reaching 24% in 1975. As unemployment increased, it put pressure on the welfare state's financial stability by increasing benefits while decreasing tax and insurance contributions. The idea of raising taxes to close the budget gap was received with fierce opposition.

The welfare states were held accountable for stifling development and causing the recession. The welfare state and the public sector have come under fire for being expensive and ineffective, which has resulted in dependency, inactivity, drug use, and crime. This upheaval provided an opportunity for a coalition of free-market and socially conservative political forces to fight back against the post-war welfare state and the power structures it had constructed (Garland, 2016). The movement's biggest voices pushed for the repeal of the welfare state and a return to free markets, self-reliance, and individual charity.

The theories and writings of eminent economists including Adam Smith (1776), Friedrich Hayek (1944), Milton Friedman (1962/2002), and Chicago School economists were all significant influences on the neoliberal ideology that arose during this period. These views were not widely held for the majority of the 20th century, but in the crisis-ridden 1970s, they became more prevalent, feeding into widespread economic unhappiness as well as concerns about social and cultural change (Duggan 2014). As a result of accelerating processes of economic globalisation, national economies have also gotten more and more entwined. The neo liberals fiercely backed open-market policies, especially the unrestricted flow of foreign capital, in order to be able to compete globally

(Smith 2017). The neoliberal challenge has had an impact on welfare states worldwide. Germany changed its approaches to the labour market, cut back on unemployment insurance, and lowered government spending. Sweden reduced taxes, partially privatised social security, and accepted historically high jobless rates. The centre of neoliberal change, however, lay in the liberal English countries of Canada, Australia, New Zealand, and, most importantly, the United States and the United Kingdom.

When the socialist government of Salvador Allende was overthrown by the Chilean military and domestic elites in 1973, that nation was one of the first to adopt neoliberal policies. The "Chicago Boys," a group of Chicago-based economists, were enlisted to advise the coup d'état leaders and assist in rebuilding the Chilean economy. From the 1950s, the US has supported the education of Chilean economists at the University of Chicago as part of a Cold War initiative to combat left-wing inclinations in Latin America. The private Catholic University in Santiago began to be dominated by economists with Chicago training. Business elites organised their opposition to Allende through a club known as "the Monday Club" in the early 1970s. With these relationships, business elites were able to support these economists' studies through research organisations. These economists were hired by Pinochet in 1975 when General Gustavo Leigh, a Keynesian and Pinochet's competitor for power, was removed from office. Their initial task was to negotiate loans with the International Monetary Fund. By privatising public assets, reducing social spending, liberalising the market, and undoing nationalisations, they reorganised the Chilean economy. Import substitution was preferred above export-led growth. The primary resource of copper was the only area set aside for the government.

Neoliberalism has since taken on many various forms and shaped the political, economic, and social landscape on a global, regional, and local scale. Early reforms were carried out by the Democratic and Labour governments of President Carter and Prime Minister Callaghan in America and Britain, respectively.

Yet, these initiatives only had the effect of decreasing their support among voters and strengthening the belief that meaningful reform would be best carried out by parties that were less intimately tied to the trade union movement and the welfare state's tax-and-spend programmes. Political parties in the United States and Great Britain consequently began to implement neoliberal policies in an effort to sustain capitalist profitability and secure the share of power held by their elites in both the economy and politics (Duggan 2014). Leading the charge were Ronald Reagan in the United States and Margaret Thatcher in Britain. They both attacked the post-war order with strong rhetorical attacks that combined neoliberal economic recommendations with neoconservative nostrums intended to reassert national "greatness" and undo the cultural shifts of the 1960s. They insisted that labour unions, left-leaning politicians, and the welfare state were to blame for the economic and moral deterioration of their countries. The answer was to limit the influence of organised labour, cut social spending, boost interest rates, lower taxes, and support free markets. They also aimed to change the state, strengthening its armed forces while minimising its influence in social and economic matters. It was intended for this new state to be modest in some ways and powerful in others. It was believed that "big government" ought to be starved, preferably by lowering taxes, and that the public sector should be kept to a minimum. But, a strong state was also required in order to protect national security overseas, enact economic reforms, reduce public spending and taxes, privatise public property, do away with regulatory controls, and cope with the opposition that these reforms sparked. In the late 1980s, India and a few other East Asian nations adopted the neo liberal approach that the west and China had proposed in 1978. The majority of countries thereafter followed this road as well.

When governments opened their economies to global markets by lowering tariffs, easing barriers, and allowing free flows of capital, money, and labour, these transnational phenomena gained importance starting in the late 1970s. Manufacturing jobs shifted to low-wage economies in developing countries, taking advantage of reduced transportation costs and the newfound freedom to invest abroad.

Advanced production methods reduced the number of workers and elevated the value of highly skilled personnel in the industries that survived. Industrial employment in the US fell from 35% in 1960 to less than 20% in 1970. (Garland, 2016). Jobs in the manufacturing sector have decreased by 50% in the UK over the same time period. Germany and Sweden, among other countries, took action to maintain a modernised industrial sector that was centred on high-skilled, high-quality output.

By the 1990s, a new "Washington Consensus" that pushed for globalisation, free trade, unrestricted capital flows, and unregulated labour markets had replaced the post-World War II welfare state settlement. Governments must now seek the approval of global markets, which are prepared to penalise wasteful social spending, high corporate tax rates, or above-average inflation, rather than relying entirely on their electorates. As a result, individual governments have less leeway in determining their social policies as well as less economic autonomy.

The social and economic orthodoxies of the post-war decades were overturned by the neoliberal reforms of the 1980s and 1990s. In order to increase revenue and give over authority from public to private hands, nationalised businesses, utilities, and assets were sold off.

Another significant development in policy was the liberalisation of banking and finance. During the 1980s, when banks lost their monopoly on lending and huge retail companies started offering financial services to customers, the economy has become more financialized, with profits coming more from credit and finance than from manufacturing. Cheap lending served as a stand-in for wage increases, increasing aggregate demand and kicking off the 1990s boom. It was 'privatised Keynesianism,' as sociologist Colin Crouch (2009) noted. Cost-cutting ministers examined every area of spending, but political wisdom made sure that cuts primarily affected discretionary social assistance programmes rather than pensions or healthcare.

Reformers aimed to eliminate all traces of "dependent culture" that could deter receivers of benefits from establishing employment or pursuing personal independence. This campaign against reliance, which was inspired by the works of intellectuals like Charles Murray and Lawrence Mead, started by introducing stricter behavioural standards and making rewards more conditional. Government expenditures favoured tax credits for the working poor more frequently than help for those out of work, forcing those in extreme poverty to rely on food banks, relatives, and various survival techniques.

Neoliberals have long argued that the market can provide services like housing, health care, education, and pensions more effectively than the government. Their ideal approach was to reform welfare institutions so that they behaved more like market players because it was impossible to remove the welfare state and go back to unregulated markets. In order to do this, a set of managerial changes known as the "new public management" were introduced. These reforms applied to government organisations certain private sector strategies such financial limitations, target setting, and performance indicators. Internal markets and competitive methods were then implemented to dismantle the 'monopolies' enjoyed by public housing, hospitals, schools, and universities as well as to encourage these organisations to operate more efficiently.

The creation of "contracting out" and "purchaser-provider" agreements was another neoliberal development. The traditional system of public agencies receiving financing, providing services, and assessing their own performance was abolished by this restructuring and replaced with a more intricate, market-based structure in which public agencies are compelled to contract out the duty of providing services to private companies that compete for the business. Most of social care was effectively privatised under the new regime.

Neoliberal programmes aimed to increase welfare and promote prosperity. U.S. and UK performance during the 1990s and early 2000s boom years was great. Neoliberal policies, however, are profoundly unequal and overwhelmingly favour large market participants. These immediate, direct advantages favour the wealthy over the poor, employers over employees, and capital over labour. Moreover, they have a party-political effect, tending to enhance support for parties that support business and markets while decreasing support for parties that promote the welfare state. They re-established the conditions for capital accumulation, restored the power of the economic elites, and tilted the balance of power and influence towards financial capital. Governments in America, Britain, and other countries took action to increase the flexibility of the labour market. Employee rights were reduced, pay stagnation persisted despite longer hours and increased productivity, and new employer-friendly industrial relations legislation were passed. But it is notable that the foundational institutions of the original welfare state have largely survived and are still in place, despite these fundamental changes, the decline in social assistance, and the emphasis on choice, consumerism, and competition. In its different manifestations, the neo liberal state developed in a way that prioritised markets while simultaneously attempting to support them through the use of the power of the state. It attempted to change the nation in some ways based on market ideas (Davies, 2018). The next section will address the specific characteristics of the neoliberal state that was created as a result of the close and complicated relationship between the market and the state.

15.3 Approaches and Features of the Neo Liberal state

Birch (2015) provides an informative list of seven approaches for comprehending neoliberalism:

1. One viewpoint is Foucauldian, which views neoliberalism as a particular type of governmentality.
2. A Marxist perspective that emphasises neoliberalism as a hegemonic or class-based initiative that benefits capital at the expense of labour.
3. An ideational analysis that sees normative neoliberal concepts advanced by think tanks and intellectuals like Hayek, Friedman, Becker, and Buchanan as the source of neoliberalism.
4. A historical and philosophical approach to economics that critiques neoliberalism by carefully tracing the development of specific schools of liberal economic thinking and the institutions created to spread them.
5. A perspective that views institutions as the major determinants of how neoliberalism has shown itself in various contexts.
6. A regulation theory perspective, which sees neoliberalism as the institutional ensemble that came together following the economic crises of the 1970s and eventually came to facilitate capital accumulation up until the "great recession" from 2008 to the present.
7. A spatial approach that views neoliberalism as a dynamic and contentious process and emphasises the unevenness and diversity that are part and parcel of it.

Readers will observe that these many interpretations of neoliberalism are highly incommensurable (Venugopal, 2015), but what is more notable is that there hasn't been much direct interaction between them. This has led to "an extraordinarily wide range" of distinct and frequently contradictory phenomena being classified as neoliberal, as a result (Venugopal, 2015: 169). Neoliberalism is frequently left undefined in empirical research, even by those who use it as a key independent or dependent variable, according to Boas and Gans-Morse (2009: 138–139). Additionally, the term is effectively used in many different ways, so its appearance in any given article offers few clues as to what it actually means.

Under this system, the state is expected to fulfil many sets of obligations, which give rise to complexity. While the state is required to provide and enforce law in order to act as the regulator and guarantee of economic competition. The neoliberal state is also necessary to promote competition and competitive dynamics in spheres of social life that are typically hostile to entrepreneurial principles and ethos, such as colleges, and to instil a respect for competition generally. On the other hand, the state's role is crucial to promote and establish conditions for the sustainability of market structures. Government institutions themselves should be reimagined along competitive principles where possible, lowering the state's monopoly power through outsourcing and attempting to make "national competitiveness" a loosely-defined teleology of all policies (Cahil et al., 2018).

Neoliberal nations focused on fostering open markets, commerce, and capital flow. Their neoliberal policies include cutting social services, welfare benefits, and education funding; privatising previously state-owned industries; opening up national economies to foreign firms and investments with the repatriation of profits; and opening up to international organisations like the World Bank, the International Monetary Fund (IMF), and the World Trade Organization. Reduced direct taxation, market liberalisation, and letting "inefficient or unproductive firms go bankrupt" are just a few of the tasks on the list. The state also has a responsibility to uphold the peace through maintaining law, order, and control, funding prison and security systems. (Grady & Harvie 2011).

The neoliberal state is in favour of strong private property rights for individuals, the rule of law, and the institutions of free markets and free trade. Thus, the state must use its exclusive use of force to protect these liberties at all costs. Entrepreneurship and private enterprise are viewed as the drivers of innovation and economic development. Neoliberal theory maintains that free markets and free trade are the greatest ways to ensure the eradication of poverty because "a rising tide lifts all boats," or "trickle down," hypothesis (Harvey, 2005). The growth of the entrepreneurial neoliberal subject, who is in charge of herself and who believes that free markets are the best way to improve human wellbeing, goes hand in hand with neoliberal behaviours. Although there is a guarantee of personal and individual freedom in the marketplace, each person is held accountable for his or her own activities and well-being. Welfare, education, healthcare, and even retirement are all subject to this guiding philosophy. Those who are incapable of competing—such as the destitute or the imprisoned—simply drop out of the system (Bockmann 2013).

The so-called "tragedy of the commons," or the propensity for individuals to carelessly super-exploit common property resources like land and water, is thought to be best avoided by enclosing land and assigning private property rights. The state must use its authority to establish or create such norms when such rules are not explicitly stated or where property rights are difficult to define.

Competition, privatisation, and deregulation are said to cut costs both directly for consumers through lower prices for goods and services and indirectly for them through lower taxes by reducing bureaucratic red tape, boosting efficiency and production, and improving quality.

The neoliberal state must continue to look for internal restructurings and fresh institutional configurations that will enhance its ability to compete against other governments on the international stage. State control over the flow of capital and commodities is voluntarily given up to the global market. Foreign competition is regarded as beneficial since it increases productivity and efficiency while lowering prices and preventing inflationary tendencies. Thus, states should work together to find and negotiate ways to lower obstacles to cross-border financial flow and market liberalisation.

Democracy is seen as a luxury that can only be enjoyed in circumstances of relative wealth and a sizable middle-class presence to ensure political stability. Neoliberals therefore frequently favour expert and elite forms of government. There is a clear preference for rule by judicial and executive order over democratic and parliamentary decision-making. Neoliberals prefer to shield important institutions from democratic demands, such as the central bank. Globalization and international competition can be utilised to control movements within individual governments that are antagonistic to the neoliberal agenda. When all else fails to quell opposition to neoliberalism, the state must turn to coercion, propaganda, or, where necessary, physical force and police power. The rights of a select few would be prioritised over the freedom of the majority.

According to Nonini (2003:166), the specific processes of cultural production are also a part of the processes of economic and political change. The State's primary tool for governing is the rhetoric of expansion, wealth, and effectiveness. The promotion of fears about threats connected with particular people, groups, and places by the state also results in the creation of new kinds of control. Credit risks, investment risks, tax payer risks, and assigning people into certain risk groupings, like into an insurance category while analysing one's health, are some examples of such risks. As a result, a "dual" or "two speed" society is created, with some people benefiting from built-in competitive mechanisms and others falling into high-risk groups because they are unable to meet these standards of competitiveness and profitability. Hence, neoliberal policies have resulted in a growing concentration of political and economic power for a small portion of the population.

Special Insights

Neoliberal state and women

The welfare, well-being, and financial security of women are severely harmed by social and economic policies that aim to increase competitiveness and growth in both economic and social spheres. The ability of women to become the kind of subject required by neoliberal policy regimes is seen to be constrained by the restrictions operating in women's life, particularly the limits of the caring and other forms of socially reproductive labour on which interdependency depends. By 2020, the living standards of the 10% of households with the lowest incomes will have decreased by an average of 21%, more than five times as much as the living standards of the top 10%. According to Women's Budget Group, 2015, households led by women, such as lone parents and single female retirees, are severely hit and will both be on average 20% worse off in 2020 (Adkins, 2018).

15.4 Neo Liberal States Across the World

The neoliberal state can take on several shapes depending on the political, social, and economic climate of the country. For instance, President Bush of the United States placed steel tariffs despite supporting free markets and free trade in order to improve his prospects of winning Ohio. President Bush's initiatives make it evident that the state plays a substantial role in the economy and that electoral compulsions occasionally play out differently (Harvey, 2005). To quell internal unrest, arbitrary quotas are imposed on international imports. Moreover, measures were implemented in several European nations to safeguard agriculture while promoting free trade in all other sectors for social, political, and even aesthetic considerations. Credits are unilaterally provided from one state to another in order to obtain political access and influence in geopolitically sensitive regions such as the Middle East. Extraordinary interventions of the state were necessary to favour particular commercial interests, for example armaments purchases.

Public-private partnerships have come to rely more on neoliberalization. In order to promote economic development, Margaret Thatcher established "quasi-governmental institutions" like urban development corporations, and this was one of her major concepts. Companies and corporations not only engage closely with government actors but also have a significant influence in crafting laws, choosing public policies, and establishing regulatory frameworks that are primarily beneficial to themselves.

The most outrageous instance of this was Vice President Cheney's steadfast refusal to divulge the names of the consultative group that developed the Bush administration's energy policy document in 2002; this group almost certainly included Kenneth Lay, the CEO of Enron, a company that was accused of profiteering by purposefully causing an energy crisis in California before collapsing in the middle of a massive accounting scandal (Harvey, 2005). The state frequently creates laws and regulatory frameworks that benefit businesses and, in some cases, particular interests like the energy, pharmaceutical, agriculture, etc. Public-private partnerships sometimes include the state bearing a large portion of the risk while the private sector reaps the majority of the rewards, particularly at the local level. The neoliberal state will also, if necessary, use coercive legislation and policing strategies (such as anti-picketing laws) to disperse or crush collective forms of opposition to corporate dominance.

Neoliberal nations frequently encourage the spread of power of financial institutions through regulatory deregulation, but they also all too frequently ensure the reliability and solvency of financial firms. This dedication is a result of the state's dependence on monetarism as the cornerstone of its policies. Even if the financial institutions are to blame for the defaults, the neoliberal state will not stand for any significant financial defaults. As a result, the state must intervene. When James Baker, Reagan's Secretary of the Treasury, discovered Mexico's imminent bankruptcy and significant losses for the major New York City investment banks that owned Mexican debt in 1982, he gave the IMF fresh life under the Reagan administration. He employed the IMF to impose structural reform on Mexico and guard against default the New York bankers. In the USA, state authority has frequently been employed to save businesses or prevent financial collapse (Harvey, 2005). A couple of instances include the 1997–1998 collapse of the hedge fund Long Term Capital Management and the US savings and loans crisis in 1987–1988. Governments have stepped in to stabilise the economy by rescuing financial institutions when they get into trouble.

States like Singapore and numerous other Asian nations rely on the public sector and state planning in close coordination with domestic and corporate capital to foster capital accumulation and economic growth for a variety of very different reasons. Infrastructures in developmental states are often given a lot of attention, both social and physical. When it comes to things like healthcare and educational possibilities, they implement much more egalitarian policies. Neoliberalization thus provides developmental states with the opportunity to strengthen their position in the global race by creating new state intervention institutions, but on the other hand, it also fosters the emergence of classes.

Developmental states find themselves being drawn farther and deeper into the neoliberal fold as new institutional arrangements begin to define the rules of global trade, for example, the opening of capital markets is now a requirement of participation in the IMF and the WTO. For instance, the Asian Crisis of 1997–1998 had the major consequence of bringing emerging states closer to conventional neoliberal methods. Over eighteen nations (including Mexico, Brazil, Argentina, Venezuela, and Uruguay) had signed agreements by 1994 that relieved them of about $60 billion in debt. Of course, the goal was that this debt reduction would spur economic growth, allowing the remaining debt to be paid off in a timely manner (Harvey, 2005). The problem was that the IMF also made sure that all the nations that benefited from this little debt forgiveness (which many considered as paltry in comparison to what the banks could afford) also had to take the lethal dose of neoliberal institutional reforms. Inevitable outcomes included the Argentine economy's complete collapse in 2001, the Brazilian crisis of 1998, and the Mexican peso crisis of 1995.

In some nations, the line separating public and private power is becoming increasingly porous. The fact that non-elected and frequently elite-led advocacy groups for different kinds of rights define and explain the principal collective methods of action under neoliberalism should not come as a surprise. Substantive advances have been made using such methods in various situations, such as consumer protections, civil rights, or the rights of people with disabilities. Under neoliberalism, non-governmental and grassroots organisations (NGOs and GROs) have also multiplied and grown significantly, leading to the notion that opposition was organised outside of the state structure.

While the benefits of competition are emphasised under the neo-liberal state, the reality is that oligopolistic, monopolistic, and transnational power is increasingly being concentrated in the hands of a small number of centralised multinational corporations. For example, the competition in the soft drink market has been limited to Coca Cola vs. Pepsi, the energy sector has been reduced to five massive transnational firms, and a small number of media tycoons dominate the news cycle.

It would appear that labour control and the maintenance of a high rate of labour exploitation have always been key components of neoliberalization given the violent attacks on all forms of labour organisation and labour rights and the heavy reliance on massive but largely unorganised labour reserves in nations like China, Indonesia, India, Mexico, and Bangladesh. As always, class power is either created or restored at the expense of labour.

The social safety net is drastically lowered in favour of a system that places a strong emphasis on individual accountability. The inevitable response to these significant changes in social policy is to rebuild social solidarities, albeit along different lines. As a result, there has been a resurgence of interest in religion and morality, new forms of associationism (such as those centred on issues of rights and citizenship), and even older political forms (fascism, nationalism, localism, and the like). The threat of authoritarian populism and nationalism has always existed when neoliberalism is practised in its purest form. Economic globalisation has reached a new phase, as Schwab and Smadja (1999), organisers of the once solely joyous neoliberal annual jamboree at Davos, warned as early as 1996. In many nations, a growing backlash against its consequences, particularly in the industrial democracies, poses a threat to social stability and economic growth. These democracies are in a state of powerlessness and worry, which helps to explain why a new breed of populist leaders has emerged (Harvey, 2000: 70).

This was especially true for states that adopted a corporatist structure, like Mexico and France. The Partido Revolucionario Institucional in Mexico had long governed under the tenet of unity of state and nation, but in the 1990s, neoliberal reforms caused this to break down, even turning much of the nation against the state. A prime example is the emergence of right-wing fascist parties in Europe, which express strong anti-immigrant views. Even more upsetting was the emergence of ethnic nationalism following Indonesia's economic collapse, which led to a vicious attack on the Chinese minority.

Nationalism of a specific kind is necessary for the survival of the neoliberal state. It mobilises nationalism in its attempt to prosper because it is compelled to act as a competitive agent in the global market and seeks to create the best possible business climate. In the Falklands/Malvinas War and, more significantly, in the push against economic unification with Europe, Margaret Thatcher exploited the nationalist card. Nationalism is necessary for the state to function effectively as a corporate and competitive entity in the global market, as shown repeatedly in the European Union, Mercosur (where integration is hampered by Brazilian and Argentine nationalisms), NAFTA, or ASEAN. This is demonstrated by the nationalism that surrounds international sporting competitions. In the fight to secure the state's place in the global economy, China openly appeals to nationalist feeling. Singapore's situation is very illuminating. Invoking moral solidarity based on the nationalist ideals of a beleaguered island state, Confucian values, and a unique form of the cosmopolitan ethic appropriate to its current position in the world of international trade, it has combined neoliberalism in the marketplace with draconian coercive and authoritarian state power.

Special Insights

Neoliberalism and the Pandemic

Millions of people's health and quality of life have been badly impacted by the commercialization of medicine and placing private interests ahead of public ones. Four major epidemics have affected the entire world since the 1980s (Ebola, SARS, MERS, and COVID-19). Even in wealthy nations like the USA, about 30 million individuals lack health insurance, and another 27 million have coverage that is incredibly inadequate. The United States has one of the lowest ratios of hospital beds per 1,000 people among OECD nations (the group of the most developed nations in the capitalist world) as a result of the nation's underdeveloped public sector. The likelihood of a swift recovery from the epidemic has also been significantly hindered by the privatisation of public services and decreases to spending on public medical care, public health, and social funding that have occurred in several European nations. For instance, the number of hospital beds per 1,000 people in Italy decreased from 3.7 in 2007 to 3.2 in 2016, and the absence of some adequate public health care services caused the system to fail during the COVID pandemic in numerous nations (Navarro, 2020).

15.5 Tensions and Contradictions

The data shows that Neo Liberal states expanded and developed in various parts of the world. According to files of national accounts data from the World Bank and the Organization for Economic Co-operation and Development (OECD), the GDP per person in North America increased from US$ 5,140.5 in 1970 to US$ 56,081.9 in 2016. (The World Bank 2017). The GDP per capita in the United States alone rose from US$ 5,246.9 in 1970 to US$ 57,638.2 in 2016. The GDP per capita in the member states of the European Union increased dramatically during the same time period, rising from US$ 1,934.8 to US$ 32,233.5.

On the other hand, contemporary neoliberal nations do experience rising economic violence and inequities within their boundaries. The Italian statistician Corrado Gini created the Gini index, which may be used to quantify inequality. The income distribution in different societies can be compared thanks to the Gini index. The Gini scale "[...] measures inequality between 0, where everyone is treated equally, and 1, when all of the nation's income is received by a single person." According to data from the U.S. Consensus Bureau, between 1970 and 2016, inequality in the United States increased quickly from 0,39 to 0,48. (United States Census Bureau 2017). Also, the U.S. Congressional Research Service's "The U.S. Income Distribution: Trends and Problems" report from 2016's major findings indicate that inequality has grown among the lower 80% of earners as well as among those at the top of the income distribution during the past four decades (Dalaker et al., 2016: 1). Therefore, significant reductions in social spending, which includes cash benefits, direct in-kind provision of goods and services, and tax breaks with social purposes, have a significant impact on the population, particularly millions of vulnerable individuals who live in low-income households or are elderly, disabled, or unemployed (Kaul, 2011). The market-driven system of profit, competitiveness, and growth also leads to exploitation, starvation, poverty, ecological collapse, human suffering, and structural inequality.

High-income nations are also rife with blatant disparities in social and medical services. For instance, health insurance coverage is "uneven" in the US, and minorities and the poor are frequently mistreated. Nearly two out of every five workers, or 40 million, lack access to paid sick leave. In 2014, it was shown that nearly 20% of people of Hispanic heritage lacked health insurance, compared to 7.6% of White people who were non-Hispanic. The system not only fosters inequality but also a variety of social issues that fuel competition for scarce resources. According to Jinkings and Guimaraes, Europe is today dealing with serious socioeconomic issues that frequently manifest as nationalist movements (2011: 11). These movements and right-wing populists, who spread anti-immigration views among other things, have become stronger in countries like Germany, Austria, the Netherlands, Hungary, Poland, and the United Kingdom.

Neoliberalism's encouraged competition frequently leads to monopolies or oligopolies when stronger parties drive out weaker ones. Neoliberalism's assumption of perfect information and an even playing field for competition comes across as either innocently utopian or an intentional concealment of the processes that would result in the concentration of wealth and, consequently, the restoration of class power. Players that are more knowledgeable and powerful have an advantage that can all too readily be used to acquire additional knowledge and relative strength. So, unless the state intervenes to balance them, asymmetric power relations tend to worsen rather than improve over time. State regulation of provision, access, and pricing appears inevitable in such a situation.

The topic of market failure is another significant area of contention. This occurs when people and businesses shed their liabilities outside the market in order to avoid paying the full expenses that are attributable to them. The typical example is pollution, where people and businesses save costs by freely disposing of toxic wastes in the environment.

As a result, productive ecosystems could be damaged or destroyed. Human health may be impacted by occupational physical threats or exposure to hazardous substances.

There is a conflict between the longing for a meaningful group existence and the tempting but alienating possessive individualism. Despite the fact that people are theoretically free to make their own decisions, they are not meant to opt for the creation of powerful collective institutions like labour unions over feeble voluntary associations like charitable organisations. The neoliberals must impose severe restrictions on democratic governance, depending instead on undemocratic and unaccountable institutions (such as the Federal Reserve or the IMF) to make important decisions in order to protect against their worst fears—fascism, communism, socialism, authoritarian populism, and even majority rule. In a society where the state is intended to be non-interventionist, this leads to the paradox of extensive governmental interventions and elite and "expert" government. So, when faced with social movements that call for collective interventions, the neoliberal state is obligated to act, often in a repressive manner, depriving the same freedoms that it is meant to preserve.

In some areas, the state's influence and involvement have grown. For instance, according to Jinkings & Guimaraes (2011), "U.S. government expenditures on public safety climbed by 466 percent from 1982 to 2001." At the same time span, spending on prisons in particular has increased by 500%. According to Jinkings and Guimares, from 1985 onward, spending on prisons outspent spending on social benefits for families with dependent children and aid for poor families.

Prisons started to be privatised in 1983, and with it came the idea of having inmates perform less complicated jobs in exchange for their accommodation. Profitability of privatised prisons depends on a constant flow of inmates. Hence, this neoliberal practise can be seen in the dramatically rising numbers of prisoners behind bars between 1980 and 2014: Over this time, the entire prison population in the United States climbed from 503,586 to 2,217,947. (WPB World Prison Brief 2017). Such "prison inflation" has also occurred in a number of European nations, including England, Portugal, and Spain (Jinkings & Guimares, 2011: 16).

It is abundantly obvious that neoliberalism does not render the role of the state or certain state institutions, such as the judiciary and police, meaningless. However, there has been a fundamental restructuring of state institutions and practises, particularly in relation to the harmony between coercion and consent, the powers of capital and popular movements, and the powers of the executive and judicial branches of government in comparison to the powers of representative democracy. The neoliberal state is anticipated to play a supporting role and only provide the framework for market functions, but it is also anticipated to actively promote an atmosphere that is business-friendly and to act as a competing force in international affairs. The issue arises because in its latter function it must operate as a collective corporation.

15.6 The Changing Dynamics of Neoliberal State

Many countries of the world now have some variation of the neoconservative state due to the inherent instability and crisis-prone nature of the neoliberal state. In light of recent Chinese events, Wang (2003:44) argues that, conceptually, discursive narratives like "neo-Authoritarianism," "neo conservatism," "classical liberalism," "market extremism," and "national modernization" all have intimate ties to the neoliberal constitution in one way or another. The convergence of neoliberalization in authoritarian governments like China and Singapore and the rise in authoritarianism apparent in neoliberal states like the US and UK, however, is interesting to notice. Neoconservatives in the US support corporate dominance, free market capitalism, and the return of class power. The neoliberal aim of elite rule, suspicion of democracy, and preservation of market liberties is thus completely congruent with neo conservatism. However, it deviates from the fundamental tenets of pure neoliberalism and has reshaped neoliberal practises in two key ways: first, in its concern for order as a solution to the chaos of individual interests, and second, in its concern for an overbearing morality as the essential social glue to keep the body politic secure in the face of external and internal threats. In its quest for order, neo conservatism appears to be merely removing the totalitarian shroud that neoliberalism attempted to cloak itself in. Yet, it also suggests unique solutions to one of neoliberalism's fundamental problems. If, as Thatcher first asserted, "there is no such thing as society, only individuals," order can simply be displaced by the anarchy of individual interests. A scenario that is increasingly unmanageable is created by the anarchy of the market, of competition, and of uncontrolled individualism (individual hopes, desires, concerns, and fears; choices of lifestyle and of sexual habits and orientation; ways of self-expression and behaviours towards others). It could even result in the dissolution of all social ties and a state that is bordering on social anarchy and nihilism. In light of this, it seems that some form of coercion is required to restore order.

Hence, militarization is stressed by neoconservatives as a remedy for the confusion caused by competing interests. Because of this, they are much more likely to draw attention to dangers to the integrity and stability of the country—real or fictitious—both at home and abroad. This incites what Hofstadter terms "the paranoid style of American politics" in which the country is seen as under siege and under threat from both within and without. Externally, radical Islam and China emerged as the top two contenders, and internal dissident movements (such as the Branch Dravidians who were burned alive at Waco, militia groups who supported the Oklahoma bombing, riots that broke out after Rodney King was beaten up, and finally the disturbances that erupted in Seattle in 1999) had to be targeted by increased surveillance and policing.

They do not deviate in any way from the neoliberal aim of building or reestablishing a dominating class power. Nonetheless, they aim to legitimise that power and exert social control by creating an environment of acceptance centred on a logical set of moral principles. This raises the issue of which moral principles ought to take precedence. Doctrines of "exceptionalism" and the lengthy history of civil rights action in the US have undoubtedly sparked moral movements about problems like global hunger, civil rights, and humanitarian involvement, as well as missionary enthusiasm. The moral principles were centred on cultural nationalism, moral rectitude, a particular brand of evangelical Christianity, family values, right-to-life concerns, and opposition to the newest social movements including feminism, gay rights, affirmative action, and environmentalism. While this cooperation was primarily tactical under Reagan, political unrest during the Clinton administration drove the morality vs. values debate to the forefront of Republicanism under Bush the younger. It currently serves as the foundation of the neoconservative movement's moral agenda. This declaration of moral principles frequently invokes national, religious, historical, cultural, and other standards inside the US, albeit these goals are by no means exclusive to the country.

It is therefore unlikely to fail in a totalizing moment of collapse because "neoliberalism" does not actually exist as a cohesive and fixed structure, as an equilibrium complex, or as a limited end-state (Peck et al., 2010). As a result, perhaps what we are seeing is a horrifying reanimation instead of the creature's eventual death (Springer, 2018). Contrarily, crises signify a continuity that provides insight into the nature of neoliberalism as an adaptive system of socioeconomic control (Peck et al., 2010). States cannot easily attain formal "independence" from neoliberalism by claiming a total qualitative departure from the past. Speaking of a "post-neoliberal" successor state seems a little premature because institutional legacies persist for a long time (Springer, 2018: 625).

15.7 Conclusion

Neoliberal theorists have consistently advocated for a more pragmatic, state-led market agenda that is aware of how dependent economic liberalism is on factors such as competition, property rights, an entrepreneurial culture, a robust police force, stringent monetary regulations, and others. Neoliberalism's commitment to a strong state that is able to fend off ideological and political threats to capitalist competition is what distinguishes it from other political ideologies and systems of thought. The 'curse of neoliberalism' according to Jamie Peck, is that it cannot exist with or without the state (Peck, 2008: 39). While neoliberalism does not reduce state authority, it does cause it to move from areas that are perceived as "political" to those that are seen as free from the hazards of politics (Davies, 2018: 274). This drive to transfer power to unelected, unconventional new bodies is known as "technocracy" in the neoliberal state era. All of this indicates that the technocratic elite of the neoliberal state, who function outside of conventional forms of professional vocation or knowledge, is a new breed. These elites differ from Weberian bureaucrats in that they frequently change jobs (and industries) and are qualified more by the analytical approaches they employ than by the knowledge they really possess. Key players in the administration of the neoliberal, anti-political state include economists, risk managers, auditors, policy "entrepreneurs," innovation "gurus," and others. The increase of outsourcing shows that the neoliberal state's teleology is not one of pure, laissez-faire privatisation. Instead, it is in the direction of new, extremely complicated alliances between the state and the market, in which authority and agency ultimately reside in an unclear area of 'governance' between the two. The state and the market are intertwined, in contrast to the liberal utopia that Polanyi decried. It is carried out by evoking liberalism and laissez-faire, but frequently entails the increase of state authority in areas like surveillance, audit, control over local government, and military power.

Keywords

Neoliberalism

State

Welfare State

Market

Review Questions

1. Neoliberal regimes may benefit certain people, yet inequality has grown. Comment.
2. How do welfare regimes and various neoliberal regimes differ from one another?
3. How the development of neoliberal regimes has been impacted by globalisation.

References

Adkins, L. 2018. Neoliberalism's Gender Order In Cahill, D. Cooper, M. Konings, M. Primrose, D. (Ed.). The Sage handbook of Neoliberalism. London: sage Publications: 469–482.

Birch, Kean (2015) We Have Never Been Neoliberal: A Manifesto for a Doomed Youth. Alresford: Zero Books.

Boas, Taylor and Jordan Gans-Morse (2009) Neoliberalism: From new liberal philosophy to anti-liberal slogan. *Studies in Comparative International Development*, 44(2): 137–161.

Bockman, J. 2013. "Neoliberalism." Contexts, 12(3). http://journals.sagepub.com/doi/full/10.1177/1536504213499873#articleCitationDownloadContainer.

Cahill, D. Cooper, M. Konings M. and Primrose D. 2018. Introduction: Approaches to Neoliberalism. In Cahill, D. Cooper, M. Konings, M. Primrose, D. (Ed.). 2018. The Sage handbook of Neoliberalism. London: sage Publications: xxv-1.

Crouch, C. 2009. Privatised Keynesianism: An Unacknowledged Policy Regime. *The British Journal of Politics and International Relations*, *11*(3), 382–399. https://doi.org/10.1111/j.1467-856X.2009.00377.x

Dalaker, J. Donovan, S. Labonte, M. 2016. "The U.S. Income Distribution: Trends and Issues." Congressional Research Service 7-5700, R44705, CRS Report. Prepared for Members and Committees of Congress. Accessed from https://fas.org on September 18, 2023.

Davies, W. 2018. The Neoliberal State: Power Against 'Politics' In Cahill, D. Cooper, M. Konings, M. Primrose, D. (Ed.). The Sage handbook of Neoliberalism. London: sage Publications: 273–283.

Duggan, L. 2014. "Neoliberalism." In B. Burgett, & G. Hendler. (Eds.), Keywords for American cultural studies. (2nd edn.), New York: New York University Press.

Garland, D. 2016. The Welfare State: A Very Short Introduction. Uk: Oxford University Press.

Grady, J. Harvie, D. 2011. "Neoliberalism." In M. Tadajewski, SAGE Key Concepts series: Key Concepts in Critical Management Studies. London, UK: Sage UK.

Harvey, D. 2005.A Brief History of Neoliberalism. New York: Oxford University Press.

Jessop, B. 2002. The Future of the Capitalist State. Uk: Polity Press.

Jinkings, I. Guimarães, Vera M. D. 2011. "The Neoliberal State and the Penalization of Misery." Latin American Perspectives, Issue 178, 38(5): 9–18.

Kaul, N. 2011. "How many zeroes are there in a trillion? On Economics, Neoliberalism, and Economic Justice" Open Democracy. Accessed from https://www.opendemocracy.net on September 18, 2023.

Mead, L. 1986. Beyond Entitlement: The Social Obligations of Citizenship. Free Press.

Murray, C. 1984. Losing Ground: American Social Policy 1950–1980. Basic Books. Navarro, V. 2020. The Consequences of Neoliberalism in the Current Pandemic. International Journal of Health services, 50(3): 271–275. http://dx.doi.org/10.1177/0020731420925449

Nonini, D. M. 2003. "American Neoliberalism, "Globalization", and Violence: Reflections from the United States and Southeast Asia." In: Friedman, J. (Ed.). "Globalization, the State, and Violence." Altamira Press. A Division of Rowman & Littlefield Publishers, Inc. 163–201.

Peck, J., 2008. Remaking laissez-faire. *Progress in Human Geography*, 32: 3–43.

Peck, J. Theodore, N. and Brenner, N. (2010).Postneoliberalism and its malcontents. *Antipode*, 41(s1): 94–116.

Schwab K. Smadja, C. 1999, "Globalization needs a human face/ International Herald Tribune. January 28th, cited in Harvey, D. 2000. Spaces of Hope. Edinburgh: Edinburgh University Press.

Springer, S. 2018. No More Room in Hell: Neoliberalism as Living Dead In Cahill, D. Cooper, M. Konings, M. Primrose, D. (Ed.). The Sage handbook of Neoliberalism. London: sage Publications: 620–630.

Springer, S. Birch, K. MacLeavy J. 2016. An Introduction to Neoliberalism. In Springer, S. Birch, K. MacLeavy J. (Ed.). The Handbook of Neoliberalism. New York : Routledge. 1–13.

Smith, N. 2017. "Neoliberalism." In Britannica Academic, Encyclopædia Britannica.

The World Bank (2017): "GDP per capita (current US$)." Data. World Bank national accounts data, and OECD National Accounts data files. Accessed from https://data.worldbank.org on September 18, 2023.

United States Census Bureau (2017): "Table H-4. Gini Indexes for Households, by Race and Hispanic Origin of Householder: 1967 to 2016". Accessed from https://www.census.gov on September 18, 2023.

Venugopal, Rajesh (2015) Neoliberalism as a concept. *Economy and Society*, 44(2): 165–187.

Wang, H. 2003. *China's New Order: Society, Politics and Economy in Transition*. Cambridge, Mass.: Harvard University Press.

Women's Budget Group (2015) *Plan F: A Feminist Economic Strategy for a Caring and Sustainable Economy*. London: Women's Budget Group. Accessed from http://wbg.org.uk on September 18, 2023.

WPB World Prison Brief 2017. "World Prison Brief Data. United States of America." Online accessible: http://www.prisonstudies.org.

CHAPTER 16

Authoritarian and Totalitarian Regimes

Ankit Tomar

Reader's Guide

Classifying political regimes has been a challenging, though important task. Classification helps to understand the political systems in comparative perspective. Based on their similarities, differences, convergences and divergences in terms of their structures and functioning, regimes are categories into democratic, authoritarian, totalitarian and transitioning systems. The trend towards democratisation has been increasing in the period following the Second World War and the Cold War as witnessed in the case of many states with an authoritarian and totalitarian past that have adopted democracy. These new waves of democratisation raise a spate of pertinent questions such as are democracies the only legitimate systems, and if so, then does it imply that all non-democratic regimes are, by nature, illegitimate? Second, why many states are still continuing with authoritarian and totalitarian rulership, what means of legitimation are available to such regimes? Third, does the future really belong to democracy? These are crucial questions, and their explanations would require a comprehensive, albeit critical engagement with the study of the classification of regimes. This chapter discusses the basis of classification and the nature of authoritarian and totalitarian regimes.

16.1 Introduction

Understanding political regimes has been a great challenge for scholars of comparative politics due to the fluidity of parameters that characterise regimes. However, since the Greek antiquity, political scientists have deliberated upon the nature of political regimes to understand the functioning of the governments and their relationships with their citizens or subjects with an aim of offering a classification. From Alexis de Tocqueville and Max Weber to Gabriel Almond and Seymour Martin Lipset to Theda Skocpol and Margaret Levi, scholars have explained the dynamics of political regimes by comparing their historical trajectories and performances. In doing so, they have suggested that the roots of major political regimes across the world often rest most fundamentally in the past. Though there is no end to the classification of political regimes as every regime is at once unique and in flux therefore, every classification of regimes is partial and temporary. Nevertheless, a classification of regimes serves to highlight similarities and dissimilarities among them, and by doing so it deepens our understanding of them.

The process of the classification of regimes as democratic, oligarchic, and tyrannical can be traced back to the fourth century BCE, when Aristotle made the first recorded attempt to describe then existing 158 Greek city-states. From the eighteenth century onwards, regimes were increasingly classified as monarchies or republics and autocratic or constitutional regimes. During the inter-war period, countries were divided into democratic and non-democratic regimes, particularly in the context of the rise of Stalinist Russia, Fascist Italy, and Nazi Germany. The Cold War gave rise to another typology of states based on their ideological orientation in terms of the capitalist and communist states, whereas on the basis of their economic development and extent of industrialisation, countries were classified into first-world, second-world and the third-world. However, in light of new developments, such as the end of Cold War, the rise of East Asia, and globalisation, such classifications have become obsolete as they are not able to capture the complexity and nuances of the political systems. The changing time and global events have been interpreted by scholars in varying ways. While some scholars view them as an indication of natural and inevitable democratisation of the world on the line of Western liberal democracy; others believe the modern world to be becoming politically more diffuse and fragmented. The critical discourses like postmodernism question the universalisation of Western liberal democracy and see it as culturally, territorially, and time bound. In fact, some of the alternative regimes and the forms of illiberal democracy are appearing as successful and enduring than expected such as Turkey, Singapore and China.

In this context, this chapter discusses the classification of contemporary political regimes on the basis of fundamental premises: who rules? How is compliance achieved? How do these systems differ in terms of citizen's rights and entitlements? What possibilities different states offer to accommodate dissent and expand the emancipatory spaces? These queries would be addressed by looking into the historical legacies of different systems with reference to their origin, evolution, nature, and scope in a comparative perspective as discussed in the sections below.

16.2 Understanding Political Regimes

Contemporary political regimes are broadly categorised as democratic (parliamentary and presidential) and non-democratic regimes (authoritarian and totalitarian). As we proceed to understand the nature of authoritarian and totalitarian regimes, it is necessary to first understand the meaning of political regimes and other related terms such as state and government which we often use interchangeably despite their differences. To understand the classification of regimes better, it is imperative to discuss the meaning of state first. The state is a historical institution that emerged in the sixteenth and seventeenth century as a political (or territorial) association and a system of centralised force that succeeded in subordinating all other competing institutions and led to an end of overlapping authority systems and groups that had characterised medieval Europe. The 'Peace Treaty of Westphalia' (1648) established the principle of territorial sovereignty, by formalising the notion of the modern state as the principal actor in domestic and international affairs. The jurisdiction of the state is geographically defined and encompasses all those who live within its borders. In other words, the state is conventionally defined as an organised political community with four important elements namely: population, definite territory, sovereignty and government. In contrast to the state, the government is the agency that acts on behalf of the state. Further, it refers to institutional processes through which collective and usually binding decisions are made and implemented. The core functions of government are law-making (legilsation), law implementation (execution), and law interpretation (adjudication) which are performed by three organs of government namely; legislature, executive, and judiciary. A political regime, however, is to be analysed from a much broader perspective in the sense that it encompass not only the organs of the government and the political institutions of the state, but also the formal and informal structures of the state, governmental roles and processes through which it interact with the civil society. It represents a set of processes, norms and culture that determines how the government functions. In short, it refers to the pattern of interactions between the various institutions, structures, the government, and civil society. A political regime is therefore, a 'system of rule' that endures despite the fact that governments come and go. The process of classification of political regimes serves three purposes: first, classification of political regimes serves as an enabling tool for the understanding of politics and government. According to Alexis de Tocqueville, 'without comparisons to make, the mind does not know how to proceed'. Second, the process of classification facilitates a meaningful evaluation of a particular political regime which leads to better governance. In other words, this process of classification allows for qualitative judgments to be made in relation to political structures and governmental forms. Third, apart from involving the normative issues and the processes, it helps in tackling the concrete questions such as whether the UK should adopt a republican form of government or not.

16.3 Traditional and Modern Systems of Regime Classification

The classification and characterisation of political regimes are as old as the study of politics itself. Beginning from the fourth century BCE onwards, there have been numerous attempts to classify the regimes, and specify the basis of classification. The earliest tradition of investigating regimes could be traced back in the writings of ancient Greek thinkers of the fourth Century BCE like Plato and Aristotle who have contributed greatly to the tradition of studying political regimes. In In those times, Aristocracy as the most desirable form of government and democracy was not a very desirable form of government, since it implied a state of rule by all, leading to orderless society. Plato distinguished law-abiding states from the lawless states. According to him, monarchy, aristocracy, and moderate democracy are the three law-abiding states whereas tyranny, oligarchy, and extreme democracy are the three forms of lawless states.

Aristotle who is regarded as the father of comparative politics, proposed classification of political regimes after studying 158 Constitutions. He classified regimes on the basis of the number of rulers and quality of rule into a monarchy, aristocracy, tyranny, oligarchy, and democracy. He believed that regimes could be categorised on the basis of two questions: who rules? and who benefits from the rule? According to him, rule could be placed in the hands of a single individual, a small group, or the many. He thus identified the six forms of regimes shown in Table 16.1. According to him, when a state is ruled by one person it is called monarchy; when it is ruled by few persons it is called aristocracy; and when it is ruled by many then it is called polity. For Aristotle, all these are the pure forms of regimes and other are the perverted forms of regimes. Tyranny, according to Aristotle, is the worst type of government because it treats its population like slaves. On the other hand, monarchy and aristocracy were unrealistic because they relied on a divine willingness to place the good of the community before the rulers' own interests. He recognised polity as the most practicable form of regime — rule by many acting in the best interests of all. Aristotle, however, criticised popular rule on the grounds that the masses would resent the wealth of the few, and too easily fall under the sway of demagogue. He therefore, advocated a 'mixed' Constitution that combined elements of both democracy and aristocracy, and left the government in the hands of the 'middle class', those who were neither rich nor poor.

In the medieval ages, attempts were made by Jean Bodin, Montesquieu, Rousseau, Kant, etc. to improve upon the Aristotelian classification but they could not carry farther. However, new modes of classification emerged with the rise of the modern nation-state (Westphalian state). The American and French revolutions gave a blow to monarchy and brought about the republican and democratic forms.

The process of decolonisation in the nineteenth and twentieth century led to the emergence of many post-colonial societies as sovereign independent states. Since then, states have been broadly categorised into democratic and non-democratic regimes. This kind of classification is often considered as a Eurocentric classification as it overrides a tendency of privileging the West and failed to take into account the socio-political realities of post-colonial states of Asia, Africa, and Latin America. The Eurocentric bias has existed and continues to exist on two levels: i) a disproportionate focus on Western European countries such as Britain, France, and Germany during the formal colonial era; and ii) the imposition of Western values

Table 16.1 Aristotle's Classification of Political Regimes

	One	Few	Many
Pure Form	Monarchy	Aristocracy	Polity
Perverted Form	Tyranny	Oligarchy	Democracy

and characteristics as the "ideal type model" for newly independent countries, pushed by American scholars. This problem was highlighted by Roy C. Macridis in 1955. Macridis argued that Eurocentric classification is parochial since it focused solely on the experience of Western Europe. In the contemporary times, the two major variables which have been employed to understand the nature of a political regime are the number of people ruling (who is ruling) and secondly the nature of power or how the ruling body exercises power over the governed and its relation to the political institutions. In the case of the second criteria, power has been a major basis of classification and a yardstick to investigate the nature of the relationship between the state and the political institutions. This kind of conceptualisation was proposed by the scholars like Plato, Aristotle, and Max Weber. There is no doubt that different political regimes have tended to priorities different sets of criteria. However, among the parameters, most commonly used to understand the nature and classification of political regimes are the following:

1. Who rules? Does the process of political participation involve only elite (privileged group), or does it encompass the entire population?
2. How is compliance achieved? Is the political regime obeyed as a result of the use of coercion, or through consensus, bargaining, and compromise?
3. Is the political power of the regime centralised or fragmented? What kind of mechanisms are needed to ensure separation of powers and checks and balances exist within the political regime?
4. How is government power acquired and transferred? Is the regime open and competitive, or is it monolithic?
5. What is the relationship between the state and the individual? What is the nature of the distribution of rights and responsibilities between the government and the citizens?
6. What is the level of material development? How materially affluent is the society, and how equally is wealth distributed?
7. How is economic life organised? Is the political economy geared to the market or to state regulation and planning?
8. Within what limits and scope the political regime operates? Whether it is a limited or unlimited government and what is the proper extent of democratic rule?
9. Under which conditions and constraints is the government operating? What are the socio-economic and cultural problems coming in the way of the functioning of the political regime?
10. How stable is a political regime? Has a particular regime survived over a considerable period of time, and does it have the capacity to respond to new demands and challenges? (Heywood, 2019, p.115)

States are also classified into unitary or federal depending on the constitutional arrangement of distribution of power between the centre and the sub-national levels of the government. In unitary systems the governing power basically resides with the central government and authority is delegated to the sub-national units to implement policy decisions as in the case of Afghanistan, Italy, China, Saudi Arabia, and United Kingdom. However, unitary states suffer from some democratic limitations due to the concentration of power in the centralised government. On the other hand, federal states like Australia, Brazil, Canada, Germany, India, and United States are marked by joint power sharing between the states and the centre. Different levels of intermediate government exist that enjoy great independence and authority guaranteed by the Constitutions of these countries. In some federal structures, the constituting territories or provinces may have their own Constitution that defines the laws of the state as in the case on the United States. According to Michael Curtis, a federal state is one in which the functions and power is shared by central government and state governments. Division of power, a written Constitution, and a judiciary with wider powers are important aspects of federal systems. However, it is important to point out that many countries cannot be neatly clubbed into any of these two categories as they lie somewhere between these two ideal types like India which is famous as a quasi-federal state with features of both the unitary and federal system.

Government systems are categorised as parliamentary or presidential depending on the degree of separation of power between legislature, executive, and judiciary. Whereas the nature of the relationship between the center and the units determine whether the state is unitary or federal, the relationship between the executive and the legislature ascertains the state to be a parliamentary or a presidential state. Parliamentary systems are characterised by the accountability of the executive to the legislature. A smooth coordination between the executive and legislature makes governance efficient and also prevents authoritarianism. Presidential systems are governed by the principle of separation of power under which all three branches of government are independent of each other. Compared to the parliamentary system, the presidential system is considered to be stable due to the fixed tenure of the president and its non-dependence on the support of the majority in the legislature.

Contrary to democratic regimes, in authoritarian systems, political power is concentrated in a leader, referred as the dictator. In such form of governments, political pluralism and freedom of expression is restricted to maintain a stronghold of the dictator. When, dictatorship tries to have complete control over all aspects of political, economic, and civil rights it may be characterised as a totalitarian regime, which will be discussed elaborately in the next section.

16.4 Authoritarianism and Totalitarianism: Nature and Characteristics

Democratic and non-democratic regimes may be distinguished both in terms of their objectives as well as the means employed to achieve them. When the power is based on people's consent, respected willingly, and recognised by wider masses, it is called legitimate and binding authority. In the democratic regimes, authority involves the legitimate exercise of power, and in that sense, it arises from 'below'. However, when a state exercises power regardless of popular consent and with the help of force it can be called a non-democratic regime. In non-democratic regimes particularly in authoritarian and totalitarian regimes, power is exercised from 'above'. The exercise of power 'from above' is also associated with monarchical absolute monarchies, traditional dictatorships, single party rule, and military regimes. They all are non-democratic in the sense that they are concerned with the repression of opposition and political liberty.

Authoritarian and totalitarian regimes are increasingly becoming an area of study for comparative political analysts in recent times. And the reason is straightforward: 'non-democratic regimes, whether by elders, chiefs, monarchs, aristocrats, military rule or one-party rule, has been the norm for most of human history' (Brooker, 2009, p.1). Authoritarian and totalitarian regimes are anti-democratic in the sense that such regimes insist on unqualified obedience, conformity and coercion. These regimes are characterised by government which has a strong command over power, often a centralised power structure. Though both regimes are anti-democratic in their nature but still they are different from each other. For understanding the differences between the two regimes, let's first discuss the meaning and nature of authoritarian regimes. Authoritarian regimes refer to a form of government in which the ruling elite decide what is good for individuals and they impose their values on the society irrespective of its members' wishes. It is in essence negation of democracy. Such regimes are characterised by limited political freedom. Under such regimes, political rights, freedom of religion and political pluralism are very limited. Also, there may be overlapping of judicial, executive and legislative functions of the state.

Box 16.1: Forms of Authoritarian Regimes

Personal Despotism: A rule by a single individual on the basis of the personal security force.
Absolute Monarchy: A ruling sovereign from the royal family.
Military Rule: Government by the military, often ruling through a *junta*.
One Party Rule: Rule by a single dominant party.
Theocracy: Rule by religious leaders.

Source: Author

Authoritarian regimes have a very controlled power structure; it usually has a centralised power structure. It is not just political power, which is centralised, even economic power may be highly centralised. In authoritarian regimes or non-democratic set up, a lot of the rules are left not on the independent bodies rather on the rulers to decide and (Linz, 2000, p.59). One of the core aspects of the authoritarian regimes is that it lacks political pluralism. Such regimes lack the spirit to accommodate any opposition or presence of alternate institutions. Authoritarian regimes are less tolerant of diverse ethnic and religious composition. Most often, such regimes sustain on use of violence or coercion. Any non-adherence to the dictates of the state may invite very harsh punishments. Secret killings, and arrests become common features, for instance, Nazi Germany, under Hitler's leadership, depended heavily on a sophisticated network for espionage and surveillance, often resorting to coercion to suppress dissenting or differing opinions. This period is marked by prolonged dominance under a singular political authority, often sustained through the misuse of power. Leaders in such circumstances don't necessarily ascend to power through democratic processes or public consent; instead, they often seize positions through coercion and populist propaganda. These leaders maintain control by spreading misinformation, exercising total dominance over mass media, and suppressing freedom of speech. Consequently, regulated media and restricted press freedom are common traits of such regimes. Authoritarian governments are characterized by limited civil liberties, and efforts are made to control them. Many authoritarian regimes exhibit a lack of mass mobilization and citizen involvement in political affairs due to the implementation of severe coercion and state repression. While history has witnessed numerous authoritarian regimes, the post-Second World War era saw many countries transitioning from authoritarianism to democracy (Gandhi and Przeworski, 2007, p.2). Factors such as the use of force or coercion alone have not been able to hold such regimes in power although it has been a crucial factor, for instance, Pol Pot was ousted out of power after killing two million Cambodians (Gandhi and Przeworski, 2007, p.2). Factors such as the process of decolonisation, end of the Cold War, the disintegration of the Soviet Union acted as a catalyst for the shift away from authoritarian regimes. Arab Spring in 2010 was another event that began in Tunisia and spread to many countries such as Libya and Egypt challenged the authoritarian regimes. However, some countries still continue with an authoritarian structure such as China. Previously, there was an assumption that all authoritarian (or totalitarian) regimes were controlled by a strongman.

In the authoritarian regimes, there are number of variations with overlapping characteristics of other regimes. The variance in the degree of authoritarianism is reflective of the fact that regimes of today use a wider range of tools to maintain themselves in power. However, political scientists have classified authoritarian regimes as oligarchic or autocratic, or rule by a one-party or the military. Alan Siaroff (2013, p.243–245), lists different kinds of authoritarian regimes which may range from traditional, military, theocratic, to electoral authoritarianism. In recent times, there is an emergence of a new form of authoritarian regime which is generally known as a 'competitive authoritarian regime'.

Box 16.2: Competitive Authoritarian Regime

Competitive authoritarian regime is a blend of democratic structures with authoritarian functioning. In a competitive authoritarian regime, unlike a fully authoritarian, electoral success forms a substantial part of the ruler's claim to authority. But election outcomes are conditioned by the ruler's influence over the media and by the use of state resources to favour his own position. This form of the regime is also known as a hybrid regime. Example: Venezuela, Malaysia, Russia

Source: Author

16.4.1 Fundamental Characteristics of Authoritarian Regimes

- Authoritarian regimes are characterised by highly concentrated and centralised authority, which is maintained through political repression and the exclusion of potential challengers.

- The political process is typically characterised by personalised leadership, a strong state, and weak opposition.
- In authoritarian regimes the decisions and power is largely exercised by those who hold authority. The political rulers often place greater emphasis on the use of force and coercion to obtain obedience.
- Those in power in an authoritarian regime claim to derive their authority not necessarily and always from the consent of the governed but from some special quality that they claim to possess.
- Political and civil liberties and rights are selectively suppressed, although no attempt is made to control every aspect of human life.
- Based on the force, authoritarian regimes are likely to use violence against the citizens who do not receive any importance in the governance. The changes in government or even of leadership, is not smooth and peaceful under authoritarian regimes. Such changes take place either by means of a coup d'etat (seizure and removal of a government by a small group of people) or as a result of revolutions.
- Authoritarian regimes are more likely to use force in their relations with other countries. Since institutions of such regimes are not based on the participation of the people, and are not accountable to people, the moderating influence of public opinion is not effective. As a result, authoritarian regimes do not help the cause of international peace.
- Authoritarian regimes are characterised by low and limited political participation and mobilisation.
- Authoritarian regimes exhibit constrained pluralism, in contrast to democratic regimes, which institutionalise unlimited pluralism.

Authoritarian regimes are distinguished from the totalitarian regimes. As discussed in the previous sections, authoritarianism in its extreme form takes the shape of a totalitarian regime. The term 'totalitarian' was first used by Gentile in 1916 to describe a seamless identification predicted on a Hegelian universalism that absorbed the elements of society within the totality of the state. It became a political term and theoretical concept after World War I. A totalitarian regime refers to a system of governance in which the state seeks to regulate and control all facets of the life of its citizens whether public or private. In other words, it seeks to direct all political, economic, socio-cultural, and intellectual activities of people towards fulfilling certain aims which are determined by the state (or leader) itself. In this type of regime, no citizen has the right or opportunity to oppose or criticise the state, or to propose new goals. It implies that the state becomes absolute, permanent and a super-natural institution, or as Hegel says, 'it is the march of God on earth'. In a totalitarian state, political authority is monopolised in the hands of a single person or the dominant party. Carl J. Friedrich and Zbigniew Brzezinski have identified totalitarian regimes as a 'six-point syndrome': 1) an official ideology, 2) one party state, usually led by an all-powerful leader, 3) a system of organised terroristic policing, 4) a monopoly of the means of mass communication, 5) a monopoly of the armed combat; and 6) state control of all aspects of economic life.

Box 16.3: North Korea: A Case Study of Totalitarian Regime

Many people consider North Korea to be one of the most repressive state in the recent times. In fact, several global standardised ratings of political repression place it at the top, and some people believe it to be the world's longest-surviving totalitarian system. The political control incorporated in the North Korea apparatus is so strong that the North Korean regime has remained stable and unthreatened by political opposition for decades. Political delegation or inaction, rejection of civil society and the free press, rejection or vilification of political opposition or political alternatives to the incumbent regime, depoliticisation or hollowing out of national identity are some of the main characteristics of the political regime in North Korea.

Table 16.2 Comparative Study of Non-Democratic Regimes

Authoritarianism	Totalitarianism
A small group of individuals exercises power over the state.	An official ideology.
Government is not constitutionally responsible to the people.	A system of terroristic policing.
People have little or no role in selecting leaders.	All activities are channeled through one dominant party or a group of power-hungry people.
Individual's freedoms are restricted.	A monopoly on the means of mass communication.
These regimes may be institutionalised or legitimate.	State control over all the aspects of an individual's life.

Source: Author

Totalitarian regime entrenches centralisation and uniform regimentation of all aspects of political, social, and intellectual life and in these respects transcending by far the earlier manifestations of absolute or autocratic or despotic or tyrannical regimes and their capacity to control and mobilise the masses. In this sense, totalitarianism is truly a phenomenon of the twentieth century. The most extreme and extensive from of intervention is found in totalitarian regimes. The essence of totalitarianism is the construction of an all-embracing state, the influence of which penetrates every aspect of human existence. This form of political regime brings not only the economy, but also education, culture, religion, family life, and so on under direct state control. The case of a totalitarian regime finds justification in philosophical interpretations as well as political practices of its exponents. The tradition of an absolutist state can be traced in the writings of Plato, Hobbes and Hegel. The classic examples of totalitarian regimes are Hitler's Germany and Stalin's Union of Soviet Socialist Republics (USSR), although in the present times, North Korea has similar characteristics. The central pillars of such regimes are a comprehensive process of surveillance and terroristic policing, and a pervasive system of ideological manipulation and control. In this sense, totalitarian regimes effectively extinguish civil society and abolish the 'private' sphere of life altogether.

Furthermore, despite the fact that totalitarian regimes are by definition authoritarian, but it does not mean that all authoritarian regimes are necessarily totalitarian. There is no doubt that the authoritarian regimes are concerned with the suppression of opposition and political liberty. However, unlike the totalitarian regime, these regimes do not aim to achieve far more radical goal of obliterating the distinction between the state and civil society. In short, authoritarian regimes tend to tolerate a significant range of economic, religious, and other freedoms.

16.4.2 Features of Totalitarian Regime

- The totalitarian regime is dictatorial in nature and as such, it is opposed to the norms of liberalism and liberal democracy.
- It imposes its official ideology on the people by the iron law of despotism.
- All means are in the hands of the ruling elite that are used for purpose of propaganda.
- It stands for the monistic character of society. It means that nothing but the state becomes everything as a result other social associations are either disallowed or made to starve.

All the above-mentioned characteristic features make it clear that the totalitarian regime presents an anti-thesis model of liberal-democratic regimes.

16.5 Authoritarian and Totalitarian Regimes in Post-Second World War Period

Though authoritarian regimes have been primarily emerged in the developing states of Latin America, the Middle East, Africa and South East Asia but developed states of the West such as Spain, Portugal, and Greece, has also experienced it in the post-World War period. These regimes have been dependent not only on the use of military power and systematic repression but also on political, economic, cultural or ideological factors. In these regimes, democratic institutions both formal and informal have been either weakened or abolished and the political and legal rights have been non-existent. These regimes have been mostly under the control of a military *junta* comprising the officers of the three wings of armed forces like in Argentina during 1978–1983 or in present day Myanmar. However, there are other forms of regimes where a military backed personalised dictatorship is established. In such cases a single individual acquires pre-eminence within the *junta* or regime often being bolstered by a cult of personality drawing on charismatic authority. The military regimes headed by Colonel Papadopoulas in Greece, General Pinochet in Chile, General Abacha in Nigeria, General Zia-ul-Haq in Pakistan, Ft. Lt. Jerry Rawlings in Ghana, Sergent Samuel Doe in Liberia are among the pertinent examples. Still another form of such a regime is one where the civil regime survives primarily due to the backing of armed forces. In such cases military often prefers to rule behind the scenes and exercise power covertly through civilianised leadership. Zaire under Mobutu, who came to power in a military coup in 1965, but later allowed the army to withdraw progressively from active politics by ruling through the popular movement of the revolution in the sixties can be cited as an example and so is the case of Egypt which experienced the transition from military regimes to authoritarian civil rule under Gamel Nasser and Anwar Sadat in the 1960s and 1970s.

Keywords

Authoritarianism
Legitimacy
Political Regimes
Totalitarianism
State

Review Questions

1. What do you understand by the term 'political regime'? Discuss the traditional and modern basis of the classification of regimes.
2. Compare and contrast between authoritarian and totalitarian regimes.
3. Do you think that authoritarian and totalitarian regimes form a stable political system? Justify your answer with help of suitable examples.
4. 'All within the state none outside the state none against state'. In the light of this statement, discuss the salient features of the totalitarian regime.
5. Is the twenty-first century destined to be defined by a struggle between democratic and non-democratic regimes? Comment.

References

Boix, Carles and Susan C. Stokes. 2011. Overview of Comparative Politics. In Oxford Handbook of Political Science edited by Robert E. Goodin. Oxford: Oxford University Press.

Brooker, P. 2014. *Non-Democratic Regimes.* Basingstoke, UK: Palgrave Macmillan.

Brownlee, J. 2007. *Authoritarianism in an Age of Democratization*. Cambridge: Cambridge University Press.

Diamond, L., M. F. Plattner, and C. Walker. (eds) 2016. *Authoritarianism Goes Global: The Challenge to Democracy*. Baltimore, MD: John Hopkins University Press.

Ezrow, N. M. and E. Frantz. 2011. *Dictators and Dictatorships: Understanding Authoritarian Regimes and their Leaders.* New York: Bloomsbury Publishing.

Gandhi, J. 2008. *Political Institutions under Dictatorship*. Cambridge: Cambridge University Press.

Gandhi, Jennifer and Adam Przeworski. 2007. Authoritarian Institutions and the Survival of Autocrats. *Comparative Political Studies* 40(11): 1279–1301.

Geddes, B. 2003. *Paradigms and Sand Castles: Theory Building and Research Design in Comparative Politics.* Ann Arbor, MI: University of Michigan Press.

Gillin, L. J. 1919. Origins of Democracy. *American Journal of Sociology* 24(6): 704–714.

Hague, R. and M. Harrop. 2004. *Comparative Government and Politics: An Introduction*. London: Palgrave McMillan.

Herb, M. 1999. *All in the Family: Absolutism, Revolution, and Democracy in Middle Eastern Monarchies*. Albany, NY: SUNY Press.

Heywood, Andrew. 2019. *Politics*. London: Macmillan Education Limited.

Hilmer, D, Jefferey 2011. Modern Democratic Thought. In *21st Century Political Science: A Reference Book* edited by Ishiyama, J. T. and Breuning, M. Los Angeles: Sage.

Juan J. Linz. 2000. Totalitarian and Authoritarian Regimes. Boulder: Lynne Reiner.

Linz, J. J. 2000. *Totalitarian and Authoritarian Regimes*. Boulder, CO: Lynne Rienner Publishers.

Siaroff, Alan. 2013. *Comparing Political Regimes- A Thematic Introduction to Comparative Politics*. Toronto: University of Toronto.

Svolik, M. W. 2012. *The Politics of Authoritarian Rule*. Cambridge: Cambridge University Press.

Webb, E. 2011. Totalitarianism and Authoritarianism. In *21st Century Political Science: A Reference Book* edited by Ishiyama, J. T. and Breuning, M. Los Angeles: Sage.

CHAPTER 17

Populist Regimes

Dr Chetna Sharma

Reader's Guide

Populism is one of the key political buzzwords of the twenty-first century. Populism, which is also the Cambridge Dictionary's 2017 Word of the Year, is considered essential to any discussion and analysis of modern politics. Populism has a history that has been global, national, and supranational at various points. The global south and the global north are traversed by this history, which highlights significant experiential contrasts while also identifying significant areas of convergence. Since regional or even global trends frequently have a significant influence on national political situations, populist players in particular places or eras might be extremely similar. Populism is a highly diverse political phenomena, despite the fact that all populists share a common rhetoric. All populist actors moralise the political discourse and attempt to (re)politicize ignored topics and groups, despite the fact that populism comes in a wide variety of forms and mobilises in very different cultural and political contexts. This chapter aims to engage many perspectives on populism and the various manifestations of it across the globe.

17.1 Introduction

The notion that "the people" are the source of political authority and have the ability to intervene in politics and seize government power gives credibility to democracy and also creates a space for populism. While political movements in the nineteenth century, employed the word populism, its origin in various parts of the world may be better explained by looking at the history of democratic legitimacy. It is essentially a contested idea that is categorised as an ideology, a movement, and a syndrome. Therefore, many academics have compared populism to a chameleon (Taggart, 2000), and in modern times, populisms denoted by adjectives or hyphens such as "ethno-populism" (Madrid, 2008) or "techno-populism" (de la Torre, 2013) have evolved (Weyland, 2017). The term "populism" is not frequently employed by people or organisations themselves, which adds to the confusion. Instead, it is attributed to others, frequently in a negative light (Mudde and Kaltwasser, 2017).

The first records of the use of populism came in US newspapers in 1891 and 1892 in connection with a movement that was opposed to political elites as well as the railroad and banking sectors for being linked with one another and dependent on special interests in an effort to divide US politics. The term populism has been used in Russia to characterise the "going to the people" movement led by the Narodniki, a group of idealistic, revolutionary students who attempted to inspire the peasantry in the countryside to overthrow the Tsarist regime in the 1860s and early 1870s. The Third Republic's political leader Boulangism undertook a campaign against the parliamentary system in an effort to overthrow it and replace it with a radical plebiscitary republicanism, displaying the populist inclinations in France (for details read Kaltwasser, Taggart, Espejo and Ostiguy, 2017).

The commonalities among the US, Russian, and French populists of the nineteenth century were the direct appeal to "the people," a feeling of resistance against an establishment, and the conviction that democratic politics needed to be done differently and more directly with the people. With the rise of Hipólito Yrigoyen in Argentina (1916 and 1922) and Arturo Alessandri in Chile (1920–1925), populism first surfaced in Latin America during the 20th century. The Great Depression of the 1930s, economic hardships, a rapid migration from rural to urban areas, and increased aspirations for the expansion of political and social citizenship all contributed to the growth of populist leaders. A few notable populist leaders in Latin America at the time were Jorge Eliécer Gaitán in Colombia, Getulio Vargas in Brazil, Victor Raul Haya de la Torre in Peru, José Maria Velasco Ibarra in Ecuador, and Juan Domingo Perón in Argentina.

Poujadism, which first appeared in France in the 1950s, was the modern manifestation of European populism. The Union de Défense des Commerçants et Artisans (UDCA), formed by Pierre Poujade, was an anti-establishment movement that supported the interests of shopkeepers and small business owners. The UDCA was successful in electing members of the National Assembly in 1956. Jean-Marie Le Pen, who started the National Front in the 1970s, was one of them. This party later came to represent right-wing populism in contemporary Europe and provided the foundation for a more resilient form of populism to emerge in France.

Scholarly literature on populism first began to appear between the 1950s and the early 1970s. One of the earliest works on the topic was the conference proceedings, which were published under the title "Populism: its definition and national Characteristics" (Inoesu and Gellner, 1969). Many scholars used the idea of populism to highlight societal issues. Shils (1956) argued that populism should be viewed as an ideology of popular resentment against elites where the people are featured as better than their rulers, while Dahl (1956) coined the term "populist democracy" to refer to a system of government that aim to maximize political equality and popular sovereignty. The term "populism" was used by Kornhauser (1959) and Germani (1978) to emphasise how the development of mass society entails the dissolution of social bonds and the formation of new multitudes that may be mobilised by movements at odds with elites. Lipset (1960), drawing on US experience, associated the growth of McCarthyism, the term made popular with reference to Republican senator Joseph McCarthy in the early 1950s to convey anti-communist mistrust and publicly accuse government employees of disloyalty, while addressing the term's negative meaning.

Ernesto Laclau challenged the premise of Marxist economic determinism and laid the foundation for a new theoretical approach to the study of populism with the release of his book Politics and Ideology in Marxist Theory: Capitalism, Fascism, and Populism (1977). In a subsequent collaboration with Chantal Mouffe, Laclau (Laclau and Mouffe, 1985) expanded on the theories of Italian Marxist Antonio Gramsci to promote a theory of radical democracy as the development of political hegemonies from a post-structuralist perspective. Margaret Canovan (1981) authored an outstanding work on populism that covered a wide range of empirical subjects and examined a seven-fold typology of many varieties, including reactionary populism, farmers' populism, peasants' populism, intellectuals' populism, populist dictatorship, populist democracy, and politicians' populism. William Riker wrote Liberalism against Populism in 1982. The 1990s saw a huge growth in scholarly work on populism due to the rise of populist radical right movements in Europe and other forms of populism in the Americas.

17.2 Core themes

Populism has three core themes: the people, the elite, and the general will.

17.3 The People

A considerable chunk of the debate around the concept and reality of populism revolves on the ambiguity of the word "the people." The fact that "the people" is a construct that, at best, corresponds to a certain perspective and simplification of reality is acknowledged by almost every approach. Populism has the capacity to frame "the people" in a way that appeals to multiple constituencies and articulates their demands, so facilitating their support for a single cause. This ability to frame "the people" can lead to the creation of a shared identity between many groups. Although the phrase "the people" is a construction that can have various meanings, it is used in association with the following three: the people as the nation, the people as the common people, and the people as the sovereign. Political clout, social standing, or nationality are the three secondary traits that are always linked to the main divide between "the people" and "the elite." Speaking to the interests and ideas of the populace is one of the most pervasive appeals that we can detect in many instances that are normally classified as populist. It's crucial to remember that this definition of the people frequently acts as both a unifying and a dividing force: not only does it aim to unite a vociferous yet enraged majority, it also aims to organise this majority against a particular enemy like "the establishment."

17.4 The Elite

Theoretically, populism divides the masses from the elite based only on morality. This contrasts the honest masses with the dishonest elite, or the good masses with the evil elites. Even while moral distinction is the main one, a variety of other variables are also used to identify the elites. Populists who utilise class or commonness to characterise the masses frequently do the same for the elite. The "latte-drinking, sushi-eating, Volvo-driving, New York Times-reading, Hollywood-loving" liberal elite, for example, is compared to the typical American by conservative populists in the United States. The majority of nativist populists categorise different groups according to both their nativism and populism. Most often than not, ethnic rather than moral factors are used to exclude immigrants and members of ethnic minorities from the people (i.e. the nation). At the same time, the cultural, economic, and political elite is frequently excluded on moral grounds.

Linking the elite to economic power is especially useful for populists in power because it enables them to "explain" their lack of political success, i.e., they project that the politically powerful still possess economic powers and hence limit their efforts for the general welfare of the masses. For instance, President Chávez regularly blamed the financial elite for his country's failure to achieve democracy, while Greek Prime Minister Alexis Tsipras, leader of the left-leaning coalition for the Radical Left (Syriza), claimed that oligarchs and lobbyists were undermining his government (Mudde and Kaltwasser, 2017).

17.5 General will

Populist politics heavily rely on the notion of a general will, which is linked to the idea of a uniform interpretation of the people. Populists support their position on a flimsy Rousseauian rationale, arguing that politics should reflect the general will of the population. By creating a moral and ideological difference between the morally upright people and the corrupt elite, populism reinforces the idea that there is a general will.

Two fundamental concepts in populist ideology that are linked to the notion of a general will of the people are common sense and special interests. Populists frequently claim that their policies are based on common sense or that they reflect the sincere, sane priorities of the (common) people. In general, populists are considered as the authentic voice of the people while the elite is generally seen as speaking for special interests. Plebiscites and referenda are two instances of direct democratic processes that populist actors frequently support. In order to project the idea that they are the authentic representatives of the will of the people, Presidents Rafael Correa of Ecuador and Alberto Fujimori of Peru both passed constitutional amendments through constituent assemblies and subsequent referendums.

Special Insights

Populist Mobilization: Role of Political party, social movement and leadership

The three primary categories of populist mobilisation are political party, social movement, and personalist leadership. Some populist figures exhibit traits from two or all three of these groupings, despite the fact that many of them can be properly categorised into just one of these three groups. The most well-known instance of populist mobilisation is when a lone candidate seeks office and attracts support wholly outside of a recognised party structure. Examples include Rafael Correa in Ecuador, Pim Fortuyn in the Netherlands, Alberto Fujimori in Peru, Beppe Grillo in Italy, and Thaksin Shinawatra in Thailand. The leaders and followers interact directly, frequently without the aid of a strong political or social institution. By establishing a personalist electoral vehicle that is unconnected to a powerful political organisation, the populist leader can depict himself as an honest actor who can speak for "the people" because there are no intermediaries in his path. For instance, Correa defeated the establishment and founded a new political party to win the Ecuadorean presidential election in 2006. Political parties, according to Correa, are fraudulent organizations (Kaltwasser and Mudde, 2017:44). In order to define a shared identity and a common enemy, social movements create a framework through which the most important social problems affecting society are identified. The major power of a populist social movement hinges on its capacity to understand a widespread attitude of animosity toward the elite and persuade people that the solution lies in the sovereign people. Examples of this include the so-called Indignados in Spain and Occupy Wall Street in the United States. Political groups that support populism argue for greater representation for social groups that are currently unheard. Different political circumstances, conditions, and incentives more or less favour the three basic types of populist mobilisation. In general, presidential systems favour personalist leadership whereas parliamentary systems support the formation of political parties.

Special Insights

What are the attributes and worldview of the populist voter?

There are a few prevalent misconceptions regarding populist voters. People that are unsatisfied with the current political system, are generally drawn to a leader's charisma, or support populist candidates for ideological grounds are a few examples. The idea that unemployed people or people from lower socioeconomic position support populist candidates is another prevalent misunderstanding about populist voters. It is also claimed that an evil elite is misleading the good people, and by merging this claim with various ideologies, both the radical right and the extreme left may exploit it to their advantage. According to Roodujin's (2017) examination of individual-level data from the European Social Survey (ESS), 2002–12, which included the supporter bases of 15 prototype populist parties and 11 political systems in Western Europe, there is no such thing as a populist voter. Voters who identify as devoted populists are the most sceptical group, according to a different survey by Angelucci and Vittori (2022).

17.6 Approaches to Understand Populism

The various approaches for comprehending populism are covered in the section that follows. Some of the approaches explain populism as purely ideological phenomenon while the other see it as both a movement and an ideology.

17.7 Ideational Approach: Clau Mudde

The ideational approach describes populism as an ideology that sees society as being split into "the pure people" and "the corrupt elite," two homogeneous and adversarial groups. In comparison to "thick" or "full" ideologies like socialism or liberalism, populism is a "thin" or "thin-centered" ideology that lacks the same level of intellectual complexity and coherence. Ideologies are a group of widely held ideas that depict the political and social reality and explain the nature of people and society, as well as its structure and aims. Thin-centered ideologies are unable to formulate a wide range of solutions to urgent socio-political problems because of their confined morphology, which invariably causes them to appear related to—and occasionally even merged into—other ideologies. For instance, while populism makes general advice for how to run politics and tackles the main societal difference (between "the pure people" and "the corrupt elite"), it offers few concrete viewpoints on political institutional or socio-economic concerns (for details read Mudde, 2017).

This approach sets up distinct boundaries, enables cross-national and cross-regional study, and satisfies one of the most important conceptualization rules—the ability to discriminate between populism and non-populism. With this methodology, it is possible to investigate a number of issues, such as whether populists tend to support populist parties in disproportionate numbers, whether populist parties are more successful in countries with populist citizens, and whether nationalist and socialist attitudes are closely related to populist attitudes. Ideological definitions of populism are sometimes criticised for being excessively expansive and having a theoretically broad applicability to all political actors, movements, and parties (Mudde and Kaltwasser, 2017).

17.8 Discursive Approach: Ernesto Laclau

Ernesto Laclau is regarded as the father of populist studies, and many populism studies are built upon his influential yet nuanced discursive methodology, as described in Politics and Ideology in Marxist Theory: Capitalism, Fascism, Populism (1977). Laclau approaches populism from a Marxist perspective. His fundamental concern is that new identities that industrialization produces would challenge the proletarian or working class identity. Populist movements provide a sense of "the people," the practical equivalent of a working class identity, which can promote harmony and cooperation among people while also uniting them against a capitalist elite. Contrary to conventional Marxist theory, Laclau argues that in order to build this identity, political action is required, and the best way to do so is through a populist movement led by a charismatic leader.

The charismatic leader is essential to this process because they provide a concrete referent, or "empty signifier," through which the otherwise disparate people can read their individual interests (Hawkins, Read and Pauwels, 2017). According to Laclau, the concept of the people is an "empty signifier," to which any specific content may be added. Political elites employ populism as a discursive tool to give meaning to the terms "the people" and "the elite" in order to win as much support from the general public as they can. Fundamentally, radical democracy is the answer to the issues plaguing society, while liberal democracy is the problem. This approach is particularly pertinent to political philosophy, critical studies, and research on politics in Western Europe and Latin America.

17.9 The Organizational Approach: Weyland

According to the organisational perspective, populism is a particular form of popular mobilisation in which leaders have direct contact with their followers. The political strategy of populism, according to Weyland (2001), is employed by a personalistic leader to gain or exercise political power based on the direct, institutionalised support of substantial numbers of largely disorganised supporters. This is a special political tactic that entails the ways and methods of obtaining and using power. The type of political actor who seeks and uses power, as well as the primary power source the political actor mobilises as a base of support, make up the two main components of this political strategy.

According to this theory, the actions of populists—particularly their methods for acquiring and retaining political power—are given greater weight than their statements (Weyland, 2017). According to populism, "the people" are the source of power, but because this diverse group is too heterogeneous and amorphous to take decisive action on their own, it is up to a charismatic leader to chart the course and motivate the followers to work toward the goals that the leader believes to be the will of the people. Most of the time, the leader appeals directly to the followers rather than through patronising or institutional intermediaries, such as through TV and large-scale rallies.

Although charisma is not a characteristic of populism, it can support the basic idea of populism—the quasi-direct interaction between a personalistic leader and their supporters. The top-down agency that acts as the centre of gravity for populism may be seen when a developing popular movement loses steam and dissolves following the death of its main figurehead, as was the case with the murders of Jorge Eliécer Gaitán in Colombia and Carlos Palenque in Bolivia (Weyland, 2017). The second component of a political strategy has to do with the primary tool that political actors use to achieve and keep power. Populists favour huge numbers to win over the support of the majority of the population. Additionally, they oppose elitism and demand political equality while denouncing advantages that stem from particular interests. As the Bolivarian populist of Venezuela declared, "Chávez is the people, and the people is Chávez," leaders also promote a strong sense of identity among their followers.

17.10 Performative or Cultural Approach: Pierre Ostiguy

Politics is defined in terms of a high-low axis in Pierre Ostiguy's cultural (or "performative") approach (2009), which essentially refers to the interactions between political actors and the populace. The high-low axis, which is related to how individuals act and think in politics, is made up of two sub-dimensions: sociocultural and political-cultural. The politico-cultural dimension refers to forms of political leadership and methods of decision-making, while the socio-cultural dimension includes manners, demeanours, ways of speaking, dressing, vocabulary, and tastes expressed in public. Although it recognises the importance of leadership qualities, it does not view populism as a purely "top-down" phenomenon. Instead, it considers it to be a two-way phenomenon, with the leader's claims and the link that develops amongst followers serving as its main distinguishing traits. This approach, which is somewhat similar to Weyland's, emphasises the importance of leaders and the people providing one another with direct, unmediated help as well as the conditions that make this relationship possible.

When populists emphasise strong personalistic leadership while acting and speaking in a popular manner, populism is classified as low on both the socio-cultural and political-cultural sub-dimensions. Leaders publicly present themselves as civil, courteous, and composed on a high axis. Low axis may cause them to appear severe, inflexible, distant, and boring. They display rawer, culturally prevalent tastes, frequently use slang or folksy idioms and metaphors, and are more demonstrative in their bodily or facial expressions as well as in their way. Low-level politicians have a tendency to behave more impolitely in public and are more likely to employ crude or colloquial language. In the United States, Ross Perot was wealthier than Al Gore, but Gore was definitely more on the high axis. George W. Bush hails from affluent and more "blue blood" families, yet in 2004, he was on the low axis (Ostiguy, 2017).

The second segment of the high-low axis of political appeals consists of political cultural appeals. At the highest levels of government, arguments are made in favour of institutionally mediated forms of authority that are formal, impersonal, legalistic, and institutionally mediated. On the low end, political appeals put a lot of emphasis on individualised leadership—typically that of men. The high is frequently said to represent formal, repeatable processes in public administration as well as procedural consistency in the conduct of public life (at least as a goal to be pursued). The personalist camp often claims that it is significantly more in touch with the people and that it represents them more effectively than those who embrace an impersonal, formal, procedural definition of authority.

Consequently, the most extreme kind of populist representation and linkage is a fusion between the leader and the people. This approach takes appeals seriously and does not limit them to only ideas or programmes. It also addresses social, cultural, and historical identities, which are important to populism.

17.11 Fuzzy-set approach: Charles Ragin

Populism has fuzzy edges because, in their pursuit of power, leaders quickly adjust to the opportunities and limitations of the setting, changing colour to suit the circumstance. In politics, however, the complexity of the context and the inventiveness of people blur or even erase the lines of demarcation. Sometimes a term's meaning is not entirely captured by the set conceptual categories. In light of this, it may be preferable to use Charles Ragin's fuzzy-set technique to explain populism (2000). This method, which includes conceptual gradations and qualitative thresholds, captures the intricacies and combinations of "real world" politics with populism. Because of politicians' propensity to shift their strategies in response to the situation, populism is sometimes compared to a chameleon.

Fuzzy sets may thus be used to represent political leaders who primarily employ one tactic but also use another one as a complement. For instance, Carlos Menem sought and wielded power in Argentina primarily as the personalist leader of a varied population. However, Menem also organised the allied labour unions as well as his Peronist Party (Partido Justicialista—PJ). In order to gain the PJ's presidential nomination for the 1989 election, he took use of union support, and for the next ten years, his government was supported by the party. The Peronist Party, however, did not offer a solid, institutionalised basis for political power. Because the PJ is generally amorphous in its methods, intellectually hazy, and often combative, Carlos Menem frequently employed a personalistic leadership style to win over the constituency (Weyland, 2017).

17.12 The Popular Agency Approach: Lawrence Goodwyn

The popular agency theory contends that populism is a democratic way of life developed via extensive political involvement. It is especially common among historians from the United States. Possibly the best illustration of the following is found in Lawrence Goodwyn's Democratic Promise: Analysis of the Populist Moment in America. According to this perspective, populism primarily serves to mobilise the (common) people and foster the development of a communitarian democratic paradigm. In contrast to most other approaches, it has a wider and more limited understanding of populist actors, which essentially include all progressive mass movements (Mudde and Kaltwasser, 2017).

17.13 The Socio Economic Approach: Rudiger Dornbusch and Jeffrey Sachs

Regarding studies of populism in Latin America in the 1980s and 1990s, the understanding based on socioeconomic technique was particularly well-liked. Economists like Rudiger Dornbusch and Jeffrey Sachs have generally viewed populism as a form of reckless economic policy. It is distinguished by a first phase of significant debt-financed overseas spending and a second era of hyperinflation and severe economic reforms. While the socioeconomic method has lost favour in the majority of other social sciences, in part because later populist presidents in Latin America began to favour neoliberal economics, it remains popular among economists and journalists, particularly in the United States.

An overview of many perspectives on populism is given by all these various strategies that were described above. However, the eminent populist experts Mudde, Weyland, and Ostiguy agree that populism shouldn't merely be characterised by a particular set of economic policies (Kaltwasser, Taggart, Espejo and Ostiguy, 2017). Along with a rise in studies on populism, the proportion of academics using broadly comparable definitions of populism has grown. The ideational approach is increasingly used in populist research around the world, even though the organisational approach to populism still has considerable appeal, particularly in studies of politics in Latin America. Additionally, the ideational approach has proven to be much more adaptable than the other approaches.

17.14 Reasons for the emergence of Populism

Populism, which is fuelled by local issues, inequality, spatial inequities, and migration, can contain either left or right-wing beliefs. Specialized narratives, many of which are based on deeply held social resentments and personal fears, are used to establish relationships between common people and populist leaders. The following section discusses some of the key hypotheses that have been advanced to explain the growth of populism in various parts of the world.

17.15 Mass Society Thesis

The decline or absence of mass-based civil society, notably organised labour or traditional religion that build a bond between people and give them a sense of collective identity, is cited by some scholars as the reason for emergence of populism. When people are unable to organise, discontent rises, and this fragmentation and inability to organise independently forces people to search for some kind of identity, especially in situations where party identification is weak, as is obvious from the example of many Latin American countries with weak party systems. According to this idea, populist politics provide people a sense of identity. Through the presentation of a wide, popular identity that declares the formerly downtrodden masses to be the true rulers, populist appeals transcend ideologies and classes. The ordinary people purported moral superiority and the claim that they have a long history of being exploited by an unethical elite help to build this popular identity in both positive and negative ways. The general people is a prime target for populist demagoguery because, according to media studies on populism, their emotional vulnerabilities and cognitive shortcomings are exploited or even made worse by modern communication technologies. As media outlets compete for viewers and readers, they usually place a greater focus on entertainment, personalization, simplicity, dramatic events, and scandals. Populist parties may easily adapt to this "media logic" since their leaders usually have individualised personalities and utilise fiery language that is more interesting for (tabloid) media than dry, mainstream speeches (Hawkins, Read and Pauwels, 2017).

17.16 Economic Thesis

According to this idea, politicians and citizens are essentially instrumental decision-makers looking to maximise their material self-interest, as opposed to weak masses acting out of a subconscious need for identification or a sense of belonging. Arguments frequently fall into one of two more specific categories; they either view populism as (1) a long-term solution to the problems of corruption and poor governance or (2) a mid-term failure of current parties to meet the needs of their electorate in the face of socioeconomic change. The role that party structure and electoral laws play in facilitating the emergence of new populist parties is covered in a third set of reasons, which frequently appears in variations of the previous two (Hawkins, Read and Pauwels, 2017).

According to Betz's "Globalization Losers Thesis," (1994) employees must be adaptable, professional, and entrepreneurial in order to thrive on the social and economic fronts in the wake of globalisation. The unemployed, underemployed, and jobless whose jobs are at risk due to technological advancement are the "losers" of globalisation. These people prefer to favour populist parties on the left and the right instead of the traditional mainstream parties because they have implemented policies that are market-oriented and support globalisation, which they disapprove of (Hawkins, Read and Pauwels, 2017). Studies showing that voters with less education tend to prefer right-wing populist parties have offered indirect support for the claim (Ivarsflaten and Stubager, 2013). Populist parties thereby fill the political void left by a shifting electorate and an unresponsive party structure (Hawkins, Read and Pauwels, 2017).

Additionally, populism is a response to the persistent problems of a corrupt democratic government. According to the relative deprivation theory, elite promises and popular expectations are out of sync, which is why populism is growing. Panizza and Miorelli (2009) contend that democratic growth produces lofty, revolutionary ideas that crumble in the face of weak democratic institutions and an unfair and arbitrary rule of law. In any case, people are disturbed by how poorly democratic institutions function and how traditional parties permit populists to thrive (Hawkins, Read and Pauwels, 2017).

17.17 Institutions and the Electoral Space Thesis

One widely stated cause for the rise of (extreme right) populist groups is the election system's openness. While proportional representation systems typically have very low electoral thresholds that should favour populist challengers, majoritarian systems have a higher threshold for newcomers. High levels of electoral instability and a large electoral field often benefit populist parties as mainstream parties disregard issues that voters find significant. Moreover, traditional parties with well-established national executive committees could resist changing their agenda, especially if doing so requires appointing new leaders. Contrarily, the majority of populist parties are new party movements led by charismatic figures that have a purely personal agenda. These parties can back popular candidates because their ideologies are more flexible.

While populism requires the appropriate context in order to make sense, it is not always clear how that context is interpreted. Therefore, populism needs a consistent stream of leaders who can spread the populist message. These politicians provide the precise populist frames that facilitate the interpretive process. In a society where citizens have limited access to information, leaders must cooperate in order to achieve their objectives. Politicians must consequently show both a rhetorical and an organisational structure. When the conditions are most conducive to populist mobilisation, such as when there is widespread corruption and significant policy failures, the broad popular agreement that supports institutions may rapidly vanish. Voters who identify as populists are not just unhappy; they are also angry, and when a sizable fraction of them direct their rage towards the current political system, they have the electoral power and motivation to overthrow it (Hawkins, Read, and Pauwels, 2017). While a small minority may constantly see the world through a populist lens, the majority of us require a combination of context, framing, and mobilizational tools to awaken and act upon our populist inclinations (Hawkins, Read and Pauwels, 2017).

17.18 Populism around the World

Populism has a long history and has at various times been global, national, and supranational. Although all populists use a similar vocabulary, populism is a highly diverse political phenomenon. Right-wing populists frequently combine populism with some type of nationalism, whilst most left-wing populists frequently combine it with socialism. As a result of the frequent and significant impact of regional or even global developments on national political situations, populist actors in some regions or times might be strikingly similar (Mudde and Kaltwasser, 2017).

17.19 Asia

Asia is a complex region with respect to its levels of political development, cultural diversity, and ethnic make-up. A few of the various types of populism that are rising in this region include authoritarian populism, progressive populism, ethno-religious populism, and redistributive populism. The basic reasons of redistributive populism are high income inequality and rural poverty, more specifically the divide between the metropolitan political and corporate elite and the rural and urban poor. The populist political movement prioritises short-term economic advantages over long-term fiscal stability. Redistributive populism has started to gain ground in Thailand and India, as well as to a lesser extent in Malaysia, Mongolia, and the Philippines.

The second kind of populism, which focuses on ethnic and religious issues, is evident in Sri Lanka, Myanmar, and, to a lesser extent, Indonesia. The primary objective of this type of populism is to elevate the dominant ethno-religious identity over other minority identities as the only legitimate one.

With prospering democracies and higher incomes than the rest of the area, South Korea and Taiwan are the birthplaces of the third model, progressive populism, which emphasises welfare policies. When people lose faith in representative democracy and prefer a strongman to address urgent national issues, as in the Philippines or Pakistan, respectively, the populist authoritarian model emerges. The reality of populist movements in Asia is more complex than what the various populism classifications imply. Numerous hybrid forms of populism also exist in this region. For instance, economic populism coexists to varied degrees with other kinds of populism in the Philippines, Indonesia, South Korea, Taiwan, Thailand, India, Mongolia, and Malaysia (Chin-en, Kaustuv, Bandyopadhyay: 2021).

17.20 Africa

African populism in the 1980s and 2000s was spurred by discontent with democratic experiments and the rise of a corrupt elite that seemed far from the disadvantaged masses. Thus, anti-elitist discourse has been prevalent at both times. The main forces driving the people's revolutions of the 1980s, however, were the military leaders who frequently had the flexibility to carry out bold plans for remaking society and who ignored the outdated bureaucratic administrative institutions in favour of new grassroots structures that were theoretically supposed to enable popular participation.

Modern presidents, however, have had a remarkably varied range of economic ideas. The (young) urban poor have been their primary supporters, and they have frequently courted traditional authority in rural areas where doing so helps them win over votes from particular ethnic and religious groupings. In Africa, democracy is still in its infancy and there aren't any organisations that can serve as mediators, therefore many political parties and their leaders are essentially interchangeable. Being largely defined by the personality of their leaders, many African parties are not afraid to disregard established laws and administrative procedures once in power for their own benefit. The late Yayi Boni of Benin, Andry Rajoelina of Madagascar, and Bingu wa Mutharika of Malawi are a few examples.

Additionally, there are cases where political figures use excluding terminology to refer to a portion of the population as the "pure people." The term "purity" has frequently been used to refer to racial, religious, or ethnic purity rather than moral purity. Leaders like Bédié and Mugabe used political parties with illustrious histories and close ties to the people of Côte d'Ivoire and Zimbabwe, such as PDCI and ZANU-PF, to organise their supporters. Leaders establish strong bonds and a strong affinity with the underclass through socio-cultural performances that highlight the connection between political strategies and ideological viewpoints in African contexts. The employment of theatrical acts, such as language, song, and dance performances, has been utilised to win over people with lower levels of education. Populist leaders have shown a particular form of intolerance for independent institutions, civil rights, and internal dissent within parties throughout the majority of the African nations.

17.21 North America

Populism in North America has frequently arisen spontaneously and been characterised by regional mobilisation and weak organisation, from the late 19th-century agricultural uprising through the early 21st-century Occupy Wall Street and Tea Party movements (Mudde and Kaltwasser, 2017). Within the Canadian and American federal systems, populist parties and leaders were successful in attaining significant local and regional power and support, but they lacked a significant national political presence. From the 1930s to the 1960s, various provincial Social Credit parties in Canada gained substantial election victories and political positions from Alberta to Quebec; nevertheless, the federal Social Credit Party of Canada (the Socreds) struggled with regional divides and never emerged as a significant national force (Mudde and Kaltwasser, 2017).

According to Laura Grattan (2016), populism in the US can be observed in social movements, political candidates' statements to a greater or lesser extent, and extra-institutional formations like economic cooperatives. Michael Kazin, argues that US populism is a "mode of persuasion." In the first 10 years of the twenty-first century, two new populist movements have appeared, both of which were propelled into action by social resentments brought on by the great recession. The government bailouts of the banking sector, which were initiated by Republican president George W. Bush and completed by his Democrat successor Barack Obama, are fiercely opposed by them.

The Occupy movement began as a left-wing protest against the Bush/Obama bailout and the connections between Wall Street and Washington, D.C., the corrupt one percent elite, and those who suffered as a result of the economic crisis, or "the 99%," the American people (Mudde and Kaltwasser, 2017). Market-driven globalisation and technocratic liberalism have undermined democratic public discourse for the last three decades, alienated the general populace, and provoked a populist response that seeks to cover the bare public square with an unpleasant, vindictive nationalism. The brutal truth is that Donald Trump won the presidency by appealing to a pool of issues, annoyances, and legitimate complaints for which the main parties lack a credible response (Sandel, 2018).

17.22 Europe

The overarching political context of the European Union (EU) significantly affects national politics, particularly populist politics, in the current European context. Even though the particular type and level of euroskepticism varies, almost all populist players within the EU are sceptical of the EU. Since the early 1990s, research on populism in Europe has focused on the electoral ascendancy and persistence of populist extreme-right parties. Some thought that the origin of these parties lay in the "silent revolution" that highlighted post-material values throughout Europe (Ignazi, 1992). Identity politics have risen as a result, not just in populist far right parties that promote a nativist perspective of who should be a part of the nation but also in Green parties that favour multiculturalism. Populist radical right parties also combine nativism and populism with their economic agenda of welfare chauvinism and their foreign policy agenda of Euroskepticism. They argue that a welfare state should be established first for their "own people" and accuse the elite of doing so in order to accommodate immigrants, who they believe would become their new electorate. They accuse their national elite of "selling over" their country and its people to the EU, calling it a "bureaucratic, socialist, undemocratic Moloch" that only pursues the interests of a cosmopolitan elite. A radical populist outburst that could endanger the liberal democratic system in European countries could be sparked by the worsening immigration problem and dwindling faith in the EU institutions' ability to govern the EU.

17.23 Latin America

Latin America has the most robust and pervasive populist tradition. History of Latin America shows that there have been three waves of populism. The first wave, which coincided with the start of the Great Depression in 1929, lasted until the end of the 1960s, when the first so-called bureaucratic authoritarian governments came into existence. A rise in rural-to-urban migration and the implementation of industrialization-spurring economic reforms caused Latin American countries to experience an integration problem during this time. Political programmes addressing social issues were promoted across the region by a number of politicians and political parties. The bulk of the countries in Latin America made progress toward communism and socialism. They also relied on the Americanismo philosophy, which rejects the interference of imperial countries and asserts that all Latin Americans share a common identity (Mudde and Kaltwasser, 2017).

The most notable examples of the second populist wave may be found in Peru (Alberto Fujimori), Brazil (Fernando Collor de Mello), and Argentina (Carlos Menem). The second populist wave was far smaller and less widespread than the first, which first arose in the early 1990s. These countries experienced major economic crises at the end of the 1980s, and populist leaders were able to win elections by attributing the bad conditions to the governing elite and claiming that the people had been cheated out of their rightful sovereignty. Once in power, they decided to cooperate with the IMF to implement strict neoliberal policies. Despite being unpopular, these initiatives helped to stabilise the economy and lower hyperinflation. This helps to explain why populist leaders such as Menem and Fujimori were re-elected.

The third wave of populism in Latin America was sparked by Hugo Chavez's political win in Venezuela in 1998 and later spread to countries like Bolivia (Evo Morales), Ecuador (Rafael Correa), and Nicaragua (Daniel

Ortega). Due to the rhetorical usage of Americanism and anti-imperialism by these politicians, these cases resemble some of those of the first wave. However, the names of the parties created by Evo Morales and Hugo Chavez, Movement toward Socialism (MAS) and United Socialist Party of Venezuela (PSUV), respectively, indicate that those associated with the third populist wave have a predisposition for using socialist doctrines. Every third-wave populist leader presents themselves as an extreme leftist who opposes free capitalism and seeks to establish a new development paradigm that will genuinely benefit the people.

Special Insights

Can there be female populist leaders?

Although the strongman image still dominates how the public perceives populism, there are a number of cases of female populist leaders. Eva Péron (1919–1952), Juan Domingo Péron's second wife from Argentina, is thought to be the first well-known female populist. Some contemporary female populists, such Yingluck Shinawatra in Thailand and Marine Le Pen in France, are also descended from populist strongmen. However, many female populist leaders have achieved success in politics as a result of their own hard work. The best example is perhaps the One Nation Party (ONP), which Pauline Hanson founded and was primarily responsible for the party's, albeit temporary, success. Additional examples are Sarah Palin, the fiery former governor of Alaska, Pia Kjaersgaard, the former leader of the Danish People's Party (DF), Frauke Petry, the leader of the Alternative for Germany (AfD) and Siv Jensen, the leader of Norwegian Progress party (FrP). Similar to populist strongmen, female populist leaders base their conception of the vox populi on gendered social constructs (Mudde and Kaltwasser, 2017:69). Invoking societal gender conventions, female populists can present themselves as reluctant politicians. When Hanson entered politics, she declared, "I come here not as a polished politician, but as a woman who has experienced her fair share of life's knocks." Many female populists highlight characteristics of the "good woman," as defined by their culture, in an effort to establish a connection with the pure people; they frequently present themselves as mothers or wives in this way. Hanson stated: "I care so passionately about this country, it's like I'm its mother, Australia is my home and the Australian people are my children" (Mudde and Kaltwasser, 2017:70).

Special Insights

Populism and Media

The relationship between populism and the media is a crucial aspect of many contemporary democracies. Political material is mediated by media, which also serves as a filter between the general public and political elites. In the era of social media, parties can forge a direct connection with voters by broadcasting their own content, eschewing the traditional function of the media. For instance, Donald Trump—who referred to himself as "the Ernest Hemingway of 140 characters"—constantly interacted online with his supporters, saturating the public debate with his presence. Matteo Renzi, the Italian prime minister, discussed national reforms via Twitter using the hashtag #Matteorisponde (Matteo Answers).

Special Insights

Why does populism appear in some countries and not in others?

In Argentina, Bolivia, Brazil, Ecuador, Peru, and Venezuela, populist leaders of different ideologies keep regaining power, but they were unsuccessful in doing so in Chile, Uruguay, Colombia, and Costa Rica. The absence of populism in a number of Latin American nations is typically attributed to strong party systems and operating liberal democracies that uphold the rule of law. Kenneth Roberts (2015: 147-8) argues that populism is caused by a crisis in political representation. Political structures that were unresponsive and unaccountable contributed to the crisis in political representation. Hugo Chavez rose up in opposition to cartel parties that were exclusive, self-serving, and self-replicating. Another scenario for a political representation crisis is when political representation and political rivalry tend to become highly personalised, voters support and identify with leaders rather than party structures or platforms, and the axes of political rivalry are also drawn between rival individuals who claim to better represent the interests of the people.

17.24 Populism and Democracy

Democracy and populism have a very intricate relationship. Populism is both an ally and a foe of (liberal) democracy, depending on the degree of democratisation. Populism has historically sought to fundamentally alter democracy as a new political system. It started off by criticising it from within before going beyond that. Populism therefore threatens democracy without actually destroying it. Once in power, populism seeks to change representative democracy by redefining its foundational principles. Populism exploits the tensions that liberal democracy unavoidably experiences when attempting to achieve a balance between minority rights and majority rule.

According to Laclau, populism promotes the "democratisation of democracy" by allowing the accumulation of demands from marginalised groups (Mudde and Kaltwasser, 2017:79). Populism takes advantage of the conflicts that liberal democracy inevitably faces as it strives to strike a balance between the rights of minorities and majority rule. The question of who controls the controllers is brought up by populism. Populism can turn into a sort of democratic extremism or, more accurately, illiberal democracy since it has a propensity to reject any unelected organisation that restricts the power of the people (Mudde and Kaltwasser, 2017:82).

By giving voice to groups that don't believe they are represented by the elite, populism raises the issue of who controls the controllers and corrects democracy. Populists promote a view of democracy that rejects unelected authorities and is based on unrestrained popular will. This is particularly crucial when looking at the successes and failings of populist actors. Even though populists frequently receive less votes than other political parties around the world, they nonetheless have a big impact on setting agendas and shaping public policy. In a world where democracy and liberalism are dominant, populism has essentially evolved into an illiberal democratic response to undemocratic liberalism. Populists ask uncomfortable questions about the undemocratic aspects of liberal institutions and practises and also give illiberal answers that are frequently embraced by sizable segments of the population (such as the reintroduction of the death penalty).

Even while populism manifests itself in many different ways and is mobilised in a variety of social, political, and cultural contexts, all populist actors strive to (re)politicize sidelined issues and individuals and moralise the political discourse. Since populism usually raises the appropriate questions but provides the wrong answers, the ultimate goal should not only be the eradication of populist supply, but also the weakening of populist demand. Only the latter will ultimately strengthen liberal democracy (Mudde and Kaltwasser, 2017). Legal, political, or socioeconomic marginalisation do not always lead to populism. However, populist interventions that politicise people's daily experiences of exclusion and humiliation remain a persistent possibility in the absence of political mediation processes and institutions of representation. A democracy's institutional structure always allows for the ascent of a strong political executive. A leader with popular support may use that support to amplify their own influence over the government. The democratic institutions have a built-in tendency toward authoritarianism, which has existed under both parliamentary and presidential governments.

Another trait that emergent, young, and developing democracies share is statism. Since power is centralised in the state, it is seen as the highest institution of authority and custodianship. This all-inclusive state takes on the responsibility of industrialization and economic expansion to steer society toward wealth accumulation and prosperity. Due to the legitimacy it acquires in this way, it has a tremendous impact on social concerns as well. A strong state encourages allegiance to the ruler, which in turn encourages devotion to the government. This populist authoritarian tendency is distinguished by its pledges to "make the country great again" and its tight paternalistic hold on the masses. Brazil's 2018 presidential campaign anthem for Bolsonaro was "Brazil above all, God above all." Putin used the campaign slogan "A strong president—a strong Russia" in Russia in 2018 (Katju). The institutional framework of democracy, the statist character of the polity, and the populist politics of the leader all contribute significantly to the emergence of authoritarian leadership that is able to maintain its hold on power. The support of a striving and "nationalistic" middle class strengthens this leadership. The regime's reliance on democratic institutions (such the legislature and political parties) and its promotion of a certain understanding of liberty that the general public supports contribute to this. Together, they keep the supreme leader in power while disguising authoritarian traits.

17.25 Conclusion

Populist forces have been gaining influence on a global scale. A greater balance between responsiveness and accountability can only be attained by comprehending the issues that the voting public has. Between liberalism and autocracy, populism occupies a middle ground (Pappas, 2019). It offers sizable electoral populations a viable and, in some cases, incredibly persuasive alternative conception of liberal democracy. The problem is that populism struggles to strike a firm balance between liberalism and autocracy. The tendency of populism in such circumstances is typically to move towards authoritarianism rather than return to the initially liberal democratic state. This should, of course, lead to a challenging conversation with populist movements to demonstrate why their remedies are typically inadequate while acknowledging the reality of the issues they identify. In the end, populist movements are correct to assert that "the people," rather than supernatural powers or the wisdom of unelected authorities, are the source of ultimate political power. But populists are incorrect when they assert that there is a single, self-evident majority will that must be upheld at all costs. Liberal democracy must take on the challenging task of identifying, detailing, and redefining not only "we, the people," but also what "we, the people" aspire to in order to counter populism.

Keywords

Populism
Elite
Masses
General will
Charismatic leader

Review Questions

1. Discuss the defining features of populist regimes.
2. Why is populism emerging as a new challenge to the liberal democracy? Discuss with reference to certain case studies.
3. 'Populism is a highly diverse political phenomena, despite the fact that all populists share a common rhetoric.' In the light of this statement discuss the history and evolution of populism

References

Angelucci, A; Vittori, D. 2022. Are All Populist Voters the Same? Institutional Distrust and the Five Star Movement in Italy. South European Society and Politics, 26(3) : 303-327. https://doi.org/10.1080/13608746.2022.2028503

Gandhi, Jennifer and Adam Przeworski. 2007. Authoritarian Institutions and the Survival of Autocrats. Comparative Political Studies 40(11): 1279–1301.

Hawkins, K.A; Read, M. Pauwels, T; 2017. Populism and its Causes in Kaltwasser, R.C; Taggart, P; Espejo, O.P; Ostiguy, P. (Ed.). The Oxford handbook of Populism.UK: Oxford University Press.

Illing, S; 2017. Why Trump's Populist Appeal is about Culture, not the Economy. Accessed from Vox. https://www.vox.com on December 21, 2022.

Kaltwasser, R.C; Taggart, P; Espejo, O.P; Ostiguy, P. 2017. Populism an Overview of the Concept and the State of the Art in Kaltwasser, R.C; Taggart, P; Espejo, O.P; Ostiguy, P. (Ed.). The Oxford Handbook of Populism.UK: Oxford University Press.

Madrid, R. 2008. "The Rise of Ethnopopulism in Latin America," *World Politics* 60(3): 475–508.

Mudde, C. 2017. Populism an Ideational Approach in Kaltwasser, R.C; Taggart, P; Espejo, O.P; Ostiguy, P. (Ed.). The Oxford Handbook of Populism.UK: Oxford University Press.

Mudde, C. Kaltwasser, R. C. 2017. Populism A Very Short Introduction. Oxford University Press.

Ostiguy, P. 2017. Populism a Socio-Cultural Approach in Kaltwasser, R.C; Taggart, P; Espejo, O.P; Ostiguy, P. (Ed.). The Oxford Handbook of Populism.UK: Oxford University Press.

Pappas, S.T. 2019. *Populism and Liberal Democracy: A Comparative and Theoretical Analysis*. UK: Oxford University Press.

Rooduijn, M. 2017. What unites the voter bases of populist parties? Comparing the electorates of 15 populist parties. European Political Science Review 10 (3): 351-368. doi:10.1017/S1755773917000145

Sandel, M; 2018. Populism, Liberalism, and Democracy. Philosophy and Social Criticism. doi: 10.1177/0191453718757888

Sato, Y; Arce, M. 2022. Resistance to populism. Democratization, 29(6): 1137-1156. https://doi.org/10.1080/13510347.2022.2033972

Sook, J.L. Chin-en, W. Bandyopadhyay. K.K. (Ed.). 2021. *Populism in Asian Democracies Features, Structures, and Impacts.* Brill: Leiden 2021.

Taggart, P. 2000. Populism. Buckingham, UK: Open University Press.

Urbinati, N; Finchelstein, F. 2018. On Populism and Democracy. Populism 1: 15-37.

Weyland, K. 2017. Populism a Political-Strategic Approach in Kaltwasser, R.C; Taggart, P; Espejo, O.P; Ostiguy, P. (Ed.). *The Oxford Handbook of Populism*.UK: Oxford University Press.

CHAPTER 18

The Security State

Dr Chetna Sharma and Dr Pushpa Singh

Reader's Guide

Modern political life is centred on the idea of security. The State is considered to be the provider of security, from defence against internal and external threats of violence to the fulfilment of basic needs. There remains a crucial question concerning how the idea of security has historically changed with the development of the state. In the context of states emerging from the aftermath of two world wars and the Great Depression, the security state was about greater internationalisation in exchange for national autonomy. Despite not necessarily endangering the existence of the state itself, the possible effects of globalisation will undoubtedly have an impact in this crucial sector. A historical sociological analysis of the development of linkages between state and citizen will assist in this process, by supplying a historical analysis of the state, in order to better articulate its continuing relevance to political life and security, its relationship with individuals and society, and the complexities of contemporary citizenship.

18.1 Introduction

Conventionally, the citizen's security is viewed as the prime concern of the state. States strive to establish and maintain the safety of their people. Whereas traditionally the idea of security was identified with the protection against war by the other state, in contemporary times the meaning has expanded to include many non-military aspects as well. With the passage of time and changing circumstances, the state's role has expanded to include socioeconomic provisions, environmental security, food security, security against international terrorism, and so on. The most recent additions are the concerns for nuclear proliferation and climate change. Thus, the state is saddled with the primary responsibility of not only providing protection from the internal and external threat of violence, but also ensuring the supply of basic needs to the people along with delivering on a range of goods and services. Globalisation has also added to the list of state's obligations in terms of monitoring the actions of Multinational Corporation and other non-state actors. All these developments have led to shifting meaning, practices and institutions of security. However, the growing understanding of security and the state's expanded role result in the latter infiltrating almost every aspect of an individual's life. The consolidation of an overpowering state gives rise to a range of challenges concerning the question of individual's rights, liberty and privacy. The discussion in this chapter aims to acquaint students with all these debates by exemplifying different cases.

18.2 Idea of State, Security and its Evolution

The concept of security is linked to the concept of state. In fact, the exigency for peace and security in the "state of nature" has led to the creation of the state. The most organised understanding of the origin and functions of the state has been offered by the social contractualists Hobbes, Locke, and Rousseau. Whereas social contractarians provided a thematic link between state and security by emphasising the inclusion of security into political discourse in terms of guaranteeing life, liberty, and security, the Treaty of Westphalia (1648) formally established security as a cardinal constituent of the state. In contrast to the divine origins of state, these theorists proposed that state is the result of a people's agreement in which individuals renounce a portion of their "personal sovereignty" and delegate it to the sovereign entity. To be safe from the insecurities that make life "solitary, nasty, short, and brutish" in the state of nature, people created government and endowed it with the responsibilities of safeguarding their life, liberty, and property. The nature of this contract differs from the thematic conceptualization of the social contractualists. Whereas for Hobbes (Leviathan, 1651) state sovereignty is unlimited, for Locke (Two Treatises on Government, 1689) the state is limited to its duties. On the other hand, for Rousseau (The Social Contract, 1762) sovereignty resides in the "general will" of the people as a corporate whole. From social contract theory onwards, people's protection has been clearly established as an obligation of the state. Whether the sovereign is the absolute monarch (for Hobbes), an organic collective (for Rousseau), a representative body (for Locke), or even a document (for example, the constitution), the idea of security has been the prime logic to create and sustain states. As a result, with changing time and context, the state has fulfilled its duty through various forms of social, political, and economic regulation.

However, meaning and the "provision of security" have historically changed with the development of the state (Mabee, 2009). The state introduced taxation to raise money for its different pursuits, which include war, but also made promises of protection to its inhabitants. Consequently, substantial bureaucracies emerged to oversee taxation, law enforcement, judicial systems, and financial record-keeping, thereby solidifying the establishment of distinct territorial states (Mabee, 2009). This process helped in the centralization of power, the elimination of rivals within a given territory, and the consolidation of state control. Overall, a cycle in European state-building centred around the ability of states to extract wealth from their subjects, which further created and reinforced the development of the substantial bureaucratic manifestations of the state, allowing even more intervention in and control over their constituent societies. Importantly, this is an international process as well, as the interaction between early state forms—that is, through military competition and war—was a crucial link in the cycle. The development of such a relationship is borne out by the two major watersheds in the state described by Mann: its increase in size in the eighteenth century and the increasing extent of its civil functions in the nineteenth century. This was also accompanied by the development of infrastructures, both material and symbolic, as exemplified by the development of roads, railways, postal services, telegraphy, and mass education—civilian functions that increased the prosperity of society but further politicised it in the sense that it could not ignore the state. At the beginning of the twentieth century, about 75 percent of state expenditure was channelled towards civilian purposes (Mann, 1993:375). As societies were clamped ever tighter within states, the state politicised societies through nationalism and sovereignty. The overall increase in civilian expenditure and the changing nature of armed forces, combined with the increased politicisation of society through the development of citizenship rights, point to the development of more advanced forms of security provision.

Gradually, with its expanding role, the modern state attained self-sufficiency in terms of its security and survival. From the origins in the policies of mercantilism pursued by early-modern European states to the more complicated arrangements that developed with the rise of liberal economics, there has long been a focus on states pursuing military autonomy. More and more of what was seen as crucial to the nation state's provision of security has been privatized, globalized, and/or civilianized. Such changes can be seen in the development of an increasingly globalised arms industry and, to some degree, in the development of private security firms and a broader privatisation of security. Security, however, sits in an awkward position between states and markets. Markets for military services are not as public as other industries, as states still try to keep some of what is seen as vital to national security.

The state holds the prerogative to decide the meaning of security and ways to ensure it. However, the term has evolved over time with parallel changes in global security threats. The conventional view of security is state-centric, as it places the state in the centre of attention and requires the state to accumulate and wield its sovereign power to protect its territorial integrity, sovereignty, and autonomy over internal affairs, to protect what it defines as the national interest, and ultimately to protect the nation(s) or group(s) that legitimately reside within it. States have been regarded as the major actors in the international system since the signing of the Treaty of Westphalia in 1648, which recognised the inviolability of borders and non-interference in the domestic affairs of the states. All states try to gain security, obtain military superiority, and improve their security status. Despite the enormous resources required, all states consistently increase their military strength in order to achieve balance of power. This perspective flows from the understanding that if the state is secure, then those living within it are automatically safeguarded (Bajpai, 2000). Traditional security concepts relied on an anarchistic balance of power, aggravating military buildup between states, and the nation-state's absolute sovereignty (Owen, 2004). Weber defines the state as "that human community which successfully lays claim to the monopoly of legitimate physical violence within a certain territory" (Weber, 1919:310–11). Security can be regarded as "freedom from imagined or real danger in the present or future" (Graham and Gregory, 2009:672). Traditionally, the states have secured themselves through military might (Collins, 2007).

The traditional theoretical perspective in security studies, such as realism, neoliberalism, and constructivism, focuses on state protection, securing it from threats to national interest. The realist theory, as seen in Hobbes and Morgenthau's work, sees the state as sovereign with a monopoly on legitimate force. The state is viewed as the ultimate legal authority to settle disputes within the state and also engage with other international actors to protect and promote its national interests. Neo-realist thinkers such as Kenneth Waltz believe that having a powerful military is essential to the security of the state because of the anarchic nature of the international system. Social constructivists, on the other hand, believe that understanding of security is dynamic and changes in response to the collective's changing orientation. It is the result of social and political interaction in which social values and norms, identities, and cultural traditions play a crucial role. In other words, security is what actors make of it. The rational approach sees the state as a utility maximizer; hence, the state responds according to the changing nature of the world and the perception of a security threat. Security has several dimensions: While states' perceptions of threats are projected as national security, countries in a region may perceive an external threat, thereby creating regional organisations like NATO and the earlier existing Warsaw Pact. On the other hand, collective security refers to an arrangement created to counter any threat to international peace and security.

Expanding the debate further, securitization theory, as developed by the Copenhagen School, led by Barry Buzan, Ole Weaver, and Jaap de Wilde (1998), understands security to be a social construct, as senses of threat, vulnerability, and (in)security are socially constructed rather than objectively present or absent. They criticised realist and neo-realist theories of international relations, which claimed that security was a power balance among nation states with rational and utilitarian agency on the side of states and their élites. "Security," according to their criticism, is not a given prerogative of states but is created through speech-acts by political élites and other actors for the legitimation of political agency and supremacy. The Copenhagen School defines security with reference to five political sectors in which securitization could take place: military, political, economic, social, and environmental (Buzan, Wver, & de Wilde, 1998). Securitization, here, means calling something a security problem and, through this, triggering the political measures to deal with it. As a result, any reference to security must also include a potential threat and the corresponding acts of securing. According to this school, any issue can be securitized or turned into a security issue if it can be heightened to the point of being portrayed and accepted as an existential danger. It is a process of turning a policy issue into a security issue by presenting it as an issue of supreme priority. The key idea is that any issue has the potential to be constructed as a security issue through a "speech act" by "security actors" when the utterance itself is the act. Buzan differentiates between two policy options: state security strategy and international security strategy (Buzan, 1991:331). The former is the more traditional approach to state security, with policymakers focusing on minimising state vulnerabilities. The second refers to attempts to address the causes of insecurity at their core through making changes in the structure of the international system. The rhetoric of security is used to promote stringent immigration laws, fortification of borders, and an emphasis on descent and blood ties for citizenship as tools to protect insiders. All these are considered to be the primary responsibilities of the state. Speech acts on a security issue by "securitizing" with words, invoking semantic resources, the so-called "grammar of security" (Buzan et al., 1998), through which a social affair can be addressed as a "problem" (for example, terrorism or migration). This then allows for exceptional measures through a centralised authority (usually the government).

From the above discussion, it is clear that all perspectives on security repose its foundational liability on the state, thereby legitimising all of the state's actions. This leads to the state being bestowed upon the "monopoly of legitimate violence" to ensure security, as Weberian understanding of the state highlights. Even Neo-Weberians like Gidden, Mann, Skocpol, and Tilly highlight that the state has authoritative, binding rule-making power backed up by organised physical force (Mann, 1986), and "a tendency to monopolise the means of violence makes a government's claim to provide protection more credible and more difficult to resist" (Tilly, 1985: 172).

18.3 Reconceptualisation of Security

The idea of security has acquired new dimensions in contemporary times by taking the individual as the primary referent as opposed to the state. New perspectives believe that the question of security cannot be solely addressed in terms of traditional security threats. Instead, other aspects of security are emphasised in order to achieve the individuals' overall well-being. These new approaches include human security, food security, environmental security, water security, energy security, security against diseases, security against climate change, cyber security, transnational security, security against global social dislocation, and so on. Human security includes protection against threats such as organised crime, terrorism, human trafficking, drug trafficking, etc. The concept of human security basically emerged from the 1994 *Human Development Report,* which explored the new frontiers of human security to address issues like global poverty, increasing population pressure, degradation of the environment, and so on (UNDP, 1994). It is also associated with the concept of sustainable human development, which tries to balance economic development with environmental regeneration and equitable distribution in society. Similarly, food security, which is defined as "physical and economic access to sufficient, safe, and nutritious food" (United Nations Committee on World Food Security), is globally accepted as one of the fundamental responsibilities to be ensured by all states. Recognizing water as the primary requirement for survival, the states are also expected to ensure the availability of water in terms of access to WASH (water, sanitation, and hygiene). Water security includes not only its availability but also managing water-related risk and capturing the opportunity related to water. Energy security focuses on diversifying energy sources, utilising renewable energy, improving energy efficiency, and minimising the carbon footprint.

One of the overpowering global phenomena impacting our understanding of security has been globalization. In this light, practises that privilege national security are not adequate to the post-Cold War, globalised world environment, as national security has merged with international security (Held et al., 1999). Therefore, "the key question to be addressed by scholars of globalisation and national security is not whether the new challenges of globalisation will overwhelm the state but in what ways they alter the state and what mechanisms the state will use to adapt to global social forces while retaining its centrality" (Ripsman and Paul 2005:224). The overall ideational impact of globalisation on security, therefore, is not just a normative rethinking of addressing security issues (or an ideology of global security), but also necessitates security to be seen as part of a broader context than just "national" security. For the promotion of a global security ideology, a more holistic security strategy is necessary.

The concept of security has adopted new conceptual and philosophical insights from the works of scholars like Ulrich Beck and Anthony Gidden. Responding to the complex reality and pervasive threat on the personal and public realms, Beck highlights modernity's projects and the crisis that results from them in his book Risk Society: Towards a New Modernity (1986/1992). Modern society's own successes carry the seeds of its failures and destruction. Products of modern times like nuclear plants, genetically modified organisms, and nanotechnology harbour within themselves the risk of an irreversible crisis if they go wrong. Beck proposed the idea of "risk society," implying that today's advanced industrialised society is primarily occupied with "debating, preventing, and managing risks that it itself has produced." The survival and security of modern societies will rest on "the ability to anticipate and endure these dangers." Anthony Giddens also highlights that in a risk society, people increasingly live on a "high technological frontier," which is beyond the complete understanding of people and may pose many potential dangers. The beginning of industrial society faced risks that were seen as "external," and these were predictable and hence manageable. However, the present world is marked by the transition to "manufactured risk," resulting from the progression of science and technology (Giddens, 1999). These risks are unpredictable and will be difficult to manage.

Expanding the debate further, Shiv Viswanathan emphasises how the development discourse and its prime instrument, transfer of technology (TOT), created new issues of security in terms of producing more refugees from development projects. The disasters caused in Chernobyl and Bhopal reminded the world of the vulnerability of humankind in the face of hazards posed by technological advancement. The development projects and scientific advances must be accompanied by a wider ethics of responsibility, the right to information and disclosure, and ideas of justice and rehabilitation beyond monetary compensation (Visvanathan, 2015). However, it emerges very clearly even from the new understanding of security that the ultimate task of providing security still rests with the state. Grappling with the new realities, the state has transformed rapidly to fulfil its role and responsibilities. In order to include the non-military components of security, eventually the state extended itself much beyond ensuring military protection and law and order. With the changing understanding of security and the state's efforts to ensure it since the post-second world war period, and further since the post-cold war period and the globalised world, the state's role, power, and control have multiplied, giving rise to the security state, as discussed below.

18.4 The Rise of Security State

The term "security state" refers to excessive surveillance, regulation, and control by the state and its agencies in everyday life. This form of state is more recent in origin and concentrates on the intelligence and security services. The whole rationale of expanding security after the Second World War assumes an expanded conception of what protection entails. Security in this sense warrants the security of the citizen and is not exclusively about the security of the state. The security state is the manifestation of a state's desire and need to participate more intensely on an international scale. The security that states provide has changed dramatically in the twentieth century, from extended ideas of citizenship at the beginning of the century to the post-Second World War development of the welfare state and social and economic citizenship rights. A combination of factors, both national and international, like wars and economic dislocations generate situations that promote the emergence of a security state (Mabee, 2009). Historical events such as the Great Depression and the Second World War had a profound impact on people's perceptions of security and social welfare. The concept was widened to include economic hardship and social protection (Mabee, 2009). In the period following the Second World War, "national security" came to be defined with reference to the internal–external divide. The term "national security" was widely utilised in policymaking circles during the 1940s (Yergin, 1977). By this time, it had become the architectonic impulse of the American security polity and subsequently of its allies (Simon, 1997:21).

The Second World War caused massive socio-economic destruction, leaving Europe in tatters. In order to revamp the economy and uplift societies, the states started focusing on reconstruction in the post-war period. In response to society's rising demand for restoration, Britain offered the 1942 Beveridge Report, outlining its social welfare provisions. The report was received with great enthusiasm and became the bestselling bureaucratic document in British history, selling over 500,000 copies. The work of John Maynard Keynes'

General Theory of Employment (1936) had already rooted policies supporting employment, welfare, and the expansion of government functions in that period. The types of social rights developed in post-war Britain included full employment, a universal national insurance scheme, a comprehensive national health service, free and compulsory education, and an extended state housing sector. This promoted the culture of increasing state control and its presence in different aspects of citizens' lives. The development of more extensive forms of security after the Second World War was part of the post-war consensus of embedded liberalism, with the compact giving citizens more security for the trade-off of the state being more integrated into the world economy and military-security system. The security state arose, at least in part, as a result of the war and the need to participate more intensely on a global and international scale, both through domestic intervention and protection from external threat.

The onset of the Cold War situated this system within an inter-systemic struggle involving two divergent social frameworks—two ideologies or viewpoints regarding the structuring of the global order (Mabee, 2009). Throughout the Cold War era, the state gained paramount importance in terms of security, particularly with the United States assuming a leading role in this evolution. To such an extent, the notion of national security was employed to promote the self-sufficiency of the state. (McSweeny, 1999). Following the conclusion of the Cold War, there arose a necessity to reassess the global security landscape. The amalgamation of a heavily militarized and centralized state for external defense, alongside the expansion of rights through increased enfranchisement and the evolution of social rights, resulted in a scenario where the state assumed a pivotal role in security matters. Despite the prominent theories put forth by Huntington and Fukuyama—namely, the concept of a "clash of civilizations" and the notion of the "end of history," (Mabee, 2009) respectively—dominated the discourse at the time, a diverse array of alternative threats was found. The environment, ultranationalism, nuclear weapons proliferation, and "rogue states" all became part of the national security agenda. In the post-Cold War multilateral world order, the military relationships among the countries were organised on a variety of principles. All of these relationships were based on degrees of internationalisation and globalisation and how nation-states redefined their national interests and strategic alliances with reference to internationalised security provisions like NATO. Nuclear weapons also changed the possibilities for total war and therefore changed the character of war in the post-Cold War era. In the post-Cold War world, new structural changes required a shift in security thinking to understand new threats that are not bound to any particular nation but rather have the capacity to cause global upheavals. Whereas there is an emergence of a new threat from mutually assured destruction due to nuclear proliferation, there is an increase in a host of new challenges due to intra-state conflicts, large-scale atrocities, and genocides. In this light, a new security agenda has been defined as including "intra-state conflict, ethnic-religious violence, landmines, terrorism, democracy, human rights, gender, crime, poverty, hunger, deprivation, inequality, diseases and health hazards, human development, economic security, markets, water, energy, migration, environmental degradation, and so on" (Brauch, 2007).

A security state lays a lot of emphasis on border demarcation to define citizens and outsiders and also develops a strong infrastructure to provide security. One of the earliest technologies used to restrict access to resources and safeguard rights for citizens within the state was the construction of walls. China's Great Wall is one such example. The notion that globalisation would lead to a world of unrestricted trade and human migration was losing ground as anti-migrant sentiments and trade protectionism became prominent political ideologies in numerous nations. While there were fewer than five border walls worldwide in 1945, the phenomenon of returning to walls really started to gain traction in the last 30 years (Jones 2018). Donald Trump's campaign to construct a wall on the US-Mexico border, the United Kingdom's attempt at BREXIT, and the additional security measures enacted by nations around the world due to concerns about migration and open borders are all examples of how border security has become a major political issue. A number of nations in Europe have built walls, implemented additional security measures, and even shut down internal border crossings that had been operational since the late 1990s. Austria, Bulgaria, Estonia, Hungary, Kenya, Saudi Arabia, and Tunisia were among the countries that declared or started building walls and fences along their borders in 2015 (Jones, 2018). From 35 in 2012 to 70 in 2017, with 40% of them in Asia, there are more border walls that target migrants rather than a potential military danger from a neighbouring country (Jones and Ferdoush, 2018: 14–22). In 2016, over 7900 people died while attempting to cross a border, the largest number ever recorded. Jones and Ferdoush (2018):14.

Special Insights

Security State: The Changing Dimensions of Border Securitization

International law recognises states based on their ability to uphold their national borders, defend their populations, and secure their regions. Along with facilitating or restricting the movement of people, the state can also control the entry and exit of products, plants, animals, and other objects. The state is now able to guarantee security using a three-dimensional framework that protects borders at ground level, through the use of drones in the air and ground-penetrating radars underground. The strict border security extends inside the state's borders as well as outside them, encompassing oceans, deserts, and neighbouring countries. To establish control and stop unauthorised movements, neighbouring states are involved. This "volumetric approach to security" extends throughout the state and internalises the borders (Elden, 2013). Reece Jones has highlighted three trends at borders: the externalisation and internalisation of border work away from the border line, the return of walls as a material and symbolic mechanism, and the militarization of border regions (2018:18). While the European Union has agreements with Turkey, Morocco, and Afghanistan that enlist these nations to patrol for possible migrants and keep them from reaching the limits of the EU, the United States has agreements with Canada and Mexico that push its borders outside of the actual borderline (Jones and Ferdoush, 2018:15).

It is noteworthy that, while the suspension of the legal order was declared in numerous states during the two World Wars, France's constitution currently explicitly regulates the declaration of a state of emergency. In contrast, most Western constitutions (such as the German, Italian, British, and American ones) do not explicitly address such a suspension (Agamben, 2005). The activation of a state of emergency in France grants extensive powers to the President of the Republic, bolsters the authority of the police forces, prohibits mass gatherings and demonstrations, and notably permits the arrest and detention of suspects without formal charges, resembling the conditions of detainees in Guantanamo. The state of emergency transforms the country into a "security state," its legitimacy founded on the cultivation of fear rather than its eradication. This state of emergency results in both "a new type of social relation, namely one of generalized, limitless control," and the depoliticization of citizens. Citizens are no longer viewed as active participants in the democratic process but rather as a group in need of state protection. This process is further reinforced by the use of a narrative framing France as "at war" with terrorists.

The terrorist attack of September 11, 2001, on the United States laced the security state with a remarkable new culture of regulation. In just six weeks following the attacks, a terrified Congress passed the **Patriot Act,** drastically expanding the government's monitoring powers. The act generally had three key provisions: stronger surveillance powers for law enforcement, including the ability to tap both domestic and foreign phones; improved interagency coordination to enable federal agencies to more efficiently deploy all resources in counterterrorism efforts; and stiffer punishments for terrorism-related crimes and a longer list of actions that would be grounds for terrorism charges. As a result, the government has unrestricted access to information about people's finances, medical histories, Internet usage, book purchases, library usage, travel habits, and any other action that leaves a record. People, generally, did not protest much against the increased regulation as non-state actors were now seen as an all-pervasive threat and capable of causing unprecedented destruction even in peacetime. This provided the states with an excuse to implement all-encompassing regulation and surveillance. In the name of security, the lives of individuals outside the West have been subjected to uncertainty, as highlighted by the situation of the inhabitants of the Federally Administered Tribal Area of Pakistan, the region where most of the US drone strikes are focused. It implies that these humans are seen as being outside the normative order. For example, the drone strikes launched by the US against what it defines as terrorists were highly questionable and unsanctioned by international law. The claim of the Obama administration that the US was exercising its right of self-defence was unaccountable and not universally accepted (Fair, 2014). In such a context, it was impossible to prove whether the targets killed were effectively al-Qaeda operatives or civilians, and the number of casualties has not been publicly released by the US. Thus, people living in the FATA are neither protected by international law, which should apply in a war zone (even though the US is not officially at war with Pakistan), nor recognised as citizens who have the right to a fair trial before being labelled as terrorists and executed. It can both account for the growing securitization which Western states are enduring as a response to the so-called global "War on Terror" and for the blurring of lines between inside and outside, legality and illegality, which is the typical feature of this century.

18.5 Transnationalism and Security State

Even though the projection of a security state may be formidable, the rising transnationalism and interdependence at the global level may lead to situations in which the states may experience a decline in sovereignty and autonomy. This raises questions about the state's capacity as a security provider. Thus, the state is not alone in monitoring and attempting to regulate risk, but works alongside other institutions to provide security to groups and individuals within society (Shaw, 1994). This shows that "risk management" and the provision of security may come through other outlets, undercutting the state's central role in security provision. In contemporary times, the monopoly of states over security has also been eroded, and a "public" military has become more and more challenged by the new realities of an independent defence-industrial base. There exist proliferating arms industries that are not specifically tied to any nation-state but exist as corporations that pursue independent policies in the production and marketing of arms and ammunition. A plethora of private firms provide a wide range of military services, causing considerable concern among nation states.

The post-war situation led to a more interconnected international system, particularly among Western allies, driven by free trade and participation in international institutions. Recent years have witnessed the expansion of the United Nations and economic organizations like the World Trade Organization, alongside social welfare initiatives, intensifying state internationalization. In a globalized economy, international financial institutions and trade systems can clash with nation-state operations. Novel threats arise due to globalization of social ties, exemplified in migration challenges originating from diverse sources that disregard national borders. National communities' identities face risks from ethnically distinct immigrants with differing values.

As security states are meant to provide quite a broad array of security functions including the provision of economic security, the impact of migrants on economic security is an important aspect of the future of the security state. Another example of these kinds of global risks is found in the difficulties surrounding environmental degradation and related problems, as they spill over national jurisdictions and require international and global solutions (Buzan, Waever and de Wilde, 1998; Held et al., 1999; Rogers, 2010). Other important issues would include terrorism, disease, organized crime, pandemic and global inequalities in wealth. This clearly represents not only a new environment of security, but also the expansion of the national security agenda from military security to other kinds of threats.

The notion of a state's unchallenged sovereign authority is under threat due to the advent of non-state entities such as multinational corporations, non-governmental organisations, and international organizations. States need the help of the "big four" of the internet: Google, Microsoft, Facebook, and Twitter, in order to exchange security information and fight against terrorist-sponsored propaganda online. In the wake of the Charlie Hebdo attacks, for instance, Microsoft claimed to have received up to 14 government requests for access to information that the government deemed valuable in tracking down the accused terrorists. What is even more astonishing is that Microsoft was able to release some of this information in less than an hour, but only after the corporation had determined that the governments followed the right procedure and that the emergency situation warranted their request (Bodoni, White, & Hodges, 2015). Microsoft does not appear to be an exception when it comes to disclosing private information to governments. Facebook also follows a "three-step" internal process before disclosing data (Senese, Mossé, Kent & Sacquet, 2017). However, what makes the Internet's position, and that of cyberspace more broadly, particularly intriguing and worth looking at is the extent to which it challenges and, at times, even competes with the traditional privileges of the state.

18.6 Security State and Mass Surveillance: Implications for Civil Liberties and Human Rights

National security shares a delicate balance with civil liberties. In response to the increasing threat of instability and destruction from a range of non-state actors, the state enlarges its defences and surveillance. Attempts towards increasing securitization have a direct bearing on citizenship and rights, as they become elements available for trade-off with greater penetration of the state into civil society. In contemporary times, states have adopted complex and subtle methods of surveillance, monitoring, and control to further consolidate their power. Transgression of civil rights occurs through various means, like discriminatory travel and immigration screening practises and social media screening. Sovereign states possess the authority to suspend the legal system and declare a state of exception if the country faces an existential threat to its integrity. In such a situation, the sovereign, i.e., the executive power, prevails over the others, and the basic laws and norms can be violated by the state while responding to the crisis. In this regard, the conceptualizations of "biopolitics" and "state of exception" by Michael Foucault in *The Birth of Biopolitics* (1979) and Georgio Agamben in *State of Exception* (2005), respectively, are illuminating.

- ***Michael Foucault and 'Biopolitics'***
  Foucault examines the ways in which the government has asserted ever-greater control over the private elements of people's lives. He coins the phrase "biopower," which serves as an instrument in the hands of the state to regulate, discipline, and control the masses (Foucault, 1991). It signifies the new technical developments that enable the state to monitor behaviour and movement and assist in a system of control. The state subjugates physical bodies and makes them behave in certain ways, creating a prototype for social control over a wider population. Discussing the nature of punishment in a historical sense, Foucault highlights that in pre-modern times, punishment was made into a public display that he calls "the culture of spectacle." However, even though the nature of punishment became more brutal in modern times, it was carried out away from public view, giving the impression of civilizational advancement. With it came a growing acceptance of various forms of punishment, which Foucault refers to as "carceral culture." In this regard, he cites the example of the panoptic model of monitoring, which has become widely accepted as a fundamental social organising principle. The panopticon, a novel prison design by Jeremy Bentham, featured a central observation tower and prison cells set around it so that inmates could possibly be under observation at any moment, but they were unable to see whether they were being watched or not. According to Foucault, this new jail design marked a fundamental evolution in the discipline of power in the late 19th century. As a result of being constantly watched, inmates had to self-monitor their behaviour, which led to their effectively disciplining themselves. The most glaring manifestations of disciplinary power are the internet, phones, cell phones, social security numbers, the census, ATMs, credit cards, and the steadily rising number of security cameras in urban areas. The development of technology, including computers, smartphones, and the internet, has also contributed to an increase in data surveillance. Private or commercialised monitoring is one component of the post-panoptic society that has become more prevalent recently. While surveillance methods are less obvious than the panoptic prison tower, they are much more effective because of their reach and control. In times of emergency, liberal states have been able to enact laws that would be unacceptable otherwise.

- **Georgio Agamben's *'State of Exception'***
  Elaborating on the significance of "biopolitical," Agamben proposes his theory of the state of exception. For Agamben, such a suspension of the law is pivotal in that it directly affects people's lives, not as subjects of politics or citizens, but as human beings as such. The key to Agamben's thought, around which the theory

of the state of exception revolves, is the indistinction, in the realm of politics, between the external and the internal, between the private life—which he calls *zoe*—and the public sphere, the one characterising life as *bios* (Agamben 2005). Exceptionalism, which refers to the situation of emergency in which civil and political liberties are suspended indefinitely, has been practised as a widespread political device in the present time. As a result of surveillance, a security state has the ability to alter people's perceptions of their private lives. The state controls all aspects of our lives. The conventional Aristotelian differentiation between the public and private domains has become obsolete, as sovereign authority blurs these demarcations to justify increased regulation over citizens' lives. This phenomenon gives rise to a vague human entity termed homo sapiens, reduced to a state of "bare life," wherein the sovereign holds complete dominion, even over their basic existence, thereby denying their right to life. Agamben identifies camps as sites where individuals are stripped down to this state of "bare life." This process corresponds with the notion of the state of exception, which validates itself through external threats necessitating extraordinary measures while also bolstering national identity by dehumanizing perceived adversaries. The implementation of exceptional measures effectively cultivates a sense of peril that unites the nation and strengthens self-identity. Simultaneously, it delegitimizes and dehumanizes the "other" by reducing them to mere "bare life." This phenomenon is apparent in instances like Guantanamo Bay and Abu Ghraib, where detainees were deprived of legal proceedings and the protections afforded by the Geneva Convention (Agamben, 2005). Agamben argues that in "modern biopolitics," the sovereign holds the power to determine the value, or lack thereof, in an individual's life (Agamben, 1998: 142). He posits that the state of exception entails "the authority to decide whether the law is applicable to a situation or if the law is suspended due to an emergency or crisis." (Salter, 2008: 366; Mabee, 2009).

The American detention facility at Guantanamo Bay has frequently been referred to as a "lawless space." The prison at Guantánamo Bay is a place where the state is granted unprecedented powers, justified by the notion of security. This place is defined as a "place of exception" by Georgio Agamben because this is the "island outside the law" where terrorist suspects could be kept without due process and probed without restriction. Since 2002, around 800 prisoners have been held in Guantánamo Bay prison cells, which have come to represent injustice, brutality, and disdain for the law. Guantanamo is seen as a suitable holding facility for the worst of the worst terrorists by those who support it. But to others who disagree with it, it is a sombre reminder of the human rights abuses committed by the state in the name of security.

- ***Digitalisation and Surveillance***

In recent times, the states have further consolidated their power by rapidly digitalizing themselves. Technology has emerged as a new medium for restricting citizens' rights and liberties. While a large part of digitalization is beneficial for people, such projects run the risk of sharing data with other agencies or commercial ventures with vested interests. Any project soliciting biometric data and other sensitive information that falls into the wrong hands would make individuals vulnerable to a range of unpleasant and harmful situations. They may also have covert goals of using data or information for unknown purposes. Few examples from around the world demonstrate the potential dangers of governments' relentless pursuit of information. In the case of the US, before the USA Patriot Act, the government needed to inform its citizens when it gathered private information about credit, student records, phone records, financial information, and so on. However, all changed after this Act, as it allows law enforcement and the intelligence agency to extract this information in hidden ways. Not only this, but people have restricted access to information available with various government agencies; many of them have even removed the content previously available from the websites (ACLU, 2001). The Social Security Number was initiated in the US in 1936 and was initially used to assess social security entitlement and keep track of the earning history of US workers. Later, it came to be used as a universal identifier, raising a host of issues related to privacy, data fraud, identity theft, and so on. In a poll conducted by the Pew Research Center in 2011, 54% of the respondents expressed that containing terrorism may not require curbing or sacrificing some civil liberties (Pew Center Research, 2011).

Similarly, the Government of India, under the Ministry of Electronics and Information Technology, created the Unique Identification Authority of India (UIDAI) in 2009 as a statutory authority to generate a database for the National Population Register (NPR). UIDAI was to assign a 12-digit unique identification number (UID) or Aadhaar to the people with the aim of delivering benefits, subsidies, and services to them. The applicant was required to submit demographic and biometric information in order for Aadhaar to be issued. Aadhaar provides a digital identity and does not guarantee any rights or entitlements. Some of the problems of such an exercise were that the data collection was not done directly by the government but by UIDAI, so the government was not the owner of the data or the database. However, the citizens were not aware of this fact, and they did not even know the implications of UIDAI being the legal owner of vital information about them. Apart from the government, this database was made available to commercial service providers. An enormous amount of revenue was generated from biometric authentication by using it for "new mobile connections, PAN cards, gas connections, passports, LIC policies, credit cards, bank accounts, airline check-in, and so on" (Ramanathan, 2013). Such digitalization initiatives are also imbued with elements of coercion, as people face the threat of exclusion from services and benefits if they are not enrolled. The state remains silent on the question of liability in cases of identity fraud or non-working systems of authentication resulting in denial of services. Mishandling and misutilisation of data can result in "tracking, profiling, tagging, the convergence of databases, and violations of privacy in ways that could threaten personal security" (Ramanathan, 2013). Some scholars like Tilly describe the unchecked powers of the state as a "protection racket," where the pursuit of power and control caused elites to monopolise the control over violence within their territories, while, furthermore, the pursuit of war caused rulers to set up systems of extraction in order to raise capital for these endeavours.

Special Insights

Citizens, Technological Advances and Security

Through instruments of statecraft such as visas, passports, and counting, monitoring, and documenting citizens, territorial coherence and control are expanded in the internal areas of states. This is accomplished by data collection, profiling, and registration techniques that also normalise political exclusion. This kind of securitization within the state is linked to a rise in what Peter Nyers (2009) refers to as "technologies of control" (detention) and "strategics of exclusion" (deportation). In order to distinguish its inhabitants from outsiders, the state keeps track of every single piece of information about its citizens. With the aid of technological breakthroughs, the state constructs its data base and erects a surveillance state using biometrics, a retina scan, and other similar facts about its citizens. With the body acting as the "password" at crucial locations of inclusion and exclusion, Benjamin Muller (2004) advances the startling argument that current securitizations have turned citizenship into a sort of "identity management." In the meantime, the state's roster of troublemakers has grown to include criminals, squatters, traffickers, terrorists, smugglers, and illegal immigrants.

18.7 Conclusion

As discussed in the chapter, the nation-states are under continuous pressure to persistently re-legitimize themselves in the eyes of their citizens. In most of the nation states, government actors employ a security state logic to maintain the powerful relationship between the nation and its governed people—positioning the country as a "homeland" under attack that must be protected with strong borders and military adroitness. This security-state logic facilitates increased militarization and the expanding hold of the state on people's lives.

Under globalisation conditions, the traditional focus of security and the nation-state becomes problematic: the security state is no longer at the centre of security concerns, as it loses the ability to solely provide insurance against contingencies, as the scope of security issues shifts (from the strictly national to include the global and local), and as state functions are integrated into institutions at other levels. Globalization has therefore potentially undercut the security state configuration through a process of restructuring, where power networks are constituted on multiple scales.

Keywords

Security State
Surveillance
Transnationalism
Rights
Borders

Review Questions

1. Citing specific examples, discuss the characteristics of the security state.
2. 'All modern states are the surveillance state.' In the light of this statement discuss the evolution of the security state.
3. "National security" is no longer separate from international security in the post-Cold War, globalised world context. What are the threats to national security in an increasingly globalised society? Explain using appropriate examples.

References

ACLU, 2001. Threats to Civil Liberties Post-September 11: Secrecy, Erosion of Privacy, Danger of Unchecked Government. Accessed from https://www.aclu.org on February 3, 2023.

Agamben G. 2005. The State of Exception translated by Kevin Attell. Chicago: University of Chicago Press.

Agamben G. 1998. Homo Sacer: Sovereign Power and Bare Life, translated by Daniel Heller-Roarzen, Stanford: Stanford University Press.

Bajpai, K. 2000. "Human Security: Concept and Measurement." Kroc Institute Occasional Paper #19.

Beck, U. 1986/1992. Risk Society towards a New Modernity. London: Sage Publications.

Bodoni, S., White, A., & Hodges, J. 2015, January 20. Microsoft Gave Data on Charlie Hebdo Probe to FBI in 45 Minutes. Bloomberg.Com. Accessed from https://www.bloomberg.com on February 4, 2023.

Brauch, H. G. 2007. Security Threats, Challenges, Vulnerability and Risks. In Ursula Oswald Spring Ed. International Security, Peace, Development and Environment, EOLSS-UNESCO, UK: Oxford. Accessed from https://www.eolss.net on February 2, 2023.

Buzan, B. 1991. People State and Fear an agenda for International Security studies in the post cold war era.UK: ECPR

Buzan, B. Waever, O. Wilde, J. 1998. Security A New Framework for Analysis. USA: Lynner Rienner Publications.

Collins, A. 2007. Introduction: What is Security Studies. In A. Collins, Contemporary Security Studies New York: Oxford University Press.1–10.

Cory, N. 2017. The Worst Innovation Mercantilist Policies of 2016. Information Technology and Innovation Foundation. Accessed from https://itif.org/publications on February 6, 2023.

Das, S. 2017, October 27. Bitcoin Banned as a Payment Method in Indonesia, Adopters Will Be "Dealt With." CryptoCoinsNews. Retrieved from https://www.cryptocoinsnews.com

Elden S. 2013. "Secure the volume: Vertical geopolitics and the depth of power" *Political Geography*, 34:35–51.

Fair, C. 2014. Fighting to the End: The Pakistan's Army Way of War. New York: Oxford University Press.

Foucault, M. 1991. Discipline and Punish: the birth of a prison. London, Penguin.

Foucault, M. 1978/2008. The Birth of Bio politics. Edited by Michel Senellart New York: Palgrave Macmillan.

Giddens A. 1985. The Nation State and Violence Volume two of A Contemporary Critique of Historical Materialism. UK: Polity Press.

Giddens A. 1999. Risk and Responsibility, The Modern Law Review, Vol.62, No.1. Available at https://courses.washington.edu/sales09/Handouts/Giddens_Risk_Responsibility.pdf accessed 02.02.23.

Graham, S. Gregory, D. 2009. Security. In: Gregory, D., Johnston, R., Pratt, G., and Watts, G. (eds)The dictionary of human geography 5th edition. Oxford: Wiley-Blackwell, pp. 672–673.

Held D. McGrew, A. Goldblatt, G. Perraton, J.1999. Global Transformations: Politics Economy and Culture. Stanford: Stanford University Press.

Hobbes T. 1651/1909. Leviathan. London: Oxford University Press.

Human Development Report, 1994.Oxford University Press available at https://hdr.undp.org/system/files/documents/hdr1994encompletenostatspdf.pdf accessed 02.02.23.

Jones R. 2018. *Violence in Asian Boderlands in* Horstmann, A. Saxer, M. Rippa, A. *Routledge handbook of Asian Borderlands. London: Routledge https://doi.org/10.4324/9781315688978*

Jones R. Ferdoush, A. 2018. "Introduction" in. R. Jones and Md. A. Ferdoush. (Ed.). *The Global Transformation of Borders and Mobility in Borders and Mobility in South Asia and Beyond*. Amsterdam: Amsterdam University press. P.11–31.

Keynes, M. J. 1936. The General Theory of Employment, Interest and Money. Cambridge: Macmillan Cambridge University Press.

Locke J. 1689/1773. An Essay Concerning the True Origin Extent and End of Civil government. Boston: Edes and Gill.

Mabee, B. 2009. *The Globalization of Security State Power, Security Provision and Legitimacy.* London: Palgrave Macmillan.

McSweeney, B. 1999. Security, Identity and Interests A Sociology of International Relations. Cambridge: Cambridge University Press.

Mangoli, D. 2017, October 23. ICO Ban in Japan a "Definite Possibility." CryptoCoinsNews. Cited in MATTIA TOMAY. The Emperor's New E-Clothes: State Sovereignty in the Cyber-era. E international Relations. Accessed from https://www.e-ir.info on September 6, 2023

Mann, M. 1986 and 1993. Sources of Social Power, Vols. I and II. Cambridge: Cambridge University Press.

Mann, M. 1997. 'Has Globalization Ended the Rise and Rise of the Nation-state?' Review of International Political Economy Vol. 4, No. 3: 472–96.

Mann, M. 2001. 'Globalization and September 11', New Left Review (Second Series), No. 12 : 51–72.

Muller B. 2004. "(Dis) qualified bodies: securitization, citizenship and 'identity management'" *Citizenship Studies*, 8:3, 279–294, DOI: 10.1080/1362102042000257005

Nyers P. 2009. (Ed.). Securitizations of Citizenship. London: Routledge.

Owen, T. 2004. Challenges and opportunities for defining and measuring human security. Human Rights, Human Security and Disarmament, Disarmament Forum, 15–24.

Pew Research Centre, 2011. United in Remembrance, Divided over Policies *Ten Years after 9/11*. Accessed from https://www.pewresearch.org on February 3, 2023.

Polatin-Reuben, D., & Wright, J. 2014. An Internet with BRICS Characteristics: Data Sovereignty and the Balkanisation of the Internet. Presented at the 4th Workshop on Free and Open Communications on the Internet, San Diego (CA). Cited in MATTIA TOMAY. The Emperor's New E-Clothes: State Sovereignty in the Cyber-era. E international Relations. Accessed from https://www.e-ir.info on September 6, 2023

Ripsman, N. M., Paul, T. V. 2005. Globalization and the National Security State: A Framework for Analysis. *International Studies Review*, 7(2), 199–227. http://www.jstor.org/stable/3699646

Rogers, P. 2010. Losing Control: Global Security in the Twenty first Century. Pluto Press.

Rousseau J.J. 1762/1893. The Social Contract or the Principles of Political Rights. London: The Knickerboker Press.

Salter, M. B. 2008. When the Exception becomes the Rule: Borders, Sovereignty, and Citizenship. *Citizenship studies*, *12*(4), 365–380.

Senese, A., Mossé, M., Kent, G., & Sacquet, M. 2017, October 9. The Internet, private actors and security challenges. Sciences Po, Paris, France.

Shaw. M. 1994. Global Society and International Relations. Polity Press.

Simon D. 1997. 'Contesting an Essential Concept: Reading the Dilemmas in Contemporary Security Discourse', in Keith Krause and Michael C. Williams. (Eds.). Critical Security Studies: Concepts and Cases.

Skocpol, T. 1979. States and Social Revolutions. Cambridge: Cambridge University Press.

Tilly, C. 1990. Coercion, Capital, and European States, AD 990–1990. UK: Basil Blackwell.

Tilly C. 1985. War Making and state making as organized crime in Peter B. Evans, Dietrich Rueschemeyer and Theda skocpol. (Ed.). Bringing the state back in. Cambridge: Cambridge University Press. 169–191.

Visvanathan, S. 2015. "Technology Transfer," in James D. Wright. (Ed.). International Encyclopaedia of the Social & Behavioural Sciences (Second Edition), Elsevier, Pages 141–145, https://doi.org/10.1016/B978-0-08-097086-8.85037-0.

Weber, M. 1919. The Profession and Vocation of Politics. In Weber 1994, Political writings, (Ed.). Peter Lassman and Ronald Speirs. Cambridge: Cambridge University Press. 309–369.

Yergin, D. 1977. Shattered Peace: The Origins of the Cold War and the National Security State. Boston: Houghton Mifflin.

UNDP 1994. Human Development Report. Available at https://hdr.undp.org. Accessed on February 4, 2023.

CHAPTER **19**

Process of Democratization in Postcolonial, Postauthoritarian and Postcommunist Countries

Chetna Sharma

Reader's Guide

US based and funded organization Freedom House that conducts research on advocacy of democracy in the world marked 2017 as another year of decline in the global freedom. Democracy faced its most serious crisis in decades. The slide began in 2006 when the basic tenets of democracy that include free and fair elections, rights of minorities, freedom of press and rule of law came under attack around the world. What was significant about 2017 was that we witnessed anti-liberal populism gaining support in France, Netherlands, Germany and Austria. The past 10 years are significant because political regimes that had installed functioning democratic institutions returned to authoritarianism (Arat 1991; Diamond 1999; O'Donnell 1999; Przeworski et al., 1997, 2000; Tilly 2003, 37). The triumph of democracy witnessed by our generation in the post-Cold War era is under threat is a question that needs to be pondered upon in the present context. This chapter is an attempt to unpack, clarify and understand the process of democratization in the postcolonial, postauthoritarian and postcommunist countries, discussing various waves of democratization and debate about democratic recession.

19.1 Introduction: Democracy and Democratization

The phenomenon of political system becoming more participatory and less authoritarian is defined as democratization. Certain essential parameters accepted by scholars to define modern democracy are rule of law; competitive political parties; free, fair and regular elections; civil and political liberties and accountability of leaders through representative institutions (Diamond et al., 1988, v. 2, xvi; Karl 1990, 2; Weiner and Ozbudun 1987, 4–5). In this list, Boyer adds legitimacy defined as political efficacy and trust and viable decentralized system of local autonomy and self-determination as requisites for sustainable democracy (Boyer 1992, 520). William W. Boyer, while reflecting on democratization, discusses some of the pertinent reasons that include human nature, decolonization, science and technology and failure of authoritarianism for this worldwide phenomenon of democratization.

Boyer stresses that the human history of the past five centuries has witnessed the struggle of humans against authoritarian empires for human rights and dignity. However, intrinsic to human beings is the quest for freedom from oppression self-realization. Democratization marks this quest for human emancipation. He further reflects that decolonization uncapped well springs of hope, aspiration and enthusiasm of many new citizens of Asia, Africa and the Caribbean Basin. It is through democratization and political participation that people of former colonies expected an end to corruption, inefficiency and oppression. New inventions in the field of science and information technology enabled people to question the set-up, enhancing their capability to question the system and government. It has made it difficult for the state to contain the information for long and that influences human desire for change and participation. The catalysing of democratization has also resulted from the failure of authoritarian governments to meet the basic needs, and aspirations of people were another reason for diffusion of democratization. Authoritarian regime exists in the world, but according to Boyer, the authoritarian regime is not compatible with intrinsic human nature that desires self-realization and self-control.

Readers might ask, how could we identify democratization? Three overlapping categories are available to identify this path towards democratization. First, substantive criteria, which focus on social relations and experience of individuals in the society; second, constitutional criteria, which emphasize the process of elections and working of institutions; third and last, political process criteria, which discuss interactions among political actors and functioning of political institutions. However, these three criteria do not elaborate on the gap between theory and practice of democratization. Charles Tilly argues that there could be multiple paths to democracy; thus, the process of democratization does not take place on the scale of millennia (with the implication that it can only happen in places that have accumulated a favourable environment very gradually) or on the scale of months (with the implication that social engineers can build it rapidly almost anywhere). The process of democratization could be measured at a scale in between, most likely over years or decades; interestingly, it may also vary from era to era and region to region (Tilly 2000, 4).

19.2 Process of Democratization: Different Waves

Samuel Huntington argued that democratization tends to occur in waves, with a series of clustered openings followed by a period of retrenchment (Huntington 1991, 3–30). This classification places period from the mid-19th century to fascist reversal in Italy around the 1920s in the first wave of democratization. The general pattern dominant in this wave was the rise of nation state, economic development and nation building. Through the process of democratization, many Western states were transformed into democracies though the pattern was different, for example, in Britain, Germany and Sweden. An interesting development during interwar years was also the crisis of liberalism that gave rise to Mussolini in Italy and Hitler in Germany.

The second wave started in the post-Second World War period and continued till the early 1960s. This was a period of the end of authoritarian regimes in Germany, Italy, Austria and Japan. In the aftermath of the war, many new states such as Yugoslavia and West and East Germany were created. The second wave was marked by the beginning of decolonization process in Asia and Africa, and countries like India, Indonesia and Algeria got independence from the colonial rule. Colonial legacy and political and economic opportunities available were the determining factors to influence the process of democratization. The important point to be noted is that despite all these developments, a part of the world was still under authoritarian regimes that includes countries under Soviet bloc as well as countries like Iran in Asia and Chile in Latin America. By the 1960s, the rise of authoritarian regime was witnessed. Illiberal juntas and military coups d'état took the control in South Korea, Indonesia, Greece and Nigeria. Countries in Latin America reverted to authoritarianism as well. Significant development in Latin America was the rise of authoritarian regimes in countries that had a long history of democracy.

The third wave of democracy began in 1974, with the number of democracies rising to 46. Electoral democracy, a system in which citizens through universal suffrage could choose and replace their leaders in free, fair and impartial elections was recorded in 30 per cent of the world's independent states. Liberal democracies of the West, along with a number of small island states that had been erstwhile, British colonies and other developing democracies of India, Sri Lanka, Costa Rica, Colombia, Venezuela, Israel and Turkey were included in the list of electoral democracies. The success of this wave was evident when the number of democracies increased every year from 1975 until 2007. The rise of democracy was witnessed in Latin America and Asia. The disintegration of the USSR and Soviet bloc was another significant development in the process of democratization. Mass movements opposing ruling cliques played a decisive role in the process of democratization during this phase. However, a number of these new 'democracies' were quite illiberal. Steven Levitsky and Lucan Way referred to some of them as 'competitive authoritarian' regimes. But one most important positive aspect of this phase was a steady and significant expansion in the levels of freedom that includes political rights and civil liberties. Distinguished scholar Larry Diamond argued that in 25 of the 32 years between 1974 and 2005, average freedom levels improved in the world, peaking at 3.22 in 2005 (Diamond 2015, 99).

As discussed earlier in this chapter, democratization is not a linear universal process and its success depends on many factors, which means that during different stages, progress could be halted, slowed or reversed. The beginning of democratization could be identified with either popular uprising or end of war. The expulsion of dictator could also be defined as the starting point of democratization. What needs to be emphasized is all the states never follow a uniform pattern of democracy, citizen's rights could be violated and institutional structure may not be democratic, and that places them in the category of 'defective democracy'. No democracy is perfect, and some of them might seem to be neither developed nor having full autocracy. These countries could be labelled as illiberal democracies, pseudo-democracies, electoral democracies and defective democracies. The classification refers to some indicators missing from the system, which includes some groups excluded from voting rights; one or more political groups excluded from elections or political liberties are limited or rule of law is not established.

Special Insights

State Building and State Capacity for Viable Democracy

Democratic government must govern, which means exercise legitimate authority and provide basic services to people. Governance and legitimacy is related in a manner that if new democracy fails to govern, it will disappoint the people and delegitimize itself. Many democracies followed the sequence of state-building prior to democratization referred as 'authoritarian transition' by Samuel Huntington. However, it does not necessarily reinforce that this is the only viable strategy for the success of democracy, attention needs to be given to state building, pushing authoritarian governments out of power.

19.3 Stages in the Process of Democratization

Three main themes identified within research on democratization according to Gerardo Munck (2007) are democratic transition, democratic consolidation and the quality of government. Transition of political institutions is referred to as democratic transition (O'Donnell and Schmitter 1986); consolidation of democratic institutions is analysed to understand democratic consolidation (Di Palma 1990; Linz and Stepán 1996); the third theme, 'quality of government', is discussed with reference to functioning of institutions (Munck 2007, 66). Denk and Silander (2012, 26) argue that, in all three themes within research on democratization, the concept of polyarchy has been central to identifying and analysing the challenges to democratization (Bollen 1990; Coppedge and Reinicke 1991; Dahl 1971; Vanhanen 2003). The concept of polyarchy was introduced by Charles Lindblom and Dahl to emphasize how democracy as an ideal system is different from institutional arrangements. The institutional arrangement and its functioning are referred as an imperfect approximation of an ideal (Dahl 1971; Dahl and Lindblom 1953). Polyarchy, to be precise, is characterized by the existence of elected officials; free, fair and frequent elections; freedom of expression; alternative information; associational autonomy and inclusive citizenship. However, if one or more of these institutions are absent, it would be interpreted as a challenge to democratization (Denk and Silander 2012, 27).

19.3.1 Transition towards Democracy

Democratic transition discerns various patterns of transition from authoritarianism to democracy. It is important to understand the thin line of demarcation of causes of authoritarian breakdown and the processes of democratic replacement. Potter et al. (1997) discuss three paths towards democracy, which includes modernization, structural and transitional. Modernization emphasizes economic prerequisites of democracy, structural focus changes in class composition and power dynamics and transition process of bargaining discuss bargaining between élites to negotiate the transition to democracy.

The successful negotiation for institutional reforms depends on five sets of factors (Pinkney 1993). These include the type of authoritarian regime to be dismantled, for example, a caretaker military regime will be easier to remove than a radical or reforming one. Another important factor is the ability and role of opposition to plan for democracy rather than just oppose authoritarianism. The configuration of institutions and political structures under authoritarianism, availability of institutions that have survived during authoritarian rule, orientations towards reform by élites and existence of civil society organizations are other significant factors. The possibility of sustenance of new democratic regimes is strengthened if the transition process is gradual and based on the consensus of objectives and balance of power between negotiating groups.

19.3.2 Democratic Consolidation

This is the process of consolidating institutional structure, strengthening structures to maintain rule of law and protection of civil rights. It is important to extend democratic processes to prevent reversal towards authoritarianism. Consolidation means democratic structure is routinized and internalized in political behaviour that restrains significant groups to pursue unconstitutional, illegal or undemocratic methods to realize their aims. At this level, democratic political culture should emerge in which trust, tolerance and compromise are the dominant political norms (Diamond 1997b, xvii; Leftwich 2000, 135; Smith 2003, 259).

19.4 Democratic Consolidation: Different Parameters

The understanding of democratic consolidation pushes us to examine factors that help in the process of democratic consolidation.

19.4.1 Economic Preconditions for Democratic Consolidation

Lipset (1959, 1960) was the first scholar to emphasize the correlation of economic affluence and social changes to improve the chances of democratic consolidation. Factors that were used as indicators of economic affluence included per capita income, the percentage of the population owning motor cars and the number of doctors, radios and telephones per 1,000 people. Industrialization was marked as an important parameter to assess democratic consolidation and so were factors such as the percentage of the population engaged in agriculture as primary economic function, literacy rates, educational qualification and levels of urbanization. To establish the relation of economic affluence and democratic consolidation, functioning of democracy and its stability in Latin America, Europe and the English-speaking world were studied. Lipset argued that his data confirmed the age-old view that he traced back to Aristotle that in a wealthy society where relatively few citizens lived in real poverty, the probability of the mass of the population participating in politics develops. It is also imperative to restrain succumbing to the appeals of irresponsible demagogues. Another contributing factor in democratic consolidation is increased wealth and education. The rising number of middle class, whose interest is in moderating conflict with the system, also plays an important role in the consolidation of democracy. What is significant to understand in terms of class composition of society is with economic affluence of the lower class, the upper class is also less inclined to deny them their political rights. According to Lipset, wealth proliferates countervailing sources of power and opportunities for political participation. With some exceptions, Larry Diamond concurs to the analysis that 'the more well-to-do the people of a country, on average, the more likely they will favour, achieve and maintain a democratic system' (Diamond 1992, 109–10; see also Rueschmeyer 1991; Rueschmeyer et al., 1992, 13–20). The study by Przeworski and colleagues from 135 countries between 1950 and 1990 also confirmed that democracy is more stable in more egalitarian societies (Smith 2003, 261).

But this assumption was challenged by some scholars who argued that for democracy to be compatible with capitalism, it has to be designed in a manner that it protects the rights of the property-owning class and not the rights of those with conflicting economic interests. Thus, under a capitalist economic system, procedural democracy is established that never initiates political reforms to protect the social and economic interests of workers. This perspective emphasizes that the consolidation of democracy works when political participation is low, citizenship rights are restricted and working class is docile, leading to a situation of absence of most of the rights required for a fully functional democracy. This is why democracy is likely to exist alongside clientelism, state repression and electoral manipulation (Cammack 1994, 1997, 253–56).

However, the most important problem of the quantitative studies of development and democracy is it fails to explain certain important reasons for breakdown of democracy. Take the example of per capita income and the consolidation of democracy. We do not have conclusive proof why a fall in per capita income is likely to reduce the chances of democratic survival. Case studies from Latin America show no simple correlation between socioeconomic development and democracy; Argentina, a relatively rich country, lost democracy in 1930, but Chile, a relatively poor country, developed democratic institutions in the first half of the 19th century. The success of India as democracy shows that democracy is not necessarily incompatible with a low level of development. The consequences of development for democracy are very ambivalent (Diamond 1989, 33–34; Smith 2003, 263). An explanation of how a relatively rich country might resist democratization is provided by Moore's 'revenue bargaining' theory of democracy which divides states into 'coercion intensive' or 'capital intensive', depending on their sources of revenue. Where the state has no need to bargain with income-earning classes and wealth creators in order to extract revenues, as in poor agricultural societies, oil-rich countries or aid-dependent states, it has no need of democracy. Thus, states that do not depend on their citizens for revenue need not take too seriously any relationship of accountability with them (Moore 1996, 59; Smith 2003, 264).

That there is no relationship between the levels of economic development and transitions to democracy has been argued by Przeworski and co-authors (1997, 2000). They base their analysis on the argument that transitions could occur for various reasons and the probability is all of which are not necessarily systematic. Gleditsch and Choun (2004) used different measures of democracy and a dataset that covers a very long time span to prove there is no direct relationship between development and transitions to democracy. Arguing from a contrary standpoint in a very important analysis that covers the time span back to 1850, Boix and Stokes (2003) argue that development does contribute to democratic transitions. Epstein et al., in their work take a position that development has a strong predictive power for transitions into and out of the category they refer to as partial democracy, but less effect on transitions from full autocracy to full democracy.

Bollen and Jackman (1985) find no correlation between democracy and inequality. However, Przeworski et al. (2000) find a strong relation between inequality (in democracies) and democratic breakdown. Significantly, this analysis does explain the correlation that exists between democracy and equality if believed so but fails to support the idea that equality makes democratization more likely. This model assumes that one reason for elites' dislike and fear towards democracy but ordinary citizens' support is they expect it would lead to some kind of redistribution. The analysis given by Lindert (1994) has shown that the expected redistribution occurred in Western Europe after the first steps towards democratization. However, the analysis given by Mulligan, Sala-i-Martin and Gil (2003) supports the argument that contemporary democracies do not on average distribute more than dictatorships. Income distribution varied greatly among the late 20th-century dictatorships. Many, both communist and non-communist countries, redistributed income and opportunities through land reform. Public education and industrialization also led to the movement of a large number of people out of agriculture and into factories.

Special Insights

David Collier and Steven Levitsky have given a remarkable understanding on how different types of political regimes in Latin America, Africa, Asia and the former communist world share important attributes of democracy and yet differ profoundly, presenting a number of subtypes of democracy. Examples from among the hundreds of subtypes that have appeared include 'authoritarian democracy', 'neopatrimonial democracy', 'military-dominated democracy' and 'protodemocracy'.

(For a detailed discussion, refer Collier and Levitsky, 1997.)

The above analysis helps us to understand that economic development is an ambiguous concept. This could cover a large number of complex processes such as industrialization, urbanization, stratification, bureaucratization and rising level of wealth, literacy and education. It is unclear how each of these contributes exactly to consolidation of democracy. We might conclude that different combinations of economic, social and cultural factors are important for the spread and success of democracy. These different combinations might give different results in different times and places. This idea was illustrated by Samuel P. Huntington. According to Huntington, democratization does not proceed as a continuous process. It works in a manner that it witnesses surges and reversals—a kind of ebb and flow or two steps forward and one step backward. Thus, our curiosity increases when in every wave, a relatively large number of non-democratic states make their first move towards democracy.

Special Insights

Democracy and Development

That economic development promotes democracy by facilitating the emergence of a middle class was first propounded by Seymour Lipset in 1959 considering the experience of Europe and Latin America (Lipset 1959).

Economic growth that tends to contribute to the creation of democracy was supported by other scholars as well (see, for example, Barro 1996; Burkhart and Lewis-Beck 1994).

Strength of civil society, egalitarian income distribution and a market-oriented economy support democratization also emerged in the thesis of scholars (Przeworski and Limongi 1997, 159–160); see also, among others, Huntington (1991).

19.4.2 Political Mediation

In 2001, the Freedom House survey of political rights and civil liberties confirmed that higher levels of political freedom are correlated with economic prosperity. But it is still possible for a state to be poor and free (for example, Benin and Bolivia) or prosperous and repressive (for example, Brunei and Libya). The process of socioeconomic development may be supportive of democracy but also depends on how élites respond to new political demands generated by increased urbanization, industrialization, education and communications. The role and positioning of new emerging groups in the political process through institutional developments, especially political parties and interest groups, and access to economic opportunities and rewards (such as land, jobs, health care and consumer goods) are important mediating factors. The history of élite competition remained a significant political factor in some Latin American countries that supports Dahl's (1971) thesis that democracy is most likely to be successful in the case of political competition becoming institutionalized before the expansion of the suffrage and other forms of political participation. The history of some of the Latin American countries supports the hypothesis that democracy is likely to be more stable if based on a historical sequence that establishes national identity, further followed by the creation of legitimate state structures and the extension of rights to political participation to all members of society (Diamond and Linz 1989, 5–9).

19.4.3 Political Culture

Following an attitude survey done in the early 1960s, significant scholars of political culture Almond and Verba postulate that there is a pattern of political attitudes that supports democracy. 'Civic' or balanced culture in which political activity, involvement and rationality exist but are balanced by passivity, traditionality and commitment to parochial values supports democracy (Almond and Verba 1963, 30). Democratic consolidation also requires attitudes which recognize the legitimacy of territorial and constitutional arrangements and a willingness to accept the outcomes when the rules of political life (especially electoral rules) have been adhered to (Leftwich 2000, 136–37). Moderation, cooperation, accommodation and bargaining are associated with the success of democracy. Moderation and accommodation infer toleration, practicality, willingness to compromise and civility in political discourse.

Latin America is an example of strengthening of democratic political cultures by the successful performance of democratic government in accommodating new interests and groups, developing education, expanding the economy and creating a structure to secure the welfare of lower classes. Studies show that the Asian society often had political cultures that could be termed as mixed. Thus, there exist countries having 'some significant values and orientations that press in a democratic direction and others that press in an authoritarian one' (Diamond 1989, 17; Diamond and Linz 1989, 11, 44). The relationship between the 'civic culture' and democracy suggests that certain values about the rightness of political structures, a high level of political competence on the part of individuals and a political system based on some sort of trust in other individuals and groups lead to a stable democracy. On the contrary, it could also be argued that all such values could be the result of the experience of a democratic government. Following de Tocqueville, Lipset argued that democratic values are more likely to be preserved at a time of great social change, for example, when democracy is first introduced. Instances from some of the African states show how the dissipation of resources by mismanagement, corruption and greed has alienated support for democratically constituted establishments. A problem for many Third World countries is that they are locked into a vicious circle of low legitimacy and ineffective performance (Diamond 1988, 16; Diamond et al., 1990, 10). Diamond argues that perception about corruption, political freedoms and the trustworthiness of leaders have an impact on attitudes about the way democracy works. Thus, when the level of satisfaction with political freedoms and political functionaries is higher, the democracy is stronger (Diamond 1998). To support this argument, India and Costa Rica could be important studies. Both the countries exhibit 'surprising democratic persistence despite low or moderate economic development' because 'political culture at both the élite and mass levels clearly plays a strong supporting role' (Diamond 1993a, 425; Smith 2003, 267).

19.4.4 Civil Society and Democratization

The informal sector of the polity that complement state and market are important pillars in any democracy. Neighbourhood associations, political parties, non-governmental organizations (NGOs), associations, private voluntary bodies, grass-roots support organizations and social movements are some of the examples of civil society. Civil society is important in a democracy because it influences policymakers and hold governments at all levels to account. It mobilizes public opinion and makes governments responsive to the expression of demands and needs of citizens. It monitors the exercise of state power, motivates political participation, educates people in democracy, represents diverse interests in society and provides an alternative to clientelism and so plays a vital role in the consolidation of democracy. By creating cross-cutting allegiances, it disseminates political information. Associational autonomy necessitates a move away from clientelism that allows people, especially the poor, to articulate their interests and so move from being clients to being citizens (Diamond 1997a, 29–42;

Fox 1994, 151–53). The development of civil society provides opportunities for the poor and disadvantaged to redress injustices as well as to practice democracy within their own associations (Diamond 1992, 123). Sustainable democracy requires 'democratic deepening' or the infusion of institutions with democratic practices (Smith 2003, 268).

Experiences indicate that even when elements in civil society are pro-democratic, it is not necessarily easy to shift from protest and political confrontation to constructive dialogue with governments (Hernandez and Fox 1995, 202–203). The positive contribution of civil society is further limited in the context of authoritarian regimes because in some of them, political organizations are traditionally monopolized by parties, and authoritarianism is deeply rooted in the system. For example, the 'democratization of social life' created a counterpoint to the state in Vietnam when in the past social organizations (trade unions, youth movements and women's organizations) have been integrated into government and party. In different democracies, though new social organizations are emerging to support the urban poor in their quest for housing, work and health care, such participation is still limited. Reasons for limited and effective participation are 'the constraints of the old centralized planning system still exist; the elements of civil society are still underdeveloped; and ways to attract and operationalize people's participation are as yet unreliable and ineffective' (Luan 1996, 1890).

19.4.5 Balance of Power

The methodology of comparative history is used to develop the balance of power approach to theorize about the necessary condition for the survival of democracy (Rueschmeyer et al., 1992). The success and survival of democracy depends on the balance of power between classes (and coalitions of classes), between the state and civil society. International and national pressures are equally crucial to determine the chances of success of democracy. The stability of democracy also varies according to different historical contexts and the overall balance of power.

The postcolonial history of Africa indicates the importance of countervailing power to that of the state. The state has been 'the primary arena of class formation' and the 'primary means for the accumulation of personal wealth', leading to corruption, concentration of power and emergence of a parasitic bureaucratic bourgeoisie. The absence of middle class as discussed earlier in this chapter to demand the expansion of democratic rights, and the limitation of state power also obstructs the process of democratization. It is extremely important that the state has to be balanced by a plurality of autonomous associations that includes intellectuals, traditional leaders, professionals, trade unions, business associations, religious groups, students and journalists. The presence of alternative autonomous groups and associations is vital for ensuring a stable, responsive, and accountable government. Similarly, in Asia, regions where bureaucratic and military control has curtailed the independence of interest groups, voluntary organizations, and political parties, a fundamental aspect of democracy has been eroded, leading to authoritarian outcomes (Diamond 1988, 21–27, 1989, 22; Diamond et al., 1990, 22–24; Huntington, 1984; Smith 2003, 270–71).

19.4.6 Institutional Development

The key attributes of democracy are institutions and associated structures to promote the rule of law, freedom, order, accountability, representation and administrative capacity (Diamond 1997b). Consociational democracy based on power sharing and institutional structure that supports the accommodation of different groups is needed to cope with ethnic demands for special treatment. Examples from Asia suggest democracy was threatened when rulers abused their constitutional powers to strengthen their position. Examples from Latin America suggest instability followed when political leadership strategies were shifted from consensus to confrontation, from accommodation to polarization.

In Latin America, the presence of stable democracies is linked to parties that meet Huntington's (1968) conditions of policy coherence, organizational complexity, state autonomy, and adaptability to societal shifts. In contrast, Africa has experienced challenges with "input" institutions, particularly political parties, which have resulted in the exclusion of a significant portion of the population from constitutional politics. This dynamic has fostered elitism and clientelism, pushing people toward informal methods of engagement (Diamond 1988: 19–20; Smith 2003: 272).

As part of this debate is to analyse comparative analysis of presidential and parliamentary system, it has been noticed that when presidential executives are combined with the personalistic and autocratic political traditions, it strengthens autocratic tendencies. Personality and tradition are used by elected presidents to claim mandates from the people that is further used to bypass elected representatives, organized interests and other mechanisms of accountability. However, the parliamentary system avoids conflicting executive interests and legislative mandates. This system provides a greater flexibility of response when the executive loses the confidence of the legislature and provides a stronger opposition and incentives for dialogue between government and opposition (Haufman 1997; Linz 1994; Mainwaring 1993). However, comparative evidence is inconclusive. Przeworski et al. (2000) through their analysis argue 'the expected life of democracy under presidential system is approximately 21 years, whereas under parliamentary system it is 73 years' (p. 129). But from a comparison of 56 transitions to democracy in the Third World between 1930 and 1995, Power and Gasiorowski (1997) could find no evidence that constitutional type 'had any significant bearing on the success of Third World experiments in democracy' (p. 144). They were forced to conclude that institutional variables generally might be less important for democratic consolidation than had been thought.

19.4.7 Foreign Influence

Finally, foreign intervention is also relevant to democratic consolidation. Such influence is supportive if the main, regional and global trend is towards democracy. When powerful external forces make the promotion of democracy and human rights direct and desired foreign policy goals, democratic consolidation process is enhanced. The influence from neighboring states and the substantial support from international governmental and non-governmental organizations have played a significant role in fostering democratic reforms (Smith, 2003). Nonetheless, external entities have the potential to subvert democracy. (Haynes 2001, 50). For example,in 2001, US politicians and officials attempted to exert influence over the Nicaraguan election through financial contributions, propaganda campaigns, and food aid. Despite the official foreign policy of the United States endorsing democratization, it has often demonstrated inconsistency when compared to its actions in the realm of international relations (Whitehead 1986). In 2002, there were widespread suspicions that the United States played a role in inciting an unsuccessful coup attempt against the democratically elected president of Venezuela (Smith, 2003).

19.5 Democratization: Some Insights from Postconflict, Postcolonial, Postcommunist and Postauthoritarian Societies

19.5.1 Democratization in Postconflict Societies

Democratization in postconflict societies is a major challenge. Though international engagement is important to push for democratization, its success or failure depends on many factors. For example, if intervening authorities try to replicate the system that exists in their society, the chances of its success are bleak. It is important to think for a system suitable for a recipient society. The possibility of acceptance of a new system increases if the natives are already familiar with the system. For example, the political system introduced in Iraq in 2004 introduced decentralization of authority through federalism. However, it was violently resisted by Sunnis and Shia groups of the country. Such examples corroborate the fact that the march towards democracy ideally should be pursued in graduated stages that begin with disarmament of contending forces to organizing political parties, local elections and finally national elections. At the same time, the success of such experiments will depend on the acquiescence of population and resources of intervening authority.

19.5.1.1 How to Structure Representative Institutions

In postconflict societies with weak democratic institutions, with a past of violence and repression, culture of gun and greed take roots deeper, and establishing a representative system of government supplanted with a political culture of discourse is a difficult and long process. Establishing political processes, civil society and free media to ensure transparency and accountability is a challenge for durable peace.

19.5.1.2 Constitution

Societies that are in serious disarray physically, socially and ideologically due to past conflict present a serious challenge of getting different political factions to agree on the text of new or revised constitution. Broader political participation, accommodating varied groups important for stability and legitimacy of constitutional process, emerges as a challenge. The role of intervening authorities becomes important to design a system that give major contending groups stakes in future political processes through sharing or devolving political power and diminishing chances of one group acquiring dominance.

19.5.1.3 Role of Civil Society

The political space between individual and government is occupied by civil society, which includes NGOs, associations and social groups. The role of civil society is important for non-violent transition from war to peace because they represent the voice of citizens, marginalized groups and minorities.

19.5.1.4 Free Media

Free, independent media is usually absent in conflict-torn societies. For building free media, establishing a legal political system that respects freedom of speech and permits independent media is a challenge. In Afghanistan, the United Nations Educational, Scientific and Cultural Organization (UNESCO) helped establish a single independent media training and resource facility, the AINA Media and Culture Centre in Kabul, which improved coordination among donors and NGOs (Dobbins et al. 2007).

19.5.1.5 Free and Fair Elections

Establishing free and fair elections for legitimate government formation is important. However, premature elections often reinforce ethnic and sectarian cleavages. Election in itself is not a guarantee that the government committed to resolving disputes and preserving democracy will be elected.

19.5.2 Democratization in Postcolonial Societies

The multireligious, multi-ethnic and multilingual characters of postcolonial societies in African and Asian countries shapes the process of democratization in very specific ways. Horowitz (1985, 8) argues, 'Issues that elsewhere would be relegated to the category of routine administration assume a central place on the political agenda of ethnically divided societies ... almost any issue, any phenomenon, can suddenly turn ethnic or turn communal' (Linder and Bachtiger 2005, 864). Ethnic or other cleavages may counterpose national unity, crucial for democratic consolidation, and might lead to the breakdown of democracy or civil war as seen in the case of Sudan and Sri Lanka. The idea of political community is based on vertical legitimacy that establishes the connection between state and society, reinforcing the notion of institutional legitimacy and horizontal legitimacy that defines the boundaries of the political community of people. The two fundamental foundations for the creation of a state are (a) the basis of territory Gesellschaft and (b) the basis of ethnicity Gemeinschaft, which were largely European and exported to erstwhile colonies in Asia and Africa. In Africa, boundaries of states were created by colonial powers according to their own convenience, though even after the independence, the border remained the same. In the postindependence period, attempts were made to construct the notion of nationalism, for example, Nyerere's Ujamaa socialism, Kenyatta's Harambee and Mobutu's authenticité. However, with a few exceptions in some countries, it was difficult to knit together diverse ethnic groups with different languages, beliefs and ways of living. There were competing interests for access to state power and resources. Electoral politics also manifested itself in complex and convoluted ways due to extremely fragmented nature of the society. The practice of majoritarian democracy produced asymmetrical representation in the parliamentary system based on first past the post system, excluding some minorities permanently from power. Therefore, losing the mandate amounts to not just being out of the government but also to denial of access to the resources of the state. This is interpreted as a sign of danger for the survival of the group. Democracy was reduced to merely being a procedure devoid of meaningful people's participation, thus losing its substantive goal. Political, cultural and institutional transformation connected with a process of democratization remained missing in these societies. For instance, Felix Houphet-Boigny, who had been the president for several decades in Cote d'Ivoire, announced elections. It was but natural that in a country where there had been no opposition activity for 30 years, the ruling president will emerge victorious. Rather than republican ethos, patron-client relations become critical for winning elections. In Ghana, Nigeria and Kenya, members of particular ethnic groups were reported to use money massively to gain votes by rewarding traditional supporters. Since the leaders' horizon is short and the focus is winning elections and being in power in Africa and most of Asia, clientelism is paramount.

These countries, due to their past experience of colonialism, are engulfed in the dilemma of an oversized state that, on the one hand, is in the hands of a small ruling elite using power positions to exploit its resources and, on the other hand, has a problem of consolidation of even minimal standards of modern statehood. When a state is ineffective to deliver socially and economically, it faces a legitimacy problem. Müller discusses three indicators from the countries of Asia and Africa to understand the process of democratization; these include ethno-linguistic homogeneity/heterogeneity, family and kinship systems and male dominance (Linder and Bachtiger 2005, 867).

On ethno-linguistic homogeneity/heterogeneity, two schools of thought exist. The group of optimist scholars (Lian and Oneal 1997) considers societal heterogeneity positively. According to this logic, the chances of conflict decreases with the presence of conflicting groups. However, most of the scholars insist that conflicts increase because of a thin ground for symbolic and direct communication between groups. Ritzen and Woolcock (2000) show that in more segmented societies, the rule of law is weak. Easterly and Levine (1997) identify high levels of ethnic heterogeneity as the most important cause of African 'growth tragedy' (Linder and Bachtiger 2005, 868).

Discussing the link between family and kinship groups and democratization, Fukuyama (1992) has coined the terms 'traditional sociability'. This refers to the situation when loyalty and identity are traced through family or kinship groups. This type of solidarity structure obstructs the process of formation of civic networks crucial for the success of democratization. Putnam (1993) claims that civil society networks make it possible for citizens to cooperate among themselves for mutual benefit. But if ties depend more on family and kinship groups, rulers use this to develop mutual distrust and defection among groups. This makes citizens' mobilization difficult, and rulers return more easily to the authoritarian regime.

Traditional societies and prevalent male dominance in them also hinder the process of democratization. Institutionalizing a political order that gives equal civil and political rights to both men and women is resisted implicitly or explicitly. Any system that jeopardizes traditional inherited privileged social status of any individual or group is faced resistance.

The setback to democracy has been experienced in ethnically divided societies, and in some of them, for example, Rwanda and Somalia, ethnic violence has led to the breakdown of not just democracy but state authority. An important justification for authoritarian regime in these societies is with reference to establishing order, stability and growth. While no dictator ever proposed the inherent and legitimate right to rule, development, order and welfare are used as key variables in defence of their regime. Thus, elections are held in many countries, but it never leads to the process of democratization.

19.5.3 Democratization in Postcommunist Countries

The collapse of communism and disintegration of the Soviet Union was a critical juncture for the political development of East European states. One significant development was the number of countries in this region increased from 9 to 27 by 1995, covering a wide spectrum of political outcomes ranging from liberal democracy to authoritarianism. There was a wide variation, ranging from liberal democracy in Poland to war and finally disintegrating of Yugoslavia. In the past few years, they are moving towards the process of democratization. Ethnic minorities are in a much better position in Romania, Slovakia and Bulgaria, and establishing relations with the European Union remained the determining factor to influence domestic politics that further facilitated democratization. Despite the presence of myriad problems with the quality of democracy, the relative progress of each state is indisputable.

While the inheritance of the old regime makes their presence felt, these countries initiated democratization from scratch. Ethnic and territorial fragmentation inherited from the communist regime was the prime reason for instability in some of them. Restrictive laws on citizenship, directed against the Russians in Estonia and Latvia or against Serbs and Croats in Slovenia, represent previous policies. Corruption is another important legacy. In former communist countries, democratization means entering into the unknown territory of the political system and a market economy. Thus, in some of them, one faction monopolized power to use it for their own political and economic gain. Elite domination and increasing popular despair also characterize Eastern Europe and in particular Russia. The old elite continues to dominate state bureaucracies, and in recent years, it has regained political power with the help of newly formed, non-communist parties. Old communists no longer represent the past; they represent the successful capitalist future. However, the positive elements prevalent in Eastern Europe are its economic and political relations with Western Europe and the attraction of cooperation with European Union. Thus, we could argue the external environment is conducive to the process of democratization.

19.5.4 Democratization in Postauthoritarian Regimes

In postauthoritarian regimes, on the one hand, military, business and political elites have hope in democracy and its norms of political competition and, on the other, disillusionment is also seen because of corruption, role of political parties and failure to control organized crime. Democratic consolidation is at risk because of demagogic populism and electoral authoritarianism. Russia and Venezuela could be cited as examples. The countries of Latin America and East Asia were ruled by a military junta, but what makes them a separate case is their fair and recent history of experience in democracy. South Korea, Philippines, Thailand, Indonesia, Pakistan, Peru, Argentina, Uruguay and Brazil all had experience in democratic institutions but in recent years experienced rule by military dictators. In some instances, the democratic government was reintroduced and yet it is doubtful to think of an uninterrupted pattern of democratization in these countries. In Venezuela and Nicaragua, the elected presidents ruled as dictators. In Honduras and Bolivia, presidents set aside court order to limit their term and ruled as autocrats. Legacy of military history, poor governance and economic issues are a challenge in Latin America. Post 2013, Latin America has also experienced soft coups, for example, controversial election of Nicolas Maduro in Venezuela. In postauthoritarian societies, democracy exhibits important deficits because of institutional decay, hyper-presidentialism, re-election, corruption and constraints to freedom of expression. The challenge is to move from an electoral democracy to a democracy of citizens and institutions.

19.6 Are We Facing Democratic Recession?

Developments in the past decade that include decline in the number of democracies in the world make, Larry Diamond laments, the worldwide process of democratic recession. Since 2006, there is a decline in the aggregate freedom house score every year (Fukuyama 2015, 2). There is no net expansion in the number of electoral democracies, which has oscillated between 114 and 119 (about 60 per cent of the world's states). The high hopes of establishing democracy in Egypt that began with Arab spring of 2011 dashed with renewed dictatorship in Egypt. Anarchy in Libya and Yemen and Islamic State in Iraq and Syria (ISIS) presence in Syria and Iraq raise doubts to the process of democratization. Francis Fukuyama who had once celebrated the victory of liberal democracy raises his voice, asking whether we are experiencing a momentary setback in a general movement towards greater democracy around the world, similar to a stock market correction, or whether the events of this year signal a broader shift in world politics and the rise of serious alternatives to democracy (Fukuyama 2015, 12). Civil society continue to raise its voice in states like Ukraine, Georgia, Tunisia, Egypt and Hong Kong, but these are not culminating in the establishment of well-functioning democracies. Larry Diamond's concern is the accelerating rate of democratic breakdown, democracy in 'swing states', that is, emerging-market countries, deepening authoritarianism and the established democracies including the United States performing poorly and most important lack of will and self-confidence to promote democracy abroad. Thus, if we compare freedom scores at the end of 2005 and the end of 2013, we see that 29 of the 49 sub-Saharan African states (almost 60 per cent) declined in freedom, while only 15 (30 per cent) improved and 5 remained unchanged (Diamond 2015, 107).

The study of African continent indicates that none of the countries has been able to consolidate and secure their democracy, South Africa and Botswana being exceptions. Overall, in the past few years, rule of law and civil and political rights have declined across sub-Saharan Africa.

Generally, every region of the world scores worse on the standardized scale of transparency and the rule of law. Performance on indicators like political rights, civil liberties and role of opposition parties varies in terms of some doing better than others, but the role of civil society, and the space of media autonomy is shrinking in the world. Weak economy and rising inequality aggravate the problems of abuse of power, rigging of elections and violation of democratic rules.

The most important worry in the present century is the deepening of authoritarianism. In Russia, space for political opposition, principled dissent and civil society activity outside the control of the ruling authorities have been shrinking. Harassment and victimization of civil society activists and human rights protectors have been witnessed in China. Both countries have been aggressively flexing their muscles in dealing with their neighbours on territorial questions. In addition, authoritarian (and even some democratic) states are becoming more resourceful, sophisticated and unapologetic in suppressing Internet freedom and using cyberspace to frustrate, subvert and control civil society.

According to Diamond, established democracies' ever-increasing cost of election campaigns, increasing role of non-transparent money in politics and low rates of voter participation are additional signs of democratic ill health. Internationally, promoting democracy abroad scores close to the bottom of the public's foreign-policy priorities. (Diamond 2015, 113). Yet, the picture is not entirely bleak concludes Diamond. Not just 'The third reverse wave' of democracy is not witnessed but also there is no erosion of public support for democracy. To undermine all forms of authoritarian forces, economic development, globalization and empowering individuals and middle class are playing significant roles. The information revolution is undermining all forms of authority. The worldwide phenomenon of greater distrust of authority and desire for accountability, freedom and political choice raise hopes high. Scholars believe that in the coming two decades, these trends will also challenge the nature of rule in China, Vietnam, Iran and the Arab states.

According to Fukuyama, one of the reasons for delegitimization of democracy is that the development of modern states has not kept pace with the development of democratic institutions. Citizens' demand for services is not being fulfilled, and at the same time, authoritarian states like China and Singapore provide efficient basic services to citizens and thus are a challenge for democracy. In postconflict societies like Afghanistan and Iraq, democratic elections started a democratic process, but modern state could not develop to provide law and order and deliver public services. The failure of the state to tackle internal insurgency and corruption undercut the legitimacy of the state to the onslaught of ISIS. Francis Fukuyama rightly argues that the legitimacy of many democracies around the world depends less on the deepening of their democratic institutions than on their ability to provide high-quality governance (Fukuyama 2015, 16). India, world's largest democracy, also suffers from pervasive clientelism and corruption. The massive victory of BJP in 2014 election was based on aspirations and hopes that Narendra Modi would provide decisive leadership and strong government in place of the feckless and corrupt Congress-led coalition.

Philippe C. Shmitter challenged Larry Diamond's analysis. He has hope and argues that the thesis of the decline of democracy is based on selective inferences. The variables used in Freedom House survey that has used the narrative of democracy in retreat since 2008 is using high upper limits, thus diminishing the chance of improvement for free regimes. Many of these regimes have no further room for decline, and many of these are 'failed states' that are locked into civil wars and have no regime at all. Thus, variation in indicators of democratization is visible for partly free or hybrid democracies. In new or established democracies, surveys reveal citizen's dissatisfaction and disillusionment with core democratic institutions, but that scepticism is visible for other institutions such as physicians, scientist and public administrators as well. According to Philippe C. Shmitter, citizens—many of whom now have access through the internet to vast sources of independent and critical information—have become better educated and more sceptical about the motives and behaviour of their politicians (Shmitter 2015, 42). Another important impact witnessed in postglobalized world is the enormous flow of North–South migration. Demographic composition has changed in a manner that substantial population have no citizen rights. Growing diversity has also led to resistance against ethnic pluralism. According to Shmitter, in post-Cold War era, democracies of the West have had to satisfy the more demanding criteria of equality, access, participation and freedom promised by democratic ideals in an era when neo-liberal reforms have failed to produce the promise of continuous growth. For Shmitter, this is not a phase of decline but transition and propose to separate the criteria for assessing the quality of democracy from those used to assess the quality of government. The quality of democracy connects the rulers to the ruled and ensures accountability, while the quality of government is exercise of power, whether democratic or not. This indicates some autocracies could outperform some democracies in terms of higher economic growth, lower inflation, better distribution of wealth, fuller employment and stricter observance of the rule of law. Much of the anecdotal evidence for the decline involves how governments—more and more of which admittedly belong to democratic regimes—are performing, not how democracy as such is doing. Carrying the debate forward, Steven Levitsky and Lucan Way argue that democracy never actually expanded as widely as Freedom House perceived, and many of the seeming failures of democracy were nothing but deteriorations of what had been competitive authoritarians. By the mid-2000s, nearly every country with minimally favourable conditions for democracy had already democratized (Levitsky and Way 2015, 70–71). Non-democracies are mainly found in the Middle East, sub-Saharan Africa and the former Soviet Union. Based on a significant amount of research, the likelihood of achieving stable democratization appears low in poor countries with fragile governments (e.g., much of the sub-Saharan Africa), dynastic monarchies supported by oil revenues and Western backing (e.g., the Persian Gulf States). Similarly, single-party regimes characterized by robust governance and rapid economic growth (e.g., China, Vietnam, Malaysia, and Singapore) present obstacles to the emergence of stable democratization retreated in Sri Lanka, Thailand and Venezuela, while it survived in a range of important middle-income countries, including Argentina, Brazil, Chile, Colombia, Croatia, India, Indonesia, Mexico, Poland, Serbia, South Africa, South Korea and Taiwan. In several countries such as Benin, the Dominican Republic, El Salvador, Ghana, Guyana, Mongolia and Romania, democracy has survived though they were middle-income countries and the condition for success of democracy was not conducive. These examples suggest an alternative way of viewing the events of the 2000s (Sadurski, 2019).

19.7 Conclusion

Is democratization historically inevitable? History is witness that some countries have never created democratic forms of government. There have been some political systems that partially succeeded in establishing democracy. Some countries after a brief stint with democracy slipped back into dictatorship and autocracy. Some theories regard democracy as a continuum and assign graded scores to each country. Other theories see a sharp distinction between consolidated and established democracies. Classification is also based on different stages of development. Reference is also made as defective, limited or partial democracies that include countries that have important democratic characteristics but suffer from a crucial democratic flaw. There are different types of democracies, and countries take different routes to democracy. Economic development as an important factor is not the only one to promote democratization. Democracy is absent in economically developed countries, but its presence is visible in poor countries as well.

Several indexes have been developed to compare the degree of democratization. The popularity of democracy could be discerned from the fact that its ideals have been appealed by most of the rulers to give some kind of legitimacy to their regime. Although the significant question remains how democratization and consolidation of democracy can be ensured. Further studies in this area engage with the context and particularities of the deeper entrenchment of democracy in the world. For example, elections and referendums have supplemented and enriched political participation (Dalton et al. 2003), and deliberative polls and citizens' juries enable active engagements (Ackerman and Fishkin 2004; Fishkin 1995; Gutmann and Thompson 1996; Smith and Wales 2000; Ward et al. 2003).

Keywords

Consociational democracy
Democratic consolidation
Political culture
Postauthoritarian societies
Postcolonial societies
Postconflict societies

Review Questions

1. How can a culture of democracy be fostered in postconflict societies?
2. Do you see any relation in economic development and consolidation of democracy?
3. Define the role of civil society in the process of democratization.
4. Discuss the debate on democratic recession in the 21st century.

References

Ackerman, B., and J.S. Fishkin. 2004. *Deliberation Day.* New Havens, CT: Yale University Press. Almond, G.A., and S. Verba. 1963. *The Civic Culture: Political Attitudes and Democracy in Five Nations.* Princeton, NJ: Princeton University Press.

Barro, Robert J. 1996. Democracy and Growth. *Journal of Economic Growth* 1(1): 1–27.

Boyer, William W. 1992. Reflections on Democratization. *Political Science and Politics* 25(3): 517–22. Bollen, K.A. 1990. Political Democracy: Conceptual and Measurement Traps. *Studies in Comparative International Development* 25(1): 7–24.

Burkhart, Ross E., and Michael Lewis-Beck. 1994. Comparative Democracy: The Economic Development Thesis. *American Political Science Review* 88(4): 903–910.

Cammack, P. 1994. Democratization and Citizenship in Latin America, in *Democracy and Democratization*, edited by G. Parry and M. Moran. London: Routledge.

Cammack, P. 1997. *Capitalism and Democracy in the Third World: The Doctrine for Political Development*. London: Leicester University Press.

Collier, David, and Steven Levitsky. 1997. Democracy with Adjectives: Conceptual Innovation in Comparative Research. *World Politics.* 49(3): 430–451. Accessed from https://scholar.harvard.edu on September 12, 2023.

Coppedge, M., and W.H. Reinicke. 1990. Measuring Polyarchy. *Studies in Comparative International Development* 25(1): 51–72.

Dahl, R. 1971. *Polyarchy: Participation and Opposition*. New Haven, CT: Yale University Press. Dahl, R.A., and C.E. Lindblom. 1953. *Politics, Economics and Welfare.* Chicago, IL: University of Chicago Press.

Dalton, R.J., B.E. Cain, and S.E. Scarroe. 2003. Democratic Politics and Democratic Institutions, in *Democracy Transformed? Expanding Political Opportunities in Advanced Industrial Democracies*, edited by B.E. Cain, R.J. Dalton and S.E. Scarroe. Oxford: Oxford University Press.

Denk, Thomas, and Daniel Silander. 2012. Problems in Paradise? Challenges to Future Democratization in Democratic States. *International Political Science Review* 33(1): 25–40.

Diamond, L. 1992. *The Democratic Revolution: Struggles for Freedom and Pluralism in the Developing World.* New York: Freedom House.

Diamond, Larry. 2015. Facing upto the Democratic Recession, in *Democracy in Decline*, edited by Larry Diamond and Marc F. Plattner. Baltimore, MD: Johns Hopkins University Press.

Diamond, L., J.J. Linz, and S.M. Lipset. 1988. *Democracy in Developing Countries: Africa*. London: Adamantine Press.

Diamond, L., J.J. Linz, and S.M. Lipset. (Eds.). 1990. *Politics in Developing Countries: Comparing Experiences with Democracy*. Boulder, CO: Lynne Rienner Publishers.

Di Palma, G. 1990. *To Craft Democracies: An Essay on Democratic Transitions.* Berkeley and Los Angeles, CA: University of California Press.

Dobbins, James, Seth G. Jones, Keith Crane, and Beth Cole DeGrasse. 2007. *The Beginner's Guide to Nation-Building*. Santa Monica: RAND Corporation.

Fishkin, J.S. 1995. *The Voice of the People: Public Opinion and Democracy.* New Haven, CT: Yale University Press.

Fukuyama, Francis. 2015. Why is Democracy Performing so Poorly, in *Democracy in Decline*, edited by Larry Diamond and Marc F. Plattner. Baltimore, MD: Johns Hopkins University Press.

Geddes, Barbara. 2007. What Causes Democratization, in *The Oxford Hand Book of Comparative Politics*, edited by Charles Boix and Susan C. Stokes. New York: Oxford University Press.

Gutmann, A., and D. Thompson. 1996. *Democracy and Disagreement.* MA: Harvard University Press. Haynes, J. 2001. *Democracy in the Developing World.* Cambridge: Polity Press.

Hernandez, L. and J. Fox. 1995. Mexico's Difficult Democracy: Grassroot Movements, NGOs and Local Government, in *New Paths in Democratic Development in Latin America.* London: Rienner Publishers.

Horowitz, D.L. 1985. *Ethnic Groups in Conflict.* Berkeley, CA: University of California Press. Huntington, S.P. 1968. *Political Order in Changing Societies.* New Haven, CT: Yale University Press. Huntington, S.P. 1984. Will More Countries Become Democratic? *Political Science* Quarterly 99 (2). Huntington, S. 1991. *The Third Wave: Democratization in the Late Twentieth Century.* Norman: University of Oklahoma Press.

Leftwich, A. 2000. *States of Development.* Cambridge: Polity Press.

Levitsky, Steven, and Lucan Way. 2015. "The Myth of Democratic Recession, in *Democracy in Decline*, edited by Larry Diamond and Marc F. Plattner. Baltimore: Johns Hopkins University Press.

Linder, Wolf, and Andre Bachtiger. 2005. What Drives Democratisation in Asia and Africa? *European Journal of Political Research* 44: 861–80.

Linz, J.J. 1994. Presidential or Parliamentary Democracy: Does It Make a Difference, in The Failure of Presidential Democracy, edited by J.J. Linz and A. Valenzuela. Baltimore, MD: Johns Hopkins University Press.

Linz, J.J., and A. Stepan. 1996. *Problems of Democratic Transition and consolidation, Southern Europe, South America and Post-Communist Europe.* Maryland: Johns Hopkins University Press.

Lipset, Seymour Martin. 1959. Some Social Requisites of Democracy: Economic Development and Political Legitimacy. *American Political Science Review* 53(1): 69–105.

Munck, G.L. 2007. Democracy Studies: Agendas, Findings, Challenges, in *Democratization: The State of the Art*, edited by D Ed. Berg-Schlosser. Opladen: Barbara Bidrich Publishers.

O' Donnell. 1999. *Counterpoints: Selected Essays on Authoritarianism and Democratization.* Notre Dame: University of Notre Dame Press.

O' Donnell, G., P. Schimitter, and L. Whitehead. (Eds.). 1986. *Transitions from Authoritarian Rule: Tentative Conclusions about Uncertain Democracies.* Baltimore, MD: Johns Hopkins University Press.

Pinkney, R. 1993. *Democracy in the Third World.* Buckingham: Open University Press.

Potter, D., D. Goldblatt, M. Kiloh, and P. Lewis. (Eds.). 1997. *Democratization.* Cambridge: Polity Press. Power, T.J., and M.J. Gasiorowski. 1997. Institutional Design and Democratic Consolidation in the Third World. *Comparative Political Studies* 30(2).

Przeworski, Adam, and Fernando Limongi. 1997. Modernization: Theories and Facts. *World Politics* 49(2): 155–83.

Przeworksi, A., E.A. Michael, A. Jose, Cheibub, and L. Fernando L. 2000. *Democracy and Development: Political Institutions and Well-Being in the World, 1950–1990.* New York: Cambridge University Press.

Putnam, R.D. 1993. *Making Democracy Work: Civic Tradition in Modern Italy*. Princeton, NJ: Princeton University Press.

Rueschmeyer, D. 1991. Different methods: Contradictory Results? Research on Development and Democracy, in *Issues and alternatives in Comparative Social Research,* edited by C.C. Ragin. Leiden: Brill.

Rueschmeyer, D., E.H. Stephens, and J.D. Stephens. 1992. *Capitalist Development and Democracy*. London: Polity Press. Shmitter, Philippe C. 2015. Crisis and Transition but not Decline, in *Democracy in Decline*, edited by Larry Diamond and Marc F. Plattner. Baltimore: Johns Hopkins University Press.

Sadurski, W. (2019). Poland's Constitutional Breakdown. United Kingdom: Oxford University Press.

Smith, Brian C. 2003. *Understanding Third World Politics Theories of Political Change and Development*, 2nd edition. New York: Palgrave Macmillan.

Smith, G., and C. Wales. 2000. Citizens' Juries and Deliberative Democracy. *Political Studies* 48 (1): 51–63.

Tilly, Charles. 2000. Processes and Mechanisms of Democratization. *Sociological Theory* 18(1): 1–16.

———. 2003. Inequality, Democratization, and De-Democratization. *Sociological Theory* 21(1): 37–43. Vanhanen, T. 2003. *Democratization: A Comparative Analysis of 170 Countries.* London: Routledge. Ward, H., A. Norval, T. Landman, and J. Pretty. 2003. Open Citizens' Juries and Politics of Sustainability. *Political Studies* 51(2): 282–99.

Weiner, M, and E. Ozbudun. (Eds.). 1987. *Competitive Elections in Developing Countries.* Durham, NC: University of North Carolina Press.

Whitehead, L. 1986. International Aspect of Democratization, in *Transition from Authoritarian Rule: Tentative Conclusions about uncertain Democracies*, edited by G. O' Donnell, P. Schmitter and L. Whitehead. Baltimore, MD: Johns Hopkins University.

CHAPTER **20**

Political Representation, Voting and Electoral Systems in Comparative Perspective

Pushpa Singh

Reader's Guide

The study of electoral process and systems forms the subject of extensive research engagements in the field of Comparative Politics. Electoral systems shape the wider political processes of representative governments and hence their comparative analysis can help in understanding a system profoundly. A cross-national examination of electoral systems enables us to understand the variants, their features and functioning. Such explorations would highly inform the choice in favour of a particular electoral system design, depending upon the specific requirement and political realities of that society. Among the two major categories available are the majoritarian system (MS) and the proportional representation (PR) system. While MSs work on the principle of plurality and have single-member constituencies, proportional systems are seen as more representative of the diverse societal groups and have multi-member constituencies. There is an increasing consensus among the scholars in favour of PR, especially from the proponents of the consociational approach who find PR as the best way to ensure representation of minority groups in a society marked by significant ethnic cleavages. This chapter aims to explore the concept of representation, elections and voting and the different models of electoral systems, upon which the entire structure of modern democracies and governments rest. It will also engage with the contemporary debates surrounding the subject of study and analyse how the similar electoral design may bear very dissimilar outcomes for different political systems.

20.1 Introduction

The modern world is distinctly marked by the global political phenomenon of democratization. At the bottom line of this magnum discourse of liberal democracy lies the indispensable idea of representation. Through the process of election and voting, the representatives are chosen by the people to hold public offices. This makes elections and electoral systems integral parts of representative democracy. Electoral system determines the arrangement for structuring the process of election and the way in which the votes translate into seats in the parliaments. Scholars and practitioners alike agree that electoral systems can play a powerful role in promoting both democracy and successful conflict management, as they help shape broader norms of political behaviour (Reilly 2002). In this way, the study of elections and electoral systems is crucial to understand the political landscape and nature of democracy in any society.

An electoral system, to a great extent, defines the inner functioning of a democracy. Hence, it is important to study it. Apparently, it has become a critical reference point in analysing politics of any country. This explains the growing interest in the study of electoral systems in recent times, as evident by the range of new scholarships on the subject. The electoral system plays a key role in all defining institutions of politics, namely elections and representation, parties and party systems and government formation and the politics of coalitions (Farrell 1995, 3). Reciprocally, it also gets conditioned by the functioning of all these institutions. It is pertinent to explore the interlinkages between concept of representation, schemas of different electoral systems, their relative advantage and disadvantage and the impact they have on political systems. As election and electoral system emanate from the idea of representation, we will examine this concept in the following section.

20.2 Representation

The idea of representation lies at the heart of modern-day democracies. It has become the fulcrum of the modern political discourse, as everyone wants to be governed by representatives, every political group or cause wants representation and every government claims to represent (Pitkin 1967, 144). Even though direct democracy as a form of government existed since Hellenic antiquities, it was not a widely prevalent system of governance. The Greek city states practised various forms of governments such as aristocracy, monarchy, oligarchy and democracy, and all these forms replaced each other in a cyclical manner. Surprisingly, in those times, democracy was seen as a lesser variant of polity. Plato, in *Republic*, Book VI, argued against the case of democracy, as he believed that governance required expertise and dexterity, and democracy appears to undermine them. For him, it stood for mediocrity and populism. The idea was relegated to the backyard of history, and the medieval world comfortably settled with monarchy as the system of governance. It was rediscovered in the modern world that was heavily informed by the spirit of renaissance and enlightenment. However, emulation of direct democracy would not have worked in light of huge population and incapacity of the people to participate in everyday governance. Also, due the growing complexities of the process of administration and governance in modern times, it became increasingly overwhelming and anachronistic for masses to participate. Therefore, people developed a system in which they chose their representatives who could ensure their interest. Pragmatism and convenience established indirect democracy as the creed of political life.

This shift from the practice of classical and direct form of democracy to the indirect and less engaging form has brought the saga of representation to the centrality of democratic discourses. Unquestionably, it is the idea of representation that makes the state and government function in modern times. The concept of representation signifies the act of standing for someone who is not present there. Among the literature that deals with the concept of representation, Fenichel Hannah Pitkin's work is highly significant. She states that representation makes things present that are not literally present. It is through this process that the vast majority choose their preferred candidates who then, on their behalf, engage with politics on a day-to-day basis. Representation is a political process that creates a channel of dual communication, projecting aspirations and generating responses between the state institutions and the people. It provides sanctity to democratic institutions. Representation is a dynamic process and calls for an understanding between the representative and the represented. The key components of representation include (a) a party that is representing, (b) a party that is represented, (c) something that is being represented (opinion, interest) and (d) the context in which it takes place. The democracy of a country to a great extent is shaped by its specific context of political representation.

Therefore, a deeper understanding of a polity solicits greater explorations of different facets of this process like the mechanism of representation, about the relationship between citizens and their formal political representatives, between who get represented and those who represent (Yadav 2010, 347).

20.2.1 Theories of Representation

Among the plethora of the political theorists writing on representation, Hobbes's account of the subject appears as very systematic. Though J.S. Mill (1861) wrote a book on the subject, Considerations on Representative Governments, he bypassed discussion on its conceptual meaning. Hanna Pitkin in her work The Concept of Representation 1967 offers the most overarching understanding of the subject. She also draws attention to the complicated, convoluted meaning of the concept that makes it very prone to all kinds of interpretations. Unable to view the concept in its entirety, at the best, theorists forward the partial picture of it, depending on what aspect is being captured by them. This cacophony adds to the complexity of its varied meaning and makes it difficult to have a unified understanding on the subject. Pitkin discusses the following types of representation:

- **Formalistic representation:** This view perceives representation as a formal arrangement which precedes and initiates it. Hobbesian position on the subject is an example of formalistic representation. It has two dimensions: authorization, meaning the authority is given to act by the represented; accountability, meaning that the constituents can penalize the representative for not securing their interests. In this arrangement, there is no mechanism for evaluating the representative. Formalistic representation may not sufficiently be able to provide a lucid understanding of the working of the concept in wake of diffusion of political power between state and the non-state actors. In the contemporary times, the formal institutional arrangements of the state may not be able to represent the views of some groups or cause of citizens as effectively as international non-governmental organizations, international movements or civic groups. In fact, the policy matters of the state are also informed and influenced by the prospects of such agencies and organizations. As the conventional understanding of politics exclusively identifies representation with the mechanism of electoral democracy and the nation state, it may fall short of capturing the other dimensions of representation. The modern analysis of politics focuses on dispersed existence of power in multiple locations making the non-formal facades of assertion and advocacy as equally representative of people that may not be possible through formalistic representation.
- **Symbolic representation:** It signifies the ways in which the representative stands for its constituent. In symbolic representation, no reflection or resemblance is needed but it works on the level of acceptance of the representatives by their constituents. The representative symbolizes the constituency and stands for it as the king symbolizes the nation.
- **Descriptive representation:** In this view, the resemblance of the representative with those it represents is crucial. It may be defined by the common interest or experiences shared by the representative and the represented. This perspective fuels the debate whether marginalized groups and weaker sections essentially need somebody from their own group to represent them in politics. There can be a case for or against it.
- **Substantive representation:** It reflects the notion that the activities of the representative must fulfil the interest of its agents in real substance by acting for others. However, the question of whether the representative is capable of knowing her/his constituent's best interest and translating them in policy matters arises.

A representative has to be dynamic in her/his thoughts and deeds, as the immense responsibility of legislation will require her/his to persistently be in tune with society and its changing configurations. The idea of representation does not just pertain to government agents or institutions. It also designates a form of political process that is structured in terms of the circularity between state institutions and civil society and is not confined to deliberation and decision in the legislative setting (Urbinati 2006). There are plenty of forces like the public opinion, political parties, interest groups and dynamics of the society that mediate this entire process.

20.2.2 Models of Representation

There are four different models of representation that discuss what representatives do or how they should act: trusteeship, delegation, mandate and resemblance models.

- **Trustee model:** Edmund Burke is seen as the key theorist of this view of representation. This model believes that representation is a moral duty of educated and privileged to represent the interest of the less fortunate. This theory works on the understanding that a representative is like a trustee who is supposed to carry the responsibility of other's property or affairs with mature judgement. In other words, the representative is expected to exercise her/his 'higher judgement' on behalf of the people she/he represents. J.S. Mill in his liberal theory of representation proposed identical views. He believed that everyone is entitled to be represented, not all political opinion is of equal value. Mill favoured the system of plural voting in which learned people will have more votes and, therefore, more say in the choosing of representatives. This view has been subjected to scathing criticism for its elitist and anti-democratic undertones. It assumes that people are ignorant and less educated, and thus incapable of wise judgement. On the other hand, those who are educated have a wiser sense of politics. However, this is a flawed argument and can be questioned. Education may not be the only or the most important factor, enabling the representative to make appropriate moral judgement about the interest of others. Representatives may get primarily concerned with furthering their own interests rather than that of those whom they are supposed to serve, as highlighted by the reports of cases of corruption and scandals in developing societies.
- **Delegate model:** A representative is required to pursue her/his constituent's preferences in the delegate model of representation in contrast to the previously discussed trustee model that rests upon the wisdom of the representative. In this model, the representative has little or no room for following her/his own judgement and preferences. Very clear guidance or directive is issued to the person who is chosen as a delegate. The views and expectations of the represented are considered as most important in this model. This model presupposes close proximity of the representative with the people she/he represents. The positive aspect of this model is that there is a wider canvas for popular participation. Many scholars think that this model comes closed to the practical application of the idea of popular sovereignty. On the negative side, as this view is based on the understanding that the delegate will strictly follow the instructions of his or her constituency, it is most likely to further regionalism, narrowness and conflicts. Additionally, it also limits the scope of leadership by not allowing the delegate to use her or his own conscience or judgement.
- **Mandate model:** This is a new model of representation developed after the arrival of modern political parties. Here, the mandate represented by the political party is the decisive factor, and depending upon the acceptability of that mandate, a party wins or loses. In other words, the representative is chosen based on the mandate or manifesto she/he presents to the electorate. As in contemporary times, the political parties virtually carry on the functioning of the system. Parties contest elections, and after winning, form government to carry on the task of legislation. This makes parties more important compared to individual politicians in present-day electoral politics, who only follow their party programme and policies. Elections are won or lost based on the mandate of the political party they stand for. The party whose agenda gets the support of the majority wins the election. The criticism of this model is that the voters are not well informed and sometimes show the tendencies of habitual allegiance. The mandate model limits the choices for combination of policies, as the electorate cannot make any change to them. They have to either to accept them in totality or reject them all together.
- **Resemblance model:** Resemblance model of representation affirms the belief that only those belonging to a particular group and having experience of that group can best represent its interests. Therefore, a representative must resemble or belong to the section that she/he claims to represent. Inherent in this idea is the concern for microcosmic representation. It means that the government should represent microcosm of larger society and should mirror the diversity of the societal spectrum. In its purest sense, this would mean that the representative should have the same social traits—gender, social class, religion, ethnicity and so forth—as their constituents and extrapolating from the social psychological perspective, the same views and attitudes

(Bara and Pennington 2009, 97). This model is criticized for its parochial speculation that only those who belong to the particular group can represent it. Politics if convened only on the separating lines of discrete groups will breed divisions, conflicts and bickering. There are always cases where people do great service to a community even though they do not belong to it.

20.3 Election and Voting

Elections are the defining institutions of modern democracy (Katz 1997, 3). They have become sine qua non of present-day representative democracies, providing political legitimacy to the government. Elections invoke huge interests, excitement and curiosity among the citizens. In fact, in some countries, elections turn into the biggest public theatre, generating the greatest public debate, strong public opinions and sometimes even lead to extreme polarization of the society. The functions of elections are of two types: 'bottom-up' functions like representing the society, political recruitment, formation of government and moulding policy and 'top-down' functions like creating legitimacy, framing public opinion, etc.

The concept of election as we understand it today is entirely distinct from its past usage. It has resulted from the vigorous demands for representative government in 17th-century Europe and North America. The most remarkable effort in this regard has been the Reform Act of 1832 of British Parliament that expanded the base of enfranchisement significantly, thus creating a large pool of voters. The newly created electorate signified the gradual shift of political power from the elitist House of Lords to the Commoners in the British Parliamentary democracy. The working class and women were still deprived of franchise right. Subsequently, the Chartist movements took up the cause for extension of the suffrage to all. Electoral politics of some counties employed obstacles like literacy rules to debar some groups from voting. Nevertheless, the deepening of democracy has made the common people the stakeholders in politics. It offers them opportunity to get recruited as political representatives and become part of governing machinery. These developments have widened the horizon of politics, thus making it more participatory and egalitarian.

Special Insights

Referendum and Plebiscite

Referendum signifies a direct voting on a public matter by the electorate. It is a way of voting in which the entire electorate is called to vote on a matter of crucial importance. Derived from Latin word *refero*, it means to carry or to be submitted to an assembly. Its earliest use is traced back to ancient Greek city-states and Rome around the 4th-century bc, though in the modern world, it has been widely practised in Swiss Canton in the 16th century as an integral part of direct democracy. Referendum is used rarely, and generally, it is through voting that different levels of government are filled. However, when there are issues of national concerns such as need for constitutional changes, then the popular vote is sought in referendum. They are most common in Ireland, France, Italy, Denmark, New Zealand and Australia, though there are countries that have never used it such as India, Japan, Israel, Germany and Argentina. Plebiscite denotes a kind of referendum held on issues of self-determination. The decision of referendum may be legally binding, while that of plebiscite may not be so.

Numerous factors that influence and determine the voting behaviour are best explained by different theories of voting: (a) party-identification model, (b) the sociological model, (c) the rational choice model and (d) the dominant ideology model. Party-identification model is the oldest model in which electors identify themselves with specific parties and vote accordingly. Family plays an important role in the political socialization, whereby partisanship decides the choice of the party. Sociological model reflects the social alignment and divisions such as class, gender, ethnicity, religion and region of the society. It suggests that people vote the group which they associate themselves with. On the other hand, rational choice model sees the voter as a rational agent who makes her/his choice based on the policies preferences and manifesto of a party. Dominant ideology model suggests that the voters vote based on the ideological inclination. Elections and voting are conditioned and determined by a variety of crucial factors and their interplay, one of them is the public opinion, which acts as a guard on the entire political process. It is measured through opinion poll, a sample survey or focus group, etc. However, it may keep on swinging and is sometimes based on inaccurate information and judgement of the scenario. Hence, it becomes a dicey variable of the electoral process. Today's politics is greatly influenced by the social media, and the parties are watchful of it.

20.3.1 Women and Electoral Process

It is true that the access to political domain and corridors of power were highly restricted to the men of aristocratic class in the ancient and medieval times. Feminists make the contention that women have been systematically and deliberately kept out of politics. It is only after consistent struggle of vigorous Suffrage movement in the United States, the United Kingdom, France and other countries of the western hemisphere that resulted in granting of female enfranchisement. New Zealand was the first country to extend franchise to women in 1894 shortly followed by Australia. Norway and Finland granted their women franchise in 1914. Paradoxically, the United States and Britain, the largest democracies of the world, did the same as late as in 1920 and 1928, respectively. This shows the inherent patriarchal bias of the society and the institutions it shapes. Even today, ensuring participation and representation of women is one of the biggest challenge as legislature remains as gendered institution. Women are under-represented in elections and parliaments across the governments in the globe. They are hardly able to make to the top tiers of government. While some nations like that of Scandinavia may portray a little better picture, the situation in the postcolonial societies is worrying. Even in present times, voter turnout is generally equal among women and men in most areas of the world but other forms of political participation, such as party activities and involvement in protest activities, are dominated by men (Adman 2009, 315). In 1995, women were only 9.4 per cent of national legislators worldwide, and women have usually lagged furthest behind in countries using majoritarian systems (MSs) (Norris 1997).

The rising level of education and employment among women has surely narrowed the gender gap. Given an equal opportunity, women and men participate similarly and perform similarly. Sometimes, women tend to participate more actively compared with man as in the case of presidential elections of the United States between 1980 and 2008, which witnessed a higher proportion of voter turnout of women. Different countries have come up with their own strategies to ensure the incorporation of more women for engendering parties and politics. More than hundred countries have adopted gender quotas in the form of reserved seats to improve women's participation in legislatures (Hague and Harrop 1982, 135). Argentina has legally binding gender quotas. Countries such as Pakistan and Rwanda mark special seats reserved for women in their governments. Europe employs voluntary party quota where women candidates are brought on board by parties to appear as gender sensitive. Whereas there is a legally mandatory legislative quota for women in Latin America that applies to all parties there. Similar mechanism can be adopted to accommodate regional, linguistic, ethnic or religious political minorities. Despite all these mechanisms to widen the contours of electoral democracy, parties and political arrangements find ways and means to evade them effortlessly. In terms of the choice of electoral system for ensuring women's higher participation in politics is the PR system, which we will discuss in detail in the following section. It will show us how women and minorities find greater chances of making to the legislature with the PR as electoral system.

20.4 Electoral Systems

Electoral system denotes a frame of rules that governs the conduct of election, and these rules vary across the countries in the world. It specifies the arrangements of the electoral process and the method of translating the votes into seats in parliamentary elections. Electoral system uses the aggregate of individual votes to work out the winners, the losers and their respective share of spoils (Bara and Pennington 2009, 94). Many voting formula and framework have been worked out in the past based on the following four principles, namely lottery, unanimity, majority and proportionality (Colomer 2004, 14). The principle of unanimity worked for small close-knit homogeneous societies like the earlier small- town hall assemblies in England and America, the ancient civilization of Mesopotamian, etc. Choosing the representatives by lottery can ensure rotation and was practised in medieval local democracies. Although majority rule was used in ancient times, it was rediscovered in recent times with the arrival of modern form of democracy. The proportionality rule is associated with fair representation. It was prevalent in the past but has been formalized in France in the 18th century. Of all the four bases, the majority and the proportionality basis have become foundational principles in the present patterns of electoral systems.

The specific ways in which the electoral system conducts this task is called electoral formula. An electoral formula decides whether the seats fetched by a party are directly proportional to the votes it secures. Based on this very feature, electoral systems have been classified into three categories: MSs, proportional systems and mixed system. This classification has been named as Electoral formula I, Electoral Formula II and Electoral Formula III, respectively (Evans 2009, 98).

20.4.1 Majoritarian Systems: First Past the Post

MS is the simplest and oldest model of electoral system and is followed by many countries in the world. Its most popular variant is First Past the Post (FPTP) system or single member plurality system. The term FPTP is derived from its similarity to horse racing, where first one to pass a particular point is declared the winner. Many countries, including the United Kingdom, the United States, India, Bangladesh, Canada and commonwealth countries, use it for the election of their lower chamber. The objective is to win the effective parliamentary majority for the government formation. It works in a way in which 'winner takes all', eliminating any competition from smaller parties and pushing them to the periphery. The territory of the entire country is divided into single member legislative districts, generally of equal size. The voters are supposed to cast their vote for their preferred candidate in single ballot meant for only one candidate. The contender securing 50 per cent + 1 vote share would be declared the winner. This setup usually does not have minimum threshold of votes.

The advantages of FPTP system are many. It offers clear choices between the contesting candidates or the political parties. This system also maintains the principle of one person, one vote. Since, only one candidate represents the entire geographical area or electoral district in this system, the onus of that constituency lies on her/him. This fosters direct connection between the representative and her/his constituency, ensuring greater yield from the former. The government formed in this context has a clear mandate and, therefore, is able to work more efficiently without any unwanted pressure, unlike in coalition government. Naturally, such government will offer greater stability to the system as there are minimal chances of internal bickering. It does not allow extreme or radical parties to secure seats and win elections. FPTP always inclines towards moderation and centrist views.

The evaluation of functioning of FPTP highlights problems of MS. As this arrangement does not need absolute majority, only a simple majority of votes for winning, the proportion of votes among three contesting candidates can be winner: 35 per cent, the other two contestants: 34 per cent and 31 per cent. In such case, MS may not be truly representative of people, as in reality it does not have mandate of even the half of the electorate. Such a scenario looks undesirable as the essence of representative politics gets diluted. Considerable portion of electorate may feel left out and unrepresented which may not be good for the system.

FPTP ends in huge wastage of votes, those cast for the losing candidate and those cast for winning candidates, over the plurality mark. This is also the reason why the voter's participation is low in those countries who employ FPTP. It results in tactical voting or compromise voting. Let us take an example of a hypothetical case where there are five contestants, A, B, C, D and E. If A and C are expected to win according to the public opinion, there may be a situation where a voter prefers D to A, B, C and E, still the voter will vote for either A or C instead of D, as she/he will not like to waste her/his vote and thus have no impact on the final verdict of the elections. (For example, the US presidential election of 2002 in which Al Gore lost very closely to G.W. Bush.) The other variant of majoritarian electoral system is the second ballot system, which is very similar to FPTP. The difference lies in the fact that the candidate is required to secure an overall majority of votes cast for winning the first ballot. In case no candidate gets a first ballot majority, the prime two candidates undergo a second, run-off ballot by which the winner is decided. Iran, Mali and Vietnam have this second ballot system or two-round system.

Plurality system sustains large parties with mass support and automatically leads to dissemination of smaller parties with narrow base. This may lead to exclusion of minorities, thus alienating them from politics. In that sense, it under-represents smaller parties due to its alignment towards duopolistic politics, tilting the electoral game in favour of two major parties. No doubt, the advantage of this system is that it appears uncomplicated and lucid compared with other variants of electoral system. On the negative side, it fails to capture the representation of wider spectrum of the society. When evaluated in terms of their representative functions, majority system may not appear as a sensible choice for a society with many competing groups. In particular, this system leads to skewed representation of women in parliaments and adds on to the practice of keeping women out of politics and power.

One of the greatest disadvantages of plurality system is the practice of jerrymandering. It is a process of defining electoral districts with an objective to give political advantage to a party or a group by playing up with the district boundaries. Usually, the party in power tries to manipulate the drawing of electoral districts in such a way so as to derive partisan benefits from it. This has been a rampant practice in many countries following the FPTP system. Election can be easily manipulated by creating the constituencies based on the concentration of the supporters of the party in power. Jerrymandering has emerged as a corrupt practice symbolic of unfair MSs.

20.4.2 Proportional Representation Systems: Party list System and Single Transferrable Vote

Proportional representation (PR) systems are different from the MSs. Here, the electoral formula is designed to ensure that the proportion of vote received by the party would be reflected in the proportion of the seats held in the legislature as far as possible (Evans 2009, 99). The major advantage of the PR system is that while it encourages the formation of parties, it also facilitates the diverse representation of the society. The disadvantage is that since there is less probability of any party getting the majority, this arrangement produces a coalition government which may not be stable. This system is more recent compared with the non-proportional system and is particularly followed in European and Latin American countries. It emerged in continental Europe towards the end of the 19th century, stimulated by associations dedicated to electoral reforms, and has become the most common choice for most democratic countries (Hague and Harrop 1982, 195). In a true proportional system, parties are accorded share of seats corresponding to the votes they fetch in the elections. For example, if a party gets 20 per cent of votes, it will receive 20 per cent of the seats. It would be too ambitious to expect the PR systems to yield the result in a purely proportional manner. The largest party still has the upper hand while smallest parties are discriminated by designs or practices. PR systems have minimum electoral thresholds that indicate a minimum vote percentage or a minimum number of seats to be won by a party to get seats in the parliament. The cardinal purpose of threshold is to prevent the concentration of too many small and radicalized parties that may excessively fragment the assembly. Turkey practises the threshold of 10 per cent, Germany practises the threshold of 5 per cent, while Denmark and Israel have the threshold of 2 per cent. By the logistics of the system, many smaller parties are decimated in this process. It is very difficult for a single party to win the majority of seats. Such an arrangement cannot produce majority government and can only produce coalitions. Post-election negotiations become usual norm in order to form government. Therefore, many people think that PR system is a method of electing the parliaments and not the government.

The dominant forms of PR system are party list system and single transferrable vote (STV). In the List PR system, there are multimember districts. Political parties prepare the list containing the names of their candidates in the form of block or slate in the descending order of preference. The electors do not vote for the individual candidates, rather they vote for the slate or the entire block of the party. Whatever percentage of votes is garnered by the party, the corresponding percentage of seats is allocated to the party. Candidates are elected based on their order of appearance in the list. For example, in a 100-seat assembly, if a political party polls 20 per cent of votes, it would fetch 20 seats and the party would be supposed to send 20 members to the assembly. These will be the first 20 members of the list and in case if some of these winning candidates withdraw, then the candidates whose names are down in the list can replace them. There are two methods in which list system operates: Open list system and closed list system. In the open list system, voters can indicate their order of preference for the candidates within the list, whereas in the closed list system, the voters vote for the complete list. The ranking of the candidates is determined by the party. Older democracies like Finland, Sweden, the Netherlands and Norway practise open list system. Newer democracies like Russia and South Africa practise closed list system. Countries like Belgium, South Africa, Israel, Portugal, Spain and Germany employ closed party lists, where electors vote only for a party. In Israel, the Netherlands and Slovakia, the whole country is treated as one constituency.

PR system promotes unity in the sense that electors tend to identify with their nation as a whole. It is bound to produce fair outcome for all parties. Additionally, it also bolsters the representation of marginalized communities such as women and minorities, by making their chances of election higher, if they are part of the party list. It has been observed that the smaller parties have more women candidates in their list in order to attract vote and appear gender sensitive. On the other hand, the stability of the government is jeopardized due to the looming risk of breaking up of understanding in the coalition. List system also leads to centralization in political party as the task of drawing up the list procures great power to the party officials who decide which candidates to be placed on the list and with what order of ranking.

Another variant of the PR system is the STV system in which there are multimember constituencies. A voter has one vote in which she/he ranks the candidates according to her/his preferences. The candidates who achieve the quota are elected. The excess votes of the elected candidates go to the other candidates according to the next preference indicated in the ballot. If candidates fail to achieve the quota, those with lowest votes are eliminated, and their votes are transferred to the next preference indicated on ballot paper. The process of eliminating candidates and transferring ballots is repeated until the required number of winners emerges.

It is also called Hare Clark system. This system employs a threshold of quota called Droop formula to elect the candidates.

$$\text{Quota} = \frac{\text{Total number of votes cast}}{\text{Number of seats to be filled} + 1} + 1$$

For example, if there 20,000 votes cast for 4 seats in a constituency, then the quota will be 20000/ (4 + 1) + 1 = 4001. After achieving this quota, candidates are declared elected. In case all seats are not filled, the candidate at the end of the list gets eliminated and her/ his vote is transferred to other candidates based on the second preference of the voter. This process continues till all seats are filled. As it is evident, this mechanism enables accomplishment of highly proportional results. It provides the electorate the opportunity to win their most desired candidate. Since there are no wasted votes, PR also leads to higher turnouts than the plurality system (Hague and Harrop 1982, 200). This system generates inner party competition among the candidates, thus motivating them to work hard and perform better. Since there are many representatives chosen from the same constituency, people have options to approach any one of them, with whom they feel comfortable, for redressal of their grievances. At the same time, since there are many representing the same district, they may try to evade their responsibility, passing the buck to others. STV is used in the following three countries: Australia, Ireland and Malta. The best feature of this system is that high degree of proportionality is achieved simultaneously along with political diversity in constituency and candidates from a number of parties or political affiliations are elected (Evans 2009, 102).

Another important concept in PR system is District Magnitude (DM). It signifies the number of seats or representatives per constituency. DM defines the degree of proportionality reflected in any electoral district. The basic factor for all proportional systems is that the larger the constituency size, the larger the DM and thus the more proportional result (Farrell 2011, 79). The system would be considered more proportional if there are more candidates elected from the districts. Minority parties also tend to face less discrimination in this setup.

The best examples are the Netherlands and Israel, where 150 members of Tweede Kamer and 120 members of Knesset are elected by the single nationalist party list and brings the most proportional system possible (Evans 2009, 100). The 2009 elections of Israel witnessed winning of 12 parties, and several of these parties had less than 5 per cent of the vote.

20.4.3 Mixed System: Additional Member System

This system combines the element of both, the MS and the proportional system. Whereas the MS generates candidate-based votes, the proportional system procures party-based votes. The adoption of mixed system makes it possible to be rewarded with the advantages of both PR and single-member district electoral arrangements ensuring 'best of both worlds' (Shugart and Wattenberg 2001). In order to incorporate the benefits of geographical representation and party representation, many countries especially in Europe have adopted the mixed system, where half the country conducts its election following the plurality system, the remaining half follows the PR. The mechanical effect of FPTP is counterchecked by the inclusive and encompassing orientation of PR system. Newer democracies like Ecuador, Hungary, Russia and Taiwan have adopted 'mixed' electoral systems, believed to combine the best of both proportional and MSs (Norris 1997). Germany presents a classic case of mixed system where half of the members of the Bundestag are elected by closed party list and rest half are elected by the single member constituency based on plurality of votes. The electors have two votes, one vote for the party list system and another vote for the constituency candidate under FPTP. This serves a dual purpose. While the constituency link is retained through plurality system, smaller parties with meagre chance of winning still find their way to the parliament.

20.4.4 Electoral System and Party System: Duverger's Law

Maurice Duverger proposed direct correlation between the electoral system and party system in his writings in the 1960s. His conceptualization is known as 'Duverger's Law' that describes how the number and strength of political parties are affected by the electoral system. Duverger proposed that nature of party system of a country is shaped by the pattern of electoral system practised there. According to him, plurality rule election system/FPTP tends to produce two-party systems, whereas PR tends to favour multiparty system (Duverger 1954, 239). The double ballot MS promotes multiple parties aligned into two camps. In other words, MS having single member districts tends to produce a bi-party system, whereas PR system with multimember districts is most likely to give rise to multiparty system. However, this interpretation would be a matter of debate. Comparative politics scholar Stein Rokkan observes that the case may be otherwise as the PR electoral system is the product of party system. He states that social cleavages produced multiparty system in Europe long before the introduction of PR system (Rokkan 1970). Similarly, Raymond Miller in his study of party politics of New Zealand states that political fragmentation and fracturing of the two-party system preceded the adoption of a PR-based voting system, and not otherwise (Miller 2005, 13). This also hints towards the fact that electoral systems get influenced and even reconstituted, as in case of New Zealand, by party system and other political circulations. On the other hand, there are interesting exceptions like India and Canada who, despite following the FPTP plurality system, have yet not gravitated into neat two-party systems. They remain vibrant multiparty systems with numerous national and regional parties. The recent developments in party politics in India tend to generate two poles represented by the BJP and the Congress and rest of the smaller parties adhere to one or the other pole. However, this would not amount to the two-party framework that Duverger is referring to.

20.5 Electoral Designs, Reforms and Representation: Some Theoretical Reflections

Charles Boix in his interesting paper 'Setting the Rule of the Game: The Choice of Electoral Systems in Advanced Democracies' (1999) states that as long as the electoral arena remains the same, and favours the ruling parties, electoral system is not changed. If there is change in electoral dynamics due to coming of new voters or alterations in voter's preference, then the ruling party reshapes the electoral setup to suit their choices (Boix 1999, 603). Therefore, the design and pattern of electoral scheme is not frequently prone to changes unless the need for it is realized by the government. However, recently there have been a lot of debates on the reforms in the electoral systems. There have been rising demand, particularly from minorities sections to make electoral systems more proportional. The unfairness of plurality, MS and the disproportionate result they produce has been a cause of constant worry in many countries. The 'Electoral Reform Society', a political pressure group of the United Kingdom, has been asking for doing away with FPTP for all elections, national and local. For a long time, this group has been emphasizing that FPTP is neither able to capture the political imaginations of all people nor conducive to the diverse spectrum of society. Similarly, electoral reform organization 'Proportional Representation Society of Australia' has been persistently advocating for PR voting systems and STV. In Canada, many provincial and national organizations have been insisting on adopting party PR. Many countries have already started moving in the direction of reforms. For example, New Zealand started its electoral reform in 1986, as it shifted from FPTP to Mixed Member Proportional Representation.

At present, there is a strong consensus in favour of PR based on the understanding that it will usually mitigate the impact of skewed representation. Parties representing minority groups and ideologies will be safeguarded. PR appears to be the safer choice for parties bargaining for reforms allowing all parties the ability to retain their stake in the system. The push for representative models of electoral designs is coming from various contemporary theoretical and philosophical sources like from the works of scholars such as Iris Marion Young, Anne Phillips, Melissa Williams, Jane Mansbridge, etc. Iris Marion Young pleads for a system that can capture the descriptive representation of racial minorities (Young 1990), while Phillips sees the possibility of enhanced legislative deliberation by representatives belonging to minority racial groups (Phillips 1995). Melissa Williams, the author of *Voice, Trust, and Memory: Marginalized Groups and the Failings of Liberal Representation* (1998), elaborates the basic problem with the models of representation. She strongly believes that a constituency with minority population can best connect and pursue its aspiration through a representative who herself/himself belongs to that race or ethnicity. As the members of the racial/ethnic groups share the same social perspective and their lives are grounded in similar experiences, it becomes more sensible for them to demand for an electoral scheme that can best capture their specificities. Jane Mansbridge, professor at Harvard, has meticulously worked in the area of democracy and models of representation discussed in her co-authored book *Deliberative Systems* (2012). She rallies for having a large number of minority representatives that should be able to consolidate common minority interests, simultaneously displaying the internal diversity of the group (Mansbridge 1999). Elizabeth Anderson in her seminal work *The Imperative of Integration* (2010) brings out the dilemmas of politics of representation. Her extensive research showcases how the racial discrimination, oppression and injustice are still pervading in all corners of the everyday lives of people in the American society. She believes that the politics of segregation may not deliver racial justice, instead comprehensive racial integration in legislative bodies and all other aspects of lives (like in workplace, schools and neighbourhood) will surely hold the key to a more equal and representative society (Anderson 2010).

Scholars, like Arend Lijphart, believe that in ethnically divided societies like that of developing countries, PR appears as the most appropriate electoral system. It would strengthen the consociational approach in the political system, as all diverse small groups will find political space for asserting their voices. Despite deep-rooted ethnic conflicts, these groups will be able to arrive at a consensus for mutual sharing of power and benefits. Like Lijphart, Benjamin Reilly also believes in the remarkability of PR in instilling inclusiveness among all sections. In terms of electoral systems, consociationalists argue that party-list PR is the best choice, as it enables all significant ethnic groups, including minorities, to 'define themselves' into ethnically based parties and thereby gain representation in the parliament in proportion to their numbers in the community as a whole (Lijphart 1990, 10). Arend Lijphart carried out a comparative study of 13 democracies between 1960 and 1980 in which he discovered that the systems with PR emerged as much more representative of different groups of their society. Of all these countries under study, nine used PR (three Scandinavian countries, Belgium, Finland, Austria, Germany, Italy and the Netherlands) and four democracies used single member plurality system (New Zealand, Australia, Britain and Canada). The countries with PR produced higher representation of women and minorities and also witnessed higher voter turnout (Lijphart 1994, 79).

However, there are scholars who might not be convinced so. Robert G. Moser, based on his study of electoral system in Russia, says that PR system may not necessarily translate into increased minority representation in a system with minimal ethnic parties.

He further says that it is the demographic and cultural characteristics of the minorities that will shape the linkages between electoral system and minority representation (Moser 2008, 273).

Special Insights

Consociational Democracy

The concept of consociational model of democracy or representation is associated with Arend Lijphart, an eminent scholar of Comparative Politics. In his work *Patterns of Democracy: Government Forms and Performance in Thirty-six Countries* (New Haven, CT: Yale University Press, 1984), he proposes that consociational democracy based on the politics of accommodation of diverse voices works best for deeply divided countries, as it develops mechanisms of elite power sharing across all major religious, cultural and social groups of that society. It also includes the feature of decentralization of political power to subnational groups.

Many countries keep on experimenting with their electoral system. The shift in the electoral system would bring drastic changes in the political institutions of a country. France adopted a highly proportional system from 1946 to 1958, thereby allowing representation of smaller and highly diverse parties in the legislature. This resulted into a very unstable and ineffective government. To overcome this problem, France reverted back to two ballot plurality system in 1959. The impact was profound. Overall, the number of parties in France decreased, smaller parties vanished away, some merged into the larger ones creating two strong parties on the left: communists and socialists and on the right UDF (Union for French Democracy Party) and Gaullists. The effect was equally visible on the office of president, making the charismatic Charles De Gaulle very strong and forcing the other parties to regroup. However, newer dynamics is again reshaping the electoral arena of France in the wake of globalization, the growing dominance of the EU, and redundancy of old political divide in old part systems (Evans 2009, 110). The example of France proves that the electoral system and party system are intrinsically linked, and change in one is bound to cause change in the other.

20.6 Reflections from Postcolonial Societies

It is quite fascinating to analyse the ways in which representative politics have unfolded in the postcolonial societies of Asia, Africa and Latin America. These societies have been under colonial subjection for a prolonged time, and the impacts are still visible on their institutional and political processes. Unfortunately, most of these countries appear to be extension of colonial state apparatus in terms of their institutional functioning, with oversized state under small ruling elite. Though these countries started their journey with representative democracy, the political leadership has been largely confined to a handful of leaders who command their allegiance to the system due to their forefathers' link to the country's independence movement. Also, the nature of representation in these countries has been formal, focusing more on the procedural aspects of democracy. With the subsequent phases of democratization, all groups in such societies, who have been denied access to mainstream, started asserting their rightful claims on public opportunities and institutions. Since these societies are ethnically and culturally divided and prone to violence, the majoritarian forms of democracy accentuate such problems by structurally excluding the minorities (Linder and Bachtiger 2005). In many developing societies, electoral competition is a bid for ownership of the state and minority groups; losing an election does not account to simply losing office, but to having no access to the resources of the state and thus losing the means for protecting the survival of the group (Makinda 1996).

From the time of their independence in the early 19th century, most of the Latin American countries made their attempts to establish electoral processes and democratic regimes. These efforts failed, unfortunately, and dictatorial and oligarchic groups took to power. Only three major electoral democracies could sustain themselves between 1900 and 1930, Argentina (1916–29), Mexico (1911–13) and Uruguay (1919–33). Surprisingly, some of the most affluent nations witnessed the subversion and breakdown of democracies in Latin America: Brazil in 1954, Argentina in 1955, and again in 1964, Chile in 1973 and Uruguay in 1963. However, by 1980, global political changes started catalysing the process of democratization in Latin America. The internalization of the finance market, receding impact of revolutionary threat, constrains of domestic policy choice and political learnings have converged at reduction in incentives and opportunities for authoritarian reversals (Remmer 1993). The mid-1980s saw the shift of Brazil and Argentina to civilian regime; in 1989, the dictatorial regime of Pinochet in Chile buckled under public pressure. This process of transition has been intermittent and incomplete as pointed by Jennifer L. McCoy. She captures the failure of the Latin American state in making democracy inclusive by granting citizenship rights and other entitlements to people. Latin American citizens are beginning to express their growing frustration with the system after two and a half decades of democracy and market reforms that promised an improvement in living standards (McCoy 2008). The challenge lies in sustaining these efforts. It is only upon the foundations of strong representative and accountable institutions that new forms of political participation would be instituted (Panizza 2005).

Interestingly, in Asia, different countries have showcased different trajectories of their engagement with democracy and electoral process. Countries such as Kazakhstan, Uzbekistan, North Korea and Myanmar continue to reel under authoritarian regimes with little or no presence of representative politics. On the other hand, India presents a case of deeper anchoring of democracy with huge celebratory ritualism around elections, while many other societies have faltered on this aspect in Asia. Scholars assign the reason to the vibrant electoral politics and accommodative framework of the country. Mass political participation of marginalized sections in the electoral politics has expanded the democratic narrative of the country. However, delivering social justice and ensuring equity to all must remain the prime commitment of the regimes.

In Africa, the promises of newly achieved independence vanished away in thin air, as charismatic leaders started playing larger than life figures after amassing powers and resources. The subversion of democratic politics began by withholding elections and other institutions of representation. If at all elections were held, they were held for the face value only and were regularly manipulated. Leaders continued to rule their countries as their feudal fiefdoms. Any kind of criticism or opposition was treated as treason in many such regimes. The dictatorial lineage and wanton brutality of colonizers were replicated in actions of postindependent leaders such as Kwame Nkrumah of Ghana, Sekou Toure of Guinea Kenneth Kaunda of Zambia and Arap Moi of Kenya (Nwauwa 1992, 378). For example, President Honsi Mubarak continued to play with the system in Egypt. He was later overthrown after Arab uprising. The changed scenario increased domestic pressures for change for better governance and to end corruption. Greater democratization required protection and promotion of civic and human rights and making the entire system conducive for a free economy (Decalo 1992, 15). Now that many African states have started afresh, electoral democracy must not remain administrative formalities. It is in this context that prospects of democracy are reshaping in African continent as ripple effect of democracy has led to greater stress on encompassing all ethnic groups and tribes in the development process in contemporary times.

At the same time, one must be also cautious of the discernible politics behind the overenthusiastic push for democratization from the western hemisphere. The implicit agenda of the West is to manage the global capitalism. However, the capitalist forces understand well that in order to make the globe more conducive to their interests, it is utmost necessary to forge democracy in the Third World. This will immediately draw developing countries into the vortex of international capital, and at the same time will allow the West to manoeuvre such engagements to their own benefit.

20.7 Conclusion

We cannot ascertain any particular model of electoral system as universally applicable and perfect for all countries. It will depend on the context and requirement of that system which will decide about the suitability. Every society adopts a discrete method of electoral process, and if that becomes widely acceptable and stable over time, it becomes institutionalized. The discussion in this chapter elaborated how the proportional system is increasingly favoured by many societies as it appears to be more representative, whereas MSs generate risk of systematically excluding the aspirations of substantial percentage of electorate, by the very design of it. For societies, which are raven by deep-rooted ethnic, religious or ethnic divisions, like Mali, Russia or Israel, the proportional system may prove more inclusive (Lijphart 2007). At the same time, proportional system may also reinforce rather than ameliorate these cleavages (Tseblis 1980). The institutional arrangements must work towards that optimum where it can capture the discrete aspirations of all groups of the society, yet at the same time, keep the system efficient and responsive.

Keywords

Consociationalism
Elections
Electoral systems
Majoritarian system
Mixed system
Proportional system
Representation
Voting

Review Questions

1. Discuss briefly the centrality of the concept of representation in the electoral democracies of the modern world.
2. Examine the majoritarian electoral system like FPTP and its relative advantages and disadvantages.
3. Critically analyse the proportional representation system. Do you think that it offers a better framework to ensure the representation of the marginalized groups of a society?
4. Illustrate the features of mixed representation system. Is it able to ensure greater representation of the diverse groups along with providing stability to the system?

References

Adman, Pere. 2009. The Puzzle of Gender-Equal Political Participation in Sweden: The Importance of Norms and Mobilization. *Scandinavian Political Studies* 32: 315–36.

Anderson, Elizabeth. 2010. *The Imperative of Integration*. Princeton: Princeton University Press.

Bara, Judith, and Mark Pennington. 2009. *Comparative Politics*. Thousand Oaks, CA: SAGE Publications.

Boix, Charles. 1999. Setting the Rules of the Game: The Choice of Electoral Systems in Advanced Democracies. *The American Political Science Review* 93(3): 609–24.

Colomer, Josep. 2004. *Handbook of Electoral System Choice*. London: Palgrave Macmillan.

Dalton, Russell J., and Andersen Christofer. 2011. *Citizens, Context, and Choice: How Context Shapes Citizens' Electoral Choices*. Oxford: Oxford University Press.

Decalo, Samuel. 1992. The Process, Prospects and Constraints of Democratization in Africa. *African Affairs* 91(362): 7–35.

Duverger, Maurice. 1986. Duverger's Law: Thirty Years Later, in *Choosing an Electoral System: Issues and Alternatives*, edited by Arend Lijphart and Bernard Grofman. New York: Praeger.

Evans, Jocelyn A.J. 2009. Electoral System, in *Comparative Politics*, edited by Bara Judith and Pennington Mark. London: SAGE Publications.

Farrell, David M. 1995. *Comparing Electoral Systems*. London: Macmillan.

Farrell, David M. 2011. *Electoral System: A Comparative Introduction*,. 2nd edition. New York: Palgrave Macmillan.

Gallagher, Michael, and Mitchell Paul. 2005. *The Politics of Electoral System*. Oxford: Oxford University Press.

Hague, Rod, and Martin Harrop. 1982. *Comparative Government and Politics: An Introduction*. New York: Palgrave Macmillan.

Katz, Richard S. 1997. *Democracy and Elections*. London, New York: Oxford University Press.

Klingemann, Hans-Dieter. 2012. *The Comparative Study of Electoral Systems*. Oxford: Oxford University Press.

Lijphart, Arend. 1977. *Democracy in Plural Society: A Comparative Exploration*. New York: Yale University Press.

Lijphart, Arend. 1984. *Patterns of Democracy: Government Forms and Performance in Thirty-six Countries*. New Haven: Yale University Press.

Lijphart, Arend. 1990. Electoral Systems, Party Systems and Conflict Management in Segmented Societies, in *Critical Choices for South Africa: An Agenda for the 1990s*, edited by Robert A. Schrire. Cape Town: Oxford University Press.

Lijphart, Arend. 1994. *Electoral Systems and Party Systems: A Study of Twenty-seven Democracies, 1945–1990*. Oxford: Oxford University Press.

Lijphart, Arend. 2007. *Thinking about Democracy: Power Sharing and Majority Rule in Theory and Practice*. New York: Routledge.

Matthew, Shugrt, and P. Martin Wattenberg. 2001. *Mixed-Member Electoral Systems: The Best of Both Worlds?* London: Oxford University Press.

Makinda, Samuel M. 1996. Democracy and Multi Party Politics in Africa. *The Journal of Modern African Studies* 34(4): 555–73.

Mansbridge, Jane. 1999. Should Blacks Represent Blacks and Women Represent Women? A ContingentYes. *TheJournal of Politics* 61(3): 628–57.

Mansbridge, Jane, and John Parkinson, eds. 2012. *Deliberative Systems*. Cambridge: Cambridge University Press.

Maurice, Duverger. 1954. *Political Parties, Their Organization and Activity in the Modern State*. London, Methuen, New York: Wiley.

McConnell, Shelley, Jennifer McCoy, and Michael McCarthy. 2015. Challenging the Norm: International Election Accompaniment in Nicaragua and Venezuela. *América Latina Hoy* 70: 109–32.

McCoy, Jennifer L. 2008. Democratic Transformation in Latin America. *The Whitehead Journal of Diplomacy and International Relations*. Accessed 17 March 2016. https://ciaotest.cc.columbia.edu. Accessed 11.09.23.

Mill, J.S. 1863 (Reprinted in 1961). *Considerations on Representative Government*. New York: Henry Holt and Company.

Miller, Raymond. 2005. *Party Politics in New Zealand*. London, New York: Oxford University Press.

Moser, Robert G. 2008. Electoral Systems and the Representation of Ethnic Minorities: Evidence from Russia. *Comparative Politics* 40(3): 273–92. DOI: 10.5129/001041508X12911362382995

Norris, Pippa. 1997. Choosing Electoral Systems: Proportional, Majoritarian and Mixed Systems. *International Political Science Review* 18(3): 297–312.

Norris, Pippa. 2002. *Democratic Phoenix: Reinventing Political Activism*. Cambridge: Cambridge University Press.

Nwauwa, Appolo O. 1992. Concepts of Democracy and Democratization in Africa Revisited. *African Studies* 30(3): 378.

Nwauwa, Appolo O., and Adekunle Julius. 2015. *Nigerian Political Leaders: Vision, Actions and Legacies*. Glassboro: Goldline and Jacobs Publishing.

Phillips, Anne. 1995. *The Politics of Presence*. Oxford: Oxford University Press.

Pitkin, Hanna Fenichel. 1967. *The Concept of Representation*. Berkeley, Los Angeles: University of California Press.

Reeve, Andrew, and Ware Alan. 1992. *Electoral Systems: A Comparative and Theoretical Introduction*. London: Routledge.

Reilly, Benjamin. 2002. Electoral Systems for Divided Societies. *Journal of Democracy* 13(2). https://devpolicy.crawford.anu.edu.au/pdf/staff/ben_reilly/breilly7.pdf.

Remmer, Keren L. 1993. The Process of Democratization in Latin America, in *Global Transformation and the Third World*, edited by Robert O Slater, Barry M. Schutz, and Steven R. Dorr. Lynne Reiner Publishers. Accessed 17 March 2016. http://link.springer.com/article/10.1007%2FBF02687137.

Riker, William H. 1982. The Two-Party System and Duverger's Law: An Essay on the History of Political Science. *The American Political Science Review* 76(4): 753–66.

Rokkan, Stein. 1970. *Citizens Election Parties: Approaches to the Comparative Study of the Process of Development: Scandinavian University Books*. New York: Mckay.

Tseblis, George. 1990. *Nested Games: Rational Choice in Comparative Politics*. Berkeley, CA: University of California Press.

Williams, Melissa. 1998. *Voice, Trust, and Memory: Marginalized Groups and the Failings of Liberal Representation*. Princeton, NJ: Princeton University Press.

Yadav, Yogendra. 2010. Representation, in *The Oxford Companion to Politics in India*, edited by Niraja Gopal Jayal and Ptatap Bhanu Mehta. Oxford: Oxford University Press.

Young, Iris M. 1990. *Justice and the Politics of Difference*. Princeton, NJ: Princeton University Press.

Web Sources

Dovi, Suzanne, "Political Representation", The Stanford Encyclopedia of Philosophy (Fall 2018 Edition), Edward N. Zalta. (Ed.). Accessed from https://plato.stanford.edu on September 11, 2023.

Linder, Wolf, and Bachtiger Andre. 2005. What Derives Democratisation in Asia and Africa. *European Journal of Political Research* 44: 861–80, 864. Accessed from http://citeseerx.ist.psu.edu on April 17, 2017.

Nwauwa, Appolo O. 2017. Concepts of Democracy and Democratisation in Africa Revisited. Accessed from https://www.kentstateuniversitypress.com on September 11, 2023.

Panizza, Francisco E. 2005. The Social Democratisation of the American Left. Accessed from https://erlacs.org on September 11, 2023.

Urbinati, Nadia. 2006. Political Representation as a Democratic Process. Accessed from https://www.jyu.fi on September 11, 2023.

CHAPTER 21

Party and Party Systems

Babita Verma

Reader's Guide

Political parties are ubiquitous actors of the modern democratic form of governance and form the core of representative politics and governments. Modern governments are basically party governments where parties perform many crucial functions and, therefore, any political system in contemporary times cannot be imagined without them. There are numerous instances where parties have become instrumental in reorganizing society. They try to mould society in a definite direction through various means of policy formulation and implementation, violence, coercion, shift in cultural practices and ideological propaganda. The political parties have become the harbinger of democratic transformations, where they have been instrumental in bringing down many authoritarian governments. The parties and party systems present in a polity help in deepening of democracy by interlinking the state and civil society, formal institutions of government and the other formal and informal institutions that operate within a polity. Party systems have also brought about accountability, stability and/or instability within representative governments depending on their structural configurations. The modern democracies are unimaginable without political parties and party systems without mobilized voters.

21.1 Introduction

Parties are the product of democracy and mass franchise. They are the storehouses of power instrumental in deepening of democracy by democratizing polity and spreading democratic values among citizens. The political parties democratize polity by organizing, coordinating and collocating political actors and issues. From the time the political parties were considered as evil, it has come a long way to become part of the democratic transformation.

The parties and types of party systems present in a polity are important for maintaining a responsible executive and accountability of the elected members to the people. They are not always the loci of relation to democratic representation; there are numerous instances where parties have also become instrumental in reorganizing society. They try to mould society in a definite direction through various means of policy formulation and implementation, political strategies, stratagems and manipulation of laws and rules. Despite the evils attached to parties, it is interesting to note that in the postcolonial societies, they play an important role in connecting the 'political society' with the state; the actors in the political society find space within parties to manipulate the government acting in their favour.

From safeguarding the interests of the party to representing the demands of the people in a representative form of governance, the party and party systems have a long and interesting lineage. As the political systems across the world have moved from simple to complex arrays of practices, the academic analysis of practices has tried to capture the complexities by producing enormous amount of literature on parties and party systems in normative and empirical terms. When the normative theories explicate the role of political parties in democratic or social transformation, the empirical works are busy finding laws and structures those govern party systems. It is definitely a herculean task to compile literature available on them within this limited space; nevertheless, a modest attempt has been made here to make students aware about the literature, issues and debates concerning parties and party systems across the countries of the world.

21.2 Defining Party

21.2.1 Sect, Factions, Interest Groups and Party

The term party was used to replace the derogatory term 'faction'. Faction is an older term than the party and derived from the Latin word *facere* (to act or to do). As a verb, it came to indicate actions of 'dire doings'. The original idea conveyed by the verb is that of 'hubris, of excessive, ruthless, and thereby harmful behaviour' (Sartori 1976, 7). The term party is derived from the Latin verb *partire*, which means to divide. According to Sartori, the term sect, which derived from the Latin word *secare*, meaning to cut, was associated with religion, and the Protestant sectarianism was gradually replaced by the term party in the political vocabulary of the politics in the 17th century.

A distinction was made between the term party and faction. The term faction is applied 'to a concrete group', the party represented 'an analytical partition' going beyond a concrete group (Sartori 1976, 9). It was Burke who first distinguished party from faction. This distinction continues till today. Madison, for instance, defines a faction as 'a number of citizens, whether amounting to minority or majority of the whole, who were united and actuated by some common impulse of passion, or of interest, adverse to the rights of other citizens, or to the permanent and aggregate interests of the community' (Madison in Fairfield 1981, 1).

In contrast to factions, the interest groups are loosely composed of self-serving individuals, those mainly aim to achieve specific interest/goal of a group and sometimes focus on the achievement of short-term public goals. Though Burke was the turning point in visualizing the concept of a party, it was in the English-speaking nation that the factions changed into the party in practice.

21.2.2 Definition

There are several definitions of the term party, but they can be clubbed under three headings: (a) normative, (b) motivational behaviour and (c) operational aspects.

The normative definition is provided by Burke for whom 'Party is a body of man united, for promoting by their joint endeavours the national interest, upon some particular principle in which they are all agreed' (Burke 1948). Epstein, in this vein, defines party as 'any group, however loosely organised, seeking to elect governmental office holders under a given label. Having a label (which may or may not be on the ballot) rather than an organisation is the crucial defining element' (Epstein 2000, 9).

The above definitions do not take into account the vital aspects of political structure and decision-making with which politics is concerned. They also ignore the role of the party as an agent of political change while defining it.

The motivational aspect has been dealt by Anthony Downs who defines party in terms of specific objectives and differentiates between 'vote seeking', 'office seeking' and 'policy-seeking' parties. The vote-seeking approach defines party as 'a team of men seeking to control the government apparatus by gaining office in a duly constituted election' (Downs 1957, 25). On the account of the second definition of party as 'office seekers', Downs states that the parties are interested in taking control over the political offices. What distinguishes the vote-seeking parties from the office-seeking parties is that the former maximizes electoral gains whereas the latter maximizes its hold on government portfolios, ministry and coalition bargaining to implement policies (Storm 1990, 567, also see Riker and Ordeshook 1968).

However, policy-seeking parties, in contrast to the aforementioned two parties, are concerned about the government portfolios and the ideological temperament of the coalition partner. It is believed that the political parties look into the policies of coalition when different political parties come together to form the government. In this perspective, Strom defines the political party as 'an organization that seeks benefits derived from public office by gaining representation in duly constituted elections' (Strom 1990, 574).

The third set of definitions follows from the operational aspect. This definition examines the party's internal functioning as the key area to understand party behaviour and goals. Important writers in this genre are Katz and Mair (1995) and Maor (1992, 2005). They define parties as institutions. Differences between parties are established in terms of patterns of internal management of parties and the way party managers run the party.

Political parties are important not only for the functions that they undertake, for example, representation, elite formation and recruitment, goal formulation, interest articulation and aggregation, socialization and mobilization and organization of government, but also because they share a complex relationship with other parties present, contesting the elections and maximizing votes for themselves (Heywood 2013, 252). The role that political parties play, the goals that they try to achieve, the decision- making procedures that happens within and outside the parties, the organizational structure of the party, the role of leadership within and outside the structure, the existence of small and big factions within the party and their influence in the decision- making procedures cannot be assigned an autonomous status. They have various kinds of patterns of political interactions. The patterns of interaction in broader sense are called party systems.

21.3 Formation of Party Systems

21.3.1 Social Cleavage Perspective

Party system is a structured and complex relationship between voters, government and relationship among different actors present within the political systems. The concept of party systems is different from what parties are. Party system is dependent on (a) a responsible government, (b) the reality of election and (c) the establishment of parties as subsystems (Sartori 1976). As a dependent variable, the process of formation of party systems has been attributed to the 'system of contrasts and cleavages within western societies', as well as to the '*model of alternative alliances and oppositions* among seven sets of actors'[1] (Lipset and Rokkan 1967, 36, italics in original). To analyse the party system, they have adopted a case study approach, as for them, the comparative study of the party system would invite the danger of succumbing to 'facile generalities and irresponsible abstractions' and each case study of specific nation would provide pattern of alliances and compromises among actors in the formation of the party system in Europe.

Following the Parsonian social stratification model with conceptual A–G–I–L paradigm, where A stands for Adaptation, G stands for Goal, I stands for Integration and L stands for Latency in social system theory. Lipset and Rokkan (1967) have developed the inventory of social and political cleavages in society, leading to the formation of party systems. They begin with the cleavages that developed during the consolidation phase of national community and subsequent conflicts in the phase of centralization and economic growth that accompanied it. They mention about four important cleavages—'centre-periphery', 'state-church', 'land-industry' and 'owner-worker'—to explain the historical trajectory of the formation of party systems. In addition to empirical developments in different countries, the authors claim that the study of the interaction between the two revolutionary processes—National Revolutions and Industrial Revolutions—must be taken into account while explaining development of parties and party systems.

They explain the social bases where the parties drew their strength from. Their three-fold analyses state that the nation-building when penetrates into the local level finds territorial resistance. The local resistances produce 'a variety of alliances' among and across the 'communities of the nation' (Lipset and Rokkan 1967, 9). In the third phase, these resistances get channelized into the formation of parties. The crystallization of parties led to the formation of a party system depending on the alliances among forces.

Taking the case study of Britain and France, they have illustrated the following cleavages: (a) between the 'nation building culture' and provincial linguistic and religious resistances of the provinces, or between 'subject vs dominant culture' and (b) between the state and the church. The Industrial Revolution contributed to the societal cleavages at two levels: between primary economy versus secondary economy (landed interest and emerging entrepreneurial class) at the one axes and between the owners and employers and labourers and workers on the other side (Lipset and Rokkan 1967, 14).

According to Lipset and Rokkan (1967), in comparison to Britain, the French Revolution produced the most profound cleavages in society. The French Revolution affected the church fundamentally by raising the moral issue of the control of the community norms and the issue of the control of education. The cleavages between the church and the state were so deep that the fights were extended into the domestic sphere, such as, marriage, granting of divorce and the organization of charities. At the education level, the conflict was over the imparting of free and compulsory education to children by the secular state and reserving religious preaching within the purview of the church. This triggered nationwide mass mobilization. There were parties of religious defence born out of this process, and it grew into mass movements after the introduction of suffrage for men.

Countering the mobilization of the religious parties were the socialist parties who built educational institutions like schools and youth movements and developed trade unions, clubs of various kinds, publication houses, and had also set up radio stations (Lipset and Rokkan 1967, 15). Similarly, in the Netherlands, there was conflict between the Protestant Columns and the Roman Catholic Columns which was the direct outcome of the French Revolution.

The tremendous production that started following the Industrial Revolution generated conflict between the primary producers in the rural and the traders and entrepreneurs in the urban areas. There were conflicts between rural estates and urban trading classes, but these conflicts were sharpened after the Industrial Revolution. This got reflected in the national legislatures across the countries of Western Europe. The economic interest was at the forefront but what made it more deeper cleavage was the 'maintenance of acquired status and the recognition of achievement' (Lipset and Rokkan 1967, 19). The conflict resulted in the formation of Conservative and Liberal parties as the merger between the interests took place subsequently with the rapprochement between the Conservative–Liberal conflict. This kind of rapprochement also took place in Germany where Liberals did not side with the working class. Despite these mergers, the rural– urban cleavages have entered the national politics even in the 20th century.

How did the birth of parties lead to the formation of 'constellations of political parties' or what is generally called party systems? Lipset and Rokkan answers through the analytical category of four thresholds such as legitimation, incorporation, representation and majority power. They discuss the third and fourth thresholds as they agree with the formulations of Weber, Tocqueville and Michels for whom the emergence of parliamentary opposition, a free press and the extension of franchise are the important factors contributing to the growth of parties and party systems. The authors focus on the thresholds of the consequences of the electoral system and the structure of the decision-making arena for the formation and functioning of party system (Lipset and Rokkan 1967, 29). The authors argue that the two cleavages of 'National Revolution' set the stage for the 'national divergences' in the European party system. The centralized nation-building project was supported by the spiritual bodies. However, this kind of nation-building project was opposed by the underprivileged sections consisting of peasants, craftsmen and workers in the provinces and were led by the political parties. The Western countries were divided to the core and without exception had strong parties defending the church explicitly or implicitly.

The Industrial Revolution produced markets. Conflicts within the market also produced divergent party alliances in Europe. In the market-driven economy that was emerging during this time, some farmers joined with the owners in the secondary sector of the economy and others chose to remain in opposition and decided to form their own parties. The labour classes in the urban areas were being mobilized by heterogeneous mass parties. The Russian Revolution also became a factor in splitting the mass parties on different lines. Gradually, the alliances and compromises resulted in an intensive identification of 'we' versus 'they' group. No communication flew 'freely over the cleavage lines but restricted and regulated to protect the movement against impurities and the seeds of compromise' (Lipset and Rokkan 1967, 11) leading to the formation of the party system and finally the 'freezing' of the party system in the Western Europe.

What is important in their model is the emphasis on the historical path, social cleavages and the alliances and compromises leading to the formation of party systems. Social cleavage theory had been emulated by scholars across the world to study party systems but they could not explain satisfactorily the development of a party system in postcolonial societies; for instance, it became highly difficult to explain what kind of social and historical cleavages led to the persistence of dominant party system in India.

21.3.2 The Sociological Law Perspective

In contrast to the social cleavage framework, Duverger has provided the 'sociological law' on the growth of party systems. This law has been famously called Duverger's Law. Duverger proposes a law and a hypothesis. Duverger's law states that 'the simple majority single-ballot system favors the two-party systems. Of all the hypotheses ... in this book, this approaches most nearly perhaps to a true sociological law' (Duverger 1963, 217). The hypothesis is 'the single-majority system with second ballot and proportional representation favors multi-partyism' (Duverger 1963, 239).

Duverger's propositions have taken into account the presence of electoral systems and their relation to the interaction between political parties. The three kinds of voting systems that Duverger draws attention to are (a) plurality voting, (b) run-off majority voting and (c) proportional representation (Riker 1982, 754). Electoral systems polarize the parties into different continuum. Electoral volatility throws conditions where different parties are formed in the continuum and share relationships with the other parties in terms of coalition or any other way of staying in the fray. The formation of a party system, in this scheme, involves not only the component parts but also involves the totality of inter-party relationships or 'streams of interaction'.

The party system can be analysed in terms of combination of the number of parties (fragmentation) with the extent of ideological distance between the parties in a party system (polarization) (Maor 1997, 33). Importance of this framework lies in its emphasis on the multiplicity of inter-relationships that include inter-relationship based on presence of parties and the electoral systems leading to different kinds of party systems.

In short, the 'pattern of relationship' that is present among different parties constitute a system only if it is characterized by stability and a 'degree of orderliness'. Based on the orderliness, we can have the party systems mentioned in the next section.

21.4 Party Systems

21.4.1 One-Party System

One-party system is different from the 'one-party state'. One-party states have a single party that represents the whole of society. It assumes that only one social interest is supreme in politics and is the unified will of the people. In a one-party system polity, on the contrary, there exists other parties but a single party has 'monopoly' over power at the expense of other parties. It excludes all other parties from power. In this sense, it is a party system where parties are present but do not match the monopolistic power of the single party.

If a party system is an interaction between different units, then a single party system is a system where the citizens, party and state machinery become a single body. The party's interest gets entrenched in the state machinery by virtue of controlling the electorate through various means. The states where one party rules by capturing state machinery is called a 'one-party state' and their units are seen as 'fused "party-state" apparatus'.

From a comparative perspective, one can find the following kinds of one-party systems. The first kind is found in socialist regimes where the communist party controls the polity. It rules all aspects of institutions of the polity. Such parties do not allow any other parties to exist. Generally, parties are ideologically motivated and committed cadre based. It has highly structured internal organization and functions on the principle of democratic centralism. The party keeps control of state, economy and society. It acts as a 'vanguard' to bring about social and political change. The controlled one-party system has been criticized for its 'elitism' and 'concealing burgeoning influence of the state bureaucracy' (Heywood 2013, 235).

The historical phenomenon of anti-colonial struggle and subsequent processes of nation-building led to the growth of a one-party system in postcolonial countries. In most of the Asian and African countries, the ruling parties were the ones that fought the anti- colonial struggles and subsequently got the support of the masses to carry forward the developmental and nation-building projects. Example of these countries were India and Pakistan in Asia and Ghana, Tanzania and Zimbabwe in Africa.

The one-party system in many other African and Asian countries had come up due to charismatic leadership and ideology that has been derived from that leadership. For example, Nkurmah of Ghana, Nyerere in Tanzania and Robert Mugabe of Zimbabwe fall under this category. These parties are less well organized and play a very marginal role in policymaking (Heywood 2013, 235).

21.4.2 One-Party Dominant Systems

Though defining a one-party dominance is extremely difficult, Kenneth J. Greene has provided a working definition of the one-party dominant system as 'hybrids that combine meaningful electoral competition with continuous executive and legislative rule by a single party' (Greene 2007, 12).

Pempel (1990, 3–4) has mentioned four characteristics of a one-party dominant system:

1. In a dominant party system, the dominant party may have the lowest share of votes in comparison to other parties but has the largest number of seat shares in comparison to plurality of parties present in a given political system.
2. The opposition parties may have the largest vote share but cannot form the government because of the strategic position that the dominant party enjoys in the polity. Sometimes, the opposition parties find it difficult to form government without the help of the dominant party.
3. The dominance of one party continues for a long period.
4. The party has a vision of a 'historical project' and a political agenda for its achievement.

One-party dominant system is different from the authoritarian form of government in that the one-party dominant system strives within what Greene calls 'meaningful electoral competition' (Greene 2007, 12ff, cited in Haren 2010, 3), whereas the authoritarian regimes, especially the 'closed authoritarian regimes', neither has meaningful election where other parties contest nor do they have opposition parties of any kind (Haren 2010, 3). For them, election is just a procedure to maintain the tag of democracy.

The problem with this formulation is that there is no clear understanding of the number of years a party should stay in power and the share of votes that it should get to qualify as a dominant party (Haren 2010, 4).

21.4.3 Two-Party Systems

There is a plethora of literature available on the presence and continuation of a two-party system. All the literature agree on the following main characteristics of the two-party systems:

1. There are a number of small parties present, but only two parties enjoy enough 'electoral and legislative strength' to have the real prospect for winning the election and forming government.
2. The largest party basically on the basis of legislature strength rules and the other party forms the opposition.
3. Power alternates between two parties as both retain the capacity to be elected alternately or what is termed as 'government in the wings' (Heywood 2013, 236).

Great Britain and the United States are the often-cited models of two-party systems. There are other countries like Canada, Australia and New Zealand who have two-party systems. Within the two-party systems, there are variations. In Britain, the two-party system was present between 1945 and 1964. Thereafter came a big lull to the two-party systems. As Hicks (1933) suggests, in America, the two-party system has the following tenets: first, is 'the tenet of originality' that is a two-party system inscribed into the electoral system of the United States. Second is the 'tenet of immutability' (Hicks 1933, cited in Disch 2007, 5), that is, it is the bedrock of democracy that is 'unmoved by partisan contest ... immune to politics it is timeless and unchanging' (Disch 2007, 5). The two-party system is hailed for its responsiveness to the demands of the voters and effective, efficient and stable government. It is also praised for providing choices to voters and accountability of parties in power and opposition. The two competing parties provide straightforward choices about alternative programmes, policies and governments. It is believed that voters support and elect the party for carrying out promises made in their manifesto. It is also supposed that two-party systems promote strong and accountable government by encouraging competition between the governing party and the opposition. The ruling party, thus, remains alert and can never relax because of the constant presence of opposition confronting it in and outside the legislature. The two-party system also guarantees moderation to capture the floating votes and prevents extreme ideological polarization. In this process, it in some way falls over conflict and argument instead of always believing in consensus and compromise.

According to Disch, the two-party system as an ideology helps democracy to progress for three reasons. First, the presence of two parties leads to a competition of formation of 'grand coalition' that accommodate the small parties within it as well. It enables citizens to trust them not because they have voted for the small segment but 'to speak for the nation as a whole' (Disch 2007, 9). Second, by providing choices, it provides clarity to the voters in terms of 'yes' or 'no' or 'continuity' or 'change' in favour of a particular party. Third, it provides for smooth transition and a responsible opposition by altering control over the government (Disch 2007, 9).

The two-party system has the following drawbacks: First, the simultaneity of choice and restriction makes it inherently problematic: on the one hand, it provides choice to voters, and on the other, it restricts the choice between two parties only (Disch 2007, 7). Second, it promotes what Disch calls 'tyranny of two-party systems' that persuades citizens to accept 'this one?' or 'that one?' system only (Disch 2007, 6). Third, it sometimes leads to class nature of the party system and ideological polarization at the grassroots level, and fourth, in order to outdo each other's electoral promises the two parties embark on populist measures (Heywood 2013, 262).

21.4.4 Multiparty Systems

A multiparty system polity is characterized by the presence of more than two parties. The small parties can coexist along with the big parties through coalitions and electoral arrangements. There are small parties within the coalition that restrict the bigger party from coming to power. The empirical evidence does not support the nomenclature of what constitutes a multiparty system. In Germany, for example, it can be called as a two- and half-party system as both Christian Democratic Union (CDU) and Social Democratic Party (SDP) have equal strength, but they are forced to work with small democratic parties as coalition partners (Heywood 2013, 264).

One of the strong points in favour of the multiparty system is that it reflects heterogeneity of social structure. The minor or major groups can organize themselves to form a political party to raise their voices. By doing this, the multiparty system prevents social rigidity and 'political immobilism' in the political system.

The second argument in favour of the multiparty system is that it creates a system of checks and balances among the parties and within the government. It encourages debates, discussions and dissensions on the one hand and dialogue, reconciliations and compromises on the other hand. It helps the government to be responsive to competing views and contending responses.

The third advantage of the multiparty system is that it challenges the two-party system for its assumption that voters rationally choose one party over the other (Holler 1987).

The pitfalls of the multiparty systems are: first, the uncertainty over the coalition government formation after the elections. In a multiparty system, the postelection arrangement brings uncertainty, excessive delay, negotiations and horse-trading. This makes coalition inherently unstable. The government instead of governing manages the squabbles in the coalition leading to policy paralyses. Second, the multiparty system cannot offer a 'clear ideological alternative'. There is a tendency towards 'moderation and compromise'. Coalition politics does not believe in conviction and 'politics of principle'. It believes in a common ground for negotiation and reconciliation to form government. In this sense, a multiparty system is democratic but simultaneously promotes populism and abandons real policy issues.

21.5 Typologies of Political Parties

Classification of parties is based on a wide variety of criteria, and it is difficult to accommodate all parties in the world following a definitive classificatory framework. Basis of classification is always a heuristic device. According to Duverger, parties can be divided on the basis of structural-organizational setup. Depending on the party's behaviour and preferences, one can distinguish among policy-seeking, vote-seeking and office-seeking parties. Many a times, the typologies ignore the parties in the Third World and pack all of them within the prevailing classificatory schema. For instance, there is hardly any answer to the question on how one is supposed to categorize the Islamic parties which have come up recently in many Islamic countries? Nevertheless, literature on classification has divided parties into the following types.

21.5.1 Mass-based Party

The mass parties can be described in reference to a 'mass party age'. According to Sartori (2005), the mass parties have the following characteristics:

1. **Openness based on political achievements:** The appeal to the masses and opening up for the people with their achievement rather than ascription.
2. **The capacity for abstraction for stable identification:** The masses identify the party as an abstract image that outlives the concrete individual and leaders of the party. It binds people and leaders on its 'own logic of inertia'.
3. **Extensive organization to manage the masses:** The mass parties are 'organizational parties'. It has sizeable permanent and bureaucratic staffing and extensive organizational structure to manage people of various shades.
4. **A relatively large following:** The label mass party definitely involves a quantitative element in that it has thousands of followers. Mass party, as a concept, is closely tied to the 'psychology of mass man,' representing an uprooted and alienated individual in an industrialized society. These masses are susceptible to mass manipulation and mobilization. The crucial element lies in these parties establishing their foundation by appealing to the masses. Mass parties tend to downplay their ideology, placing greater emphasis on recruitment and organization. They attract not only influential figures and those representing special interests but also any citizen willing to join the party. Mass parties can acquire both direct and indirect memberships. Even if a party starts with a small following, it has the potential to evolve into a mass party (Sartori 2005).

According to Duverger, in the continental Europe, the socialist parties started organizing themselves on a mass basis. The under-classes became politically significant owing to the extension of suffrage by the end of the 19th century. The main aim of the socialist parties thus was to educate and organize the industrial labourers and wage earners to mobilize them for propaganda and bring about a qualitative change in the system. This was achieved through membership campaigns, where every member would pay a party fee. When the large number of members made the party a powerful organization and mobilizing machine, then the party gradually collected and managed its own funds and infused new ideas among the party members and different sections of the population. It definitely had a rigid organizational structure. The best example of mass party was German Democratic Socialist Party that had more than one million members by the year 1913 (Duverger 2016).

The workers' participation in strikes and other union activities gradually enabled them to become more disciplined, but managing workers at different levels favoured the development of a complex party organization and hierarchies within the party. The hierarchical party organization became an important source for development of certain oligarchic tendencies because people at different levels of hierarchy became influential. The socialist parties tried to control this tendency by trying to make the organization internally democratic: electing leaders from among the members. The local party groups present across different areas would conduct election to select a delegate to represent party members in the regional and national congress to decide party policies and debate about the national, as well as regional policies. Many non-socialist and cadre parties in Europe imitated this kind of party management and tried to organize themselves similarly. Where the Christian Democratic Parties became successful in imitating, many liberal parties did not succeed in setting up of a disciplined party organization along similar lines (Duverger 2016).

21.5.2 Cadre-based Parties

What distinguishes a mass and cadre party is the numbers versus selection procedure: 'what mass party secures by numbers, the cadre party achieves by selection' (Duverger, 1967, 78).

According to Koole, the following are the main characteristics of the cadre parties:

1. **predominance of professional leadership:** The cadre-based parties are basically dominated by the committed set of activists who work whole time for the party. The parties recruit them and make them permanent members who are highly accountable to the lower rung of party leaders and workers.
2. **Lower level of voting member's ratio:** In contrast to the mass-based party which has a high level of voter and member ratio, the cadre-based party has a low member/voter ratio. The members are important for mobilizing funds for meeting party expenditures, recruiting candidates for offices and different bodies to help the party to remain functional.
3. **Broad-ranging orientation to voters:** The cadre-based parties have a strong orientation to the voters. Their strategy is not to become a catch-all party nor are they interested in 'focusing classe gardee', that is, a specific social class.
4. **Vertical organization with internal democracy:** The cadre parties maintain the structure of the mass parties by retaining vertical organizational structure but it maintains a specific image of the party by making it internally democratic. It relies for financial resources on a combination of donations from the members and public (Koole 1994, cited in Wolinetz 2002, 5).

For Duverger, the growth of cadre parties in the Europe and America was reflective of the ideological conflict between the aristocracy and the bourgeoisie. In Europe, a violent conflict started between them. Both the classes developed their own ideology. Bourgeois ideology followed Lockean liberal principles of legal equality and accepted the 'inequities of circumstances' and reflected interest of bourgeoisie. However, the Conservative Party had a considerable impact on people because their ideology was based on religion. The Conservative Cadre Party was basically dominated by the clergy. In America, political parties were no different from the European counterparts except that they were less violent and had thin ideological appeal, nevertheless all political parties shared the same liberal ideology, irrespective of whether they were Federalists, Anti-Federalists or Republicans.

In terms of party structure, the parties were similar to that of the European cadre party dominated by local notables. The decentralized structures in America enabled a quasi-dictatorial system to develop at the local level that gradually spread into different parts of government. This process was the beginning of the original cadre party, according to Duverger. Subsequently, the nature of cadre parties changed. The new cadre parties like that of Labour Party recruited members who were highly 'political individuals' brought together because of their desire to change the power relation, through an affiliated body, such as, trade unions.

21.5.3 Revolutionary Parties

It may be difficult in theory to distinguish the Revolutionary Political party, mostly present in the Third World countries from that of the other aforementioned parties. Nevertheless, certain characteristics can be identified to distinguish it from the other parties.

These parties do not follow the constitutional path to come to power. They believe in underground and clandestine activities of a revolutionary nature. They rely on highly motivated cadres to mobilize and recruit the local population. They also have a hierarchical structure which is more centralized in organizing their party activities. The core committee in the party discusses what plans would be carried out. This is followed by the other subcommittees which are set up at different local units. They use clandestine plots to destabilize the government. Sometimes, they use disruptive activities to show the powerlessness of the government that helps to mobilize the masses and cadres. Their propaganda and campaign are conducted by well-organized ideological wings and writings. The resources are mobilized through contributions of local units present in both rural and urban areas. The revolutionary parties such as Communist Parties of Marxist and Leninist in India are examples.

21.5.4 Catch-all Parties

In the Western European countries, Germany in particular, there are palpable functional changes in the composition of parties, especially after the world wars. The following are the changes and concerns as stated by Otto Kirchheimer (1966): first, there was the waning of parliamentary democracy with simultaneous disappearance of 'principled opposition'; second, the beginning of dissociation of parties from their bases leading to management by professional politicians; third, 'professionalization of party organization' and the personalization of party–voter relationship started in a big scale and fourth, the practice of politics devoid of substance and depoliticization of masses. The political parties that came up during this time which manifested these changes within their organization were labelled as Catch-all Party (Krouwel 2003, 24).

Kirchheimer (1966) has provided the following characteristics of a Catch-all Party:

1. Parties do not carry much of 'ideological baggage'.
2. The strength of leadership is judged on the basis of how she/he contributes to the efficient functioning of the whole social system. They do not identify goals to be achieved for the organization.
3. There is the obscuring of the role of the individual party member.
4. Playing down of the role of 'the class-gardée', that is, a specific social class and recruiting voters from population across the territory.
5. Increasing access given to various interest groups for financial support during elections.

In short, Catch-all Parties are an opportunistic vote-seeking and a leader-centred party which is highly tied to the interest groups and lack ideological commitments and programmes.

21.5.5 Other Bases of Classifications

According to Gunter and Diamond, there are two problems involved in the aforementioned kind of classifications. The first involves what they call 'concept stretching', that is, there are problems of inappropriately labelling parties which have emerged recently and markedly depart from the characteristics of the aforementioned parties. For instance, it is difficult to label Green Party as a cadre-based or a mass-based party. The second problem that they site against the conventional classification is that of overpacking: adding a wide variety of parties into one fold (Gunther and Diamond 2003, 168). They provide three criteria for classification of parties across the world. They are 'formal organization', 'programmatic commitments' and the strategy that the parties adopts to promote values in society and control behaviour of party members.2 Accordingly, they have divided parties into 15 different 'species'. They have borrowed from biology and defined party organization as a 'genus' that encompasses several species of political parties. The five genera are *'Elite-Based Parties', 'Mass-Based Parties', 'Ethnicity-Based Parties', 'Electoralist-Parties' and 'Movement-Parties'* (Gunther and Diamond 2003, 173).

Gunther and Diamond though classified parties into 15 varieties, they have categorized the Islamist party within the fundamentalist party, which for Saleem (2014) is highly contentious. Saleem states that Islam is not a monolithic religion. The assertion is made that there is no singular entity termed 'Islam'; rather, there exist multiple 'Islams.' Similar to other major religions, Islam, too, 'defies a single interpretation.' According to this perspective, Islamic teachings possess a multivocal nature, open to diverse interpretations that can be employed for contrasting purposes. Additionally, the distinction between Islamist parties and others solely based on allegiance to Islam, Islamic principles, or Shariah is deemed challenging (Saleem, 2014, 1). The author questions the rationale behind defining political parties that fail to accommodate entities from Islamic countries, such as 'Salafis' or global Islamist groups like the Muslim Brotherhood, which transcend national boundaries within the Muslim world. This perspective challenges the oversimplification of categorizing political entities solely based on their allegiance to Islam, highlighting the complexity and diversity within the Islamic spectrum.

21.5.6 Islamist Party

The importance of Islamist party has increased in Muslim majority countries, especially after 9/11 attack in the United States and winning of election by the Muslim Brotherhood Party in Egypt and the subsequent development. Generally, the Islamist Party has been defined in terms of its belief in the Islam and the mode of its propagation to woe Muslims in its favour. The definitions do not construe the proper meaning of Shariah. Many have defined the so-called Islamist party as a party that believes in and propagates Islam as a solution to all Muslim's woes. However, these definitions ignore the differences among Muslims on what Shariah is. To understand Islamist Party, one has to take into account the differences between them and the 'Islamist' programmes. Thus, for example, one cannot discern among the Freedom Party, Justice Party and Al-Nour Party in Egypt without understanding their politics and what they stand for; though both are committed to Shariah and both are labelled as Islamists, their politics differ. There are as many Shariahs as there are many Islams (Saleem 2014, 2).

In Indonesia, there are four types of parties: 'nationalist-religious, secular-nationalist, pluralist-Islamic and Islamist parties'. Though the first two categories fit into Gunther and Diamond's typology, the latter, that is, pluralist-Islamist and Islamist parties do not fall into the typologies. The latter two are 'ideologically religious', but we cannot place them under the fundamentalist categories nor can they be placed within the movement and elite parties. According to Saleem (2004), the revised Gunther and Diamond Chart would add Islamist party to the movement party as well (pp. 5, 6).

21.6 Emerging Trends in Party System

21.6.1 National Party System or Local Party System

The first trend that we witness in the party systems in many matured democracies is that there is a tendency among the parties to become more nationalized. Many claim that, for an effective democracy, there has to be an efficient party system, that is, the party system should be able to respond to the needs of the electorates and deliver according to their requirement. Thus, for an efficient and stable party system, the role of electoral system, voting behaviour and orientation of voters are important factors. Party system size is a function of party aggregation, that is, 'the coordination of candidates or voters across electoral districts into national political parties' (Chibber and Kollman 1998, 330). Put simply, the capacity of the party to bring together competitors of different districts under a single party banner is called party aggregation. Where aggregation is poor, there is a proliferation of political parties, and where aggregation is high, there is a trend towards nationally oriented parties, that is, there is a national party system (Chibber and Kollman 1998, 2004).

This trend has been clearly brought out by Pradeep Chibber and Ken Kollman. They have attempted to explain why in the United States, two parties dominate the political landscape while in a similar situation—single-member, simple-plurality voting system for the lower house of the parliament—in countries like India, Canada and Great Britain, party systems vary. They argue that the answer lies in the nature of federalism that has an influence over the dynamics and stability of a party system (Chibber and Kollman 2004, 3).

For them, while a party system means 'an enduring pattern of electoral competition between parties for public office', a national party system is 'one in which the same parties compete at different levels of vote aggregation'. In practice, this means that party systems at the constituency level or at the state or provincial levels look similar to the national party systems (Chibber and Kollman 2004, 4). The party system is highly nationalized when the vote share of major parties do not vary across different provinces. In the case of the weak national party system, the vote share of national parties vary. Hence, the authors conclude that party systems at different levels—the constituency or state—show a similar trend to the national party system (Chibber and Kollman 2004, 4).

Recently, there has been bucking of trend of national party system in India where at the provincial level, the ruling party is being replaced by the regional parties. Many regional parties have come to power to challenge the national parties. At the provincial level, the national party has been forced to enter into coalition with the small parties.

21.6.2 Ethnicism or Regionalization of Party System

The studies that Chibber and Kollman have taken up constitute well-established democracies of the world. What about the party system in African countries?

In one of the interesting studies, Horowitz (1985) stresses on the ethnic party system in Africa. For him, ethnic party is a party that receives 85 per cent of its support from a single group.[3] Taking cue from him, many labelled the African party system as an ethnic party system (Norris and Mattes 2003). In a recent study, Matthias Basedau challenges this assumption and states that though 'ethnicity matters', recently, the impact of ethnicity on formation of party and party system has weakened considerably (Basedau and Stroh 2011, 1). For him, there has been a shift towards regional party formation in Africa where voters and parties work in tandem through personal networks around same geographically contiguous areas which 'allows leaders to exploit personal networks in their region of origin rather than the idea of shared ethnic identity' (Basedau and Stroh 2011, 13). He concludes that, in Africa, there is a tendency towards the regionalization party system in the 21st century.

21.6.3 Programmatic or Clientelistic Party System

In Latin America, in the later half of the 20th century, most countries have witnessed the transition to political democracy. According to Kitschelt et al. (2010), Latin America stands out as 'the most uniformly democratic region behind the established Western democracies. Because of prevalence of democracy in Latin America the focus of research has started to shift from political regime change to 'empirical quality" of democratic institutions and processes of authoritative decision making' (Kitschelt et al. 2010, 1–2). The earlier studies on parties focused on the relation of citizens and politicians on the basis of 'democratic accountability'. The studies highlighted the shallowness of the roots of parties and lack of alternative policy programmes based on social development and distributive justice especially during the globalization process. According to this formulation, Latin American parties generate 'at most relations of accountability around clientelistic-selective material inducements' (Kitschelt et al. 2010, 2). However, with the countries adopting liberalization process, the political system has changed from 'clientelist-selective system' to 'programmatic alternatives'. The authors argue that the party is structured around the linkage of 'programmatic coordination' as well as 'programmatic linkages'. Programmatic party system is indicative of the way the party develops procedures for formulation and implementation of coherent and alternative policies and deploys this as an instrument of attracting the masses to vote for it. The parties are arranged according to their preference to the policy and programmes, thus forming a programmatic party system.

21.7 Conclusion

The nature of the party and party systems are undergoing tremendous change in the neo-liberal era. The bases of the traditional parties are shifting, as there is movement of people across the world. The stable two-party systems are giving way to multiparty system in some established democracies because of transformed social and political situations. It remains to be seen what shape the party system would take once European Union witnesses the Brexit. In many postcolonial countries, different kinds of party systems are evolving. The party system is changing from regional to national, ethnic to regionalization, from clientelistic to programmatic.

There has been a major shift in the nature of representative form of government in established democracies recently. Some of the matured and established democratic countries, like the United States, Brazil and India, are witnessing 'Electoral Authoritarianism', where the party leaders are being elected by manipulating the established electoral practices and 'Illiberal Democracy', where the leaders after getting elected are suppressing minorities of all hues (Slater 2018). In this situation, it remains to be seen what would be the nature of the parties and party systems in matured, established and fledgling representative democracies across the world.

Keywords

Factions
Interest groups
Party
Party system
Social cleavages

Review Questions

1. What do you understand by the term party? Critically examine the different kinds of party systems.
2. Distinguish between party and party system. Discuss historical processes of formation of party and party system in the Western European countries.
3. What do you understand by a party system? Do you think that the multiparty system is better than the two-party system? Justify your answer with suitable examples.
4. Discuss different ways of classifying parties in the world.
5. Discuss the emerging trends in the party system in the contemporary world.

Appendix

Synoptic View of Party Systems in Some Matured and Postcolonial democracies

<table>
<tr><th colspan="2">Country/Form of Government</th></tr>
<tr><td>Britain/Prime Ministerial Form</td><td>Brief history of parties and party system:
Two-party system: From the late 17th century, the United kingdom has been a two-party system with Whigs and Tories being the two major parties. The two parties were replaced by Liberals and Conservatives after the Reform Act of 1832 was enacted. Subsequently, the Labour Party replaced the Liberal Party in 1906. The Conservative Party was formed from the erstwhile Tory party in 1894.
Support Base
Conservative Party: The Church of England and the Church of Scotland, older voters, women, geographically southern England and the Midland.
Labour Party: The main membership comes from trade unions, cooperatives and young socialist societies/groups.</td></tr>
<tr><td>The United States/Presidential Government; Two-party system</td><td>Brief history of parties and party system:
Two-party System: Republican Party and Democratic Party.
Date of Formation: Republican Party: 1854; and Democratic Party: 1790s.
Support Base
Republican Party: Higher socioeconomic strata, college educated, business houses and persons, professionals, protestants (especially Evangelicals) and recently in Mountain West.
Democratic Party: Self-identification by stating 'I am a Democrat'. African Americans, Catholics, Jews, lower social-economic classes, Hispanics, Asians, unions and north-eastern urban voters.</td></tr>
<tr><th colspan="2">Postcolonial States and party system</th></tr>
<tr><td>India/prime Ministerial: Multiparty system</td><td>Important parties
• The Indian National Congress (INC): 1885
• Communist Party of India (CPI): 1925
• Communist Party of India (Marxist) (CPI (M)): 1964
• The Bharatiya Janata Party (BJP): 1980
• Bahujan Samaj Party (BSP): 1984
• All India Trinamool Congress (AITC): 1998
• Nationalist Congress Party (NCP): 1999
Support Base
INC: Mainly a conglomeration of minorities including, Scheduled Caste, Scheduled Tribes, landless along with upper caste and upper and middle class people. Now, the base has changed drastically.
BJP: Mainly upper-caste religious majority living in urban areas, intermediate castes like Yadavs or other OBCs, urban youth, middle class and professionals and geographically the Hindi-speaking areas, western India, and recently, it has its presence in the eastern and north-eastern part of India.
CPI: Rural landless and middle peasants and landless and urban working class.
The CPM: Like CPI, it also draws its strength from the urban industrial working class, landless and middle peasants, intellectuals and university students.</td></tr>
</table>

	BSP: Mostly dalits of rural and urban areas of Hindi-speaking belt. NCP: Primarily commercial agricultural belt and urban areas of Maharashtra. It has also its presence in the northern India. AITC: Geographically spread over in rural and urban West Bengal. It also has its presence in north-eastern states of India and other neighbouring states.
Brazil/Presidential System: Multiparty System:	**Important Parties** Worker's Party (PT): 1979 Democratic Labour Party (PDT): 1980 Brazilian Social Democracy Party (PSDB): 1988 Party of the Brazilian Democratic Movement (PMDB): 1979 **Support Base** PT: Active unions, peasant movement Catholics, and non-fundamentalist Protestant Churches, students, workers, intellectuals and white collar employees. Geographically, it is strong in industrial hub around São Paulo. PDT: Basically, the association of the members of black movement, labour women associations and its members, the labour syndicates and socialist youths. Geographically, it is centred around Rio Grande de Sul and Rio de Janeiro. PSDB: Essentially, middle class, left leaning but non-radical academics and intellectuals. PMDB: Apart from having some support in the most-developed regions, recently, the party is strong in the interior and less-developed regions and rural membership.

Notes

1. The seven sets of actors symbolically put are N, C, R, D, L, U, and P where N stands for nation builders, C stands for ecclesiastical body, R for Roman Curia and the Pope, D stands for dissidents to C and R, L stands for the landowners, U stands for the urban commercial and industrial entrepreneurs and P stands for the Periphery where a movement of protest against 'Central National Control' starts.
2. The party norms include tolerance towards opposition, respecting plural and other democratic values. Sometimes, parties also inculcate 'proto-hegemonic' values among their cadres. They are intolerant to democratic rules and values and established institutions and attempt to change them in favour of the authoritarian regime. The tampering with the system is aimed at achieving 'their programmatic objectives' (Gunther and Diamond 2003, 171).
3. Horowitz defines, 'Ethnicity is based on a myth of collective ancestry, which is usually carries with it traits believed to be innate. Some notion of ascription, however diluted, and affinity deriving from it are inseparable from the concept of ethnicity' (Horowitz 1985, 52).

References

Basedau, Matthias, and Alexander Stroh. 2011. How Ethnic Are African Parties Really? Evidence from Four Francophone Countries. *International Political Science Review* 33(1): 5–24.

Burke, Edmund. 1948. Thoughts on the Cause of the Present Discontent, in *Prose of Edmund Burke*, edited by Sir Philip Magnus. Accessed 15 August 2018. https://www.ourcivilisation.com/smartboard/shop/burkee/extracts/chap2.htm

Chibber, Pradeep, and Ken Kollman. 1998. Party Aggregation and the Number of Parties in India and the United States. *American Political Science Review* 92(2): 329–42.

———. 2004. *The Formation of National Party System: Federalism and Party Competition in Canada, Great Britain, India, and the United States*, Princeton and Oxford: Princeton University Press.

Disch, Lisa Jane. 2007. *The Tyranny of the Two Party System*. New York: Coulumbia University Press.

Downs, Anthony. 1957. *An Economic Theory of Democracy*. New York: Harper.

Duverger, Maurice. 1963. *Political Parties: Their Organization and Activity in the Modern State*. London: Methuen.

———. 1967. *The concept of Membership in Jean Blondel edited Comparative Politics: A Reader*. UK: MacMillan Education (pp. 77–85).

———. 2016. *Political Party, Encyclopaedia of Britanica*. Accessed from https://www.britannica.com on 25 November 2017.

Epstein, Leon D. 2000. *Political Parties in Western Democracies*. New Brunswick and London: Transaction Publishers.

Fairfield, Roy P. (Ed.). 1981. *The Federalist Papers*. Accessed from http://www.houseofrussell.com on November 6, 2018.

Greene, Kenneth F. 2007. *Why Dominant Parties Lose—Mexico's Democratization in Comparative Perspective*. Paperback Edition. New York: Cambridge University Press.

Gunther, Richard, and Larry Diamond. 2003. Species of Political Parties: A New Typology. *Party Politics* 9(2): 167–99.

Gunther, Richard, Jose Ramon Montero, and Juan J. Linz. 2002. *Political Parties and: Old Concepts and New Challenges*. Oxford: Oxford University Press.

Haren, Sebastian. 2010. Explaining One-Party Dominance: The Case of Liberal Democratic Party of Japan, 4. Accessed from http://lup.lub.lu.se on November 18, 2017.

Heywood, Andrew. 2013. *Politics*. New York: Palgrave MacMillan.

Hicks, John D. 1933. The Third Party Tradition in American Politics. *Mississippi Valley Historical Review* 20(1): 3–28.

Holler, Manfred J. (Ed.). 1987. *The Logic of Multi-Party Systems*. Dordrecht, Boston: Kluwer Academic Publisher.

Horowitz, Donald L. 1985. *Ethnic Groups in Conflict*. Berkeley, CA: University of California Press.

Katz, R. S., and Peter Mair. 1995. *Changing Models of Party Organizations and Party Democracy: The Emergence of the Cartel Party, Party Politics* 1 (5): 28.

Kirchheimer, Otto. 1966. The Transformation of the Western European Party Systems, in *Political Parties and Political Development*, edited by Joseph La Palombara and Myron Weiner. Princeton, NJ: Princeton University Press.

Kitschelt, Herbert, Kirk A. Hawkins, Juan Pablo Luna, Guillermo Rosas, and Elizabeth J. Zechmeister. 2010. *Latin American Party Systems*. Cambridge: Cambridge University Press.

Koole, Ruud. 1994. The Vulnerability of the Modern Cadre Party in the Netherlands, in *How Parties Organize: Change and Adaptation in Party Organization in Western Democracies*, edited by Richard S. Katz and Peter Mair. London, Thousand Oaks, CA: SAGE.

Krouwel, Andre. 2003. Otto Kirchheimer and the Catch-All-Party. *West European Politics* 26(2): 23–40. Accessed from https://www.researchgate.net on October 16, 2017.

Lipset, Seymour P., and Stein Rokkan. 1967. Cleavages Structures, Party Systems, and Voter Alignments: An Introduction, in *Party Systems and Voter Alignments: Cross-National Perspective*, edited by Seymour P. Lipset and Stein Rokkan, 1–64. New York: Free Press.

Maor, Moshe. 1992. Intraparty Conflict and Coalitional Behavior in Denmark and Norway: The Case of 'Highly institutionalized' Parties. *Scandinavian Political Studies* 15(2): 99–116.

———. 1997. *Political Parties and Party Systems: Comparative Approaches and the British Experience*. London, New York: Routledge.

Norris, Pippa, and Robert Mattes. 2003. Does Ethnicity Determine Support for the Governing Party? The Structural and Attitudinal Basis of Partisan Identification in 12 African Nation. Accessed from https://sites.hks.harvard.edu on November 11, 2018.

Pempel, T. J. (Ed.). 1990. *Uncommon Democracies: The One-Party Dominant Regimes*. New York: Cornell University Press.

Riker, William H., and Peter C. Ordeshook. 1968. A Theory of the Calculus of Voting. *The American Political Science Review* 62(1): 25–42.

Saleem, Raja M. Ali. 2014. Identifying Islamist Parties Using Gunther and Diamon's Typology. *Sage Open* (July–September): 1–8. doi: 10.1177/2158244014544288

———. 2005. Party Types, Organisation and Functions. *West European Politics* 28: 5–32.

Sartori, G. (1976). Parties and Party Systems: A Framework for Analysis, Volume 1, London: Cambridge University Press.

Slater, Dan. 2018. After Democracy: What Happens When Freedom Erodes? Foreign Affairs. Accessed from https://www.foreignaffairs.com on November 12, 2018.

Strom, Kaare. 1990. A Behavioral Theory of Competitive Political Parties. *American Journal of Political Science* 34(2): 565–98.

Wolinetz, Steven B. 2002. Beyond the Catch-all-party: Approaches to the Study of Parties and Party Organisation in Contemporary Democracies. Accessed from http://www.olemiss.edu on November 12, 2018.

CHAPTER 22

Brazil: Tracing the Constitutional Development and Political Economy

Tripta Sharma

Reader's Guide

Brazil is generally associated with its rich natural and cultural capital. While Amazon has attracted peoples' imagination ranging from natural beauty, mythology to contemporary literature, carnivals, samba and soccer are equally incredibly popular in the world. However, to students of comparative politics, Brazil presents a different set of issues and concerns. This chapter, in the context of comparative political analysis, seeks to provide an analysis by highlighting some general trends of Brazilian politics and economy. It attempts to underline important events of Brazil's history which have shaped Brazil's present polity and economics. The chapter begins by discussing the process of colonization, fall of Portuguese empire and the most important event in Brazil's history—the 1930 revolution. Then, it discusses populist and bureaucratic authoritarianism after which Brazil transited to democracy and continued its journey to become one of the world's largest economies. It then describes the process of constitutional development and political economy of the country along with its rich tradition of social movements, an important feature of Brazilian social and political scenarios. It is followed by a discussion on challenges the country is facing with kinds of solutions it is providing. Thus, the chapter seeks to provide an anatomy of the politics of a rising power—Brazil.

22.1 Introduction

The largest and most populous country in South America, Brazil gained its independence in 1822 after three centuries of Portuguese rule. Initially, after independence, it followed a monarchical system of government until 1889. After that, with a proclamation by the military, it became a republic. The coffee exporters of Brazil politically dominated the country until Getulio Vargas' rise to power in 1930. Subsequently, for almost half a century, Brazil had populist and military governments till 1985. Since 1985, Brazil has been under a democratic rule and is seen as one of the world's strongest emerging economies.

Brazil

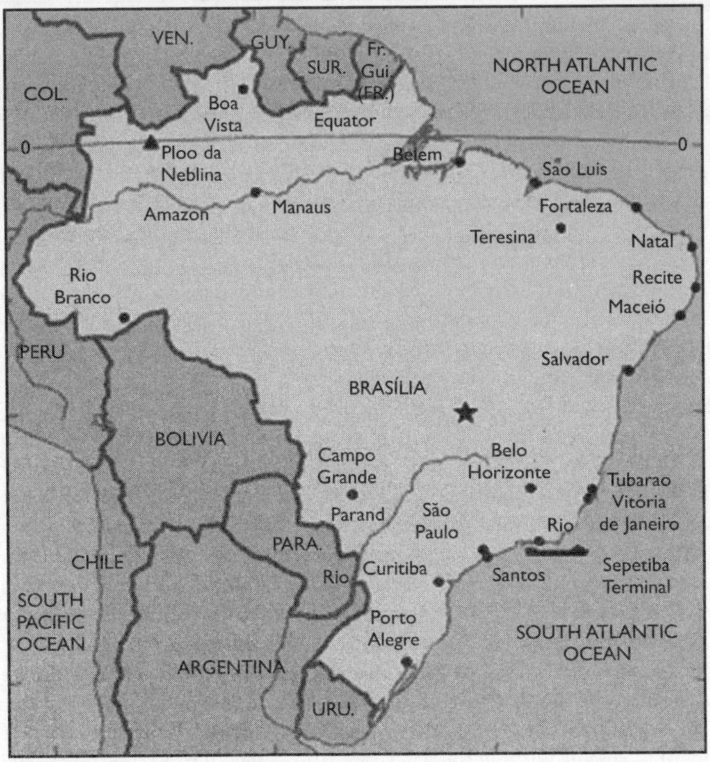

Disclaimer: This figure is not to scale. It does not represent any authentic national or international boundaries and is used for illustrative purposes only.

Key Facts

Capital	Brasilia
Area	8,515,770 sq. km
Population	208,846,892 (July 2018 est.)
Official Language	Portuguese
Major Religion	Roman Catholic (64.6%); Protestants (22.2%)
GDP (Purchasing Power Parity)	$ 3.248 Trillion (2017 est.)
GDP Real Growth Rate	1% (2017 est.)
HDI Ranking	79
Political System	Federal Republic; Presidential System

Sources: CIA, World Fact Book (2018) and UNDP (2018).

The following sections of the chapter describe the country's journey from a colony to military regime to finally democracy.

22.2 Colonization

The Treaty of Tordesillas of 1494 (a treaty dividing newly found lands between Spain and Portugal) gave Portugal only a land strip along the west coast of today's Brazil to be able to access the American continent. According to the treaty, the huge land mass of today's Brazil belonged to Spain; yet, Portuguese exploration in Brazil went largely unresisted, as much of the territory apart from the Amazons was unexplored and scarcely populated. From Portugal, the first time a fleet of 13 Portuguese ships that accidently reached Brazil on 22 April 1500, under the command of Pedro Álvares Cabral, was supposedly headed for India. This arrival was the first step towards European settlement in present-day Brazil. Álvares left some of his men in Brazil to express dominion of Portugal over the territory. This first arrival gave birth to the 'pau-brasil' (Brazil wood) trade. Since the Portugal explorers were introduced to Brazil wood dye at a time of growing interest in textiles and dyes in Europe, harvesting Brazil wood proved to be a lucrative enterprise. In this entire process, the indigenous people became victims of the Brazil wood trade, as they were used as workers for they knew the forest. After a few years, this trade gained pace, and Portuguese royalty established its 'monopoly to prevent the factors, as Brazilian merchants were called, from developing too much independence and stepping outside the boundaries of the colonial taxing and revenue collection system' (Meade 2010).

Machado and Figueiroa (2001) divided the Brazilian economic history of three centuries (16th–19th) into seven major cycles of production and trade, starting from trade of Brazil wood, sugar, gold, diamond, coffee and rubber. The first European settlement in Brazil was founded in 1532, and effective colonization began very shortly after the first settlement. In 1534, King John III divided Brazilian territory into 15 private and autonomous captaincies (the Portuguese system of dividing land into noblemen). However, the decentralized character of captaincies proved to be difficult to organize administratively; hence; in 1549, the Portuguese king restructured them into a more centralized system under the Governorate General of Brazil (Meade 2010, 4–42).

By the middle of the 16th century, sugarcane became Brazil's most important resource for export. Due to increased demand of Brazilian cane in the international market, Portugal had to step in the slave trade with Sub-Saharan Africa to meet up the demand of labour in crop production. It is said that Brazil could have not been able to meet the international demands of sugarcane without the slave population of western Africa (Boxer 1962). It has been estimated that more than 30,000 Africans were imported to Brazil during the 16th century. More than half a million slaves came during the 17th century. Over a period of about 350 years, an estimated 3–4 million African slaves were bought to the country (Greenbaum 2003). Due to such large slave population, Brazil could produce quantity of sugarcane that would serve as the sole contributing factor in Brazilian economy for a period exceeding 150 years. Actually, in the middle of the 17th century, Brazil was the world's largest sugarcane producer. More or less simultaneously, cattle grazing also became an important economic factor in Brazil (Machado and Figueiroa 2001).

However, by the end of 17th century, sugarcane export declined heavily, and Portuguese turned to gold mining. In the early 1690s, gold was discovered by Bandeirantes (17th-century settlers and fortune hunters in Brazil) after which gold trade picked up so rapidly that it soon became the backbone of the economy leading to a phenomenon called Brazilian Gold Rush (Boxer, 1962, 22–30). During this time, Brazil was contributing to 50 per cent of the world's gold and diamond, promoting the prosperity and luxury of the Portuguese crown (Machado and Figueiroa 2001).

Both Boxer and Meade describe how the history of Brazilian colonization, as elsewhere, is the history of exploitation of people and resources. While Meade gives us a detailed account of exploitation of indigenous people, Boxer focuses more on 17th- and 18th-century Brazil and underlines the fact that without ample supply of slaves from West Africa, Portugal would be unable to maintain a colony like Brazil. In each economic cycle of Brazilian colonial history, exploitation of indigenous people or slaves or both is evident.

On one hand, Brazil, because of its resources, was attracting other colonial powers, and on the other hand, many resistances for autonomy by the settlers and also from slaves in many regions of Brazil had started. These resistances raised their voice against the Portuguese administration. The colonial rule had to address both the concerns in order to uphold its monopoly in Brazil. However, the resistance movements were not a sign of a 'national consciousness'; they were an administrative concern that had to be dealt with (Pimenta 2016). Amid this, in 1808, Napoleon Bonaparte invaded Spain and Portugal, following which Prince Regent Joao, the Portuguese king, moved the royal court from Lisbon to Brazil. In 1814, the courts of Europe demanded that the Portuguese royal court be shifted back to Portugal, as it is not fit for an ancient European monarchy to stay out of its own kingdom. Prince Regent Joao then decided to upgrade Brazil's status from colony to a part of kingdom and named it as the United Kingdom of Portugal, Brazil and the Algarves (Meade 2010, 69).

While many resistances were picking up pace, for people wanted some qualitative changes in their lives, a section of Portuguese leadership kept emphasizing on moving back to Lisbon and keeping Brazil a colony of Portugal. It created severe tension between Portuguese Cortes and resisting populations. Prince Pedro I, the son of Prince Regent Joao, sided with Brazilians in this conflict and declared Brazil free from the Portuguese empire on 7 September 1822 and took the new title of emperor of Brazil. Thus, Pedro I became the first emperor of Brazil. The constitution for Brazil was drafted 2 years later in which the monarch would act as a moderating power among different interest groups. The emperor was endowed with the job of managing executive, legislative and judicial branches of state along with the class of landed elite (Montero 2007, 419). Brazil's first constitution was modelled upon the French Constitution of 1814. It introduced a centralized unitary system of government with hereditary monarchy. The central government was divided into four powers: legislative, executive, judicial and moderating with the emperor exercising both executive and moderating power (Encyclopedia.net). This constitution continued until the fall of the empire in 1889 (Table 22.1).

Table 22.1 Head of the States in Brazil (Civilian and Military)

Name	Period	Party
Deodoro da Fonseca	February 1891–November 1891 (military regime)	NA
Floriano Peixoto	1891–94 (military regime)	NA
Prudente de Morais	1894–98	Federal Republic Party
Campos Sales	1898–1902	Sao Paulo Republican Party
Rodrigues Alves	1902–1906	Sao Paulo Republican Party
Afonso Pena	1906–1909	Mineiro Republican Party
Nilo Pecanha	1909–1910	Rio Republican Party
Hermes da Fonseca	1910–14	Conservative Republican Party
Venceslau Bras	1914–18	Mineiro Republican Party
Delfim Moreira	January 1919–July 1919	Mineiro Republican Party
Epitacio Pessoa	July 1919–November 1922	Mineiro Republican Party
Artur Bernardes	1922–26	Mineiro Republican Party
Washington Luis	1926–30	Sao Paulo Republican Party
Julio Prestes	Never took office	Sao Paulo Republican Party
Military Junta	October 1930–November 1930	NA
Getulio Vagas	1934–45 (from 1930 to 1934, Vargas was the provisional head of the state)	Liberal Alliance

Name	Period	Party
Jose Linhares	1945–46	None. As the president of the Supreme Court, he was in line of succession
Gaspar Dutra	1946–51	Social Democratic Party
Getulio Vargas	1951–54	Brazilian Labour Party
Café Filho	September 1954–January 1956	Social Progressive Party
Carlos Luz	8 November 1955–11 November 1955 (the time during which Café Filho declared himself unable to preside over the post of president due to his illness)	Social Democratic Party
Neeru Ramos	11 November 1955–30 January 1956 (the time during which Café Filho declared himself unable to preside over the post of president due to his illness)	Social Democratic Party
Juscelino Kubitschek	1956–61	Social Democratic Party
Janio Quadros	January 1961–August 1961	National Labour Party
Ranieri Mazzilli	August 1961–September 1961	Social Democratic Party
Joao Goulart	1961–64	Brazilian Labour Party
Ranieri Mazzilli	2 April 1964–14 April 1964	Social Democratic Party
Humberto Castelo Branco	1964–67 (military regime)	National Renewal Alliance
Artur da Costa e Silva	1967–69 (military regime)	National Renewal Alliance
Military Junta	August 1969–October 1969 (military regime)	NA
Emilio Medici	1969–74 (military regime)	National Renewal Alliance
Ernesto Geisel	1974–79 (military regime)	National Renewal Alliance
Joao Figueiredo	1979–85 (military regime)	Democratic Social Party
Tancredo Neves	Died before taking office	Brazilian Democratic Movement Party
Jose Sarney	1985–90	Brazilian Democratic Movement Party
Fernando Collor de Mello	1990–92	Party of the National Reconstruction
Itamar Franco	1992–94	Brazilian Democratic Movement party
Fernando Henrique Cardos	1995–2002	Brazilian Social Democracy Party
Luis Inacio Lula da Silva	2003–2010	Workers' Party
Dilma Rousseff	2011–16	Workers' Party
Michel Temer	2016–18	Brazilian Democratic Movement Party

22.3 Post-empire Developments

22.3.1 Fall of empire and Beginning of Old Republic

The year 1889 was a critical juncture in Brazil's history marking peaceful demise of the empire. Exile of the King Dom Pedro II, the son of Pedro I, and emergence of a republic rule began the era of dominance of land-owning oligarchy in Brazilian politics. This was again a shift from centralized to decentralized authority. What is interesting to note here is that the republican regime was brought through a military coup (Montero 2007, 420). The year 1889 also succeeded another very important historical event in Brazil as it, following the British anti-slavery law, abolished slavery as an institution in Brazil. The anti-slavery law came as the consequence of turn in the Brazilian economy. After 1830, focus of business in Brazil was shifted from sugarcane plantation to coffee production which did not require heavy labour or large work force. The anti-slavery law was passed in May 1888.

The 'old republic', from 1889 to 1930, as it is popularly known, consolidated the political rise of coffee oligarchy in the state. Coffee oligarchy went one step further to establish liberal republican values. For instance, the 1891 constitution provided for direct elections, franchise was expanded to all literate males and secularism became a foundational principle of governance. Policymaking was still in the hands of a few elites, but now these elites were not chosen on hereditary basis. Power in the old republic was rather decentralized. States got much greater authority regarding policy formulation and taxation system and were also free to maintain their own military. The basis for rule was more constitutional, and a legitimate rule of law was established in Brazil. However, the larger operation of state by and large relied on patrimonialism. Also, contrary to the established rule of law, the landed oligarchy in rural Brazil vigorously suppressed any dissent to manipulate local political activities. Hence, local politics became de facto focal point of state manifesting itself in 'Politics of Governors' who were empowered elites of caffe and latte regimes. The following three states were the key players during the old republic: Sau Paulo (coffee), Minas Gerais (coffee and ranching) and Granda do Sul (ranching). The presidency alternated so frequently among these regions that this period of Brazilian history is known as the rule of café com leite (coffee with milk), reflecting the predominance of Sau Paulo and Minas Gerais (Montero 2007, 420–21). The old republic continued till the Revolution of 1930.

22.3.2 The Revolution of 1930

The early republic of Brazil was filled with instabilities. At the international level, Brazil got involved in the First World War. Also, at the domestic front, regional rivalries were springing up followed by severe economic crisis due to the Great Depression. Political arena of Brazil was going through a lot of upheavals making its way again towards another centralized system and then to military regime. In 1930, Vargas had lost the elections but took advantage of the instability in Brazil and overthrew the government with the help of military to become the provisional president of the county (Greenbaum 2003).

Vargas' victory had been the work of a complex coalition. This coalition consisted regional rivalries; establishment of strong opposition party—Democratic Party (Partido Democratico); rebellion of tenants against both military and civilian governments; angry coffee growers who did not get compensation for their loss due to Great Depression; all these were among the reasons leading to Vargas' victory. 'He observes a heterogeneous coalition was obviously unstable, with potential strains that were bound to appear as soon as the provisional government started to make decisions' (Skidmore 1999, 108). However, Skidmore noticed that lives of common Brazilians were more affected by the Great Crash than the change of government at the centre level in Brazil. 'Nor had the revolution of 1930 brought any major change in property relations or working conditions, despite the creation of a federal Ministry of Labour, Industry and Commerce in 1930. Brazil was still a country where landowners, merchants, industrialists, and bankers controlled power. The source of most wealth was still rural and there was still no talk of serious land reform' (ibid.).

The Great Depression cost Brazilians their jobs and businesses and pushed the country towards despair. Vargas took this opportunity to take full control of the political system in his hands. In 1937, he dissolved the Congress and imposed an emergency regime. Policymaking powers got concentrated in Vargas' hands (Greenbaum 2003). Role of state shifted from being an arbiter to the sole determining factor where people get a limited and controlled exposure to political processes. Within the next 8 years, Vargas became an uncontested figure in Brazil and was known as Pai Do Povo (father of the people). During this time, state corporatism approach was consolidated through labour codes and establishment of public firms for producing strategic commodities like steel and oil. The period of 1937–1945 was called Estado Novo (New State) in which Vargas became the primary agent of the state. Policies in this period were influenced both by the United States as much they were influenced by fascist Italy or Nazi Germany (Montero 2007, 421).

22.3.3 Populist Republic

The results of the Second World War, and mounting resistance of both working and middle classes as well as US diplomatic pressures, forced Vargas to hold democratic elections. Elections were held in December 1945 with three political parties—Social Democratic Party (PSD), Brazilian Labour Party (PTB) and National Democratic Union (UDN). While the PSD and PTB were pro-Vargas and were more or less created by the state itself, UDN was alliance of various regional forces dedicated to liberal constitutionalism. Vargas at this time resigned from president's post due to mounting military pressure, and in 1946, Brazil returned to democracy. The new democratic regime, however, guaranteed some fundamental democratic practices, that is, periodic elections, etc., yet most important economic and social policies were still to be decided by the state bureaucracy rather than by elected representatives of the national legislature.

In the next election of 1950, Vargas returned to power as elected president. He promised people a widespread social insurance system which brought him a lot of workers' support. However, this time, Vargas could not prove himself an undisputed leader. He faced accusation of attempted assassination of his adversary and very popular Brazilian journalist. This raised unrest among people as well as the state machinery against Vargas following which Vargas committed suicide in August 1954. For the next 10 years, Brazil faced various interim governments till another military coup took place in 1964. The period from 1964 to 1985 in Brazil was a period of Bureaucratic Authoritarianism (ibid.).

22.3.4 Bureaucratic authoritarianism

As happens with claims of all military regimes, the military regime of Brazil too was intended to be transitory but through 1968 Act—Fifth Institutional Act—military secured a long-term intervention in government's day-to-day functions. Many scholars suggest that the military regime in Brazil, despite all its brutalities, was very popular, as economically Brazil was performing very well. Brazilian economic boom was also known as 'economic miracle'.

Special Insights

Bureaucratic Authoritarianism

World over and especially in Latin America, the 20th-century military regimes, including Brazil, Mexico, Chile, Peru, etc., emerged in the backdrop of rising dilemmas of development. Military regime thus came in picture by portraying itself as 'protector' of constitutional order and as an institution that could achieve set development goals. This phenomenon led scholars to redefine military regimes as 'bureaucratic authoritarianism' and also, as Collier (2001) suggests, a complete political system rather than just a regime type.

The economic miracle, however, did not sustain for long, and military succumbed to pressures of economic crisis on one hand and mounting civilian opposition on the other hand. In 1979, Amnesty law (a law allowing exiled politicians, trade unionists and other activists to return) was brought resulting into slow return to democracy in 1985 with democratically elected president Jose Sarney. Initial civilian governments faced many problems, as it was hard to deal with economic instabilities they inherited from earlier military regimes. Despite this, the governments have been shifting hands within various parties. Elections are regularly held since 1985, and people are allowed to express themselves. This is evident in the numerous protests people staged against their governments. The democratic system in Brazil is continuing and maturing; however, they are facing problems on many political and economic fronts.

22.4 Constitutional Development in Post-independence Brazil

22.4.1 From decentralization to Centralization (1824–1937)

Brazil got independence on 7 September 1822 and commenced its first constitution in 1824. This constitution gave enormous powers to the emperor, including control over legislature and provincial governments. The 1824 constitution lasted till 1889 when Pedro II was overthrown to establish a republic. Thereafter, the first republican constitution was established in 1891. This document was highly influenced by the US constitution providing for a presidential system and voting rights to males. It also provided a bicameral system and a system of checks and balances for a smooth functioning of republican government. Post 1930 revolution, Vargas' government created a new constitution in 1934. After few years, Vargas faced a counter revolution leading Vargas to lead a counter coup in 1937. The 1937 Vargas regime came up with a new authoritarian constitution. It centralized all legislative and executive powers of the president and established the president as the supreme authority. During this regime, Congress was shut down and political parties were dissolved. The president had the power of appointing governors who could further appoint mayors completing the line of command and execution of orders. Individual rights were suspended. The 1937 constitution allowed Vargas to claim a dictatorship that Vargas call 'Estado Novo', the New State. Vargas enjoyed this dictatorial powers for almost a decade.

22.4.2 1946 Constitution: A Step Towards Federalism

The next Constitution in Brazil came in 1946 following the overthrow of Vargas' government and replacing the 'Estado Novo' constitution. Through this constitution, a representative government was established that appointed a constituent assembly to draft a more balanced and liberal constitution. The constitution was heavily influenced from the US constitution especially with regard to federalism. Along with individual's rights, this constitution, however, also established active role of state in economic policy formation and implementation. The president, though, still could enjoy a lot of power, but this time, executive head's powers were not as unlimited as they were in the previous Estado Novo constitution (constitution.net 2016).

22.4.3 Military Regime, Constitution and authoritarianism

After Vargas' death in 1954, Brazil faced many ups and downs. The autocratic regime substantially changed constitution through Institutional Acts. In 1967, the constitution was changed and then it was changed again in 1969. In both the constitutions, power was centralized in the executive (in the president in particular) as the constitution aimed at institutionalization of military regime. Term of the president was increased from 4 to 5 years. The president was given more powers with regard to decree laws for creating laws related to taxation, creation of public employment, determination of civil servants' salaries, etc. Institutionalized acts were also used by military bodies to remove opposition leaders from Congress. When the economic growth slowed down and military regimes faced many protests and resistances, military felt the pressure to return to democracy. The transition to democracy started in 1974. The first important measure was the organization of free Congressional elections. In 1982, military allowed direct elections for state governors and gradually increased federal transfers of municipal governments (ibid.).

Following the small steps for advancement of democracy, in 1985, the government established National Constituent Assembly to draft a new constitution. The 559-member assembly, with public hearings and deliberations, drafted the 1988 'Citizens Constitution'. On the principles of federalism, the document provided that every state should rewrite its constitution. Further, each municipality should elaborate its own organic laws.

22.4.4 1988 Constitution: Era of Redemocratization

It is important to understand the 1988 constitution, as it launched democratic regime for the longest time, which is still being followed with various amendments. This constitution declared Brazil a presidential federal republic with 26 states and 1 federal district. Also, with the constitutional amendment of 1996, Brazil incorporated municipalities as part of its federal structure. The following paragraphs show the detailed features of the constitution of 1988.

In the executive branch, president is directly elected and heads both state and the government. Through the 1997 amendment of the constitution, the term of president, which was earlier limited to two terms, was extended to any number of contesting elections. However, the amendment provided that the president cannot serve for more than two consecutive terms. The president in the new constitution was authorized to appoint ministers of state, military officers and judges, though the appointments now, unlike an authoritarian regime, must be approved by the senate.

With the 1988 constitution, legislative branch became bicameral consisting of chambers of deputies and senate. The Chamber of Deputies consists of 513 federal deputies—three members from each state and one federal district are to be elected for an 8-year term. In the senate, 81 senators are elected through proportional representation to serve a term of 4 years.

The federal judiciary of Brazil contains one federal court and the superior court of justice. Apart from this, the federal judiciary has regional federal courts, labour courts, electoral courts and military courts. The highest court, the Supreme Federal Court, contains 11 judges appointed by the president after due approval of the Senate.

22.5 Organization of Brazilian State

The Brazilian state since colonial times has been going through the phases of centralization and decentralization. It has affected creation and institution of postcolonial Brazil as well. Centralization of state authority, for instance, can be traced back to colonial times. Paradoxically, decentralization can be similarly traced back to colonial rule. Even in the 1988 constitution, contradiction remained as the president remained the authority to legislate on social and economic matters undermining democratic credentials of a democratic system. However, the 1988 constitution provided for a democratic system.

The constitution provided for compulsory voting for literate citizens between the age of 18 and 69 years. Citizens of 16, 17 and above 69 years of age who are illiterate can choose whether to vote or not. Brazil at present has 27 states and more than 550 municipalities. Each municipality is run by a mayor. The country has opted for different electoral systems for different layers of governance. The president, state governors and mayors of cities are elected through direct elections. States with less than two lakh voters elect for the afore- mentioned positions by a simple 'first past the post' system but states having more than two lakhs voters require more than 50 per cent votes for a candidate to win. In case no candidate acquires 50 per cent and above votes, a runoff election is held between the top two contestants. Federal and state deputies and local councillors are elected by another system, open list proportional representation. This proportional system has a unique feature of the 'open list'. It means that the voters, and not the political parties, have the power of setting preferences of candidates through votes. Usually, the preference setting is the discretion of the party; however, in Brazil, it is the other way round. Adding to this, if a party drops a candidate out of the list, the candidate possesses the right to nominate him- self or herself in party's ballot or through another party's ballot list. This right to candidate is called *candidato nato* (birth right candidate) (Hagopian 2001, 548).

22.5.1 executive

The democratic republican system of Brazil grants significant power to the president. The president has a very strong hold on the executive and appoints the cabinet and judges of the Supreme Court; however after 1988 constitution, it is done with the approval of the Senate. The president is also the commander-in-chief of the armed forces. President has the powers to appoint or dismiss ministers, managing the higher level of federal administration; president possesses complete or partial veto powers on bills. The president has the power of appointing judges, governors, prosecutor general, director of the central bank and many other powers flowing from the aforementioned function.

22.5.2 legislature

The legislative branch of Brazil, the national congress, is constituted of the federal senate. It has 81 members elected through a system of proportional representation for a 4-year term. The second part of the legislative branch is Chamber of Deputies having 513 members directly elected for an 8-year term. The national congress of Brazil is bicameral with federal senate as the upper house and Chamber of Deputies as the lower house. The Congress has its annual meeting from 2 February to 27 July and from 1 August to 22 December. The Senate is constituted of three representatives directly elected for an 8-year term. Every three years, one-third or two-thirds of the senate gets renewed.

The Lower house, known as Chamber of Deputies, represents people of each state on the basis of proportional representation. Lower house members' strength is decided on the basis of state's population. The seats in Chamber of Deputies vary from a minimum of 8 to maximum of 70 seats. Members of this house are elected for a term of 4 years.

The president of the Upper House is the ex-officio president of the National Congress and, thereby, authorized to preside over joint sessions of Congress.

22.5.3 Judiciary

Brazilian judicial system works at three levels—courts of 1st instance, 2nd instance and 3rd instance (Figure 22.1). All these levels are present in both legal and special courts, the two types of courts dealing different types of cases. Courts of first instance are divided into two parts—courts of state and federal state. State courts are to be supervised by Courts of Justice, the courts of 2nd instance. While 1st instance courts at federal level come under Federal Regional Courts. Both 2nd instance courts, namely Courts of Justice and Federal Regional Courts, are supervised by the 3rd instance court known as Superior Court of Justice.

Similar hierarchy can be seen in special courts as well. Military courts have state military court as 1st instance court that comes under State Military Court of Justice at the second instance level, while the military first instance court is supervised by the third instance of military court. However, the first level of electoral and labour courts do have 2nd instance level in the form of Regional Electoral Court and Regional Labour Court which have 3rd instance level as Superior Electoral Court and Superior Court of Labour. The intra-constitutional and jurisprudence appeals can be made to Supreme Federal Court from 2nd instance courts. Constitutional appeals, however, in case of legal courts can be made from 2nd instance to Superior Court of Justice. All the instances of appeal in both legal and special courts are bound by the singular command of the Supreme Federal Court.

The Supreme Federal Court is the highest court of appeal and the constitutional court in the Brazilian judiciary. As guardian of the constitution, Supreme Court has the power to analyse the constitutionality of federal and state laws.

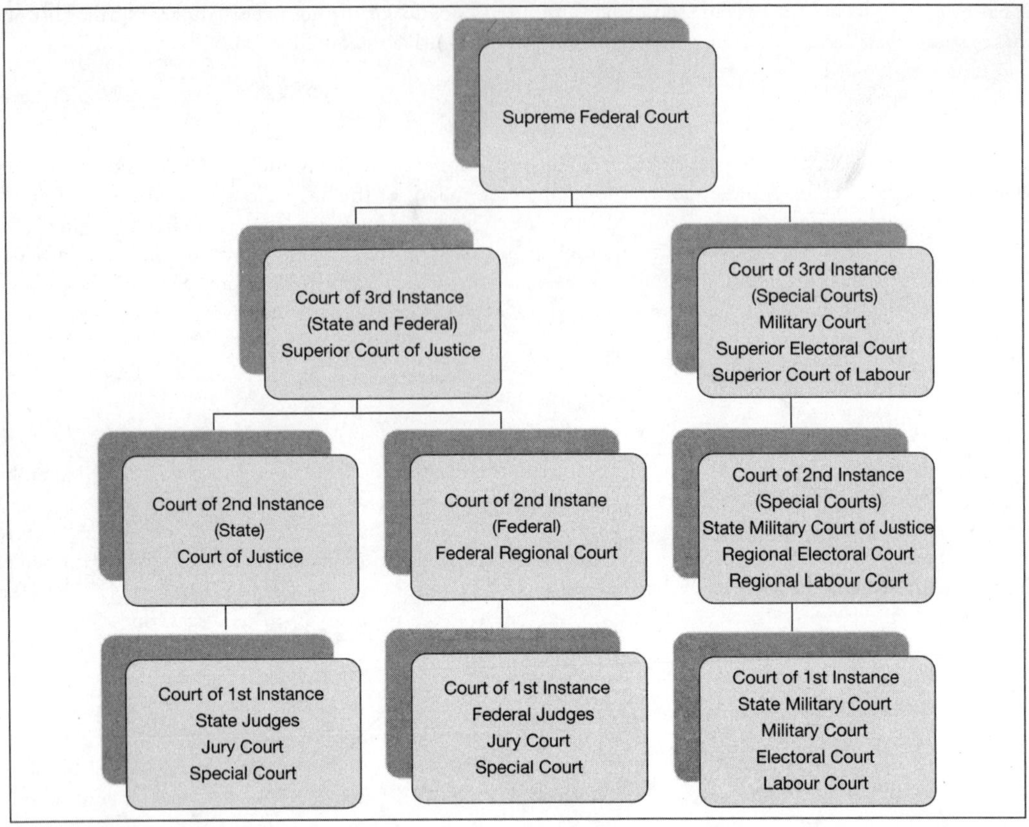

Figure 22.1 Brazil Judicial System

Despite such complex network of judicial system, there are severe problems in the Brazilian judiciary. First and foremost, Brazilian judiciary does not have a system of judicial review which limits its power in many aspects and creates obstacles for judiciary to work as citizen-oriented system. Though the judicial system seems to work under a single command system, the lower courts are not obliged to follow the precedents from the higher courts and, therefore, makes it an ambiguous structure.

The judiciary has also been criticized for its unresponsive character towards social problems of Brazilian society, particularly problems of rural areas where poor people are more than often denied their right to fair trial. A corrupt system involving 'powerful landowners', police and local-level judicial system work hand in hand to save people indulged in criminal activities like child prostitution, pornography and 'murder of street urchins' (Montero 2007, 446).

However, two major initiatives were taken in 2004 to deal with the problems of judicial system. For instance, the commission of National Council of Justice, created by the 45th amendment in the constitution, has been given the charge of overall supervision on administrative and financial matters of judiciary. Second, with the judicial reforms of 2004, the principle of 'binding precedent' also came into force. This principle dealt with the problem of ambiguity at 1st and 2nd instance levels. According to a Supreme Court judge, the principle of 'binding precedent' provides that a 'two-thirds majority of the votes at the Supreme Court (eight votes); it must deal with constitutional matters that have been the object of repeated decisions by the Court.

It has the goal of overcoming any controversy over the validity, interpretation and efficacy of specific norms that may generate legal insecurity and a significant multiplication of court cases' (Mendes 2009, 5).

Constitutionally, federalism of Brazil is the strongest among the other Latin American countries. However, in practice, it is eclipsed by many problems emerging from both constitution and implementation of federal practices at the ground level. For instance, 1988 constitution secures judiciary's power of judicial review through a plethora of procedure, yet the judiciary has not been able to play 'the ultimate arbiter of the balance of power between the states and the national government' (Rosenn 2005, 584). Many scholars argue that representation system provided by the 1988 constitution is heavily biased against more populous states. For instance, for the National Congress, every federal district elects three senators. Rosenn argues that 'this constitutional rule, coupled with a history of eliminating old states and creating new states for partisan advantage, has given Brazil one of the most "malapportioned" upper chambers in the world' (2005, 587). Second, the maximum number of representatives in House of Deputies can be 70. This renders a severe inequality in terms of representation of people, as the most populous states are proportionally under represented and scarcely populated states are over-represented. Further, fiscal federalism provided by the 1988 constitution accounts for many economic problems in Brazil, including high debts and inflation rates. The federal government and/ or the states had the political responsibility for levying and collecting the taxes, but the municipalities had only the responsibility for spending much of what were essentially free funds. Adding to this, the Tax on Circulation of Goods is the primary source of states' revenues. This tax is levied in the state of production rather than where goods are being consumed. This flaw has produced competition among the states to attract investment from other states by selectively reducing the tax rates and has the unfortunate effect of failing to exempt exports of goods and services, thereby making Brazil less competitive in world markets and affecting its overall growth (ibid.).

22.6 Political Parties in Brazil

The Brazilian political party system is one of the 'most mercurial' in the world. Party names, affiliations, and structures of party alliances have constantly been in flux (Montero 2007, 450). Frequent interruptions by military regimes have adversely affected the growth of party system in Brazil. According to Hagopian (2001), the party system in Brazil has been transient, undisciplined multi-class but non-ideological-based system that heavily relies on clientelism in which local bosses arrange and manipulate votes and local polity for their states oligarchs. Frequent shifting of parties by politicians leaves voters more person centric rather than party oriented.

22.6.1 Post Estado Novo: Challenges of Creating Democracy Through Parties

The real growth of political parties as a party system can be seen in post Estado Novo period. During the period of electoral politics after 1945, few parties made their mark. Local sections in interiors of Brazil that were largely aligned with Vargas government made PSD while the PTB, a pro-Vargas group, organized itself in the urban areas. On the other hand, groups opposing Vargas consolidated themselves into UDN. In next 15 years, Brazil saw a slow progression towards multi-party system. By 1960, Brazilian Congress had 13 parties; however, it soon received a jolt in 1965 when president Costello issued a decree to end the existing multi-party system following adverse result for himself in 1965 elections. In this context, two parties—National Renewal Alliance and Brazilian Democratic Movement (MBD)—were born. The then president Costello Branco's objective was to organize a strong majority support party and a loyal opposition. In 1979, the party system was again changed to multi-party system after General Golbery do Couto e Silva, who was the architect of much of the regime's political evolution from 1964 to 1981, called for a party realignment. The reason for this was that most voters due to prolonged military regime started identifying themselves as pro- or anti-government. On the other hand, this was also the period when social movements against regime in Brazil were gaining strength that gives political mileage to opposition party in the institutional politics. Thus, with abolition of the two-party system, the military regime intended to split the advancing of MBD (Hagopian 2001, 540).

In 1985, Congress passed another legislation regarding party system. In this law, the Congress ceased the requirement of organization of new parties. As a result, only 11 parties could participate in the national assembly in 1987 that grew up to 19 parties in 1991 and to 18 in 1995. Despite the multi-party system, it is interesting to note that Brazilian presidents come largely from two parties—Workers' Party (PT) and Brazilian Social Democracy Party (PSDB)—which are not the largest parties in Brazil. Carlos R. Melo explains why since 1989, most of the times, PT and PSDB are winning the presidential seat (see Melo 2015).

However, as Brazil is increasingly moving towards a stable democracy, party system suffers many weaknesses. One of them, according to Scott Mainwaring, explains that rules make it very easy to change parties, particularly to income their access to patronage (Mainwaring, cited in Montero 2007, 451). These frequent shifts of political leaders from one party to other party led to many other problems. Levin Lucas and David Samuel argue that this messes up with the ideological spectrum of political parties which in turn creates a confused voting population. Voting becomes more person centric, as it is not in interest of political leaders to generate public opinion on ideological basis. This situation has become graver after Lula regime (Lucas and Samuel 2013).

Other problem is the mix of presidential system with the multi-party system. Given the political fragmentation and weaknesses of party system in Brazil, presidents generally are not able to gain majority in Congress. Following this problem, often, the Brazilian president attempts to govern the aforementioned parties by dispensing favours to key congressional politicians to get a legislation passed. It is more often argued that the Brazilian party system now has become more ideologically oriented and vote in favour of economic reforms. On the other hand, many scholars argue that support for economic agenda is not due to ideological coherence but because of the president's patronage to many congress members. Despite this factor, scholars such as Timothy Power argue that political parties are inclining more and more to neo-liberal reforms (ibid.).

22.7 Political Economy of Brazil

Brazil has shown interesting trends in economy since its advent in the world market system. In the first three major economic cycles, as explained in the aforementioned section, has almost monopolized the trade of commodities like sugarcane, gold and coffee. However, after every cycle, Brazil has had to witness a period of decline as well. The most evident decline was seen after the coffee trade cycle. Brazilian coffee was not only popular in European markets but it had also monopolized the market. By 1924, coffee was contributing for 75 per cent of the total export income of Brazil. It is important to know as demand for coffee in the world market structured Brazilian economy in such a way that it ensured minimum intervention by the state as the trade was largely being done by the oligarchs. As the Great Depression appeared, demand for coffee declined heavily in the world market. The decline in export also resulted in the decline in import, and as a result, Brazilian economy had to produce many goods domestically which they were earlier importing through international trade. This model of Brazilian economy is known as 'Import Substitution model' or 'Import Substitution Industrialization' (Montero 2007, 429).

Due to the Great Depression of 1929, economic dimensions changed in Brazil leading to a change in the polity as well. The Revolution of 1930 took place and, as Boxer (1962) suggests, one of the very important causes of the success of revolution and Vargas' victory was the dissatisfaction among the coffee growers.

After this revolution, 'Old Republic' gave way to a regime led by Vargas who launched his 'Estado Novo' programme, rebuilding economy on new principles. Vargas' regime provided the initial phase of import substitution with subsidies and tariff protection to protect the import substitution-based industrialization (Montero 2007, 429).

The Great Depression and Second World War put Latin American economies under enormous pressure due to heavily constrained export–import, but European recovery afterwards provided foreign capital to these countries that along with domestic capital and focus on basic industries could have lighten up the road to development provided the presence of a strong state in economic sphere. Brazil fulfilled these conditions quite well. The state promoted quick growth in selected sectors like heavy industries through planning, subsidies and financial support system. It created institutions with a centralized command system with minimum accountability to people. Therefore, institutions like National Development Bank and National Public Firms could support the import substitution model very smoothly. Along with this, state also promoted private investments by extracting and distributing resources like raw materials at much cheaper prices than international markets to advance production (Montero 2007, 430).

As a result of economic policies, Brazil performed excellently on growth scale during the 1950s, 1960s and 1970s. However, it was also the period when many problems emerged that had a long-term effect on the Brazilian economy. State protection fostered non-competitiveness and inefficient use of government resources. Industries deeply relied on state subsidies and constantly went into loss while looking up to the state for their revival. Further, the import substitution model also became 'import-intensive'. Business used government finances to avail imported technology and machinery. Government helped them by over-valuing currency to make import price cheaper. This in turn affected the export sector, as it could not provide the state enough revenues to sustain the growth. Owing to this, during the 1970s, the industrial sector was mainly growing on international loans which led to a crisis in 1982. Problems and failures of import substitution model inspired new thinking about development. This school of thought in the realm of development theory is known as the 'dependency school' (Montero 2007, 430). Dependency theory, articulated by scholars like A.G. Frank, categorically talks about the unfair terms of trade between developing and developed countries. The under-developed 'periphery' provides resources to developed 'core' that benefits the latter rather than the former, making peripheries poorer in international trade regime. Therefore, 'dependistas' advocated delinking of Third World countries, like Brazil, from the world economy.

Military-led governments in the 1960s and 1970s adopted reforms, but to further intensify import substitution model through state-led development methods (primarily para-statals) and with help of multi-national firms ready to transfer their investments and technology to large products envisaged by the military. By the 1970s, the military regime realized the importance of international markets in order to deal with huge expenditure in public dealings. Therefore, the military started export of many agricultural products, that is, coffee, cereals, iron ore, etc. Export of agricultural products rejuvenated the Brazilian economy for some time. Period from 1968 to 1974, as Hagopian notes, produced an 'economic miracle' (2001, 520).

Nonetheless, frequent regime changes have adversely affected Brazil's economy leading to many fiscal problems. For instance, with complexities of economic system in post-1960 Brazil, informal economy emerged as a significant means of evading tax. A large population working outside the tax regime and even big firms were sub-letting their works to informal sector in order to breach taxes. Federal structure of the government also posed many challenges to the fiscal situation in Brazil. While the central government was spending less than its collected taxes between the 1960s and 1990s, the municipal governments were spending manifolds more than their earnings. Use of public sector banks' money to finance expenditure pushed Brazilian states to severe debts, so much so that by 1992, half of Brazil's total debt was held by its states (Montero 2007, 432). However, a very significant factor of deteriorating economy was 1974 oil crisis and then hike in the same sector in 1979. Brazil struggled with this economic crisis with traditional economy until the 1990s till the government began to implement market-oriented neoliberal reforms. The biggest problem of Brazilian economy was finally tamed in 1994 by the 'Plano Real' or 'Real Plan' (Hagopian 2001, 520). 'Plano real' was about taking measures to stabilize the Brazilian economy in 1994. It intended to stabilize the domestic currency in nominal terms after a string of failed plans to control inflation.

Collor, Cordoso and Lula governments brought some stringent measures to revive Brazilian economy from its severe fiscal problems. With sustained efforts of reviving economy, Brazilian leadership was able to take the country at international level as a big market player. The growth of Brazilian economy is reflected by the fact that despite 2008 crisis, Brazil successfully promoted itself as an 'investment grade' country which indicates international confidence in Brazilian economy and wish to trade. Brazil has also diversified its foreign markets by joining trade regimes like Mercosur or Southern Common Market, a South American Trade Bloc, and BRICS, an association of five major emerging economies, namely Brazil, Russia, India, China and South Africa. In this process, Brazil has made China its largest trade partner, a position earlier enjoyed by the United States (Meade 2010).

Many scholars argue that Brazil can be studied as an important case of 'boom and bust' economy. It has been facing cycles of growth and decline in its economy. In its post-reform period only, it has encountered three major economic crisis—2001–2003, 2008 and 2014–16. Despite these crises, Brazil tried to overcome and rectify its economy. However, problems in the economy persisted and demanded a rather holistic solution which will not only stabilize the economy but also solve other problems associated with it. For instance, in the 2007–2017 period, Brazil's public debt increased from 43.9 per cent of the GDP to 84 per cent of the GDP. The rate of unemployment also went up from 9.8 per cent to 12.8 per cent in the same period. (CIA, World Fact Book 2018), and as per UNDP calculation, 30.5 per cent of the youth between 15 and 24 years of age are unemployed, which indeed is a worrisome concern. Higher rate of unemployment has led Brazilian cities to multiple social problems, that is, crimes, illegal drug trade and class violence especially in densely populated cities (Meade 2010). Apart from this, the problem of corruption has adversely affected Brazilian economy especially after impeachment of President Dilma Rouseff in 2016 that has really shaken the international confidence of doing business. However, Temer administration has implemented a series of fiscal and structural reforms in order to gain credibility for the Brazilian government but their effects are yet to be seen.

Despite being one of the largest economies, economic inequality in Brazil has reached extreme levels, and it is listed as one of the most unequal countries. Oxfam international reports that the rich continue to benefit the most from the economic growth. For instance, between 2001 and 2015, the richest 10 per cent in Brazil accounted for 61 per cent of economic growth. Brazil's six rich men have the same wealth as poorest 50 per cent of the population, that is, around 100 million people. Meanwhile 16 million people live below the poverty line (Oxfam International 2018).

Nevertheless, the key long-time concerns of Brazilian economy appear to be macro-economic stability, booms and busts, unemployment, corruption and huge inequality owing to a lopsided distribution of key resources.

22.8 Social Movements

Brazil had witnessed a very impressive phase of social movements during the 1970s and 1980s till democratic government according to the new constitution took place. The reason for such overwhelming social movement scenarios lied in the significantly reduced possibilities of opposition from within the political system due to a long-standing military regime of two decades. Therefore, the opposition to the state expressed itself through various social movements. However, resistance to the military regime came both through violent and non-violent methods; violent streams were rather easily repressed by the state while non-violent movements gained pace by increasingly involving larger sections of society (Bethell 2008, 184). During this period, new forms of trade unionism, grass-roots social movements, neighbourhood movements and groups of many professional associations along with domestic and international NGOs became active (Montero 2007, 459).

Social movements in pre-redemocratization phase concentrated on democracy as their sole objective. Therefore, the master frame of social movement was 'democratization' or 'opposition to military'. Such a frame was big enough not only to include people facing destitution by the state but also other political institutions like political parties cutting across the ideological lines. This was the time when public arena of Brazil witnessed unprecedented networks of both formal and informal formations both 'within and across their sectoral issues' (Hochstetler 1997).

Church played a very special role in protest cycles, as it enjoyed a widespread cadre and ability of door-to-door mobilization. National Conference of Bishops of Brazil (Conferencia Nacional dos Bispos do Brasil) launched a series of manifestos appealing for non-violent opposition to the regime and denouncing the imprisonment of priests and the general lack of freedom in the country (Bethell 2008). Brazilian Catholic Church formed Pastoral Land Commission to work with poor in rural areas with an aim to end widespread violence of landowners and the state through non-violent means. Bishops at regional levels were personally leading the protests and giving public speeches against state's exploitation (Bruneau and Hewitt 1989). In post re-democratization period too, the Church has 'nurtured the MST's formation by building network of activists engaged in different land struggles across Southern Brazil' (Carter 2010, 194).

Post 1980, Movement of Rural Landless Workers (MST) has been working for creating awareness among the rural populations in favour of landless workers. It has been working specially for changing land tenure patterns which are under the control of handful of land owners. MST, in its fairly long history, has adopted variety of tactics including non-violent protests, to militancy to now advocacy and participation in the government at various levels (Navarro 2005). In 1984, the MST had a remarkable show of strength encouraging farmers to occupy little used land. This movement was in response to the neoliberal policies adopted by the state leading to a shift from agro-economy to industry-based economy forcing peasants to migrate to urban areas. MST is expanding in multiple dimensions for benefits of farmers. Currently, it is also working as the Brazilian branch of international farmers' movement—La Via Campesina (the peasants' way)—to create awareness for producing food without pesticides or genetically modified organisms (GMOs); it has involved itself over 90 agri-businesses to improve farmers' income and also works to make education accessible to at least 160,000 children (Zakin 2016).

Apart from the rural poor, women from rural and urban areas participated in resistances in large numbers. Along with their own issues, women were participating in leading popular initiatives on a wide variety of issues ranging from employment to other provisions of basic services. Out of 5,324 urban unions, 14.8 per cent unions had elected women directors. In rural areas, women constituted 78 per cent of active memberships (Montero 2007, 460). During the military regime, the women's movement was working under the umbrella frame of 'democratization'. This brings to women a 'double struggle' leading them to participate in struggle for issues concerning whole society at large as well as issues specific to women in Brazil (Sardenberg and Costa 2014). As an effect of women's participation in variety of social movements, the 1988 constitution had to include gender equality as a constitutional value despite opposition in the constituent assembly (Machado 2016). However, the larger challenge remains to execute constitutional provisions at ground level, especially for Afro-Brazilian women who constantly raise the questions of prejudice and discrimination from race perspective. A major part of feminist movement in Brazil is now dealing with the race question, arguing that black women have a different agenda vis-à-vis white feminist activists, as they have an additional exploiter in form of race (Lovell 2000). Race and class, by and large, overlap with each other in which black people have to suffer more. The suffering aggregates for black women. The Oxfam reports explain how black women are located at the last platform of receiving state's social policies. Stating data collected from various sources, it highlights that black women alone constitute 10 per cent of the poorest 20 per cent population of Brazil and that regressive fiscal policies adopted by the state discriminate most against the black women (Oxfam Fact Sheet 2018). Despite such bleak circumstances, black women are raising their voice in streets, Congress and many other official and unofficial platforms through social movements and NGOs (Rodrigues and Prado 2012).

Special Insights

Women's Rights and Austerity Measures in Brazil

The Oxfam reports that women are the worst sufferers of austerity measures taken by Brazilian government. Its fact sheet shows the following points:

- Women Rights have suffered budget cuts.
  - Up to 40 per cent budget reduction in 2014 and 2016.
- Femicides and other forms of violence against women are extremely high in Brazil.
  - Around 13 Brazilian women die every day due to violence against women.
- Black women are disproportionately affected by severe femicide scenario.
  - While some progress is made in case of white women, crimes against black women jumped to 54 per cent.

Along with the fact that Brazil is the eighth largest economy and has acute income inequality, the country has another peculiar characteristic that it is a country with most profound environmental degradation. Amazon has attracted a worldwide attention in the 1980s and 1990s due to heavy deforestation affecting climate, not only of Brazil but also of the entire region. The conflict between environmentalists and groups having vested interests in status quo reached severe levels. It is reflected in the number of murders committed around this issue. In 2017, according to an estimate, more environmental activists were killed in Brazil than in any other country. Brazilian environmentalist movement also has to deal with strong lobbies juxtaposing ecological concerns and development, putting environment as a less important issue in the dominant political discourse (Picanco, Prado, and Allen 2018).

Notwithstanding such challenges, environmentalist movement in Brazil has covered a long journey from the phase of participating into 'democratization' through which the movement could make it a point to bring environment issues in public discourse to the early 1990s when the movement began to positively participate in parliamentary politics (Viola 1998). Further, The Earth Summit of 1992—United Nation's Conference on Environment and Development—provided enormous opportunity of networking among the environmental groups from all over the world but more importantly to Brazilian ecological movement to work on environmental issues with much more rigour (Alonso, Costa, and Maciel 2005).

Post 1985, the significance of the earlier master frame of 'democratization' got diminished as the goal was achieved through 1988 constitution leading the social movements assume a different form and role. After 1988, the frame of democratization was replaced by frame of citizenship. Many organizations focusing on citizenship rights have chosen to work on specific aspects. For example, Viva Rio (a Rio de Janeiro-based organization) works on violence in the city and tries to bridge gaps between middle classes and their poor neighbourhood (Hochstetler 1997) and organization of Union of Housing Movement (Levy 2005). Other than urban areas movements, Brazilian civil society is also bringing up the issues and concerns of indigenous people and Human Rights violations not only in Brazil but also in areas where Brazil is showing increasing business interest (Abelvik-Lawson 2014). Despite emergence of social movements in various sectors, Brazil has yet to fully acknowledge problems of racial discrimination. Scholars such as Alfred P. Montero mention that not acknowledging problems related to racial discrimination can be due to the absence of legally sanctioned discrimination after abolition of slavery in 1888 and mixing up the racial issue with class issues (2007, 460). However, in 2001, the Brazilian government recognized the problem and introduced affirmative action for Afro-Brazilians by providing them quota in government jobs and higher education (Htun 2004).

22.9 Conclusion

Such rich presence of social movements in Brazil since the 1970s undoubtedly indicates towards a vibrant civil society hitherto specifies the persistent problems of Brazilian society, politics and economy. The government has been focusing primarily on development without considerably working towards the problems it creates. Acute income imbalances in both rural and urban areas leading to many other social problems of unemployment, violence, growing crime rate, drug trafficking, etc., are major problems in Brazilian society. On the other hand, women's movements in Brazil are still struggling for equality rights in both social and economic spheres. Environment degradation is a severe problem that emerges from the development agenda and practices of the state, yet Brazilian state does not do much except for paying lip service to the issue.

The structure of the state, on the other hand, presents a different set of difficulties, making Brazil a curious case of comparison in the arena of politics. Brazil is a presidential system with multi-party political arrangement where large-scale representatives are elected on 'open list proportional representation system'. This causes a great deal of instability along with incoherent policymaking and execution for the political party, and representation system is largely corrupted through clientelism. Additionally, the complex judicial arrangement, without a 'national mission', creates chasm between state and people making state further distanced for people.

That is the reason why the world's eighth largest economy that marks its presence on most of world's powerful platforms—economically and otherwise—is still not able to help people at the grassroots. In this regard, what Boxer (1962) said for Brazil about 1930 revolution seems true even today that many changes are taking place only superficially rather than bringing qualitative change in peoples' life. How a surging economy like that of Brazil copes with such grave problems with its ongoing economic reform agenda is yet to be seen.

Keywords

Clientelism
Colonization
Economic reforms
Estado Novo
Import substitution
State corporatism

Review Questions

1. What do you understand by 'bureaucratic authoritarianism'? Explain its role in Brazil's politics.
2. Explain the various systems of representations presented in Brazilian polity. What are the implications of such a system?
3. Describe Brazil's journey from a long-standing military regime to democracy.
4. Discuss major challenges faced by Brazilian political systems along with the role of social movements in dealing with these challenges.

References

Abelvik-Lawson, Helle. 2014. Sustainable Development for Whose Benefit? Brazil's Economic Power and Human Rights Violations in the Amazon and Mozambique. *International Journal of Human Rights* 18(7/8): 795–821.

Alonso, Angela, Valeriano Costa, and Débora Maciel. 2005. The Formation of the Brazilian Environment. IDS Working Paper 259. Accessed from https://citeseerx.ist.psu.edu on September 18, 2023.

Bethell, Leslie. 2008. Brazil. In *Cambridge History of Latin America*, Vol. 9. Cambridge: Cambridge University Press.

Boxer, C.R. 1962. *The Golden Age of Brazil 1695–1750: Growing Pains of a Colonial Society.* Berkley, CA: University of California Press.

Bruneau, Thomas C., and W. E. Hewitt. 1989. Patterns of Church Influence in Brazil's Political Transition Transforming Rights into Social Practices? *Comparative Politics* 22(1): 39–61.

Carter, Miguel. 2010. The Landless Rural Workers Movement and Democracy in Brazil. *Latin American Research Review* 45(Special Issue: Living in Actually Existing Democracies): 186–217. Central Intelligence Agency (CIA). 2018. Brazil, in *The World Fact Book*. United States. Accessed from https://www.cia.gov on December 5, 2018.

Constitutional History of Brazil. Accessed from http://constitutionnet.org on November 10, 2017.

Collier, David. 2001. Bureaucratic Authoritarianism. In *The Oxford Companion to Politics of the World*, edited by Joel Krieger. London: Oxford University Press.

Greenbaum, Harry. 2003. *Brazil.* Philadelphia, PA: Modern World Nation, Chelsea House Publication.

Hagopian, Frances. 2001. Politics in Brazil. In *Comparative Politics Today*, edited by Gabriel A. Almond, G. Bingham Powell, Russell J. Dalton, and Kaare Strom. Pearson Education Asia.

Hochstetler, Kathryn. 1997. Democratizing Pressures from Below? Social Movements in New Brazilian Democracy. *Latin American Studies Association XX International Congress*, Guadalajara, Mexico, 17–19 April.

Htun, Mala. 2004. From Racial Democracy to Affirmative Action: Changing State Policy on Race in Brazil. *Latin American Research Review* (January). Vol. 39, No. 1 (2004), pp. 60–89.

Levy, Charmain. (2005). The Housing Movement in the City of São Paulo: Crisis and Revival. In Collective Action and Radicalism in Brazil: Women, Urban Housing and Rural Movements (pp. 97–129). Toronto: University of Toronto Press. https://doi.org/10.3138/978144267309-006

Lovell, Peggy A. 2000. Gender, Race and Struggle for Social Justice in Brazil. *Latin American Perspective* 27(6): 85–103.

Lucas, K., and D. Samuel. 2010. The Ideological Coherence in the Brazilian Party System: 1990–2009. *Journal of Politics in Latin America* 2 (3): 39–69.

Machado, I.F., and S.F. Figueiroa. 2001. 500 Years of Mining in Brazil: A Brief Overview. *Resources Policy* 27: 9–24.

Machado, Lia Zanotta. 2016. Brazilian Feminism in Their Relations with the State: Context and Uncertainties. *Cadernos Pagu* (47), Compinas 2016. Accessed from http://www.scielo.br on February 27, 2019.

Meade, Teresa A. 2010. *Brief History of Brazil.* New York: Library of Congress.

Melo, Carlos Ranulfo. 2015. The 2014 Elections and the Brazilian Party System. *Brazilian Political Science Review* 9(1): 93–114.

Mendes, Gilmar. 2009. *Framework of Brazilian Judiciary and Judicial Review.* Accessed from http://www.stf.jus.br on September 9, 2023.

Montero, Alfred P. 2007. Brazil. In *Introduction to Comparative Politics*, edited by Mark Kesselman, Joel Krieger, William A. Joseph. Boston, MA: Houghton Miffin Company.

Navarro, Zander. 2005. Transforming Rights into Social Practices? The Landless Movement and Land Reforms in Brazil. *IDS Bulletin* 36(1): 129–37.

Oxfam Fact Sheet. 2018. Brazil: Human Rights in Times of Austerity. Accessed from https://www.cesr.org on December 12, 2018.

Oxfam International. 2018. Brazil: Extreme Inequality in Numbers. Accessed from https://www.cesr.org on September 11, 2023.

Picanço, Lara Bartilotti, Mariana Nozela Prado, and Andrew Allen. 2018. Accessed from Environmental Concerns—Brazil, Understanding the Issues. https://www.wilsoncenter.org on December 5, 2018.

Pimenta, Joao Paulo. 2016. *Brazilian Independence: Continuity and Change.* Accessed from http://oxfordre.com/latinamericanhistory on September 11, 2023.

Rodrigues, Cristiano, and Marco Aurelio Prado. 2012. A History of Black Women's Movement in Brazil: Mobilization, Political Trajectory and Articulation with the State. *Social Movement Studies* 12(2): 158–77.

Rosenn, Keith S. 2005. *Federalism in Brazil.* University of Miami Law School. pp. 577–98.

Sardenberg, Cecilia M.B., and Ana Alice Alcantara Costa. 2014. Contemporary Feminisms in Brazil: Achievements, Challenges and Tensions. *Revista Feminismos* 2(2): 53–82.

Skidmore, Thomas E. 1999. *Brazil: Five Centuries of Change.* New York: Oxford University Press.

United Nations Development Programme (UNDP). 2018. Brazil. *Human Development Indices and Indicators: 2018 Statistical Updates.* Accessed from http://hdr.undp.org on November 9, 2018.

Viola, Eduardo J. 1998. The Ecologist Movement in Brazil (1974–1986): From Environmentalism to Ecopolitics. *International Journal of Urban and Regional Research.* onlinelibrary.wiley.com.

Zakin, Zoe. 2016. A Brief History of Landless Workers' Movement. *Alternatives International Journal.* Accessed from www.alterinter.org on July 10, 2018.

CHAPTER 23

Nigeria: The Troubled Giant of Africa

Praveen Dhanda

Reader's Guide

The most populous country of Africa, Nigeria is a tropical land located in West Africa. It was a British colony before it gained independence on 1 October 1960. After independence, politics of Nigeria has witnessed both civilian and military rules. The death of a military head of the state in 1998 allowed for a political transition. A new constitution was adopted in 1999 and a peaceful transition to civilian government was completed. However, the democratic venture is still considered fragile. The present chapter commences by a quick marking of the important aspects and underpinnings of the Nigerian state of affairs. The next section traces the historical trajectory of the region of what is today known as Nigeria. By focusing on the pre-colonial and colonial periods, the attempt here is to identify those aspects which carry bearings for the present-day developments. The chapter then presents the trajectory of postcolonial Nigeria which has seen four democratic republics and numerous coups and counter-coups.The fourth republic, which began in 1999, is discussed in somewhat detail. In the next section, the important aspects of Nigerian political economy are highlighted including the oil turmoil. Towards the end, some other important issues of the Nigerian state and society, including the challenge posed by Boko Haram, are discussed. Thus, this chapter seeks to provide introductory analysis about a country which, according to Campbell and Page, possesses 'extraordinary potential' but is also a 'troubled giant of Africa' (2018, 5).

23.1 Introducing Nigeria

At first sight, most things do not dovetail in Nigeria for a casual outside observer. For instance, in December 2018, the challenge facing Nigeria's incumbent president was an allegation that he was dead. The controversy, which gripped Nigeria and made headlines in world media, was that whether Nigeria's president is really Nigeria's president or was clone. 'It's the real me, I assure you', claimed the president Muhammadu Buhari (see *The Indian Express* 2018; Parkinson 2018). However, incongruences in Nigeria are not all comical, but offer classic problematiques for students of comparative politics. For instance, why more than half a century after the independence Nigerians are still debating about the basic political structures of the country, what they call 'national question', including who will rule and how and even whether the country should remain united or not. Nigeria is also a case which can squarely tell what is not to be done in the governance of a complex multi-ethnic country. It is also a case study where what happened during the colonial past still casts a long shadow over the present enigmas of the country. Nigeria also illuminates the lasting implications of an 'unfinished state' in the governance of the country. In terms of resources, Nigeria is not a poor land and yet it is one of the poorest countries where millions are living in abject poverty. Further, why a country continuously neglects agriculture, the source of livelihood, for its masses and in many ways a mainstay of the economy and imports those agro-commodities for which it was once globally known? These questions may appear puzzling, but that is Nigeria!

Nigeria

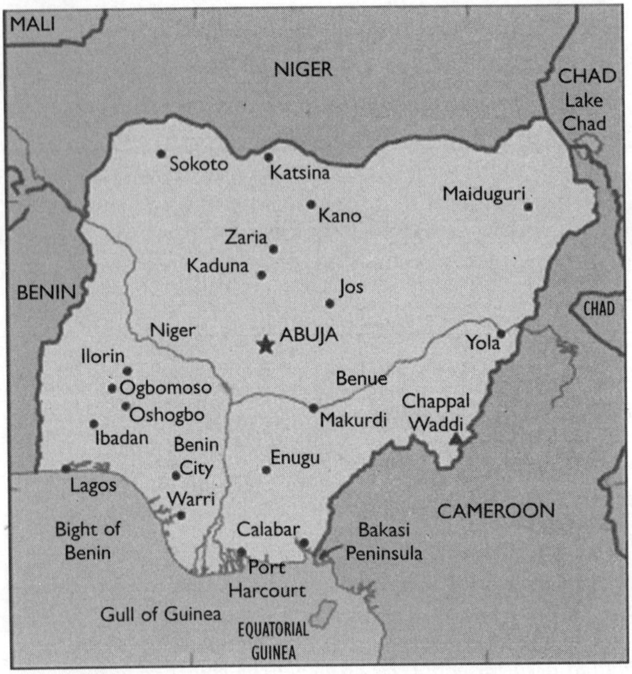

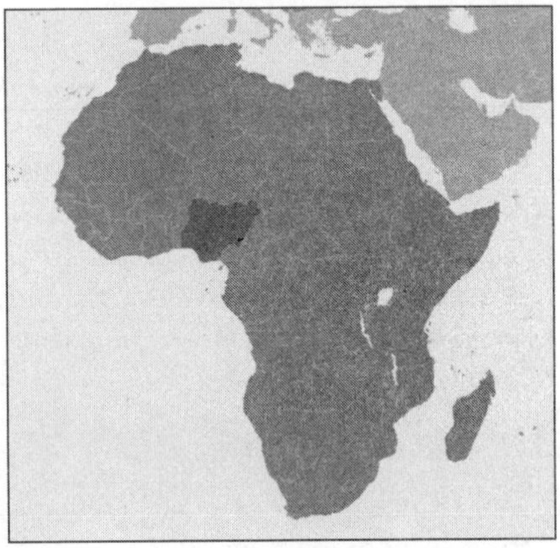

Disclaimer: This figure is not to scale. It does not represent any authentic national or international boundaries and is used for illustrative purposes only.

Key Facts

Population	203,452,505 (July 2018 est.)
Area	923,768 sq. km
Capital	Abuja
Currency	Naira
Official language	English
Major religions	Islam (51.6%), Roman Catholic (11.2%) and other Christian (35.7%) (2013 est.)

GDP (purchasing power parity)	$1.121 trillion (2017 est.)
GDP real growth rate	0.8% (2017 est.)
Labour force—by occupation	Agriculture (70%), industry (10%) and services (20%) (1999 est.)
Population below poverty line	70% (2010 est.)
Corruption perception index rank	148
Political system	Federal presidential republic

Sources: CIA, World Fact Book (2018), Transparency International (2018) and UNDP (2018).

Though Nigeria appears to be a proverbial 'riddle wrapped in a mystery inside an enigma', there are numerous reasons for its immediate importance (Campbell and Page 2018, 5–8). These reasons, in addition to the aspects indicated in the preceding paragraph, are important for the students of comparative politics. First, Nigeria is huge. In terms of population, it is not only the largest country in Africa, there are credible estimates that Nigeria's population will approach 440 million by mid-century, making it the third most populous country after China and India. Second, it functions as a social and political laboratory, providing examples and lessons for other multi-ethnic, religiously pluralistic societies. It is an experiment in state-building and domestic peacemaking among a range of ethnic groups and between Christianity and Islam. Third, Nigeria plays an important role in international energy markets. Fourth, Nigeria has long been Africa's political leader. It was one of the founders of African Union and it lobbies vigorously for a permeant seat in the United Nations Security Council. Fifth, Nigeria makes major contribution in the field of arts and has led the way in developing a postcolonial African cultural identity that is distinct from that of the continent's former colonial masters. Finally, Nigeria's internal security challenges spillover into the West African region. These reasons, inter alia, make Nigeria an important country to engage with and a case study to derive cues about comparative politics.

23.2 Broader Contours and Underpinnings of Nigerian State of Affairs

At the outset, it shall be helpful to chalk out certain broader contours which shape the present state of affairs in Nigeria. Colonialism played an important role, like most other countries of Africa, in the formation of this country. The British created Nigeria out of territories which had little in common. Artificial boundaries of the state, drawn out of the dynamics of colonial and imperial expansion, as they brought together distinct ethno-cultural groups into one political territory, carry salient implications for political development in Nigeria. Owing this, Nigeria has been described as an 'unfinished state', 'geographical expression', 'ethnic mosaic' and 'artificial creation'. In general, there is a weak identification by the Nigerians with the state, and that translates into minimal loyalty towards it, and thus, Nigeria presents a case of 'fragile collective identity' (Kew and Lewis 2007, 533).

Nigeria is a country with a complex and diverse ethnic composition. There are three largest ethno-linguistic groups in Nigeria—Hausa-Fulani (two are distinct but are closely interconnected), Yoruba and Igbo. These are respectively concentrated in the north, southwest and southeast of the country and have distinct language, material culture, norms about governance and traditional religion. There are almost 300 other ethnic groups. The key challenge of Nigeria since the colonial period has been to manage and balance these ethnic groups. With this, religion has been a constant cleavage in Nigeria which often overlaps with ethnic cum regional fault lines. North is dominated by Islam and south by Christianity. Thus, ethnic, regional and religious factors, which often overlap, determine the texture of Nigerian politics. 'In the Nigerian case study, the reconfiguration, formation of political parties, distribution of human and material resources and even crisis (coups, civil war, and religious impasse) are hinged on ethno-religious politics', providing Nigeria with a chequered history (Brown 2013, 172). Thus, the division between north and south is overlaid with numerous ethnic divisions across the nation, which both the civilian and military governments have manipulated for selfish ends.

Cultural divisions within Nigeria have been continually exacerbated by the triple threats of clientelism or patron–client networks, corruption and unstable authoritarian governing structures. These together foster ethnic group competition and hinder economic potential (Kew and Lewis 2007, 552–53). The toxic mix of corruption and ethnic politics has become a key feature of Nigerian state of affairs. The country is characterized by a type of corruption in which government or public officials seek personal gain at the expense of those being governed, a kleptocracy (Campbell and Page 2018, 2–3). Scholars have also called Nigeria a 'patrimonial' state where the rulers treat the state as personal property. The peculiarly Nigerian version of corruption, theorized as prebendalism, remains one of the persistent challenges for Nigeria (see Joseph 1987). It involves disbursing of public offices and state rents to one's ethnic clients. It is an extreme form of clientelism that refers to the practice of mobilizing cultural and other sectional identities by political aspirants and officeholders for the purpose of corruptly appropriating state resources. It has been argued that as long as prebendalism remains the norm of Nigerian politics, a stable democracy will be elusive. These practices are now deeply embedded in Nigerian society and are therefore more difficult to uproot.

After independence in 1960, frequent regime changes, oscillating between civilian governments and military regimes, have been a feature of Nigerian polity. However, even the democratic pursuits in Nigeria are marred by electoral malfeasance. Of late, since 1999, under the fourth republic, democracy appears to be stabilizing in Nigeria.

Seen from the perspective of political economy and development, Nigerian situation has largely been in doldrums. The distortions caused by the discovery of sudden oil wealth, in the absence of the institutions to channel it productively, has made Nigeria a classic case study of 'paradox of plenty' (Karl 1997) and 'natural resource curse' (Sala-i-Martin and Subramanian 2013).

With this background, a brief look at the history of Western Africa and the process through which Nigeria emerged in its present form is important to understand contemporary Nigeria.

23.3 Pre-Colonial and Colonial Nigeria: Enduring Imprint of the Past

Nigeria's history is filled with twists and turns that have taken it from tribal kingdoms to a British colony, from a colony to a military dictatorship and from a dictatorship to a developing democracy (Phillips 2004, 10). It must be stated in the beginning that there was no Nigeria before 1914, when British created a political entity through an amalgamation of the southern and northern protectorates. Mundt and Aborisade (2000), by borrowing from anthropologist Clifford Geertz, have called the 'old societies and new states' as an apt characterization for Nigeria.

Evidence of Nok culture, an Iron Age culture in North Nigeria, was discovered in 1928. This culture existed for about 600 years, from 400 BC until the second century AD and was quite advanced as evident from the relics. With the disappearance of the Nok, things seemed to fall silent for the next thousand years. Little information exists on this 'silent millennium' in Nigeria's history. In the first half of the second millennium, various rich and powerful kingdoms emerged within the region. They were independent from one another, each having its own political structure, cultural traditions and social patterns. These early cultures formed the roots for some of the cultural groups existing in Nigeria today. Each of the kingdoms functioned as a separate political unit (Phillips 2004, 30–32).

In northern Nigeria, between 1000 and 1200 AD, Hausa people began forming city- states. Over the time, another ethnic group, Fulani, became so intertwined with Hausa that dominant culture of northern Nigeria came to be known as Hausa-Fulani. The kingdoms in this area grew constantly from 15th to 18th century. However, due to frequent wars, internally and externally, they were exhausted. Later, these were incorporated under the Sokoto caliphate, an independent Islamic Sunni caliphate. The British defeated the caliphate and put the area under the Northern Nigeria Protectorate in 1903. In the forest regions of southwest, the Yoruba and Bini peoples began forming kingdoms at Benin, Oyo and Ife between 1100 and 1400 AD. By the 17th and 18th centuries, Oyo kingdom, by subverting other kingdoms, extended its control over the entire area of southwest Nigeria. Some of the people in Nigeria, for example, the Igbo in the southeast, were organized only at the village or extended family level. In this sense, there were many political units and hence 'many' Nigerias in the pre-colonial period (Mundt and Aborisade 2000, 682–83).

Against this background, one should note that the immediate cause for British interest in this part of the world, as everywhere else, was trade. First such international trade of any importance was in slaves. Coastal groups began exchanging captives for goods with Europeans as early as the 16th century. Wars among the various kingdoms ensured ample supply of captives, in particular in southwestern Nigeria. For next 300 years, this trade was continued and Benin, Lagos, Bonny and Calabar thrived as slave trade centres (Mundt and Aborisade 2000, 683). Europeans developed a lucrative pattern of triangular trade that served, of course, the economic interests of the colonial European powers.

The first leg of the triangle was slaves who were loaded on ships, often in ports such as Lagos, and taken to the New World and sold. Cotton, tobacco, sugar and other raw materials were then shipped from the New World to the European colonial power. This formed the second leg of the triangular trade. Then, to complete the triangle, manufactured goods, weapons and other raw goods were shipped to Africa to trade for more slaves. The whole process was then repeated. The main beneficiary of all this were the European nations. England, Spain, France, Portugal and the Netherlands sought and developed colonies in order to advance their efforts in this triangular trade (Phillips 2004, 36–37). However, the impact of slave trade on this part of Africa was deep. Economically slave-trade era meant 'a barren three centuries' for this part of the world (Crowder 1978, 68). Those who profited from the slave trade spent their earnings on imports. Slave trade not only negatively impacted the general trade and technological development but also provided an effective barrier against the development of agriculture and industry (Ekundare 1973). The practice also led to great divisions and intensification of disharmony between various ethnic groups and regions.

In 1807, the British parliament outlawed the slave trade. However, the trading patterns that had been established already through slave trade gradually converted to other goods and British colonial presence remained strong in this part of Africa. English consuls established themselves on the coast and began to intervene in the politics of local communities, favouring those candidates for ruling positions who would give them commercial advantages over other Europeans. The British succeeded in obtaining treaties of British protection and trade along the coast. These were treaties between unequals, increasingly favourable to the British as they first established commercial and then political control (Mundt and Aborisade 2000, 683). Thus, the strategy employed to gain political control, in many ways, was similar to that used by the British in many other parts of the world including India.

In order to avoid the danger of war resulting from the competition for colonies, the European powers met at the Conference of Berlin in 1884–85 and divided Africa into spheres of influence. Berlin Conference, also known as West Africa Conference, paved way for the European powers to seize control of the continent of Africa rather than merely trade with it. In a wave of negotiations, imperialist wars and conquests, their efforts were successful. By 1914, that is, beginning of the First World War, Africa showed clearly drawn lines with areas colour-coded according to the European power claiming control (Mundt and Aborisade 2000, 683–84). The outcome of Berlin Conference can be seen as formalization of 'Scramble for Africa'.

Post Berlin Conference, the British government furthered much serious efforts to colonize the areas which are today known as Nigeria. Lord Frederick Lugard, a British colonial administrator, played a key role in shaping British colonialism in this part of Africa. In 1897, he was appointed as the commissioner of northern Nigeria. He started the process of putting all of Nigeria into British hands and left the country in 1903. Others followed his work and consolidated southern Nigeria into a protectorate by 1906. Lugard returned to Nigeria in 1912 and accomplished the task of uniting the northern and southern protectorates into one political entity in 1914. However, it brought together multiple cultures which in turn brought many complexities in establishing a modern state. Further, despite the unification, Lugard and the British preferred to rule indirectly through their local puppet leaders. Especially in the north, existing authority structures were used by the British, and a strategy of 'indirect rule' was adopted, which had consequences for state building in Nigeria (Phillips 2004, 42–43). This terminated the creation of a cohesive state.

The British in Nigeria opted for weak centralization, indirect personal rule and subordination rather than assimilation—the opposite of what was needed to create a modernizing state. Colonial rule tried to bring in some characteristics of modern state, but even those features came through negotiations with tribal chiefs; therefore, it could never really develop a strong state system during colonial times.

This minimal state was organized along laissez-faire lines, responsible for little more than preserving law and order and for promoting infrastructure and commodity exports (Kohli 2004, 300–301). Even though all of Nigeria was brought together in the early 20th century, little meaningful contact took place between the regions. Differences in environment, history and culture between the north and south were enormous. These differences continue to plague the country even today (Phillips 2004, 42–43). Thus, the different regions of Nigeria came to be ruled differently and over time came to develop fairly distinct socio-economic characteristics.

Special Insights

Colonial Policies and Impact on State Formation: Cases of South Korea and Nigeria

The sharpest contrast in the pattern of colonialism was evident in the role of the Japanese and the British in Korea and Nigeria, respectively. Of decisive impact instead was the fact that the Japanese sought to control and exploit Korea while transforming it, whereas the British pursued similar goals while squeezing Nigeria. These contrasting strategies proved to be of considerable long-term significance: The Japanese created and left behind the building blocks of a cohesive-capitalist state, while the British left a legacy that included the rudiments of a neopatrimonial state.

Source: Kohli (2004, 409).

Subsequently, the British governed Nigeria through Clifford Constitution of 1922, Richard's Constitution of 1946 and Lyttleton's Constitution of 1954. Under these constitutions, gradually, some constitutional elements and structures to create an impression of rule of law, which had far-reaching consequences, were adopted. A more direct involvement of Nigerians in political decision-making was allowed. This led to the formation of Nigerian political parties which also ignited a spirit of Nigerian nationalism. Political parties like Lagos-based Nigerian National Democratic Party (NNDP), led by Herbert Macauley, who is widely regarded as the father of Nigerian nationalism, were formed. Such parties argued for greater Nigerian participation in the government. Though political parties tended to be regional and often culture based, the efforts of Macauley helped to develop and extend the spirit of Nigerian nationalism. Despite this spirit of Nigerian nationalism, immense regional cultural fragmentation continued to exist, in fact intensified, as each major ethnic group—Hausa, Yoruba and Igbo—developed their own political parties. The British played off ethnic and social divisions to keep Nigerians from developing organized political resistance to colonial rule. They ensured that ethnicity would remain the primary element in political identification and mobilization. Finally, in order to create a constitution, British divided the country into three administrative regions, namely the Hausa north, the Yoruba southwest and the Igbo southeast. However, at the national level, the problem of division still existed—an aspect which set the tone for post-independence politics in Nigeria. Thus, colonialism left its imprint on all aspects of Nigeria's existence. The dual standard adopted by the British left a conflicted idea of democracy in Nigeria (Kew and Lewis 2007, 526–27; Phillips 2004, 43–44).

Further, the Western educated elite that emerged in Nigeria came largely from the south of the country. The division between the north and south was multifold, including ethnic and religious dimensions as north was overwhelmingly Muslim. Moreover, Nigeria got its independence due to mounting pressures on the colonial power, though not so much from a strong nationalist movement but more from the international political context and domestic politics of Britain along with declining legitimacy of colonialism across the world. All these aspects—competition among ethnic and regional groups, creation of a weak colonial state, relatively fragile national identity and an underdeveloped economy—were to have an enduring imprint on the post-independence trajectory of Nigeria. In this context, the discovery of oil triggered a new turmoil.

23.4 Postcolonial Nigeria: A House Divided

23.4.1 First Republic (1960–66) and the story of Coups and Counter-coups (1966–79)

Due to gradual move towards greater autonomy and federalization of Nigeria through various constitutions as well as international circumstances, Nigeria got its independence from colonial rule on 1 October 1960. However, since its independence, Nigerian political trajectory has been about its struggle for democracy with frequent coups and counter- coups. Moreover, each of these regimes—whether military or democratic—has by and large been person centric (see Tables 8.1 and 8.2).

Following the footsteps of many other British colonies, Nigeria first adopted a parliamentary system. However, in 1963, the constitution was amended, and Nigeria changed its parliamentary form of government to a republican political system, though even the changed political system could not get Nigeria a very stable government. During the first election, northerners dominated the parliament because of their population. This region was dominated by Northern Peoples' Congress (NPC), a party of Hausa-Fulani elites. NPC started a policy of 'northernization' of resources and infrastructure claiming deprivation during the colonial period.

Table 23.1 Nigerian Government Leaders (Civilian)

Name	Party	Period
Prime Minister Abubakar Tafawa Balewa	Political coalition	1 October 1960–15 January 1966
President Nnamdi Azikiwe	National Council of Nigeria and the Cameroons	1 October 1963–16 January 1966
President Shehu Shagari	National Party of Nigeria	1 October 1979–31 December 1983
President Ernest Shonekan	Independent	26 August 1993–17 November 1993
President Olusegun Obasanjo	People's Democratic Party	29 May 1999–29 May 2007
President Umaru Musa Yar'Adua	People's Democratic Party	29 May 2007–5 May 2010
President Goodluck Jonathan	People's Democratic Party	5 May 2010–29 May 2015
President Muhammadu Buhari	All Progressive Congress	29 May 2015–incumbent

Table 23.2 Nigerian Government Heads (Military)

Name	Period	Way Out
Johnson Thomas Aguiyi-Ironsi	16 January 1966–29 July 1966	Overthrown
Yakubu Gowon	29 July 1966–29 July 1975	Overthrown
Murtala Mohammed	29 July 1975–13 February 1976	Assassinated
Olusegun Obasanjo	13 February 1976–1 October 1979	Resigned
Muhammadu Buhari	31 December 1983–27 August 1985	Overthrown
Ibrahim Babangida	27 August 1985–26 August 1993	Resigned
Sani Abacha	17 November 1993–8 June 1998	Died in office
Abdulsalami Abubakar	8 June 1998–29 May 1999	Resigned

This brought NPC into direct confrontation with its southern counterparts, particularly the Action Group (AG) controlled by the Yoruba people and later with National Convention of Nigerian Citizens (NCNC) dominant in the eastern part with Igbo ethnicity. Trust deficit among various political parties and rivalries intensified over the years (Kew and Lewis 2007, 527–28). The problem was further complicated by other issues like loopholes in the constitution. For instance, emergency provisions could be imposed with simple majority in provinces leading to major human rights violation in the name of security of the state. In addition, the constitution provided that the parliament can take over the lawmaking function of regional legislative assemblies by a two-thirds majority. In a country with strong ethnic cleavages, this provision created 'enormous potential for intimidation' (Diamond 1995, 424).

A complex of political and ethnic problems led to a very chaotic political situation as law and order collapsed and army had to intervene. So much so that president Nnamdi Azikiwe (NCNC) and prime minister Tafawa Balewa (NPC) separately approached the military to ensure that if it came to conflict, they could count on its loyalty. In the name of breaking down of system and election-related misconduct and fraud, the military intervened to end the first republic with the January 1966 coup. Through this coup, a group of largely Igbo officers seized power, and their Igbo leader Aguiyi Ironsi became head of the state (Kew and Lewis 2007, 527–28). The constitution was suspended, and the country came under the rule of military dictates. The stated reasons for the coup were prevailing corruption, nepotism, gangsterism and disorder. This coup witnessed a large- scale bloodshed. Many political leaders and military officials were killed including the Prime Minister Tafawa-Balewa.

The January coup of Nigeria had to face a counter-coup within a period of few months. The second coup of 1966 started in July and is therefore known as 'July rematch'. The coup was executed by northern military officers under the leadership of Murtala Muhammed. It was said to be a reaction to the killings of northern politicians and officers primarily by Igbo soldiers. This counter-coup resulted in the assassination of Nigeria's first military heads—General Ironsi and Lt. Colonel Fajuyi. Lt. Colonel Yakubu Gowon became the head of the state as the consequence of the second military coup. Gowon headed the Nigerian state from 1966 to 1975. As head of the state, he faced a civil war (1967–70). The war was fought between the government of Nigeria and Biafra, geographical southeastern Nigeria, which represented nationalist aspirations of the Igbo people. The political economy of oil, in this context, as elaborated ahead in this chapter, played a fundamental role. Though the conflict between Igbo and other prominent ethnic communities had existed during colonial Nigeria, the counter-coup of July 1966 gave a strong reason to Igbo leadership to make a case for separate state as there were too many economic, political and cultural differences. The movement was supported by many countries like France, Spain, South Africa and Israel. Nigerian state run by Yokubu Gowon won the civil war by crushing the secessionist movement. It resulted in around a million killings by military (see Siollun 2009).

After the civil war, Gowon initiated efforts of national reconciliation, which preceded fairly smoothly with the aid of oil revenues. Under this policy, Yokubu Gowon divided the major three regions into 12 states. Alongside, he strengthened the armed forces by two and half times from what it was in 1966. Senior officials from security forces were the direct beneficiaries of oil boom.

Military head Gowon had promised a return to civil rule by 1976, but enormous political and economic power in the hand of military increased its stakes in the status quo and arrival of democracy was postponed. This led to the overthrow of Gowon by Murtala Muhammed, another military ruler (Kew and Lewis 2007, 529). Despite his promise of reactivation of democracy, like his predecessor, Muhammed halted the process of democratization, leading to his assassination and another military coup. General Olusegun Obasanjo assumed power after Muhammed and peacefully ceded power to a civilian government in 1979.

23.4.2 Second Republic (1979–83),Third Republic (1993) and the Military Rule (1983–93, 1993–99)

On 1 October 1979, Nigeria returned to a democratic rule. Though the elections were considered successful, various political parties complained of fraud, victimization and all kinds of electoral malpractices (Diamond 1995, 434). Despite allegations, the government was formed, and a new constitution came into practice. This marked the beginning of the second republic (1979–83) in Nigeria. The new regime tried to establish a system through which people could participate in making of the new constitution. The new constitution declared

Nigeria a federal system with the presidential form of government with all executive powers vested in the president who was to be both head of the state and head of the government. The provision of removing the president was also mentioned in the constitution. Both president and vice-president could be removed from the office through the process of impeachment. The National Assembly was bicameral which consisted of the Senate and House of Representatives. Most importantly, the constitution provided for the system of checks and balances and a clear-cut division of power which also gave judiciary the power to interpret the law and judicial review.

Shehu Shagari was appointed as executive president, who remained president from 1979 to 1983. Major support base of his party—National Party of Nigeria (NPN)—was drawn from the northern region. NPN captured outright majorities in 1983 state and national elections through massive fraud and violence. His government did little to reduce the mistrust between various parts of the federation. Multiple problems like ethnic polarization, deteriorating economy and conspicuous misconduct of politicians eroded the legitimacy of civilian rule. Few months later, military dictatorship emerged, this time under the leadership of Major General Muhammadu Buhari. Buhari refused to pledge a rapid return to democratic rule and failed to revive the economy. As a result, his popular support diminished, and in August 1985, General Ibrahim Babangida seized power. Babangida quickly announced a programme of transition. The constitution of the Third Republic was drafted in 1989; however, the date for election was pushed to 1993. In the election, Chief Moshood Abiola won, but to remain in power, Babangida annulled the election. This led to severe reactions from people and Babangida had to resign. On his way out, he put a successor, Ernest Shonekan, as the head of the caretaker civilian government who remained in power from 26 August 1993 to 17 November 1993. Soon, General Sani Abacha ousted the caretaker government and remained in power till his death in 1998. His death saved the country from certain crisis as his scheme to orchestrate the outcome of the transition to produce his own 'election' as president became clearer. Abacha's successor Abdulsalami Abubakar quickly established a new transition programme and promptly handed it over to an elected civilian government led by president Olusegun Obasanjo in May 1999 (Diamond 1995, 433–60; Kew and Lewis 2007, 529–31).

23.4.3 Fourth Republic (1999–Present): A Delicate Democratic Venture

The fourth republic initiated its journey in May 1999 with President Olusegun Obasanjo, the leader of Peoples' Democratic Party (PDP). After 16 years of military rule, Nigeria transitioned back to civilian governance. The presidency of Olusegun Obasanjo from 1999 to 2007 was technically civilian, even though he had previously served as a military chief of state, and his governing style often resembled that of a military ruler. However, his attempt to secure an unconstitutional third term in office was foiled in the National Assembly. This incident indicates a growing elite consensus against having presidents serve for extended, undemocratic periods. The 2007 elections were marred by blatant rigging in favor of Obasanjo's chosen successor, Umaru Yar'Adua. Nevertheless, Yar'Adua's presidency from 2007 to 2010 marked a genuine shift toward a more civilian style of governance and outlook. Notably, Yar'Adua adhered to the principle of enforcing judicial decisions even if they ran counter to his administration's preferences. This was in contrast to Obasanjo, who had disregarded inconvenient court rulings. When Yar'Adua passed away while in office, his vice-president, Goodluck Jonathan, assumed the presidency without military intervention, adhering to the rule of law and maintaining the democratic transition. (Campbell and Page 2018, 1–2). This was certainly a step towards a mature democracy.

Thus, the democratization process started with Obasanjo continued with the elections of Goodluck Jonathan (president from 2010 to 2015) and Muhammadu Buhari (president since 2015). Nigeria is increasingly moving on the democratic path since 1999, and its trajectory towards democracy is regarded broadly positive. However, for many, despite witnessing a series of elections, it is yet to show profound evidence of a growing democracy (Dhikru 2011, 1). If elections are taken as milestones towards democracy, then most of these were problematic. The 2015 election in Nigeria represented an improvement over previous elections, although it was not without its flaws. This time, Muhammadu Buhari's victory was widely accepted, reflecting increasing concerns about the overall security breakdown caused by the jihadist terrorist group Boko Haram and widespread dissatisfaction with the corruption within the administration of Goodluck Jonathan. In a noteworthy display of a maturing democratic culture, Jonathan publicly conceded defeat rather than challenging the election results. This marked the first instance in Nigeria's history where the civilian opposition came to power through the democratic electoral process, arguably advancing the country's democratic development. (Campbell and Page 2018, 2).

23.4.3.1 Constitutional Structure Under the Fourth Nigerian Republic

Since the fourth republic of Nigeria has been the longest civilian government, it is important to have a glance at the key features of the constitutional arrangements. The constitution of Nigeria, under the fourth republic, is a federal presidential republic. The bicameral National Assembly consists of 'Senate' and 'House of Representatives'. Senate has 109 seats—3 each for 36 states and 1 for Abuja—Federal Capital Territory. Members of the Senate are directly elected in single-seat constituencies by a simple majority vote to serve a 4-year term. House of Representatives has 360 seats, and members are directly elected in single- seat constituencies by simple majority vote to serve a 4-year term. President of Federal Republic of Nigeria is directly elected by qualified majority popular vote, and at least 25 per cent of the votes are cast in 24 of Nigeria's 36 states. President is elected for a 4-year term and is eligible for a second term. Federal Executive Council, the cabinet, is appointed by the president but constrained constitutionally to include at least one member from each of the 36 states. The highest court is the Supreme Court which consists of the chief justice and 15 justices. Judges are appointed by the president on the recommendation of the National Judicial Council, a 23-member independent body of federal and state judicial officials, and appointments are confirmed by the senate. Judges serve until the age of 70. Nigeria has a mixed legal system of English common law, Islamic law (in 12 northern states) and traditional law (CIA, World Fact Book 2018).

Thus, similar to the American federal system, the senate of the National Assembly is organized on the principle of equality. Apart from its usual functions, Nigerian senate has some special powers.

The constitution also provides for a federal legislative list. The national assembly has the sole authority on matters mentioned under this list. The national assembly can also make laws on subjects mentioned under the concurrent list. Along with the responsibilities of general policy making on domestic and international relations-related issues, the executive has the duty of preparing the annual budget, decides about the use of armed forces and under extraordinary circumstances, the executive can also declare emergency. The ministries are also responsible for different 'parastatals' (government-owned corporations). During the successive military regimes, judiciary suffered heavily as junta demonstrated a profound disdain for judicial practices, and eventually, it undermined not only the autonomy but also the very integrity of judiciary as a third branch of government. However, the courts have slowly begun to restore some independence and credibility in the fourth republic. In the early 2002, for instance, the Supreme Court passed two landmark judgements. The first struck down a 2001 election law that would have prevented new parties from contesting the general election in 2003—a decision that contravened the wishes of the president and the ruling PDP. The court also decided against the governors of Nigeria's coastal states over control of the vast offshore gas reserves, declaring these to be under the jurisdiction of the federal government. However, despite the very modern synchronized system in place, traditional authorities have maintained heavy influence in the judicial system. This became a point of conflict between Muslim and other communities. It has been said that official recognition to one community is divisive and not in benefit of the state itself (Kew and Lewis 2007, 554).

Bureaucracy in Nigeria also shows traits of postcolonial countries. Present bureaucracy flowed from the colonial administrative system that relied on much expanded bureaucracy to run the country. In postcolonial Nigeria, bureaucracy 'became a way to reward individuals in the patrimonial system ... increasingly individuals were appointed on the basis of patronage, ethnic group and regional origin rather than merit' (Kew and Lewis 2007, 252–53).

23.4.3.2 Rights of Citizens

Nigerian constitution guarantees a set of rights to its citizens. Given the context that life of citizens under the previous governments has often been precarious, constitution explicitly grants right to life and provides a constitutional guarantee to keep this right sacred. Other major rights of citizens protected by the constitution include the following: the right to privacy in communications and in their home; freedom of thought, conscience and religion; freedom of expression (this includes the right to speak freely without harming others and implies freedom of the press and media); freedom of assembly and association, meaning the right to form groups whether they are political or non-political; freedom of movement within Nigeria; the right to own property and the right to a fair trial. Citizens are also protected in the constitution from torture, slavery and inhumane treatment. Equality is promoted for all citizens regardless of ethnic group, gender, religion, disability or any other status. With all of the religious and ethnic tensions existing in the country, the enforcement of these rights is a very important—and often difficult—function of the national government. Citizens also have responsibilities which are specifically spelled out in the constitution (Phillips 2004, 82–85).

23.4.3.3 Federalism in Nigeria

In Nigeria, federalism can be an important strategy for realizing the national moto of 'unity in diversity'. Technically, Nigeria, like the United States, has a federal structure comprising 36 states and 774 local government units. Thus, there are three levels of government which together constitute a single national entity. The federal units are empowered to enact their own laws within their individual jurisdictions, but limited in scope by the constitution and federal laws. Yet, unlike a true federation, in Nigeria the legacy of colonial rule and many years of military domination have yielded a unitary system in federal guise: a system with an all-powerful central government surrounded by weak and economically insolvent states. Institutions have been created top-down by military fiat. The 1999 constitution retains enormous powers with the federal government and the executive in particular. The control over oil by this centralized command structure has further increased economic and political control of the centre. This results into a skewed federalism in which states enjoy nominal powers but, in reality, are totally dependent on the central government. The state and local governments receive virtually their entire budget from the federally determined share of oil revenues (Kew and Lewis 2007, 532, 548). Another key characteristic of federalism in Nigeria is the 'federal character'—in principle an affirmative action programme to ensure representation of ethnic and religious groups in civil services and the military. It seeks to ensure that appointments to public service institutions fairly reflect the linguistic, ethnic, religious and geographic diversity of the country (see Ekeh 1989). However, it is argued that application of the principle in the federal civil service and the military has amounted to a confused balancing of the merit principle and the quota system having adverse consequences for both institutions and overall effectiveness and efficiency (Adamolekun, Erero, and Oshionebo 1991).

23.4.3.4 Political Parties in Nigeria

Social structure, in particular ethno-regional aspect, of Nigeria has heavily affected the formation of political parties as well as the political culture of the state. With the provision of Clifford Constitution of 1922, Herbert Macaulay formed the first modern political party in Nigeria—the NNDP—in 1923. Under the colonial rule, several such movements contended for power at the local level, and a diverse national movement emerged in 1944 under the leadership of Macaulay and Nnamdi Azikiwe, the National Council of Nigeria and Cameroons (NCNC). This was later renamed as National Convention of Nigerian Citizens in 1959. However, when the British introduced a more decentralized constitution in 1951, the NCNC broke up along ethnic lines. The 1951 constitution mandated indirect elections in houses of assembly in three regions.

Lagos was the Western Region, where Yoruba were in majority. An opposition party Action Group, emerged under the leadership of Obafemi Awolowo, a young Yoruba, with an initial organization base in a Yoruba cultural society. Although NCNC won in multi-ethnic Lagos, AG won the majority of the seats in the Western region. The NCNC won overall in the eastern region where Igbo ethnic group, to which Azikiwe belonged, was in majority. However, from the beginning, there were forces within both the NCNC and AG arguing for multicultural, issue-based and cross-regional movement. But the fact that elected offices were established first at the regional level, and only later (in 1957) at the national level, favoured the forces of regionalism. It became clear that a regional power base would be essential to the subsequent contestation for control at the national level. Azikiwe, who particularly was committed to action at the national level, was also constrained to centre his party on its strength in the east. In the north, Britain's successful application of indirect rule has resulted in an alliance between the colonial administration and the traditional emirs that impeded the formation of modern political movements (Mundt and Aborisade 2000, 713–14). The Northern People Congress, NPC, was found in 1946 as a 'pro-tradition, pro-northern association' (Brown 2013).

Thus, the structure of colonial rule and constitutional development under it created ground for ethno-regional mobilization, a trend which has only intensified with time.

Governments, particularly the military ones, have tried to force Nigerians to express their will through cross-ethnic parties. However, the political leadership has succeeded in subverting the goal of truly national parties through their calls to ethnic identity. Typically, a political career is started in a local community on ethnic basis. In this situation, a cross- ethnic party is nothing more than a coalition of ethnic interests. The Hausas have been the most successful in this situation as they got the big prize as presidency each time this was filled by election until Obasanjo's victory in 1999 (Mundt and Aborisade 2000, 716).

With this trend, politicians who feel aggrieved for whatever reason dump one party for another—in a bid to remain politically relevant in the niche carved or intended. This can explain the plethora of political parties in Nigeria (Brown 2013, 174). Splits, mergers and coalitions are also a marked feature of the Nigerian party system. All Progressive Congress (APC), to which the current president Muhammadu Buhari belongs, was formed in 2013 as a result of an alliance between many parties—Action Congress of Nigeria (ACN), Congress for Progressive Change (CPC), All Nigeria Peoples Party (ANPP) and a faction of the All Progressive Grand Alliance (APGA)—to take on the PDP.

23.5 Political Economy of Nigeria

Nigeria's economic status is a peculiar one as despite being a recourse rich country, it remains one of the poorest countries in the world. Nigeria has many riches in terms of natural resources and is considered as a potential power by many analysts. Yet, it could not, so far, exploit its potential. The major source of livelihood for Nigerians is agriculture, and it contributes 24.18 per cent in terms of GDP (NDP 2016). It has been argued that agriculture sector, though historically remained neglected, is the most critical and basic sector that has significant potentials for the transformation of the Nigerian economy (Ogbalubi and Wokocha 2013).

23.5.1 Agriculture: Neglected Mainstay of the economy

Given Nigeria's geographical location, which makes it rich in agro-diversity, agriculture becomes an important sector in Nigeria's economy. Nigeria has not utilized its agricultural potential and this has negatively impacted the development and poverty reduction in Nigeria. There are various reasons why agriculture did not get its due. First, neglect of agriculture in Nigeria is rooted in colonial history. The British forced Nigerian farmers to grow crops useful as raw material for British products. Due to colonial policies, Nigeria came to independence with typical of Africa and other third-world areas. The economy was based on production and export of agricultural production. Nigeria though tried to break away from colonial economic policies, but the need for foreign exchange meant that the emphasis on agriculture would remain on exportable commodities. The country had to carry on producing same crops as was in colonial time in order to run the economy. Further, immediately after independence also, due to the prevailing views amongst the economists in both the industrial and Third World countries, agriculture was seen as a sector from which to extract savings for investment in other sectors (Mundt and Aborisade 2000, 687–88). After independence, 'for close on a decade, Nigeria existed only through the exploitation of her farmers' (Dudley 1982, 230, as quoted in Mundt and Aborisade 2000, 688). However, Nigeria, despite all this, was self-sufficient in food at the time of independence, and agriculture was the central component of the national economy in the First Republic. This sector received a setback during the Biafran War (1967–70), which negatively impacted the agricultural commodity production in the east, and also during a severe drought in 1969. Finally, the development of oil industry dealt a blow to the agriculture in terms of both labour and capital investment. Agriculture, which accounted for 80 per cent of exports in 1960 plummeted to 2 per cent by 1980. Food imports surged by 700 per cent between 1970 and 1978 (Watts 1987, 71). Nigeria, once known as the 'land of palm oil', started importing even this agro-commodity.

Further, rural forces never had a significant influence on Nigerian politics. The 'nonelite and rural elements continue to be marginalized and manipulated by elite and urban groups' (Kew and Lewis 2007, 567). Parties use ethnic identity and traditional authority as political devices to mobilize voters. During the British colonial era also, peasants were marginalized economically and politically as they had no political organizations or parties that defended peasants' economic and political interests (Arif 2018). Needless to say, therefore, peasant interests continue to be marginalized in the policy discourse in Nigeria. Despite this, it is now increasingly believed that 'farming-led strategies are particularly important in the agriculture-based countries, where farming is the main livelihood for a large share of rural households, as many as 71 per cent in Nigeria' (World Bank 2007, 75).

Special Insights

Significance of Agriculture in African Nations Abundant in Minerals

Agriculture plays a significant role in the economies of mineral-rich African countries, accounting for one-third of their economic activity. Interestingly, between 1985 and 1999, agriculture contributed on average twice as much as the industrial sector to their overall economic growth. However, despite having higher average per capita GDP compared to mineral-poor countries, poverty remains prevalent in these nations.

The divergent experiences of Indonesia and Nigeria, both large oil-exporting countries, before 1997 illustrate this point. Indonesia supported its agriculture sector, both indirectly through regular devaluations of the exchange rate that incentivized agricultural tradables, and directly through investments in rural infrastructure, irrigation, agricultural credit, and fertilizer subsidies funded by windfall oil revenues. In contrast, Nigeria had policies that hindered agriculture. This was done directly through the operation of marketing boards and indirectly through a fixed exchange rate system that heavily taxed agricultural exports and subsidized inexpensive imports.

The results were striking: In Indonesia, the poverty rate at $1 a day declined from 47 percent in 1981 to 14 percent in 1996, demonstrating significant poverty reduction. In Nigeria, during the same period, the $1-a-day poverty rate increased from 58 percent to 70 percent. The differing treatment of agriculture played a crucial role in explaining these divergent outcomes.

23.5.2 Political economy of Oil and Turmoil

Oil politics has become a critical issue in Nigeria's body politics. Since the discovery of the black gold in 1956, oil has become a determining factor in the economy (Clark 2016, 76). The source of Nigeria's hard currency shifted dramatically from agricultural products to petroleum in the early 1970s, and since that time, petroleum has accounted for over 90 per cent of export earnings (Mundt and Aborisade 2000, 689). However, oil and politics have been inextricably linked in Nigeria, and this relationship has proven more harmful than beneficial. Oil made Nigeria a prominent player in the international market. Nigeria has been a member of Organization of the Petroleum Exporting Countries (OPEC) since 1971. It is the biggest oil producing country in Africa. In Nigeria, politics around oil has also led to a situation of 'resource curse', creating severe problems in the state.

First, oil in Nigeria is concentrated in Niger delta, forming just 8 per cent of the countries' geographical area. This concentration of such an important natural resource presents a classic problem of distributive justice. Awareness of oil's potential value was an important motivation behind the Eastern region's declaration of independence as Biafra in 1966. However, simultaneously, the rest of the country was so obstinately determined to keep the region with Nigeria. Even though the federal government won the civil war, these regions in general wonder why the riches should be shared by the distant north. Further, the oil-producing region is the least developed in Nigeria, and unrest will continue until the delta people believe they have been fairly treated (Mundt and Aborisade 2000, 690). Nigeria's crude oil wealth paradoxically became an impediment to its democratic development, as it incentivized the country's military to seize and retain political power (Siollun 2009, 2). Thus, the most important question in Nigerian economy has been related to distribution of oil revenues.

Second, oil politics and its impact on state have led to neglect of other key sectors of development. Agriculture, as indicated earlier, was the most obvious and prime casualty of this approach. Agriculture introduced a healthy competition amongst different geographical regions where each region was exploring its own strength for both domestic and international markets. It received a major setback from oil-based political economy. One of the impacts was notably the 'Dutch Disease', where the non-oil tradable sector (agriculture) declined in response to appreciation of the domestic currency. By 1975, Nigeria had become a net importer of food for the first time (Fosu 2008, 149). Nigerian elites used the oil money to reproduce their interests in infrastructural and industrial development at the expense of peasant producers (Arif 2018).

Third, oil took corruption at a different level. Patron-client relationships were encouraged to amass wealth for individuals at the expense of state. Corruption in Nigeria was closely linked with oil economy and let the state to 'resource curse' where state has been losing its wealth due to the resource it has. Xavier Sala-i-Martin and Arvind Subramanian (2013) have argued that Nigerian experience provides telling confirmation of the assertion that some natural resources—oil and minerals in particular—exert a negative and nonlinear impact on growth via their deleterious impact on institutional quality. Waste and corruption from oil has been held responsible for Nigeria's poor long- run economic performance.

Special Insights

Resources and Economic Development

The scholarship on the relationship between rich endowment of resources and economic development has attempted to explain why do some resource-abundant countries succeed while others do not? (see, for instance, Karl 1997; Ross 1999; Sala-i-Martin and Subramanian 2013). Karl (1997) contends that in oil countries, dependence on petroleum leads to disproportionate fiscal reliance on petrodollars and public spending at the expense of statecraft. Oil booms, which create the illusion of prosperity and development, actually destabilized regimes by reinforcing oil-based interests and further weakening state capacity.

There is a complex relationship between rich resource endowment and economic development as there are so many other variables which determine the outcomes. However, historically, at the risk of simplification, it can be observed that richness in natural resources is neither essential nor sufficient for economic progress, though it can be tremendously beneficial. Rich in agricultural, mineral and energy resources, the United States is one of the strongest and most diversified economies of the world. Japan, not a rich country in terms of natural resources, primarily through its unique developmental strategies, is one of the most advanced economies of the world. Nevertheless, by contrast, almost always, states which rely on one or two natural resources for export and growth for a long time often fail to generate a wider momentum in the economy. Nigeria is a case in point. Here oil overshadowed all other sectors of the economy. It relied on petroleum exports and even became a net importer of the agricultural products for which it was the leading exporter. By contrast, countries like Indonesia and Malaysia managed to diversify their export basket. In this comparative context, Nigeria's case study allows us to emphasize one basic point that richness in terms of resources is not sufficient for economic growth, and consolidated political systems along with sound economic policies are often a prerequisite to harness the potential of rich endowment of resources.

23.5.3 Towards Liberalization: SAPs and Needs

Nigeria adopted planned economy even before its independence. The first plan was adopted for 10 years in 1946. After independence also, Five Year Plans were common from 1962 to 1985. In 1985, Nigeria opted for Structural Adjustment Programmes (SAPs), which were endorsed by International Financial Institutions (IFIs). These programmes, as everywhere else, were intended to reduce government role in the economy and develop free markets by encouraging economic liberalization and promoting private enterprises. It was argued that during the planned economy period, Nigeria faced perpetually growing debt burden, balance of payment crisis, lack of fiscal discipline and declining oil revenues. However, the SAP outcomes showed only partial success in terms of putting the economy back on path. The performance of Nigeria as measured by conventional indices was discouraging even after SAPs (Ekpo 1992), and they failed to revitalize the economy.

With the fourth republic came some hopes of stability in economic processes. President Obasanjo started a new economic initiative—National Economic Empowerment and Development Strategy (NEEDS). It is a medium-term planning strategy with claims of a blueprint for new order in Nigeria. Based on a macroeconomic plan document, it presents a comprehensive vision, goals and principles that would be made possible through four key policies of wealth creation, employment generation, poverty eradication and value reorientation. On the similar line of NEEDS, states have also designed similar programmes—State Economic and Empowerment Development Strategies (SEEDS). However, despite a catchy nomenclature, it has been argued that NEEDS is not different from previous development plans in Nigeria, and despite the claim to be a home-grown plan, it is very much in line with the wishes of the international agents of developed capitalist economies (Marcellus 2009).

Manufacturing has not taken off in Nigeria. As commented by Kew and Lewis, 'on domestic level, Nigerian entrepreneurs have found that trading, government contracting and currency speculation offer more reliable yields than manufacturing. Potential foreign investors remain hesitant to risk significant capital in an environment characterized by social and political instability, unpredictable economic policies and endemic corruption' (2007, 538).

23.5.4 Political Economy of Nigeria's Elusive Progress

But what is the political economy explanation for Nigeria's elusive progress? Commenting on the role of ideas, institutions, circumstances and interests, as these components form the core of political economy, Olu Fasan (2017) opined why economic progress continues to deceive Nigeria. In terms of ideas, there is hardly any normative consensus about anything in Nigeria. Since the pre-independence period, when there was a national consensus around the need for Nigeria to become independent from Britain—even then the north demurred on timing—there has been no prevailing idea driving change in Nigeria. There is no consensus, for instance, on the need to restructure the country, even though that is badly needed. Similarly, while institutions drive policy change in many countries, in Nigeria, they lead to 'path dependency'. Further, despite going through several existential crises—the civil war, economic devastation, deep political divisions and tensions, etc.—Nigeria is not a country that typically responds to crisis by undertaking radical reforms. The core explanation lies in terms of vested interests. Nigeria is a deeply fractured country where powerful interest groups hold sway. Any attempt to change is thwarted by these powerful interests. It becomes impossible to achieve change when there are too many vested interests with sectional and narrow agendas.

Unlike countries like Brazil, the regime type—military or civilian—does not matter much in terms of economic performance in Nigeria. In fact, in the whole of Africa, the most serious single episode of looting, a situation in which assets, whether private or public, are stripped outside the context of the rule of law and due process, was indeed under the auspices of democracy, namely the Shagari regime in Nigeria, 1979–83. This period was the peak of the oil boom, potentially providing the country with massive finance for productive investment. This opportunity, probably the most important in Africa, was missed due to looting during democracy (Collier and O'Connell 2008, 93).

Atul Kohli (2004) has emphasized the state's role in both promoting and hindering industrialization. He has argued that some states have simply proved to be more effective agents of economic development than others. Nigerian state's failure to industrialize, in particular, is rooted in its neopatrimonial character. Such states can variously be described as clientelistic, corrupt or predatory. In states exhibiting neopatrimonial characteristics, several key features become evident. First, leadership tends to prioritize personal or sectional objectives over broader public goals such as nation building, economic development, or industrialization. Second, these neopatrimonial states often have a civil service staffed by individuals with relatively low levels of competence and professionalism. Third, the relationship between state elites and business in these settings tends to be marked by mutual corruption, with state resources bolstering private gains, while private gains in turn reinforce the power position of the ruling elite. Fourth, the state's influence typically has limited reach downward. Even if decision-making within the government is highly centralized, these states often lack meaningful connections to various societal groups, including workers and rural populations. Finally, despite the potential presence of various ideological stances, such as socialism or economic nationalism, in the leadership's rhetoric, ideologies tend to play a minimal role in guiding policy, legitimizing the state elite, or fostering a shared project between the state and society. Kohli notes that while a "pure" neopatrimonial state may be rare in reality, Nigeria closely approximates many of the characteristics associated with this form of governance. (Kohli 2004, 394).

Additionally, what is wrong, with reference to many African states in particular, is that they repeatedly distort markets and serve the urban interests. Due to this, there are serious economic failures and neglect of agriculture. One important consequence of this is low agricultural production having a multiplier negative impact in a predominantly agrarian society (see Bates 1981). In Nigeria also, particularly in the initial years, agriculture was seen as a 'cash cow' from which to extract savings for investment in other areas. Governments also tried to satisfy urban demands for cheap basic food products by holding down the prices of food crops paid to the farmers. 'This contributed to the unattractiveness of agricultural work, and enhanced the lure of the cities' (Mundt and Aborisade 2000). The urban bias has distorted economic progress and has increased and reinforced the urban crises as well (Anochiwa and Michael 2016).

23.6 Some Other Issues: Terrorism and Human Development Challenges

Since 2010, Boko Haram, a militant/terrorist organization based in north-east of the country, has dominated the security discourse in Nigeria and nearby areas. It is believed that the members of the group commonly known as Boko Haram actually prefer to be referred to by their Arabic name, which is 'Jama'atu Ahlis Sunna Lidda'awati Wal-Jihad,' signifying 'People Committed to the Propagation of the Prophet's Teachings and Jihad.' However, in the town of Maiduguri, located in northeastern Nigeria, where the group is thought to have originated, the local residents commonly refer to them as 'Boko Haram.' This term is a combination of the Hausa word 'boko,' meaning 'Western education,' and the Arabic word 'haram,' which figuratively conveys 'sin' and literally means 'forbidden.' 'Boko Haram' has thus been frequently translated as 'Western education is sacrilege' or 'Western education is a sin.' Some argue that the use of this expression is meant to convey that the group is opposed not just to Western education but to Western civilization as a whole. In essence, their opposition extends beyond education to encompass Western civilization, which includes Western education but is not limited to it. (Adibe 2013, 10–11).

In 2014, according to 'Global Terrorism Index' (GTI), Nigeria faced intense challenge from terror as the country witnessed the largest increase in terrorist deaths ever recorded by any country. Boko Haram was reported to be the 'most deadly terrorist group in the world' (IEP 2015, 2). However, in 2016, GTI has reported that terrorism deaths attributed to Boko Haram decreased by 80 per cent in this year following interventions from the Multinational Joint Task Force. This coincided with the splintering of the group into three separate groups, significantly improving Nigeria's GTI ranking. Despite this, Nigeria is likely to continue to face terror challenges as 13 separate groups undertook attacks in 2016 including the attacks in Nigerian delta as well as Fulani extremists in the middle belt (IEP 2017, 3).

Nevertheless, many issues about Boko Haram remain unclear and contested. Some scholars say that primary conflict in Nigeria is religious and not ethnic. Academics working on state theories and postcolonial studies understand Boko Haram as a symptom of Nigeria's failing state. Many sociologists and several social anthropologists attribute it to poverty. Southern Nigerian politicians and lobbyists blame Northerners' domination of the state. Counter-terrorism and security experts focus on the international linkages of the group and the threat it poses to the stability of Western Africa (Mantzikos 2013, 7). Whatever may be the case, Boko Haram has attracted global attention of the security analysts along with the academics and policymakers interested in Nigerian and African politics during recent years.

In terms of social and human development, there are numerous challenges in front of Nigeria. Not only poverty is rampant in Nigeria, but it is a country of huge inequalities. According to Oxfam International (2018), more than 112 million people are living in poverty in Nigeria, paradoxically the country's richest man would have to spend $1 million a day for 42 years to exhaust his fortune. The amount of money that the richest Nigerian man can earn annually from his wealth is sufficient to lift 2 million people out of poverty for 1 year. Further, the combined wealth of Nigeria's five richest men—$29.9 billion— could end extreme poverty at the national level in Nigeria. The country also faces an alarming growth in youth unemployment; more than 42 per cent are unemployed, and nearly two-thirds of them live in poverty (FAO 2018). The latest Human Development Index (UNDP 2018) presents Nigeria as a state struggling with a lot of problems especially in terms of human security of its people. Though Nigeria presents features of both traditional and modern society, women as elsewhere do not enjoy much socio-economic freedom. The role of women differs according to geographic, ethnic and religious factors with women in north more likely to be secluded in home.

23.7 Conclusion

The trajectory of precolonial and colonial history of Nigeria has shaped its troublesome present polity and its key features. As a political unit, Nigeria was a colonial creation in which distinct groups were willy-nilly brought together primarily for colonial interests. British policies of dealing with ethnic complexities intensified these cleavages, resulting into a fragile national identity along with, of course, a retarded economy. All these aspects percolated into a postcolonial state. After an early debacle of democracy, the state kept oscillating between civilian and military regimes. While military regimes severely weakened democratic institutions, ethnicity-based polity has also been responsible for the pitfalls and travails of Nigeria. The discovery of oil, in the absence of proper institutions and amidst ethnic competition for resources, earned only problems for Nigeria. Further, through misplaced policies in economy, Nigeria—within the framework of patrimonial and prebendalist Nigerian state, society and economy—brought more miseries for its masses. Seen from the perspective of comparative politics, Nigerian case study allows us to engage with themes and issues including, inter alia, the role of colonialism in the postcolonial state formation, experimentations in handling ethnically and religiously pluralistic societies, interface of ethnicity and politics, civil-military dynamics and troubles of establishing a successful democracy in postcolonial conditions, value of federalism in managing diversities, the entanglement of democracy and development, state's capacity and necessary and sufficient conditions for economic development, the problem of 'resource curse' and so on. Nigerian experience, though troublesome it is, offers lessons for other similarly placed societies and those which are grappling with predicaments alike to that of Nigeria.

In the above context, for a stable state of affairs in Nigeria, it is important that the so-called 'national question' must be settled concussively once and for all. With this, modern democratic institutions should be allowed to work on secular and neutral basis, and a more representative mode of politics based on the idea of true federalism is called for. In terms of political economy, Nigeria must not repeat the mistakes of the past. Along with diversifying its economy, a new impetus to the agriculture sector is required. Above all, when democracy appears to be stabilizing under the fourth republic, Nigeria must turn from a system of politics which is dominated by an oligarchy of ethnic elite and few 'big men'. In essence, the current state of politics, based on ethnic, regional and religious lines, must give way to politics based on real issues of livelihood for the masses. All this is also important because 'as Nigeria goes, so goes the rest of sub-Saharan Africa'.

Keywords

Ethnic conflicts
Kleptocracy
Patrimonialism
Political economy of Nigeria
Politics of Nigeria
Prebendalism
Resource curse
Unfinished state

Review Questions

1. Why is the case study of Nigeria important for the students of comparative politics?
2. The long shadow of colonialism still shapes the state of affairs in Nigeria. Do you agree?
3. Almost every aspect of politics and political economy in Nigeria revolves around regional and ethno-religious politics. Explain.
4. Write an essay on the fourth republic of Nigeria.
5. Nigerian political economy presents a classic case of 'resource curse'. Elucidate.
6. How is agriculture the neglected mainstay of Nigerian economy? Also explain its implications.

References

Adamolekun, Ladipo, John Erero, and Basil Oshionebo. 1991. 'Federal Character' and Management of the Federal Civil Service and the Military. *Publius: The Journal of Federalism* 21(4): 75–88.

Adibe, Jideofor. 2013. What Do We Really Know about Boko Haram? In *Boko Haram: Anatomy of a Crisis*, edited by Ioannis Mantzikos. Bristol: e-International Relations. Accessed from https://www.e-ir.info on October 5, 2018.

Anochiwa, L.I., and Enyoghasim Michael. 2016. Urban Bias, Urban Crisis, and Development in Nigeria: Controversies and Contending Issues. *EPRA International Journal of Economic and Business Review* 4(6): 5–11.

Arif, Sirojuddin. 2018. Cursed by Oil? Rural Threats, Agricultural Policy Changes and the Impact of Oil on Indonesia's and Nigeria's Rural Development. *Journal of International Development*. Accessed from wileyonlinelibrary.com on December 9, 2018.

Brown, Grace Malachi. 2013. Nigerian Political System: An Analysis. *International Journal of Humanities and Social Science* 3(10): 172–79.

Campbell, John, and Matthew T. Page. 2018. *Nigeria: What Everyone Needs to Know*. Oxford: Oxford University Press.

Central Intelligence Agency (CIA). 2018. Nigeria. In *The World Fact Book*. United States. Accessed from https://www.cia.gov on December 5, 2018.

Clark, Esekumemu Victor. 2016. The Politics of Oil in Nigeria: Transparency and Accountability for Sustainable Development. *American International Journal of Contemporary Research* 6(4): 76–82.

Collier, Paul, and Stephen A. O'Connell. 2008. Opportunities and Choices. In *The Political Economy of Economic Growth in Africa: 1960–2000*, edited by Benno J. Ndulu, Stephen A. O'Connell, Robert Bates, Paul Collier, and Chukwuma C. Soludo, Vol. 1. Cambridge: Cambridge University Press.

Crowder, Michael. 1978. *The Story of Nigeria*. London: Faber and Faber.

Dhikru, Adewale Yegboyaju. 2011. Nigeria's Forth Republic and the Challenges of a Faltering Democratization. *African Studies Quarterly* 12(3): 93–106.

Diamond, Larry. 1995. Nigeria: The Uncivic Society and the Descent into Praetorianism, in *Politics in Developing Countries*, edited by Larry Diamond, Juan Linz, and Seymour Martin Lipset. London: Lynne Rienner Publisher.

Dudley, Billy. 1982. *An Introduction to Nigerian Government and Politics*. Bloomington, IN: University of Indiana Press.

Ekeh, Peter. 1989. The Structure and Meaning of Federal Character in the Nigerian Political System. In *Federalism and the Federal Character in Nigeria*, edited by Peter Ekeh and Eghosa E. Osaghae. Ibandan: Heinemann Publisher.

Ekpo, Akpan H. 1992. Economic Development under Structural Adjustment: Evidence from Selected West African Countries. *Journal of Social Development in Africa* 7(1): 25–43.

Ekundare, R. Olufemi. 1973. *An Economic History of Nigeria: 1880–1960.* New York: Africana Publishing Company (Holmes and Meir).

Fasan, Olu. 2017. The Political Economy Explanation for Nigeria's Elusive Progress. Accessed from https://www.businessdayonline.com on November 15, 2018.

Food and Agriculture Organization (FAO). 2018. Boosting Youth Employment in Nigeria. Accessed from http://www.fao.org/partnerships/resource-partners on December 12, 2017.

Fosu, Augustin Kwasi. 2008. Anti-Growth Syndromes in Africa: A Synthesis of the Case Studies. In *The Political Economy of Economic Growth in Africa: 1960–2000*, edited by Benno J. Ndulu, Stephen A. O'Connell, Robert Bates, Paul Collier, and Chukwuma C. Soludo, Vol. 1. Cambridge: Cambridge University Press.

The Indian Express. 2018. Double Trouble. *Editorial Page*, 4 December.

Institute for Economic and Peace (IEP). 2015. Global Terrorism Index. Accessed from http://economicsandpeace.org on October 23, 2017.

Institute for Economic and Peace (IEP). 2017. Global Terrorism Index. Accessed from http://visionofhumanity.org on November 16, 2018.

Joseph, Richard A. 1987. *Democracy and Prebendal Politics in Nigeria: The Rise and Fall of The Second Republic.* Cambridge: Cambridge University Press.

Karl, Terry Lynn. 1997. *The Paradox of Plenty: Oil Booms and Petro-States.* Berkeley: University of California Press.

Kew, Darren, and Peter Lewis. 2007. Nigeria. In *Introduction to Comparative Politics,* edited by Mark Kesselman, Joel Krieger, and William A. Joseph. New York: Houghton Miffin Co.

Kohli, Atul. 2004. *State-Directed Development: Political Power and Industrialization in the Global Periphery.* Cambridge: Cambridge University Press, Cambridge.

Mantzikos, Ioannis. 2013. Introduction. In *Boko Haram: Anatomy of a Crisis*, edited by Ioannis Mantzikos. Bristol: E-International Relations.

Marcellus, Ikeanyibe Okey. 2009. Development Planning in Nigeria: Reflections on the National Economic Empowerment and Development Strategy (Needs) 2003–2007. *Journal of Social Sciences* 20(3): 197–210.

Mundt, Robert J., and Oladimeji Aborisade. 2000. Politics in Nigeria. In *Comparative Politics Today: A World View*, edited by Gabriel A. Almond and G. Bingham Powell. Delhi: Pearson Education. Nigeria Data Portal (NDP). 2016. Nigeria Agriculture. Accessed from http://nigeria.opendataforafrica.org on December 7, 2018.

Ogbalubi, L.N., and C.C. Wokocha. 2013. Agricultural Development and Employment Generation: The Nigerian Experience. *Journal of Agriculture and Veterinary Science* 2(2): 60–69.

Oxfam International. 2018. Nigeria: Extreme Inequality in Numbers. Accessed from https://www.oxfam.org on December 28, 2018.

Parkinson, Joe. 2018. Nigeria Gripped by Whether President is a Clone: 'It's the Real Me, I Assure You'. Accessed from https://www.wsj.com on December 9, 2018.

Phillips, Douglas A. 2004. *Nigeria.* Philadelphia, PA: Chelsea House Publishers.

Ross, Michael L. 1999. The Political Economy of the Resource Curse. *World Politics* 51 (2): 297–322.

Sala-i-Martin, Xavier, and Arvind Subramanian. 2013. Addressing the Natural Resource Curse: An Illustration from Nigeria. *Journal of African Economies* 22(4): 570–615.

Siollun, Max. 2009. *Oil, Politics and Violence: Nigeria's Military Coup Culture.* New York: Algora Publishing.

Transparency International. 2018. Nigeria, in *Corruption Perception Index*. Accessed from https://www.transparency.org on December 7, 2018.

United Nations Development Report (UNDP). 2018. Human Development Report. Accessed from http://hdr.undp.org on December 11, 2018.

Watts, Michael J. 1987. *State, Oil and Agriculture in Nigeria.* Berkeley: University of California Press.

World Bank, World Development Report. 2007. *Agriculture for Development.* Washington, DC: The World Bank.

CHAPTER 24

China's Constitutional Development and Political Economy Since 1949: Perspectives and Trends

Rityusha Mani Tiwary and Shivani Sharma

Reader's Guide

The chapter begins by outlining the history of China's constitutional development, salient features of the Chinese constitution, major debates around political reform in China and amendments in its constitution. In the next section, the chapter elaborates the debates behind China's transformation from planned to market economy, focusing on questions pertaining to economic reforms, modernization and industrialization in China. The chapter traces the phases of industrialization and modernization in Chinese economy and, in the last part, the impact of China's rise on a globalized market economy is briefly discussed.

24.1 Introduction

Since 1949, China has shown an alternate path of development for the Third World countries, and with the opening up and reform in 1978, it has proven to be an eclectic experiment of integrating socialism with market economy. Its ever-deepening links with world politics and economy invite a closer scrutiny of its development path. This chapter outlines the debates surrounding China's political and economic reforms and focuses on its constitutional development since 1949, phases of industrialization and modernization, integration with world market economy and its current role. Post USSR world politics and the end of Cold War, economic globalization has been ever expanding. In this backdrop, China's case has huge resonance with the discussion around the negative and positive impacts of economic globalization, the economic strategies adopted by developing economies and the imbalances of development. The next section focuses on the constitutional development of China and paves the way for further insights into domestic political reforms and their interlinkages with globalization.

Key Facts

Capital	Beijing
Area	9,596,960 sq. km
Population	1,384,688,986 (July 2018 est.)
Official language	Mandarin
Major religion	Buddhists (18.2%), Christians (5.1%) and Muslims (1.8%)
GDP (purchasing power parity)	$23.21 trillion (2017 est.)
GDP real growth rate	6.9% (2017 est.)
Government type	Communist party-led state

Sources: CIA, World Fact Book (2018) and UNDP (2018).

24.2 History of Constitutional Development of China

A conscious constitution-making was a 20th-century phenomenon in China. The imperial dynasties that ruled China from the 3rd century BC until 1912 had developed a large collection of sophisticated statutes, describing the structures, principles and functioning of the various agencies of the empire. The statutes were also supplemented by customs, traditions and precedents. However, unlike in the West, China did not experience a single document charter of government until the very last years of the ailing Manchu dynasty. Admiring Japan's success after the adoption of the Meiji constitution, the Manchu government accepted the demands of the reformers to emulate Japan and grudgingly announced an introduction of a Western-style constitution, a monarchy of the parliamentary type over the period of a decade (Cohen 1979, 58).

The process of constitution-building, however, got stalled due to the objections raised by the reformers who disappointingly noted that, despite the promises, the government was steadily concentrating powers in the hands of the royal family. Thus, the failure of the Qing dynasty to carry out extensive economic and political reforms led to a successful uprising in the state. The revolution which began with the Wuchang Uprising of 10 October 1911 slowly spread over to other cities and provinces and ended over 2,000 years of imperial rule in China. The uprising successfully overthrew the Manchu dynasty and announced the establishment of the Republic of China (ROC).

ROC was born in 1912 with the promulgation of a provisional constitution under the Nanjing Provisional government led by Sun Yat-sen (Teon 2016). The provisional constitution bestowed upon the parliament the responsibility of writing and producing a permanent constitution. Sun Yat-sen proposed an incremental process of constitutional development. In his work, 'The Three Stages of Revolution', Sen suggested three stages of constitutional development (Yat-sen 1918) (see Box 24.1). Sun Yat-sen was succeeded by Chiang Kai-shek in the year 1925. Chiang's rise to nominal national power in 1928 directed his efforts to frame the constitution for the country. A new provisional constitution was introduced under Chiang's leadership in 1931. The new provisional constitution mostly confirmed itself with the provisions and arrangements of the previous constitution and kept all government agencies under the control of the generalissimo's authoritarian Nationalist Party (Cohen 1979). The constitution followed Sun Yat-sen's principle of 'political tutelage', for the de facto dictatorial powers of the Guomindang government to precede the true constitutional era. The process was considered to have accelerated the stage for the establishment of a constitutional government in which political power gets restored to a popularly elected government (Teon 2016).

Box 24.1 Special Insights

The Three stages of Revolution by sun Yat-sen

First Stage of revolution: It is a period of destruction. The revolutionary army unites against the Manchu dynasty and enforces martial law.

Second Stage of revolution: It is known as the transitional period or what Sun Yat-sen calls as 'political tutelage'. During this stage, provisional constitution is enacted and the government is promoted to encourage the exercise of political rights by the people.

Third Stage of revolution: The third phase is the completion of the reconstruction process. During this period, constitutional government is introduced.

Source: http://afe.easia.columbia.edu/ps/cup/sun_yatsen_revolution.pdf

However, the continuous process of framing constitutions was opposed by various groups of people, who not only rejected Sen's theory of the need for a period of tutelage but also demanded the promulgation of a permanent constitution. The opposition leaders made the said demand in order to curb the dictatorial powers of the nationalist party, whereas the demand for embracing constitutionalism instilled the ruling nationalist party with fear of losing power.

The constitution of the ROC was finally passed in the year 1946 by the National Assembly. The framing of the constitution was considered a unilateral act of the Chinese Kuomintang Party as the Chinese Communist Party (CCP), the largest organized opposition party in China, refused to participate in the drafting of the new constitution and withdrew its delegation from participation in April 1946. One of the most eminent leaders of CCP, Zhou Enlai, showed his disgruntlement over the new constitution and grudgingly noted that, 'in spite of the fact that the so-called "National Assembly" has already been held and a so-called constitution has been passed; its nature is still that of a "Chiang Kia-shek" constitution. We and the democrats of the whole country will determinedly not recognise it as legal and valid' (Tkacik 2004).

Therefore, the new constitution did not bring about much change in the nature and character of the nationalist party's dictatorial rule in the state. The organization and management of the party continued to remain more important than the formal structures and processes of the government in the ROC. Constitutionalism failed to take roots in the state, and the policy documents did not bring about much stability as hoped by their advocators.

Hence, the monopolization and the growing dictatorial power of the nationalist party aggrieved the people of the country. The disgruntlement of the communists against the nationalists finally led to a civil war. During the war, the communists marked their victory against the nationalists and declared the formation of the People's Republic of China (PRC) in 1949.

24.3 Constitutional Development of PRC Since 1949

Unlike the constitutions in the West, Chinese constitution does not establish or describe the apparatus of the government. The constitution document merely signals a change in the power position or in the political and economic conditions of the country. It indicates the direction in which the country is to be governed, by notifying the basic ideological statement and declaring the actions that the government intends to take. Therefore, the Chinese constitution can be referred to as 'particularized statements of policy' (Jones 1985, 714).

The ideological statement in the constitution serves as the basis for all economic and social policies. Thus, Chinese constitutions are more like a reflection of social, economic and political conditions that existed in the country at the time of the promulgation of the constitution and actions taken and contemplated by those who promulgated them. Therefore, in order to comprehend and trace the constitutional history of China, it is imperative to understand the processes of the stages of development in the country.

Communist's victory in the civil war led to the establishment of a completely new government in China. The cooperation among the CCP and other political parties and social organizations (*minzhu dangpai*) resulted in Chinese People's Political Consultative Conference. The conference concluded with the constitution of a 'Common Program', which served as the main guiding principle for the new state (Common Program of the PRC 1949–54). China, in the opinion of the communists, was experiencing the revolutionary transformation from a semi-feudal and semi-colonial state into a new democratic society (Chang 1956, 523).

Based on Mao's New Democracy, the Chinese State turned into what is referred to as 'People's Democratic Dictatorship' (Karunakaran 1952, 38). The people's democratic united front was composed of the Chinese working class, peasantry, petty bourgeoisie, national bourgeoisie and other patriotic democratic elements. Although based on an alliance of workers and peasants, the united front was led by the working class. However, cognizant of the challenges towards the transition to a socialist state, Mao rallied the inclusion of petty bourgeoisie and national bourgeoisie under the leadership of the working class. He considered them as forces capable of helping in the struggle against imperialism.

Therefore, in order to fight the imperialist forces as well as the landowning and the bureaucratic capitalist class, the newly independent state took upon itself the task of confiscating the bureaucratic capital to return it to the ownership of the democratic society.

However, with an intention to seek support from the national bourgeoisie, the party declined to undertake the process of nationalization and refused to carry out the confiscation of private industrial capital and its enterprises. Though the intermediate position of the national bourgeoisie was of a temporary nature. For instance, as early as June 1952, Mao made a reversal on his policy position and no longer recognized the national bourgeoisie as an intermediate class. He declared that, 'with the overthrow of the landlord and the bureaucratic-capitalist class, the contradiction between the working class and the national bourgeoisie has become the principal contradiction in China' (ibid.).

The Common Program, therefore, paved the way for the first constitution in China in the year 1954. The 1954 Constitution defined China as 'People's Democratic State', a broad people's democratic united front, led by the working class and based on the alliance of workers and peasants. The period from the founding of PRC to the attainment of socialism was referred to as the period of transition. The period was recognized as the earlier stage of people's democracy en route to socialism, advancing from 'people's democracy' to 'socialist transformation of agriculture, handicrafts and capitalist industry and commerce' (Chang 1956).

The Chinese constitution of 1954 reflected the Soviet model. Like the Supreme Soviet, the National People's Congress, although unicameral, became the highest organ of the state and, along with local people's congresses, practised democratic centralism. According to Mao Zedong, democratic centralism 'is centralized on the basis of democracy and democratic under centralized guidance' (Gasper 1982, 162). More so, the long list of fundamental rights and duties of citizens paralleled with that of the Soviet Constitution. And lastly, as in the Soviet-bloc countries, courts in China too were not granted the power to invalidate legislation on the grounds of constitutional violation (Cohen 1979, 63).

However, very little effort was made to implement some of the provisions of the constitution. For example, Article 87 of the 1954 constitution guaranteed the citizens the right to exercise freedom of speech, press, assembly, association, procession and demonstration. This right was complemented by Mao's movement/policy of 'Let a hundred flowers bloom, let the hundred schools of thought contend' (MacFarquhar 1960, 3), encouraging China's intellectuals to submit different ideas, even offering criticism of the party and its policies. However, not being receptive of the growing criticism of the party, the policy was soon withdrawn. The party leaders not only turned against the critics and condemned them as 'bourgeois rightists' but launched an anti-rightist campaign (1957–59) in the country.

The next constitution in China was introduced in the year 1975. The 1975 constitution declared China as a 'Socialist State of the Dictatorship of the Proletariat' led by the working class and based on an alliance of workers and peasants. The constitution primarily laid emphasis on party's leadership and organization and declared the Communist Party of China (CPC) as a 'vanguard' for the working class (Article 2). It included the support for the leadership of the CPC as one of the fundamental rights and duties of its citizens (Article 26). Moreover, the command of the country's armed forces and people's militia was given in the hands of the chairman of the party central committee (1975 Constitution Preamble).

The constitution also reflected upon the economic transformation in the country. The articles enshrined in the constitution notified the provision for the ownership of the means of production. For example, Article 5 of the constitution specified two kinds of ownership: the 'socialist ownership by the whole people' and 'socialist collective ownership by the working people'. The constitution also inserted the socialist principle declaring, 'He who does not work, neither shall he eat' and 'from each according to his ability, to each according to his work' (Article 9) (1975 Constitution). However, the 1975 constitution did not last for long and was soon replaced by the 1978 constitution. The 1978 constitution did not make many changes in the realm of property relations but introduced some potential checks upon executive powers and actions.

China finally realized the socialist system in its 1982 constitution and declared the PRC as a 'Socialist State under the People's Democratic Dictatorship' led by the working class and based on an alliance of workers and peasants. The 1982 constitution was essentially considered a Dengist constitution based on Deng Xiaoping's ideas of modernizing China. The preamble of the constitution emphasized upon the country's road to 'Socialist modernization'. It aimed at modernizing the industrial, agricultural, defence and science and technology sectors step by step to transform China into a socialist country with a high level of culture and democracy' (Constitution of the PRC 1982).

With the drive towards socialist modernization and opening up, many of the provisions of the 1982 constitution were revised in the following years. In China, revisions of constitutional provisions are based on party's will and policies. For example, CPC's suggestions at the 14th congress in 1992 were dutifully adopted by the NPC. Revisions were carried out in the 1982 constitution in which the term 'socialist market economy' was added in place of 'planned economy', while the terms 'state-run economy' and 'state-run enterprises' were replaced with 'state-owned economy' and 'state-owned enterprises' (SOEs), respectively. Moreover, the proposal at the 15th Party Congress in 1997 was accepted at the second session of the 9th NPC word by word. The proposal to incorporate Dengist version of socialism into the constitution was accepted and amendments were made in the constitution in regard to 'the Four Fundamental Principles', a Chinese version of the 'Rule of Law' and a politico-economic version of 'socialism with Chinese characteristics'. The next amendment in the constitution took place in the year 2004, following the 16th Party Congress in 2002. The revision mainly included the adoption of the idea of 'Three Represents' (see Box 24.2), an explicit recognition of human rights and further protection for private property (Chen 2004, 2).

Box 24.2 Special Insights

The Three Represents

It is a guiding sociopolitical theory credited to Jiang Zemin, who talked about fulfilling the requirements of three represents:

- Representing development trend of China's advanced productive forces.
- Representing the orientation of China's advanced culture.
- Representing fundamental interests of the overwhelming majority of the Chinese people.

Source: *Selected Works of Jiang Zemin*, Eng. (Ed.). FLP, Beijing, 2013, Vol. III, pp. 1–2.

24.4 Salient Features of the Constitution of China

The salient features of the constitution are as follows:

- **People's Republic:** Article 2 of the Chinese constitution declares China as People's Republic. All power belongs to the people. The National People's Congress and the local people's congresses at various levels are the organs through which the people exercise state power.
- **Democratic Centralism:** The principle of Democratic Centralism was first promulgated by Mao in his essay on 'New Democracy' in 1940. By declaring no impassable gulf between democracy and centralism, Mao suggested that only by adopting democratic centralism can a government be really strong. Democracy will ensure that the government in power be truly representative of the popular will and, on the other hand, the centralization of administrative power will smoothen up the process of carrying out the policies in accordance with the people's will (Mao Vol. II: 57–58). Article 3 of the Chinese constitution states that the state organs of the PRC apply the principle of democratic centralism. The NPC and local people congresses at various levels are constituted through democratic elections. They are responsible to the people and are subject to their supervision. The division of functions and powers between the central and local state organs is guided by the principle of giving full scope to the initiative and enthusiasm of the local authorities under the unified leadership of the central authorities.
- **Fundamental Rights (Articles 33–56):** Chapter II of the Chinese constitution lays down the provisions of the fundamental rights and duties for its citizens. It guarantees freedom of speech, press, association, assembly, procession and treats all citizens equal before the law.
- **Flexible Constitution (Article 64):** The constitution of PRC is a flexible constitution as amendments to the constitutions can be proposed by the standing committee of the NPC or by more than one-fifth of the deputies of the NPC and adopted by a vote of more than two-thirds of all the deputies to the congress. Laws and regulations are to be adopted by a majority vote of all the deputies to the NPC.
- **Unicameral Legislature:** National People's Congress is the highest organ of state power and meets in session once a year. Elected for a period of 5 years, the NPC and its standing committee exercise the legislative power of the state. The legislative body is composed of deputies elected by the provinces, autonomous regions and municipalities directly under the central government and by the armed forces. NPC is a unicameral legislature with additional powers to oversee the work of the government and to elect major officials. The state constitution vests in NPC a wide range of powers and functions such as the power to amend the constitution, supervise the enforcement of constitutional and legal enactments, decide on questions of war and peace and examine and approve the national economic plan and the state budget and report on their implementation. Formally, it has a significant role in the appointment of senior state officials as it elects the president and vice-president and decides upon the name of the Premier of the State Council on the nomination by the president (Saich 2015, 2). The standing committee of the NPC also enjoys many powers such as the right to interpret the constitution, supervise its enforcement, enact and amend statutes with no exception of those which should be enacted by the NPC and enact when the NPC is not in session.
- **Socialism with Chinese Characteristics:** Socialism with Chinese characteristics is a product of the integration of the basic tenets of Marxism with Chinese realities and the primary stage of socialism in China, marked by reform and opening up (see Box 24.3).

Box 24.3 Special Insights

Socialism with Chinese Characteristics

Proposed by Deng Xiaoping and incorporated in the 1982 constitution, the principle of 'Socialism with Chinese characteristics' laid down the path of socialist modernization in China and paved the way for the establishment of a 'Socialist Market economy'. The term socialism with Chinese characteristics represents a broad theoretical category which represents adaptation of Marxist–Leninist thought to Chinese circumstances at specific times. For instance, according to one view, 'Xi Jinping Thought' represents Marxist-Leninist policies suited for China's present condition, while 'Deng Xiaoping Theory' was considered relevant for the period when it was formulated (He 2001). Socialism with Chinese characteristics is not the same socialism as envisaged by Marx and Engels. Although upholding the basic tenets of scientific socialism, China establishes a basic economic system in which socialist public ownership stays dominant but different types of ownership develop side by side. It meant adopting essentials of market economics as a means to promote growth using foreign investment and to increase productivity (especially in the villages where 80% of China's population lived) while the CPC kept its hold on both the official loyalty to communism and the control on political power.

For further reading: Xiaoping, Deng (1984). 'Building Socialism with a Specifically Chinese Character'. *People's Daily,* 1 October.

China declares 'market economy' as its present stage of development in which markets play a primary role in resource allocation under macro-adjustment and stay under the control of the state (Wu 2008, 48–49). Thus, socialism with Chinese characteristics discounts the assumption that socialism can be only achieved through planned economy and realizes that market economy can operate within socialism too by controlling economic activity. Hu Jintao at the 17th National Congress of the party defined socialism with Chinese characteristics as 'localization of Marxism'. He stated, 'the state under the leadership of the CPC and in light of China's basic conditions will take economic development as its central task, adhere to the Four Cardinal Principles and preserve in reform and opening up, release and develop the productive forces, consolidate and improve the socialist system, develop the socialist market economy, social democracy, and make China a prosperous, strong, democratic, culturally advanced and harmonious modern socialist country' (Xinhua 2007).

24.5 Major Debates in the Context of Political Reforms in China

China has been engulfed with many challenges coming from within. Debates within China have sparked off around the issue of political reforms and constitutionalism. Demands have been raised in the country for carrying out reforms in the country to ensure better implementation of constitutional provisions and to keep in check the growing powers of CCP and its leadership. The liberals in China allege the government of having a constitution without the spirit of constitutionalism. They assert scepticism over party's willingness to enact constitutional reforms in its true spirit.

One of the major debates in China surfaced around the time of political and economic reforms in the country which led to a subsequent debate on the issue of human rights. China faced a major setback in the form of a Democratic movement in 1989. The pro-democratic student movement had deep roots in the political, economic and social reforms undertaken by China in the post-1978 period. Divided into two stages, the initial stage of reform introduced decentralization, advocated high consumption and generated rapid economic growth and unrealistic high expectations among both the leaders and the people. The second stage, however, introduced economic reforms calling in for a transformation from a planned to a market economy.

In order to make that transformation, the state undertook price reforms as the first step for establishing market discipline. In 1985, the CCP decided to decontrol the prices of the means of production. Leveraging their political power, the state officials managed purchasing products directly from producers below the market price and made huge profits selling them in an open market. This policy action benefitted the high officials and their family members or relatives who got the opportunity to set up their own firms. The practice of 'official profiteering' gave rise to a new class, the 'third echelon cadres', which highly benefitted the offspring of high officials. Therefore, widespread corruption and practice of official profiteering raised discontent amongst the people of China (Shi 1990, 1188–91).

Adding to this, the State Educational Commission in 1988 announced a reform shedding all responsibility on the part of the state to assign jobs to students. The reform aggrieved the student community who believed that the new policy was introduced to benefit the progeny of high officials. Furthermore, arrangements to prevent newly graduate students from going abroad reinforced the tensions between students and the government and paved the way for a democratic movement.

The movement appealed to the government for admission of guilt, demanding to lift control over news media and student's right to open their own organizations. The Chinese authorities who have for long deprived the right of association to its people and maintained control over news media decided to suppress the growing democratic movement in the country.

However, the major crackdown on student demonstrators in Tiananmen Square in 1989 sparked a new debate on the issue of human rights in China. Due to persistent international pressure and condemnation for its actions, China revised its constitution, adding a paragraph to Article 33 which reads, 'The State respects and preserves human rights'.[1]

Despite the constitutional guarantees, human rights violation has been a recurring theme in China. The government in China has been long suppressing the fundamental rights of its citizens. For example, the constitution of China guarantees some of the fundamental rights to its citizens such as freedom of speech, press, assembly, association, procession and demonstration (Article 35) and gives the citizens the right to criticize and make suggestion to any state organ or functionary (Article 41). However, these rights are far from being realized. The Tiananmen Square tragedy of 1989 and the more recent case of Liu Xiaobo (see Box 24.4) highlight the curbing of dissent.

Box 24.4 Special Insights

Demand for Democratic Reforms in China

- **1989 Democracy Movement:** The 1989 Tiananmen Square protests were studentled demonstrations in Beijing in 1989. The protests were forcibly suppressed by the Chinese Premier Li Peng who declared martial law and ordered the troops to fire at the demonstrators trying to block the military's advance towards Tiananmen Square. The movement was loosely organized and had varied goals where student protestors called for democracy, greater accountability, freedom of the press and freedom of speech.
- **Charter 08:** Liu Xiaobo is one of the drafters of a manifesto published in 2008 named Charter 08 and signed by more than 350 Chinese intellectuals and activists. He was punished with an 11-year jail sentence for 'subverting state power' for his suggestions on seeking imposition of constitutional government, electoral democracy and the elimination of one-party rule.
- **Counter currents:** *Global Times*, a party newspaper, ran an editorial criticizing constitutionalism as a roundabout route to repudiating China's development path. Moreover, in 2013, a memo named Document No. 9 was distributed within the CCP, outlining seven threats to party's control, which included 'Western constitutional democracy', human rights, pro-market 'neoliberalism' and 'Western-inspired ideas of media independence and civic participation' (Eleanor and Xu 2018).

For further reading: 1. Nathan, Andrew J. 2001. "The Tiananmen Papers." *Foreign Affairs*, January- February. http://files.foreignaffairs.com/legacy/attachments/PC12_Tiananmen.pdf.

Congressional Executive Commission on China, US, Annual Report. 2010. https://www.cecc. gov/publications/annual-reports/2010-annual-report.

The growing demand for political and constitutional reforms in the country has been suppressed and kept under check by the counter-attack movement led by party conservatives. In order to maintain its control over the rising dissent in the country, the CCP attempts to embed itself across layers of Chinese society and economy. It does so by restricting the growth and movement of religious groups, media organizations, human rights activists and lawyers and stakes a much harder line against corruption that has led to the downfall of influential politicians, military officers and businessmen (Eleanor and Xu 2018).

China is also confronted with another challenge around its model of 'political constitutionalism'. In China, the constitutionality of legislative actions is determined by the country's legislative body (the NPC and standing committee), instead of courts. Though, in the past 15 years or more, the issue of constitutional enforcement has become an important topic of deliberation in China. Many see this as an emerging wave of 'popular constitutionalism' as a group of scholars, lawyers, citizens and the media are attempting through litigation not only to assert their constitutional rights but also to bring about a change in the very understanding of the structure of their government (Kellogg 2009, 218).

On the other hand, many significant Chinese scholars have promoted the debate on the idea of 'judicial constitutionalism' in which the courts help determine the unconstitutionality of legislative acts. As prevalent in most of the countries, such as India and the United States, judicial activism is promoted for primarily two reasons: (1) courts are better equipped at interpreting laws, and since constitution is primarily a legal document, courts seem necessarily drawn to constitutional interpretation; (2) constitutional enforcement requires objectivity and decision makers who act independently from ordinary politics. Thus, courts are usually more independent than political entities themselves. Therefore, constitutional enforcement without objectivity and professional expertise lacks real enforcement.

The monopolization of power in the hands of one party has stalled the process of constitutionalism. The overwhelming powers of the CCP supersede the powers of the constitution. President Xi Jinping has proposed to cut through this challenge by suggesting to establish a coexistence between the party and the constitution. Recommending the party to function within the scope of the constitution, he stated, 'The Party leads the people in formulating the constitution and the law, the party leads the people in implementing the constitution and the law, the Party itself must act within the scope of the constitution and the law' (Jinping 2014). However, it is too early in the day to conclude whether the practice will be realized in the true spirit or, like any other provision of the constitution, be violated.

Moreover, the party organization primarily dominates the legislative wing of the country. Unlike the parliaments in the West, NPC acts as a ceremonial legislature and functions like a rubber stamp authority for the CCP. With having 70 per cent of its delegates as party members, the NPC hardly enjoys a status of an independent legislature. NPC does not exercise most of the powers given to it. For example, major decisions and appointments in China are made by the CCP and are passed on to the NPC only for its consideration. The recent NPC's ratification over the constitutional amendment proposed by the CCP for ensuring a lifelong tenure for President Xi Jinping is a prime example. Given 70 per cent of the communist party's representation in the National People's Congress, the parliament unanimously elected Xi Jinping as president and chairman of the Central Military Commission through a majority vote of 2,970 out of 3,000 in the first session of the 13th National People's Congress of the fifth plenary session held in 2018 (*Outlook* 2018).

24.6 China's Development Strategies: The Debate Over Economic Reforms

There have been various debates and controversies on the question of economic reforms in most of the developing states that were also the erstwhile colonies in many cases. This was true in case of China as well since any unfavourable developments in its economy were viewed by the political class in China as major roadblocks leading to disagreement and internal bickering in the party. The debate around reform started in 1978 when

Deng Xiaoping opened up China's economy. This also meant doing away with Mao's conceptualization of China's economy and his narrative of what should be a favourable path to development for the country (see Boxes 24.5 and 24.6). Mao tried to explain the economy of China by highlighting the contradiction and 10 major relationships. In October 1984, the Chinese leaders released schematic economic reform in the Central Committee of the CCP (Almanac of China's Economy 1985). This was a result of long drawn debate over the nature of reforms (Sung and Chan 1987, 17–24). First, the reforms were initiated as the local-level experiments (for instance, Sichuan province[2]) later implemented by central authorities—a process that developed a circuitous relationship between the local experiments in different provinces and the national reform programme (Ling 1981, 54–62). Second, owing to the macro-economic and structural imbalance that national economy was suffering from, economic readjustment (retrenchment) was suggested as an immediate action rather than economic reforms (ibid.).

There is also a debate regarding the factors that pushed China's reform and opening up. According to one perspective, China's reform began in the early 1970s against a realigned international context.[3] First, by the 1970s, changed international circumstances facilitated overseas Chinese capital investments in southeastern coastal China via Hong Kong. Second, Taiwan and Japan formed a significant industrial relationship with China (Yuhai 2006, 2206–12). The Sino-Soviet split and the disbanding of the world socialist bloc in the early 1960s led China to reject the Soviet model of emphasizing on developing heavy industry, instead adopting the 'Four Modernizations' policy of 1975, which put industry, defence, agriculture and science and technology (in that order) as major areas of modernization (ibid.).

Box 24.5 Special Insights

On Contradictions

Mao wrote *On Contradiction* (1937), and along with *On Practice*, it forms the philosophical base of Maoism. It was an attempt by Mao to interpret dialectical materialism who suggested that all life and movement is a result of contradiction. It entailed the following points:

- **Two World Outlooks:** the metaphysical and dialectical concepts of the world.
- **Universality of Contradiction:** Mao believed in absoluteness of contradiction, which means that the process of development of all things has inherent contradictions where a movement of opposites exists from the beginning to end.
- **Particularity of Contradiction:** In each form of motion of matter, there is a particular contradiction which is the essence of a thing. Universality and particularity of a contradiction can be understood as common and individual characters of a contradiction.
- **Principal Contradiction and Principal Aspect of Contradiction:** Principal contradiction is the one that allows other contradictions to exist despite its centrality. For example, in a capitalist society, the contradiction between the proletariat and the bourgeoisie allows the other contradictions, such as the one between imperialists and their colonies.
- **Identity and Struggle of Aspects of Contradiction:** Mao defines identity as two different thoughts: the two aspects of contradiction coexist and contradictions can transform into one another.
- **Place of Antagonism in Contradiction:** In the Maoist theory, the two primary classes, the working class/proletariat and bourgeoisie, have insurmountable differences, and there is no way to reconcile the two. Non-antagonistic contradictions may be resolved through debate, but antagonistic contradictions can only be resolved through struggle.

Source: https://www.marxists.org/reference/archive/mao/selected-works/volume-1/mswv117.htm

Box 24.6 Special Insights

On the Ten Major Relationships

'On the Ten Major Relationships' is a speech by Mao Zedong, delivered during an enlarged session of a Politburo meeting of the CCP on 25 April 1956. It outlined the unique characteristics of PRC's socialism, different from that of the Soviet Union. These served as the guiding principles for PRC's political economy till 1978 after which Deng Xiaoping initiated the opening up of China's economy. Following are the 10 major relationships:

1. Relationship between heavy industry on one hand and light industry and agriculture on the other.
2. Relationship between industry in the coastal regions and industry in the interior.
3. Relationship between economic construction and defence construction.
4. Relationship between the state, the units of production and the producers.
5. Relationship between the central and the local authorities.
6. Relationship between the Han nationality and the minority nationalities.
7. Relationship between Party and non-Party.
8. Relationship between revolution and counter-revolution.
9. Relationship between right and wrong.
10. Relationship between China and other countries.

Source: https://www.marxists.org/reference/archive/mao/selected-works/volume-5/mswv5_51.htm

24.7 Various Phases of Industrialization and Modernization in China

As a result of the Sino-Soviet rift, the first round of industrial reforms in China in 1975 was based on the management model of Yugoslavia where more independence was given to enterprises. Under Mao's influence, the importance of labourers' participation in enterprise management was also given equal importance. Most importantly, till the 1980s, in its official stance towards development, China has put 'socialism' before 'modernization' and 'social development' before 'economic development', which has also been referred to as 'Chinese characteristics' (see Box 24.2).

As a result of early emphasis on modernization, by 1972, China had achieved a triple average life expectancy, economic growth of 6 per cent as an average annual, the universalization of education, the establishment of cooperative rural healthcare, 74 per cent decline in infant mortality, a better status of labourers and an overall social equality (Yuhai 2006). China's industrialization was marked by promotion of local and small-scale industrial production. This was in coordination with sustained agricultural investment in basic rural infrastructure, seeds, agricultural machinery, fertilizers and increased grain price. This in turn allowed for a more balanced development of the rural heartland, checking rapid urbanization and its associated challenges.

The 'Open-door Policy Reforms' of the foreign trade/foreign investment sector and the agricultural sector need to be discussed briefly as later these heralded large-scale changes in other sectors. The CCP's Third Plenum in December 1978 gave official approval to the open-door policy, favouring autonomy to agricultural production teams and facilitating private plots and sideline production. At the same time, the division of land for family farming and the fixed output quotas on a household basis were prohibited (Chinese Agricultural Yearbook 1980, 58). Agricultural decollectivization was undertaken in the Anhui province on a large scale in 1978, as a result of peasant pressure (Shiqi 1982, 3). The Shekou Special Industrial Zone (later subsumed under the Shenzhen Special Economic Zone) was established in January 1979, and the Shenzhen, Zhuhai and Shentu Special Economic Zones were authorized in the late 1979. Many elements of the open-door policy, including foreign aid, loans and investment (from the Soviet Union), technology imports, had been in place since the 1950s even during the Great Leap Forward and collectivization of agriculture (see Box 24.7A). After the Sino-Soviet split of the early 1960s, China replaced its trade from the Soviet bloc with the advanced capitalist countries and began to import complete industrial plants from Japan and Western Europe, which stopped for a brief period between 1966 and 1970 due to the Great Cultural Revolution (see Box 24.7B). As China improved its relations with the United States, and the Cultural Revolution ended, the import of industrial plants was resumed in 1970.

The outreach of enterprise management reform in 1978–80 was impressive as it was adopted by six enterprises in Sichuan in October 1978, 100 in early 1979, 4,000 throughout the country by the end of 1979 and over 6,600 by the end of 1980 (Sung and Chan 1987). This was equivalent to 16 per cent of all industrial enterprises covered by the state budget, accounting for 60 per cent of the total output and 70 per cent of the total profits (Zerong 1986). In 1981, enterprise reform was made mandatory for all state industrial enterprises. In the second half of 1980, the economic reforms slowed down owing to worsening balance of payment deficit, government budget deficit, the decentralization of the foreign trade with uncontrolled expenditures and imports and foreign debt (Davie and Carver 1982, 30).

Box 24.7 Special Insights

A. Great Leap Forward

After China's first Five Year Plan, in 1958, Mao initiated 'grass-roots socialism' to build a modern industrialized state. Mass mobilization of the people into collectives and establishment of people's communes in the rural China with the goal of doubling the 1957 agricultural production in the next year; all these marked the Great Leap Forward (GLF) policy. Steel Production was assigned to many communities. This resulted in mass-scale amateurish attempts by uneducated farmers who used their garden furnaces to produce poor quality and mostly useless steel. The Great Leap reduced harvest sizes and led to a decline in the production of most goods except substandard pig iron and steel. In the meantime, bad weather, disorder in the collectives and exports of food products necessary to procure hard currency resulted in the Great Chinese Famine.

Source: The People's Republic of China: II, The Great Leap Forward, 1958–60. http://www.chaos. umd.edu/history/prc2.html

B. Great Proletarian Cultural Revolution

Initiated by Mao, the Cultural Revolution, or the Great Proletarian Cultural Revolution (GPCR), was a sociopolitical movement in China from 1966 until 1976. It aimed at ameliorating capitalist and traditional elements and establishing communism from Chinese society. The revolution marked Mao's return to power after the failures of GLF. Mao alleged that bourgeois elements had infiltrated the government and society at large, aiming to restore capitalism, who he termed the 'revisionists'. Red Guard groups were formed across China to resume the class struggle and had massive impact. It also led to the ouster of 'corrupt' senior officials like Liu Shaoqi and Deng Xiaoping from power.

Mao officially declared the end of GPCR in 1969, but it lasted until the death of military leader Lin Biao in 1971. After Mao's death and the arrest of the Gang of Four (leaders of GPCR) in 1976, reformers led by Deng Xiaoping gradually replaced the policies associated with the Cultural Revolution. In 1981, the party declared that the Cultural Revolution was 'responsible for the most severe setback and the heaviest losses suffered by the Party, the country, and the people since the founding of the People's Republic'.

Source: Roderick MacFarquhar and Michael Schoenhals. 2008. *Mao's Last Revolution*. Cambridge, MA: Belknap Press.

With such experiences, the leadership concluded that economic reform should follow, not precede, economic balance. In the next 2 years, the restoration of economic balance and focus on agricultural reforms favoured the resumption of the urban reforms since 1983 in the form of contract system. SOEs pushed for greater autonomy, direct taxation of SOEs and greater director/manager responsibility. This trend in urban/industrial reforms continued till 1993.

In 1997 and 1998, massive privatization was unleashed in which most SOEs (except petroleum and banking) were disinvested. China joined the WTO in 2001, and between 2001 and 2004, the number of SOEs decreased by 48 per cent, triggering massive lay-off of workers; tariffs, trade barriers and regulations were reduced; banking system reformed; social welfare system shrunk and inflation reduced (Loren, Rawski, and Sutton 2008). The domestic private sector first exceeded 50 per cent of GDP in 2005, and in 2010, China became the second largest economy in the world (*The Guardian* 2010). The Chinese government under Hu Jintao adopted more egalitarian and populist policies by increasing subsidies and control over the health care sector, halted privatization, adopted a loose monetary policy and promoted the rise of large 'national champions' which could compete with large foreign corporations (Chovanec 2009).

Under Xi Jinping and his administration, the government has increased its control over SOEs and private enterprises. It is reported that in 2017, around 288 firms amended their company charter to allow a greater hold of the CPC in corporate management (*Nikkei Asian Review* 2018).

The legacy of reforms has been variously debated with the recent reversal of some reforms in 2008 as marking the 'third anniversary of the end of reforms'. Despite bringing poverty levels down and increasing the national income, China's New Left has been critical of the reforms due to increasing inequality and purchase of state assets at reduced prices by private entrepreneurs (Li 2015, 46–49). The demands of the New left were accommodated by the Chinese government under Hu Jintao and Wen Jiabao, who adopted populist and egalitarian measures including a flexible monetary policy, increasing subsidies and control over the health care sector, halting privatization and promoting the rise of large 'national champions' which could compete with large foreign corporations (Chovanec 2009). Some Chinese economists have criticized these measures that advocate a policy of deregulation, tax cuts and privatization and point out that SOE dominance and technology transfers laws need reform for faster growth (CNBC 2018). There are criticisms against reforms from the environmental perspective too which points out the negative impact of rapid industrialization on environment and public health. It is pointed out that environmental measures and the air quality in China are 'better than those in developed countries, such as the United States and Japan, at the same level of development' (Perkins and Rawsk 2008). It is also pointed out that rising regional disparities, unemployment and the failure to resettle the displaced workers could create social uncertainty and instability (Li 2001), if not addressed in the next phase of reforms.

24.8 Impact of China's Rise on Globalized Market Economy

China's economic rise has led to many concerns about its impact on other economies and whether its phenomenal success will have negative ripples. This impact assessment is closely linked with the sustainability and equity challenges in front of China's current growth and development strategies. Reliance on exports and investment has been an important aspect of China's economic growth which contributed to numerous structural problems within China as well as the global imbalances in recent decades. During recent decades, an increased foreign direct investment (FDI) in China has attracted the scrutiny of critics with regard to the negative impact on other developing Asian economies. This fear was allayed in the backdrop of Asian financial crisis as studies found out that there has been a positive 'China Effect' on investment-creation in the Asian region during 1992–2008; the increased resource demand by Chinese economy contributed to greater production-networking activities within Asia, in turn, deepening Asian integration (Golley and Song 2010).

While not all of the concerns related to global/regional imbalances can be addressed by China, a rebalancing of growth of domestic consumption and productivity is required. China's first 30 years of reform and transformation have laid the foundation for deeper institutional reforms during the next stage of its development. It has been suggested, for example, that an effective way of increasing domestic demand is to 'accelerate the pace of "urbanizing" migrant workers (estimated to have reached 160 million in China in 2009) by granting these workers urban residency, which would change their consumption behavior' as higher wages will lead to higher consumption and therefore higher import demands (ibid.). The institutional reforms that impact the aforesaid goals are labour mobility laws, social security system, exchange rate regime and land management system. The government in China has been moving in the direction of these reforms as is evident from the US$282 billion current account deficit of China in the first quarter of 2018, its first in 17 years which, it has been argued, is due to increase in import of goods but more services by China (Taylor 2018).

A rising crop of Chinese companies mainly in the technology sector is redefining the flow of capital and business in the world economy. Companies like Alibaba, Xiaomi, Tencent and Baidu represent an unparalleled growth of entrepreneurialism in China (Tse 2015) and add to innovation capacities that create premier products and services, heralding a new age of global competition. The rising power of China in Asia and Latin America can be accounted by the fact that 21 per cent of exports coming to Southeast Asia in 2015 were from China, which is also the largest importer of goods and the main trade partner for neighbouring countries. In 2018, China is among the top five export markets for 12 of the Latin American region's 20 countries. The Belt and Road Initiative by China is another indicator of its deepening influence across Asia.

24.9 Conclusion

The dynamics of China's rapid development and economic rise are complex. The Chinese case is one response to the political economy debate on what must gain precedence: economic reforms or political reforms? Associated with the rise are the scenarios of Great Powers competition for resources in developing and underdeveloped countries. These perspectives also lead to the implications of Chinese hegemony in the region and beyond as there are many criticisms of China's 'predatory economic practices' (Harrington 2018). On the other side, the US hegemony constantly strengthened through neoliberal finance capital is seen as the reason behind current trade and currency wars between China and the United States. China's role as a leader in global trade and investor in Asia and Africa has strengthened the *renminbi* (Chinese currency: RMB). China's economic success and increasing soft power make an interesting case for centralized power and authoritarian practices even though the twin threats of political instability and economic sustainability question the longevity of authoritarian models of policymaking.

Keywords

Constitutional development in China
Economic reforms
Globalization
Industrialization and modernization
Market economy
Political reform

Review Questions

1. To what extent the political system of China has helped promote rapid growth?
2. Highlight some salient features of China's constitutional development.
3. Explain how rural reform became the driving force of China's economic reform in its initial phase.
4. Indicate some major features of economic strategies of development pursued by China.
5. Examine the impacts of globalization on China's socialist political economy.
6. Discuss the role of 'opening-up' in China's economic reform. In this context, what do you understand by 'Socialism with Chinese characteristics'?

Notes

1. Amendment to the Constitution of PRC, http://www.npc.gov.cn
2. The Sichuan initiatives emphasized on enterprises over central planning, which was not in sync with the national-level discourse among leaders and economists who preferred unified national planning (Sung and Chan 1987).
3. Factors like Richard Nixon's 1972 visit to China in the backdrop of US withdrawal from Vietnam and China's long-term support for Vietnam, breaking up of 'New Crescent Containment' (composed of the Southeast Asian Treaty, the Baghdad Treaty and the Japan-US Security Accord), India and Indonesia's advocacy of 'Bandung Spirit' led to, what some believed as, the revival of 'Chinese civilization sphere', earlier split up by East Asia's Cold War order.

References

Almanac of China's Economy. 1985. *Central Committee of the CCP*, 1–12. Beijing.

Brandt, Loren, Thomas G. Rawski, and John Sutton. 2008, China's Industrial Development, in *China's Great Economic Transformation*, edited by Loren Brandt and Thomas G. Rawski. Cambridge: Cambridge University Press.

Chang, Yu-Nan. 1956. *The Chinese Communist State System under the Constitution of 1954*, 524. Chicago, IL: University of Chicago Press.

Chen, Jianfu. 2004. The Revision of the Constitution in the People's Republic of China: A Great Leap Forward or a Symbolic Gesture. *China Perspectives* 53: 1–22.

Chinese Agricultural Yearbook. 1980. p. 58. Beijing: Nongye Chubanshe.

Chovanec, Patrick. 2009. China's Real Estate Riddle. *Far East Economic Review*. Accessed from http://www.feer.com on September 11, 2023.

CNBC. 2018. China's Economic Reform is Falling Short—and Patience is Growing Thin, Says Report. Accessed from https://www.cnbc.com on September 11, 2023.

Cohen, Jerome Alan. 1979. China's Changing Constitution. *Northwestern Journal of International Law & Business* 14(57): 58–59.

Common Program of the People's Republic of China. 1949–54. Accessed from http://www.commonprogram.science on September 11, 2023.

Constitution of the People's Republic of China. 1982. US-China Institute Press. Accessed from https://china.usc.edu on September 11, 2023.

Davie, John, and Dean W. Carver. 1982. China's International Trade and Finance, in *China Under the Four Modernizations Joint Economic Committee*, 30, edited by US Congress Joint Economic Committee.

Eleanor, Albert, and Benia Xu. 2018. *The Chinese Communist Party*. Council on Foreign Relations Press. https://www.cfr.org/backgrounder/chinese-communist-party.

Golley, Jane, and Ligang Song. 2010. Chinese Economic Reform and Development: Achievements, Emerging Challenges and Unfinished Tasks, in *China: The Next Twenty Years of Reform and Development*, edited by Ross Garnaut et al., 1–18. Sydney: Australian National University Press.

Harrington, Kent. 2018. *The Gift that Keeps on Giving—to China*. Accessed from Project Syndicate. https://www.project-syndicate.org on September 11, 2023.

Jinping, Xi. 2014. Explanation Concerning the 'CCP Central Committee Decision concerning Some Major Questions in Comprehensively Moving Governing the Country According to the law Forward'. *China Copyright and Media*. Accessed from https://chinacopyrightandmedia.wordpress.com on September 11, 2023.

Jones, William C. 1985. The Constitution of the People's Republic of China. *Washington University Law Quarterly* 63(4): 704–14. Accessed from https://openscholarship.wustl.edu on September 11, 2023.

Karunakaran, K.P. 1952. New Democracy—The Chinese Communist Concept. *The Australian Quarterly* 24(3): 33–42.

Kellogg, Thomas E. 2009. Constitutionalism with Chinese Characteristics? Constitutional Development and Civil litigation in China. *International Journal of Constitutional Law* 7(2): 215–46. https://doi.org/10.1093/icon/mop001

Li, He. 2015. *Political Thought and China's Transformation*, 46–49. London: Palgrave Macmillan.

Li, Kui Wai. 2001. The Two Decades of Chinese Economic Reform Compared. *China and World Economy*, No. 2. Accessed from http://unpan1.un.org on September 11, 2023.

Ling, Lin. 1981. Sichuan's Reform of the Industrial Management System, in *Almanac of China's Economy*, 54–62. Beijing: Jingji Guanli Zazhishe.

MacFarquhar, Roderick. 1960. *The Hundred Flowers Campaign and the Chinese Intellectuals*, 3. New York: Frederick A. Praeger.

Nikkei Asian Review. 2018. Chinese Enterprises Write Communist Party's Role into Charters. Accessed from https://asia.nikkei.com on August 18, 2017.

Outlook. 2018. China's Rubber-Stamp Parliament Re-Elects Xi Jinping as President. Accessed from https://www.outlookindia.com on September 18, 2023.

Perkins, Dwight H., and Thomas G. Rawsk. 2008. Forecasting China's Growth to 2025, in *China's Great Transformation*, edited by Loren Brandt and Thomas G. Rawski. Cambridge: Cambridge University Press.

Saich, Tony. 2015. *The National People's Congress: Functions and Membership*. Cambridge: Ash Centre for Democratic Governance and Innovation, Harvard Kennedy School.

Shi, Tianjian. 1990. The Democratic Movement in China in 1989: Dynamics and Failure. *Asian Survey* 30(12): 1186–205.

Shiqi, Xu. 1982. A Debate that Has Aroused Widespread Attention. *Nongye jingji wenti [Issues in Agricultural Economics]* 4: 3.

Sung, Yun-Wing, and Thomas M. H. Chan. 1987. China's Economic Reforms: The Debates in China. *The Australian Journal of Chinese Affairs* 17: 29–51.

Taylor, Timothy. 2018. China Now Has a Trade Deficit. *Conversable Economist*. Accessed from https://conversableeconomist.blogspot.com on September 18, 2023.

Teon, Aris. 2016. Provisional Constitution of the Republic of China (1931). *The Greater China Journal*. Accessed from https://china-journal.org on September 18, 2023.

The Guardian. 2010. China Overtakes Japan as World's Second-Largest Economy. Accessed from https://www.theguardian.com on September 18, 2023.

The National People's Congress (NPC), (c) Embassy Of The People's Republic Of China In The Republic Of Bulgaria All Rights Reserved, http://bg.china-embassy.gov.cn/eng/zgzt/lh/200502/t20050215_2368881.htm, accessed on 11 August 2023

Tkacik, John. 2004. History's Implications for Taiwan's Constitution. *China Brief* 4(21). Accessed from https://jamestown.org on September 18, 2023.

Tse, Edward. 2015. *China's Disruptors*. New York: Penguin.

Wu, Yuanliang. 2008. Socialism with Chinese Characteristics in a Comparative Vision. *Social Sciences in China* 29(2): 46–55.

Xinhua. 2007. Hu Jintao Delivers Report to CPC Congress, Stressing Socialism with Chinese Characteristics. Accessed from http://www.chinaembassy.org.nz on September 18, 2023.

Yat-sen, Sun. 1918. Selections from a Program of National Reconstruction: The Three Stages of Revolution. Accessed from http://afe.easia.columbia.edu on September 18, 2023.

Yuhai, Han. 2006. Assessing China's Reform. *Economic and Political Weekly* 41(22): 2206–2212.

Zerong, Zhang. (Ed.). 1986. *Diary of China's Economic System Reform*. Chengdu, China: Sichuan Kexue Jishu Chubanshe.

CHAPTER 25

Britain: Constitutional Development and Political Economy

Shivali Aggarwal

Reader's Guide

Why do we need to study the British constitutional development and the political system? This simple question can be answered by unfolding the history and relevant chronological accounts of the political developments that led to the formation of the most modern operating political system in the world. Britain has influenced various countries and inspired them to adopt ideas such as rule of law, personal freedom, toleration, political modernization, bicameralism, two major political parties' systems and organization of a vigilant society to name a few. Since the British system has been an epitome of the institutional endurability and systemic stability supplemented with a high degree of political culture, these features make Britain the archetype of a political system that can hardly be missed. The British system is also instructive for the scholars of comparative politics and for those who are interested in understanding modernization, evolution and political underpinnings of the societal changes and economic transformations.

The chapter tries to trace the political, legal and social factors involved in the constitutional history of Britain. Certain indispensable characteristics and the importance of statutes, common law and conventions played a dominant role in the formation of the British constitution. The first part of the chapter is devoted to unravelling the trajectory of evolution along with the understanding of the political institutions such as monarchy, executive, legislature and political parties.The second part of the chapter focuses on the British economy in the postindustrial world order where the mixed economy model is well operative with the social welfare system of the state placed well in order. Britain has been a landmark study in the neo-liberal phase of global economy as it has now become the cornerstone in understanding the reversing trends of the globalization with the 'Brexit'.

25.1 Introduction

Britain is the most significant political and economic political system in the world. British political system has been a benchmark for the newer democracies because of its legacy of having strong and stable political institutions that have endured for centuries (Rutland 2000). Unlike any other countries of Europe, Asia and Latin America that have gone through many political upheavals and tread uneasily on the path of their relatively newly acquired democracy, Britain transformed to parliamentary system in a smooth and gradual evolution. Britain has strong and stable political institutions, a deeply acknowledged national identity and an open society in which individual freedoms are safeguarded and social interests are defended. In the views of John Mc Cormick, 'Britain is quite distinct from other countries in its record of evolutionary development; it has suffered civil wars and political conflict, but the modern British political system is the product of changes and developments dating back centuries' (2007, 112).

It is also interesting to see that Britain has entered the 21st century with the 19th-century political institutions. Although the political institutions in Britain enjoy a highly stable atmosphere, we cannot ignore the fact that these institutions have never been static. Important constitutional reforms have always paved a better way for the British political system with a scope for reforms. *Sun Never Sets for the British Empire* does not hold true for the British system anymore. However, the kind of influence the British system has left on the 49-member Commonwealth also proves that there are unique features in the constitution of Britain. In order to understand the value of these influences, it is important to look at the organization of the institutions, framing of the constitution and mechanism of the political economy in Britain.

This chapter will explore the history of constitutional developments and political economy of Britain through the study of social, political and economic institutions and their changing dynamics. The functioning of the executive and judiciary and presence of social movements are also pertinent for understanding the polity and society of the modern British politics.

25.2 Nature and Evolution of the British Constitution

The British political system is termed as the 'mother'[1] of all the modern democratic political systems, and the constitution forms its heart and soul. Unlike the constitutions of the United States and India, the British constitution was not drafted by constituent assembly formally. Many scholars eulogize the uniqueness of the British constitution. Munro finds it as a complex mixture of institutions, principles and practices augmented by the judicial decisions and common law of precedents, usages and traditions. British constitution is not a single set of documents rather hundreds of documents clubbed together. Prof. Munro has also called its evolution as guided by sometimes accident and other times by serious thinking. It encompasses ages of wisdom of the British system. Its elasticity and porousness is enriched by the commonsense of statesmen instead of conjectural inconsistencies.

The British political tradition has been able to develop a different type of political system where every institution is linked directly or indirectly with its tradition in one way or the other. Britain pioneered the liberal democratic system that has become the inspiration for many countries of the world. For instance, the United States calls itself the most pristine model of democracy because of its written constitution in 1787. Britain is unique, as it lacks a formal written constitution. Unlike other counties, there is no codification of law that happened in Britain. The *unwritten* constitution is a jumble pack of acts of parliament, judicial pronouncements and conventions.

Britain (the United Kingdom)

Disclaimer: This figure is not to scale. It does not represent any authentic national or international boundaries and is used for illustrative purposes only.

Key Facts

Population	67.081 million UK (July 2020)
Total geographical area	243,610 sq. km. Land: 241,930 sq. km. Water: 1,680 sq. km
Urban population	83.4% of the total population
Gross domestic product (GDP) purchasing power parity	$41.600 data in 2017 dollars (2020 est.)
Overseas territories	14 territories with 1,727,570 sq. km area
Temperature	Temperate
Official language	English
Infant mortality rate	4.2 deaths/1,000 live births
Official religion	Christianity
Main occupation of the people	Service Industry with 79.2% of total GDP
Largest ethnic group	Asian or Asian British; Indian: 2.3%
National minorities	Scottish, Walsh, Irish and Cornish people

Sources: CIA, World Fact Book, UNDP 2021.

One of the main virtues of the British model is its capacity to adapt gradually over the time. When we say that the British Constitution is 'evolutionary', we mean that the formation of the British constitution is a never-ending exercise. There is almost no system in the British political traditions which is not related to the ancient system. According to Prof. Munro, the British constitution is the *child of wisdom and chance.* The passage of the evolution of the British constitution and parliament was a gradual and evolutionary process, and it also witnessed few revolutions. Under the leadership of Oliver Cromwell, the parliament fought a civil war from 1642 to 1648 in defence of the rights. Charles I was executed as a result of this civil war. However, the monarchy was restored subsequently. This was said to be the last political upheavals in Britain which on one hand curtailed the powers of the king and on the other hand established the concrete structures of the individual liberties and the parliamentary supremacy.

Being unwritten, the British constitution is the most *flexible* one. There is no procedure of amending the constitution of Britain. The element of flexibility makes the British constitution as one of the most modern constitutions. The British parliament can make changes by simple majority even in all important matters like abolition of monarchy, abolition of House of Lords, changes in the basic structures of the House of Commons, etc. The best example is the Indian Independence Act 1947. By a simple majority, the then Prime Minister Atlee liquidated the British empire from India.

Britain was the first country where the *Parliamentary government* was successfully experimented and implemented. Parliamentary sovereignty rests on the notion of the popular sovereignty, where voters choose their leaders through frequent and fair direct/indirect elections. The British cabinet is responsible to the House of Commons. Unlike in the United States, in Britain, instead of separation of powers, there is centralization of responsibilities. Another salient feature of the British constitution is that the monarch is the head of the state, but not the head of the government. All the executive powers are used by the prime minister who is the real head of the government. Thus, the British political system shows the features of *limited Monarchy.* With passage of time, the importance of the throne has decreased and the ultimate sovereignty lies with the parliament or with the cabinet.

There are number of structural characteristics of the British political system that can be regarded as almost 'constitutional' in their significance and centrality. The *unitary* feature is one such feature. There is no sharing of sovereignty between the national government and the government at the intermediate levels. The second structural characteristic is that of the *Westminster model.* This Westminster model of government differs significantly from the American system in that there is no clear separation of powers between the legislative and executive branches of the government under the British system. The concern and practice of the US constitutional system of *checks and balances* is completely absent in the British constitutional tradition.

Democracy in the United States and Britain

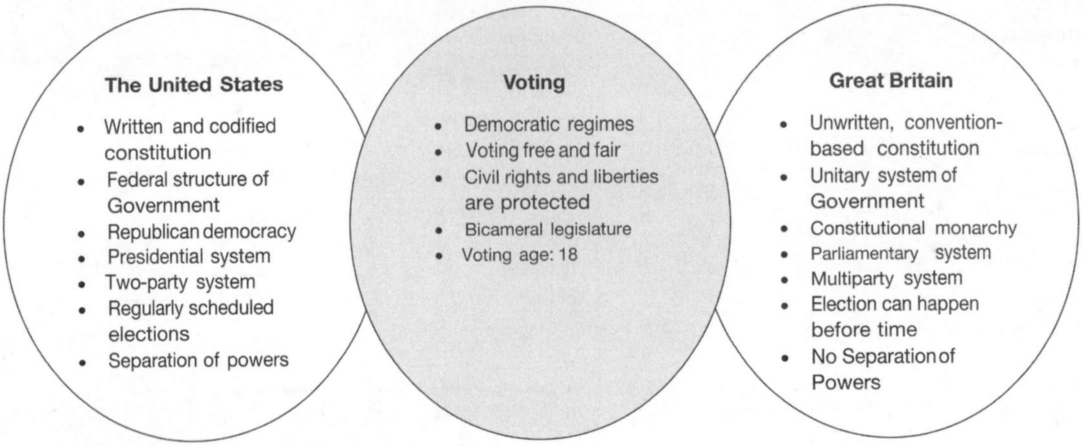

Another major significant political structure in the British constitutional system is that of the political parties. It is impossible to imagine the functioning of the British political system without the functioning of the political parties. Parliamentary form of government has survived because of party discipline, votes of confidence, responsible government, etc. From the above discussion of the salient features of the constitution, it becomes clear that the principles which govern the working of the constitution have been scattered into the history and present circumstances. The citizens of Britain enjoy maximum liberties and rights. Being dynamic in its orientation, the constitution has the capacity to cope with all kinds of situations.

Lord Bryce had once remarked that the 'British constitution works by understanding which no writer can formulate'. French writer Tocqueville once stated that it is sure that 'Britain has no constitution' as nothing exists in a written concrete manner. Despite the scattered resources, the sources of the British constitution can be found in two ways, the written and the unwritten. The written part includes the statutes, acts and charters, whereas the unwritten sources comprised of the conventions and the common law traditions.

25.2.1 The Sources of the British Constitution

25.2.1.1 The Great Charters

The main sources of the constitution can be located in the traditions and the great constitutional landmarks like the Magna Carta 1215, the Petition of Rights of 1628, the Bill of Rights of 1689, the Act of Settlement of 1710, the Parliament Act of 1911, etc. Many of these acts were never fully implemented, yet their significance in evolving the constitution can never be ignored.

The Magna Carta: It is called as an important document of the constitutional history of Britain although it has nothing to do with the common man. For scholars such as Peter Rutland, the story of the framing of the British Constitution and political consolidation actually began with the Magna Carta of 1215.[2] The story of the legacy of the British constitution can be roughly said to 'began with defeat of the English in the battle of Hastings in 1066. Duke William of Normandy defeated the English and extended its control over entire Britain except for Scotland' (Kesselman 2013, 49). The king's control increased after 1066, but the conduct of King John (1199–1216) evoked opposition from the side of feudal lords. In 1215, the regional feudal lords forced King John to sign a charter which will ensure that there will be no abuse of powers from the king's side and the king will provide security to the feudal lords in return of the army troops and monetary help (Rutland 2008, 42). In 1236, the term 'parliament' was used for the first time officially where the king used to summon feudal lords in order to decide about the taxes and implementation of certain laws. By the 15th century, parliament had fought with the monarch for making the laws.

The Magna Carta paved the way for the establishment of limited monarchy and constitutional government in Britain. The Magna Carta affirmed the rule of law, mainly indicating that there should be limits to the king's soverign powers and that the monarch was subjected to the law of the land. Magna Carta is a detailed charter which has 63 articles and 3 major sections. The first section was concerned with the barons, and it mentions the conditions under which the king can borrow money from the barons; the second section deals with the courts and their supremacy. The second section mentions that the king can neither confiscate anybody's property nor order anyone for an exile. Moreover, the king cannot arrest anybody in the absence of the court. The third section deals with the restrictions of imposing new taxes without the advice of archbishops and barons who constituted the council.

Chatham termed Magna Carta to be the 'Bible of the British Constitution', and scholars like Gregory S. Mahler opined that although the major parts of the British constitution are unwritten, the most significant written part is Magna Carta which has prescribed a legislative process for the British constitution (Mahler 2008, 194). This document laid down the basis for the supremacy of Rule of Law with a powerful check on the king's autocracy. The importance of Magna Carta lies in the fact that the rights and privileges which were granted to the barons were subsequently extended to the common man. This charter is extremely important, as it provides the strength to the people to fight for their rights in case they feel that rights are being curtailed. This has become all the more significant with the gradual evolution of the British political system as it shapes the institutions that has to be obeyed by the king as well as the government. The Magna Carta also establishes an important principle for the British political organization that in case of the denial of rights from the government or the king; the people of the Britain have the power and rights to overthrow such kind of a government.

The Petition of Rights 1628: This was another historic charter of rights after the Magna Carta. It was approved by Charles I on 7 June 1628. This was not passed as an act of parliament. The charter made it necessary that no individual should be taken, imprisoned or fortified without proven guilty. It also states that no free individual can be forced to pay or contribute to taxes, compensation or any charges not set by the parliament. This charter also abolishes the provision that soldiers and sailors should be punished by the martial law. 'The petition also prohibited that no person can be compelled to make any gift, loan, benevolence etc' (Bouvier 1914, 2579). The king agreed to all the conditions, and in a way, the common man got many more liberties.

The Bill of Rights 1689: The Bill of Rights was a watershed development in the history of British constitution as it increases the powers of the Parliament. It was another major document after the Magna Carta and the Petitions of Rights 1628, which has been detrimental in regulating the Crown. The bill also aimed at establishing a constitutional monarchy in Britain. By the 16th century, Britain was embroiled in a complex interplay of religious conflicts, national rivalries and the struggle between rulers and the parliament. 'In the Glorious Revolution of 1688, the Protestant William of Orange replaced Roman Catholic James II' (Rutland 2008, 42). On 12 February 1689, a declaration was drawn affirming the rights and liberties of the people. This was constitutionally passed by the parliament and hence it became the 'statute'.

The main provisions of the Bill of Rights include defining the powers and limitations of the crown. The same article also defines the rights of the common man and those of the House of Commons. The bill clearly states that the sessions of the parliament should be convened regularly, and there should be free and fair elections for the House of Commons. Special safeguards were also mentioned so that members of both houses—the House of Lords and the House of Commons—should feel free to speak up their minds. It also warned the king against keeping the army in the times of peace and increasing or levying new taxes without the permission of the parliament. It was also mentioned that it is the prerogative of only the parliament to dispense or suspend any law. The most sensitive part of the Bill deals with prohibiting useless cruel punishments, torture and excessive fines upon the individuals under any circumstances.

The Bill of Rights has the status of being the 'core' constitutional law which has deserved and received particular respect and special honour. It was also mentioned in the Bill of Rights documents that the bill shall stand and remain as 'law' forever. According to Geoffrey Lock, 'this expression was included in the Bill of Rights in order to add solemnity and weight' (Lock 1989, 555). Geoffrey Lock also states that the Bill of Rights forms the basis of many substantive laws of the British constitution and it acts like an indication that the parliament must refer to these topics in the future in order to make more such full-scale statutes (Lock 1989, 541).

Act of Settlement 1707: The Act of Settlement of the parliament of Britain was an act passed in 1701 according to which only a protestant can be the legal heir to the throne in Britain. In addition to the settlement about the crown, the Act contains some other significant provisions. All the future kings were bound to join in communion with the Church of England, and if a future king is not a native of England, then England is not obliged to engage in any war for the protection of the territories not belonging to the crown of England. The judges must be in the office irrespective of the will of the crown; they can only be removed by impeachment by both the houses of parliament. It was also added in the Act that no person who is not born in England, Scotland or Ireland, except born of English parents, shall be capable to be a member of the Privy Council. Such a person cannot be a part of either house of parliament nor can enjoy any important office of trust. However, by the act of 'Naturalization' in 1870, this clause was omitted for all those who have obtained a certificate of naturalization.

25.2.1.2 Statutes

One of the other important sources of the British constitution is the large number of statutes[3] passed by the British parliament from a long time. Acts of the parliament have been collectively called as statutes. When the parliament passes a bill and it gets a Royal accent, it becomes an Act of Parliament and it comes on record as 'on the statute book'. These statutes are the main source of the British constitutionalism because they are known as the written part of the constitution. These statutes mainly deals with the extension of franchise and regularization of the election system.

Some examples of the statutes are the Reform Acts of 1832, 1867, 1884, 1918 and 1928. The Representation of the People Act of 1948 abolished the University Constituencies where a person was debarred from voting on the criteria of 'business premises qualifications'. The Habeas Corpus Act 1671 is still prevalent in British constitution which guarantees that no one can be imprisoned unlawfully.

The Reform Act 1832: It has been known as The Great Reform Act. The British electoral system was criticized for being unfair and partial. People across the Britain had revolted at several places for removing disparities in the voting system. King William IV had become unpopular as he stood in between the electoral reforms. Eventually, he agreed to remove the anomalies present in the electoral system. Rotten boroughs were removed and the right to franchise was extended to the new towns to elect their respective members of parliament. The size of the constituencies was still not acceptable to the people. The men who had property could vote. This decision marginalized the working classes, women and the middle class from the right to vote. It was a systematic step towards empowering the House of Commons where the representatives are now being selected by new industrial towns and cities.

The 1867 Reform Act: This act gave the right to franchise to the middle class and the working class of the cities. The people living outside the municipalities were still not given the franchise. In 1884, the right to franchise was also given to the people residing in municipalities.

The Judiciary Act of 1873: It brought together many tribunals and created the Court of Appeal and the High Court of Justice.

The Representation of People's Act of 1918: This is popularly known as fourth Reform Act. It was an act to reform the electoral system by giving franchise to all the men irrespective of the property they own and to all the women over the age of 30 years with minimum property qualifications. During the First World War, many soldiers who were returning to Britain had no property left with them. Thus, they demanded the extension of franchise, omitting the clause of property ownership condition. This act allows conducting of the general elections on a single day and also keeping the records of the voters.

The Equal Franchise Act of 1928: It enabled both male and female of 21 years of age for the franchise. By the Act of 1948, 'one person one vote' formula was established and special votes for the universities and the industrial cities were eliminated. Finally, in Representation of People's Act 1967, every British citizen, who had attained the age of 18 years was given the right to vote irrespective of the gender.

The Parliament Act of 1911: In order to reform the working of parliament and make the House of Commons more powerful, certain provisions were passed in the form of an Act in 1911. It was decided that once the budget is passed by the House of Commons, it will be sent to the House of Lords for the discussion. After one month, the bill will be considered as passed if the House of Lord does not respond. The decision of the speaker of the House of Commons will be final in the case of deciding if a bill is a money bill or not. Any other bill can become a law by getting the royal consent, once the House of Commons has passed it thrice in 2 years and the House of Lords has not done anything for the suggestions. The tenure of the House of Commons is fixed at 5 years rather than 7 years.

The Ministry of Crown Act 1937: It clears the remunerations and salaries of the ministers in the government as well of the ministers of the opposition.

Similarly, many other Acts can be mentioned as a source of the British constitution like the Abdication Act of 1936; Septennial Act of 1716; the Irish Free State Act of 1922; the Municipal Elections Act of 1872; the Judicature Acts of 1873–76; the Local Government Acts of 1888, 1884, 1929 and 1933; the Public Order Act of 1937 and the Statute of Westminster of 1931, which are also a part of the constitution.

25.2.1.3 Judicial Interpretations

Various judicial decisions are also a convincing source of the British constitution. Though the judiciary in Britain does not have the power of judicial review, yet the judiciary sets the limits of the charters and defines the limits of the statutes by interpreting them. In their vital judgements, they have interpreted the constitutional laws and fixed their directions. References can be made of *Brainbridge vs Postmaster General, Beatly vs Fagg, Ashley vs White, Entick vs Carrington, Local Government Board vs Arlidge, O' Kely vs Harway, De Keyser's Royal Hotel Co. vs Attorney General*, etc. For example, in the case of *Wilkies vs Wood*, it was ruled that a general warrant to search for and capture the papers of an unnamed author was illegal. Similarly, the case of Somerset made the institution of slavery to be illegal in Britain. Between 1771 and 1772, British judiciary dealt with a case where James Somerset—who was a slave—was taken forcibly from England to the other colonies. The court ruled that no man can be taken to the foreign lands and sold by the masters. The slaves, mainly the blacks, interpreted the decision as freedom from slavery and celebrated the historic decision.

The judiciary needs to be safeguarded against all pressures, and this was ensured by the case of Bushell 1670. It was quite confirmed from the Bushel's case that the court of common pleas could issue a writ of habeas corpus in the ordinary criminal cases. Immunity of the judges was taken care of by case of Howell.

25.2.1.4 Common Law and the Rule of Law

Another major source of the British constitution is the 'common law'. According to Prof. Munro, 'a common law like statutory law is continual in process of development of judicial decisions' (Munro 1954, 18). It is like a body of judge-made rules which have never been ordained by a king or enacted by a parliament. The common law consists of those precedents and customs which have been prevalent in the society since time immemorial and have been accepted by the law courts. While giving the judgements, the courts take the common law tradition into their considerations. These are uncodified and unwritten. The unwritten nature of the common law empowers the British constitution to be more flexible as it can be interpreted according to the changing circumstances. The common law forms the basis of the prerogatives of the Crown and the monarchy, the right of trial by jury in all the criminal cases, the rights pertaining to the freedom of speech and to form association and also the rights to have redressal against the government officers.

Another important tradition of the British constitution is the *Rule of Law.* According to Laski, it is through the rule of law that the British parliament has sought to avoid any danger of unregulated executive. He added, 'Britain has sought to assure that the citizens shall have his right decided by a body of men whose security of tenure is safeguard against the shifting currents of public opinion' (Laski 2014, 35). This means that the law of the land is supreme in Britain, and nobody can be punished unless he/she has violated the law. Rule of Law also means that no arbitrary punishment can be given to anybody, and all are equal before the law. This principle requires that the law should be of general application and capable of being obeyed.

25.2.1.5 Conventions

Conventions are the most important sources on which the constitution of Britain is based. According to Ogg, 'the conventions can be said practices, understandings, and regular habits which are prevalent in public life and they govern the actual behaviour and implementation of the public authorities' (Ogg and Zinc 1949, 29). On the account of following conventions, and that too unwritten conventions, the British constitution is accused of being traditional and orthodox.

There is a clear distinction between a 'law' and a 'convention'. The conventions have the force of law, although they cannot be termed as law. Laws are enacted by the legislature whereas the conventions are not. In future, conventions may become law. Unlike laws, conventions are not enforced by the courts. Conventions are dynamic in the sense that they kept on altering with time, but laws are fixed. Laws need to be introduced and passed, whereas conventions have their own momentum of growth. There is as such no punishment for not following conventions, but, there is definitely a strong conduct for any breach of law. The conventions are not punishable, but there is a very strong lineage of the obedience to them. The sanction and strength of this obedience, according to A.V. Dicey, lie in the fear of impeachment[4] and the force of the public opinion. Impeachment for any office of position has not been practised since long in Britain and is not likely to be revived, so the force of the public opinion itself puts a lot of pressure in terms of following the conventions. Public opinion will not tolerate the continuance of a ministry which has lost the confidence of the representatives of the people.

Similarly, the public expects that the king will not veto a bill which has been passed by the House of Commons and the House of Lords. There is parliamentary supremacy in Britain which means that any convention can be altered or discontinued by the act of parliament. For example, until 2009, the House of Lords stood at the apex of Britain's legal system as the highest court of appeal for the entire country in civil cases, and for England, Wales, and Northern Ireland (not Scotland) in criminal cases. However, a government backed constitutional reform act passed in 2005 created a new Supreme Court of the United Kingdom, which will take over the judicial functions of the House of lords as well as other judicial responsibilities.

There are different kinds of conventions: those related to monarch, to cabinet, to the parliament, and to the dominions. The conventions covered the whole constitutional system of Britain as they provide social and moral lubricant for the smooth functioning of the governmental machinery. The parliament does not repeal the conventions because of their utility and reasonableness. If any convention loses its utility, it dies a natural death. According to Neumann, 'the validity of constitutional conventions will be determined by the political realities' (1951, p. 27).

The British political system is a traditional one. If the circumstances change, the conventions also change accordingly. It is thus been suggested to distinguish between the constitution and the *principles* that underlie it. The principles are in one sense more crucial than the constitution itself. 'There is a possibility that the constitution may change through the above discussed statutory laws, common law traditions, judicial interpretations, or conventions- but the principle remain' (Mahler 2008, 195). The two fundamental principles are the *rule of law* and the *Parliamentary Sovereignty*.

25.2.2 The Structure and Functions of Political Organizations in Britain

Along with understanding the features and the sources of the constitution, we must understand the structure of the government. In everyday political conversations, British people talk about the government and not the constitution.

25.2.2.1 The Executive

According to Bagehot, there is a difference between the dignified and efficient parts of the political system. Some institutions were important for symbolic reasons, while the others exercised the real powers. The British executive is the same where the head of the state is the *monarch*, who reigns but not rule. The real political power lies with the *Prime Minister* and the *Cabinet*.

The Monarchy: The monarchy in Britain is as old as Britain itself. Although its powers have been curtailed down to practically nothing and its more ceremonial, Britain's Thousand year old monarchy is very important with respect to British politics. It is symbolic of the long continuity of the Britain's glorious history, institutions and the practices. Although Monarchy has been widely appreciated and celebrated by British people still since few years it has been subjected to criticism because of the lavish life style and amount of money which goes into the maintenance of the British monarchy. In 1992, the queen thus, agreed to pay the income tax.

'The monarchy survived in Britain because the sovereign became a constitutional monarch, neither exercising the wide powers of the crown nor being responsible for their exercise' (Needler and Wrigth 1990, 68). According to the conventions, the crown usually obeys the will of the government, although the monarch is free to give his/her opinion on any decision. Constitutionally, the monarch is the part of the parliament. The monarch has the legal powers to designate the prime minister, dissolve the parliament and calls for parliamentary elections. The monarch is the commander-in-chief of the armed forces and the head of the British Commonwealth. (source 289). With time, all these powers have been ultimately given to the prime minister and the cabinet. And thus, it is the government which actually takes all the important decisions on the behalf of the crown.

Where there is a clear majority and there exists a leader who can be the best person to control the majority in the House of Commons, there is nothing for the crown to do, but in case where there is a dilemma, the crown has the ultimate authority to decide. The monarchy has a limited, symbolic and ceremonial role today.

The Government: The real power is exercised by the Government, composed of the political ministers among whom, the most crucial is the prime minister and his cabinet. 'Ministers are individually responsible to Parliament for the work of their departments' (Mahler 2008, 198). Ministers introduce legislative bills, show the demands of their department, and ask for funds and form inter-departmental committees. Ministers coordinate with other interest groups and represent popular public opinion for policy matters in the parliament. The defeat of one single minister may lead to the collapse of the whole ministry.[6]

The Cabinet: The cabinet system emerged after the Norman kings established the two councils—Magnum Concilium or the Great Council and the Curia Regis or the King's Council—in order to help and advise the king in administrative matters. Curia Regis became strong as its meetings were held regularly unlike that of the King's council. The Curia Regis ultimately got converted into the House of Commons in the times of Tudor kings. The idea of the cabinet was accepted during the times of George I and George II. In Modern British system, the *cabinet government* comprises the most significant members of the government. The prime minister selects ministers for the cabinet. The member of the cabinet must be either a member of parliament or, less commonly, a member of the House of Lords.

'The cabinet has replaced the Privy Council[7] which was the chief source of executive power since the eighteenth century' (Rose 2008). The cabinet has many executive and legislative functions. Executive functions of the cabinet include giving suggestions for all important appointments and policies. The cabinet has the duty to prepare budget, and the imposition of new taxes and reduction in the existing tax rates are also governed by the cabinet or the Chancellor Exchequer. So far, as the main legislative functions are concerned, parliament is summoned by the cabinet in consultation with the king.

Cabinet serves as one and only routine check on the prime minister; the only other constitutionally mandated mechanism for checking the prime minister is the fall out on the floor on a 'no confidence motion'[8] in the House of Commons. The paucity of time prevents many discussions and debates in the parliament over many laws and thus the bills are passed with the 'delegated legislation'[9] which ought to increase the powers of the cabinet. Most cabinet ministers are formally called as the secretaries of the state, though a few have more prestigious titles such as the chancellor of the exchequer and the lord chancellor. The British political system rests on the principle of parliamentary supremacy, but in actual practice it is the government which dominated the legislative process.

The British cabinet meets more frequently than that of the United States of America and involves the cabinet members in greater collective role in debating and deciding the government policies. The Prime Minister is not formally bound to obey all the decisions suggested by the cabinet, but even very strong Prime Ministers such as Thatcher or Blair cannot go against the wish of the cabinet. Once a common decision is being made and the prime minister enunciates it, the principle of collective responsibility is being followed which demands that all the cabinet ministers must fall in line behind the policy in their public statements. (pg. 288)

The Prime Minister: In Britain, the prime minister is the formal head of the executive. The office of the British prime minister is based on the conventions. The first 'modern' British prime minister was Robert Walpole (1721–42); he started the tradition of linking cabinet with the crown. The prime minister was once regarded as the *primus inter pares* (first among the equals) in the cabinet. The prime minister is fully responsible for composition, organization and dissolution of the council of ministers. All the decisions related to the foreign matters and financial importance are taken by him. He has to appear in the House of Commons after every two weeks to answer parliamentary questions. Ramsay Muir has correctly termed that no head of any other democratic country of the world has more powers than the prime minister of Britain. He/she can be removed by the 'no-confidence motion' passed in the House of Commons. The Prime Minister steers the government. His powers are derived from the customary practices and are not codified in the legal statutes. The manner in which he controls the cabinet and the government brought the position of 'elective dictatorship' to the British Prime minister.

The Structure of Government in Britain

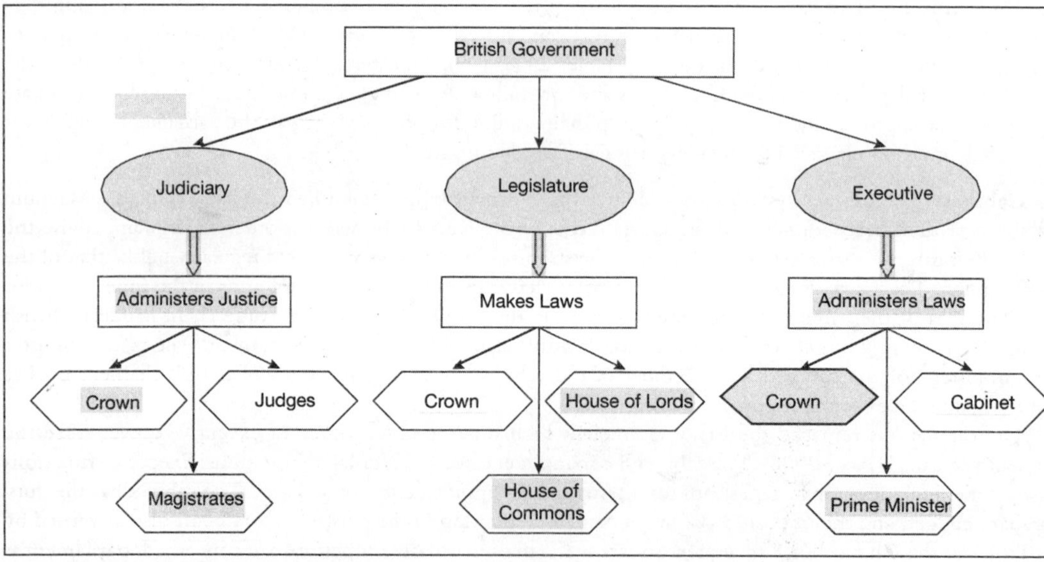

25.2.2.2 The Legislature

Parliament: It is the supreme legislative body in Britain. Parliament has the power to even reverse the decisions of the courts. In 1911, by the Parliamentary Act, the term of the parliament is fixed at 5 years, but it can be dissolved earlier also. The opening of the British parliament is the most celebrated ritual of the British

Political life. Usually it takes place every autumn as the parliament begins the new session and it also occurs when the new government assumes the office after the elections. The monarch deliver the speech outlining the priorities of the government for the coming years. The parliament in Britain consists of two houses: the House of Lords and the House of Commons. The House of Commons consists of people's representatives and the composition of the House of Lords is hereditary.

To become a law, the bill has to be passed by a majority of those present and voting in both the houses. The bill introduced in one house can not be debated and discussed in the other house until it has been passed. Unlike the US congress the British houses can not consider the two bills simultaneously. Because of its direct elections, the House of Commons enjoys much privilege in British politics. Like most of the parliamentary democracies, the British legislative process adhere to the party discipline. Which means all the members of a parliamentary delegation are expected to vote together on the bills introduced in the parliament. The members who do not fall in the party lines are penalized. The leader of the opposition in the parliament is called as the shadow prime-minister. The task of the shadow prime minister is to challenge the governing prime minister. In case the opposition party came to power, the shadow cabinet is ready with portfolios and they are ready to take charge immediately.

House of Lords is the upper chamber. This house consists of seven categories of members like the princes of the royal blood, the hereditary peers, the Scottish peers, lords spiritual, law lords, life peers and Irish peers. The House of Lords enjoys a share in the executive powers. The membership of the house was near about 1000 members, out of which the membership included various bishops of the Church of England and so called hereditary peers who can pass on their membership to their heir. In early 1999 there were 26 "lords spiritual" and 759 hereditary peers. Laws were passed in 1876 and 1958 permitting creation of the "life peers", who can serve the house only till they are alive and they can not pass their membership to their heir. Life peers are suggested by the monarch in consultation with the Prime Minister as a reward for those who have contributed exceptionally in the field of politics and their professions. There has been attempts by various governments in order to reduce the size of the House of Lords and also to make its membership based on elections.

Although the House of Lords has a significant role in approving legislations, its legislative powers are curtailed by the Parliament Acts of 1911 and 1949. By these acts, the House of Lords can only delay the passage of this bill if the members do not accept the legislation. The delay cannot be for more than a month and in some cases it can be for more than a year. If the House of Lords failed to pass the disputed bill in the stipulated time frame, the bill becomes the law automatically. The House of Commons has evoked this power since 1949. The legislative importance of the House of Lords had decreased with time, still it managed to influence and impact the legislative passage. For example, it has managed to amend the bills proposed by the government in the House of Commons on pertinent issues such as antiterrorism, personal identity cards, acts of racial and religious hatred and the banning of the fox hunting.

The House of Lords is criticized for various reasons. The first is that this house has members who are not democratically elected. Second, it is famous for delaying decisions on the basis of the party ideology. Sidney and Beatrice Webb have summed up the case in following words: 'its decisions are vitiated through its composition. It contains absolutely no members of the manual working class, teachers or clerks and none from the religious non-conformity (Catholics), or art, science or literature' (Mahler 2008, 210).

House of Commons consists of the elected members. The House of Commons is elected for 5 years. The House of Commons has tried to accommodate the Britain's non- white community as well. What types of people get elected to the House of Commons? House of Common has the diversified composition. From lawyers, to teachers, civil servants, college professors, manual workers, businessmen etc. the representation of women has undergone slow but observable change over few years. From the years 1964–1983, women held only 19 seats, in 1987 the figure jumped to 41 women representatives in order to increase the women representation, the Labor party in 1990s adopted a selection procedure of the candidates which aimed at electing women to half the party's seats in the House of Commons. Since then, the number has been on the rise.

The House of Commons has various legislative committees. Some of the important committees are Committee of the Whole House, Standing Committees, Sessional Committees, Committees on Private Bills and Select Committees on Public Bills. The most important legislative function of the House of Commons is the *law making.* All money bills can be introduced only in the House of Commons. The House of Commons controls the executive. The House of Commons is the best forum to redress the anguish and grievances of the people.

There are many types of legislations in the British House of Commons. 'The primary among them are the *Government Bill* and the *private members bills*' (Mahler 2008, 213). Government bills are those bills which are introduced, sponsored and formulated by the members of the cabinet. The private member's bills are proposed by non-cabinet members and opposition party members also. In the words of Mahler, there is another basis of understanding of the scope of the bills that is: *Public Bills* and *Private Bills.* 'Public bills tend to introduce new laws such as tax laws, criminal laws, regulation policy etc. Private bills have specific and individual application for example special act of citizenship' (Mahler 2008, 215).

Political System: A Comparison

	The United Kingdom	Germany
Parliament	• Dictated by House of Commons • Second Chamber almost powerless	• Two chambers • Both Chambers have veto powers • Parliament bound by constitution
Elections	• First past the post • Results in a strong single party majority	• Mix Member proportional • Normally coalition governments
Veto players	• Prime Minister is the agenda setter • Majoritarian system	• Coalitional partners • Second Chamber, member states • Consensus democracy

25.2.2.3 The Judiciary

In Britain, unlike the United States, there is no system of judicial review. 'British Judges have long had the reputation of being impartial and neutral' (Needler and Wright 1990, 86). There different subjects like immigration, industries, race relations, powers and functions of police and the human rights on which we have observed that the British judiciary have shown a conservative approach based on tradition and precedents. Judges in Britain are used by the government to chair tribunals of inquiry or Royal Commission.[10] Nevertheless, the courts in British history have played a major role in controlling the executive and maintained the supremacy of the individual rights. British judiciary has ratified the European Convention on Human Rights, and the British citizens can appeal to the European Courts on the concerned matters (Needler and Wright 1990, 90).

25.2.3 Political Processes

25.2.3.1 Political Parties and the Party System

The British system has often been quoted as the perfect example of the two-party system (the Conservative Party and the Labour Party). 'Since the national elections of 2010, it had been a strong opinion that the Two-Party system is no more practiced in Britain as per the classical understanding' (Keselman; 76). Till the formation of the Social Democratic Party (SDP) in 1981, no party, except for the nationalists, have succeeded in the British parliament. SDP argued that it was committed to the supremacy of parliament and democracy, no class war, controlled trade unionism and favored the membership of Britain in the European Union and NATO.[11]

The 'class-line' have been an important benchmark to explain the formation of the two major political parties. In the 19th century, the rich, aristocratic and the affluent classes were interested in the Conservative Party which was an ardent advocate of traditions and precedents. The Liberal Party had been the party of the reform change and used to construct its policies along the middle-class thinking. With changing times, the parties have adopted a very pragmatic approach which cut across the class lines. The two-party systems in Britain have officially established the role of the opposition in the parliament (Rose 2008, 194). Owing to the well-balanced and vigilant party system, institutions in Britain are stable, coherent, popular and dignified (Rose 2008, 193).

25.2.3.2 The Conservative Party

The formation of the Conservative Party can be traced from the 18th century. 'This party was dominated by landlords, bankers, clergymen and merchants and the basic orientation of the party used to be conservative in nature' (Kesselman 2013, 77). The social institutions propagated by the conservative party are the continuation of the power of the church, freedom of private property from the state interference and existence of a powerful governing class. Its pragmatism, flexible approach and organizational capacities have made the Conservative Party as the most successful and innovative centre-right party in Europe.

25.2.3.3 The Labour Party

The Labour Party was established in 1900 and comprised the peasants and the labourers. The aim of the party is to bring about the best possible equitable distribution of the nation's wealth among all the classes. It has also seen growing disaffection with even the moderate social democracy associated with the Keynesian welfare state and Labourism. The era of the 1980s and 1990s saw healthy relations within the party fragments.

Under the effective leadership of Tony Blair, Labour party was renamed as "New Labour". Tony Blair tried to reinvent the party and mould its functioning according to the changing demands of the middle class and other sections of the society' (Kesselman 2013, 77).

Special Insights

Principles of the Labour Party

Old Labour	New Labour
• Pressurize on the importance of nationalization of Coal and Steel industries to increase employment • Focus on welfare state in order to tackle poverty and enhance social justice • Fast track implementation of pro-working class policies (even if it is at the cost of the 'Rich') • Legislation—important for ensuring equality legislation. • Social Housing schemes. • Keynesist Economics- Top Down Spending to encourage economic growth.	• Part Privatized/Public ownership schemes e.g. National Health Service Trusts and Banks. • Focus on welfare schemes such as Child-Tax Credits. • Broader policies to appeal to all groups. • With growth and legislation equality can be achieved • Empowering local councils • 3rd Way Economics in Public Sector.

25.2.3.4 The Liberal Party

The Liberal Party was important once, but after the emergence of the Labour Party, this party was somehow neglected. 'Through the 1970s, the Liberals were the only prominent challenger to the Labour and the Conservative parties' (Kesselman 2007, 77). When SDP was formed out of a split within the Labour Party, the Liberal Party and the most of the 'Social Democrat Party merged together to form the Social and Liberal Democratic Party which is presently called as the Liberal Democrats' (Mahler 2008, 218). Liberal Democrats had no major issues left for criticizing the Labour Party as Tony Blair from the Labour Party tried to inculcate the policies and issues backed by the Liberal Democrats in the New Labour Party. 'In 2007, Nick Clegg tried to redirect the party with his policies like "knocking million doors to connect citizens", but all in vain' (Kesselman 2013, 78).

25.2.4 Voting and Elections in Britain

After the Second World War, either the Labour or the Conservative Party got the clear sweep at polls. After 1951 elections, there has been a decline in the electoral support for the two major parties because there has been a rising tide of the nationalist sentiments within the masses on the account of Liberal Social Democratic support (Needler and Wright 1990, 50). The rate of polling in Britain shows that after the Second World War, there has been almost 70 per cent voting happened in every general election. 'There has been a strong correlation between the "class" and the "party voting". Labour Party gets on average two- third votes of the working class' (Needler and Wright 1990, 53–54).

In Britain, voting is done mainly on the basis of the psychological commitment and identification with any political party. Since the 1970s and 1980s, there is a shift in this pattern; proportional representation system is demanded mainly by the Liberal Democrats. This change could give a way to the smaller parties to come to the power. 'Under the rubrics of the parliamentary supremacy if there is a political will to introduce Proportional Representation, system it can be changed' (Kesselman 2013, 79).

25.3 Political Economy

Britain was the world's first industrialized country. The process of industrialization had been initiated by the end of the 18th century in Britain, and it grew into a full-fledged industrial model by the middle of the next century. Agriculture became the second choice in terms of employment, whereas industrialization was becoming an attractive option. When the Corn Law[12] was repealed in 1846, Britain adopted the free trade policies. The import of the cheap food items became easier, and as a result, Britain became a hub of international business and exchange of currency and became a medium of the international trade.

Special Insights

Corn Laws and Crisis

- Rural areas given more representation than the cities.
- In 1795, bad harvest and corn laws led to food crisis and riots.
- Napoleonic Wars increased the price of food grains; landlords profits increased.
- Corn laws 1850: tariffs on imported food grains to bring prices back up.

Anti-Corn Law League

- Manufactures organized the league; call for lower prices and no higher wages.
- British manufactured goods prices could be of lower prices which will improve the position of Britain.

Repeal of Corn Laws 1846

- Corn laws finally repealed in 1846 with pressures from the middle class and manufactures.
- Improved government aid to make British agriculture efficient and profitable.

With expansion in exports of machines and technological innovation, Britain became highly industrialized. Industrial Revolution[13] brought about many social and economic changes in British state. With Industrial Revolution, there was an exchange of ideas, institutions and practices. Industrial Revolution improved the economic standard of the people on one hand but also rendered thousands of skilled craftsmen unemployed and vulnerable. Huge dependence on the raw material and reliance on the overseas markets made Britain an expansionist country. By 1870, Britain was dominating almost one-fourth of the world trade, and by the virtue of trade, Britain was able to rule over more than 50 colonies, including India. With prominence of the Industrial capital,[14] the economic power was shifted from landowners to businessmen and industrialists. This was an important shift with respect to the increasing plea for democratization.[15] The rich businessmen lobby compelled the parliament by the 1820s to expand certain rights like the right to vote. Since the 1820s till the passing of The Representative of the People Act, there was a long history of the struggle for rights in Britain, and the economic compulsions became the chief motivation for these Acts.

Britain has been the most successful example of capitalist economic system. With its industries growing, its foremost priority was cheap labour, raw materials and markets for the products. This resulted in colonialism, and the British empire was established in almost one-fourth of the world. The four century-long domination of the British empire was challenged after the First World War. The Economic Depression of the 1930s and the political and economic developments between the two World Wars like rise of the Soviet Union and the United States challenged the domination of Britain. Britain entered the scene of the Second World War in 1939, and by the end of the war, its economy was almost shattered and ruined. British economy suffered heavy loses due to de-colonization movement and independence of rich colonies like India. The postwar period saw the rise of the welfare state and mixed economic model in Britain which was thought to get away with the economic slowdown faced by the economy. The subsequent section discusses the mixed economy and welfare state as practiced in Britain.

25.3.1 The Mixed Economy and the Welfare State in Britain

Britain adopted a mixed economy model like many European countries under which the private and the public sectors both operate in the country. After the Second World War, the two major political parties of Britain, namely the Labour and the Conservative, have tried to influence the working of the economy in such a way in which there are chances to implement social principles like creation of a welfare state, decreasing unemployment and more investments into the public distribution systems. Since then, there has been an increase in the investments in industries and government is giving more credits to private and public sectors in order to increase avenues of wages. 'This approach where state was taking a direct control of the economy was termed as *Keynesianism*' (this approach was named after British economist John Maynard Keynes who emphasized that the state economic policies must be utilized to control and stabilize the economic growth and the markets) (Kesselman 2013, 59).

'In Britain, the Public sector includes three distinct sectors like Central Government, Local Government and the nationalised industries, three sectors have different areas to invest into and govern the expenditure' (Needler and coworkers 1990, 88). For example, the central government takes care of the social security benefits, defence, trade and commerce, foreign exchange mechanisms, housing, education and law and order. The local government incurs its income from the property taxes and aids given by the central government. It takes care of education, transportation and maintenance of law and order. 'The nationalised industries sector is accountable for giving employment to almost two million people' (Needler, 88). The nationalized industries govern industries such as coal, electricity, iron and steel. Denationalization has negatively affected this sector and resulted in cutting of jobs in significant number.

Special Insights

John Maynard Keynes

John Maynard Keynes was a British economist who fundamentally challenged the theory and practice of the Macro Economic model and altered the economic policies of the government. During the time of Great Depression of the 1930s, Keynes challenged the neo-classical model of economics that believes that *free markets* would generate full employment for the workers. He argued that *Aggregate demand* determined the overall level of economic performance and can solve the problem of unemployment for a longer period of time. In a paper titled 'The General Theory of Employment, Interest and Money', he favoured full government intervention instead of laissez-faire as a way to deal with economic recession. He also suggested the use of monetary and fiscal policies to avert the adverse consequences of economic recessions.

He was followed by Western economics before the Second World War. The advent of global financial crises of 2007–2008 called for bringing back the Keynesian thought. The then US president Barack Obama and Prime Minister Gordon Brown of Britain recognized the strength of Keynesian economic thought.

Once it was being felt that the Keynesianism was not reaping out the desired benefits, it was realized that *Monetarism*[16] has to be adopted as the new economic policy (Kesselman 2013, 59). It was realized that the labour market must run on the 'natural rate of employment' (ibid.). The state intervention must be restrained to only money supply and keep rates of inflation low. Margaret Thatcher became the prime minister in 1979, and with that victory, a new era of economic policy formation got introduced into the British political system. She was fed up of the sick nature of the public sector enterprises. In the 1979 electoral campaign, she called for a radical counter revolution:

> the last two decades have seen an inexorable rise in government spending, accounting for 33 percent of the nation's GDP in 1959 and 41 percent in 1978; a dangerous growth in trade union power; a diminution in freedom of choice; a decline in the moral standards and law and order. The country is becoming an Eastern European style socialist state. (Mahler 2008, 206)

The Thatcher government started with the process of privatization of number of government industries. It also pressurized the local governments to take care of the sectors which central government was not controlling any more. She tried her level best not to integrate British economy with that of European economy. When she won the elections in 1983, she continued with her economic reforms. She had believed that privatization would enable the industrial sector to come out of the interference of the officials, will become much more efficient and profitable in competitive markets. Her successor John Major who won the elections in 1990 abolished many of the taxes created by her and was extremely unpopular. He once again re-united Britain with the European and the world politics.

By the mid-1990s, the Conservative Party lost the support of the citizens, and 'New Labour' policies of the Labour Party candidate Tony Blair became rather more attractive than that of the Conservative Party. The trade unions have been weakened by the Thatcher government; 'the share of manufacturing in total employment fell from 38 percent in 1956 to 19 percent in 1990' (Kopstein and Lichbach 2008, 75). Tony Blair tried to redefine labour's identity so that he can appeal to the middle class that Labour would never come to power by seeking support of the workers or peasants alone, rather the party would now think of every class and its needs. The New Labour accepted Thatcher's policy that the state must not interfere in the economic management and should keep on investing in the sectors such as education and welfare. New Labour also agreed with Thatcher's policy of giving space to free markets. Old styled socialism was replaced by the slogan of 'pro-business pro-enterprise' face of the party (ibid.). New Labour evoked the sense of pride in being British and also encouraged women candidates to participate more openly in elections. New government jobs were created for the youth, and no new welfare initiatives were planned in order to stabilize the economic condition. One of the most noticing acts of the New Labour government was the granting of independence to the Bank of England. Now, the board of directors of the bank could fix the interest rates and can control the inflation. The head of the Treasury, Gordon Brown followed a tight monetary and fiscal policies on one hand, and on the other, he spent heavily on sectors such as health, education and welfare.

Comparative Study of British Economy During Different Prime Ministers

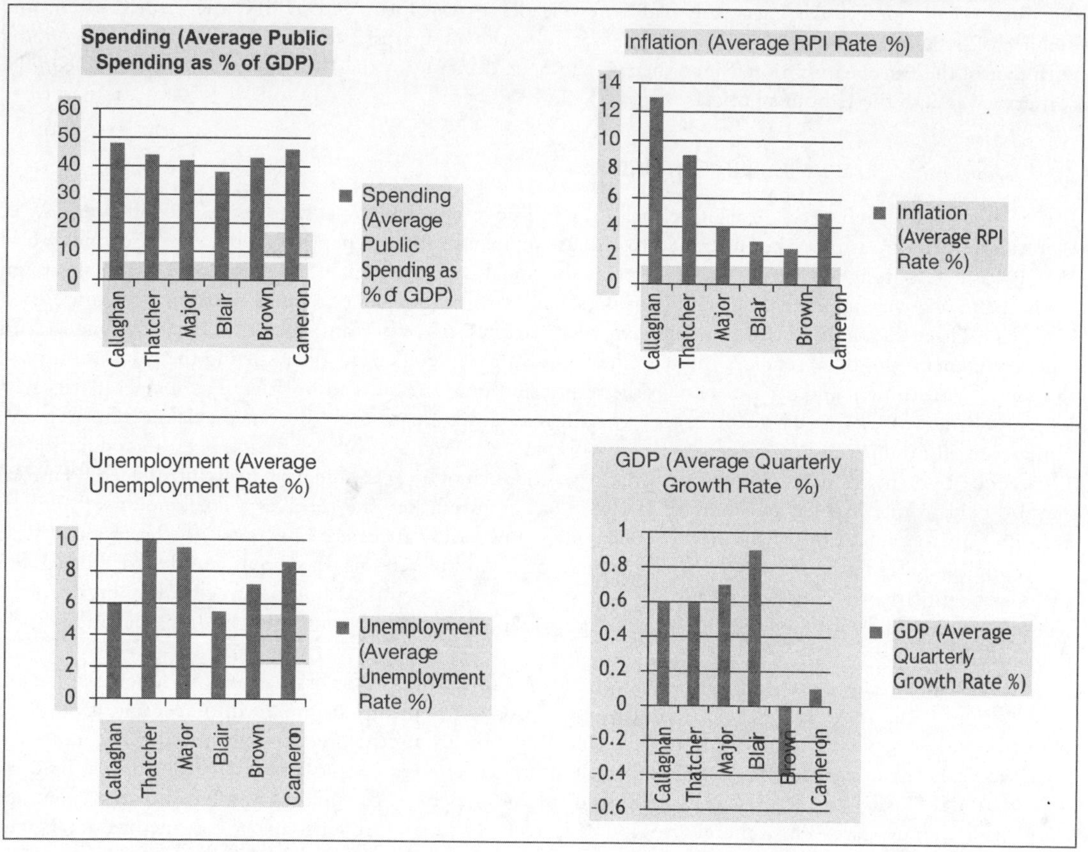

Source: Adapted and modified from Durden, T. (2013). Thatcher's Legacy. Zerohedge (April 17, 2013). Accessed from https://www.zerohedge.com on September 12, 2023.

New Labour could only keep few of their promises in delivering the improved public services through decentralization and increased competition. The privatized railway track met with a serious accident in 2001, and the status of health and education sector was also dissatisfactory. The Tony Blair government pressurized the universities to charge less from the students. The new labour policies were showing positive results in form of declining pensioner poverty to one-third and child poverty by one-sixth. 'Labour Party continued to spend heavily on public spending especially the sectors of health and education which caused rising government spending to 42 percent in 2006 from 39 percent in 1997' (Rutland 2008, 80).

With the waves of globalization and liberalization[17] sweeping through the world, Britain, like many other states, had to move away from national economic policy. The British Political system in the 2000s started moving away from the collective interest's politics of the 1950s and 1960s and focused on the citizen and consumer. Labour Party started losing out its regular constituencies of the workers who cut down the contribution given to the party and kept on protesting against the policy of privatization (ibid.). The membership of the Labour Party too fell down in wake of the pro-European policies of Blair's government.

After Tony Blair's economic reforms and disillusionment from the New Labour polices, Brown became the new prime minister in 2007. He was closer to the traditional labour policies than his predecessors. The British economic scenario seemed confused as the two major political parties kept on swinging between being more globalized and being traditionally conservative. This dilemma can be substantiated by the fact that in 2007, 'Conservative Party too had a new leader in the form of David Cameron' (Kopstein and Lichbach 2008, 81). Cameron was a neoconservative who was against the integration of British economy with that of the European Union. Since then, it had been difficult for the British people to opt between the conservatives' and the Labour's policies.

25.3.2 Social Security Measures in Britain

Britain has always been keen on welfare measures and poverty alleviation. Before the Second World War, there were many measures like insurance to the unemployed, old-age pensions, etc. 'After Second World War British state designed various welfare plans for social improvement' (Needler, 93). During the reign of the Labour government in 1945–50, pension schemes were introduced which continued for more than 45 years. 'Three elements of this scheme have been particularly important: social security, national health scheme and personal social services' (ibid.). The first two parameters have always being the responsibility of the central government and the third one is the responsibility of the local authorities. The social security nets are very strong in Britain. Various categories of allowances like maternity allowances, sickness, retirement, injuries during industrial accidents, deaths at workplace, unemployment, etc. have been introduced after 1945. Since 1946, pensions to women of 60 years age and men of 65 years age have been introduced. Pensions are also paid to the disabled people, and if a worker is injured, he/ she receives a fair amount of pension according to the condition of his/her disablement. Family allowances are also given to the mothers who have children going to schools till the time they pass out from the schools. In schools, children are also given various benefits like free milk up to the age of 7 years, medical examinations and free healthy meals in the school. The families with fairly low income are also supported through rents and children education while their parents work.

Britain spends a lot on various social services. A fair amount of gross national product is spent on social schemes and services. 'If health education, retirement pensions are taken into account, around 23 percent of GNP is spent every year' (Needler, 94). Expenditure on the government treasury has increased over the years because of high numbers of single mothers, old age people and retired persons in Britain. The National Health Service (NHS) introduced in 1946 has been considered as a jewel in the crown of the British welfare state. This scheme provided a universal and comprehensive low cost medical facility to all British citizens, and this has been one of the most sought after right of the British people. This service gives freedom to the patients to choose their doctors, hospitals and the kind of facilities they want to avail. The doctors in the service receive a basic minimum pay along with the fee prescribed for individual patients. All the residents of Britain can avail the benefits by choosing their dentists, pharmacist, specialists and hospitals. 'This scheme provided huge employment to the doctors and accounts for 10 percent of the public expenditure of the GDP' (ibid.). This welfare scheme has brought tremendous results in not only providing the medical facilities to the ailing but has also contributed in creating awareness in prevention of diseases and promotion of health benefits.

Special Insights

The National Health Service (NHS)

- Formed nearly 49 years ago
- Based on 'treating all equally'
- Irrespective of the financial status-all facilities regarding health is given to all citizens
- Basic medical services are guaranteed to all residents of the UK
- Quality treatment and that too free of cost.

Welfare state model in Britain was pushed forward by the New Labour government at the centre. The government invested a huge chunk into training and broader social investment as more positive third way alternatives. In the wake of globalization, when markets have overpowered the working of the state, Britain too faced difficulty in order to create an egalitarian social order. The policy instruments and strategic capacities to pursue targets such as eliminating childhood poverty seem a far cry. Ethnic minorities suffer a huge income gap in Britain. Ethnic minorities, particularly young men, are subjected to inhuman and unequal treatment by the police, and they also lack opportunities in job markets. Women's contribution and participation in the job markets also witness huge chunk of inequalities. 'In 2008, a higher portion of men (79 percent) than women (70 percent) of working age were employed in the Britain' (Kesselman 2013, 63).

In response to the COVID-19 pandemic which was one of the biggest challenge for the Global society, the British government introduced various public health care services and economic safeguards for its citizens. As soon as the cases of COVID-19 were confirmed in January 2020, the government announced advice for the travelers coming from affected countries. The government introduced societal restrictions in form of Lockdowns. Prime minister Boris Johnson announced the first lockdown in 2020 and then the parliament introduced the Corona virus Act 2020, which granted the emergency – powers to the government and empowered the police to enforce public health care measures in the areas of NHS, social care, schools, Border Force, local councils, funerals and the courts.

The Government began introducing laws for those who were exposed to the virus and the rules on *face masks* as well as the efforts to expand testing for COVID-19 cases. The country wide COVID-19 vaccination programme began in December 2020, after Margaret Keenan became the first person in the world to receive her first dose of the two of Pfizer- BioNtech COVID-19 vaccine. The British rollout response for the vaccination was among the fastest in the world. After initiating the vaccination for old and then young population; the vaccination was then extended to the children.

During the third wave driven by *Delta variant*, the British government lifted most the restrictions. At the time of *Omicron variant*, the British government reintroduced restrictions with a "living with COVID" plan announced by the government. Massive economic support was extended to the struggling businesses and to the employees of the companies in order to mitigate the damage caused by the pandemic. Because of its financial impact, the Chancellor of the Exchequer Rishi Sunak (the present British Prime Minister) was asked to rapidly help the Shadow Chancellor, John Mcdonell. Rishi Sunak then announced the *Corona Virus Job Retention Scheme* in early 2020. The scheme provides grants to the employers to pay 80% of a staff wage and employment costs each month.

The welfare state in Britain has been quite concern in order to avoid or defer mass redundancies, company bankruptcies and potential unemployment levels. In September 2020, the British government also announced another scheme to protect jobs in the country, called the *Job Support Scheme*. The scheme enabled the employees to get financial support where their firms have been closed. The Government also announced a six- months delay on tax payments. In order to ensure the stability in the market, the government announced a *Retail Hospitality and Leisure Grant Fund* and *the small Business Grant Fund*. Various other schemes and efforts such as *Eat Out to Help Out* has been an attempt by the present Prime minister of Britain Rishi Sunak in order to save the food sector. Because of lockdown and social distancing during the pandemic, restaurants, pubs, food joints cafes etc has witnessed massive slowdown. The scheme thus involved the Government subsidizing food and non-alcoholic drinks at participating cafes and restaurants.

25.3.3 Britain in Neo-liberal Economy

In the views of Richard Rose, British national identity and economy have been overshadowed by the legacy of 'empire' and the victory against Germany in the Second World War which were the finest phases for the Britain (Rose 2009, 42). This psychic supremacy has created more difficulties for Britain to adjust to the changing global order. However, Britain is one of the best destinations for Foreign Direct Investment (FDI)[18] where there are lots of opportunities for expansion of markets. Britain offers a friendly environment for private entrepreneurs; stable political climate and cooperative trade unions are suitable for the large pool of foreign direct investments in the era of globalization. In terms of growth competitiveness and international comparisons of microeconomics stability,

UK population COVID-19 vaccine coverage, by dose, of those aged 12 and over as of 16 February 2022

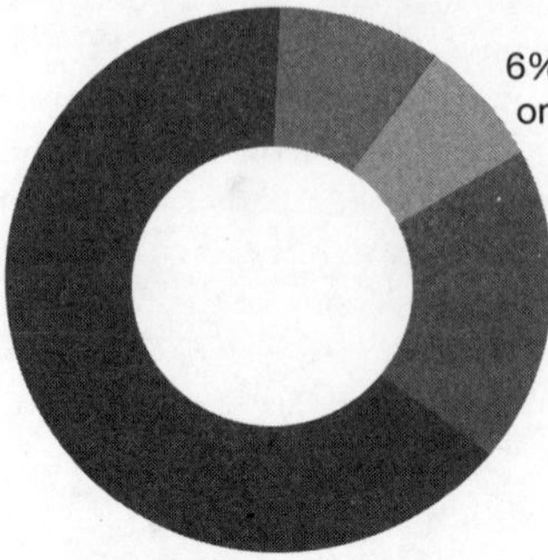

Source: COVID-19 Response: Living with COVID-19 - GOV.UK (www.gov.uk)

Britain scores well. The use of technology and quality production techniques has positioned Britain on the highest platform in comparison with any other European country.

Until the global recession of 2008, British economy runs on a 'two-track' pattern of growth (Kesselman 2007, 58). A strong service sector and industrialization made it possible for Britain to exhibit an overall strength by sustained growth, low unemployment rates, controlled inflation and low interest rates. 'The recession of 2008[19] influenced Britain as the industrial performance was showing slight negative trends towards the mid of 2000s' (Kesselman 2013, 87). Gordon Brown framed a globalization-friendly environment of the British economy where labour laws are flexible in comparison with the other countries of Europe. Britain assured the international markets that Britain would accept FDIs but at the same time would also maintain domestic stability. Britain called for a strict control over the inflation and tough limits on public expenditure which could save employment opportunities.

25.3.4 Brexit: Reversal of Globalization?

As a significant and historic decision, Britain announced its exit from the European Union in July 2017. This phenomenon is also termed as *Brexit*.[20] There were lots of speculation as to why Britain took this stand and what could be the possible outcomes of this historic move.

Britain became the member of the European Community (EC) on 1 January 1973 through an act of the British parliament called the European Communities Act under the Conservative Prime Minister Edward Heath. The opposition Labour Party had reservations regarding the integration of Britain with the EC. Once the Labour Party won elections in 1975, they called for a referendum to know the will of the people that whether they want to continue with the EC or they want Britain to withdraw. Overall, 67.2 per cent of the electorates wished to continue with EC and a sharp contrast could be seen in the 2016 referendum. EC got converted into the European Union on 1 November 1993 which had a clear signal that it is no more an economic organization, rather it is now a political organization. The call for exit was strongly put forward by the UK Independence Party since its inception in 1993. The Conservative Party which won the general elections of 2015 favoured remaining a part of the EU and Prime Minister David Cameroon promised to negotiate with the EU on the terms like sufficient safeguards for the non-Euro zone member countries, single market for non-Euro zone countries, reduction of corruption and red tapism, exempting Britain from 'ever-closer union' and putting tight security check on EU immigration. Prime Minister Cameron could not negotiate these promised terms from the EU, and majority of citizens were distressed. He proposed to trigger the Article 50 process as soon as possible following a leave note, and of the 'two-year time period to negotiate the arrangements for exit'. The referendum results show a clear majority in favour of leaving the EU.[21]

Inspired by the Britain, many other countries such as the Netherlands too initiated a referendum asking people to vote for continuation of relations with the EU. With Theresa May becoming the new Prime Minister of Britain, the way for the Exit from the EU was almost confirm. There were many reasons for the British citizens to decide to vote for leaving the EU. Voting to leave the EU was also associated with showing solidarity with conservatism, opposing cosmopolitanism and having an opinion that life in Britain is worse since it has joined the EC.

According to John Van Reenen, there will be long-run economic effects on the British economy. There will be higher cost for trade with rest of the European countries. This may amount to lower foreign investment and lower income for Britain. 'If the leaving from EU is "soft Brexit",[22] then the results may not be that worse, but in case the exit is "hard Brexit" then things could be worse' (Minford 2015). The bottom line of this exit will impact harshly on the income avenues of the Britain. This could result adversely on the welfare state modality of Britain. If the consequence of this reversal of globalization can result in low trade deficit and less income to the state, then why did the people vote to leave? People were aware of the greater sovereignty that this exit would result. Fewer immigrants would also result in less pressure on opportunities and resources of the country.

According to Thomas Sampson and John Van Reenen, 'the process of Brexit may result in making the goods and services cheaper for the UK consumers and it will be friendlier for the businesses in terms of export. Britain was contributing heavily into the budget of EU' (Sampson et al. 2017). The economic benefit will result into less contribution into the EU budget and spending more on welfare state activities. On a softer note, Britain, like Norway, has attained access to British market and can still trade with EU countries. Being outside the EU, Britain would not be able to achieve benefits from the deals proposed by the United States and Japan. Britain could weaken certain regulations like social, employment-related policies and environment protection modes to some degrees.

As per the study conducted by Iain Begg and Fabian Mushovel in 2022, there will be a long term loss of GDP for the British economy. The main reason for this fall of GDP lies in the assumption made about shifting from the current access that the Britain has to the EU single market to a new regime in which the Britain faces restrictions. The Bank of England, in particular, has warned that Brexit could lead to financial instability because of the financial openness of the Britain. The lower level of GDP in macroeconomics terms will mean a lower level of employment in the country. There are some sectors which can witness loss of jobs, while the others like import may witness increase in the jobs. Exit from the EU means that some import competing industries which will become more competitive because they can avoid regulations that impair their competitiveness. The jobs in the service sector may witness a decline. The regional distribution of jobs could be influenced by the shifts in the destinations of the foreign direct investment into the Britain. Migration from the Britain can have both positive and negative consequences. The supply of workers from the EU to Britain has been significant in contributing to public finances. The migrants from some origins do remit some of their income to their home countries and this can be regarded as a loss for the British Economy. Migration will put pressure on public service and housing. International

Advantages and Disadvantages of Brexit for UK

Advantages	Disadvantages
• Independent trade – More control over trade laws	• Less access to EU funds & programs (research, science, Infrastructure)
• EU independent international politics & immigration laws	• Limited trade – No access to EU single market. Need to renegotiate trade deals. Customs controls.
• Costs – not paying EU membership fee	• Employee shortage – outflow of skilled workers.
• Border control – Less competition from immigrants.	• Influence – Less influence in international matters.

organizations such as IMF have warned that the risk factor after Brexit will be more for Brexit and lasting effects on the economy will be negative. The effect will also be dangerous for the other partners of EU and it will take years to stabilize the economic scenario of EU and its partner countries. There is definitely lot of uncertainties regarding who would gain or lose domestically in Britain after Brexit, but unfortunately there are strong indications that the burden would fall more heavily on the low-income groups. The trends have already started showing that inequality have persisted more deeply in Britain.

25.4 Conclusion

After analysing the constitutional history and changing patterns of the political economy of Britain certain broad conclusions can be drawn.

Politically, the Westminster model is still looked forward and appreciated among other successful models of governance. The presence of a strong parliamentary system of governance and support of the two strongest parties competing for the office has showed that Britain has the capacity to produce strong governments which are meticulous, decisive and strong in tackling various socio-economic problems.

Socially, Britain has a flexible class system that comprises different races and heterogeneous mix of population. It has been evident that British civil society forums are one of the strongest and the polity gives lots of credit to the vibrant public opinion. Economically, Britain has demonstrated the success of adopting a mixed economy model. In 2017, with a historic decision of exit from the European Union, Britain has opened up lots of avenues for speculation, debates and results of this move in the future. This exit will have the political and economic consequences not only for the British economy but also for the globalized world.

Keywords

Brexit
British Commonwealth
Cabinet
Centralization
Crown
Delegated legislation
European community
European Union
Glorious revolution
Keynesian model
Mixed economy
North Atlantic Treaty Organization
Privatization
Thatcherism
Westminster

Review Questions

1. Write an essay on the evolution of British constitution.
2. Explain the contribution of various written and unwritten sources in the making of the British Constitution.
3. How is British society and polity engaging with the changing economy of Britain in the contemporary times?
4. Is it correct to say that the British constitution is a balance of tradition and modernity? Explain with suitable examples.
5. What are the factors which led to Britain shifting from 'Mixed' economic model to that of 'Neo-liberal' model in the age of globalization?
6. Explain the phenomenon of 'Brexit' with special reference to Britain. Is it correct to say that Britain has initiated a phase of 'de-globalization' in the recent world order?
7. Discuss the possible consequences of 'Brexit' for the political economy of Britain.

Notes

1. The term 'mother' signifies the origin of the idea or the beginning of the idea.
2. The rule of King John shows what usually happened in the Middle Ages when a king lose a war and his authority got completely submissive. The barons in England rebelled, and on 15 June 1215, they forced King John to sign a series of demands through which the barons can limit the powers of the king. The king agreed to govern England and deal with its people according to the customs of feudal laws.
3. A written law or rule.
4. A process where a public official is held unfit for the post and thus is removed through a set procedure which is lengthy and complicated.
5. Those countries are called Dominions, which were once in the British Empire and were governed by the British Crown, but later on, achieved independence. For example, Australia, New Zealand and Canada.
6. In this manner, the British Cabinet system differs from the French government. In the French system, the responsibility of the minister is individual and not collective.
7. It is an advisory body that gives advice to the head of the state of a nation. The word 'privy' means 'private' or 'secret' and thus this council originally used to be close to the monarch to assist him/her on the matters related to utmost confidentiality.
8. A motion of no confidence, vote of no confidence or unsuccessful motion is a statement of vote which refers to a condition in which the person in the position of authority or responsibility is no longer deemed fit to hold the position. In the parliament, it means that the head of the state of the elected parliament no longer enjoys the confidence in the appointed government. No confidence motion leads to resignation of the council of ministers and it is directed against the entire cabinet. A no confidence motion may not require reasons to be specified for its introduction to the house.
9. It is also called as Subordinate legislation. It is made by the act of parliament. It includes statutory rules, by-laws, ordinances, orders in council and various other mechanisms made by the executive.
10. In Britain, a commission of inquiry appointed by the crown but on the recommendation of the head of the government to gather information about the operation of existing laws or to investigate any social, political or educational matter.
11. North Atlantic Treaty Organization is a formal alliance between the territories of North America and Europe. Its main aim was to defend the member countries against Soviet control. It's an inter-governmental military alliance between 29 North American and European countries and was signed on 4 April 1949.
12. This law was enforced in Great Britain between 1815 and 1846. This was regarding tariffs and other trade restrictions on imported food grains mainly 'corn'. This was in order to keep the rates of the grain prices high and benefit domestic producers. This law was designed as a symbol of British mercantilism.
13. In the middle of the 18th century, this was the era of speedy and destabilizing social, economic and political changes caused by the introduction of large-scale factory production, resulting in lots of low cost finished products. Industrial revolution improved the living standard of the people and often is associated with the disruption of old ways of life.
14. Industrial capital is what is used in actual industrial manufacturing or producing goods or services. These are the physical things that make the production possible like factories, electricity, water systems and roads.
15. Democratization is the transition to a more democratic political regime. It may be the transition of an authoritarian regime to a full democracy or a semi-democracy. The result can be in the form of *consolidation* as happened in Britain or reversal to another regime as happened in Venezuela.
16. It is an approach to economic policy that assumes a natural rate of unemployment in the labour market. It rejects the state and government funding in order to manage budget deficits for stimulating the economy and creating new jobs.
17. It is a term used for showing a scenario where the state lifts up most of the restrictions in the economic activities of the individual and the market.
18. It is the investment made by a company or enterprise in another country and in return the mother firm controls the business proportion of the country concerned.
19. The Recession of 2008 is also known as the Recession of the late 2000s or the Great Recession. It was a major economic downturn that was initiated in 2008 and lasted till 2010. This financial crisis was the most severe crisis which originated from banks which were under great mortgages.
20. *Brexit* is a combination of 'British' and 'exit'. It was derived by the analogy from Grexit, referring to a hypothetic withdrawal of Greece from the Euro zone. The term *Brexit* was first coined by Peter Wilding in the reference of the withdrawal of Britain from the European Union.
21. National referendum results showed that 51.9 per cent of voters (17,410,742) were in favour of leaving the EU while 48.1 per cent (16,141,241) wanted to continue the association with the EU.
22. The terms 'hard Brexit' and 'soft Brexit' are used unofficially in order to define the relationship between the EU and Britain once Britain decides to quit the EU. If the exit is hard then, free movement of people is not allowed and Britain

has to trade with the EU like any other non-EU- member country prescribing the WTO rules. If the exit is soft, then it can result in retaining membership of the EU single markets for goods and services and some free movement of the people.

References

Blondel, Jean, Michael Curitis, and Martin C. Needler. (Eds.). 1990. *Introduction to Comparative Government*. New York: HarperCollins Publications.

Bouvier, John. 1914. *Bouvier's Law Dictionary and Concise Encyclopedia* (p. 2579), Third Revision Volume 2. Kansas City: Vernon Law Book Company.

Dunt, Ian. 2016. *BREXIT—What the Hell Happens Now?* UK: Canbury Press.

Gourevitch, Peter. 2006. Political Economy, in *Readings in Comparative Politics—Political Challenges and Changing Agendas*, edited by Mark Kesselman and Joel Krieger. Boston, MA: Houghton Mifflin Company.

Head, Simon. 1999. The Death of British Business. *NYR Daily*, London.

Hennessy, Peter, and Anthony Seldon. 1987. *Ruling Performances: British Governments from Atlee to Thatcher.* New York: Blackwell.

Sampson, Thomas, John Van Reenen, Swati Dhingra, and Gianmarco Ottaviano. 2017. The Consequences of Brexit for UK trade and Living standards. Centre for Economic Performance, Paper Brexit 2.

Jeffrey Jowell, Jeffrey. 2011. The Rule of Law and its Underlying Values, in *The Changing Constitution*, edited by Jeffrey Jowell and Dawn Oliver, 7th edition. Oxford: Oxford University Press.

Kesselman, Mark, and Joel Krieger. 2013. *Introduction to Comparative Government and Politics-Political Challenges and Changing Agendas*. Wadsworth: Cengage Learning.

Kesselman, Mark, Joel Krieger, and William A. Joseph. (Eds.). 2010. *Introduction to Comparative Politics—Political Challenges and Changing Agendas*, 47–89. UK: Wadsworth.

Kopstein, Jeffrey, and Mark Lichbach. (Eds.). 2008. *Comparative Politics: Interests, Identities and Institutions in a Changing Global Order.* New York: Cambridge University Press.

Laski, Harold J. 2014. *Parliamentary Government in England*, 35Routledge.

Lock, Geoffrey. 1989. The 1688 Bill of Rights. *Political Studies* XXXVII(4): 555.

Macshane, Denis. 2016. *BREXIT—How Britain Left Europe.* UK: I.B Tauris.

Mahler, Gregory S. 2008. *Comparative Politics—An Institutional and Cross National Approach*, 192–220. New Delhi: Pearson Education and Dorling Kindersley Publishing Inc.

Mc Cormick, John. 2007. Britain, in *Comparative Politics in Transition.* UK: Wadsworth.

Minford, Patrick. 2015. Evaluating European Trading Arrangements. Cardiff Economic Working Paper No. E2015/17, Cardiff Business School.

Mukherjee, Subrata, and Sushila Ramaswamy. 2017. *Theoretical Foundations of Comparative Politics*, Chapters 14 and 19. New Delhi: Orient Blackswan.

Munro, William Bennett. 1954. *The Governments of Europe*, 18. New York: Macmillan.

Neumann, Robert G. 1951. *European and Comparative Government*, 27. New York: Mc Graw Hill.

Ogg, Frederic A., and Zink, Harold. 1949. *Modern Foreign Government*, 29. New York: Macmillan.

Palekar, S.A. 2009. *Comparative Politics and Government*, 15–80. New Delhi: PHI Learning Private Limited.

Rose, Richard. 2004. Politics in England, in *Comparative Politics Today: A World View*. (Eds.). Gabriel A. Almond, G. Bingham Powell, Kaare Strom and Russell J. Dalton. Singapore: Pearson Education Pte Ltd.

Rutland, Peter. 2008. Britain, in *Comparative Politics: Interest, Identities and Institutions in a Changing Global Order*, edited Jeffrey Kopstein and Mark Lichbach. Cambridge: Cambridge University Press.

Sampson, Thomas. 2015. Dynamics Selection: An Idea Flows Theory of Entry, Trade and Growth. *Quarterly Journal of Economics* 131(1): 315–80.

Schwellnus, Cyrille, and Isabelle Mejan. 2009. Price Convergence in the European Union: Within Firms or Composition of Firms? *Journal of International Economics* 78(1): 1–10.

Stanworth, Philip, and Anthony Giddens. (Eds.). 1974. *Elites and Power in British Society.* London: Cambridge University Press (Toronto: Macmillan of Canada).

Van Reenen, John, Thomas Sampson, et al. 2017. The Consequences of Brexit for UK Trade and Living Standards, Centre for Economic Performance, Paper Brexit- 2.

Glossary

Antecedent: A thing that existed before or logically precedes another.

Approach: It is a world view that provides a particular direction or angle to study the politics in a comparative setting.

ARENA: A political party of the military in Brazil between 1965 and 1979. Post 1964 coup, Brazilian military did not abolish the Congress but created a party through which it can select someone to rule.

Asymmetrical federalism: Asymmetrical federalism is federalism based on unequal distribution of powers between different units of the government. It is preferred as a solution when some states feel different needs from the others because of ethnic, linguistic or cultural differences. For example, Article 370, which provides for some special provisions for Jammu and Kashmir in India.

Authoritarianism: It is a form of government characterized by blind submission to authority. It denotes a political system that concentrates power in the hands of a leader or a small elite that is not constitutionally responsible to the body of the people.

Authority: It is the legitimate power of a person or group over other people.

Ballot: It signifies the input or choice from the voter to be cast as vote in the election in a secret manner. The design of ballot depends on the method of election used by the political system; for example, there may be requirement of choosing one candidate or an entire slate or even rank the candidates in sequence of preference of the voters.

Bandeirantes: Primarily the 17th-century Portuguese settlers in Brazil who made treasure hunting their job. With their explorations in interiors of Brazil, they were the first to find gold that eventually became the backbone of Brazilian economy in the 17th century.

Behaviouralism: It is a school of thought that emerged during the post-war period, especially in the United States. It stressed on the study of individuals rather than institutions, for instance, the focus was on votes rather than elections, legislators rather than legislatures and the role of judges rather than judiciary.

Biafra: Geographical southeastern Nigeria which represented nationalist aspirations of the Igbo people.

Boom and bust cycle: Refers to economic growth and decline where boom shows the positive growth of economy while bust reflects overheating of boom phase of economy. In this phase, GDP turns negative and high rate of inflation occurs with high rates of unemployment.

Bourgeoisie: This term has been used by the Marxist theorization on class war denoting the property-owning class in the capitalist system.

Brexit: It is a term used for the process of departure of the Britain from the European Union. This has become a reality but was assumed to be a hypothetical phenomenon as it goes against the rules of globalization.

British Commonwealth: It is also termed as the Commonwealth of Nations. It is an inter-governmental organization of 53 member nations consisting of the United Kingdom and other former territories/colonies which are now sovereign, but still pay allegiance to the British Crown.

Capital: land, property, money, labour and organization.

Capitalism: It is an economic system in which a country's trade and industry is owned by private players, sometimes named as the capitalist class.

Captaincy: During the trans-Atlantic exploration period, kings or prince of Portuguese were to depute people to control and administer an area on their behalf. Such responsibility was to be given to the men of noble origin. Brazil, when initially explored, was divided into 15 captaincies.

Centralization: It is the process by which the activities related to the planning and decision-making became concentrated in one power centre.

Class struggle: This concept constitutes the foundational idea of Marxism that denotes the antagonism and irreconcilable differences between the capitalist class and the working class present in capitalism. It will come to end with the abolition of class in the communist society.

Clientelism: A political or social system based on patron–client relationship, where client gives political or financial support to a patron in exchange of special privilege.

Clientelism: The tendency of politicians as patrons to respond to political competition by excessively favouring one group of clients over another in return for political advantage. Examples include providing supporter group with free public services or public employment.

Cold War: The ideological polarization between the Western capitalist Block and the Communist Block under the leadership of the Soviet Union that took the shape of indirect confrontation for a stretch of four decades. From 1945 to 1990, there was an international conflict between democratic capitalist countries and non-democratic communist countries.

Colonialism: Colonialism denotes the theory as well as practice of establishing control over a foreign land. It leads to division of countries, namely the powerful countries as colonial powers and the ruled countries as colonies.

Command economy: A system in which the production system, the prices of the produce and other related decisions are taken by the government and not by the market forces.

Communism: The system of political and economic arrangement of the society which is based on community ownership and will be a stateless, classless and just society.

Comparative government and politics: Refers to the study of governments across the world. Here, the emphasis is on the government, its institutions and its functioning, although it may be interchangeably used with comparative politics or comparative political analysis.

Comparative politics: Covers a wide range of studies from the formal political institutions of the governments to the other crucial aspects of society that may not be a part of the government but yet relevant for political analysis and understanding. It includes the study of all forms of political activities.

Comparativists: Are the scholars engaged in the research and studies in the field of comparative politics. They particularly adopt meticulous comparison in their approach and study politics of different countries.

Confederation: It is a system of government in which the sovereign power is held by the regional governments, and there is no superior central government. They enter into a confederation for reasons of mutual security and convenience. The central government derives its powers from component states. States enjoy a larger degree of autonomy and could freely leave the union when they decide to do so.

Consociationalism: It denotes an approach of accommodative politics that ensures democratic power sharing of all ethnically divided diverse groups of a society. This term is associated with Arend Lijphart who has extensively researched different political systems to find that concessional model of democracy can ensure greater level of stability and representativeness in vulnerable and volatile developing societies.

Constitutionalism: It is the theory, ideology and practice of constitutions. In its most hegemonic sense, it has been defined as restraint on the powers of the state by the instrument of constitution.

Cooperative federalism: Cooperative federalism is a system in which the national and state governments work together to solve common problems facing the country. It believes that all units of the government are partners in governing. It is opposed to the strict separation of powers or some unitary kind of government. The federal government can use its financial resources as a bargain tool to coax states to implement its policies, for example, GST in India.

Coup d'état: A quick and decisive extra-legal seizure of governmental power by a relatively small but highly organized group of political or military leaders typically by means of the unexpected arrest or assassination of the incumbent chief executive and his principal supporters within the government.

Crown: The crown refers to the institution which is the legal embodiment of executive, legislature and judicial governance in the monarchy of Britain.

Cultural ambivalence: Showing or having mixed and conflicting feeling towards one's culture. It may signify simultaneously harbouring the feeling of adherence, pride and alienation from one's own culture.

Decolonization: It is the act or process of overcoming colonialism through anti-colonial struggle.

Delegated legislation: Delegated legislation is also known as secondary legislation and subordinate legislation. It is a law made by an executive authority to which the parliament has delegated law-making authority.

Democratization: Transition towards democratic regime from authoritarian regimes to full democracy, from authoritarian political system to semi-democracy and from semi-authoritarian political system to democratic political system.

Dependency theory: It is an approach to understand the economic underdevelopment by illustrating that resources from the 'periphery' of underdeveloped states to the 'core' of developed and wealthy states, enriching at the expense of the former.

Development: It refers to the socio-economic, political and cultural changes that bring about improvement and progress in the situations of life.

Dialectic Contradiction: A contradiction that arises when the same topic is considered from different vantage points, but each vantage point by itself does not violate the law of non-contradiction.

Dutch disease: A phenomenon wherein natural resource-rich countries witness uneven growth across sectors (say agriculture or manufacturing). When a resource-rich country exports its natural resources, it causes a significant appreciation of its currency. This in turn affects other sectors by discouraging their exports while encouraging the import of cheaper alternatives.

Economic reforms: The reforms aim at achieving economic efficiency in terms of tax policies and promoting competition in the market. These are associated with privatization, deregulation and minimum control by the state in the economic sphere, often being seen as goalposts of neo-liberal economic regimes led by the World Bank and International Monetary Fund. These reforms focus on limiting subsidies and removing tariffs (both of which are taken as distortions in economy, caused by the interventions of the government) rather than on equity or employment.

Election: A formal decision-making process by which a population chooses an individual to hold public office. It is a mechanism by which modern representative democracy has operated since the 17th century. This process is also used in voluntary associations and corporations to choose leaders.

Elections: It is a process of casting of votes in order to select our representatives to form government and govern the political system.

Electoral systems: These are the frameworks of set of rules that determine the ways in which the votes are translated into the seats in the parliament.

Environmental rights: They are composed of substantive rights (fundamental rights) and procedural rights (tools used to achieve substantial rights). Substantive are those in which the environment has a direct effect on the existence or the enjoyment of the right itself.

Eurocentrism: It is a worldview biased towards Western civilization. It reflects the tendency to interpret the world regarding European experiences. It also refers to a set of traditions based on a system of knowledge that challenges the superiority of the West.

European Community: The European Community was formed in 1967 after the Second World War. It was an opinion that a more united Europe would try to avert war. Initially, the European Community comprised three organizations, the European Economic Community, the European Coal and Steel Community and the European Atomic Energy Community. They deal with the governance and policies of all the member states. In 1993, European Community was changed to the European Union. At present, there are 28 countries which are members of the European Union.

Excentrism: It is a worldview that is asymmetrically placed against the centre. It moves away from 'Eurocentrism' and reflects the experience of non-European regions.

Faction: They can be called as 'parties within party' revolving around persons and personalities with the aim of fulfilling either party interests or individual leader's interests within the party.

Federalism: Federalism is a system of government in which power is divided between the national and state governments, with the central government having more power over the state. Federalism allows regional units to have their own legislature and executive branches as long as they are not contradicting the constitution. The powers of both the levels of government are specified in the constitution.

Federation: A federation is a political system in which different units of the government come together under the aegis of a central authority. In most of the cases, different units enter a federation voluntarily as a result of the long historic process or the transformation of a confederation (temporary arrangement) into a federation. States do not lose their independence of framing separate laws for themselves, but the central government has authority over major issues like defence and foreign policy. For example, United States and Canada.

Feminism: A range of socio-political movements and ideologies that aim to define and establish the political, economic, personal, and social equality of the sexes.

Fundamental rights: They are a group of rights that have been recognized by a high degree of protection from encroachment. These rights are specifically identified in a constitution, or have been found under due process of law.

Gender Equality: It is the state of equal ease of access to resources and opportunities, including economic participation and decision-making; and the state of valuing different behaviours, aspirations and needs equally, regardless of gender.

Gini coefficient: This concept is used to measure income inequality by studying the wealth distribution in a given population.

Global South: The countries belonging to the continents of Asia, Africa and Latin America, most of which were colonized by the European powers.

Globalization: It explains the emergence of a complex web that illustrates the growing inter-connectedness between the local, national and global. Due to globalization, geographical distance and territorial boundaries have lost their significance.

Globalization: It is a process where the labour, goods and material flow freely from one country to the other without any hindrance.

Glorious Revolution: The Glorious Revolution is also called as 'The Bloodless Revolution' or 'The Revolution of 1688'. It took place in England from 1688 to 1689. The Catholic King James II was overthrown and was replaced by his Protestant daughter Mary and her Dutch husband, William of Orange. It was a demonstration of the right of people in order to initiate the process of change in the government if they believe that the government no longer protected their rights.

Imperialism: A policy of extending a country's power and influence through colonization, use of military force or other means. Imperialism implies absolute control over the colonies through use of military. The establishment of empire is crucial for imperialism. For example, British Empire which ruled over India and many other Third World countries; another example is the scramble of Africa in the late 19th century.

Import Substitution Model: A model of development which focuses on replacing foreign imports with domestic production in order to reduce its dependency on foreign trade.

Institutional Act: Institutional Acts are the highest decree by the military which can even overturn constitutional guarantees, as they are issued on behalf of the supreme command of the Revolution. This Act in particular came in response to events like 'March of over fifty thousand people in Rio de Janeiro'. The regime's oppression after the 5th Act was extended to institutional opponents like artists, journalists and other parts of civil society.

Institutionalism: Known as the traditional approach that had the study of political institutions as it central focus.

Institutions: They are the social practices and norms that define the organization of the society. They may include any social activity or administrative structure or any bureaucratic organization.

Instrumental Marxism: It believes that the structure of the government exists to serve the interest of the ruling or bourgeoisie class.

Interest group: Group of people sharing similar interests and goals come together to influence the government to enact policies or laws in their favour.

Keynesian Model: It is an economic model created by the British economist John Maynard Keynes during the 1930s at the times of the Great Economic Depression. He advocates that government should increase expenditures and lower the taxes to stimulate demand and pull the global economy out of the depression.

Kleptocracy: A type of corruption in which government or public officials seek personal gain at the expense of those being governed.

Labour: A person who adds value to a product or produces a product with the help of physical labour or with the help of instrument.

Legitimacy: Acceptance of leaders and governmental officials by people on the grounds of accepted procedures.

Leninism: This denotes the doctrine of organizing and carrying out socialist revolution by the communist vanguard party. The communist party would act as the guardian and caretaker of the socialist political systems.

Liberalism: As an ideology, it stresses upon the liberty of an individual as the first and foremost. It stands for formal equality and political freedom. Some of its proponents were John Locke, J.S. Mill, etc.

Majoritarian system: Also known as Plurality System, it is the electoral design based on the principle of plurality and has single member constituencies, for example, FPTP.

Maoism: This stands for the socialist thoughts of Mao Zedong that saddled the peasant class of China the responsibility of bringing out the socialist revolution by improvising upon the philosophy of Karl Marx.

Market economy: This refers to a system where output and cost are determined by competition between private businesses, and there is no intervention by the government in the processes of production, distribution, investment and pricing.

Market: A regular gathering of people for the purchase and sale of provisions, livestock and other commodities.

Mercosur: Brazil is a member of the Common Market of the South America (also known as Mercosur). It is a trade bloc that includes Argentina, Paraguay and Uruguay. Earlier, Venezuela was also a member of this group; however, Venezuela's membership was suspended in August 2017. After the Asian and Russian financial crises, Mercosur adopted a protectionist stance to guard against exposure to volatile foreign markets, and it currently is negotiating Free Trade Agreements with the European Union and Canada.

Metanarratives: It is based on the premise of a pervasive theory, which defines a definitive way of interpreting events.

Method: Denotes a process of providing tools in inquiry for testing a theory. There are different kinds of methods such as comparative method, experimental method, statistical method, linguistic method and case study method.

Methodology: Is the study of different methods, concepts and rules for shaping our study and testing the theory and is used in a specific area of study. It also signifies a particular way of organizing a research. Different methodologies are applied in qualitative and quantitative methods.

Mid-range theory: This refers to a theory of middle range based on empirical data that does not attempt large-scale theorizations but emphasis on situations that have recurrent patterns in distinctive contexts.

Minority: It indicates groups of people who are lesser in number in a society; it may denote religious/ethnic/racial minority.

Mixed economy: It is described as an economic system where elements of market economies are blended with that of elements of the planned economies. Both the sectors operate here, private and public. This system symbolizes common aspects of both capitalism and socialism. It allows the freedom to use capital but at the same time also allow government to interfere in the economic activities of the market in order to achieve social aims.

Mixed system: When there is simultaneous adoption of the plurality principle and the proportional representation, the electoral system is called mixed system. It has been adopted in number of countries in Europe to achieve a balanced outcome from the electoral system.

Mode of production: This is the sum total of means of production (tools, equipment, knowledge, technology and materials), labour power and the relations of production.

Modernity: It refers to a particular historical period and sociocultural norms that arose in the backdrop of renaissance.

Modernization theory: It rests on the belief that the difference between traditional and modern societies is the level of development which is a result of systematic rationalization of societies, values, social structure and technology.

Modernization: This refers to the process of societies transitioning from traditional to modern era in the realm of economic, social, political and technological systems and values.

Multiparty systems: A political system where there are more than two parties who rule either by coalition or through support of the partner parties.

Nation: A large body of people united by common descent, history, culture or language, inhabiting a particular state or territory.

NEEDS (National Economic Empowerment and Development Strategy): A medium-term planning strategy with claims of a blueprint for new order in Nigeria. Based on a macro-economic plan document, it presents a comprehensive vision, goals and principles that would be made possible through four key policies of wealth creation, employment generation, poverty eradication and value reorientation.

Negritude: The concept is used as an attitude in the African context to affirm the black identity. Its use started in the 1930s in the literary theory.

Neocolonialism: Neocolonialism is an indirect control by the developed countries over the developing countries. Kwame Nkrumah used this concept especially for the former colonies which are eventually dependent economically.

New institutionalism: Formal organizational structure reflected not only technical demands and dependencies on resource but was also shaped by institutional forces, rational myths, knowledge legitimated through the educational system and by the professions, public opinion, and the law.

One-party dominant systems: A system where despite the presence of the opposition parties, a single party dominates over the rest and rules over a prolonged period of time.

One-party systems: A political system where a single party continues to rule either because there are no other political parties or the other political parties cannot match up to the ruling party's strength or the party absorbs other parties within its fold.

Orthodox Marxism or vulgar Marxism: It signifies the economic determinism and materialist interpretation of the world.

Para-Statals: Military regime worked on the development project through 'para-statals'. Para-statals are public firms involved in large-scale development projects such as ship-building, mining, steel, oil and bauxite production, etc. These para-statals were often managed by bureaucratic agencies and state firms. They also in most cases, after reforms, involve foreign investors and domestic capitalists. The state in this alliance, however, remained the dominant player.

Parochial: Characterized by general ignorance about the political subject, it also indicates lack of involvement in the political activity.

Party system: The pattern of structured relationship between parties, government and citizens.

Patrimonialism: A system of government where the ruler treats the state as personal property.

Political party: An organized large political group of individual members having ideological agreement on policies, goals of social change/transformation functioning within a hierarchical/bottom-up organizational setup, who select candidates to represent people as well as the organization in the parliament.

Political reforms: The reforms aimed at the improvements in constitutional and legal machinery. These reforms also include expanding the scope of transparency, accountability, justice, expediency in legal, legislative and executive functions of the government, the electoral process of the state and delivery of public goods and services. The goalposts of political reforms vary owing to the type of political system and political consensus of the people in question.

Postbehaviouralism: It came as a critique of behaviouralism which was rigorously scientific that mostly led to abstraction. Postbehaviouralism emphasized on 'relevance' and 'action' and believed that knowledge should be value-based. They believe that knowledge should help in times of crisis and engage in reshaping the society.

Postcolonialism: It is a catch-all term that refers to the range of developments that happened after the end of European colonial system like social movements, political projects and research agendas. It denotes a theoretical approach in various disciplines of social sciences and humanities to study the lasting impact of colonialism on the former colonies.

Postmodernism: Postmodernists argue that the idea of absolute and universal truth is a myth. For them, there is no such thing as certainty, and they place importance on democracy, debate and discourse.

Prebendalism: A pattern of political behaviour where state offices are utilized for personal benefits of the officeholders and their clients.

Privatization: It is a process where the public sector units are transferred to the private hands. This is done in order to increase efficiency and profits. The disadvantage of privatization is that the government regulation is decreased significantly.

Proletariat: The working class in the capitalist system who is conceived as being responsible to carry out socialist revolution.

Property: The assets that have exchange value in market.

Proportional system: It denotes a schema in which the votes secured by the political parties get translated into the seats in the legislature in more proportional ways.

Protestant reformation: A religious reform movement that swept through Europe in the 1500s. It resulted in the creation of a branch of Christianity called Protestantism.

Race: A tribe/community/group of people sharing common biological heritage and may be exposed to structural and institutional segregation in society leading to racial injustices, for example, the case of African Americans in the United States.

Real plan: A policy Brazil opted in 1994 to correct the course of economy. This plan was brought primarily to deal with problems like hyper-inflation by stabilizing the domestic currency, Real.

Relations of production: This is a set of all social relationships that human beings enter into in order to survive, produce and reproduce their means of life.

Religious Schism: It occurs when a single religious body divides and becomes two separate religious bodies.

Representation: It is an act of standing for or acting on behalf of other, in order to carry on the mandate given to the representative.

Residual category: Something that is not taken to formally constitute or be represented in a system of classification. For example, earlier culture was not taken as a formal unit of analysis as it was thought to be constituting only the background.

Resource curse: A paradoxical situation in which countries with an abundance of natural resources experience stagnant economic growth and even economic contraction.

SAPs (Structural Adjustment Programmes): A set of economic policies introduced by the International Monetary Fund (IMF) and World Bank (WB). SAPs often involve privatization, trade liberalization and fiscal restraint by the target country.

Simple majority: It means more votes compared with the votes fetched by any other candidate, but not necessarily 50 per cent.

Socialism: A dominant political and economic theory that advocates for state ownership and control of the means of production and distribution.

State: A state is a compulsory political organization with a centralized government that maintains a monopoly on the legitimate use of force within a certain geographical territory.

Subject: Is a form of political culture that characterized widespread knowledge about the political processes but disinterest of individuals to participate in the political processes.

Suffrage: It stands for the right to vote.

Third World: The countries of Asia, Africa and Latin America which underwent colonialism and got their political independence in the post-Second World War period through decolonization.

Two-party systems: A system where two parties rule alternately, one forming the ruling party and the other playing the role of a responsible opposition.

Underdevelopment: Underdevelopment refers to that state of an economy where the levels of living of masses are extremely low due to very low levels of per capita income resulting from low levels of productivity and high growth rates of population.

Unfinished state: A state characterized by instabilities and uncertainties that may render it susceptible to collapse as a coherent political entity.

USSR: The Union of Soviet Socialist Republics also known as Soviet Russia; it stands for the socialist federation of Russia, formed after the Bolshevik revolution.

Variables: Are concepts whose values change depending on other factors and have qualitative (such as educated population and law abiding citizens) or quantitative (such as age and size) attributes. The variables may be 'dependent variables' (if they depend upon or are tied with another variable) or 'independent variable' (if they are not tied to any other variable).

Voting: It signifies the activity of casting vote on the ballot paper in election.

Westminster: 'Westminster' is an area of central England, where the parliament of Britain is situated. It is a democratic parliamentary system of government modelled after the British system of parliament.

World-systems theory: It suggests that the world economy divided into core, periphery and semi-periphery is an interlocking capitalist system. The interrelationships between these parts is of structural inequalities based on exploitation.

Index